Scalable Fuzzy Algorithms for Data Management and Analysis:
Methods and Design

Anne Laurent
LIRMM, University Montpellier 2, France

Marie-Jeanne Lesot
LIP6, University Paris 6, France

T0321688

Information Science REFERENCE

INFORMATION SCIENCE REFERENCE

Hershey · New York

Director of Editorial Content: Kristin Klinger
Senior Managing Editor: Jamie Snavely
Assistant Managing Editor: Michael Brehm
Publishing Assistant: Sean Woznicki
Typesetter: Mike Killian, Sean Woznicki
Cover Design: Lisa Tosheff
Printed at: Yurchak Printing Inc.

Published in the United States of America by
Information Science Reference (an imprint of IGI Global)
701 E. Chocolate Avenue
Hershey PA 17033
Tel: 717-533-8845
Fax: 717-533-8661
E-mail: cust@igi-global.com
Web site: http://www.igi-global.com/reference

Library of Congress Cataloging-in-Publication Data

Scalable fuzzy algorithms for data management and analysis : methods and design / Anne Laurent and Marie-Jeanne Lesot, editors.

     p. cm.
  Includes bibliographical references and index.
  Summary: "This book presents up-to-date techniques for addressing data management problems with logic and memory use"--Provided by publisher.

   ISBN 978-1-60566-858-1 (hardcover) -- ISBN 978-1-60566-859-8 (ebook) 1.
Database management. 2. Fuzzy logic. 3. Algorithms. 4. Machine learning.
I. Laurent, Anne, 1976- II. Lesot, Marie-Jeanne, 1978-
   QA76.9.D3S267 2009
   006.3'1--dc22
            2009028581

British Cataloguing in Publication Data
A Cataloguing in Publication record for this book is available from the British Library.

List of Reviewers

Sadok Ben Yahia, *Faculty of Sciences of Tunis, Tunisia*
Sandra Bringay, *LIRMM, Univ Montpellier 3, France*
Guillaume Cleuziou, *LIFO, Orléans University, France*
Thanh Ha Dang, *LIP6, University of Paris 6, France*
Federico Del Razo Lopez, *Instituto Tecnológico de Toluca, Mexico*
Nicolas Labroche, *LIP6, University of Paris 6, France*
Dominique Laurent, *ETIS, Cergy-Pontoise University, France*
Cécile Low Kam, *LIRMM, Univ Montpellier 2, France*
Christophe Marsala, *LIP6, University of Paris 6, France*
Jordi Nin Guerrero, *CSIC, Spanish National Research Council, Spain*
Yoann Pitarch, *LIRMM, Univ Montpellier 2, France*
Marc Plantevit, *GREYC, Université de Basse-Normandie, France*
Pascal Poncelet, *LIRMM, Univ Montpellier 2, France*
Julien Rabatel, *LIRMM, Univ Montpellier 2, France*
Chedy Raïssi, *National University of Singapore, Singapore*
Liva Ralaivola, *LIF, Université de la Méditerranée, France*
Maria Rifqi, *LIP6, University of Paris 6, France*
Mathieu Roche, *LIRMM, Univ Montpellier 3, France*
Fatiha Saïs, *LRI, INRIA-Saclay, France*
Paola Salle, *LIRMM, Univ Montpellier 2, France*
Maguelonne Teisseire, *CEMAGREF Montpellier, France*

Table of Contents

Section 1
Introductory Chapters

Koldo Basterretxea, Universidad del País Vasco/Euskal Herriko Unibertsitatea
(UPV/EHU), Spain
Inés del Campo, Universidad del País Vasco/Euskal Herriko Unibertsitatea (UPV/EHU), Spain

Lawrence O. Hall, University of South Florida, USA
Dmitry B. Goldgof, University of South Florida, USA
Juana Canul-Reich, University of South Florida, USA
Prodip Hore, University of South Florida, USA
Weijian Cheng, University of South Florida, USA
Larry Shoemaker, University of South Florida, USA

Section 2
Databases and Queries

François Deliège, Aalborg University, Denmark
Torben Bach Pedersen, Aalborg University, Denmark

Section 3
Summarization

Section 4
Real-World Challenges

Detailed Table of Contents

Section 1
Introductory Chapters

Chapter 1

Koldo Basterretxea, Universidad del País Vasco/Euskal Herriko Unibertsitatea
(UPV/EHU), Spain
Inés del Campo, Universidad del País Vasco/Euskal Herriko Unibertsitatea (UPV/EHU), Spain

This chapter presents a comprehensive synthesis of the state of the art and the progress in the electronic hardware design for the fuzzy computation field over the past two decades, in particular for the implementation of fuzzy inference systems. The authors show how fuzzy hardware has evolved, from general purpose processors (GPPs) to high performance reconfigurable computing (HPRC), as well as the development of the hardware/software codesign methodology. The last part of the chapter is dedicated to research directions for the development and improvement of architecture to directly implement and thus speed up fuzzy data mining algorithms.

Chapter 2

Lawrence O. Hall, University of South Florida, USA
Dmitry B. Goldgof, University of South Florida, USA
Juana Canul-Reich, University of South Florida, USA
Prodip Hore, University of South Florida, USA
Weijian Cheng, University of South Florida, USA
Larry Shoemaker, University of South Florida, USA

This chapter considers the scalability issue from the machine learning and data mining point of view, to extract knowledge from huge amounts of data, studying in turn both supervised and unsupervised learning and thus providing an introduction to the sequel of the book. It focuses on ensemble based approaches that learn classifiers on subsets of data, to reduce the amount of data that must be fit in computer memory at any time. In the unsupervised learning case, the authors concentrate on data streams: they offer an overview of existing algorithms to deal with such data and propose an online variant of the classic fuzzy c-means, experimented on datasets containing up to 5 millions magnetic resonance images.

Section 2
Databases and Queries

Chapter 3

François Deliège, Aalborg University, Denmark
Torben Bach Pedersen, Aalborg University, Denmark

This chapter considers the framework of data warehouses when managing large collections of music data, in the purpose of designing music recommendation systems. A fuzzy representation through the concept of fuzzy songs is introduced and several solutions for storing and managing fuzzy sets in general are studied: three options are considered, namely tables, arrays and compressed bitmaps. Theoretical cost estimates are built for these alternatives that are also studied experimentally for various data collection sizes. Furthermore an algebra to query the built data cubes is defined; the operators are examined both from a theoretical and a practical point of view.

Chapter 4

Nicolás Marín, University of Granada, Spain
Carlos Molina, University of Jaen, Spain
Daniel Sánchez, University of Granada, Spain
M. Amparo Vila, University of Granada, Spain

In the framework of data warehouses and OLAP systems, this chapter investigates the particular topic of on-line analytical mining (OLAM) which aims at coupling data mining and OLAP. The authors consider association rules which are one of the most used data mining techniques to extract summarized knowledge from data, focusing on the case of data cubes for which they must be further studied. The authors propose methods to support imprecision which results from the multiple data sources handled in such applications and constitutes a challenge when designing association rule mining algorithms. They study the influence of the fuzzy logic use for different size problems, both in terms of the cube density (number of records) and topology (number of dimensions), comparing the results with a crisp approach. Experiments are performed on medical, financial and census data.

Chapter 5

Giorgos Stoilos, National and Technical University of Athens, Greece
Jeff Z. Pan, University of Aberdeen, UK
Giorgos Stamou, National and Technical University of Athens, Greece

This chapter considers a data model that is in particular adapted to databases in the form of ontology, namely the fuzzy description logic format: which is of particular use to handle fuzziness in Semantic Web applications whose high current development makes such works crucial. The authors show that its high expressivity does not come at the expense of efficiency and that there exist methods capable of scaling up to millions of data. The authors study the two main inference services, which are query answering and classification. They show how the Fuzzy DL-Lite language provides scalable algorithms for expressive queries over fuzzy ontologies, and how Fuzzy EL+ leads to very efficient algorithms for classification, extended to fuzzy subsumption.

Chapter 6

Jonathan Lawry, University of Bristol, UK
Yongchuan Tang, Zhejiang University, PR China

Focusing on the issue of query formulation, this chapter deals with quantified linguistic data queries, for which a new interpretation based on a combination of the random set theory and prototype theory is proposed: concepts are defined as random set neighborhood of a set of prototypes, which means that a linguistic label is deemed appropriate to describe an instance if the latter is sufficiently close to the prototypes of the label. Quantifiers are then defined as random set constraints on ratios or absolute values. These notions are then combined to a methodology to evaluate the quality of quantified statements about instances, so as to answer expressive quantified linguistic queries.

Chapter 7

Gloria Bordogna, CNR IDPA, Italy
Alessandro Campi, Politecnico di Milano, Italy
Stefania Ronchi, Politecnico di Milano, Italy
Giuseppe Psaila, Università di Bergamo, Italy

This chapter considers a specific type of queries, namely those submitted to search engines: it tackles the more and more crucial problem of managing the results from search engines and automatically extracting hidden relations from these results that can be very large. Assuming that the set of retrieved documents is given in the form of a set of clusters, the authors propose a flexible exploratory language for manipulating the groups of clustered documents returned by several engines. To that aim, they define various operators among which refinement, union, coalescing and reclustering and propose several ranking criteria and functions based on the fuzzy set theory. This makes it possible to preserve the interpretability of the retrieved results despite the large amount of answers obtained for the query.

Section 3
Summarization

This chapter studies how to mine huge volumes of data for user-friendly summaries, through the use of the natural language and a fuzzy logic based model. The focus is laid on the interpretability of the summaries, defining scalability as the capability of algorithms to preserve understandable and intuitive results even when the dataset sizes increase, at a more perceptual or cognitive level than the usual "technical scalability." The authors offer a general discussion of the scalability notion and show how linguistic summaries answer its perceptual definition, detailing their automatic extraction from very large databases.

This chapter provides a description of the order weighted averaging operator (OWA) that generates summarizing statistics over large datasets. The author details its flexibility derived from weight generating functions as well as methods to adapt them to the data analysts, based on graphical and linguistic specifications.

This chapter considers the framework of summaries based on association rules, and focuses on its computationally most complex part, namely the problem of mining frequent itemsets. In order to improve its scalability, the authors propose efficient data structures and processing schemes, using a split and merge technique, that can be applied even if all data cannot be loaded into the main memory. Approximation is introduced by considering that missing items can be inserted into transactions with a user-specified penalty. The authors study the behavior of the proposed algorithm and compare it to some well-known itemsets mining algorithms, providing a comprehensive overview of methods.

This chapter considers the domain of association rules learning when huge amount of data are to be handled, focusing on the case where the data are grouped into hierarchically organized categories. The aim is then to extract rules to describe relations between these categories; fuzziness allows avoiding the difficulties raised when crisp separations must be defined. A new definition of fuzzy confidence is proposed to be consistent with the framework addressed in the chapter.

This chapter explores data summarization, through fuzzy clustering. The authors propose to combine two approaches to decrease the computation time and improve the scalability of the classic fuzzy c-means algorithm, based on a theoretical analysis of the reasons for the high complexity, both for time and memory, and on an efficient data structure. The authors combine a modification of the fuzzifier function with a suitable data organization exploiting a neighborhood representation to significantly speed up the algorithm. The efficiency of the proposed method is illustrated through experiments.

This chapter considers fuzzy clustering focusing on the selection of the appropriate number of clusters: the latter is classically determined in a procedure that consists in testing several values and choosing the optimal one according to a validation criterion, which can be very time consuming. The authors propose to address this problem as an integrated part of the clustering process, by making the algorithm insensitive to too high values for this parameter: they modify the update equations for the cluster centers, to impose a repulsive effect between centers, rejecting the unnecessary ones to locations where they do not disturb the result. Both the classic fuzzy c-means and its Gustafson-Kessel variant are considered.

Section 4
Real-World Challenges

This chapter addresses the problem of detecting as early as possible problems on cars by managing data stored in a warranty database which contains customer claims recording information on dealer location, car model, car manufacturing and selling dates, claim date, mileage to date, complaint code, labor code, and so on. Warranty databases constitute massive stream data that are updated with thousands of new claims on a daily basis. This chapter introduces an original approach to mine these data streams by proposing a fuzzy method for the automatic detection of evolving maintenance problems. For this purpose, the authors propose to study frequency histograms using a method based on a cognitive model of human perception instead of crisp statistical models.

This chapter proposes to use forests of fuzzy decision trees to perform automatic indexing of huge volumes of video shots. The main purpose of the chapter is to detect high-level semantic concepts such as "indoor," "map," or "military staff" that can then be used for any query and treatment on videos. This data mining problem requires addressing large, unbalanced and multiclass datasets and takes place in the highly competitive context of the TRECVid challenge organized by NIST. The authors report the success of the fuzzy ensemble learning approach they propose, that proves to be both tractable and of high quality. They also underline the robustness advantage of the fuzzy framework that improves the results as compared to other data mining tools.

This chapter considers a fuzzy clustering issue with very large relational datasets, in the framework of bioinformatics to extract information from micro-array data. It describes the whole process of how such problems can be addressed, presenting the theoretical machine learning methods to be used as well as the practical processing system. The considered three-step approach consists in subsampling the data, clustering the sample data and then extending the results to the whole dataset. The practical system describes the methods applied to select the appropriate method parameters, including the fuzzifier and the number of clusters, determined using a cluster validity index. It also describes the adjustments that appear to be necessary to handle the real dataset, in particular regarding the sampling step. The experiments are performed with real data containing around 37,000 gene sequences.

Foreword

Scalability is one of the main problems practitioners have to cope with when grasping a real-world application in data management or information analysis. The size of databases and data warehouses, associated with incompleteness of information and missing values has been a major difficulty from the early beginning of their studies. Modern digital devices, Internet possibilities, and distributed networks are among the most powerful means of storing, retrieving, and sharing information. The amounts of documents and data available for the users are continuously increasing, whatever their nature may be: text, video, music, images, multimedia, Web. The ways to access these documents and data are also diverse: exchanges within communities, social networks and peer to peer communications have increased the complexity of transfers from data repositories to users.

To increase the efficiency of existing algorithms is a necessity. Dimension reduction or dynamic treatment of data avoiding their storage is for instance a solution to large scale learning systems. Moreover, alternative approaches to classic information retrieval, knowledge discovery and data analysis need to be created, in order to cope with the complexity of the problem to solve, due to the size, the heterogeneity, the incompleteness of data and their access paths. Thinking differently is also a necessity since classic statistics or machine learning methods have their limits. System science provides interesting paradigms for the handling of complex systems, always taking the user into account, in a holistic involvement of all components of the system. Active learning involving the user is for example a solution to the difficulty of using supervised learning in huge training sets. Another lesson from systems science is the exploitation of synergies between components of the system, and this capacity is well understood in the complementarity between medias, for instance between text and image.

Fuzzy knowledge representation and logic are among the efficient tools for the management of complex systems, since they bring solutions to the incompleteness, inaccuracy and uncertainty, inherent to large scale and heterogeneous information reservoirs, taking into account synthetic descriptions of isolated elements and reducing individual treatments. Providing an interface between numerical data representations by computers and symbolic representations well understood by humans, fuzzy logic fills in the gap between technological needs and usability requirements. Concepts such as fuzzy categories, fuzzy quantifiers, fuzzy prototypes, fuzzy aggregation methods, fuzzy learning algorithms, fuzzy databases, and fuzzy graphs have proved their utility in the construction of scalable algorithms.

The present book is certainly of particular interest for the diversity of addressed topics, covering a large spectrum in scalability management. Anne Laurent and Marie-Jeanne Lesot are experts in theoretical and methodological study of fuzzy techniques, and they have moreover coped with various real world large-scale problems. The group of experts they have gathered to prepare this volume is unquestionably qualified to provide solutions to researchers and practitioners in search of efficient algorithms and models for complex and large dataset management and analysis.

Scalability is understood in this book from several points of view. The first one is the size of available data implying difficulties in their tractability, with regard to memory size or computation time. This aspect is strongly related to the complexity of involved algorithms.

The second point of view regards the form of the algorithm results and the capability of human users to understand and grasp these results, through summaries and visualization solutions. This aspect is more related to a cognitive framework.

The scalability of knowledge representation is at the crossroads of these points of view, dealing with ontologies or formal languages, as well as a variety of concepts in a fuzzy setting.

The classic scalability problem in hardware is another point of view, revisited here in the light of modern electronic solutions and fuzzy computation.

This book deals with all these aspects under a fuzzy logic based perspective. A sample of applications is also presented as a showcase, pointing out the efficiency of fuzzy approaches to the construction of scalable algorithms. Potential applications of such approaches go far beyond the domains tackled here and this book opens the door to a vast spectrum of forthcoming works.

Bernadette Bouchon-Meunier
LIP6 / UPMC / CNRS, France

Bernadette Bouchon-Meunier *is the head of the department of Databases and Machine Learning in the Computer Science Laboratory of the University Paris 6 (LIP6). Graduate from the Ecole Normale Superieure at Cachan, she received the degrees of B.S. in Mathematics and Computer Science, Ph.D. in Applied Mathematics and D. Sc. in Computer Science from the University of Pierre and Marie Curie. Editor-in-Chief of the International Journal of Uncertainty, Fuzziness and Knowledge-based Systems, she is a co-founder and co-executive director of the International Conference on Information Processing and Management of Uncertainty in Knowledge-based Systems (IPMU) held every other year since 1986. She is an IEEE senior member and chair of the IEEE French Chapter on Computational Intelligence.. Her present research interests include approximate and similarity-based reasoning, as well as the application of fuzzy logic and machine learning techniques to decision-making, data mining, risk forecasting, information retrieval and user modeling.*

Preface

The fuzzy logic and the fuzzy set theory have been proposed by Lotfi Zadeh in 1965, and largely developed since, in various directions, including reasoning, control, data representation and data mining. They now provide numerous tools to handle data in a very relevant and comprehensive way, in particular offering theoretically well founded means to deal with uncertainty and imprecision. Furthermore, they constitute an interface between numerical and linguistic representations, increasing the interpretability of the developed tools and making it possible to *compute with words*, using the expression proposed by L. Zadeh in 1996.

Despite these advantages, fuzzy approaches often suffer from the opinion that they cannot address huge amounts of data and are inappropriate because of scalability difficulties: a high computational complexity or high memory requirements are feared, that might hinder their applications to very large datasets, as occur more and more frequently nowadays. Now this is not the case, as many applications, including industrial success stories, have shown that fuzziness and scalability are not antagonistic concepts. This book aims at highlighting the relevance of fuzzy methods for huge datasets, considering both the theoretical and practical points of view and bringing together contributions from various fields.

This book gathers up-to-date methods and algorithms that tackle this problem, showing that fuzzy logic is a very powerful way to provide users with relevant results within reasonable time and memory. The chapters cover a wide range of research areas where very large databases are involved, considering among others issues related to data representation and structuring, in particular in data warehouses, as well as the related querying problems, and the extraction of relevant and characterizing information from large datasets, to summarize them in a flexible, robust and interpretable way that takes into account uncertainty and imprecision. The book also includes success stories based on fuzzy logic that address real world challenges to handle huge amounts of data for practical tasks. The databases considered in the various chapters take different forms, including data warehouses, data cubes, tabular or relational data, and different application types, among which multimedia, medical, bioinformatics, financial, Semantic Web or data stream contexts.

The book aims at providing researchers, master students, engineers and practitioners the state-of-the-art tools to address the new challenges of current applications that must now both remain scalable and provide user-friendly and actionable results. The readers will get a panorama of the existing methods, algorithms and applications devoted to scalability and fuzziness. They will find the necessary material concerning implementation issues and solutions, algorithms, evaluation, case studies and real applications. Besides, being the very first reference gathering scalable fuzzy methods from various fields, this book contributes to bridging the gap between research communities (e.g., databases, machine learning) that are not always enough combined and mixed.

The book is organized in four complementary sections: after two introductory chapters that provide general overviews on fuzziness and scalability from two different points of view, the second section, entitled "Databases and Queries," is devoted to methods that consider data structuring as the core of the approach and propose either flexible representations, through the incorporation of fuzzy components in the data, or flexible queries that make interactions of the user with the database easy and intuitive thanks to linguistic formulations. The third section, called "Summarization," tackles the complexity of huge datasets through the extraction of relevant and characteristic information that provide summaries of the whole data. In this context, fuzzy approaches offer a linguistic interface to increase the interpretability of the results, flexibility and tools to handle imprecision and uncertainty. Lastly, the fourth section, entitled "Real-World Challenges," presents success stories involving fuzzy approaches, considering various domains such as stream, multimedia and biological data. In the following, we detail each section in turn.

The first two chapters of the book introduce general overviews, respectively from the hardware point of view, and from a machine learning perspective.

The chapter "*Electronic Hardware for Fuzzy Computation,*" by Koldo Basterretxea and Inés del Campo, presents a comprehensive synthesis of the state of the art and the progress in the electronic hardware design for the fuzzy computation field over the past two decades, in particular for the implementation of fuzzy inference systems. The authors show how fuzzy hardware has evolved, from general purpose processors (GPPs) to high performance reconfigurable computing (HPRC), as well as the development of the hardware/software codesign methodology. They discuss their relationships with the scalability issue, and the new trends and challenges to be faced. The last part of the chapter, dedicated to the architectures proposed to speed up fuzzy data mining processing specifically, constitutes a promising research direction for the development and improvement of implementation of fuzzy data mining algorithms.

Chapter 2, entitled "*Scaling Fuzzy Models*" by Lawrence O. Hall, Dmitry B. Goldgof, Juana Canul-Reich, Prodip Hore, Weijian Cheng and Larry Shoemaker, considers the scalability issue from the machine learning and data mining point of view, to extract knowledge from huge amounts of data, studying in turn both supervised and unsupervised learning. It focuses on ensemble based approaches that basically consist in learning classifiers on subsets of data, to reduce the amount of data that must be fit in computer memory at any time. This approach is also used in Chapter 15 in the case of fuzzy random forests to handle large multimedia datasets. In the unsupervised learning case, the authors concentrate on data streams that are more and more common nowadays and can lead to very large datasets to be handled incrementally. They offer an overview of existing algorithms to deal with such data and propose an online variant of the classic fuzzy c-means. Their experimental results, performed on datasets containing up to 5 millions magnetic resonance images, illustrate the possibility to apply fuzzy approaches to data mining from huge datasets.

The chapters of the second section, Chapters 3 to 7, address the topic of databases and queries coupled with fuzzy methods: they consider the scalability issue from the point of view of data structuring and organization, as well as for the querying step. Chapters 3, 4 and 5 mainly focus on the data storing issue, respectively considering data warehouses adapted to fuzzy set representation (chapter 3), fuzzy data cubes following the OLAP model (Chapter 4) and fuzzy description logic to both represent and exploit imprecise data in a logical reasoning framework (Chapter 5). Chapters 6 and 7 concentrate on queries, considering two different types: chapter 6 considers linguistic data queries and more specifically quantified linguistic queries, proposing a framework to model and answer them. Chapter 7 focuses on the results provided by queries submitted to search engines and tackles the problem of managing them through a flexible exploratory language.

More precisely, Chapter 3, entitled "*Using Fuzzy Song Sets in Music Warehouses*" by François Deliège and Torben Bach Pedersen, considers data warehouses used to manage large collections of music data, in the purpose of designing music recommendation systems. The authors introduce a fuzzy representation through the concept of fuzzy songs and study several solutions for storing and managing fuzzy sets in general, considering three options, namely tables, arrays and compressed bitmaps. They construct theoretical estimates for the cost of each solution that are also studied experimentally and compared for various data collection sizes. Furthermore, they discuss the definition of an algebra to query the built data cubes and examine the operators both from a theoretical and practical point of view. Thus this chapter provides both an insight on theoretical works on scalability issues for storing and managing fuzzy sets, and an example of a real world challenge.

In the same framework of data warehouses and OLAP systems, the chapter "*Mining Association Rules from Fuzzy DataCubes*," by Nicolás Marín, Carlos Molina, Daniel Sánchez and M. Amparo Vila, investigates the particular topic of on-line analytical mining (OLAM) which aims at coupling data mining and OLAP, bridging the gap between sections II and III of the book. The authors consider association rules which are one of the most used data mining techniques to extract summarized knowledge from data, focusing on the particular framework of data cubes for which they must be further studied. The authors propose methods to support imprecision which results from the multiple data sources handled in such applications and constitutes a challenge when designing association rule mining algorithms. The chapter studies the influence of the fuzzy logic use for different size problems, both in terms of the cube density (number of records) and topology (number of dimensions), comparing the results with a crisp approach. Experiments are performed on medical, financial and census data.

In Chapter 5, entitled "*Scalable Reasoning with Tractable Fuzzy Ontology Languages*," Giorgos Stoilos, Jeff Z. Pan, and Giorgos Stamou consider another data model that is in particular adapted to databases in the form of ontology, namely the fuzzy description logic format. The latter offers the possibility to both model and reason with imprecise knowledge in a formal framework that provides expressive means to represent and query information. It is of particular use to handle fuzziness in Semantic Web applications whose high current development makes such works crucial. The authors show that the increased expressivity does not come at the expense of efficiency and that there exist methods capable of scaling up to millions of data. More precisely, the authors study the scalability of the two main inference services in this enriched data description language, which are query answering and classification (i.e., computation of the implied concept hierarchy). To that aim, they consider two languages: on one hand, they show how Fuzzy DL-Lite provides scalable algorithms for expressive queries over fuzzy ontologies; on the other hand, they show how Fuzzy EL+ leads to very efficient algorithms for classification and extend it to allow for fuzzy subsumption.

Focusing on the issue of query formulation, in particular for expressive queries, Chapter 6, entitled "*A Random Set and Prototype Theory Model of Linguistic Query Evaluation*" by Jonathan Lawry and Yongchuan Tang, deals with linguistic data queries, that belongs to the *computing with words* domain introduced by Zadeh in 1996. More precisely the authors consider quantified data queries, for which a new interpretation based on a combination of the random set theory and prototype theory is proposed: concepts are defined as random set neighborhood of a set of prototypes, which means that a linguistic label is deemed appropriate to describe an instance if the latter is sufficiently close to the prototypes of the label. Quantifiers are then defined as random set constraints on ratios or absolute values. These notions are then combined to a methodology to evaluate the quality of quantified statements about instances, so as to answer quantified linguistic queries.

The chapter "*A Flexible Language for Exploring Clustered Search Results*," by Gloria Bordogna, Alessandro Campi, Stefania Ronchi and Giuseppe Psaila, considers specific types of queries, namely those submitted to search engines: they tackle the more and more crucial problem of managing the results from search engines that can be very large, and automatically extracting hidden relations from them. Assuming that the set of documents retrieved by a search engine is given in the form of a set of clusters, the authors propose a flexible exploratory language for manipulating the groups of clustered documents returned by several engines. To that aim, they define various operators among which refinement, union, coalescing and reclustering and propose several ranking criteria and functions based on the fuzzy set theory. This makes it possible to preserve the interpretability of the retrieved results despite the large amount of answers obtained for the query.

The chapters in the next section, Chapters 8 to 13, consider a different approach on the problem of scalability and fuzziness and address the topic of exploiting fuzzy tools to summarize huge amounts of data to extract from them relevant information that captures their main characteristics. Several approaches can be distinguished, referring to different types of data mining tools, as detailed below. Chapter 8 considers linguistic summaries, and uses fuzzy logic to model the linguistic information, Chapter 9 proposes an aggregation operator relevant to summarize statistics in particular. Chapters 10 and 11 consider the association rules to summarize data. Chapters 12 and 13 belong to the fuzzy clustering framework. It must be underlined that Chapter 4 also considers association rules, in the case where data are stored in a structure as fuzzy cubes.

More precisely, Chapter 8, entitled "*Linguistic Data Summarization: A High Scalability through the Use of Natural Language?*" by Janusz Kacprzyk and Sławomir Zadrożny, studies user-friendly data summaries through the use of natural language, and a fuzzy logic based model. The focus is laid on the interpretability of the summaries, defining scalability as the capability of algorithms to preserve understandable and intuitive results even when the dataset sizes increase, at a more perceptual or cognitive level than the usual "technical scalability." The authors offer a general discussion of the scalability notion and show how linguistic summaries answer its perceptual definition, detailing their automatic extraction from very large databases.

The summarization process is also the topic of Chapter 9, "*Human Focused Summarizing Statistics Using OWA Operators*" by Ronald R. Yager, that provides a description of the order weighted averaging operator (OWA). This operator generates summarizing statistics over large datasets. The author details its flexibility derived from weight generating functions as well as methods to adapt them to the data analysts, based on graphical and linguistic specifications.

Another common way to summarize datasets consists in extracting association rules that underline frequent and regular relations in the data. Chapter 10, entitled "*(Approximate) Frequent Item Set Mining Made Simple with a Split and Merge Algorithm*" by Christian Borgelt and Xiaomeng Wang, considers this framework and focuses on its computationally most complex part, namely the problem of mining frequent itemsets. In order to improve its scalability, the authors propose efficient data structures and processing schemes, using a split and merge technique, that can be applied even if all data cannot be loaded into the main memory. Approximation is introduced by considering that missing items can be inserted into transactions with a user-specified penalty. The authors study the behavior of the proposed algorithm and compare it to some well-known itemsets mining algorithms, providing a comprehensive overview of methods.

The chapter "*Fuzzy Association Rules to Summarise Multiple Taxonomies in Large Databases*," by Trevor Martin and Yun Shen, also considers the domain of association rules learning when huge amounts of data are to be handled, focusing on the case where the data are grouped into hierarchically organized categories. The aim is then to extract rules to describe relations between these categories; fuzziness allows avoiding the difficulties raised when crisp separations must be defined. They propose a new definition of fuzzy confidence to be consistent with the framework addressed in the chapter.

Chapter 12, entitled "*Fuzzy Cluster Analysis of Larger Data Sets*" by Roland Winkler, Frank Klawonn, Frank Höppner and Rudolf Kruse, explores another method for data summarization, namely fuzzy clustering. The authors propose to combine two approaches to decrease the computation time and improve the scalability of the classic fuzzy c-means algorithm, based on a theoretical analysis of the reasons for the high complexity, both for time and memory, and on an efficient data structure. Indeed the high computational cost of the fuzzy c-means is basically due to the fact that all data belong to all clusters: the membership degrees can be very low, but do not equal 0, which also implies that all data have an influence on all clusters. The authors combine a modification of the fuzzifier function to avoid this effect with a suitable data organization exploiting a neighborhood representation of the data to significantly speed up the algorithm. The efficiency of the proposed method is illustrated through experiments.

Chapter 13, entitled "*Fuzzy Clustering with Repulsive Prototypes*" by Frank Rehm, Roland Winkler and Rudolf Kruse, also considers fuzzy clustering, focusing on the selection of the appropriate number of clusters: the latter is classically determined in a procedure that consists in testing several values and choosing the optimal one according to a validation criterion. This process can be very time consuming, the authors propose to address this problem as an integrated part of the clustering process, by making the algorithm insensitive to too high values for this parameter. To that aim, they modify the update equations for the cluster centers, to impose a repulsive effect between centers, rejecting the unnecessary ones to locations where they do not disturb the result. Both the classic fuzzy c-means and its Gustafson-Kessel variant are considered.

The last section of the book, Chapters 14 to 16, is dedicated to real world challenges that consider the scalability of fuzzy methods from a practical point of view, showing success stories in different domains and using different techniques, both for supervised and unsupervised data mining issues. Chapter 14 considers massive stream data describing car warranty data. Chapter 15 addresses the indexation of huge amounts of multimedia data using random forest trees, following the same approach as the one presented in Chapter 2. Chapter 16 belongs to the bioinformatics domain that is among the domains that currently give rise to the largest datasets to handle, it more precisely focuses on micro-array data. Chapter 3 that describes a data warehouse used to manage large collections of music data also belongs to this real world challenges section.

Chapter 14, entitled "*Early Warning from Car Warranty Data using a Fuzzy Logic Technique*" by Mark Last, Yael Mendelson, Sugato Chakrabarty and Karishma Batra, addresses the problem of detecting as early as possible problems on cars by managing data stored in a warranty database which contains customer claims recording information on dealer location, car model, car manufacturing and selling dates, claim date, mileage to date, complaint code, labor code, and so on. Warranty databases constitute massive stream data that are updated with thousands of new claims on a daily basis. This chapter introduces an original approach to mine these data streams by proposing a fuzzy method for the automatic detection of evolving maintenance problems. For this purpose, the authors propose to study frequency histograms using a method based on a cognitive model of human perception instead of crisp statistical models. The obtained results reveal significant emerging and decreasing trends in the car warranty data.

The problem of video mining is tackled in Chapter 15, entitled "*High Scale Fuzzy Video Mining*" by Christophe Marsala and Marcin Detyniecki, where the authors propose to use forests of fuzzy decision trees to perform automatic indexing of huge volumes of video shots. The main purpose of the chapter is to detect high-level semantic concepts such as "indoor," "map," or "military staff" that can then be used for any query and treatment on videos. This data mining problem requires addressing large, unbalanced and multiclass datasets and takes place in the highly competitive context of the TRECVid challenge organized by NIST. The authors report the success of the fuzzy ensemble learning approach they propose, that proves to be both tractable and of high quality. They also underline the robustness advantage of the fuzzy framework that improves the results as compared to other data mining tools.

Chapter 16, entitled *"Fuzzy Clustering of Large Relational Bioinformatics Datasets"* by Mihail Popescu considers a practical problem of fuzzy clustering with very large relational datasets, in the framework of bioinformatics to extract information from micro-array data. It describes the whole process of how such problems can be addressed, presenting the theoretical machine learning methods to be used as well as the practical processing system. The considered three-step approach consists in subsampling the data, clustering the sample data and then extending the results to the whole dataset. The practical system describes the methods applied to select the appropriate method parameters, including the fuzzifier and the number of clusters, determined using a cluster validity index. It also describes the adjustments that appear to be necessary to handle the real dataset, in particular regarding the sampling step. The experiments are performed with real data containing around 37,000 gene sequences.

The book thus gathers contributions from various research domains that address the combined issue of fuzziness and scalability from different perspectives, including both theoretical and experimental points of view, considering different definitions of scalability and different topics related to the fuzzy logic and fuzzy set theory use. The variety of these points of view is one of the key features of this book, making it a precious guide for researchers, students and practitioners.

Anne Laurent and Marie-Jeanne Lesot
Editors

Acknowledgment

The editors would like to express their gratitude to all authors, for their precious and high quality contributions that made this first book on scalability and fuzziness possible. We are honored that the authors, key researchers from various research communities that address this issue, accepted to participate to this book, offering a survey on this topic covering a wide range of perspectives on scalability and fuzziness.

The editors' gratitude also goes to Bernadette Bouchon-Meunier who accepted to write the foreword of this book, sharing her expertise, in-depth knowledge and hindsight on all aspects of the fuzzy logic domain in the introduction to this book.

The editors would also like to warmly thank the reviewers whose valuable comments helped to improve the quality of the book: Sadok Ben Yahia, Sandra Bringay, Guillaume Cleuziou, Thanh Ha Dang, Federico Del Razo Lopez, Nicolas Labroche, Dominique Laurent, Cécile Low Kam, Christophe Marsala, Jordi Nin Guerrero, Yoann Pitarch, Marc Plantevit, Pascal Poncelet, Julien Rabatel, Chedy Raïssi, Liva Ralaivola, Maria Rifqi, Mathieu Roche, Fatiha Saïs, Paola Salle, Maguelonne Teisseire.

Finally the editors would like to acknowledge the IGI Global publishing company for having accepted to publish this book on Scalable Fuzzy Algorithms for Data Management and Analysis: Methods and Design. Special thanks go to Joel Gamon who followed the whole process from the first call for chapters to the publication and whose help was so precious.

Anne Laurent and Marie-Jeanne Lesot
Editors

Section 1
Introductory Chapters

Chapter 1
Electronic Hardware for Fuzzy Computation

Koldo Basterretxea
Universidad del País Vasco/Euskal Herriko Unibertsitatea (UPV/EHU), Spain

Inés del Campo
Universidad del País Vasco/Euskal Herriko Unibertsitatea (UPV/EHU), Spain

ABSTRACT

This chapter describes two decades of evolution of electronic hardware for fuzzy computing, and discusses the new trends and challenges that are currently being faced in this field. Firstly the authors analyze the main design approaches performed since first fuzzy chip designs were published and until the consolidation of reconfigurable hardware: the digital approach and the analog approach. Secondly, the evolution of fuzzy hardware based on reconfigurable devices, from traditional field programmable gate arrays to complex system-on-programmable chip solutions, is described and its relationship with the scalability issue is explained. The reconfigurable approach is completed by analyzing a cutting edge design methodology known as dynamic partial reconfiguration and by reviewing some evolvable fuzzy hardware designs. Lastly, regarding fuzzy data-mining processing, the main proposals to speed up data-mining workloads are presented: multiprocessor architectures, reconfigurable hardware, and high performance reconfigurable computing.

INTRODUCTION

Electronic hardware development for fuzzy inference-based computing systems (fuzzy hardware) has been an active research area almost since the first papers on successful fuzzy logic applications, mainly fuzzy controllers, were published in the early eighties. Although historically, due to the greater flexibility and compatibility, as well as the advantages and easiness of using high level languages, the majority of fuzzy inference system (FIS) implementations have been software developments to be run on general purpose processors (GPP), only concurrent computation architectures with specific processing units

DOI: 10.4018/978-1-60566-858-1.ch001

can take greatest advantage of fuzzy computation schemes. The development of fuzzy hardware has been mainly motivated by real-time operation demands, or by low power and/or small area occupation requirements. In this sense, the first fuzzy hardware researchers basically tried to design fuzzy chips capable of processing fuzzy control laws in a more efficient manner in terms of processing speed, occupied area and consumed power. But not only is computing efficiency a concern for fuzzy hardware designers; system programmability, compatibility of input/output signals and scalability at various levels (word-length, partition of the input and output domains, number of rules, or overall throughput gain) are also important features to be considered.

Design of fuzzy hardware is strongly conditioned by the target application it is addressed to. In consequence, many different application-specific designs have been reported, each of them showing characteristic features, strengths and weaknesses. The choice of the development platform and implementation technology is closely linked with this issue, and may itself bias the obtainable final features. Despite this, implementation of a general purpose fuzzy ASIC (Application Specific Integrated Circuit) suitable for any fuzzy rule-based application has been somehow sought but never achieved by fuzzy hardware designers, both in academic and in commercial contexts. It has been the arrival of high capacity reconfigurable hardware and the drastic changes in the design processes of complex digital systems associated with this technology that has finally made obsolete the general purpose fuzzy hardware objective. Last generation reconfigurable hardware platforms allow the implementation of optimized complex hardware/software codesigned adaptive and on-the-fly reconfigurable systems for application specific computation. The combination of reconfigurable hardware with the use of standardized hardware description languages (HDL) has entailed the transference of the task of achieving desirable features such as flexibility, scalability, reusability, etc from the hardware itself to the description or modeling of this hardware.

Fuzzy data management and analysis methods do not rest normally on a rule-based inference scheme, so the development of hardware for fuzzy data-mining has usually little to do with what is referred to as "fuzzy hardware". In fact, fuzzy data-mining algorithms have been traditionally implemented by software applications running on GPPs, since there were not usually tight requirements for computation time, occupied silicon area or consumed power. On the contrary, flexibility, scalability and good interaction with data base storage systems were the only concerns. Nonetheless, nowadays, due to the increasing complexity of data-mining algorithms and the growing amount of data to be processed by them, sometimes with time constraints, more attention is being paid to the hardware acceleration of this kind of application. This field can be considered, together with scientific computation, a natural target for high performance computing (HPC). Consequently, specific hardware development for parallel processing or coprocessing of data-mining algorithms has been gaining relevance in recent years.

The chapter is organized as follows: Section 2 introduces the main hardware implementation variants performed since first fuzzy hardware chips were published and until the consolidation of reconfigurable hardware for complex digital system implementation. First of all, the distinctive characteristics of fuzzy inference-based computation that pushed researchers to find specifically designed hardware are described. Secondly we summarize the general pros and cons of the two main design approaches used for fuzzy hardware realizations, the digital approach and the analog approach; the performance indexes used for fuzzy hardware characterization are also briefly discussed. The bulk of the section follows by analyzing the different solutions proposed by hardware designers both for digital and analog approaches in a taxonomical way, giving examples of the most representative publications in the area. In Section 3 the evolution of fuzzy hardware implementations based on reconfigurable hardware and its relationship with the scalability issue are explained. A short description of the FPGA (Field Programmable Gate Array) technology and the repercussions of the development of hardware description languages are given, and the fruitful synergism between FISs and FPGAs are enumerated. The section continues with the description of the hardware/software codesign methodology and its contribution to the fuzzy hardware design, and introduces the associated concept of System on Programmable Chip (SoPC), giving examples of reported designs in this area. The Section is completed by analyzing the cutting edge design methodology known as Dynamic Partial Reconfiguration and by reviewing some evolvable fuzzy hardware designs, and is closed by highlighting the new trends and challenges to be faced by the reconfigurable hardware technology. Lastly, Section 4 is devoted to the hardware implementation proposals for fuzzy data-mining processing, as it presents very distinct characteristics and requirements compared to fuzzy rule-based inference systems. Section 5 concludes this chapter summing up the described main concepts and giving some concluding remarks.

HARDWARE IMPLEMENTATION OF FUZZY INFERENCE SYSTEMS

As mentioned in the introduction, design and implementation of a FIS strongly depends on the requirements of the target application. When the hardware implementation of a FIS is considered, this is due to the special requirements of computation time, occupied area and/or power consumption that the application to be performed may demand. Each application field of FISs has its own characteristics which condition the system design: process control, industrial automation, embedded control, signal processing, pattern recognition, or data analysis and decision making –when making use of fuzzy rule-based schemes– all share a common computational scheme but all show specific processing and interfacing requirement,. In order to understand the reasons that have pushed researchers to investigate new hardware architectures for fuzzy systems, it is worth to briefly analyzing the specificities of fuzzy computation.

Distinctive Characteristics of Fuzzy Computation

There are three main aspects of fuzzy computation that have motivated the design of ad-hoc hardware to overcome the limits imposed by the processing on general purpose processors: parallelism, use of specific non-standard operators, and the intensive computation of non-linear functions.

Parallelism: The typical three processing stages of a fuzzy inference, that is, fuzzification, inference, and defuzzification, are performed sequentially (see Figure 1). However, at each stage internal operations can be carried out in parallel. At the fuzzification stage parallelism is possible because several membership degrees at a time must be computed for an input value, and there may be more than one input. At the inference stage the computation of the degrees of truth of several rules are performed in parallel, since more than one rule may be activated at the same time. Finally, to compute the output value, which is usually crisp, the partial conclusions of the rules must be obtained from the consequents, and these values are combined to obtain the final general conclusion and the defuzzified value. GPPs are sequential machines, so all these operations are performed serially. It is obvious that the more input variables in the input domain and the more rules defined in the inference engine, the more time-consuming is a fuzzy inference in a sequential processor and the more worthwhile it is to parallelize it.

Specific non-standard operators: Fuzzy computing requires intensively performing some basic operations that cannot be efficiently executed by GPPs. Maximum and minimum operations and de-

Figure 1. Basic computational scheme of a fuzzy rule-based system

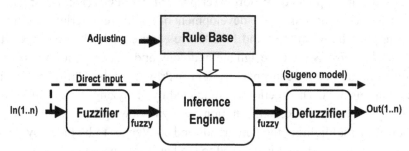

fuzzification functions, for instance, are very time-consuming on GPPs. While some software solutions have been proposed by adding new instructions implemented as microprograms to the microprocessors, implementation of dedicated fuzzy functional blocks is the most efficient solution regarding the computation time.

Computation of non-linear functions: Any fuzzy computing system is based on fuzzy logic theory, and the core concept of this logic is the concept of membership degree to a given set. To represent the membership degrees, fuzzy logic uses membership functions (MF), which are, in the most general case, monotone smooth non-linear functions such as sigmoidal functions, Gaussians, generalized bells and so on. The computation of such functions is very demanding for any processor and hence this has been one of the most analyzed aspects of fuzzy hardware design. In fact, to overcome this problem, many fuzzy hardware designs rested on simple triangular or trapezoidal membership function representations. This is a valid approach, as it is demonstrated that FISs keep their universal approximation property even when simple piecewise-linear (PWL) MFs are used (Castro, 1996), but this is a property based on an existence theorem that does not consider quantitative implications. For a given number of MFs and rules, the system's plasticity –capability of representing information– is degraded when using simple PWL MFs, so simpler MFs imply a more complex rule base (Basterretxea et al., 2007).

Hardware implementations must always be oriented to achieve maximum simplicity. There are of course some "tricks" that hardware designers have developed to adapt the computation of fuzzy algorithms to the characteristics of hardware technologies. Hardware engineers have often modified mathematical operations or other computational features to produce more hardware-friendly algorithms. Sometimes this means reducing the accuracy, in the sense that produced processing does not replicate exactly the underlying mathematical functions. This is the case of the diverse circuits designed for approximating the non-linear functions used to represent MFs, or the reduction of quantization levels when memory-based solutions are implemented. At other times accuracy is not affected but some limitations are imposed on the system, such as the allowed maximum overlapping degree of MFs or their configurability, for instance. Sometimes however, a closer and more detailed study of how an electronic circuit processes data can lead to discovering regularities that can be exploited, or ways to avoid useless or repetitive calculations, with no impact on computational accuracy or system flexibility. One example of this is the use of register files to store truth tables obtained from the computation of the degree of truth of an antecedent, since the same antecedent is usually repeated in several rules (Ascia & Catania, 1998). Another common example is a technique consisting in the implementation of "active rule detectors", that is, for each input, detecting which rules will be activated and which rules will produce no output (not active), so only those rules with a positive degree of truth in their antecedents are processed (see

Hamzeh et al., 2009 and references herein). Sometimes the search for hardware-friendly algorithms has pushed researchers to work on the mathematical basis of fuzzy logic, hence inducing the definition of new operators such as the operators used for piecewise-linear or -multilinear (PWM) fuzzy systems (Rovatti & Borgatti, 1997; Sasaki & Ueno, 1994), as well as parameterized defuzzification methods such as the height method, weighted fuzzy mean, Yager´s method, etc. (Baturone et al, 2000). In the next subsection we examine some of these design strategies, described by fuzzy hardware researchers in papers and books, the most significant of which are referenced in the text.

Hardware Design Strategies and Implementation Technologies

Traditionally there have been two main approaches to the implementation of FISs: using GPP based machines and the development of dedicated hardware. Obviously, using pure software solutions running on GPPs –microprocessors, microcontrollers or digital signal processors– is the least expensive and more flexible procedure, but generally it is the slowest one. On the contrary, the development of ad-hoc hardware for high performance fuzzy processing implemented in ASIC technology requires a longer design time and much more effort, in order to culminate in a faster system, although very often with poor generality. Halfway approaches are also possible though. One option is to customize GPPs by introducing fuzzy dedicated instructions, which sometimes is referred to as *software expansion*. Another option consists in splitting fuzzy operations from the CPU instruction-set and developing an external fuzzy coprocessor to execute those operations faster, which is called *hardware expansion*. The main problem in using fuzzy coprocessors is that the I/O signal transmission between the processor and the coprocessor is usually a bottleneck that impedes fast operation. This section is devoted to describing the most representative design solutions for dedicated fuzzy hardware reported in the last two decades, leaving the GPP-based approaches and the direct memory mapping-based implementations aside. However, each reported hardware design is unique, generally differing the ones from the others in various aspects, so it is not possible to make a complete catalogue of developed fuzzy processors over the years. Yet there are some common characteristics of different reported solutions that can be, and will be, emphasized and that allow us to make a somewhat taxonomical description of fuzzy hardware design.

The first fuzzy processing device was implemented in 1985 by Togai and Watanabe (1986), from the AT&T Bell laboratories. It was a digital VLSI chip with one input and one output capable of executing 250,000 FRPS (Fuzzy Rules Per Second) with no defuzzification. Previously Yamakawa had built the first analog fuzzy circuits based on bipolar transistors, but it was not until 1988 that he reported the first analog fuzzy controller chip (Yamakawa, 1988). The controller was implemented in bipolar technology and was capable of evaluating 1 Mega FIPS (Fuzzy Inference Per Second) including defuzzification, or 10 MFIPS without it. These two works represent, respectively, the beginning of the race to produce the fastest, smallest and/or the least power-consuming fuzzy chip in the two main design methodologies. These are directly linked to implementation technology: the analog hardware and the digital hardware. Both approaches have their own pros and cons, which are summed up below.

Digital FIS Hardware vs. Analog FIS Hardware

When facing the designing of fuzzy hardware, both in the analog and the digital approaches, some designers have developed very specific dedicated architectures with the aim of achieving the higher processing speed together with an efficient use of silicon for a given application. Other designers have tried to make more flexible, general purpose fuzzy chips. The more dedicated circuits implement quite simple computation algorithms on simple architectures. The more general application targeted circuits include programmability options by implementing different MF shape and/or inference method selection capabilities, various defuzzification methods and also scalability features to some extent (bit level scalability, MF level scalability, selectable number of rules etc.). In any case, the selection of the digital or the analog approach itself may bias the achievable features. The main characteristics of both approaches are:

Digital Hardware

- Use of well known and well characterized target technology.
- Structured and systematic design process and availability of EDA (Electronic Design Automation) tools to obtain reliable and lower cost integrated circuits.
- Connectivity to other digital processing conventional units.
- More flexible devices with easy programmability and external parameter selection.
- Adjustable accuracy and resolution.
- High area occupation. This is due to the big quantity of transistors required to implement fuzzy operators (max, min, etc.), the coded representation of the membership functions by bit sequences, and the probable need of A/D (Analog to Digital) and D/A (Digital to Analog) converters to transform the input and output signals.

Analog Hardware

- Better speed/area ratio.
- No need for A/D and D/A interfaces (controllers).
- Lower power dissipation.
- Analog design is a costly long-cycle, generally manual process, although some automated design tools have been developed (Lemaitre et al., 1993; Manaresi et al., 1996).
- Lower precision due to noise and temperature drifts.
- Lower flexibility.

Characterization of Fuzzy Hardware Performance

When referring to the performance of fuzzy hardware implementations we have used the term *speed*, but we have not defined exactly what the term speed means in this context. We have even used the more specific terms FIPS and FRPS, as the majority of authors do, in order to characterize their designs. However, different authors may use different performance indexes, and sometimes these indexes can be misleading when employed to compare the performance of systems with different architectures and functionalities. The most used performance indexes in the related literature are:

- Maximum clock frequency (digital and mixed signal designs).
- Number of fuzzy logic inferences per second (FLIPS) or fuzzy inferences per second (FIPS), where the concept *fuzzy inference* is fuzzy itself or ill-defined.

- Number of fuzzy rules per second (FRPS).
- Number of basic fuzzy operations per second.

None of these terms is a reliable measure of the real system performance, especially in the digital approach, as far as other factors such as the parallelism, the on-chip fuzzification or defuzification operations and others may be involved. In (Patyra et al., 1996) a more realistic speed measure is proposed to characterize any fuzzy hardware design. This index is the *input/output delay time* of the system –which is often used in analog designs–, defined as the total delay time from the moment of providing the input variable to the FIS device until the generation of a crisp action at the output[1]. But in order to make a performance comparison of different designs, more performance indexes have to be added to the bare processing speed. The author proposes the following set of index parameters:

- Number of inputs.
- Number of outputs.
- Number of linguistic rules in the knowledge base.
- Number of MFs in the input universe of discourse.
- Number of MFs in the output universe of discourse.
- Number of binary vectors characterizing the membership function (resolution of the input universe of discourse for digital designs).
- Number of bits in a single binary vector (resolution of the membership degree for digital designs).
- Input-to-output time delay.

This set of parameters, which was defined to make a comparative study of the state-of-the-art dedicated digital fuzzy logic controllers at the time of publication, summarizes perfectly the main architectural characteristics to be considered in the design of a fuzzy chip. To complete the picture, dissipated power should be also considered.

Digital Implementations

The first digital hardware realizations, such as the above mentioned pioneering work of Togai and Watanabe, used parallel rule processing architectures by providing a data path for each rule (Figure 2). This configuration allows fast operation but is very area consuming and imposes a maximum number of rules, so its scalability, in this sense, is limited. The provided fuzzy inference method was the max-min inference rule, so circuits for maximum and minimum operators were implemented. Max and min operations were performed serially to save silicon area, since the max-min operator structure had to be replicated for each rule. Membership functions were implemented by storing the function values in memory look-up tables. By using memories any membership function shape can be stored, but occupied memory grows exponentially with the resolution, and hence memories are only used with low resolutions. Obviously, decreasing the resolution in the discretization of the input values and the membership degrees negatively affects the system performance (del Campo & Tarela, 1999; del Campo et al. 2001). Moreover, in a parallel processing architecture the memory size required to store the MFs is proportional to the number of rules, so severe limitations were imposed on the processing engine.

Figure 2. Pure parallel implementation scheme of a three-input-one-output FIS with n rules (min-max operation blocks replicate the graphically depicted input processing). MFs are linked to the rules and stored individually for parallel processing.

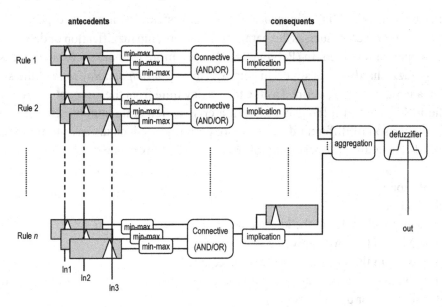

To overcome the above described limitations, many designers have implemented sequential rule processing architectures. Serialized architectures are more flexible but do not exploit all the parallelism of fuzzy systems and, since the number of clock-cycles required for processing the rules is proportional to the number of the latter, they are generally slower. The rule base is stored symbolically in a memory, and the generation of the membership functions is performed by circuitry that is shared by all the rules,

Figure 3. Serialized implementation scheme of a three-input-one-output FIS with single data-path for all rules (min-max operation blocks replicate the graphically depicted input processing). Rules are stored in memory using labels of antecedent and consequent MFs, and only one rule can be addressed every clock cycle.

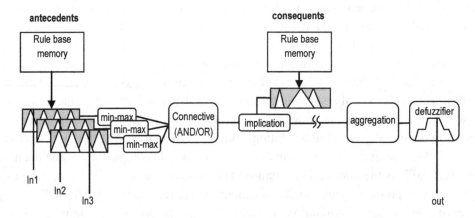

that is, there is a fuzzy partition of the universes of discourse for each input variable (Figure 3). For sequential fuzzy processors, memory size is still a problem for systems with a high input dimensionality (many input variables), as memory size grows exponentially with the dimensionality of the input domain. There have been proposed some alternative memory organization proposals that optimize memory usage and achieve a linear proportionality between memory size and input dimensionality (Eichfeld et al., 1992; Eichfeld et al., 1995; Hollstein et al., 1996), although these optimized organizations apply severe restrictions to the allowed MF overlapping degree.

Input Stage: Pure memory approach to the MF representation is very flexible, but is very memory demanding too. An alternative approach that saves memory resources consists in storing only some values that define the shape, usually piecewise-linear, of the MFs. These values may represent both the breakpoints and the slopes of the interpolating linear functions. The operations required to calculate a membership degree are usually a search of the domain segment the input value belongs to, and the computation of the linear function defined for each domain segment. The amount of linear functions needed to describe a MF is limited, and the more complex shape is wanted the more memory must be used to store the function parameters. There are very simple designs restricted to represent elementary Λ, S or Z shapes (Ascia et al., 1997), and other more developed implementations capable of representing more complex PWL functions (Eichfield, 1996; Halgamuge, 1994; Hollstein et al., 1996). The allowed overlapping between MFs is also a concern, but in any case, the required memory is much lower than for a look-up-table approach.

The drawback is the need for additional though quite simple, membership function circuits (MFC) to compute the membership degrees. The use of pure MFCs (circuits that directly compute the MF through an algorithm) to process the membership degrees in digital implementations, unlike in the analog approach, is quite rare. These circuits approximate, with adjustable accuracy and full programmability, continuous nonlinear functions like Gaussians, sigmoidals or generalized bells that boost the knowledge representation capability of the FISs with almost no memory cost (Basterretxea et al., 2002; Basterretxea et al., 2006).

Rule processing: A common strategy that improves the performance of serial processing architectures consists in evaluating only the active rules, that is, the rules with non-zero output. The active rules are detected after calculating the membership degrees of the antecedents or by comparing the input values with the supports of the MFs. When a non-zero fuzzified data is detected, the number of active MFs and their degrees of membership are saved. Then, an associative memory in which the rule antecedents address their consequents is accessed to retrieve the consequents of active rules. Any rule that shares a MF that is not activated by a system input will have a null output, so there is no need for it to be processed and computation time is saved. The active rule selection operation is critical for the active rule driven processors and different implementations have been reported. Some of them perform the detection of active rules in parallel with fuzzification (Weiwei et al., 2004), saving clock-cycles and reducing latency, but are static non-adaptable selectors for predefined MFs. In the majority of designs, hence, the selection begins late after fuzzification, as explained above (D'Amore et al., 2001; Ikeda et al., 1992; Watanabe et al., 1990). In (Ascia & Catania, 2000), an active rule selector that uses two fuzzification units to operate in parallel is described, obtaining a process two times faster than for simple selectors. Another limitation imposed by these designs is a severe restriction in MF overlapping, usually allowing the overlapping of just two MFs. Moreover, these selectors are not scalable in terms of the number of inputs, MFs or bit-width. Recently, some more sophisticated algorithms have been proposed to obtain fully scalable, faster and overlapping restriction-free active rule detectors (Hamez et al., 2008).

As an increase in the dimensionality of the input space causes an exponential growth in the complexity of the system when using grid partitions -this problem is known as the *curse of dimensionality*-, some designers have searched for alternative architectures in order to tackle this problem. This is the case of the above mentioned PWL and PWM fuzzy systems (Rovatti, 1998). In piecewise linear and multilinear systems the inference procedure is reformulated to have a complexity $O(n.\log n)$, being n the number of input variables. The underlying idea is a sort of active rule processing scheme applied to a restricted fuzzy modeling. Imposed restrictions are as follows: the MFs are triangular shaped, they are normalized, and they overlap in pairs. These constraints guarantee that, given an input vector, only two antecedents per input dimension provide non-zero activation values, so a corresponding "active cell" is defined in the input domain partition. Once this active cell is identified and its corresponding parameters loaded, a single inference kernel processes the output (del Campo et al., 2008; Rovatti et al., 1998;). Of course, this improvement in performance means storing many intermediate pre-computed results, so memory requirements are notably increased. Similar architectures are proposed in (Baturone et al., 1998; Vidal-Verdú et al., 1998) for mixed analog/digital fuzzy chips.

Output Stage: The last of the processing units in a FIS, that is, the defuzzification stage, is of main importance, as it is one of the most time-consuming operations. Generally speaking, defuzzification requires multipliers, adders, substracters, accumulators and a divider. There are many defuzzification methods proposed. The most common defuzzification method for hardware implementations is the Center-of-Area, but it is not very hardware-friendly itself –although not so time consuming as the more extended centroid of area–, so several alternatives to optimize the hardware have been proposed, usually with the aim of avoiding the multipliers (Watanabe et al., 1990) or the divider (Ruiz et al., 1995). In any case, defuzzification operations are not easily subject to rigorous mathematical analysis, so alternative non Mamdani-like fuzzy inference systems that do not employ fuzzy consequences, such us the very popular Sugeno-type fuzzy inference systems, have been widely used both in software and hardware implementations.

With the aim of simplifying the implementation of fuzzy operators and reduce occupied area, some researchers have worked on alternative representations of digital numbers that allow their serial processing. These are the so-called pulse-based techniques, including stochastic computation, pulse-width modulation and bit-serial arithmetic. In these alternative approaches, numbers are represented as streams of individual bits and system precision is controlled in time rather than in area. With the present gigahertz clock rates, it is possible to compute numbers serially with highly pipelined architectures and achieve good throughput while hardware complexity is dramatically reduced for high accuracy number representations –see (Dick et al., 2008) and references herein–. Depending on the representation, arithmetic operations like multiplication, probabilistic sums, and probabilistic negation in the stochastic representation, or maximum, minimum, and difference in pulse-width modulation are performed by simple two-input one-output logic gates. Bit-serial arithmetic operators are also much simpler than parallel-bit implementations. The major drawback of these approaches is the high clock frequencies required, only achievable by state of the art devices that may imply higher power consumption.

Analog Implementations

In spite of their design complexity and lower accuracy, analog realizations have sometimes been preferred for their high speed, low area, and low power consumption, mainly for highly parallel and high input/output dimensionality. Input-output delay times reported for various analog designs are as low as tenths

Figure 4. Current-mode analog fuzzy circuit examples: (a) transconductance membership function circuit, (b) max operator (concept diagram), (c) min operator (concept diagram). Analog circuits use much less transistors than their digital counterparts: an 8 bit resolution MF occupies 256 bytes of memory, and around 430 transistors are needed to implement an 8 bit MAX/MIN CMOS digital circuit.

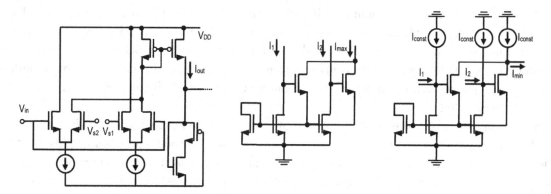

of microseconds (D'Amore et al., 2001; Peters et al., 1995), or even less –63 ns in (Amirkhanzdeh et al., 2005)–. As they process the fuzzy rules in parallel, time response does not depend on the complexity of the inference engine. When input signals are taken from sensors and output signals excite actuators, using fuzzy analog chips avoids the use of A/D and D/A converters, since the majority of sensors and actuators cope with analog signals. On the other hand, compared to the digital approach, analog designs are less efficient with regard to rearrangement and programmability, and show relatively low accuracy, although analog designers sometimes claim that this is not a severe limitation in view of the typical demands of fuzzy control applications.

The first analog fuzzy chips were designed by Yamakawa (1988) in bipolar technology. Analog design is much more "artistic" than digital design since it is less hierarchical and structured, and the same specifications can be reached in many different ways. Consequently, it is more difficult to make a taxonomical description of analog fuzzy chips, which are almost exclusively fuzzy controllers. In any case, in the continuous-time analog design framework, two main design styles can be distinguished: current-mode circuits and voltage-mode circuits. There are also some designs with transconductance blocks, which work with voltages as inputs and currents as outputs. Current-mode circuits appear to be the best suited option since basic fuzzy operations can be implemented with very few transistors. Adding and subtracting operations are simple wire connections, and multiple input maximum and minimum operators are also very simple circuits (Baturone et al., 1994; Lemaitre et al., 1994), as depicted in Figure 4. Another advantage of current-mode circuits is that they are capable of operating with very low voltage supplies. However, current-mode MFCs use current mirrors to replicate their outputs, as their fan-out is 1. From the technological point of view, most current-mode designs use MOS (Metal Oxide Semiconductor) transistors.

Voltage-mode circuits interface much better than current-mode circuits do with the majority of sensors and transductors, which usually have voltage-mode output signals. Another advantage is that the input and output signals of the circuits can drive various inputs at the same time with no need of additional circuitry. Voltage-mode fuzzy chips usually use transconductance-mode MFCs based on differential-pairs of transistors operating in weak inversion (Dick et al., 2008) or in strong inversion (Baturone et al. 1994 ; Guo et al., 1996; Landlot, 1996; Lemaitre et al., 1994; Ota & Wilamowski, 1996; Peters et al., 1995; Rojas et al., 1996; Ruiz et al., 1995;.Vidal-Verdú & Rodríguez-Vázquez, 1995) to produce smooth non-linear MFs, although there are some pure voltage mode designs, such as those circuits of Yamakawa (1993) implemented in bipolar technology. Some researchers have exploited the subthreshold operation mode of MOS transistors with floating gates to obtain very low consuming building blocks with the ability to store information in the MOSFET (MOS Field Effect Transistor) gates (Marshall & Collins, 1997). Voltage-mode designs are usually implemented with single ended amplifiers, resistors and capacitors (RC-Active), or with differential amplifiers and capacitors (MOSFET-C). Transconductance designs use OTAs (Operational Transconductance Amplifiers) and capacitors as basic building blocs. The OTA-based design is more structured, but it occupies more silicon area (Indue et al., 1991; Tsukano & Inoue, 1995).

An alternative to continuous-time analog design is the use of switched circuits or discrete-time circuits. The aim of switched circuits is to obtain a superior precision and better programmability compared to the classical analog designs, but maintaining a high processing speed with less area occupation and power consumption than a digital counterpart. Switched design is based on the use of a clock-signal to control the operation of switches, so the behavior of the circuit is controlled by the clock-period. A drawback of switched design is that basic operations are not implemented at transistor level, but with operational amplifiers or comparators, so the occupied silicon area is bigger. There are two main discrete-time analog design techniques: switched capacitors (SC), which are voltage-mode and switched current (SI), which are current-mode. Some discrete-time analog FIS implementations were published in the nineties (Huertas et al., 1993; Fattaruso et al., 1994; Çilingiroglu et al., 1997). Going further, hybrid analog/digital implementations such as those described in (Amirkhanzdeh et al., 2005; Baturone et al., 1997, Bouras et al., 1998; Miki & Yamakawa, 1995; Yosefi et al., 2007) have been presented as a good alternative to pure analog circuits, combining the strengths of both analog and digital approaches. In these designs, analog circuitry is used to perform a highly parallel fuzzy inference engine with low area, high speed and low power consumption, and digital circuitry is used to provide high programmability and long term storage for the system parameters.

SCALABILITY AND NEW TRENDS IN FUZZY HARDWARE

As is clear from the preceding section, a great research effort was dedicated in the decade of the 1980s and early 1990s to the design and implementation of fuzzy hardware. Many of those works were developed by means of ASIC technology with the aim of achieving high performance requirements for real-time applications. As exposed above, this technology is suitable to fit the specificities of fuzzy computation, but it suffers from several drawbacks such as low flexibility, long development cycles, and a complex design methodology that results in expensive solutions that rapidly become obsolete. However, the present situation of fuzzy hardware design is other than it was ten to fifteen years ago, as is the design of any other complex digital system. Nowadays flexible solutions for high-performance fuzzy computation may be easily developed and updated by means of user-friendly CAD (Computer Aided Design) tools. This is a consequence of the development of new hardware platforms and new design paradigms that have broaden the implementation choices by giving new freedom degrees and new tools to the design process.

With regard to the platforms, the use of reconfigurable hardware –mainly FPGAs– and the integration of whole digital systems –processors, dedicated circuits, memory and other peripherals– on a single chip (System on Chip or SoC) has narrowed the gap between general purpose hardware and dedicated hardware approaches, and between software and hardware. General-purpose fuzzy hardware implementations are rarely published nowadays, and there are no reports of new commercial fuzzy chips. Instead, ad-hoc solutions targeted to specific applications are designed and implemented on configurable hardware platforms. If the target application or its requirements change, the system is redesigned and rapidly implemented by reconfiguring the hardware. In this sense, the present availability of synthesizers based on standard HDLs enhance desired properties of hardware architectures such us *modularity*, *reusability* and *scalability*.

The scalability of a fuzzy system is closely related to the technology of reconfigurable hardware; it measures the ability of the system to improve its performance after adding hardware, proportionally to the new resources. This property is closely linked to the fraction of parallelism allowed by the algorithms and the availability of resources in the target platform. Concerning fuzzy computation, a scalable fuzzy system is efficient and practical when applied to complex situations such as multidimensional problems with a large number of membership functions and a large rule base. A useful tool in designing for scalability is the well known Amdahl's Law (Amdahl, 1967) which gives a measure of the speedup that can be achieved by exploiting parallel processing. It states that the maximum speedup that can be achieved by adding new functional modules to the parallelizable fraction of an algorithm is limited by the fraction of the calculation that is sequential. For instance, the inference algorithm in a FIS allows a certain degree of parallelism but it necessarily involves a fraction of serial computation (the same states for defuzzification algorithms). In summary, hardware designers have to carefully analyze the performance and scalability issues before making decisions about the system architecture. Finally, note that the scalability property, applied to electronic systems, is sometimes used to quantify specific requirements for a particular dimension such as load, precision, etc.

Reconfigurable Hardware

With the aim of better understanding the state-of-the-art in reconfigurable hardware for fuzzy computation, let us briefly introduce some background concepts concerning FPGA technology. An FPGA is a *semiconductor* device which can be configured by the user, after the chip is manufactured, to implement virtually any digital function as long as its available resources are adequate.

Figure 5 illustrates the general structure of a typical static random access memory (SRAM)-based FPGA. Most FPGAs consist of a matrix of configurable logic blocks (LBs), a configurable routing structure, and I/O blocks that drive the I/O pads of the chip. A circuit is implemented in the FPGA by programming each LB to implement a small part of the logic and by programming the routing structure to make the necessary connections between LBs, while the I/O blocks are programmed to operate as either input pads or output pads. The programming information is a string of '0' and '1' (bitstream) generated after automatic mapping of the design onto the FPGA. This information, commonly referred to as *configware*, is stored in SRAM cells during the configuration process of the device (the configuration memory is not shown in Figure 5). The actual circuit is easily updated by reconfiguring the device with a new bitstream.

The whole development cycle of FPGA solutions is supported by user-friendly CAD tools, developed by the vendors or third party companies, which dramatically reduce the development time. The inherent reconfigurability of FPGAs, without additional costs, eases system prototyping and architecture update. Although FPGAs cannot match ASICs in performance, the former delivers a better performance/cost

Figure 5. Structure of a typical SRAM-based FPGA

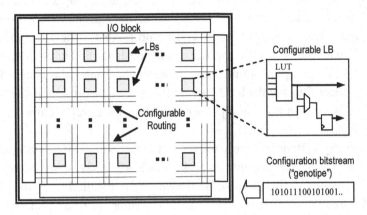

ratio than the latter whenever the parallelism can be exploited. Undoubtedly FPGAs outperform ASICs in terms of the flexibility (in a broad sense) and development time.

Reconfigurable Fuzzy Processing

Since first fuzzy chips based on FPGAs were reported in the literature in the early 1990s (Manzoul & Jayabharathi, 1994; Hossain & Manzoul, 1993), both the capacity and the performance of FPGA devices have been greatly improved due to the rapid evolution of microelectronic technology over the past years. Those preliminary works were devoted to the development of small scale fuzzy controllers, with no strict requirements in performance or in power dissipation. Most of them used simplified approaches, mainly look-up tables, to implement either the whole system or the most time-consuming operations (Hung & Zajak, 1995; Manzoul & Jayabharathi, 1994: Manzoul & Jayabharathi, 1995). To overcome the capacity limitations imposed by early FPGA technology, some researchers proposed the partition of the system functionality into multiple programmable devices –e.g. FPGAs and EPROMs (Erasable Programmable Read Only Memory)– (Hollstein et al., 1996; Hung & Zajak, 1995). In addition, FPGAs were also used at that time with prototyping purposes, as a previous step to the fabrication of ASIC fuzzy chips with better performance (Hossain & Manzoul, 1993).

Beside the technological evolution, FPGA design tools and methodologies have also evolved from a design flow based on schematics to a more flexible design flow centered on HDLs. Standard HDLs, namely VHDL and Verilog, are nowadays the most widely used mean to describe, simulate and synthesize digital circuits. With the integration of HDLs into the design flow, the reconfigurable approach has gained in flexibility, portability and scalability; HDL allows the designer to define generic and parameterizable architectures which can be easily resized and resynthetized. Therefore, the scalability problem associated with FPGA solutions has to do more with system modeling –i.e. HDL model– than with electronic design. Towards the middle of the 90s, some researchers began to exploit the benefits of HDL specifications to develop fuzzy hardware. Some of them went a step further by developing CAD tools, mainly based on VHDL, for rapid prototyping of fuzzy hardware (Hollstein et al., 1996; Kim, 2000). The ultimate goal of these tools is to fulfill the requirements of a wide range of applications in terms of fuzzy model type –fuzzy operators, inference mechanism, fuzzification and defuzzification strategies–, complexity –number of I/O variables and size of the rule base–, and performance.

However, despite the methodological advances introduced by HDLs in the past decade, large fuzzy systems still exceeded the size of a single device so they had to be split into several FPGAs. In this situation, another way to tackle the problem of capacity limitation was proposed: the *global run-time reconfiguration method* where the computation of the fuzzy system is divided into several temporally independent tasks (Kim, 2000). Each task is configured onto a single FPGA, one task at a time, while a memory board is used for storing the intermediate results between consecutive configurations. This work can be seen as the first precedent in the field of fuzzy computation of the method nowadays known as *partial run-time reconfiguration method.*

In the framework of present FPGA technology, previous drawbacks have been largely overcome and current technology provides a realistic approach to the development of hardware for high-performance fuzzy computation. Let us outline some significant examples. For instance, fuzzy logic has been successfully applied to controlling the behavior of mobile robots. In (Li et al., 2003) the authors present an FPGA-based car-like mobile robot which uses fuzzy rules to model the experience of a skilled driver to perform the parking task. Two FISs were implemented on a single FPGA of the Altera's FLEX family, one to control the steering angle and the other to control the speed of the car. Fuzzy hardware based on FPGAs has also been used in the field of image processing. In (Louverdis & Andreadis, 2003) the authors propose a fuzzy processor suitable for morphological color image processing. The processor is capable of performing the basic morphological operations of standard and soft erosion/dilation for color images with 24-bit resolution. The prototype (54 rules) was implemented on a FLEX10K device of Altera and provided a performance of 601 KiloFLIPS with a typical clock frequency of 65 MHz. A survey of FPGA-based intelligent controllers for modern industrial systems can be found in (Monmasson & Cirstea, 2007). This review includes the implementation of a fuzzy controller for a synchronous stand-alone generator. The proposed design aims to improve the efficiency of diesel-engine-driven generators by allowing optimum speed operation. The fuzzy controller was modeled and simulated using VHDL and the prototype was synthesized and implemented into a low-cost Xilinx XC4010 FPGA. This solution greatly improved the control performance while keeping a high level of flexibility. Finally, another perspective of the suitability of FPGA to develop fuzzy computation is provided in (Chowdhury et al., 2008). This work presents the development of a smart processing FIS for clinical diagnostic applications in rural areas of Third World countries. The authors point out that FPGA technology is very useful in these countries due to low investment, portability, short design cycle and the scope of reprogrammability for improvement without any additional cost. The whole system has been realized on an Altera's Cyclone II chip which can be interfaced with a wireless transceiver and other telecommunication media for telediagnostic applications.

The Synergism between FISs and FPGAs

Summing up, in addition to the well known advantages of FPGAs, there are several specific advantages of reconfigurable hardware technology that make it specially suited to implementing real-time scalable fuzzy algorithms:

• Some FPGA families (e.g. Xilinx's Virtex family) incorporate internal RAM blocks to the generic structure depicted in Figure 5. These memory blocks are very useful for implementing large fuzzy systems because of the huge amount of information involved in the definition of membership functions and rules that demands large on-chip memory resources. Distributed RAM blocks are also useful for mapping memory-based approximations.

- The availability of a dense and flexible interconnection architecture (i.e. configurable routing in Figure 5) fits the requirements of high performance FISs. Most fuzzy models can be viewed as a layered structure, similar to an artificial neural network, where each layer consists of several parallel processing units densely connected with the neighboring layers. The interconnection scheme of such systems requires high flexibility in the segmentation of the routing paths to avoid additional propagation delays.
- Modern FPGA families include higher level functionalities, such as multipliers or generic DSP (Digital Signal Processing) blocks, embedded into the silicon. These resources are very useful for implementing both the inference engine (e.g. Sugeno type fuzzy inferences) and the defuzzification stage because they are faster and occupy less area compared to if building them from primitives.
- The capacity of FPGAs has increased according to Moore's Law since the first families appeared on the market, so, even very large fuzzy systems (e.g. data mining applications) may soon be implemented on a single FPGA, provided that the architecture is scalable enough.
- Rapid prototyping on FPGAs is a useful feature in developing for scalability. Reconfigurable devices and tools allow the designer to develop fuzzy systems with different sizes and compare the achieved performance in order to experimentally verify the scalability of the architecture.

In what follows we will continue to uncover potential advantages of FPGAs for fuzzy computation, especially those concerning the latest advances in reconfigurable technologies.

Hardware/Software Codesign

In the last decade new design methodologies and tools have emerged to deal with the challenges of new electronic platforms. In this sense, hardware/software (HW/SW) codesign (De Micheli, 1997; Wolf, 2003) has been proposed as an optimal solution for many systems where a trade-off between versatility and performance is required. This approach proposes the partition of the computation algorithms into HW and SW blocks by searching for the partition that optimizes the performance parameters of the whole system. A recent work in the field of fuzzy computation (Cabrera et al., 2004) concludes that HW/SW solutions, with an adequate partition, can often outperform classical solutions, based either on HW or SW, for designing high-speed and low-consumption fuzzy control systems. In this work the authors implement the inference mechanism and a simplified defuzzification method in the hardware partition whereas the remaining tasks (initialization, I/O processing, etc) are implemented in software. On the basis of this partition of tasks, the authors present two HW/SW prototypes: i) a medium complexity FPGA interfaced with an external microcontroller, and ii) a single Xilinx's Spartan2 FPGA with an embedded microcontroller core. The main advantage of the second approach, where all the parts of the fuzzy system are integrated in a single chip, is the direct interfacing of HW and SW modules with the consequent savings in I/O delays and hardware resources.

Meanwhile, a milestone in the evolution of reconfigurable hardware has been to combine the logic blocks and interconnects of traditional FPGAs (logic fabric) with embedded microprocessors and related peripherals to form a system-on-a-programmable chip (SoPC). Some examples are the Excalibur family of Altera (Altera Corp., 2002) which incorporated an ARM processor core, and the Virtex-II Pro, Virtex-4, and Virtex-5 families manufactured by Xilinx, which include one or more *PowerPCs* embedded within the logic blocks (Xilinx Inc., 2008a). A similar approach, but less efficient in terms of area and performance, consists in using soft-processor *cores* instead of hard-cores that are implemented within the FPGA logic; two widely used soft-cores are the Xilinx's MicroBlaze (Xilinx Inc., 2008b) and the Altera's NIOS processors (Altera corp., 2008). These new features of reconfigurable hardware have been exploited to develop a new enhanced generation of fuzzy systems.

The analysis of the above mentioned works shows that to obtain efficient HW/SW architectures the regular and recurrent computations have to be implemented in the hardware partition and the irregular or less frequent computations are better suited to a software development (see Figure 6). For example, the implementation of a PWL fuzzy controller using a SoPC of the Altera's Excalibur family has been reported in (Echevarría et al., 2005). The system is a three-input single-output PID (Proportional-Integral-Derivative) fuzzy controller with a cellular architecture. The main processing blocks of the proposed architecture are a hyperplane generator and a preprocessing module. On the one hand, since the hyperplane generator is a typical sum of products, it has been efficiently implemented in the hardware partition. On the other hand, the preprocessing module, which involves a sorting algorithm, has been developed by simple software procedures. The ARM processor operates up to 200 MHz and the hyperplane unit performs the evaluation of the output in only two clock cycles with a maximum frequency of 84 MHz. Another approach to SoPC-based fuzzy computation can be found in (Sánchez-Solano et al., 2007) where a complete design methodology and tool chain is presented. The proposed design flow combines standard FPGA implementation tools with a specific environment (*Xfuzzy*) for the development of fuzzy controllers as IP (Intellectual Property) modules. The design flow has been used to develop a fuzzy controller, on a Xilinx's Spartan device, for solving the navigation tasks of an autonomous vehicle. 60% of the FPGA resources are dedicated to implementing the MicroBlaze soft core and its associated components, and the remaining 40% corresponds to the fuzzy inference IP core. Both the processor and the fuzzy core operate with a 50 MHz clock; the fuzzy core completes one inference in 16 clock cycles.

However, the impact of using configurable hardware and HW/SW codesign techniques is greater when hybrid systems, based on the synergism of fuzzy logic and other computational intelligence tech-

Figure 6. HW/SW co-design for fuzzy computation: a SoPC-based solution

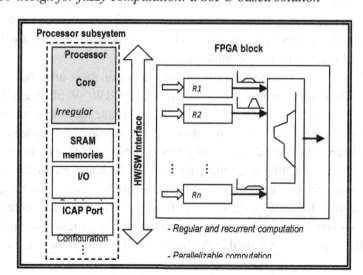

niques (mainly neural networks), are considered. Hybrid neuro-fuzzy systems combine typical fuzzy systems with the learning algorithms of neural networks. The latter are used to adapt parameters of the fuzzy system as membership functions or rules. A few years ago, Reyneri (2003) performed an in-depth analysis of the implementation issues of neuro-fuzzy hardware. This work points out the limitations, advantages and drawbacks of different implementation techniques and draws attention to HW/SW code-sign as the most promising research area concerning the implementation of neuro-fuzzy systems, since it allows the fast design of complex systems with the highest performance/cost ratio. Recently, several publications account for HW/SW solutions for neuro-fuzzy computation (del Campo et al., 2008, Kung & Tsai, 2007; Reyneri & Renga, 2004).

In (del Campo et al., 2008) an efficient HW/SW implementation of an adaptive neuro-fuzzy system based on a SoPC is presented. The Excalibur device family, which embeds an ARM processor core, has been used to prototype a neuro-fuzzy architecture. The microprocessor performs the learning algorithm (gradient-descent method plus least-square estimator) and the I/O data processing, while a Sugeno-type inference algorithm is implemented in the FPGA logic fabric. The main motivation to develop a hetero-geneous HW/SW solution is the nature of neuro-fuzzy algorithms: the embedded processor provides flexibility and high precision to implement the learning algorithms, while the logic fabric allows the development of parallel hardware for high-speed fuzzy inferences. Along the same line is the adaptive fuzzy controller for speed control of a permanent magnet synchronous motor drive developed in (Kung & Tsai, 2007). The authors argued that the modules requiring fast processing but simple computation are suitable to be implemented by hardware, whereas control algorithms with heavy computation can be realized by software. They selected a device of the Altera's Cyclone family and a soft processor core, the NIOS II IP core, to develop the prototype.

Another recent proposal in HW/SW fuzzy computation is the context switchable fuzzy inference chip (Qao et al., 2006). The authors have developed a reconfigurable fuzzy inference chip (RFIC) on a Virtex II FPGA which allows for online changes in the rules. The RFIC uses a formatted memory map to encode the fuzzy relational knowledge and the inference model. Any change in the rules (context switch) is achieved via a loadable register, so there is no need to reconfigure the FPGA. A remarkable feature of this work is the suitability of the RFIC to develop evolvable fuzzy hardware. The block architecture suggested by the authors consists of the RFIC as fuzzy processing unit and an evolution module that generates the new context. The evolution module (i.e. genetic algorithms) can be developed by using a processor core. If the architecture is developed as a SoPC, it supports intrinsic hardware evolution (real hardware is used during the evolutionary process). The potentiality of this trend will be analyzed later after introducing partial reconfiguration techniques.

Although HW/SW solutions enhance reconfigurable hardware, there are also a few drawbacks that have to be considered. The main drawback is the bottleneck of the HW/SW interface. The communication overload between the microprocessor and the HW block can reduce the whole system performance. To avoid this problem, the transfer rate of data and parameters has to be high enough to take advantage of the parallelism of hardware. The limited bandwidth of the HW/SW interface is also an important obstacle in designing for scalability, no matter what the scalability of the hardware or the software may be. In this sense, a different kind of architecture known as network-on-chip (NOC) has been proposed recently to deal with the communication problem in an efficient way. NOCs feature a router-based network for on-chip communication among different cores (i.e. processor cores, memories and specific IP cores). This emerging paradigm, as yet unexploited in the field of fuzzy computation, is suitable for the design of reconfigurable fuzzy systems with a high level of parallelism, better performance and enhanced scalability in comparison with a conventional bus-based architecture.

Dynamic Partial Reconfiguration

Dynamic partial reconfiguration is a new design methodology for reconfigurable hardware that consists in the ability to reconfigure selected parts of an FPGA anytime after its initial configuration while the device is still active (run-time reconfiguration). Potential advantages of partial reconfiguration for fuzzy hardware are multiple: self-reconfiguration, adaptability, scalability, reduction of power dissipation, and reduction of device size, among others.

The most popular partially reconfigurable architecture is the Virtex II series of Xilinx. These SRAM-based FPGAs have a fine-grained architecture, similar to that depicted in Figure 5, but improved with the addition of RAM blocks and hardware multipliers. Parts of the hardware on the reconfigurable device can be changed at run-time by reprogramming only selected SRAM cells of the configuration memory, while all other parts stay unaffected and operative. The device has different internal and external reconfiguration interfaces of which the internal configuration access port (ICAP) is of particular interest because it is accessible from the components within the FPGA (see Figure 6). Thus, a processor core embedded in the FPGA can be used to control the internal configuration port during run-time. Since the system itself decides to load new configuration data and initiates the reconfiguration task, this reconfiguration style is known as *self-reconfiguration*. The above ideas have inspired the development of new approaches for fuzzy computation, the evolution of reconfigurable hardware being the most innovative.

The configuration bitstream of a FPGA determines the function implemented by each logic block and each interconnection switch (see Figure 6). Adaptation of the circuit functionality is achieved by modifications in the bitstream, in the same way that evolution of living beings is accomplished by modification in the DNA strings. In this sense, there is an analogy between the bitstream in a FPGA and the genetic sequence in living beings that has pushed researchers to apply the principles of artificial evolution to reconfigurable hardware design. Concerning FPGA, evolvable fuzzy hardware uses genetic algorithms for searching for a bitstream (i.e. genome) that configures the device with a circuit that satisfies the design specification. Upegui (2005) proposes three methodologies for evolving hardware by means of dynamic partial reconfiguration of the Virtex II family. Each methodology is related to a different level of abstraction and granularity in the elementary components used to evolve the circuit: modular evolution, node evolution, and bitstream evolution.

Node evolution methodology has been applied to evolve fuzzy computation hardware in the pioneering work by Mermoud et al. (2005). They use the *difference-based reconfiguration flow* (Eto, 2007) where the designer is able to change the configuration of FPGA components such as LUTs (Look-Up Tables), multiplexers, RAM blocks or I/O resources. After the modifications have been performed, a partial bitstream can be generated including only the differences between the initial and modified bitstream. Since only a limited number of bits are changed, the reconfiguration time is considerably reduced if compared with the reconfiguration of a full bitstream. In this application, system evolution implies the modification of LUT functions. The proposed implementation co-evolves two species (i.e. MFs and rules) in a 4-input single-output FIS with 3 triangular MFs per input and a total of 20 rules. The genome describing the FIS consists of two individuals; the first one encodes the vertices of the triangular antecedents while the second one encodes the connections between the antecedents and the rules, the fuzzy operators and the consequents. The genome encoding is a key feature of the scalability of the system; it can be easily extended to increase the number of inputs and/or rules of the FIS. The main drawback of this solution is that each partial bitstream has to be generated externally by the FPGA vendor tool. However, to overcome this limitation, the authors are refining the implementation in order to allow on-chip evolution (Upegui, 2006). Performing on-chip evolution on FPGAs is a promising trend for fuzzy computation and adaptable systems, however, there is still much research effort to be done in this area.

HARDWARE FOR FUZZY DATA-MINING

Fuzzy data-mining techniques such as fuzzy clustering or fuzzy decision-tree algorithms are not fuzzy rule-based processing schemes. In fact these algorithms are used to find structure in raw data, so very often are useful for generating fuzzy rules not from expert knowledge but from non-directly interpretable data sets. Hence, hardware design for fuzzy data-mining algorithm processing, except for the possible need of input fuzzification or the use of common fuzzy operators such us max or min, has little to do with the systems previously analyzed in this chapter. In any case, data-mining algorithms have been traditionally implemented by software applications running on GPPs, since flexibility, scalability and good interface with data-bases is more important for these systems than computation time, area or power consumption. However, due to the increasing amount of data to be processed by data-mining algorithms and the more and more frequent high speed processing specifications, the hardware development for parallel processing or coprocessing of data-mining algorithms is gaining relevance. A few papers and reports on hardware design and implementations for fuzzy data-mining algorithms speed up have seen the light in the last few years, mainly related to fuzzy clustering algorithms. Let us review some of them in this section.

Multiprocessor architectures: One of the characteristics of data-mining algorithms to be exploited for process acceleration is their intrinsic parallelism, so the first steps to speed up data-mining applications have been oriented to algorithm parallelization. The main data-mining algorithms, fuzzy set theory-based ones included, have been investigated with the aim of speeding up their processing: association rule-based (Agrawal & Shafer, 1996; Shen et al., 1999), decision trees (Kubota et al., 2000) and fuzzy decision trees (Kim et al., 1999), clustering (Boutsinas & Gnardellis, 2002), and fuzzy clustering (Modenesi et al., 2007; Rahimi et al., 2004). The hardware implementation of the parallelized algorithms has been performed in various manners using conventional processors, such as by using distributed memory (Modenesi et al., 2007; Xu et al., 2003) or shared memory multiprocessor architectures (Jin et al., 2005; Modenesi et al., 2007; Syeda et al., 2002;), or in grid environments (Cannataro et al., 2004). All of them report good scalability figures.

Regarding fuzzy data-mining algorithms, in (Modenesi et al., 2007) for instance, a fuzzy C-means-based parallel cluster analysis is performed in two multiprocessor architectures: a PC cluster and a multiprocessor machine. Unlike in previous published parallel implementations, where only strategies to distribute the iterative process to find cluster centers are considered, this work describes how to parallelize the entire cluster analysis, including the determination of cluster centers and the optimal number of clusters by computing a cluster validity index. This is an iterative process where the clustering algorithm is computed for a range of number of clusters and the performance index is computed for every partition generated. When all partitions have been computed, the partition corresponding to the maximum performance index is chosen. The algorithm begins by splitting the data equally among the available processors. Each processor computes de geometrical center of its local data and communicates this center to a master processor, which sets the initial centers and broadcasts them so that all processors have the same centers values at the beginning of the fuzzy C-means clustering algorithm. After convergence is achieved in a processor, a distance factor needed to calculate the global validity index is computed in its local data and this value is sent to the master, where the validity index is calculated and stored. If the range of number of clusters is covered, the algorithm stops, otherwise returns to the set of initial centers performed by the master processor. This whole procedure is repeated as many times as the desired range of number of clusters to obtain the partition with the best performance index. The authors conclude that the bigger the datasets are, the more variables implied and the more number of clusters to be generated, the higher the speeding up of the algorithm in multiprocessor computation is, that is, it behaves in a scalable manner.

The same research team has investigated a multiprocessor based parallelization of fuzzy rule based classifiers by deriving a fuzzy rule based classifier for each input variable to aggregate the partial conclusions into a global one (Evsukoff et al., 2005). In this case, a single variable classifier is assigned to a different processor in a parallel architecture, and partial conclusions are synchronized and processed by a master processor. This approach is applied to a very large database and results are compared with a parallel neural network architecture.

Reconfigurable hardware: In recent years some efforts have been focused on designing ad-hoc hardware accelerators to speed up data-mining workloads. As clustering algorithms are, to some extent, data streaming applications, experimentation on their implementation on data streaming targeted off-the-shelf hardware can be found, as in (Harris, 2005), where a fuzzy C-means adaptive algorithm is programmed on a commercial graphic processing unit. With the maturing of FPGA technology, researchers working on intensive data-mining applications immediately became aware of the benefits of exploiting the fine-grain parallelism and scalability easiness of reconfigurable logic devices as hardware coprocessors: exploring the properties of a FPGA coprocessor system in the domain of query processing for computation-intensive data mining applications (Leung et al., 1999), implementing clustering algorithms on reconfigurable fabrics (Baker & Prasanna, 2005; Estlick et al., 2001), improving the data transfers for large data sets (Zhang et al., 2004) or developing text mining IP-cores for FPGAs (Freeman & Jayasooriya, 2006) . In (Choundary et al., 2007), for instance, the authors describe a generic data-mining system architecture that can be customized for specific applications. This is achieved by implementing kernels with very time-consuming data-mining specific calculations on reconfigurable hardware (FPGAs). Once the critical kernels of various data-mining algorithms are identified, specific hardware can be implemented to process them in a processor/coprocessor architecture. Since kernels remain the same for a given application, the required logic can be loaded before the process begins by programming the FPGA. In the case study performed by these researchers, the fuzzy C-means is one of the analyzed algorithms. The kernels identified as critical for this algorithm are the clustering process, the distance calculation and the fuzzy sum. Ad-hoc hardware logic for these kernels is designed and programmed in a FPGA. The system has been tested with datasets of various sizes, and it has been observed that the bigger the dataset the bigger the improvement in the speed up. The authors report overall speed ups from 11x to 80x in the fuzzy C-means algorithm. Besides this, the experimental results strongly suggest that the designed system is scalable.

High performance reconfigurable computing: A relatively new and very promising research field on high performance computing that can be naturally targeted to intensive and/or real-time data-mining applications is the one known as high performance reconfigurable computing (HPRC). HPRC combines parallel processing theory and techniques used in high end supercomputers and computer clusters with state-of-the-art hardware acceleration devices, such as the most advanced FPGAs. These systems are able to exploit coarse-grained functional parallelism as well as the fine-grain parallelism intrinsic to the FPGA internal architectures (Buell et al., 2007). Nearly all major high performance computing vendors such as SRC Computers (SRC-7family), Cray (XR1) or Silicon Graphics (RASC Technology) now have HPRC highly scalable product lines, reflecting a clear belief in the huge potential of reconfigurable computing. The first parallel-computing architectures including FPGAs were not designed to be scalable, but recent HPRC computers use stackable crossbar switches connected to parallel buses that allow for implementing different, highly scalable topologies. Commercial firms such as Nallatech, for instance, have introduced a family of scalable cluster optimized FPGA HPRC products to either upgrade existing HPC cluster environments or to build new clusters with off-the-shelf FPGA computing technology (Cantle, 2006).

Some vendors like Exegy have developed specific data mining targeted systems by combining software with reconfigurable hardware to produce applications that perform at hardware processing speeds, while retaining the flexibility of software (Dutcher, 2006). Exegy claims its systems have virtually zero latency and near linear throughput gains by adding appliances (linear scalability). For the highest performance systems, where I/O band and FPGA interface latency requirements are higher than standard parallel buses (PCIx) can offer, specific solutions for data I/O management are implemented. Some examples are Silicon Graphics' RASC blade technology and NUMAlink® interconnect with its Scalable System Port solution, SRC's Hi-Bar Switch for its SRC-7 family, and Cray's SeaStar2+ for its XR1 Reconfigurable Processing Blade. HPRC provides performance increases that are often of orders of magnitude compared to scalar microprocessors-only-based solutions. In addition, power consumption per gigaflop (floating-point operation per second) is dramatically reduced, form factors are diminished, and the overall price/performance ratio is notably lower. All these promising features make us think HPRC will soon be a preferred option for cutting edge fuzzy (and non-fuzzy) data-mining algorithm processing of large data-bases.

CONCLUDING REMARKS

In this chapter we have seen that electronic hardware design for fuzzy computing has been a very active research field during the last twenty years, beginning early after the first successful applications of fuzzy inference systems were published. Specificity of fuzzy processing computational characteristics combined with high speed, small area, and/or low power requirements have pushed designers to investigate into new hardware implementations to obtain high performance fuzzy ASICs targeted to specific applications, which generally have been fuzzy controllers. Both the digital approach and the analog approach have been followed in the design process, producing fuzzy chips with distinctive performance characteristics, strengths and weaknesses. However, in the last decade the number of reported works on FIS analog implementations has suffered a progressive decay that clearly shows a loss of interest in this technology for applications in this area. This tendency is closely related to the never ending and comparatively much faster advances in digital technologies, and more precisely, to the rapid development of digital reconfigurable devices and the associated drastic changes in design and implementation methodologies.

The consolidation of reconfigurable hardware, particularly FPGA technology, together with the standard use of hardware description languages for digital system modeling have revolutionized the field of digital system design in many areas, particularly in fuzzy hardware design. New design methodologies such as the hardware/software codesign, and bioinspired techniques such as the genetic algorithms have produced novel and more efficient and flexible hardware designs and have broadened the research perspectives in this field:

- HW/SW co-design techniques, applied to the development of SoPCs, make it possible to implement a complete fuzzy inference system, including system peripherals, on a single chip with the consequent savings in size, cost and power consumption.
- Several present applications of fuzzy computation require enhanced capabilities to deal with complex problems. This feature involves the hybridization of the fuzzy algorithm with other techniques poorly suited for hardware implementation. Thus, the heterogeneity (HW/SW) of SoPCs is tailored to the computational demands of hybrid fuzzy systems.
- Current design methodologies for FPGAs promote the use of soft IP cores (i.e. netlist or HDL) as building blocks for complex hardware design. The availability of reliable and previously tested IP cores addresses the needs for rapid prototyping, design reuse and scalability.
- Partial hardware reconfiguration is emerging as a promising solution to enhance digital fuzzy hardware with the capability of self-adaptation. Although this technology is not yet mature, it is expected that over the next few years FPGA manufacturers improve design tools to fully support dynamic partial reconfiguration.

Hardware design for fuzzy data-mining, which traditionally has been implemented on general purpose machines, has become the object of investigation in the last few years as a consequence of the huge amount of data to be processed and the more frequent requirements for high speed applications. On the one hand, various hardware coprocessors for speeding up data-mining algorithms have been recently published. On the other hand, recent advances in high performance reconfigurable computing foretell a very promising outlook for low cost, high performance, linearly scalable data-mining processing environments. Nevertheless, there are still some challenges for HPRC applications that must be faced: double-precision floating-point performance, memory bandwidth and ease of use of development tools for HPC programmers not familiarized with electronic engineering computing EDA tools are some of these.

REFERENCES

Agrawal, R., & Shafer, J. C. (1996). Parallel mining of association rules. *IEEE Transactions on Knowledge and Data Engineering, 8*(6), 962–969. doi:10.1109/69.553164

Altera Corporation. (2002). *Excalibur device overview (ver 2.0, May 2002), data sheet*. Retrieved December 1, 2008, from http://www.altera.com/literature/ds/ds_arm.pdf

Altera Corporation. (2008). *NIOS II processor reference handbook (ver 8.1, Nov 2008)*. Retrieved December 1, 2008, from http://www.altera.com/literature/lit_nio2.jsp

Amdahl, G. M. (1967). Validity of the single processor approach to achieving large scale computing capabilities. In *Proceedings of the AFIPS spring joint computer conference* (Vol. 30, pp. 483-485).

Amirkhanzdeh, R., Khoei, A., & Hadidi, Kh. (2005). A mixed-signal current-mode fuzzy logic controller. [AEÜ]. *International Journal of Electronics and Communications*, *59*, 177–184. doi:10.1016/j. aeue.2004.11.019

Ascia, G., & Catania, V. (1998). A parallel processor architecture for real-time fuzzy applications. In A. Kandel, & G. Langholz (Eds.), *Fuzzy hardware architectures and applications* (pp. 182-196).

Ascia, G., & Catania, V. (2000). A pipeline parallel architecture for a fuzzy inference processor. In *Proceedings of the Ninth IEEE International Conference on Fuzzy Systems* (pp. 257-262).

Ascia, G., Catania, V., Ficili, G., Palazzo, S., & Panno, D. (1997). A VLSI Fuzzy expert system for real-time traffic control in ATM networks. *IEEE transactions on Fuzzy Systems*, *5*(1), 20–31. doi:10.1109/91.554444

Baker, Z. K., & Prasanna, V. K. (2005). Efficient parallel data mining with the apriori algorithm on FPGAs. In *Proceedings of the 13th IEEE Symposium on Field-Programmable Custom Computing Machines* (pp. 3-15).

Basterretxea, K., Tarela, J. M., & del Campo, I. (2002). Digital design of sigmoid approximator for artificial neural networks. *Electronics Letters*, *38*(1), 35–37. doi:10.1049/el:20020008

Basterretxea, K., Tarela, J. M., & del Campo, I. (2006). Digital Gaussian membership function circuit for neuro-fuzzy hardware. *Electronics Letters*, *42*(1), 44–46. doi:10.1049/el:20063712

Basterretxea, K., Tarela, J. M., del Campo, I., & Bosque, G. (2007). An experimental study on non-linear function computation for neural/fuzzy hardware design. *IEEE Transactions on Neural Networks*, *18*(1), 266–283. doi:10.1109/TNN.2006.884680

Baturone, I., Barriga, A., & Sánchez-Solano, S. (1994). Current-mode multiple-input maximum circuit. *Electronics Letters*, *30*(9), 678–680. doi:10.1049/el:19940510

Baturone, I., Barriga, A., Sánchez-Solano, S., & Huertas, J. L. (1998). Mixed-signal design of a fully parallel fuzzy processor. *Electronics Letters*, *34*(5), 437–438. doi:10.1049/el:19980392

Baturone, I., Barriga, A., Sánchez-Solano, S., Jiménez-Fernández, C. J., & López, D. R. (2000). *Microelectronic design of fuzzy-logic-based systems*. Boca Raton, FL: CRC Press LLC.

Baturone, I., Sánchez-Solano, S., Barriga, A., & Huertas, J. L. (1997). Implementation of CMOS fuzzy controllers as mixed-signal integrated circuits. *IEEE transactions on Fuzzy Systems*, *5*(1), 1–19. doi:10.1109/91.554443

Bouras, S., Kotronakis, M., Suyama, K., & Tsividis, Y. (1998). Mixed analog-digital fuzzy logic controller with continuous-amplitude fuzzy inferences and defuzzification. *IEEE transactions on Fuzzy Systems*, *6*(2), 205–215. doi:10.1109/91.669017

Boutsinas, B., & Gnardellis, T. (2002). On distributing the clustering process. *Pattern Recognition Letters*, *23*, 999–1008. doi:10.1016/S0167-8655(02)00031-4

Buell, D., El-Ghazawi, T., Gaj, K., & Kindratenko, V. (2007). High-performance reconfigurable computing. *IEEE Computer*, 23-27.

Cabrera, A., Sánchez-Solano, S., Brox, P., Barriga, A., & Senhadji, R. (2004). Hardware/software codesign of configurable fuzzy control system. *Applied Soft Computing, 4*(3), 271–285. doi:10.1016/j.asoc.2004.03.006

Cannataro, M., Congiusta, A., Pugliese, A., Talia, D., & Trunfio, P. (2004). Distributed data mining on grids: Services, tools, and applications. *IEEE Transactions on Systems, Man and Cybernetics . Part B, 34*(6), 2451–2465.

Cantle, A. (2006). Scalable cluster-based FPGA HPC system solutions. *Xcell Journal*, (58), 35-37.

Castro, J. L. (1996). Fuzzy logic controllers are universal approximators. *IEEE Transactions on Systems, Man, and Cybernetics, 25*(4), 629–635. doi:10.1109/21.370193

Choudhary, A., Narayanan, R., Özisikyilmaz, B., Memik, G., Zambreno, J., & Pisharat, J. (2007). Optimizing data mining workloads using hardware accelerators. In *Proc. of the 10ʰ Workshop on Computer Architecture Evaluation Using Commercial Workloads (CAECW)*.

Chowdhury, S. R., Chakrabarti, D., & Saha, H. (2008). FPGA realization of a smart processing system for clinical diagnostic applications using pipelined datapath architectures. *Microprocessors and Microsystems, 32*(2), 107–120. doi:10.1016/j.micpro.2007.12.001

Çilingiroglu, U., Pamir, B., Günay, Z. S., & Dülger, F. (1997). Sampled-analog implementation of application-specific fuzzy controllers. *IEEE transactions on Fuzzy Systems, 5*(3), 431–442. doi:10.1109/91.618278

D'Amore, R., Saotome, O., & Kienitz, K. H. (2001). A two-input, one-output bit-scalable architecture for fuzzy processors. *IEEE J. Design Test Computation, 18*, 56–64. doi:10.1109/54.936249

De Micheli (Ed.). (1997). Special issue on hardware/software codesign. *Proceedings of the IEEE, 85(3)*.

del Campo, I., Echanobe, J., Bosque, G., & Tarela, J. M. (2008). Efficient hardware/software implementation of an adaptive neuro-fuzzy system. *IEEE transactions on Fuzzy Systems, 16*(3), 761–778. doi:10.1109/TFUZZ.2007.905918

del Campo, I., & Tarela, J. M. (1999). Consequences of the digitization on the performance of a fuzzy logic controller. *IEEE transactions on Fuzzy Systems, 7*(1), 85–92. doi:10.1109/91.746317

del Campo, I., Tarela, J. M., & Basterretxea, K. (2001). Quantisation errors in digital implementations of fuzzy controllers. In R. S. H. Istepanian & J. F. Whidborne (Eds.), *Digital controller implementation and fragility. A modern perspective* (pp. 253-274). Berlin, Germany: Springer.

Dick, S., Gaudet, V., & Bai, H. (2008). Bit-serial arithmetic: A novel approach to fuzzy hardware implementation. In *Proceedings of the Fuzzy Information Processing Society, 2008. NAFIPS 2008. Annual Meeting of the North American* (pp. 1-6).

Dutcher, B. (2006). Mining data without limits. *Xcell Journal*, (57), 64-66.

Echevarría, P., Martínez, M. V., Echanobe, J., del Campo, I., & Tarela, J. M. (2005). Design and HW/SW implementation of a class of piecewise-linear fuzzy system. In *Proceedings of the XII Seminario Anual de Automática, Electrónica Industrial e Instrumentación, SAAEI 05* (pp. 360-364).

Eichfeld, H., Klimke, M., Menke, M., Nolles, J., & Künemund, T. (1995). A general-purpose fuzzy inference processor. *IEEE Micro, 15*(3), 12–17. doi:10.1109/40.387677

Eichfeld, H., Künemund, T., & Menke, M. (1996). A 12b general-purpose fuzzy logic controller chip. *IEEE transactions on Fuzzy Systems, 4*(4), 460–475. doi:10.1109/91.544305

Eichfeld, H., Löhner, M., & Müller, M. (1992). Architecture of a CMOS fuzzy logic controller with optimized organisation and operator design. In *Proceedings of the First International Conference on Fuzzy Systems, FUZ-IEEE* (pp. 1317-1323). Washington, DC: IEEE Computer Society Press.

Estlick, M., Leeser, M., Szymanski, J., & Theiler, J. (2001). Algorithmic transformations in the implementation of k-means clustering on reconfigurable hardware. In *Proceedings of the Ninth Annual IEEE Symposium on Field Programmable Custom Computing Machines 2001 (FCCM '01)* (pp. 103-110).

Eto, E. (2007). *Difference-based partial reconfiguration (ver 2.0, 2007), application note: Virtex architectures*. Retrieved December 1, 2008, from http://www.xilinx.com/support/documentation/application_notes/xapp290.pdf

Evsukoff, A. G., Costa, M. C. A., & Ebecken, F. F. (2005). Parallel implementation of a fuzzy rule based classifier. In M. Daydé et al. (Eds.), *Proceedings of the VECPAR 2004* (LNCS 3402, pp. 184-193). Berlin, Germany: Springer-Verlag.

Fattaruso, J. W., Mahant-Shetti, S. S., & Barton, J. B. (1994). A fuzzy logic inference processor. *IEEE Journal of Solid-State Circuits, 29*(4), 397–402. doi:10.1109/4.280687

Freeman, M., & Jayasooriya, T. (2006). Hardware support for language aware information mining. In B. Gabrys, R.J. Howlett, & L.C. Jain (Eds.), *Proceedings of the KES 2006, Part III* (LNAI 4253, pp. 415-423). Berlin, Germany: Springer-Verlag.

Guo, S., Peters, L., & Surmann, H. (1996). Design and application of an analog fuzzy logic controller. *IEEE transactions on Fuzzy Systems, 4*(4), 429–438. doi:10.1109/91.544303

Halgamuge, S. K., Hollstein, T., Kirschbaum, A., & Glesner, M. (1994). Automatic generation of application specific fuzzy controllers for rapid-prototyping. In *Proceedings of the IEEE International Conference on Fuzzy Systems* (pp. 1638-1641).

Hamzeh, M., Mahdiani, H. R., Saghafi, A., Fakhraie, S. M., & Lucas, C. (2009). Computationally efficient active rule detection method: Algorithm and architecture. *Fuzzy Sets and Systems, 160*(4), 554–568. doi:10.1016/j.fss.2008.05.009

Harris, C. (2005). *Using programmable graphics hardware to implement the fuzzy c-means algorithm*. Unpublished honors dissertation, The University of Western Australia.

Hollstein, T., Halgamuge, S. K., & Glesner, M. (1996). Computer-aided design of fuzzy systems based on generic VHDL specifications. *IEEE transactions on Fuzzy Systems, 4*(4), 403–417. doi:10.1109/91.544301

Hossain, A., & Manzoul, M. A. (1993). Hardware implementation of fuzzy replacement algorithm for cache memories using field-programmable gate arrays. *Cybernetics and Systems, 24*(2), 81–90. doi:10.1080/01969729308961701

Huertas, J. L., Sánchez-Solano, S., Barriga, A., & Baturone, I. (1993). A fuzzy controller using switched-capacitor techniques. In *Proceedings of the IEEE International Conference on Fuzzy Systems* (pp. 516-529).

Hung, D. L., & Zajak, W. F. (1995). Design and Implementation of a hardware fuzzy inference system. *Information Sciences-Applications, 3*(3), 193–207. doi:10.1016/1069-0115(94)00042-Z

Ikeda, H., Kisu, N., Hiramoto, Y., & Nakamura, S. (1992). A fuzzy inference coprocessor using a flexible active-rule-driven architecture. In *Proceedings of the IEEE International. Conference on Fuzzy Systems* (pp. 537-544).

Indue, T., Motomura, T., & Matsuo, R. (1991). New OTA-based analog circuits for fuzzy membership functions and maximum operations. *IEIC Transactions on Communication Electronics, 74*(11), 3619–3621.

Jin, R., Yang, G., & Agrawal, G. (2005). Shared memory parallelization of data mining algorithms: Techniques, programming interface, and performance. *IEEE Transactions on Knowledge and Data Engineering, 17*(1), 71–89. doi:10.1109/TKDE.2005.18

Kim, D. (2000). An implementation of fuzzy logic controller on the reconfigurable FPGA system. *IEEE Transactions on Industrial Electronics, 47*(3), 703–715. doi:10.1109/41.847911

Kim, M. W., Lee, J. G., & Min, C. (1999). Efficient fuzzy rule generation based on fuzzy decision tree for data mining. In . *Proceedings of the IEEE International Fuzzy Systems Conference FUZZ-IEEE, 99*, 1223–1228.

Kubota, K., Nakase, A., Sakai, H., & Oyanagi, S. (2000). Parallelization of decision tree algorithm and its performance evaluation. In *Proceedings of the Fourth International Conference on High Performance Computing in the Asia-Pacific Region, Vol. 2* (pp. 574-579).

Kung, Y.-S., & Tsai, M.-H. (2007). FPGA-based speed control IC for PMSM drive with adaptive fuzzy control. *IEEE Transactions on Power Electronics, 22*(6), 2476–2486. doi:10.1109/TPEL.2007.909185

Landlot, O. (1996). Low power analog fuzzy rule implementation based on a linear MOS transistor network. In *Proceedings of the 5th International Conference on Microelectronics for Neural Networks and Fuzzy Systems* (pp. 86-93).

Lemaitre, L., Patyra, M. J., & Mlynek, D. (1993). Synthesis and design automation of analog fuzzy logic VLSI circuits. In *Proceedings of the IEEE Symposium on Multiple-Valued Logic* (pp. 74-79).

Lemaitre, L., Patyra, M. J., & Mlynek, D. (1994). Analysis and design of CMOS fuzzy logic controller in current mode. *IEEE Journal of Solid State Circuits, 29*(3), 317–322. doi:10.1109/4.278355

Leung, K. T., Ercegovac, M., & Muntz, R. R. (1999). *Exploiting reconfigurable FPGA for parallel query processing in computation intensive data mining applications* (UC MICRO Technical Report). University of California, Los Angeles, Computer Science Department.

Li, T. H. S., Chang, S. J., & Chen, Y. X. (2003). Implementation of human-like driving skills by autonomous fuzzy behavior control on an FPGA-based car-like mobile robot. *IEEE Transactions on Industrial Electronics, 50*(5), 867–880. doi:10.1109/TIE.2003.817490

Louverdis, G., & Andreadis, I. (2003). Design and implementation of a fuzzy hardware structure for morphological color image processing. *IEEE Transactions on Circuits and Systems for Video Technology, 13*(3), 277–288. doi:10.1109/TCSVT.2003.809830

Manaresi, N., Rovatti, R., Franchi, E., Guerrieri, R., & Baccarani, G. (1996). A silicon compiler of analog fuzzy controllers: From behavioral specifications to layout. *IEEE transactions on Fuzzy Systems, 4*(4), 418–428. doi:10.1109/91.544302

Manzoul, M. A., & Jayabharathi, D. (1994). CAD tool for implementation of fuzzy controllers on FPGAs. *Cybernetics and Systems, 25*(4), 599–609. doi:10.1080/01969729408902344

Manzoul, M. A., & Jayabharathi, D. (1995). FPGA for fuzzy controllers. *IEEE Transactions on Systems, Man, and Cybernetics, 25*(1), 213–216. doi:10.1109/21.362948

Marshall, G. F., & Collins, S. (1997). Fuzzy logic architecture using subthreshold analogue floating-gate devices. *IEEE transactions on Fuzzy Systems, 5*(1), 32–43. doi:10.1109/91.554445

Mermoud, G., Upegui, A., Peña, C. A., & Sanchez, E. (2005). A dynamically-reconfigurable FPGA platform for evolving fuzzy systems. In *Computational Intelligence and Bioinspired Systems* (LNCS 3512, pp. 572-581). Berlin, Germany: Springer-Verlag.

Miki, T., & Yamakawa, T. (1995). Fuzzy inference on an analog fuzzy chip. *IEEE Micro, 15*(4), 8–18. doi:10.1109/40.400638

Modencsi, M. V., Costa, M. C. A., Evsukoff, A. G., & Ebecken, N. F. F. (2007). Parallel fuzzy c-means cluster analysis. In *Proceedings of the High performance computing for computational science – VEC-PAR 2006* (pp. 52-65). Berlin, Germany: Springer.

Monmasson, E., & Cirstea, M. N. (2007). FPGA design methodology for industrial control systems – a review. *IEEE Transactions on Industrial Electronics, 54*(4), 1824–1842. doi:10.1109/TIE.2007.898281

Ota, Y., & Wilamowski, M. (1996). CMOS implementation of a voltage-mode fuzzy min-max controller. *Journal of Circuits . Systems and Computers, 6*(2), 171–184.

Patyra, M. J., Grantner, J. L., & Koster, K. (1996). Digital fuzzy logic controller: Design and implementation. *IEEE transactions on Fuzzy Systems, 4*(4), 439–459. doi:10.1109/91.544304

Peters, L., Guo, S., & Camposano, R. (1995). A novel analog fuzzy controller for intelligent sensors. *Fuzzy Sets and Systems, 70*, 235–247. doi:10.1016/0165-0114(94)00221-R

Qao, Q., Lim, M. H., Li, J. H., Ong, Y. S., & Ng, W. L. (2006). A context switchable fuzzy inference chip. *IEEE transactions on Fuzzy Systems, 14*(4), 552–567. doi:10.1109/TFUZZ.2006.876735

Rahimi, S., Zargham, M., Thakre, A., & Chhillar, D. (2004). A parallel fuzzy c-means algorithm for image segmentation. In *Proceedings of the IEEE Annual Meeting of the Fuzzy Information NAFIPS '04* (Vol. 1, pp. 234-237).

Reyneri, L. M. (2003). Implementation issues of neuro-fuzzy hardware: Going toward HW/SW codesign. *IEEE Transactions on Neural Networks, 14*(1), 176–194. doi:10.1109/TNN.2002.806955

Reyneri, L. M., & Renga, F. (2004). Speeding-up the design of HW/SW implementations of neuro-fuzzy systems using the CodeSimulink environment. *Applied Soft Computing, 4*(3), 227–240. doi:10.1016/j.asoc.2004.03.003

Rojas, I., Pelayo, F. J., Ortega, J., & Prieto, A. (1996). A CMOS implementation of fuzzy controllers based on adaptive membership function ranges. In *Proceedings of the Fifth International Conference on Microelectronics for Neural Networks and Fuzzy Systems* (pp. 317-321). Washington, DC: IEEE Comp. Soc. Press.

Rovatti, R. (1998). Fuzzy piecewise multilinear and piecewise linear systems as universal approximators in Sobolev norms. *IEEE transactions on Fuzzy Systems, 6*(2), 235–249. doi:10.1109/91.669022

Rovatti, R., & Borgatti, M. (1997). Maximum-throughput implementation of piecewise-linear fuzzy systems. In *Proceedings of the Sixth IEEE International Conference on Fuzzy Systems. Vol. 2* (pp. 767-772).

Rovatti, R., Ferrari, A., & Borgatti, M. (1998). Automatic implementation of piecewise-linear fuzzy systems addressing memory-performance trade-off. In A. Kandel & G. Langholz (Eds.), *Fuzzy hardware* (pp. 159-179). Amsterdam: Kluwer Academic Publishers.

Ruiz, A., Gutiérrez, J., & Felipe-Frenández, J. A. (1995). A fuzzy controller with an optimized defuzzification algorithm. *IEEE Micro, 15*(6), 76.40-76.49.

Sanchez-Solano, S., Cabrera, A. J., Baturone, I., Moreno-Velo, F. J., & Brox, M. (2007). FPGA Implementation of embedded fuzzy controllers for robotic applications. *IEEE Transactions on Industrial Electronics, 54*(4), 1937–1945. doi:10.1109/TIE.2007.898292

Sasaki, M., & Ueno, F. (1994). A novel implementation of fuzzy logic controller using new meet operation. In *Proceedings of the Third IEEE International Conference on Fuzzy Systems* (pp. 1676-1681).

Shen, L., Shen, H., & Cheng, L. (1999). New algorithms for efficient mining of association rules. *Information Sciences, 118*, 251–268. doi:10.1016/S0020-0255(99)00035-3

Syeda, M., Zhang, Y.-Q., & Pan, Y. (2002). Parallel granular neural networks for fast credit card fraud detection. In *Proceedings of the 2002 IEEE international Conference on Fuzzy Systems* (pp. 572-577).

Togai, M., & Watanabe, H. (1986). Expert system on a chip: An engine for real-time approximate reasoning. *IEEE Expert, 1*(3), 55–62. doi:10.1109/MEX.1986.4306980

Tsukano, K., & Inoue, T. (1995). Synthesis of operational transconductance amplifier-based analog fuzzy functional blocks and its application. *IEEE transactions on Fuzzy Systems, 3*(1), 61–68. doi:10.1109/91.366571

Upegui, A. (2006). *Dynamically reconfigurable bio-inspired hardware*. Unpublished doctoral dissertation, École Polytechnique Fédérale de Lausanne, Switzerland.

Upegui, A., & Sanchez, E. (2005). Evolving hardware by dynamically reconfiguring Xilinx FPGAs. In *Evolvable systems: From biology to hardware* (LNCS 3637, pp. 56-65). Berlin, Germay: Springer-Verlag.

Vidal-Verdú, F., Navas-González, R., & Rodríguez-Vázquez, A. (1998). Multiplexing architecture for mixed-signal CMOS fuzzy controller. *Electronics Letters*, *34*(14), 1437–1438. doi:10.1049/el:19980968

Vidal-Verdú, F., & Rodríguez-Vázquez, A. (1995). Using building blocks to design analog-fuzzy controllers. *IEEE Micro*, *15*(4), 49–57. doi:10.1109/40.400633

Watanabe, H., Dettlof, W. D., & Yount, K. E. (1990). A VLSI fuzzy logic controller with reconfigurable, cascadable architecture. *IEEE Journal of Solid State Circuits*, *25*(2), 376–382. doi:10.1109/4.52159

Weiwei, J., Dongming, J., & Xun, Z. (2004). VLSI design and implementation of a fuzzy logic controller for engine idle speed. In *Proceedings of the 7th International Conference on Solid-State and Integrated Circuits Technology* (pp. 2067-2070).

Wolf, W. (Ed.). (2003). A decade of hardware/software codesign. *Computer*, *36*(4), 38–43. doi:10.1109/MC.2003.1193227

Xilinx Inc. (2008). *Microblaze processor reference guide (ver 9.0, 2008)*. Retrieved December 1, 2008, from http://www.xilinx.com/support/documentation/sw_manuals/mb_ref_guide.pdf

Xilinx Inc. (2008). *Virtex-5 family overview (ver 4.4, 2008), data sheet*. Retrieved December 1, 2008, from http://www.xilinx.com/support/documentation/data_sheets/ds100.pdf

Xu, B., Lu, J., Zhang, Y., Xu, L., Chen, H., & Yang, H. (2003). Parallel algorithm for mining fuzzy association rules. In *Proceedings of the 2003 International Conference on Cyberworlds* (pp. 288-293).

Yamakawa, T. (1988). High-speed fuzzy controller hardware system: The mega-FIPS machine. *Information Sciences*, *45*, 113–128. doi:10.1016/0020-0255(88)90036-9

Yamakawa, T. (1993). A fuzzy inference engine in nonlinear analog mode and its application to a fuzzy control. *IEEE Transactions on Neural Networks*, *4*(3), 496–522. doi:10.1109/72.217192

Yosefi, G., Khoei, A., & Hadidi, K. (2007). Design of a new CMOS controllable mixed-signal current mode fuzzy logic controller (FLC) chip. In *Proceedings of the IEEE International Conference on Electronics, Circuits and Systems* (pp. 951-954).

Zhang, Q., Chamberlain, R. D., Indeck, R., West, B. M., & White, J. (2004). Massively parallel data mining using reconfigurable hardware: Approximate string matching. In *Proceedings of the 18th Annual IEEE International Parallel and Distributed Processing Symposium (IPDPS'04)*.

ENDNOTE

[1]   In pipelined designs attention must be paid, of course, to possible variations in the system throughput when new inputs are introduced to the system.

Chapter 2
Scaling Fuzzy Models

Lawrence O. Hall
University of South Florida, USA

Dmitry B. Goldgof
University of South Florida, USA

Juana Canul-Reich
University of South Florida, USA

Prodip Hore
University of South Florida, USA

Weijian Cheng
University of South Florida, USA

Larry Shoemaker
University of South Florida, USA

ABSTRACT

This chapter examines how to scale algorithms which learn fuzzy models from the increasing amounts of labeled or unlabeled data that are becoming available. Large data repositories are increasingly available, such as records of network transmissions, customer transactions, medical data, and so on. A question arises about how to utilize the data effectively for both supervised and unsupervised fuzzy learning. This chapter will focus on ensemble approaches to learning fuzzy models for large data sets which may be labeled or unlabeled. Further, the authors examine ways of scaling fuzzy clustering to extremely large data sets. Examples from existing data repositories, some quite large, will be given to show the approaches discussed here are effective.

INTRODUCTION

Scaling fuzzy learning systems can be a challenge, because the search space for fuzzy models is larger than that of crisp models. Here, we are concerned with scaling fuzzy systems as the size of the data grows. There are now many collections of data that are terabytes in size and we are moving towards petabyte collections such as a digital Sloan sky survey (Giannella et al., 2006, Gray and Szalay, 2004).

DOI: 10.4018/978-1-60566-858-1.ch002

If learning fuzzy models requires more computation time than learning crisp models and it is a struggle to enable crisp learning models to scale, can we scale fuzzy models of learning? The good news is that scalability is certainly possible as the number of examples grow large or very large. We do not examine the issues with large numbers of features which are a significant problem, for at least supervised fuzzy learning.

Methods for scaling supervised fuzzy learning methods and unsupervised fuzzy learning methods (though only clustering algorithms) will be discussed. An obvious approach is to subsample the data such that each subset is a size that is amenable for learning, but captures the information inherent in the full data set. It is a good approach, but one that has pitfalls in knowing when to stop adding data to the training set (Domingos and Hulten, 2000). Some good papers in the area of subsampling are (Provost and Kolluri, 1999, Wang et al., 2008, Provost et al., 1999, Pavlov et al., 2000). Decomposition of the data is the other major approach one can envision. It is this approach, leading to an ensemble or group of models that is the focus of this chapter.

For labeled data which enables supervised learning, We will show that an ensemble approach can be used to increase the accuracy of the fuzzy classifier. This is a necessary condition to working with disjoint subsets to enable the construction of fuzzy classifiers on very large data sets. However, we will focus on relatively small data sets where the goal is to increase accuracy, not to scale. The same approach using disjoint subsets will allow for scalable fuzzy classifiers to be developed. For unsupervised learning, examples will be given which show that the clustering approaches presented here produce data partitions which are comparable to those obtainable when clustering all of the data.

Ensembles

An ensemble, for our purposes, is made up of a set of models. The models may be created through supervised or unsupervised learning. The models in the ensemble need to be diverse. The idea of diversity is that they make different types of errors and in the aggregate errors are corrected (Banfield et al., 2005).

The models may be created from different underlying learning algorithms. However, the most common way to create an ensemble is to use different data sets and the same underlying learning algorithm. A common approach is to use bootstrap aggregation or bagging (Breiman, 1996), which is selection with replacement to create different training data sets. This has the effect of weighting the data, as some of it is left out (0 weight) and some of it is duplicated (doubled, tripled or more in weight). On average about 63% of the training data will be in a given bag which is the same size as the training data. The assumption that the training and test data are independently identically distributed is implicit in bagging. The use of bagging to create an ensemble typically improves the classification accuracy (Banfield, et al., 2007, Dietterich, 2000).

Boosting is another popular algorithm for creating ensembles of classifiers (Freund and Schapire, 1996). It focusses on misclassified examples by giving them a higher weight. For our purposes, it is a sequential algorithm (you do not know what is incorrect until the next model/classifier in the ensemble is built). There have been efforts to make it scalable (Chawla, 2004), but they have not been applied to fuzzy classification approaches.

As fuzzy learning algorithms typically scale poorly with the number of training examples, methods that allow for minimal training data set sizes, but produce accuracy comparable to all the data are desirable. Recent work has shown that an ensemble can be created from disjoint training data sets or data sets that have no overlap and obtain accuracy on unseen test data that is equivalent (or sometimes better) than training on all of the data (Chawla, et.al. 2001). For large data sets, this means you can build classifiers in parallel on subsets of the training data to get the same accuracy as training with all of the data. Now, you can train on data that would not fit in main memory, for example.

Scaling Supervised Fuzzy Learning

There are a number of ways to scale learning. Subsampling the data for a smaller training set is an important approach. As the number of fuzzy rules grow with the number of features, effective feature selection can be a big help. Other approaches are to optimize the learning algorithm or develop algorithms which scale better, at perhaps the cost of some precision.

In this section, we focus on one particular approach using ensembles. Essentially, this is the subsampling approach with a twist that all of the training examples are used by the union of classifiers in the ensemble. Each learning algorithm will get a unique set of training examples. It is certainly also feasible to give them overlapping sets, but for true scalability to very large or extreme data unique or disjoint sets are likely the best. You will overall use less data with the disjoint data sets, which may be important when the size of the data is very large. A disjoint data set can be given to each learning algorithm for building a classifier which will almost certainly result in a diverse set of classifiers.

In order to be confident that the combination of classifiers built on disjoint data sets will result in accuracy comparable to building a single classifier on all the data, it is useful to look at experiments with smaller data sets. We will present experiments using 20 smaller data sets and bagging to show that bagging can improve the accuracy of fuzzy classifiers. Where bagging works, one can expect that classifiers built from disjoint data subsets of reasonable size can be combined to produce accuracy comparable to learning on all the data (Shoemaker et al., 2008). So, our experiments here show that bagging can be applied to increase the accuracy of fuzzy classifiers.

The classifiers in the ensemble do not need to be of the same type. However, the most typical configuration is to use classifiers that are all of the same type. We will illustrate the idea of an ensemble of classifiers by using the ANFIS (Adaptive Neuro-Fuzzy Inference Systems) fuzzy neural network (fl-toolbox, 2006) learning algorithm to generate classifiers. It is widely available as part of the MATLAB Fuzzy Logic Toolbox.

An adaptive network can be considered as a superset of feed-forward neural networks with supervised learning. ANFIS is a type of Neuro-fuzzy network which has the fuzzy rules embedded within the neural network. Figure 1 shows the structure of an adaptive network. Node functions are represented by squares if they have parameters, which make them adaptive, and by circles if they do not have parameters. The links have no associated weights and they only represent direction flow. For further details on ANFIS, see (Jyh and Roger, 1993).

The ensemble building approach here is simple. It is a modification of bagging (bootstrap aggregation) (Breiman, 1996) in which training sets are selected from the overall data by selecting data, with replacement, until a bag of the chosen size (usually 100%) is created. This essentially re-weights the examples in the training set for each classifier.

For scalability, one would simply divide the data into *n* disjoint subsets of tractable size. Learn *n* classifiers using ANFIS. Then, given a test example you will get *n* fuzzy predictions. These need to be combined. They can be combined by using a majority vote (e.g. harden each decision and take the class that most often has the highest fuzzy membership). Perhaps a better combination is to add up all the fuzzy memberships and average them. Then take the higher average membership. The reader can

Figure 1. Structure of an adaptive network

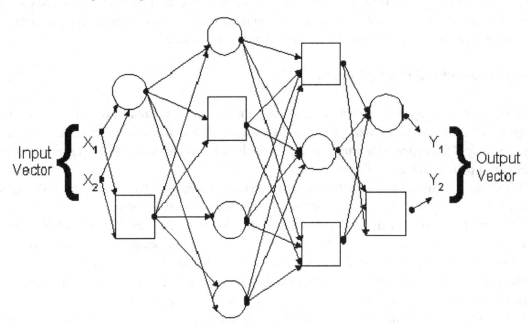

certainly think of other possible, combination methods which may be better, but we will present the above two.

The approach of building *n* classifiers trained on disjoint subsets of data and then combining them has been shown to provide accuracies comparable to those obtained using all the data (Shoemaker et al., 2008). The advantages are that each classifier can be trained in parallel on tractable size data sets. This can enable learning from data which cannot be fit in computer memory or that will require calculation time that is not feasible for the problem. It allows for using more data in the training process (all of it for example) than you could if you subsample to enable timely learning. Experimental evidence has shown that this approach is successful with decision trees and neural networks as the underlying base classifiers. As long as the classifiers make different errors (have a diversity of responses) and have "reasonable" accuracy, one can expect that any underlying learning algorithm can be exploited to produce the classifiers (Kuncheva, 2004). If fuzzy classifiers which make different errors, but generally have comparable accuracy, can be constructed an ensemble approach may work for them.

There has not been very much work on ensembles of fuzzy classifiers and no work that we are aware of on scaling fuzzy classifiers for really large data sets. A clear reason for this is the fact that fuzzy classifiers have been found most useful for their explanation capabilities. That is, they are very good at producing understandable sets of rules (Klawonn et al., 1996). If you have very large data sets where you get lots of fuzzy rules and even worse have to combine them, you will lose the understandability. Then the question becomes did you get a fast, accurate overall classifier. People have either not obtained more accuracy through ensembles of fuzzy classifiers or not tried this approach to get higher accuracy. Perhaps because of the loss of interpretability.

In the following subsection, we will show up some results from bagging ANFIS classifiers. The positive aspect of the results is that you can get a statistically significant increase in accuracy on a number of data sets using bagging and a fuzzy learning approach. Of course, an interpretable set of rules no

Table 1. The 20 data sets used. The number of attributes used, the total attributes, number of instances and classes are shown

Data Set	Attributes used	Total Attributes	# Instances	# Classes
balance_scale	4	4	625	3
breast	6	9	699	2
cmc	6	9	1473	3
dermatology	6	34	366	6
glass	6	9	214	7
haberman	3	3	306	2
heart-statlog	6	13	270	2
Ionosphere	6	34	351	2
iris	4	4	150	3
monks1	6	6	432	2
monks2	6	6	432	2
newthyroid	5	5	215	3
page-blocks	6	10	5473	5
phoneme	5	5	5404	2
pima (5)	5	8	768	2
satimage_test (6)	6	36	2000	6
Tae	5	5	151	3
vehicle (6)	6	18	846	4
wine (6)	6	13	178	3
yeast (4)	4	8	1484	10

longer exists. The results also suggest that scalability using disjoint training data sets without a loss in accuracy is attainable.

Experiments and Results

The ANFIS classifier was tested on twenty data sets, both without bagging and with 2 types of vote counting for the bagged ensemble (Canul-Reich et al., 2007). Each bag of training data was of the same size as the original training data, often called bagging at 100%. So, each of training data sets consisted of examples chosen at random with replacement from the original data. The data sets were all public domain mostly from the UCI repository (UCIrepository, 2006). ANFIS results are typically poor for datasets with more than six features due to the size of the fuzzy search space. In the data mining tool, Weka (Weka, 2006), the gain ratio feature selector was used to choose the best 6 features for data sets with more than six features. Table 1 shows the characteristics of the data sets used.

Each experiment on a data set begins with a stratified separation of the data into approximately 2/3 of the examples for training, and the remaining examples (approximately 1/3) for testing. The stratification process is intended to preserve the class distribution present in the original data set for both training and testing sets. Then for each of 100 bags, the bag of data was created by randomly drawing with replacement from the stratified training set until the number of examples in the bag equals the stratified training set size. This bag probably will have numerous instances of examples that are in the bag more than once. Conversely, some of the examples in the stratified set will not be drawn and put into the bag. These **out-of-bag** examples are used for the checking or validation set. The checking set is used by ANFIS to prevent overfitting the training data, especially if the data has noise or if the number of training epochs is large.

In order to evaluate both methods of bagging with a single classifier that does not use bagging, one instance of each unique example in the stratified training set was used to create the training data set. This can also be viewed as simply removing all duplicates or multiple instances of examples from the bag. This method uses the same checking set used for the bagging trials, which should provide a fair comparison of bagging vs. no bagging.

ANFIS was run using the data in the newly formed training set (either a bag or that bag with duplicates removed) as an input to train the FIS (Fuzzy Inference System). A separate checking FIS is generated that captures the parameters of the training FIS in the epoch of minimum error, which results in a more accurate model. When the training process is complete, the checking FIS is used to classify the unseen test data.

The above process was repeated in each experiment for the number of bags we chose to use for experiments, which was 100. Each new bagged and non bagged classifier was formed from the same stratified training set that was selected from the entire data set before the first bag was formed.

When all 100 classifiers have been created, two different types of ensemble voting were performed on the outputs generated by the checking FIS for test examples. In the first type of voting, the predictions for each test example consisted of the defuzzified outputs from the checking FIS. These real numbers are rounded to crisp values (whole numbers) and any resulting value that is invalid or out-of-range is changed to the closest valid class value. Then the 100 crisp votes are counted and the predicted class for the example is the one with the majority of votes. In the case of ties, the class with the lower number wins.

Here, we note that just one output is used to discriminate among classes. In the other type of ensemble voting, the 100 defuzzified votes are simply added. Then the mean or average value is determined. This value is then rounded to a valid, crisp class value and is designated as the class predicted by the ensemble. For example, consider the case of 3 classifiers predicting 0.4, 1 and 0.4 respectively for a sample (prediction ≤ 0.5 means class 1 and prediction > 0.5 means class 2). Under the majority-of-votes criteria, these individual predictions are clearly 1, 2, 1, resulting in a majority of votes for class 1. Under the mean-of-defuzzified-votes criteria, the mean of the three original predictions is calculated, that is 0.6, resulting in a combined prediction for class 2 for the sample.

The process described above was performed 25 times and average accuracies are reported.

Analysis of Results

In Table 2 the average test accuracies are shown for 25 test runs using the ANFIS checking FIS for 10 epochs. A visual representation of these results is shown in Figure 2.

Figure 2 shows higher accuracy was achieved with the defuzzified ensemble voting method on fifteen out of twenty test data. The worst accuracy consistently came from the majority vote bagging ensemble method.

In Table 3 the average test accuracies are shown for 25 test runs using the ANFIS checking FIS for 20 epochs.

Table 3 and Figure 3 indicate that higher accuracy was achieved on the glass and yeast data sets with bagging using the defuzzified mean.

Figure 4 shows a head-to-head comparison of 10 vs. 20 epochs for test accuracies using defuzzified voting of predictions from the checking FIS generated using bags of data. The accuracy with 20 epochs was greater than or equal to that of 10 epochs, except for the iris and newthyroid datasets.

The significance of the accuracy difference between bagging and a single classifier was evaluated using the Friedman-Holm Test, which was discussed in (Demsar, 2006). The procedure allows the comparison of two or more classifiers over multiple data sets and determines whether there is a statistically significant difference in the accuracies. It uses the ranks of the classifier on each data set, ranging from 1-3 here. Ties of 1, for example, are each given 1.5, and smaller is better.

Briefly, the Friedman test is a "non-parametric equivalent of the repeated-measures ANOVA" (Demsar, 2006). ANOVA is a statistical method for testing differences between the performances of classifiers measured on the same test environment with the null-hypothesis being that there is no differences between them. When the null-hypothesis is rejected, a post-hoc test follows. Holm's procedure was applied in our work. It consists of sequentially testing ordered hypotheses starting from the most significant p

Table 2. Average test accuracies in % for 25 runs using checking FIS for 10 epochs with standard deviations in (). A bold value indicates the highest accuracy for that data set

Data set	No bags	Bags majority vote	Bags mean defuzzified
Balance_scale	71.229 (2.34)	69.627 (2.75)	**71.522** (2.14)
breast	92.769 (0.90)	81.236 (2.48)	**93.579** (1.25)
cmc	**31.801** (1.68)	28.318 (1.91)	31.479 (1.92)
dermatology	51.825 (1.07)	50.426 (3.05)	**52.262** (1.07)
glass	**48.602** (3.98)	41.556 (4.05)	48.167 (6.93)
haberman	73.739 (1.19)	72.078 (3.18)	**73.882** (1.81)
heart-statlog	74.189 (2.73)	70.133 (3.28)	**75.467** (4.09)
ionosphere	85.733 (1.59)	70.598 (2.0)	**87.111** (2.18)
iris	95.642 (2.26)	92.960 (3.01)	**96.080** (3.13)
monks1	69.271 (2.68)	56.889 (2.15)	**74.083** (3.13)
monks2	76.247 (2.47)	54.806 (3.27)	**78.722** (3.47)
newthyroid	86.863 (1.63)	79.944 (4.11)	**88.000** (1.92)
page-blocks	86.992 (0.78)	82.692 (0.96)	**87.163** (0.88)
phoneme	79.603 (0.77)	78.735 (0.77)	**79.847** (0.86)
pima	74.484 (1.7)	71.125 (1.6)	**75.484** (1.87)
satimage-test	61.110 (1.02)	56.102 (1.02)	**61.985** (1.48)
tae	**46.013** (4.31)	41.961 (5.0)	44.863 (5.56)
vehicle	47.869 (1.70)	**53.475** (2.45)	49.418 (2.44)
wine	81.667 (2.63)	51.667 (5.09)	**90.200** (4.01)
yeast	32.693 (1.65)	**36.065** (2.08)	32.630 (1.94)

Figure 2. Average test accuracies for 25 runs using checking FIS for 10 epochs

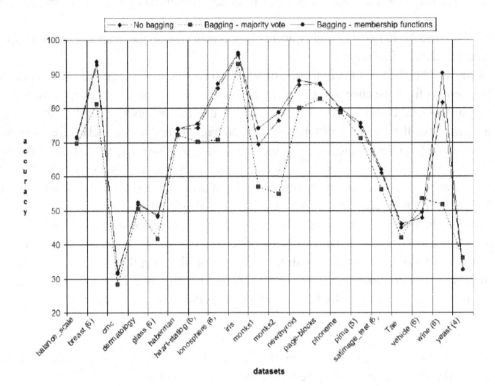

value, if its corresponding hypothesis is rejected the procedure goes on with the next *p* value, which is tested and so forth until a null hypothesis that cannot be rejected is found.

The Friedman-Holm test results show that using ANFIS, the bagging approach with the membership function based combination method was statistically significantly better than a single classifier, at the 95% threshold.

SCALING UNSUPERVISED FUZZY LEARNING

Clustering streaming data presents the problem of not having all the data available at one time. Further, the total size of the data may be larger than will fit in the available memory of a typical computer. If the data is very large, it is a challenge to apply fuzzy clustering algorithms to get a partition in a timely manner. In this section, we present an online fuzzy clustering algorithm (OFCM) (Hore et al., 2008) which can be used to cluster streaming data, as well as very large data sets which might be treated as streaming data. OFCM can provide partitions equivalent to fuzzy c means (FCM). It processes the data as each independent chunk of data arrives. That is, the algorithm can perform well even if the data is evolving over time. Results on several large volumes of magnetic resonance images show that the new algorithm produces partitions which are very close to what you could get if you clustered all the data at one time. That shows that this algorithm is an accurate approach for online clustering.

Clustering streaming data has become an important issue due to the increasing availability of large amounts of data collected over time. Due to the reducing costs of recording data, the sources of stream-

Table 3. Average test accuracies in % for 25 runs using checking FIS for 20 epochs with standard devia-
tions in (). A bold value indicates the highest accuracy for that data set

Data set	No bags	Bags majority vote	Bags mean defuzzified
balance_scale	72.484 (2.23)	72.057 (2.41)	**72.632** (2.40)
breast	92.764 (0.91)	81.270 (2.47)	**93.614** (1.23)
cmc	**32.006** (1.65)	28.554 (1.85)	31.796 (1.89)
dermatology	52.139 (0.98)	50.787 (2.98)	**52.361** (1.12)
glass	42.284 (2.55)	40.444 (4.00)	**50.833** (5.95)
haberman	73.736 (1.21)	72.078 (3.02)	**74.000** (1.72)
heart-statlog	74.801 (2.6)	68.178 (3.11)	**78.044** (3.74)
ionosphere	86.007 (1.51)	71.179 (2.13)	**87.282** (2.21)
iris	95.365 (1.97)	91.040 (3.75)	**95.920** (2.2)
monks1	71.224 (1.80)	56.694 (2.57)	**75.556** (2.57)
monks2	82.601 (2.99)	62.083 (2.75)	**84.806** (4.23)
newthyroid	86.279 (2.32)	80.278 (5.26)	**87.333** (3.24)
page-blocks	88.140 (0.75)	82.323 (0.90)	**88.743** (0.83)
phoneme	80.096 (0.75)	79.119 (0.87)	**80.391** (0.82)
pima	74.516 (1.69)	71.125 (1.59)	**75.500** (1.84)
satimage-test	61.403 (1.02)	56.492 (1.01)	**62.309** (1.4)
tae	**46.049** (4.31)	41.961 (5.0)	45.098 (5.55)
vehicle	48.326 (1.72)	**53.887** (2.42)	49.773 (2.38)
wine	82.099 (2.45)	52.933 (5.68)	**90.267** (4.58)
yeast	34.386 (1.64)	34.537 (1.83)	**35.515** (2.58)

ing data are growing rapidly. Features of streaming data are that it arrives at different times and the size of the streaming data can be so enormous that we cannot store all of it. Instead, we must process the data as it arrives, or in chunks, and delete it to free memory for incoming data. In many cases, the streaming data cannot be revisited due to its evolving nature (Aggarwal et al., 2003, Aggarwal et al., 2004, Yang, 2003, Cao et al., 2006, Nasraoui et al., 2003, Hore et al., 2007a). That is, random access is impossible. To find meaningful clusters under these constraints, a number of clustering algorithms based on the single pass approach (O'Callaghan et al., 2002, Guha et al., 2003, Hore et al., 2007b) have been proposed. The single pass approach can work well for scaling classical clustering algorithms, but may not fit for clustering streaming data (Aggarwal et al., 2003). The reason is that streaming data might evolve over time and a single pass view of the entire stream tends to make algorithms insensitive to an evolving distribution (Aggarwal et al., 2003, Hore et al., 2007b).

A good streaming algorithm should not only extract meaningful information from the entire data set, but also respond to dynamic changes. As stated in (Aggarwal et al., 2003), a streaming clustering algorithm should be able to produce a good quality partition even if data is evolving considerably over time. Streaming methodology may also be used for scaling purposes when clustering very large stored data sets. One advantage of streaming algorithms over many single pass and other scalable algorithms (Farnstrom et al., 2000, Pal and Bezdek, 2002, Hathaway and Bezdek, 2006, Hore et al., 2007a) is that they don't require random access to data and process data in whatever order it may arrive.

Figure 3. Average test accuracies for 25 runs using checking FIS for 20 epochs

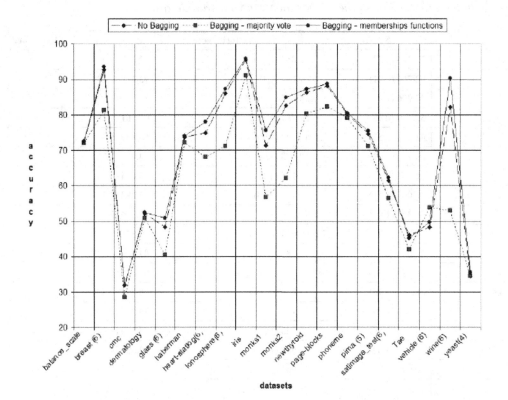

Short Review of Algorithms for Clustering Streaming Data Sets

Recently a number of algorithms have been proposed for clustering streaming data sets (Aggarwal et al., 2003, Aggarwal et al., 2004, Yang, 2003, Cao et al., 2006, Nasraoui et al., 2003, O'Callaghan et al., 2002, Hore et al., 2007a, Dai et al., 2004, Beringer and Hullermeier, 2006). Most of them address the crisp case, clustering streaming data by using either hard c means or its variants or other crisp algorithms. In (O'Callaghan et al., 2002) a streaming algorithm was proposed using a k-Median algorithm called LOCALSEARCH. They showed that their LOCALSEARCH algorithm was better in quality but computationally expensive compared to hard-c-means. They viewed the streaming data as arriving in chunks and then, after clustering, memory was purged by representing the clustering solution by weighted centroids. Then they applied the LOCALSEARCH algorithm to the weighted centroids obtained from chunks to obtain weighted centroids of the entire stream seen so far. They showed that their algorithm outperformed BIRCH (Zhang et al., 1996) in terms of quality measured in sum of squared distance. This method of freeing the memory is similar to the method of creating a discard set in the single pass hard c means algorithm (Farnstrom et al., 2000). OFCM summarizes clustering results in a similar way (Hore et al., 2008). The difference between (O'Callaghan et al., 2002, Farnstrom et al., 2000) and our approach is in the fact that in fuzzy clustering an example may not completely belong to a particular cluster. Our method of summarizing clustering results involves a fuzzy membership matrix and fuzzy centroids, which do not exist for the crisp cases. So in (O'Callaghan et al., 2002), clustering streaming data was approached using a single pass view of the data.

Figure 4. Average test accuracies for 25 runs using 100 bags, and defuzzified checking FIS outputs for 10 and 20 epochs

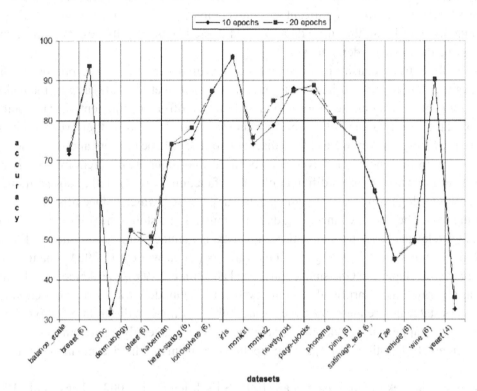

In (Aggarwal et al., 2003), it was pointed out that a streaming algorithm may not be viewed as single pass clustering problem because they are generally blind to evolving distributions and a single pass algorithm over an entire stream will be dominated by outdated history. They proposed a framework for analysis of clusters over different time frames. They stored summary statistics describing the streaming data periodically using micro-clusters which was the online component of their algorithm, and later analyzed these summary statistics of clusters, known as the offline components, over a user provided time horizon. They showed the superiority of their algorithm compared to (O'Callaghan et al., 2002) on data with an evolving distribution.

In (Hore et al., 2007b), a streaming FCM (SFCM) algorithm was proposed. When the first chunk of data arrives, the algorithm will cluster the chunk of data into c cluster centroids using FCM. Memory is freed by summarizing cluster centroids into c weighted points using the fuzzy matrix obtained during the clustering. When a second or later chunk of data comes, it will be clustered with the weighted points of previous clustered chunks. How many chunks of history to use for clustering with a new chunk is predefined by the users. The first chunk's cluster centroids are initialized randomly while the other chunks' are initialized as the last chunk's cluster centroids. Their experiments showed this method could provide results comparable with FCM only in the case the amount of clustering history to use is selected properly.

In (Hore et al., 2007a), a single pass FCM (SPFCM) method was proposed. They separated the large data into several partial data accesses (PDA). The first PDA was clustered into c cluster centroids. Then the data in memory was condensed into c weighted points. Those weighted points will be clustered with new points in the next PDA. In their experiments, the method provided excellent partitions, almost the same as FCM's. There was a significant speedup compared with FCM. However, single pass FCM requires randomly reordering the entire data to avoid unpredictable results. So, its performance drops when processing data in the order it arrives.

In (Cao et al., 2006) a density based streaming algorithm DenStream was proposed. The design philosophy of the DenStream algorithm was similar to (Aggarwal et al., 2003) as they too had an online component for summarizing cluster information and then an offline component later to combine clusters. They used the density based DBSCAN algorithm (Ester et al., 1996) in their work. Using a density based clustering algorithm they were able to discover arbitrary shape clusters and show the robustness of their algorithm towards noise. However, density based algorithms are different from fuzzy clustering algorithms as they try to optimize a different objective function. In (Cho et al., 2006) a framework for efficiently archiving high volumes of streaming data was proposed, which reduces disk access for storing and retrieving data. They grouped incoming data into clusters and stored them instead of raw data.

Many other relevant single pass or scalable algorithms include using hard c means, EM (Jain and Dubes, 1988), Hierarchical Clustering and their variants (Aggarwal et al., 2004, Zhang et al., 1996, Bradley et al., 1998, Gupta and Grossman, 2004, Neal and Hinton, 1998, Karkkainen and Franti, 2007). A streaming algorithm using artificial immune system (AIS) models was also proposed in (Nasraoui et al., 2003). As stated before the fuzzy c means algorithm optimizes a different objective function and also the single pass approach may not be suitable for clustering an evolving stream.

Non-incremental algorithms for speeding up fuzzy c means or hard c means (Pal and Bezdek, 2002,

Hathaway and Bezdek, 2006, Zhang et al., 1996, S.Eschrich et al., 2003, Cheng et al., 1998, Guha et al., 1998) are not generally applicable to clustering streaming data sets because they assume all the data can be loaded into memory. In (J. Lazaro and Cuadrado, 2003) a modified FCM was proposed to simplify hardware implementation and obtain parallelism for real time video processing, but it is very application specific and not applicable for data streams. In (Liu and Meng, 2004) a data driven fuzzy clustering method based on the Maximum Entropy Principle was proposed for a real time robot-tracking application. It is application specific and does not have the same objective function as FCM.

Thus some work has been done for hard-c-means and fuzzy-c-means clustering applied to streaming data and large data. However, as stated in (Hathaway and Bezdek, 2006), the crisp clustering methods may not be easily generalized to their fuzzy counterparts. The fuzzy methods we examined above have constraints including having to select a properly predefined history and an inability to handle evolving streams.

Online Fuzzy C Means

Due to the constraints of limited memory and computation time, a streaming algorithm may be able to load only a relatively small amount of the data at a time depending upon the speed of the stream and hardware capability. As in (O'Callaghan et al., 2002), we assume the data is both arriving and processed in chunks, that is, n_1 data points arrive at time t_1, n_2 at t_2, and so on.

We cluster data in each chunk by fuzzy c means (FCM), and we have to decide the number of clusters c for each chunk. In the worst case, all data in a given chunk might come from one class only and in the best case data might come from all n classes. If we set the number of clusters to be always c (highest resolution under the assumption we know the upper bound on the number of clusters), there are 2 cases:

Case A: If less than c classes arrive in a chunk, then we are overclustering. Overclustering may not cause any information loss. Information loss is only certain to occur when we undercluster.
Case B: If exactly c classes come in a chunk, then we are partitioning the data correctly, that is, neither overclustering nor underclustering.

In both cases, setting the number of clusters to be equal to c, the maximum number of classes in the data set, will likely not cause any information loss. So we set the number of clusters to be c in each chunk.

Data in each chunk is clustered by FCM. The objective function (J_m) minimized by FCM is defined as follows:

$$J_m\left(U,V\right) = \sum_{i=1}^{c}\sum_{k=1}^{n}U_{ik}^m D_{ik}\left(x_k,v_i\right) \tag{1}$$

U and V can be calculated as:

$$U_{ik} = \left[\left[\sum_{j=1}^{c}\frac{D_{ik}\left(x_k,v_i\right)^{\frac{2}{m-1}}}{D_{jk}\left(x_k,v_j\right)^{\frac{2}{m-1}}}\right]\right]^{-1} \tag{2}$$

$$v_i = \frac{\sum_{j=1}^{n}\left(u_{ij}\right)^m x_j}{\sum_{j=1}^{n}\left(u_{ij}\right)^m} \tag{3}$$

where U_{ik} : is the membership value of the kth example, x_k, in the ith cluster, v_i : is the ith cluster centroid, n: is the number of examples, c: is the number of clusters, $D_{ik}\left(x_k,v_i\right) = \left\|x_k - v_i\right\|^2$: is the distance metric. We have used the Euclidean distance.

After data in one chunk is clustered by FCM, memory is freed by condensing the clustering solution in the memory into c weighted examples. The c weighted examples are represented by the c cluster centroids obtained after clustering. Their weights are calculated using the membership matrix as follows:

$$w_i = \sum_{j=1}^{n_1}u_{ij}, 1 \leq i \leq c \tag{4}$$

n_1 is the number of examples in memory.

The weighted centroids of each final partition are saved with weights as calculated above. The weighted centroids of all chunks form an ensemble of weighted clustering solutions. The ensemble is then merged into c final clusters. The merging operation is done by clustering all the weighted centroids in the ensemble using their weights. Weighted FCM (WFCM) is used for this purpose:

We modified the objective function of FCM (similar to [Karkkainen and Franti, 2007]) to take into effect the weighted examples.

Assuming there are n_c weighted examples in total, the cluster centroids for WFCM are calculated as:

$$V_i = \frac{\sum_{j=1}^{n_c} w_j (u_{ij})^m x_j'}{\sum_{j=1}^{n_c} w_j (u_{ij})^m}, \quad 1 \leq i \leq c, \quad x_j' \in X'.$$

x_j' may be an original example or a weighted centroid and X' is the union of the original examples and all weighted examples (centroids). The w_j are calculated from equation (4) for any added centroids and are 1 for the original examples. The weights of the n_c weighted examples are calculated from condensation/summarization of clustering at previous time instants.

The membership matrix is calculated as follows:

$$u_{ij} = \left[\sum_{l=1}^{c} \left(\frac{\left\| x_j' - v_i \right\|}{\left\| x_j' - v_l \right\|} \right)^{\frac{2}{m-1}} \right]^{-1}, 1 \leq i \leq c \text{ and } 1 \leq j \leq n_c.$$

It should be noted that the modification of the objective function does not change the convergence property of FCM because a weighted example can be thought of as many identical singleton examples.

To speed up clustering, we initialize the clustering process for each chunk with the final centroids obtained from clustering the previous chunk. This knowledge propagation allows for faster convergence, provided the distribution does not change rapidly, which might often be the case.

The size of the ensemble of weighted centroids is not likely to be large because it consists of only weighted centroids. If in any case it becomes large, similar to (O'Callaghan et al., 2002) the weighted centroids from the ensemble can be incrementally loaded and reclustered into c weighted centroids. This will decrease the ensemble size, which can be finally merged into c partitions in memory.

Data Sets for Experiments

Nine real data sets were used, including Iris, KDD98, Plankton and 6 magnetic resonance image data sets (MRI-4, MRI-5, MRI-6, MRI-7, MRI-8, and MRI-9). Below we list details of those data sets. Note that value of m used in FCM was m=1.2 for the KDD98 data set and m=2 for the other 8 data sets.

The Iris plant data set consists of 150 examples each with 4 numeric attributes (Merz and Murphy, n.d.) and 3 classes of 50 examples each. One class is linearly separable from the other two. We clustered this data set into 3 clusters. KDD98 is the data set used in the 1998 KDD contest (kddcup08, 1998). This data set is about people who gave a charitable donation in response to direct mailing request. It was used

Table 4. Summary of data sets. The number of attributes used, number of instances and classes are shown

Data Set	Attributes used	# Instances	# Classes
Iris	4	150	3
KDD98	56	95412	10
Plankton	26	419358	12
MRI-4	3	3621971	3
MRI-5	3	1248595	3
MRI-6	3	4948180	3
MRI-7	3	4031593	3
MRI-8	3	1236969	3
MRI-9	3	1504594	3

in (Farnstrom et al., 2000), and has been pre-processed in the same way. After processing the original data, it has 95412 examples and 56 features. As done in (Farnstrom et al., 2000), we clustered this data into 10 clusters. The code for preprocessing is available at http://www-cse.ucsd.edu/users/elkan/skm. html. The Plankton data set (Luo, et al. 2005) consists of 419358 samples of plankton images from the underwater SIPPER camera which records 8 gray levels. There are 26 features extracted. The samples were taken from the twelve most commonly encountered classes of plankton during acquisition in the Gulf of Mexico. The class sizes range from about 11,337 to 74,053 examples. We clustered this data set into 12 clusters. Table 4 summarizes all the data sets.

With the MRI data set, we fetched data for the experiments along the axial plane, from the bottom of the brain (neck) to the top of the skull. The distribution of tissues in the human brain naturally evolves as we go up or down along the axial plane, and there also will be different amounts of tissues at different locations. So we believe MRI images provide good data sets to study our streaming algorithm in a real life scenario. Specific details include (1) The MRI-4 data set was created by concatenating 96 slices of MR images, T1 weighted, of size 512X512 from a single human brain. The magnetic field strength was 1.5 Tesla. After air and skull were removed using the brain extraction tool (BET2) (Jenkinson et al., 2005), there were 3,621,971 examples. The code for the BET2 is available at http://www.fmrib.ox.ac. uk/analysis/research/bet/. We clustered this data set into 3 clusters. (2) The MRI-5 data set was created by concatenating 144 slices of MR images, T1 weighted, of size 256X256 from a single human brain. The magnetic field strength was 3 Tesla. After air and skull were removed using the brain extraction tool (BET2) (Jenkinson et al., 2005), there were 1,248,595 examples. Intensity homogeneity on this data set was corrected using an implementation of the bias correction algorithm from (Cohen et al., 2000). We clustered this data set into 3 clusters. (3) The MRI-6 data set was created by concatenating 96 slices of MR images, T1 weighted, of size 512X512 from a single human brain. The magnetic field strength was 1.5 Tesla. After air and skull were removed using the brain extraction tool, BET2 (Jenkinson et al., 2005), there were 4,948,180 examples. We clustered this data set into 3 clusters. (4) The MRI-7 data set was created by concatenating 96 slices of MR images, T1 weighted, of size 512X512 from a single human brain. The magnetic field strength was 1.5 Tesla. After air and skull were removed using the brain extraction tool, BET2, there were 4,031,593 examples. We clustered this data set into 3 clusters. (5) The MRI-8 data set was created by concatenating 144 slices of MR images, T1 weighted, of size

256X256 from a single human brain. The magnetic field strength was 3 Tesla. After air and skull were removed using the brain extraction tool, BET2, there were 1,236,969 examples. Intensity homogeneity on this data set was corrected using an implementation of the bias correction algorithm in (Cohen et al., 2000). We clustered this data set into 3 clusters. (6) The MRI-9 data set was created by concatenating 144 slices of MR images, T1 weighted, of size 256X256 from a single human brain. The magnetic field strength was 3 Tesla. After air and skull were removed using the brain extraction tool, BET2, there were 1,504,594 examples. Intensity homogeneity on this data set was also corrected. We clustered this data set into 3 clusters.

Experimental Setup and Results

In (Hathaway and Bezdek, 2006) a reformulated optimization criteria R_m (mathematically equivalent to J_m in equation (1)) was given as:

$$R_m\left(V\right) = \sum_{k=1}^{n}\left(\sum_{i=1}^{c}D_{ik}\left(x_k, v_i\right)^{\frac{1}{(1-m)}}\right)^{(1-m)}$$

(5)

The new formulation has the advantage that it does not require the U matrix and can be directly computed from the final cluster centroids. For large data sets, where the whole data set cannot be loaded into memory, R_m can be computed by incrementally loading examples from the disk.

For KDD98, Plankton and the 6 MRI data sets, 5% of the data was loaded in each chunk. For the Iris data set, we fetched 25 examples in each chunk. So, it required 6 time instants to fetch the full data set. We will compare the performance of streaming FCM (Hore et al., 2007b) and OFCM under this setting. We also compared the results of the single pass FCM (SPFCM) algorithm on these data with the same chunk size as used for SFCM and OFCM experiments. Results of experiments on the single pass algorithm (SPFCM) running with and without scrambling (randomly reordered) the data is also reported.

The results of OFCM and SPFCM were compared with the clustering quality obtained at the end of the stream for the SFCM algorithm. The difference in quality is computed according to:

$$DQ = \left(\frac{m_2 - m_1}{m_1}\right) * 100$$

(6)

m_1 is the mean R_m value for experiments with FCM and m_2 is the mean R_m value for experiments with OFCM, SPFCM and SFCM.

That is, the difference in R_m value expressed in percentage, of the OFCM, SPFCM, and SFCM algorithms from the quality obtained by clustering all the data at once using FCM.

All results are an average of 32 random experiments, each starting with a random initialization at the beginning of the stream. On each data set all algorithms had the same random initializations. Table 5 shows the performance of the SFCM, OFCM, and SPFCM algorithms compared to clustering the entire stream at once.

Table 5. Difference in Quality (in percentage) of the SFCM, OFCM, and SPFCM algorithms compared to clustering all the stream at once with FCM. SPFCM" means clustering without scrambling the data

	HIS1 (%)	HIS2 (%)	HIS3 (%)	HIS4 (%)	HIS5 (%)	SPFCM" (%)	SPFCM (%)	OFCM (%)
MRI-4	0.7082	1.0378	6.654	12.9819	17.6392	8.8818	0.0026	0.17447
MRI-5	2.4084	3.8948	11.1541	18.0348	23.1885	10.4976	0.0011	0.17691
MRI-6	6.7014	4.2827	10.2577	15.7393	19.5325	8.2708	0.0009	1.1098
MRI-7	1.2444	22.0437	69.0189	109.1186	141.9229	84.72	0.0065	0.439
MRI-8	0.584	15.7915	41.5251	63.6055	82.3348	47.623	0.0027	0.2398
MRI-9	0.5464	13.0416	35.9483	53.7082	67.0518	40.582	0.0141	0.2995
Iris	5.2772	2.3517	90.083	91.2483	91.565	79.6733	0.1117	0.21661
KDD	-0.0567	-0.0585	0.0169	0.0127	0.0098	-0.1315	-0.0324	-0.07934
Plan-Kton	14.2393	11.7439	10.1547	8.7612	8.6569	4.02337	0.0046	2.95274

In the table, HISn means SFCM using a history of n chunks. For the single pass experiments, in the table SPFCM denotes clustering was done on the randomly reordered data set, while SFCM" means data was clustered the way it comes: the way SFCM and OFCM algorithms fetches data.

In Table 5, we see SPFCM, as expected, provides unpredictable clustering quality when it processes data as it comes. When the same data sets were scrambled, it always produced excellent quality. For processing data in a typical stream setting (processed as it comes), either SFCM (with appropriate history) or OFCM can be used. The results in Table 3 show that OFCM is always superior to SFCM in producing a clustering solution as good as clustering the full stream at once. OFCM always obtained good quality partitions; even for the Iris experiment the quality difference is only 0.21661%. Generally, usage of history greater than or equal to 2 resulted in poor partitions, at least in the context of producing clustering quality (at the end of stream) as good as clustering the entire data stream at once. On the KDD98 data set, any amount of history usage gives good quality; however, with HIS1 and HIS2 average quality was even better than the average quality of FCM. OFCM varied from FCM by 1% for MRI-6 and 2.9% for Plankton. There are still small variations on large data sets. The quality of OFCM always was better than SFCM in producing a partition as good as clustering the full data set. Thus, OFCM can be thought of as a generalized single pass FCM algorithm that like streaming algorithms can process data as it comes, while at the end of the stream it can produce clustering quality as good as clustering the entire data stream.

Summary

In this chapter, we have focused on ways of dividing data to enable fuzzy learning systems both supervised and unsupervised to scale. The approaches focused upon do not throw away any of the data, but instead they use disjoint subsets of the data to build individual classifiers or data partitions.

We have briefly discussed other approaches, based on subsampling, to building scalable fuzzy learning systems. The issues with subsampling are in selecting the right subsample or right set of examples which enable learning a good model. Typical approaches stop too early when they use things like the chi-squared test. Subsampling is an area deserving of further research.

For supervised learning to show the possibilities of ensembles, we have compared ANFIS with and without bagging to classify twenty data sets. Results were computed two different ways:

a)   Ensemble class votes for each example from the defuzzified output of the FIS for each bag were individually converted to crisp class values. Then, the predicted class for each test instance was found using a majority vote of these crisp values.

b)   The mean of the sum of the defuzzified FIS outputs for each bag was converted to a crisp class prediction for the ensemble.

c)   Feature reduction was done via the gain ratio feature selector in Weka for all data sets with more than 6 features. Other sets of features chosen differently would result in different accuracies, but similar conclusions.

The mean defuzzified output gave the most accurate results. It is advisable not to make crisp the defuzzified outputs of each FIS before these values are combined in a vote. Otherwise, the benefit of the fuzzy membership functions is lost and lower accuracies result.

The Freidman/Holm test for determining significance of differences in accuracies for our classifier methods was performed, resulting in the conclusion bagging is statistically better than a single classifier at the 95% level.

It is interesting that fuzzy models have enough variability to benefit from an ensemble formulation. This suggests that ensembles of fuzzy classifiers where each is built on a disjoint subset of data can be used to generate an accurate scalable fuzzy classifier.

For unsupervised learning, we have shown that tractable size data subsets, or chunks of the stream, can be clustered in the usual way. You get an ensemble of data partitions which must then be combined. One way to combine them is to simply cluster weighted class centers, centroids, of the data in each partition. Using online fuzzy clustering, the centroids of the individual data partitions are given weights based on the membership of the examples assigned to the clusters they represent. The centroids then form weighted examples which can be clustered to obtain the centroids of final data partition. Any future data can be assigned to the nearest cluster. If one needs to assign all of the data to the final clustered centroids, this can be done by sending the clustered centroids to processors where the data resides and to determine their class.

The online fuzzy clustering process results in cluster centers that are very similar to those obtained by clustering all of the data using fuzzy c-means. So, in cases where you could not possibly cluster all the data at once due to its size one may expect that the partition will be similar to a venerable, well-known clustering algorithm. Hence, there is evidence that scaling fuzzy clustering algorithms can be effective.

This chapter has outlined methods of using ensembles to enable fuzzy learning systems to scale whether the data is labeled or unlabeled. In the case of labeled data there will be many fuzzy rules (for instance) reducing the interpretability of the system. For clustering, there should be no loss in interpretability. The ensemble approaches outlined here are viable ways of scaling fuzzy learning systems.

ACKNOWLEDGMENT

This research was partially supported by the Department of Energy through the ASCI PPPE Data Discovery Program, Contract number: DE-AC04-76DO00789 and the Department of Defense, National Functional Genomics Center Project, under award number DAMD 17-02-2-0051. Views and opinions of, endorsements by, the author(s) do not reflect those of the US Army or the Department of Defense. Partial support was also received from the National Institutes of Health under grant number 1 R01 EB00822-01.

REFERENCES

Aggarwal, C. C., Han, J., Wang, J., & Yu, P. S. (2003). A framework for clustering evolving data streams. In *VLDB '2003: Proceedings of the 29th international conference on Very large data bases* (pp. 81-92). VLDB Endowment.

Aggarwal, C. C., Han, J., Wang, J., & Yu, P. S. (2004). A framework for projected clustering of high dimensional data streams. In *VLDB '04: Proceedings of the Thirtieth international conference on Very large data bases* (pp. 852-863). VLDB Endowment.

Banfield, R., Hall, L., Bowyer, K., & Kegelmeyer, W. (2005). Ensemble diversity measures and their application to thinning. *Information Fusion, 6*, 49–62. doi:10.1016/j.inffus.2004.04.005

Banfield, R. E., Hall, L. O., Bowyer, K. W., & Kegelmeyer, W. P. (2007). A comparison of decision tree ensemble creation techniques. *IEEE Transactions on Pattern Analysis and Machine Intelligence, 29*(1), 173–180. doi:10.1109/TPAMI.2007.250609

Beringer, J., & Hullermeier, E. (2006). Online clustering of parallel data streams. *Data & Knowledge Engineering, 58*, 180–204. doi:10.1016/j.datak.2005.05.009

Bradley, P. S., Fayyad, U., & Reina, C. (1998). Scaling clustering algorithms to large databases. In *Proceedings of the International Conference on Knowledge Discovery and Data Mining* (pp. 9-15).

Breiman, L. (1996). Bagging predictors. *Machine Learning, 24*, 123–140.

Canul-Reich, J., Shoemaker, L., & Hall, L. (2007). Ensembles of fuzzy classifiers. In *Proceedings of the IEEE International Conference on Fuzzy Systems*.

Cao, F., Ester, M., Qian, W., & Zhou, A. (2006). Density-based clustering over an evolving data stream with noise. In *Proceedings of the 2006 SIAM Conference on Data Mining* (pp. 328-339).

Chawla, N., Moore, T. E., Bowyer, K. W., Hall, L. O., & Kegelmeyer, W. P. (2001). Bagging is a small-data-set phenomenon. In *Proceedings of the International Conference on Computer Vision and Pattern Recognition (CVPR)* (pp. 68-69).

Chawla, N. V., Hall, L. O., Bowyer, K. W., & Kegelmeyer, W. P. (2004). Learning ensembles from bites: A scalable and accurate approach. *Journal of Machine Learning Research, 5*, 421–451.

Cheng, T. W., Goldgof, D. B., & Hall, L. O. (1998). Fast fuzzy clustering. *Fuzzy Sets and Systems, 93,* 49–56. doi:10.1016/S0165-0114(96)00232-1

Cho, K., Jo, S., Jang, H., Kim, S. M., & Song, J. (2006). DCF: An efficient data stream clustering framework for streaming applications. In *Database and expert systems applications* (pp. 114-122). Berlin, Germany; Springer.

Cohen, M., DuBois, R., & Zeineh, M. (2000). Rapid and effective correction of RF inhomogeneity for high field magnetic resonance imaging. *Human Brain Mapping, 10,* 204–211. doi:10.1002/1097-0193(200008)10:4<204::AID-HBM60>3.0.CO;2-2

Dai, B.-R., Huang, J.-W., Yeh, M.-Y., & Chen, M.-S. (2004). Clustering on demand for multiple data streams. In *Proceedings of the Fourth IEEE International Conference on Data Mining, 2004. ICDM '04* (pp. 367-370).

Demsar, J. (2006). Statistical comparisons of classifiers over multiple data sets. *Machine Learning, 7,* 1–30.

Dietterich, T. (2000). An experimental comparison of three methods for constructing ensembles of decision trees: Bagging, boosting, and randomization. *Machine Learning, 40,* 139–157. doi:10.1023/A:1007607513941

Domingos, P., & Hulten, G. (2000). Mining high-speed data streams. In *Proceedings of the Sixth International Conference on Knowledge Discovery and Data Mining* (pp. 71-80).

Eschrich, S., Ke, J., Hall, L. O., & Goldgof, D. (2003). Fast accurate fuzzy clustering through data reduction. *IEEE transactions on Fuzzy Systems, 11,* 262–270. doi:10.1109/TFUZZ.2003.809902

Ester, M., Kriegel, H.-P., Sander, J., & Xu, X. (1996). A density-based algorithm for discovering clusters in large spatial databases with noise. In *Proceedings of 2nd International Conference on Knowledge Discovery and Data Mining (KDD-96)* (pp. 226-231).

Farnstrom, F., Lewis, J., & Elkan, C. (2000). Scalability of clustering algorithms revisited. *SIGKDD Explorations, 2,* 51–57. doi:10.1145/360402.360419

fltoolbox. (2006). *The mathworks - fuzzy logic toolbox.* Retrieved from http://www.mathworks.ch/access/helpdesk r13/help/toolbox/fuzzy/fuzzy.html

Freund, Y., & Schapire, R. (1996). Experiments with a new boosting algorithm. In *Proceedings of the International Conference on Machine Learning* (pp. 148-156).

Giannella, C., Dutta, H., Borne, K. D., Wolff, R., & Kargupta, H. (2006). Distributed data mining for astronomy catalogs. In *Proceedings of the 9th Workshop on Mining Scientific and Engineering Datasets, Proceedings of the SIAM International Conference on Data Mining.*

Gray, J., & Szalay, A. (2004). *Where the rubber meets the sky: Bridging the gap between databases and science* (Tech. Rep. MSR-TR-2004-110). Redmond, WA: Microsoft.

Guha, S., Meyerson, A., Mishra, N., Motwani, R., & O'Callaghan, L. (2003). Clustering data streams: Theory and practice. *Knowledge and Data Engineering . IEEE Transactions on, 15*(3), 515–528.

Guha, S., Rastogi, R., & Shim, K. (1998). CURE: An efficient clustering algorithm for large databases. In *Proceedings of ACM SIGMOD International Conference on Management of Data* (pp. 73-84).

Gupta, C., & Grossman, R. (2004). GenIc: A single pass generalized incremental algorithm for clustering. In *Proceedings of the Fourth SIAM International Conference on Data Mining (SDM)* (pp. 22-24).

Hathaway, R. J., & Bezdek, J. C. (2006). Extending fuzzy and probabilistic clustering to very large data sets. *Computational Statistics & Data Analysis, 51*(1), 215–234. doi:10.1016/j.csda.2006.02.008

Hore, P., Hall, L., & Goldgof, D. (2007a). Creating streaming iterative soft clustering algorithms. In *Proceedings of the Fuzzy Information Processing Society, 2007. NAFIPS '07. Annual Meeting of the North American Fuzzy Information Processing Society* (pp. 484-488).

Hore, P., Hall, L., Goldgof, D., & Cheng, W. (2008). Online fuzzy c means. In *Proceedings of the Fuzzy Information Processing Society, 2008. NAFIPS 2008. Annual Meeting of the North American Fuzzy Information Processing Society* (pp. 1-5).

Hore, P., Hall, L. O., & Goldgof, D. B. (2007b). A fuzzy c means variant for clustering evolving data streams. In *Proceedings of the IEEE International Conference on Systems, Man and Cybernetics,* Montreal (pp. 360-365).

Jain, A., & Dubes, R. (1988). *Algorithms for clustering data*. Englewood Cliffs, NJ: Prentice Hall.

Jenkinson, M., Pechaud, M., & Smith, S. (2005). BET2: MR-based estimation of brain, skull and scalp surfaces. In *Proceedings of the Eleventh Annual Meeting of the Organization for Human Brain Mapping*.

Jyh, S., & Jang, R. (1993). Anfis: Adaptive-network-based fuzzy inference system. *IEEE Transactions on Systems, Man, and Cybernetics, 23*, 665–685. doi:10.1109/21.256541

Karkkainen, I., & Franti, P. (2007). Gradual model generator for singlepass clustering. *Pattern Recognition, 40*(3), 784–795. doi:10.1016/j.patcog.2006.06.023

kddcup08. (1998). *Kdd cup data*. Retrieved from http://kdd.ics.uci.edu/databases/kddcup98/kddcup98.html

Klawonn, F., Gebhardt, J., & Kruse, R. (1996). *Foundations of fuzzy systems*. New York: John Wiley and Sons.

Kuncheva, L. I. (2004). *Combining pattern classifiers: Methods and algorithms*. New York; Wiley-Interscience.

Lazaro, J., Arias, J., Martin, J. L., & Cuadrado, C. (2003). Modified fuzzy c-means clustering algorithm for real-time applications. In *Field-programmable logic and applications* (pp. 2778). Berlin, Germany: Springer.

Liu, P., & Meng, M.-H. (2004). Online data-driven fuzzy clustering with applications to real-time robotic tracking. *IEEE transactions on Fuzzy Systems, 12*(4), 516–523. doi:10.1109/TFUZZ.2004.832521

Luo, T., Kramer, K., Goldgof, D. B., Hall, L. O., Samson, S., Remsen, A., & Hopkins, T. (2005). Active learning to recognize multiple types of plankton. *Journal of Machine Learning Research, 6*(Apr), 589–613.

Merz, C., & Murphy, P. (n.d.). *UCI repository of machine learning databases Univ. of CA., Dept. of CIS, Irvine, CA*. Retrieved from http://www.ics.uci.edu/~mlearn/MLRepository.html

Nasraoui, O., Uribe, C., Coronel, C., & Gonzalez, F. (2003). Tecno-streams: Tracking evolving clusters in noisy data streams with a scalable immune system learning model. In *Proceedings of the Third IEEE International Conference on Data Mining, 2003. ICDM 2003* (pp. 235-242).

Neal, R. M., & Hinton, G. E. (1998). A view of the em algorithm that justifies incremental, sparse, and other variants. In *Learning in Graphical Models* (pp. 355-368).

O'Callaghan, L., Mishra, N., Meyerson, A., Guha, S., & Motwani, R. (2002). Streaming-data algorithms for high-quality clustering. In Proceedings of the 18th IEEE International Conference on Data Engineering (pp. 685-694).

Pal, N., & Bezdek, J. (2002). Complexity reduction for "large image" processing. *IEEE Transactions on Systems, Man, and Cybernetics . Part B, 32*(5), 598–611.

Pavlov, D., Chudova, D., & Smyth, P. (2000). Towards scalable support vector machines using squashing. In *Proceedings of the sixth ACM SIGKDD international conference on Knowledge discovery and data mining* (pp. 295-299).

Provost, F., Jensen, D., & Oates, T. (1999). Efficient progressive sampling. In *Proceedings of the Fifth International Conference on Knowledge Discovery and Data Mining* (pp. 23-32). New York: ACM Press.

Provost, F., & Kolluri, V. (1999). A survey of methods for scaling up inductive algorithms. *Data Mining and Knowledge Discovery, 3*, 131–169. doi:10.1023/A:1009876119989

Shoemaker, L., Banfield, R., Hall, L., Bowyer, K., & Kegelmeyer, W. P. (2008). Using classifier ensembles to label spatially disjoint data. *Information Fusion, 9*(1), 120–133. doi:10.1016/j.inffus.2007.08.001

UCIrepository. (2006). *Uci machine learning repository*. Retrieved from http://www.ics.uci.edu/mlearn/MLRepository.html

Wang, L., Bezdek, J. C., Leckie, C., & Kotagiri, R. (2008). Selective sampling for approximate clustering of very large data sets. *International Journal of Intelligent Systems, 23*(3), 313–331. doi:10.1002/int.20268

Weka. (2006). *Weka 3 - data mining with open source machine learning software in java*. Retrieved from http://www.cs.waikato.ac.nz/ml/weka/

Yang, J. (2003). Dynamic clustering of evolving streams with a single pass. In *Proceedings of the 19th International Conference on Data Engineering, 2003* (pp. 695-697).

Zhang, T., Ramakrishnan, R., & Livny, M. (1996). BIRCH: An efficient data clustering method for very large databases. In *Proc. of the ACM SIGMOD Int'l. Conf. on Management of Data* (pp. 103-114). New York: ACM Press.

Section 2
Databases and Queries

Chapter 3
Using Fuzzy Song Sets
in Music Warehouses

François Deliège
Aalborg University, Denmark

Torben Bach Pedersen
Aalborg University, Denmark

ABSTRACT

The emergence of music recommendation systems calls for the development of new data management technologies able to query vast music collections. In this chapter, the authors present a music warehouse prototype able to perform efficient nearest neighbor searches in an arbitrary song similarity space. Using fuzzy songs sets, the music warehouse offers a practical solution to three concrete musical data management scenarios: user musical preferences, user feedback, and song similarities. The authors investigate three practical approaches to tackle the storage issues of fuzzy song sets: tables, arrays, and compressed bitmaps. They confront theoretical estimates with practical implementation results and prove that, from a storage point of view, arrays and compressed bitmaps are both effective data structure solutions. With respect to speed, the authors show that operations on compressed bitmap offer a significant grain in performances for fuzzy song sets comprising a large number of songs. Finally, the authors argue that the presented results are not limited to music recommendations system but can be applied to other domains.

INTRODUCTION

Automatic music recommendation systems have recently gained tremendous popularity. To provide pertinent recommendations, music recommendation systems use fuzzy set theory (Zadeh, 1965) to combine user profiles, music features, and user feedback information. However, at the current growing speed, the database element of any recommendation system will soon become a bottleneck. Hence, appropriate musical data management tools, able to manipulate fuzzy sets and scale to large music collection

DOI: 10.4018/978-1-60566-858-1.ch003

and growing user communities, are needed. Music Warehouses (MWs) are dedicated data warehouses optimized for the storage and analysis of music content.

The contributions of this chapter are fourfold. First, based on a previous case study (Deliège & Pedersen, 2006), we propose three generic usage scenarios illustrating the current demands in musical data management. To answer these demands, we define fuzzy song sets and develop a query algebra for them. Second, to demonstrate the usefulness of fuzzy song sets, a prototypical MW composed of two multidimensional cubes is presented. Fuzzy song sets prove to be an adequate data representation to manipulate musical information. Third, we discuss three solutions for storing fuzzy song sets and fuzzy sets in general. We construct theoretical estimates for each storage solution. A practical implementation shows that the storage overhead represents a major part of the storage consumption and that two solutions are viable for large music collections. Fourth, we benchmark and compare the performance of the main operators previously presented for various sizes of both data structures. Experiments are conducted on a real music collection.

This chapter demonstrates how fuzzy set theory can be used in the context of music recommendation systems. All results presented in this chapter can be directly applied to standard fuzzy sets; the presented storage solutions remain generic and can thus be applied to a vast range of domains besides music recommendation and user preferences.

The remainder of this chapter is organized as follows. After presenting the related work on fuzzy sets for the management of musical data, we present three information scenarios that are commonly treated by music recommendation systems. We proceed by defining fuzzy song sets and an algebra. Two prototypical multidimensional cubes are presented; they illustrate the use of the algebra through query examples. Storage solutions are then discussed and precise storage estimates are proposed and experimentally validated. Next, a comparison of the performance of the fuzzy song set operators on the bitmap and array representations is conducted. Finally, we conclude and describe promising future research directions.

RELATED WORK

Research on music recommendation systems has received a lot of attention lately. Current trends on playlist generation are focused on how to improve recommendations based on user-specific constrains. For example, a playlist generator that learns music preferences by taking user feedback into account was presented by Pauws & Eggen (2001). Other new interesting approaches concentrate on aggregating different music features; for instance, Bosteels & Keere (2007) study the use of generalized conjunctions and disjunctions of fuzzy sets theory for combining audio similarity measures. However, fewer researchers have addressed the scalability issues raised by these methods in terms of storage and performance (Aucouturier & Pachet, 2002; Pampalk, 2005). This chapter focuses specifically on the storage and performance issues and proposes to manipulate a large collection of musical data where song similarities, user preferences and user feedbacks are represented with fuzzy sets.

A traditional database approach is to use a relational model such as the one proposed by Rubenstein that extends the entity-relationship data model to implement the notion of hierarchical ordering, commonly found in musical data (Rubenstein, 1987). A multimedia data model, following the layered model paradigm that consists of a data definition layer, a data manipulation layer, a data presentation layer, and a control layer, is presented by Wynblatt & Schloss (1995), but no query language is proposed. None of those models adopts a multidimensional approach by representing data in cubes, a very convenient structure for performing on-the-fly analysis of large volumes of data that has already proved its strengths in data warehouses (Pedersen & Jensen, 2001). Finally, a music data model, its algebra and a query language are presented by Wang, Li, & Shi (2004). The data model is able to structure both the musical content and the metadata but does not address performance optimization issues. In particular, it does not provide an adequate framework to perform similarity based search. Jensen et al. address this issue and offer a multi-dimensional model that supports dimension hierarchies (Jensen, Mungure, Pedersen, & Sørensen, 2007). We extend that multidimensional model by integrating fuzzy sets and addressing additional usage scenarios. Furthermore, this implementation proves to be able to handle a much larger music collection of a realistic size in the context of an MW.

The use of bitmaps in multidimensional databases is frequent. Different compression schemes exist to reduce the storage consumption of bitmaps. The Word Align Hybrid (Wu, Otoo, & Shoshani, 2006), WAH, and the Byte-aligned Bitmap Compression (Antoshenkov, 1994), BBC, are two very common compression algorithms. BBC offers a very good compression ratio and performs bitwise logical operations efficiently. WAH performs bitwise operations much faster than BBC but consumes more storage space. We propose a modified version of WAH compression technique to represent fuzzy sets. We show how fuzzy set operators can be adapted to directly manipulate the compressed representations in order to preserve the performance.

Significant efforts have been made in representing imprecise information in database models (Codd, 1979). Relational models and object oriented database models have already been extended to handle imprecision utilizing the fuzzy set theory (Prade & Testemale, 1984; Bordogna, Lucarella, & Pasi, 1994). This chapter proposes pragmatic solutions to store and manipulate fuzzy sets within multidimensional data cubes. It significantly extends our previous work (Deliège & Pedersen, 2007) in several ways: improving the WAH compression algorithm, revising size estimates, and implementing and benchmarking the operators. While our focus is on musical data, we believe our approach can easily be generalized to the similarity matrices extensively used in fuzzy databases, e.g., to perform fuzzy joins.

QUERY SCENARIO

The data obtained from a music recommendations system has to be organized to answer specific queries. Examples of such query scenarios are presented below.

User Feedback

The user's opinion about the system's previous recommendations is a valuable piece of information for improving the future suggestion, e.g., by reinforcement learning. For each song played, the user can grade if the suggestion was wise based on the criteria provided, referred to as the query context. The query context can be the artist similarity, the genre similarity, the beat similarity, or any other similarity measure available to the system to perform a selection. The grading reflects if a proposed song was relevant in the given query context. For example, it is possible to retrieve the list of songs Mary liked when she asked for a list of rock songs or the ten songs she liked the most when she asked for similar songs to a song made by "U2".

Typically, the data obtained should contain:

- the profile of a registered user in the system;
- the query context provided by the user; and
- the list of songs and marks so that for each song proposed, the user can grade how much he liked a particular song being part of the proposition.

Grades are given on a per song basis, they reflect if the user believes the song deserves its place among the suggested list of songs: strongly disagrees, neutral, likes, and loves. While the grade must not be a numerical value, we assume that a mapping function to the interval [0,1] exists so that when a user believes a song definitely deserves its place in the list, a high value in the interval should be given.

User Musical Profile

Regardless of any given query context, some songs should never be proposed to Mary as she simply can't stand them or, on the contrary, some songs should be proposed more often as they are marked as Mary's favorites. Therefore, recommendation systems often offer to their users the possibility to rate any song on a *fan-scale* ranging from "I love it" to "I hate it" depending if they like the song or not. Such information is useful for building network based on users having similar musical taste. The database backend of the recommendation system should be able to find users similar to Mary based on his favorite and loathed songs.

The User Musical Preferences contains two different pieces of information:

- a reference to a user registered; and
- a list of songs associated with their respective grades on the fan-scale.

As above, we assume the mapping to the interval [0,1] so that if Mary hates a song, a low score is assigned; and if she loves it, a value close to 1 should be used. So, musical profiles can be used to modify the frequency a given song appears as a recommendation and build recommendation based on profile similarities.

Songs Similarities

Finally, music recommendation system should be able to compare songs. For each pair of songs, the system is able to provide a similarity value with respect to a given aspect of the song such as the release year, the genre, the theme, the lyrics, or the tempo. The similarity values should indicate if two songs are "very different", "different", "somewhat similar", or "very similar" from the perspective of any given aspect of the song. For example, the song "We will rock you" by Queen is "very different" from the song "Twinkle, twinkle little star" with respect to their *genre similarity aspect*.

To compare songs, three pieces of information are necessary:

- a pair of compared songs;
- a similarity function that maps to a pair of songs to a similarity value; and
- a similarity value reflecting how similar the two songs are.

Again, we assume that the similarity values can be mapped to the interval [0,1] so that if two songs are very different, a value close to 0 should be used, and if they are very similar, a value close to 1 should be used instead.

The scenario is very generic; very few assumptions are made about the properties of the functions used to compute the similarity values. In particular, the similarity functions do not have to fulfill the mathematical properties of a metric: the non-negativity, the identity of indiscernibles, the triangular inequality, and the symmetry properties. They do not have to be defined over the whole domain of song pairs. This allows similarities to be based on a wide diversity of song attributes.

AN ALGEBRA FOR FUZZY SONG SETS

In this section, we introduce fuzzy song sets as well as operators and functions to manipulate them.

Let X be the set of all songs. Then, a fuzzy song set, A, is a fuzzy set defined over X such that:

$$A = \left\{ \mu_A\left(x\right) / x : \ x \in X, \ \mu_A(x) \in \left[0,1\right] \right\}$$

and is defined as a set of pairs $\mu_A\left(x\right) / x$, where x is a song, $\mu_A\left(x\right)$, referred to as the membership degree of x, is a real number belonging to [0,1], and / denotes the association of the two values as commonly expressed in the fuzzy logic literature (Galindo, Piattini, & Urrutia, 2005). When $\mu_A(x) = 0$, song x does not belong to A, and when $\mu_A(x) = 1$, x completely belongs to A.

Operators

The following operators are classically used in order to manipulate song sets.

Equality

Let A and B be two fuzzy song sets. A is equal to B iff for all song the membership degree of a song in A is equal to the membership degree of the same song in B.

$$A = B \Leftrightarrow \ \forall x \in X, \ \mu_A\left(x\right) = \ \mu_B\left(x\right)$$

Subset

Let A and B be two fuzzy song sets. A is included in B iff for all song, the membership degree a song in A is lower than the membership degree of the same song in B.

$$A \subseteq B \Leftrightarrow \forall x \in X, \mu_A\left(x\right) \le \mu_B(x)$$

Note that the empty fuzzy song set defined with the null membership function, i.e., $\forall x \in X, \mu\left(x\right) = 0$, is a subset of all fuzzy sets.

Union

Let A and B be two fuzzy song sets over X. The union of A and B is a fuzzy song set with, for each song, a membership degree equal to the maximum membership degree associated to that song in A and B.

$$A \cap B = \left\{ \mu_{A \cap B}(x) / x \right\}$$

$$\mu_{A \cap B}(x) = \max\left(\mu_A(x), \mu_B(x) \right)$$

Intersection

Let A and B be two fuzzy sets over X. The intersection of A and B is a fuzzy song set with, for each song, a membership degree equal to the minimum membership degree associated to that song in A and B.

$$A \cap B = \left\{ \mu_{A \cap B}(x) / x \right\}$$

$$\mu_{A \cap B}(x) = \min\left(\mu_A(x), \mu_B(x) \right)$$

Negation

Let A be a fuzzy set over X. The negation of A is a fuzzy song set with the membership degree of each song equal to its symmetric value on the interval [0,1].

$$-A = \left\{ 1 - \mu_A(x) \right\}$$

Reduction

Let A be a fuzzy set over X. The reduction of A is a subset of A such that membership degrees smaller than α are set to 0.

$$\text{Reduce}(\alpha, A) = \{ \mu_{A\alpha}(x) / x \}$$

$$\mu_{A\alpha} = \begin{cases} \mu_A(x) & if \ \mu_A(x) \geq \alpha \\ 0 & if \ \mu_A(x) < \alpha \end{cases}$$

The reduction operator changes the membership degree of songs below a given threshold to 0. It allows the construction of more complex operators that allow the reducing the membership degree granularity over ranges of membership degrees.

Top

Let A be a fuzzy set over X. The Top$_k$ subset of A is a fuzzy song with the membership degree of all elements not having the k highest membership degree set to 0 and the membership degree of the k highest elements of A set to their respective membership degree in A.

$$\text{Top}_k\left(\alpha, A\right) = \left\{\mu_{Ak}(x) / x \mid \forall x_i, x_j \in X, 1 \leq i < j, \ \mu_A\left(x_i\right) \geq \mu_A(x_j)\right\}$$

$$\mu_{Ak} = \begin{cases} \mu_{Ak}(x) & if \ i \leq k \\ 0 & \text{otherwise} \end{cases}$$

Note that the Top$_k$ subset of A is not unique, e.g., when all elements have an identical membership degree. The Top$_k$ operator returns a fuzzy song set with all membership degrees set to zero except for k elements with the highest membership degrees that remain unchanged. Top$_k$ is a cornerstone for the development of complex operators based on relative ordering of the membership degrees. Note also that Top$_k$(A) can not be defined as the subset of A having all its elements having a membership greater or equal to the one not included since Top$_k$(A) contains all the elements of A.

Average

Let A$_1$,...,A$_i$ be i fuzzy song sets. The average of A$_1$,...,A$_i$ is a fuzzy song set that assigns to each song a membership degree equal to the arithmetic mean of the membership degrees of that song in the given sets.

$$Avg_{A_1,...,A_i} = \{\mu_{A_1,...,A_i}\left(x\right) / x\}$$

$$\mu_{A_1,...,A_i}\left(x\right) = \frac{\sum_{j=1}^{i} \mu_{A_j}\left(x\right)}{i}$$

The average operator in fuzzy sets is the pendant of the common average operator and is very useful to aggregate data, a common operation in data warehousing in order to gain some overview over large datasets.

Functions

The following functions are defined on song sets. They extract information from the song sets to real values or crisp sets.

Support

The support of A is the crisp subset of X that includes all the elements having a non-zero membership degree in A.

$$\text{Support}\left(A\right) = \{x \in X : \mu_A\left(\mathrm{x}\right) > 0\}$$

Cardinality

The cardinality of A is the sum of the membership degrees of all its elements.

$$\# A = \sum_{x \in X} \mu_A(x)$$

Distance

The Minkowski distance of order $p \geq 1 \in \mathbb{R}$ between two song sets is defined as follows.

$$d_p\left(A, B\right) = \left(\sum_{x \in X}\left|\mu_A\left(x\right) - \mu_B\left(x\right)\right|^p\right)^{\frac{1}{p}}$$

The 1-norm distance is the Manhattan distance, the 2-norm distance is the Euclidean distance, and the ∞-norm is the Chebyshev distance.

THE MUSIC WAREHOUSE CUBES

This section presents two data cubes built to serve queries introduced in the scenarios. In data warehouses, data are logically organized in cubes. A cube is a generalization of a flat two-dimensional spreadsheets to multiple dimensions. While spreadsheets have rows and columns that are combined to form cells, cubes have dimensions that are combined to form facts. Each fact has numeric measures attached to it. To capture the context of a fact, dimensions are organized into hierarchies. Hierarchies define groupings and aggregation functions to be performed, e.g., a counter or an average. The two cubes presented below show how fuzzy song sets can be integrated into a multi-dimensional model and how they can be queried.

The Song Similarity Cube

The Song Similarity cube captures similarity between songs with respect to selected similarity functions. The cube is composed of two dimensions: a song dimension and similarity dimension; they are represented in Figure 1. The song dimension captures all the details about a song, including editorial

Figure 1. Dimensions composing the Song Similarity Cube

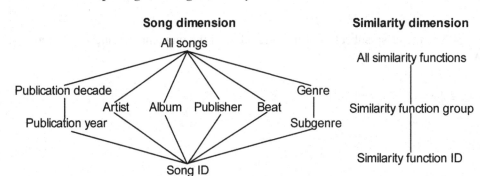

information such as the artist name, the publication year or any acoustic information such as the beat of the song or its genre. For each of these attributes, similarity functions can be created, e.g., an artist similarity function that gathers information from external web sites and social networks, or a similarity function that compares the genre wherein songs have been classified, aware that some genres are more similar than others, or the timbre comparison that uses low-level extracted information to provide a full comparison matrix.

Each dimension has a hierarchy, which defines how the data can be aggregated to provide different degrees of granularity, e.g., the similarity of songs between sub-genres and the similarity of songs between coarsely defined genres. Similarity function of coarser granularity can also span over different attributes, e.g., to provide some average similarity values out of attributes obtained using different extraction algorithms.

At its most detailed level, the cube is organized based on a star schema, using three tables: the song dimension table, the similarity function table and the closest songs fact table. The closest songs fact tables is composed of three attributes: a reference to a song (referred to as the seed song), a reference to a similarity function, and a fuzzy song set. The notion of similarity between a song and the seed song is represented by the fuzzy song set membership degree. The closest songs take a high membership degree while the farthest songs have a low membership degree.

Data of the Song Similarity are shown in Tables 1, 2, and 3.

Typical queries involve the intersection, union, and reduction operators. The queries can be performed on the song seeds using pieces of information such as the artist or the creation year. Closest Songs Cube usage examples are presented below. The example assumes the creation of a new SQL data type, called FZSET, using object-relational extensibility functionality like found in PostgreSQL. For example, the closest songs attribute in the fact table is of type FZSET. The FZSET implementation details will be discussed further.

Example 1:

"What are the songs that have a similar beat to the song "One" by U2?"

```
SELECT SUPPORT(REDUCE(0.6, c.songs)
FROM closest_songs c
INNER JOIN songs as a USING (song_id)
INNER JOIN similarity_functions as b USING (c.sim_id)
WHERE a.title = 'one' AND a.artist = 'U2' and b.sim = 'beat 1'
```

Table 1. CubeSong dimension

song id	title	Artist	album	beat	genre
1	One	U2	Achtung Baby	DATA	DATA
2	One	U2	Miss Sarajevo	DATA	DATA
3	Paint it black	Rolling Stones	Aftermath	DATA	DATA

Table 2. Similarity function dimension

Sim id	Sim function	Sim type
1	beat 1	beat
2	beat 2	beat
3	genre 1	genre

Table 3. Closest songs fact

song_id	sim_id	Closest_songs
1	1	{ 1.0/1; 0.5/2; 0.0/3 }
1	2	{ 1.0/1; 0.7/2; 0.1/3 }
1	3	{ 0.9/1; 0.4/2; 0.1/3 }
2	1	{ 1.0/1; 0.5/2; 0.4/3 }
2	1	{ 1.0/1; 0.5/2; 0.3/3 }
3	1	{ 1.0/1; 0.5/2; 0.5/3 }

In a star schema, the fact table and the 2 dimensions tables are joined to form the cube. Retrieving the similarities between a song and all the others simply requires selecting a song and a similarity function from the dimension tables and retrieving the corresponding FZSET in the closest song table. The *support* function transforms an FZSET data type into a regular SQL crisp set of elements having non-zero membership degrees.

Example 2:

"Find the beat similarity between two songs; the first song is identified with the artist, album, and title attributes from the song dimension, the second is identified using its unique key."

```
SELECT MU(c.songs,el)
FROM closest_songs c
INNER JOIN songs as a USING (song_id)
INNER JOIN similarity_functions as b USING (sim_id)
WHERE a.artist = 'U2' AND a.album='Achtung Baby' AND a.title='One' and b.sim = 'beat 1'
GROUP BY a.album_id
```

The *mu* function returns the membership value associated to a given element. The similarity between two songs can be obtained by retrieving the full fuzzy song set representing song similarities for the first song, and filtering out the results to only return the element matching the second song. However, with such an operation being so common, optimization based on the physical storage structure of the fuzzy song set can be performed, thus motivating the need for creating a specific element search function within a fuzzy song set.

Example 3:

"Retrieve the 100 songs having the most similar beat to the songs made by U2."

```
SELECT SUPPORT(TOP(100, UNION(c.songs))
FROM closest_songs c
INNER JOIN songs as a USING (song_id)
INNER JOIN similarity_functions as b USING (sim_id)
WHERE a.artist = 'U2' AND b.sim = 'beat 1'
GROUP BY a.album_id
```

Aggregation functions allow multiple fuzzy song sets to be retrieved and combined. In Example 3, multiple songs are matching the selection criteria in the song dimension, causing multiple fuzzy song sets to be retrieved from the closest song table. The fuzzy song sets are then combined using the union operator; finally the elements with the 100 highest membership degrees are returned.

Example 4:

"Return the similar songs to the given song across the different beat similarity functions available."

```
SELECT SUPPORT(AVG(songs))
FROM closest_songs c
INNER JOIN songs as a USING (song_id)
INNER JOIN similarity_functions as b USING (sim_id)
WHERE a.title = 'one' AND a.artist = 'U2' and b.sim = 'beat'
GROUP BY a.albumid, b.similarity_function_group
```

As in a spreadsheet, aggregation can be performed on both dimensions. Example 4 retrieves all the versions of a song in the different albums of an artist and returns an average over similarity functions of the same type, such as the beat, the genre, or the mood.

The User Feedback Cube

The User Feedback Cube collects relevance statistics about the songs proposed to users by the music recommendation system. As illustrated by Figure 2, the User Feedback Cube is composed of two dimensions: the user dimension and the query dimension. For each user and query, the user feedback is stored. The feedback given for a particular played song is stored as a membership degree representing how relevant the proposed song is in the context of the query. A very low membership degree is given when a user believes the song should not have been proposed. The Feedback and the Favorite Songs attributes are both defined using the FZSET abstract data type. The user dimension is composed of a hierarchy allowing users to be aggregated along the various attributes composing their profiles. One of these attributes is a fuzzy song set representing the user's favorite songs; it becomes thus simple to

Figure 2. Dimensions composing the User Feedback Cube

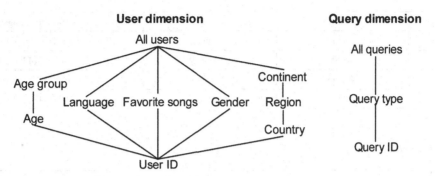

compare groups of users created based on the users' musical tastes. The hierarchy on the query dimension permits to obtain overview along group of semantically close queries.

Example 5:

"What are the favorite songs three users have in common?"

```
SELECT SUPPORT(REDUCE(0.8, INTER(Favorite songs))
FROM users
WHERE user_id = 1 OR user_id = 2 OR user_id = 3;
```

Retrieving the songs three users like is an immediate query using the proposed algebra; only the user dimension table is required. Here, the aggregation form of the intersection function allows straight-forward selection of the intersection between three multiple sets. The Reduce operator selects only the songs resulting from the intersection with a membership degree above 0.8. The support operator transform the fuzzy song set object into a crisp set that can be manipulated with the regular SQL algebra.

Data from the User Feedback Cube are shown in Tables 4, 5, and 6.

Example 6:

"Who are the 100 users that have the most similar taste to John's taste?"

```
SELECT b.user_id
FROM users as a, users as b
WHERE a.user_id = 1
ORDER BY distance(a.favorite_songs, b.favorite_songs) ASC
LIMIT 100;
```

Example 6 illustrates how, using a self-join, the user dimension can be used to find similarities between users based on their favorite songs.

Example 7:

"Per query type, what are the songs users born in the 80's were usually happy to hear?"

```
SELECT SUPPORT(REDUCE(0.8, AVERAGE(uf.feedback)), q.query_type
FROM user_feedbacks as uf
INNER JOIN users as u USING (user_id)
```

Table 4. Users dimension

User id	Name	DOB	Favorite songs
1	John	01 Jan 80	{ 1.0/1; 0.5/2; 0.0/3 }
2	Nadia	02 Feb 70	{ 1.0/41; 0.7/42; 0.1/43 }
3	Natalie	03 Mar 60	{ 0.9/11; 0.4/22; 0.1/33 }
4	Adam	04 Apr 83	{ 0.2/1; 0.47/; 0.13/23 }

Table 5. Queries dimension

Query id	Query	Query type
1	Rock songs	Genre
2	Pop songs	Genre
3	Songs marked as favorite by users with similar music profiles	Social
4	New song releases	Editorial

Table 6. User feedbacks fact

User id	Query id	Feedback
1	1	{ 1.0/1; 0.5/2; 0.0/3 }
1	2	{ 1.0/1; 0.7/2; 0.1/3 }
3	1	{ 0.9/1 0.4/2; 0.1/3 }

```
INNER JOIN queries as q USING (query_id)
WHERE '1 JAN 80' <= u.DOB AND u.DOB <= '31 DEC 89'
GROUP BY q.query_type;
```

Using the user dimension, only the users born in the 80's are selected, and the average feedback per query type is then calculated. Again, using the reduce and support operators, only the songs with a high membership degree are output as crisp sets.

Example 8:

"What are the 100 songs that fans of 'Elvis' liked the most when they asked for Rock songs?"

```
SELECT SUPPORT(TOP 100(AVERAGE(uf.feedback)))
FROM user_feedbacks as uf
INNER JOIN queries as q USING (query_id)
WHERE u.user_id IN (
SELECT user
FROM songs
WHERE SUPPORT(TOP(10,favorite song)) = song_id AND artist = 'Elvis'
) AND q.query = 'Rock songs'
```

Example 8 performs an aggregation of the user feedback. The selection of the users for the aggregation is performed using the favorite songs in the user dimension. Thus, both fuzzy song sets in the user dimension table and the fact table are used.

STORAGE OPTIONS

In this section, three different storage options for representing fuzzy song sets in the MW are presented: tables, arrays, and bitmaps. A prototypical MW where song elements are uniquely identified using 32 bits is used to illustrate the discussion. The proposed MW can reach a size of over 4 billion songs and at least 100 different membership degrees.

Table

The first solution is to represent the fuzzy song set attribute as a table with three columns: *(seed song, song, membership degree)*. Let s be the size of the seed song set, e the size of the song set, and m the size of the set of all the values the membership degree can take. The size of the payload, i.e., the size of the data when not considering the overhead due to the DBMS, denoted p, can be calculated as follows.

$$p = s.\ e(log_2 s + log_2 e + log_2 m)$$

where $log_2 s$, $log_2 e$, and $log_2 m$ are the minimum number of bits required to store respectively a seed song, a song, and a membership degree.

The quadratic growth can be limited by admitting only k songs for each seed song to be physically stored in the table and letting the remaining songs take a default membership degree. The selection of which song should be represented is dependent on the application. Here, we assume that the elements with the highest membership degree are interesting; this is performed using the Top_k operator. The size of the payload can then be estimated as follows.

$$p = s.\ k(log_2 s +\ log_2 e + log_2 m)$$

When 2^{32} seed songs are present, the database reaches its maximum capacity. In such case, the size of the payload, if only the 1000 elements with the highest membership degree are physically stored, reaches 36 TB. On a data set composed of 10,000,000 seeds, the payload attains 84 GB.

Array

A second approach is to use one-dimensional arrays containing the songs and their associated membership degrees for representing fuzzy song sets. The data is stored in a table with two columns: *(seed song, array)*. As with tables, only the k ($\leq e$) most similar songs should be physically stored. The size of the payload grows as follows.

$$p = s(log_2 s + k(log_2 e + log_2 m))$$

When storing the 1000 closest songs of 2^{32} song seeds, the size of the payload is reduced to 19 TB; on a data set composed of 10,000,000 song seeds, the payload reaches a size of 44 GB However, since the probability of having no songs for a particular membership degree is small, ordering the fuzzy song set by membership degrees allows membership degrees to be stored using one bit relatively to each other: a bit set means to move to the next lower membership degree, a bit unset means to keep the same membership degree. In the unlikely case of a gap in the sequence of membership degrees, a dummy element, referred to as the *empty element*, is used to jump to the next membership degree. For large gaps, successive empty elements are used.

For example, the fuzzy song set {100 / 1234,100 / 2345,99 / 3456,97 / 4567,96 / 5678} is represented by the array [{1234,100}, {2345,100}, {3456,99}, {4567,97}, {5678,96}] that is compressed as [{1234,0}, {2345,1}, {3456,1}, {0,1}, {4567,1}, {5678,0}], where only one bit is required to capture a decrement of the membership degree, and 0 is the empty element.

The compression ratio, r, obtained is as follows.

$$r = \frac{k(log_2 e + log_2 m)}{(k + x)(log_2 e + 1)}$$

In order to be efficient, i.e., $r > 1$, the number of empty elements, noted x, in the data set has to remain limited.

$$x < k \frac{log_2 m - 1}{log_2 e + 1}$$

The compression ratio in the best (no empty element) and worst ($m - 1$ empty elements) case scenarios are:

$$r^+ = \frac{log_2 m + log_2 e}{log_2 e + 1} \quad , \quad r^- = k \frac{log_2 m + log_2 e}{(k + m - 1)(log_2 e + 1)}$$

For high k values, the likelihood of using empty elements vanishes, therefore causing r^- to asymptotically converge to r^+ as k increases. Figure 4 shows the compression ratio r^+ and r^- for membership degrees represented on 7 bits (128 different values), and fuzzy song set and song seeds represented using

Figure 3. organization of a compressed array

seed	elem	elem	elem	elem	elem	elem	elem	elem
elem	elem	elem	gap	elem	elem	elem	elem	elem
elem	elem	elem	elem	elem	gap	elem	elem	elem
elem	elem	gap	elem	elem	elem	elem	elem	elem

Figure 4. best and worst compression ratio for the arrays

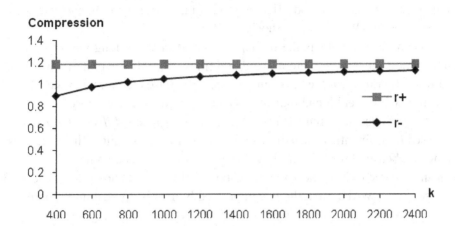

32 bits. For $k = 1000$, the compression ratio ranges between 1.04 and 1.18. The full similarity matrix represented with compressed arrays takes 17 TB.

Bitmap

A third option is to use bitmaps to represent fuzzy song sets. In a bitmap (Chan & Ioannidis, 1998), each element is represented by a position in a sequence of bits. Typically, in a bitmap index, a bitmap for each attribute value is created. The size of each bitmap is equal to the cardinality of the indexed elements. Fuzzy song sets can be constructed using the same structure. A fuzzy song set is composed of a bitmap for each membership degree an element can have. As illustrated in Figure 5, each song element is represented with a bit set in the bitmap corresponding to its membership degree.

A fuzzy song set where the membership degree has a cardinality of m is represented with m bitmaps of song elements, where each bitmap has a size of e bits. Thus the size of a fuzzy song set using bitmaps is as follows.

$$p = s(\log_2 s + m\ e)$$

Figure 5. representation of a fuzzy song set with an array of bitmaps

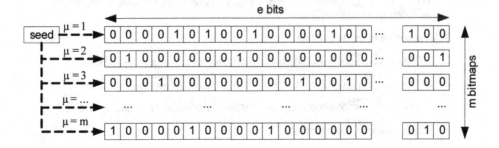

The bitmap size can be dramatically reduced using compression algorithms. The Word Aligned Hybrid (WAH) bitmap compression method offers a good compression ratio on sparse bitmaps while preserving query performances (Wu, Otoo, & Shoshani, 2006).

Briefly, in a WAH-compressed bitmap, the bitmap is divided in 32 bit long words. The first bit of each word is used to mark if the word is a literal word or a fill word. If the first bit of a word starts with a unset bit, the word is a literal word; the remaining bits are then used to store a classical 31 bit long bitmap. A fill word starts with a set bit and indicates the presence of a run composed of homogeneous 31 bit long groups of set or unset bits; thus, fill words are of two kinds: *0-Fills* or *1-Fills*. The second bit of a fill word is used to differentiate runs of unset bits from runs of set bits. The remaining 30 bits are used to count the number of homogeneous 31 bit long groups the run contains.

Figure 6 shows an example of how the bitmap composed of 9*0, 3*1, 56*0, 69*1, 98*0, 3*1 and 6*0 can be compressed using WAH. First, the uncompressed bitmap is divided into groups of 31 bits. If a group forms a literal word, an unset bit is prepended to it. Otherwise, the group is replaced by an appropriate fill word and a counter of the number of identical consecutive groups following the current group.

The WAH compression becomes effective when many consecutive zeros or ones can be represented with fill words. In the worst bit distribution, i.e., a random bitmap, the WAH algorithm reduces the size of the bitmap as follows.

$$p_{wah}\left(n, d, w\right) = \frac{n}{w-1}\frac{w}{}\left(1 - \left(1 - d\right)^{2w-2} - d^{2w-2}\right)$$

Figure 6. The WAH bitmap compression

Uncompressed bitmap:

```
00000000 01110000 00000000 00000000 00000000 00000000 00000000 00000000
00001111 11111111 11111111 11111111 11111111 11111111 11111111 11111111
11111111 10000000 00000000 00000000 00000000 00000000 00000000 00000000
00000000 00000000 00000000 00000000 00000000 00011100 0000
```

Uncompressed bitmap organized in groups of 31 bits:

```
0000000001110000000000000000000   0000000000000000000000000000000
0000001111111111111111111111111   1111111111111111111111111111111
1111111111111000000000000000000   0000000000000000000000000000000
0000000000000000000111000000       0000000000000001111000000
```

Merging consecutive homogenous 31 bits groups

```
0000000001110000000000000000000  x 1    0000000000000000000000000000000  x 1
0000001111111111111111111111111  x 1    1111111111111111111111111111111  x 1
1111111111111000000000000000000  x 1    0000000000000000000000000000000  x 2
0000000000000000000111000000     x 1
```

WAH encoding in words of 32 bits

```
          Literal word                              0 - Fill word, counter = 1
00000000001110000000000000000000       10000000000000000000000000000001

          Literal word                              1 - Fill word, counter = 1
00000001111111111111111111111111       11000000000000000000000000000001

          Literal word                              0 - Fill word, counter = 2
01111111111111000000000000000000       10000000000000000000000000000010

          Literal word
00000000000000000000111000000
```

where n is the size of the bitmap in bits, d is the bit density, i.e., the fraction of bits set, and w is the word length, (32 bits in our example). Using the top_k operator, the bit density is $d = k/e$. On a fuzzy song set of 2^{32} songs where only 1,000 songs are physically stored and $n = 2^{32}$, $d = 1,000 / 2^{32}$, the size of each bitmap is 64,000 bits.

As previously illustrated by Figure 5, a bitmap is constructed for each of the membership degree a song element can possibly take. The fuzzy song set is then represented using an array composed of 100 bitmaps, but this does not affect the size of the overall bitmap as the bit density of in each bitmap will proportionally decrease, maintaining the bit density in the full bitmap unchanged.

$$p \approx s \left[\log_2 s + \ p_{wah}\left(e.\ m, \frac{k}{e.\ m},\ w\right) \right]$$

In an MW of 2^{32} songs, where 1,000 song elements with the highest membership degree are physically stored, the size of the payload reaches 33 TB. On a data set composed of 10,000,000 song seeds, the payload size is 76 GB.

Payload Estimate Comparison

Figure 7 shows the expected size for storing a Fuzzy Song Set Attribute (FSSA) for each of the 2^{32} song seeds and for different values of k. The linear growth of the WAH bitmap with the number of stored elements is explained by considering $k / n \ll 1$ and applying a binomial decomposition. The payload can then be approximated by $p_{wah} \approx 2.k.w$.

$$p_{wah}\left(n,d,w\right) \begin{vmatrix} = \dfrac{n\ w}{w-1}\left(1-\left(1-d\right)^{2w-2}-d^{2w-2}\right) \\ \approx \dfrac{n\ w}{w-1}\left(1-\left(1-\left(2w-2\right)d\right)-0\right) \\ \approx \dfrac{n\ w}{w-1}\left(2w-2\right)d \approx 2\,w\,n\,d = 2\,k\,w \end{vmatrix}$$

Figure 7. estimated payload storage requirements

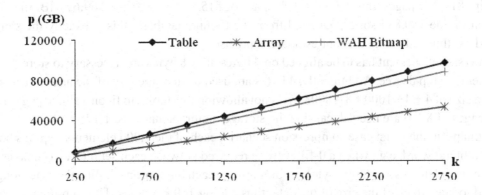

In arrays, the seed elements only have to be stored once per FZSET. Arrays take thus half the storage requirements of tables. With arrays, however, the data need to be compressed and reorganized, thus leading to an overall increase in complexity. The array compression scheme is focused on compressing the membership degree. The compression occurs on the 7 bits used to represent the membership degree but leave the 32 bits representing each element untouched; thus limiting the maximum compression performance that can be achieved. Bitmaps, on the other hand, are focused in compressing the 32 bits representing the elements; this is done by imposing a position to each song element. These important structural differences will have an impact on the implementation of operators and functions.

Storage Estimates and Benchmark

This section describes the storage requirements for the implementation of the Song Similarity Cube fact table. Therefore, some parts of the following are dependent on the DBMS chosen for implementing the cube. We calculate some storage requirements estimates for each of data structure. As our estimates match experimental results, we proceed on predicting the size of each storage option depending on the number of fuzzy elements they contain.

The experience was conducted on PostgreSQL 8.3, well-known for its scalability. As already explained, the songs can be uniquely identified using 32 bits and the membership degree of each song element has a granularity of 100. The dataset used for the implementation consists of 150,834 songs, gathered from the Intelligent Sound project. Song similarities are computed using a genre classifier collecting acoustic features from a popular media player (Lehn-Schiøler, Arenas-García, Petersen, & Hansen, 2006)

The expected table overhead in PostgreSQL can be estimated by considering tuple overhead and page overhead (PostgreSQL, 2008). In our configuration, pages have a fixed size of 8 KB. Since tuples are not allowed to span over multiple pages, PostgreSQL uses secondary storage tables, referred to as The Oversized-Attribute Storage Technique (TOAST) tables, to store large attributes. Using TOAST, large field values are compressed and/or broken up into multiple physical rows. TOAST tables use the Lempel-Ziv, briefly LZ, compression technique to reduce their size (Ziv & Lempel, 1977). The compression of 'toasted' attributes being optional, we will compare the different possible setups.

In a table, the number of rows is the product of the number of seeds and the number of elements per seed: $150,834.1000 = 150,834,000$ rows. Each page has a size of 8KB, with a header of 24 bytes, thus leaving 8,168 bytes of free space. Each row has a payload of $4 + 4 + 4 + 1 = 17$ bytes. Each tuple is stored after a 20 bytes long header, and is aligned to start on the 32nd byte. Therefore, the size of each row in the table is $31 + 17$ bytes. Thus, each page can accommodate 185 rows, and 150,834,000 rows will require 815,319 pages, thus taking a disk space of $815,319 * 8$ KB $= 6,369.67$ MB. In our storage experiment on the 150,834 songs, gathered from the iSound database, this is exactly the storage size taken on disk; thus indicating that our estimate is precise.

For arrays, each element has to be aligned on 4 bytes, thus 8 bytes are necessary to store the element and the membership degree. Additionally, 4 bytes are used to store the size of the array. Each array has therefore a size of $4 + 4 + 1000 * 8 = 8008$ bytes not allowing two tuples to fit on a single page. Therefore 150,834 pages of 8 KB are needed, causing the storage requirements to be 1,178 MB.

For bitmaps, in the worst case compression scenario, each of the 1,000 elements requires both a fill-word and a literal word, e.g., when a 0-fill word is required between each set bit. A word takes 4 bytes, thus 8 bytes per elements and 8,000 bytes per bitmap. For each bitmap, an additional 4 bytes long integer is required to keep track of the size of the data, thus adding $100 * 4$ bytes. Thus a bitmap cannot fit on a page and has to be moved to an auxiliary toast table, where each bitmap is split into chunks of 2,000 bytes. In that case, 4 rows per bitmap attribute are required in the auxiliary table. Storage estimates show that in the most pessimist case 1,472 MB are required to store the bitmaps. In the selected dataset, 183,184 pages are required to store the bitmaps. The total space taken by the WAH compressed bitmap storage representation is therefore: 1,431 MB.

If the number of element increases, a similar storage technique using an auxiliary TOAST table is required for the array data structure. As with bitmaps, data larger than 2,000 bytes is split into 2,000 bytes chunks. Each array is therefore divided into 5 chunks, and 150,834*5 chunks are needed. For each data chunk, a 31 bytes long header has to be added. Since 8,168 bytes of storage are available per page, only 4 chunks can be stored per page and 188,543 pages are needed. The total size of the array data structure is 1,472 MB when stored using a TOAST table.

Further compression of TOAST data using standard LZ algorithm can be performed. The compression ratios are data depending.

Table 7 shows the storage requirements for the three storage options. In addition, the space required to index seed songs and similarity functions using a standard B-Tree and storage requirements for LZ-compressed data are presented.

Our experiments show that the real size requirements match the estimates. While table are certainly the most straightforward solution, they are a bad choice for data storage requirements and indexing purposes. With respect to the payload, the arrays are very promising but suffer from an important overhead that makes arrays and WAH compressed bitmaps very comparable in term of storage size. Furthermore, since array elements are aligned on 8 bytes, compressing the array does not bring any storage benefit

Table 7. Comparison of the storage options

		Size (MB)
Table	Payload estimate	1,852
	Overhead estimate	4,518
	Total estimate	6,370
	Real size	6,370
	B-tree Index	3,231
	Total	**9,601**
Array	Payload estimate	666
	Overhead estimate	511
	Total estimate	1,178
	Real size	1,178
	Real size + LZ	794
	B-tree Index	3
	Total	**1,181**
WAH Bitmap	Payload estimate	1,151
	Overhead estimate	296
	Total estimate	1,447
	Real size	1,447
	Real size + LZ	719
	B-tree Index	3
	Total	**1,450**

and adds unnecessary complexity. LZ compression works better on bitmaps, therefore creating a sensible difference in favor of bitmaps; this is observation might, however, be data dependent. Finally, with respect to the implementation of the two new data types, WAH-bitmaps are a more complicated data structure to build; the compression requires some particular attention and the variable length nature of the bitmap brings additional complexity.

Using identical storage estimates, we predict the size of tables, arrays, and bitmap with respect to k. Considering that k elements are required in order for the data to be useful, we can thus choose what data structure is the most appropriate. The results of the size estimates are shown in Figure 8. For all values of k, tables are the worst solution. For $k > 2,000$, arrays and WAH-compressed bitmaps tend to behave very similarly. For lower values of k, due to the data organization in pages, results vary sensibly depending on k. However, arrays always keep a slight advantage.

FZSET FUNCTIONS AND OPERATORS

We now compare the array and bitmap storage structure with respect to the performances of their operators.

WAH Bitmap Operations

The original WAH compression method has been slightly adapted in order to manipulate bitmaps of different lengths. First, the last word, i.e., the remainder of the uncompressed bitmap is stored as if the bitmap is extended with extra unset bits to finish the last word. So a bitmap composed of: $10*0$'s, $21*1$'s, and $4*1$'s becomes <001FFFFF> <78000000> and not <0001FFFF> <0000000F> as in the original algorithm. This allows no particular treatment for the last word and allows expanding existing bitmaps without any extra manipulations.

Logical operations on WAH-compressed bitmaps can be performed without decompressing the bitmaps. Operations are performed by scanning both inputs word by word. If two fill words are met, the

Figure 8. estimated storage requirements including PostgreSQL overhead

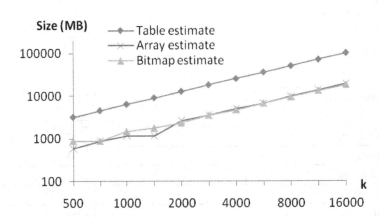

result will be a fill word of type resulting from the operation; its length is the minimum length of the two input fill words. If two literal words, or a literal and a fill word are met, the result will be a literal corresponding to the operation.

Listing 1. Pseudo C implementation of the bitwise logical AND operator on two WAH compressed bitmaps

```
struct wah32run_struct {
    unsignedint it; // iterator
    unsignedint data; // decompressed data
    unsignedint nWords; // group counter
    bool isFill;
};
staticinline void wah32_run_decode(wah32run run, unsigned int word) {
    if (WAH32_ISCOUNTER(word)) {
        run->data = (word > WAH32_ONECOUNTER ?
                WAH32_ALLONES : WAH32_ALLZEROES);
        run->nWords = word & WAH32_MASK_COUNTERVALUE;
        run->isFill = 1;
    }
else {
        run->data = word & WAH32_MASK_LITTERAL;
        run->nWords = 1;
        run->isFill = 0;
    }
}
// input: 2 bitmaps represented with 2 dynamic arrays of integers
// output: 1 bitmap represented with 1 dynamic array of integers
voidwah32_and(Intlist x, Intlist y, Intlist rtnBitmap) {
    unsignedint nWords = 0; // minimum counter
    wah32run xrun, yrun;
    xrun = wah32_run_init(); // initialize data struct
    yrun = wah32_run_init(); // initialize data struct
    while (xrun->it < intlist_size(x) && yrun->it < intlist_size(y))
{
        if (xrun->nWords == 0) // load a new word from x
                wah32_run_decode(xrun,*intlist_getp(x,xrun->it));
        if (yrun->nWords == 0) // load a new word from y
                wah32_run_decode(yrun,*intlist_getp(y,yrun->it));
        if (xrun->isFill && yrun->isFill) {
                // appends a fill word with counter = minimum counter
                nWords = min(xrun->nWords, yrun->nWords);
                wah32_appendFill(rtnBitmap, nWords,
                        xrun->data & yrun->data);
                xrun->nWords -= nWords;
                yrun->nWords -= nWords;
        }
        else {
                // append a literal word to the bitmap
                wah32_appendLit(rtnBitmap, xrun->data & yrun->data);
                (xrun->nWords)--;
                (yrun->nWords)--;
        }
        if (xrun->nWords == 0)(xrun->it)++;
        if (yrun->nWords == 0)(yrun->it)++;
    }
    wah32_run_free(xrun);
    wah32_run_free(yrun);
}
```

Intersection and Union

The computation of the intersection or the union of two fuzzy song sets represented in arrays is performed by a modified sort-merge. The arrays are first decompressed and sorted by element. In our experiment, the sorting of the array with respect to its elements is done using the quicksort algorithm. Once sorted, the membership degrees of identical elements are compared. For an intersection, if both elements are present, the minimum membership degree is placed in the array; for a union, the maximum membership degree of both elements or the membership degree of the existing element are placed in the return array.

The computation of the WAH union is performed as follows. In the WAH bitmap representation, the elements are organized per membership degree. For each membership degree starting from the highest, we perform a logical OR on the compressed bitmaps. To prevent future operations to set a bit already set previously for another membership degree, we have to maintain a history of bit, also represented using a WAH-bitmap. This costs two additional operations on the bitmaps, a compressed NOT-AND to check that a bit was not previously set, and a compressed or, to maintain the history up to date as we scan through the various membership degree. Pseudo C code for performing the union is shown in Listing 2, results are shown in Figure 9. The computational cost of the "OR", the "NOT-AND", and the "OR" for maintaining the set bit history are shown in Figure 9. The WAH union is the sum of the three operations.

No update of the history is needed when handling the last bitmap, thus the CPU time reaches a ceiling when no more elements are added to a bitmap corresponding to a level higher than 1. After 2000 elements, all the bitmaps have elements. New elements are added in the last bitmap corresponding to the lowest membership degree.

For sparse bitmaps, the number of elements grows linearly with the number of elements. As the density of bits set increases, the proportion of literal words increases, thus increasing the likelihood of new element being added to existing literals rather than splitting fill words into literals. Figure 10 shows the average input and output length of the bitmaps used for benchmarking the CPU time of the "OR" operation. After 2000 elements, the length growth diminishes due to the increase in the number of literals.

The union of arrays is highly efficient for low numbers of elements. As expected, their performances decrease as the number of elements increases. Additionally, the sort operation significantly increases the computation time. Note, however, that the resulting set is sorted, thus preventing successive sort

Listing 2. Pseudo C implementation of the union of fuzzy song sets represented with two arrays of WAH compressed bitmaps with membership degree ranging from 0 to 100

```
wahbitmap * union(wahbitmap *x, wahbitmap *y) {
    wahbitmap tmp, history; // temporary and history bitmaps
wahbitmap z[101]; // z is the return array of bitmap
    unsignedshort mu; // membership degree
    for (mu = 100; mu >= 2 ; mu--) {
        tmp = wah_or(x[mu],y[mu]); // logical or, save in tmp
        z[mu] = wah_notand(history,tmp); // check with history
        history = wah_or(history,tmp); // update history
    }
    // for mu = 1, no history update
    tmp = wah_or(x[mu],y[mu],); // logical or
    z[1] = wah_notand(history,tmp); // check with history
    return z;
}
```

Figure 9. CPU time required for the various steps of a union of fuzzy song sets represented with bit-maps

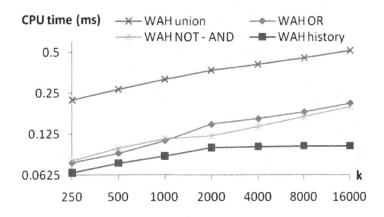

operations to be necessary, e.g., in case the function is used for an aggregation. But, even in the best case scenario, when no sorting of the elements is required, the CPU time spent on the union of arrays is proportional to the number of elements in the sets. Bitmap operations, however, are linearly proportional to the number of words in the input bitmap and not directly to number of elements, i.e., the number of bits set. As the number of elements increases, bitmaps will keep a nearly constant processing time where arrays will be proportional to the number of elements. Efficiency of the array and bitmaps union operations on the song similarity dataset is shown in Figure 11.

Top

The top operation for the array data structure requires ordering the elements with respect to their membership degrees. Since the number of membership degrees is limited, the sort is performed using a bucket sort whose complexity is linear in the number of elements.

Figure 10. Input and output length depending on the number of song elements stored

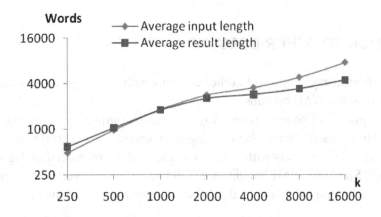

Figure 11. comparison between the performances of the union operator for arrays and WAH bitmaps

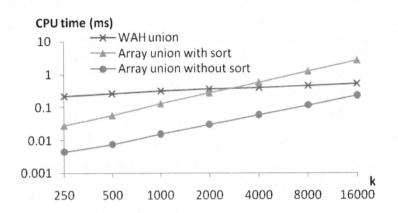

For WAH bitmaps, the elements are already grouped by membership degree. The only operation required is to scan the compressed bitmap, starting with the highest membership degree. As soon as k elements are found, the scan stops. The number of operations is thus only depending on the number of words needed to be read during the scan before k set bits are found. Unlike arrays, the operation is independent from the total number of elements in the bitmaps. Pseudo C code for performing the top is shown in Listing 3.

Finally, returning the resulting WAH bitmaps is performed simply by copying the input bitmaps and truncating it at the right place. Sorting the array is a slower process as it requires copying elements one by one. The CPU time spent for performing top operations depending on the size of the fuzzy song set are shown in Figure 12.

Reduce

On an array, the reduce operation requires scanning the elements of the array; the computational cost is therefore proportional to the number of elements. In a WAH bitmap, since the elements are already organized per membership degree, the operation only consists of deleting the bitmaps corresponding to membership degree lower than alpha from the input bitmap. Pseudo C code for performing the reduce operation is shown in Listing 4. The computation time results are shown in Figure 13.

GENERALIZATION TO OTHER DOMAINS

The generalization from fuzzy song sets to other domains with respect to the storage solutions is immediate for both arrays and WAH bitmaps.

For fuzzy sets requiring a fine level granularity, i.e., a high cardinality of membership degrees, the number of bits used to represent the membership degree on uncompressed arrays grows logarithmically. On compressed arrays, for fuzzy sets with at least one element per membership degree, no size difference will be noticed. Similarly, WAH bitmaps are well known to scale very well with high cardinality attributes as their size is bounded by the total number of elements and not the number of bitmaps.

Listing 3. Pseudo C implementation of the top operation of a fuzzy song set represented by an array of WAH compressed bitmaps with membership degree ranging from 0 to 100

```
wahbitmap * wah_top(wahbitmap * x, unsignedint k) {
    for (mu = 100; mu >= 0; mu--) {
        if (k > 0) wah_truncate_k(&k,x[mu]);
        else x[mu] = 0;
    }
    return x;
}
wahbitmap wah_truncate_k(unsignedint *k, wahbitmap x){
    while (xrun->it < bitmap_size(x)) {
        tmp = bitmap_get(x,xrun->it); // get new word
        wahrun_decode(xrun,*tmp); // decode the current word
        nWords += xrun->nWords; // update the word counter
        if (xrun->isFill && xrun->data == ALLONES) {
            if (setbitcount + 31 * xrun->nWords > *k) {
                // append trailing fills then a literal
                // set k = 0 and leave
                // ...
            }
            setbitcount += 31 * xrun->nWords;
        }
        else {
            if (setbitcount + bitCount(xrun->data) > *k) {
                // need to find which bit exactly is the k
                // override trailing bit with 0
                // set k = 0 and leave
                // ...
            }
            setbitcount += bitCount(xrun->data);
        }
        xrun->it++; // point to next word
    }
    *n-=setbitcount; // remaining number of bits not found
}
```

Figure 12. Comparison between the performances of the top operator for arrays and WAH bitmaps

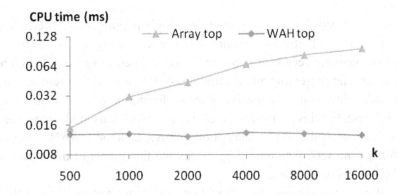

Listing 4. Pseudo C implementation of the reduce operation of a fuzzy song set represented by an array of WAH compressed bitmaps with membership degree ranging from 0 to 100

```
wahbitmap * wah_reduce(wahbitmap *x, unsignedint alpha) {
    for (mu = alpha - 1; mu > 0; mu--) {
        x[mu] = 0;
    }
    return x;
}
```

Figure 13. comparison between the performances of the reduce operator for arrays and WAH bitmaps

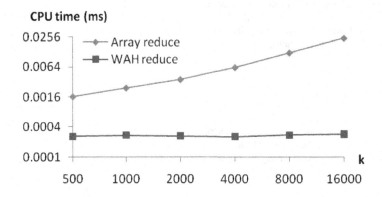

Finally, the performance studies of the previously presented operators are directly applicable to fuzzy sets. For other operators, e.g., intersections defined using different t-norms, new performance studies are required. For WAH bitmaps, the computational time will be proportional to the number of logical bitwise operations required on the compressed bitmaps.

CONCLUSION AND FUTURE WORK

As music recommendation systems are becoming increasingly popular, new efficient tools able to manage large collections of musical attributes are urgently needed. Fuzzy sets prove to be well suited for addressing various problematic scenarios commonly encountered in recommendation systems. After defining fuzzy song sets and presenting an algebra to manipulate them, we demonstrate the usefulness of fuzzy song sets and their operators to handle various information management scenarios in the context of a music warehouse. For this purpose we create two multidimensional cubes: the Song Similarity Cube and the User Feedback Cube. Three data options, arrays, tables and WAH bitmaps, are envisioned for representing fuzzy song sets. We proceed by discussing the impact of these data structures on the storage space and operators performance.

With respect to storage, while arrays first show to be a very good choice from a theoretical point of view, they suffer from a significant overhead. Estimates taking into account DBMS overheads show that the differences between WAH bitmaps and arrays vanish as the number of elements grows. The different data organizations in WAH bitmaps and in arrays cause operators to behave very differently depending on the number of elements. Arrays are very efficient when the number of elements remains limited. However, due to frequent sorting operations, arrays behave poorly for larger sets. Requiring more complex management, bitmaps suffer from a higher starting overhead that is mostly visible when the number of elements is low. As the number of elements grows, operations on bitmap are faster than on arrays. In our experiment with the largest number of elements, the *Union* operator on WAH bitmaps is performed 5 times faster than on arrays, the speedup factor is 7 for the *Top* operator and 85 for the *Reduce* operator.

Future research directions include the development of methods for the transparent manipulation of arrays and bitmap and the automatic selection of a data structure option during the query plan optimization phase. Further research on how to improve the WAH compression performance by using a longer alignment without diminishing the compression ratio seems also promising, e.g., for 64 bits system architecture.

ACKNOWLEDGMENT

This work was supported by the Danish Research Council for Technology and Production, through the framework project "Intelligent Sound"[1] (STVF No. 26-04-0092).

REFERENCES

Antoshenkov, G. (1994). *U. S. Patent No. 5363098*. Washington, DC: U.S. Patent and Trademark Office.

Aucouturier, J.-J., & Pachet, F. (2002). Scaling up music playlist generation. In *Proceedings of the IEEE International Conference on Multimedia and Expo (ICME'02)* (pp. 105-108).

Bordogna, G., Lucarella, D., & Pasi, G. (1994). A fuzzy object oriented data model. In *Proceedings of the IEEE Conference on Fuzzy Systems* (pp. 313-318).

Bosteels, K., & Kerre, E. E. (2007). Fuzzy audio similarity measures based on spectrum histograms and fluctuation patterns. In *Proceedings of the International Conference on Multimedia and Ubiquitous Engineering (MUE07)* (pp. 361-365).

Chan, C.-y., & Ioannidis, Y. E. (1998). Bitmap index design and evaluation. In *Proceedings of the ACM SIGMOD 1998* (pp. 355-366). New York: ACM Press.

Codd, E. F. (1979). Extending the database relational model to capture more meaning. *ACM Transactions on Database Systems, 4*(4), 397–434. doi:10.1145/320107.320109

Deliège, F., & Pedersen, T. B. (2006). Music warehouses: Challenges for the next generation of music search engines. In *Proceedings of the International Workshop on Learning the Semantics of Audio Signals* (pp. 95-105).

Deliège, F., & Pedersen, T. B. (2007). Using fuzzy song sets in music warehouses. In *Proceedings of the International Conference on Music Information Retrieval (ISMIR'07)* (pp. 21-26).

Galindo, J., Piattini, M., & Urrutia, A. (2005). *Fuzzy databases: Modeling, Design and implementation.* Hershey, PA: IGI Publishing. *Intelligent sound.* (n.d.). Retrieved from http://www.intelligentsound.org

Jensen, C. A., Mungure, E. M., Pedersen, T. B., & Sørensen, K. (2007). A data and query model for dynamic playlist generation. In *Proceeding of IEEE-MDDM* (pp. 65-74).

Lehn-Schiøler, T., Arenas-García, J., Petersen, K. B., & Hansen, L. K. (2006). A genre classification plug-in for data collection. In *Proceedings of the International Conference on Music Information Retrieval (ISMIR'06)* (pp. 320-321).

Pampalk, E. (2005). Speeding up music similarity. *Report on the Music Information Retrieval Evaluation EXchange (MIREX'05).*

Pauws, S., & Eggen, B. (2001). PATS: Realization and user evaluation of an automatic playlist generator. In *Proceedings of the International Conference on Music Information Retrieval (ISMIR'02)* (pp. 179-192).

Pedersen, T. B., & Jensen, C. (2001). Multidimensional database technology. *IEEE Computer*, *34*(12), 40–46.

Postgre, S. Q. L. (2008). *Postgresql manual.* Retrieved November 2008, from, http://www.postgresql.org/docs/8.3/interactive/storage-toast.html

Prade, H., & Testemale, C. (1984). Generalizing database relational algebra for the treatment of incomplete or uncertain information and vague queries. *Information Sciences*, *34*, 115–143. doi:10.1016/0020-0255(84)90020-3

Rubenstein, W. B. (1987). A database design for musical information. In *Proceedings of ACM SIGMOD* (pp. 479-490).

Wang, C., Li, J., & Shi, S. (2004). A music data model and its application. In *Proceedings of the International Conference on Multimedia Modeling (MMM'04)* (pp. 79-85).

Wu, K., Otoo, E. J., & Shoshani, A. (2006). Optimizing bitmap indices with efficient compression. *ACM Transactions on Database Systems*, *31*(1), 1–38. doi:10.1145/1132863.1132864

Wynblatt, M. J., & Schloss, G. A. (1995). Control layer primitives for the layered multimedia data model. In *Proceedings of the ACM International Conference on Multimedia* (pp. 167-177).

Zadeh, L. A. (1965). Fuzzy sets as a basis for a theory of possibility. *Information and Control*, *8*, 338–353. doi:10.1016/S0019-9958(65)90241-X

Ziv, J., & Lempel, A. (1977). A universal algorithm for sequential data compression. *IEEE Transactions on Information Theory*, *23*(3), 337–343. doi:10.1109/TIT.1977.1055714

ENDNOTE

[1]   http://www.intelligentsound.org

Chapter 4
Mining Association Rules from Fuzzy DataCubes

Nicolás Marín
University of Granada, Spain

Carlos Molina[1]
University of Jaen, Spain

Daniel Sánchez
University of Granada, Spain

M. Amparo Vila
University of Granada, Spain

ABSTRACT

The use of online analytical processing (OLAP) systems as data sources for data mining techniques has been widely studied and has resulted in what is known as online analytical mining (OLAM). As a result of both the use of OLAP technology in new fields of knowledge and the merging of data from different sources, it has become necessary for models to support imprecision. We, therefore, need OLAM methods which are able to deal with this imprecision. Association rules are one of the most used data mining techniques. There are several proposals that enable the extraction of association rules on DataCubes but few of these deal with imprecision in the process and give as result complex rule sets. In this chapter the authors will present a method that manages the imprecision and reduces the complexity. They will study the influence of the use of fuzzy logic using different size problems and comparing the results with a crisp approach.

INTRODUCTION

As defined by OLAP Council (2007) *"On-Line Analytical Processing (OLAP) is a category of software technology that enables analysts, managers and executives to gain insight into data through fast, consistent, interactive access to a wide variety of possible views of information that has been transformed from*

DOI: 10.4018/978-1-60566-858-1.ch004

raw data to reflect the real dimensionality of the enterprise as understood by the user". According to Han (1997), the use of OLAP systems in data mining is interesting for the following three main reasons:

- Data mining techniques need integrated, consistent and clean data to work with (Fayyad, Piatetsky-Shapiro, Smyth, & Uthurusamy, 1996). The data processing performed when building a data warehouse guarantees these qualities in data and converts data warehouses into good data sources for data mining.
- Users frequently need to explore the stored data, selecting only a portion of them, and might want to analyze data at different abstraction levels (different levels of granularity). OLAP systems are designed to ease these operations in a flexible way . The integration of data mining techniques with OLAP provides the user with even more flexibility.
- It is difficult to predict what knowledge is required a priori. The integrated use of OLAP and suitable data mining methods allows the user to obtain this knowledge using different approaches and representations.

Information in decision support systems usually has an ill-defined nature. The use of data from human interaction may enrich the analysis (Gorry & Morton, 1971) and, nowadays, it is common for companies to require external data for strategic decisions. These external data are not always compatible with the format of internal information and even if they are, they are not as reliable as internal data. Moreover, information may also be obtained from semi-structured or non-structured sources.

In addition, OLAP systems are now being used in new fields of knowledge (e.g. medical data) that present complex domains which are difficult to represent using crisp structures (Lee & Kim, 1997). In all these cases, flexible models and query languages are needed to manage this information.

These reasons, among many others, justify the search for multidimensional models which are able to represent and manage imprecision. Some significant proposals in this direction can be found in the literature (Laurent, 2002; Jensen, Kligys, Pedersen, & Timko, 2004; Alhajj & Kaya, 2003; Molina, Sánchez, Vila, & Rodríguez-Ariza, 2006). These proposals support imprecision from different perspectives. In (Molina, Sánchez, Vila, & Rodríguez-Ariza, 2006), we propose a fuzzy multidimensional model that manages imprecision both in facts and in the definition of hierarchical relationships. These proposals organize imprecise data using DataCubes (imprecise DataCubes) and it is therefore necessary to develop data mining techniques that can work over these imprecise DataCube models.

Our aim in this chapter is to study the influence of using fuzzy logic in the scalability of a method to extract association rules from a fuzzy multidimensional model that can represent and manage imprecision in different aspects: COGARE. As we have already mentioned, previous proposals in the literature are directed towards obtaining as many associations as possible. However, they produce complex results (e.g. a high number of rules, rules that represent the same knowledge at different detail levels, etc.). In contrast, this proposal has two main goals:

- Firstly, to manage data imprecision throughout the entire process.
- Secondly, to reduce the complexity of the final result using both the fuzzy concepts and the hierarchical relation between elements, without reducing the quality of the rule set.

In the literature there are some other approaches to reduce the complexity of the results (closed itemsets, maximal itemsets, etc.) but they work on another way because these methods try to reduce the number of rules shown to the user but been able to recover all the association rules. Our approach will try to reduce the global number of association, not only the way to represents them.

During all the process fuzzy logic is used. This introduces complex calculation along with the high time consuming process of data mining. What we want to do in this chapter is study the influence of the use of the fuzzy logic in the process of extraction association rules over fuzzy DataCubes and the overload.

Next sections present the data mining method proposed, and after that, the data used for the study and the results of the experiments.

ASSOCIATION RULE EXTRACTION

In this section, we will briefly describe the main published approaches for association rule extraction. We will first discuss classical methods. As the multidimensional models usually define hierarchies, the multi-level association methods are interesting when studying the association rule extraction over them. The final subsection introduces the proposed method to work on both crisp and fuzzy DataCubes.

Association Rules

Agrawal et al. (Agrawal, Imielinksi, & Swami, 1993) formalized the problem of association rule extraction. Let $I= \{i_1, i_2, ..., i_m\}$ be a set of literals called items and D be a set of transactions, where each transaction T is a set of items such that $T \subseteq I$. A transaction T contains the set of items X if $X \subseteq T$.

Definition 1. Let $I= \{i_1, i_2, ..., i_m\}$ be a set of literals and D be a set of transactions defined over I. An association rule is an implication $X \rightarrow Y$, where $X \subset I$, $Y \subset I$, and $X \cap Y = \emptyset$.

The quality of the rules is usually measured in terms of the confidence and the support of the rule. The confidence is computed as the percentage of transactions that contain both X and Y with respect to the transactions that contain X, while the support of the rule is the percentage of transactions that contain XY in the entire dataset. First approaches considers interesting only the rules with a confidence and support greater than a threshold. These rules are called strong rules.

The association rule extraction process is divided into two phases:

- Discover the frequent item sets, i.e. the sets of items with a support greater than a given threshold.
- Build the association rules using the previously obtained frequent item sets.

Since the first step is the most time-consuming, there are proposals which focus on the optimization of the frequent item set calculation (Agrawal & Sritkant, 1994; Park, Chen, & Yu, 1995; Brin, Motwani, Ullman, & Tsur, 1997; Savasere, Omiecinski, & Navathe, 1995; Han, Pei, & Yin, 2000).

Multiple-Level Association Rules

The use of taxonomies over the data is interesting because the desired associations may not appear at the most detailed level but at higher levels. Researchers have also paid attention to this approach, and a first proposal (Srikant & Agrawal, 1995) applies a rule extraction process to all the levels. The authors

Figure 1. Frequent item sets at different levels using the same support threshold

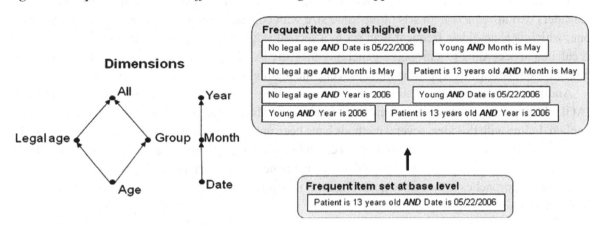

define an interest measure that is used to prune the rule set. In this way, a rule is deleted if a rule defined at a higher level exists and the first does not give more information. This approach considers the same support threshold for all the levels.

When the taxonomy is complex or when a relatively high number of levels is considered, a high number of rules appears. Let us explain this with a naive example. Figure 1 represents a possible taxonomy over data. Let us suppose that the item set *{Age is 13, Date is 05/22/2006}* is frequent; then all the items that group one of the values will be frequent, and all the combinations of these values will also be frequent.

This circumstance will imply that the following item sets will be frequent: *{Young, Date is 05/22/2006}*, *{Age is 13, May}*, *{Young, May}*, *{No legal age, Date is 05/22/2006}*, *{No legal age, May}*, *{Age is 13, Year 2006}*, *{Young, Year 2006}* and *{No legal age, 2006}*.

Therefore, for a single item set we obtain another 8 frequent item sets that represent exactly the same information at different abstraction levels. When the method finishes, it will produce a high number of rules that are redundant (i.e. they represent the same information at different abstraction levels). This fact only increases the complexity for the user.

The method uses an interesting measure to reduce redundant rules if other rules at a higher level give at least the same information. However, it allows redundant rules if the concrete ones are of a higher quality.

Han and Fu (1995) proposed a top-down approach using a single taxonomy: an item set is considered to be frequent if the support is greater than a threshold and all the ancestors are also frequent. The items belonging to an item set are all defined at the same detail level. Later the authors adjust the algorithm to work with different details level (1999). The authors used different support thresholds for each level that must be established by the user (if the taxonomy is complex, this involves a large number of parameters), and do not consider multiple taxonomies over the items. Thus, if the domain is complex, it may not be modeled well.

Shen and Shen (1998) proposed another method that extracts all the strong rules which are defined at all the combinations of detail levels using different taxonomies, considering the same threshold. Yen (Yen, 2000) used a graph structure to obtain the relationships between elements at all the detail levels. Both approaches present the same problems as those mentioned for Srikant and Agrawall's proposal: a large number of rules with redundant information.

The method proposed by Lui and Chung (2000) uses a bottom-up approach. In this case, the method considers two infrequent item sets of the same size with common items, and generalizes them to a new one, which is a candidate frequent item set in a second stage. The support threshold for each item set is calculated according to a proposed generality measure. As the generalization process is applied only once, if the relationships appear at higher levels, the method will not discover them.

Another approach to association rule extraction using taxonomies is attribute-oriented induction (AOI). In this case, the taxonomies are used to raise the abstraction of the items before the process is applied. In line with this idea, several methods have been proposed (Han, Cai, & Cercone, 1993; Muyeba & Keane, 2000) and these have recently been extended to use fuzzy hierarchies (Angryk & Petry, 2005). The idea is to reduce the number of rules decreasing the number of items to consider. The main problem of all these approaches is that since generalization is applied before rule extraction, information is lost in the process.

Association Rules over DataCubes

Let us now briefly describe some proposals for association rule extraction on DataCubes. The first approach can be found in (Kamber, Han, & Chiang, 1997). The authors proposed a method that works over a very simple multidimensional model (there are neither hierarchies on the dimensions nor grouping mechanisms to change the granularity of the data) and which focuses on frequent item set calculation to speed up the process using DataCube operations.

Zhu (1998) proposed a more complex approach, with the definition of three different associations:

- Intra-dimensional association: the association is found between elements in the same dimension (item dimension), using another dimension to calculate the support (transaction dimension).
- Inter-dimensional association: in this case, the associations hold between elements in different dimensions.
- Hybrid association: this association is the result of merging the two previous types. The method first looks for intra-dimensional frequent item sets and then for inter-dimensional frequent item sets, merging the resulting sets in order to obtain the rules.

In all the cases, the method works over a single abstraction level, and the support threshold is therefore a single value. For multi-level association rules, the user must run the method for all the level combinations required, defining the same number of support thresholds as executions (something which may be very complex for the user) or using the same value for the entire process. As the final result is the union of all of the obtained rule sets, there may be a high number of rules and repeated associations expressed at different abstraction levels (as in Srikant and Agrawal's proposal as mentioned in the previous section).

Finally, Kaya and Alhajj (2003; 2005) propose a method that works over a simple fuzzy multidimensional model. The proposed DataCube structure defines fuzzy relations at the lowest abstraction level and does not support imprecision in hierarchies or facts, as well as the normal operations over DataCubes (e.g. changing the detail level, reducing the dimensionality of the DataCube, etc.). Under these circumstances, users would have less flexibility since they cannot explore the data. The proposed method extracts association rules at all abstraction levels, obtaining intra-dimensional and inter-dimensional associations as previously presented. The user must establish a support threshold for each level in the DataCube and the threshold for an item set will be the minimum of the threshold established for each item. The authors use an interesting measure to reduce certain problems of confidence when measuring the quality of the rules, but do not control the redundant associations defined at different abstraction levels.

THE FUZZY MULTIDIMENSIONAL MODEL

Although there is no standard multidimensional model, we shall briefly introduce the common characteristics of the first models proposed in literature. In classical multidimensional models, we can distinguish two different types of data: on the one hand, we have the facts being analyzed, and on the other, the dimensions that are the context for the facts. Hierarchies may be defined in the dimensions (Agrawal, Gupta, & Sarawagi, 1995;Kimball, 1996;Cabibbo & Torlone, 1997;Cabibbo & Torlone, 1998).

The different levels of the dimensions allow us to access the facts at different levels of granularity. In order to do so, classical aggregation operators are needed (maximum, minimum, average, etc.). Other models, which do not define explicit hierarchies on the dimensions, use other mechanisms to change the detail level (Li & Wang, 1996; Datta & Thomas, 1999). The model proposed by Gray et al. (Gray, Chaudhuri, Bosworth, Layman, Reichart, & Venkatrao, 1997) uses a different approach. This model defines two extensions of the relational group by (rollup and cube) that are used to group the values during the aggregation process.

As the models that define hierarchies usually use many-to-one relations, one element in a level can only be grouped by a single value of each upper level in the hierarchy. This makes the final structure of a DataCube rigid and well defined in the sense that given two values of the same level in a dimension, the set of facts relating to these values have an empty intersection. The normal operations (roll-up, drill-down, dice, slice, and pivot) are defined in almost all the models. Eventually, some of the models define other operations in order to provide the end user with additional functionality (Agrawal, Gupta, & Sarawagi, 1995; Gray, Chaudhuri, Bosworth, Layman, Reichart, & Venkatrao, 1997; Datta & Thomas, 1999).

A Fuzzy Multidimensional Structure

In this section, we will briefly introduce a fuzzy multidimensional model which we have already developed to manage data imprecision (Molina, Sánchez, Vila, & Rodríguez-Ariza, 2006). The model is provided with explicit hierarchies that can use fuzzy relations between elements in two levels.

Definition 2. A dimension is a tuple $d=(l, \leq_d, l_\perp, l_\top)$ where $l=\{l_i, i=1,...,n\}$ so that each l_i is a set of values $l_i=\{c_{i1}, ..., c_{in}\}$ and $l_i \cap l_j = \emptyset$ if $i \neq j$, and $\leq_d$ is a partial order relation between the elements of l so that $l_i \leq_d l_k$ if $\forall c_{ij} \in l_i \Rightarrow \exists c_{kp} \in l_k | c_{ij} \subseteq c_{kp}$. $l_\perp$ and $l_\top$ are two elements of l so that $\forall l_i \in l \ l_\perp \leq_d l_i$ and $l_i \leq_d l_\top$

We use level to denote each element li. In order to identify level l of dimension d we will use $d.l$. The two special levels $1_\perp$ and $1_\top$ will be called the base level and top level, respectively. The partial order relation in a dimension is what gives the hierarchical relation between the levels. An example of dimension on the ages can be found in Figure 2.

The domain of a dimension will be the set of all the values that appear in all the defined levels.

Definition 3. For each dimension d, the domain is $dom(d) = \bigcup l_i$

In the above example, the domain of the dimension Age is $dom(Age) = \{1, ..., 100, Young, Adult, Old, Yes, No, All\}$.

Figure 2. Example of hierarchy over ages

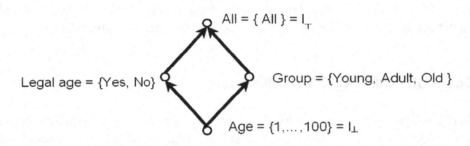

Definition 4. For each l_i, the set

$$H_{l_i} = \{l_j \; / \; l_j \neq l_i \wedge l_j \leq_d l_i \wedge \neg \exists l_k \quad l_j \leq_d l_k \leq_d l_i\}$$

is called the set of *children of level l_i*.

This set defines the set of all the levels which are below a certain level (l_i) in the hierarchy. In addition, this set gives the set of levels whose values or labels are generalized by the ones included in li. Using the same example of the dimension on the ages, the set of children in level All is H_{All} = *{Group, Legal age}*. In all the dimensions defined for the base level, this set will always be empty (as the definition shows).

Definition 5. For each l_i the set

$$P_{l_i} = \{l_j \; / \; l_i \neq l_j \wedge l_i \leq_d l_j \wedge \neg \exists l_k \quad l_i \leq_d l_k \leq_d l_j\}$$

and we call this the *set of parents of level l_i*.

For a certain level, this set shall give all the levels that group or generalize the values of the level. In the hierarchy we have defined, the set of parents in level Age is P_{Age}=*{Legal age, Group}*. In the case of the top level of a dimension, this set shall always be empty.

In the case of fuzzy hierarchies, an element can be related to more than one element in the upper level and the degree of this relationship is in the interval [0,1]. The kinship relationship defines this degree of relationship.

Definition 6. For each pair of levels l_i and l_j such that $l_j \in H_i$, we have the relation

$$\mu_{ij} : l_i \times l_j \rightarrow [0,1]$$

and we call this the *kinship relationship*.

The degree of inclusion of the elements of a level in the elements of their parent levels can be defined using this relation. If we only use the values 0 and 1 and we only allow an element to be included with degree 1 in a unique element of its parent levels, this relation represents a crisp hierarchy.

Figure 3. Example of the calculation of the extended kinship relation. a) path All-Legal Age-Age b) path All-Group-Age

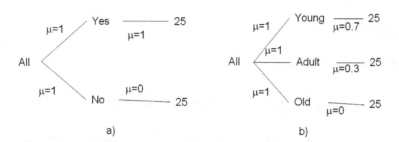

If we relax these conditions and we allow values to be used in the interval [0,1] without any other limitation, we have a fuzzy hierarchical relationship. This allows several hierarchical relations to be represented in a more intuitive way. An example can be seen in Figure 3 where we present the group of ages according to linguistic labels. Furthermore, this fuzzy relation allows hierarchies to be defined where there is imprecision in the relationship between elements of different levels. In this situation, the value in the interval shows the degree of confidence in the relation.

Using the relation between elements in two consecutive levels, we can define the relation between each pair of values in different levels in a dimension.

Definition 7. For each pair of levels l_i and l_j of dimension d such that $l_i \leq_d l_j \wedge l_i \neq l_j$

$$\eta_{ij}(a,b) = \begin{cases} \mu_{ij}(a,b) & si \quad l_j \in H_{l_i} \\ \underset{l_k \in H_{l_i}}{\oplus} \underset{c \in l_k}{\oplus} (\mu_{ik}(a,c) \otimes \eta_{kj}(c,b)) & otherwise \end{cases}$$

where $\otimes$ and $\oplus$ are a t-norm and a t-conorm, respectively, or operators from the families MOM and MAM defined by Yager (1994), which include the t-norms and t-conorms, respectively. This relationship is called the extended kinship relationship.

This relation gives us information about the degree of relationship between two values in different levels within the same dimension. In order to obtain this value, it considers all the possible paths between the elements in the hierarchy. Each one is calculated by aggregating the kinship relationship between elements in two consecutive levels using a t-norm. The final value is then the aggregation of the results of each path using a t-conorm.

By way of example, we will show how to calculate the value of $\eta_{All,Age}(All, 25)$. In this situation, we have two different paths:

- *All -Legal age -Age*. In Figure 3.a it is possible to see the two ways of reaching 25 from All through the level legal age. The result of this path is $(1 \otimes 1) \oplus (1 \otimes 0)$.
- *All -Group -Age*. This situation is very similar to the previous one. In Figure 3.b it is possible to see the three different paths going through the level Group. The result of this path is $(1 \otimes 0.7) \oplus (1 \otimes 0.3) \oplus (1 \otimes 0)$.

We must now aggregate these two values using a t-conorm in order to obtain the final result. If we use the maximum as t-conorm and the minimum as t-norm, the result is

$$((1 \otimes 1) \oplus (1 \otimes 0)) \oplus ((1 \otimes 0.7) \oplus (1 \otimes 0.3) \oplus (1 \otimes 0)) =$$

$$(1 \oplus 0) \otimes (0.7 \oplus 0.3 \oplus 0) = 1 \oplus 0.7 = 1$$

Thus, the value of $\eta_{All,Age}(All, 25)$ is 1, which means that the age 25 is grouped by All in level All with grade 1.

Definition 8. We say that any pair (h, α) is a fact when h is an m-tuple on the attribute domain we want to analyze, and $\alpha \in [0, 1]$.

The value α controls the influence of the fact in the analysis. The imprecision of the data is managed by assigning an α value that represents this imprecision. When we operate with the facts, the aggregation operators must manage these values in the computations. The arguments for the operator can be seen as a fuzzy bag (Yager, 1986; Delgado, Martin-Bautista, Sanchez, & Vila, 2003) since they are a set of values with a degree in the interval [0,1] that can be duplicated. The result of the aggregation must also be a fact. So, in the fuzzy case, the aggregation operators may be defined as follows:

Definition 9. Let $\tilde{B}(X)$ be all the possible fuzzy bags defined using elements in $\tilde{X}$, $\tilde{P}(X)$ be the fuzzy power set of X, and D_x be a numeric or natural domain. We define an aggregation operator G as a function $G : \tilde{B}(X) \rightarrow \tilde{P}(X) \times [0,1]$

When we apply an aggregation operator, we summarize the information of a bag of values into a single value and it is not always possible to undo this operation. If we want to undo operations that reduce the level of detail in a DataCube, we therefore need something to prevent this problem and so we define the object history that stores a DataCube's aggregation states.

Definition 10. An object of type history is the recursive structure

$$H^0 = \Omega$$
$$H^{n+1} = (A, l_b, F, G, H^n)$$

where:

- Ω is the recursive clause,
- F is the fact set,
- l_b is a set of levels $(l_{1b}, ..., l_{nb})$,
- A is an application from l_b to F $(A:l_b \rightarrow F)$,
- G is an aggregation operator.

This structure enables detail levels of the DataCube to be stored while it is operated on so that it may be restored to a previous level of granularity.

We can now define the structure of a fuzzy DataCube. A DataCube can be considered to be the union of a set of facts (the variables to analyze) and a set of dimensions (the context of the analysis). In order to report the facts and dimensions, we need a correspondence which for each combination of values of the dimension gives us the fact related to these coordinates in the multidimensional space defined by the dimensions.

In addition to these DataCube features, we also need the levels that establish the detail level that the facts are defined with, and a history-type object that keeps the aggregation states during the operations. The DataCube is therefore defined in the following way:

Definition 11. A DataCube is a tuple $C = (D, l_b, F, A, H)$ such that

- $D = (d_1, ..., d_n)$ is a set of dimensions,
- $l_b = (l_{1b}, ..., l_{nb})$ is a set of levels such that lib belongs to d_i,
- $F = R \cup \varnothing$ where R is the set of facts and $\varnothing$ is a special symbol,
- H is a history-type object,
- A is an application defined as $A : l_{1b} \times ... \times l_{nb} \rightarrow F$ that gives the relation between the dimensions and the facts defined.

If for $\vec{a} = (a_1, ..., a_n)$, $A(\vec{a}) = \varnothing$, this means that no fact is defined for this combination of values. Normally, not all the combinations of level values have facts. This situation is shown by the symbol $\varnothing$ when application A is defined.

The basis of the analysis will be a DataCube defined at the most detailed level. We shall then refine the information while operating on the DataCube. This DataCube is basic.

Definition 12. We say that a DataCube is basic if $l_b = (l_{1\perp}, ..., l_{n\perp})$ and $H = \Omega$.

Operations

Once we have the structure of the multidimensional model, we need the operations to analyze the data in the DataCube. Over this structure we have defined the usual operations of the multidimensional model:

Roll-Up

Going up in the hierarchies to reduce the detail level. In this operation we need to know the facts related with each value in the desired level. The set of facts is obtained using the kinship relationships as follows:

Definition 13. For each value c_{ij} belonging to l_r, we have the set

$$F_{c_{ij}} = \begin{cases} \bigcup_{l_k \in H_{l_r}} F_{c_{kp}} \ / \ c_{kp} \in l_k \wedge \mu_{ik}(c_{ij}, c_{kp}) > 0 & if \ \ l_r \neq l_b \\ \left\{ h \ / \ h \in F \wedge \exists \vec{c} A(\vec{c}) = h \right\} & if \ \ l_r = l_b \end{cases}$$

where $\vec{c} = (c_b^1, ..., c_{ij}, ..., c_b^n)$.

Once we have the facts for each value, we must aggregate them to obtain a new fact according to the new detail level. The influence of each fact in the aggregation will depend on the relation of the fact with the value considered and the α value assigned to the fact. Fuzzy operators are needed for this process.

This operation may be defined in the following way:

Definition 14. The result of applying roll-up on dimension d_i, level l_{ir} $(l_{ir} \neq l_{i\perp})$, using the aggregation operator G on a DataCube $C=(D, l_b, F, A, H)$ is another DataCube $C' = (D, l'_b, F', A', H')$ where

- $l'_b = (l_{1b}, ..., l_{ir}, ..., l_{nb})$,
- $A'(c^1_b, ..., c^i_r, ..., c^n_b) = G\left(\left\{ h \mid h \in F_{c^i_r} \wedge \exists c^i_b A(c^1_b, ..., c^i_b, ..., c^n_b) = h \right\} \right)$,
- F' is the range of A',
- $H'=(A, l_b, F, G, H)$.

Drill-Down

This operation implies go down in the hierarchies to increase the detail level. In this operation, we use the history-type object. Since this structure stored the initial aggregation state when roll-up operations were applied, by using the information stored in this structure we can therefore get to a previous detail level. The operations may therefore be defined as:

Definition 15. The result of applying drill-down on a DataCube $C=(D, l_b, F, A, H)$ where $H = (A', l'_b, F', G', H')$ is another DataCube $C' = (D, l'_b, F', A', H')$.

Dice

This operation consists on a projection over the DataCube using a condition. In this operation we must identify the values in the dimension that satisfy the condition or that are related with a value that satisfy the condition. This relation is obtained using the kinship relationship. Once we have reduced the values in the dimension, we must eliminate the facts for which the coordinates have been removed.

Definition 16. The result of applying dice with the condition β on level l_r of dimension d_i in a Data-Cube $C =(D, l_b, F, A, H)$ is another DataCube $C' = (D, l'_b, F', A', \Omega)$ where

- $D' = d_1, ..., d'_i, ..., d_n$ with $d'_i = (l'_i, \leq_{d_i}, l_b, l_\top)$ where $l' = l_j \mid l_b \leq_d l_j$ and

$$
d'_i.l'_j = \begin{cases}
\left\{ c_{jk} \mid c_{jk} \in l_j \wedge \beta(c_{jk}) \right\} & if \quad l'_j = l_r \\
\left\{ c_{jk} \mid c_{jk} \in d_i.l_j \wedge \delta_{rj}(c_{jk}) \right\} & if \quad l'_j \leq_d l_r \\
\left\{ c_{jk} \mid c_{jk} \in d_i.l_j \wedge \delta_{jr}(c_{jk}) \right\} & if \quad l_r \leq_d l'_j
\end{cases}
$$

where $\delta_{ij}(c) = \exists c_r \in l_r \beta(c_r) \wedge \eta_{ij}(c_r, c) > 0$,

- $A'(c^1_b, ..., c^i_b, ..., c^n_b) = (h, \alpha) \mid c^1_b \in d'_1.l'_b \wedge ... \wedge c^n_b \in d'_n.l'_b \wedge A(c^1_b, ..., c^n_b) = (h, \alpha)$,
- F' is the range of A'.

Slice

The slice operation reduced the dimensionality of the DataCube. When we apply this operation, we eliminate one of the DataCube's dimensions and so we must adapt the granularity of the facts using a fuzzy aggregation operator.

Definition 17. The result of applying slice on dimension di using the aggregation operator G in a DataCube $C = (D, l_b, F, A, H)$ is another DataCube $C' = (D, l_b', F', A', \Omega)$ where

- $D' = (d_1, ..., d_{i-1}, d_{i+1}, ..., d_n)$,
- $l_b' = (l_{ib}, ..., l_{i-1b}, l_{i+1b}, ..., l_{nb})$,
- $A'(c_b^1, ..., c_b^{i-1}, c_b^{i+1}, ..., c_b^n) = G\left(\left\{h \mid \exists c_b^i A(c_b^1, ..., c_b^{i-1}, c_b^i, c_b^{i+1}, ..., c_b^n) = h\right\}\right)$,
- *F'* is the range of *A'*.

Pivot

This operation implies to change the order of the dimensions. This operation does not affect the facts, only the order of the coordinates that defined them.

Definition 18. The result of applying pivot on dimensions d_i and d_j in a DataCube $C = (D, l_b, F, A, H)$ is another DataCube $C' = (D', l_b', F, A', \Omega)$ where

- $D' = (d_1, ..., d_{i-1}, d_j, d_{i+1}, ..., d_{j-1}, d_i, d_{j+1}, ..., d_n)$,
- $l_b' = (l_{1b}, ..., l_{i-1b}, l_{jb}, l_{i+1b}, ..., l_{j-1b}, l_{ib}, l_{j+1b}, ..., l_{nb})$,
- $A'(c_b^1, ..., c_b^{i-1}, a_b^i, c_b^{i+1}, ..., c_b^{j-1}, c_b^j, c_b^{j+1}, ..., c_b^n) = A(c_b^1, ..., c_b^{i-1}, a_b^j, c_b^{i+1}, ..., c_b^{j-1}, a_b^i, c_b^{j+1}, ..., c_b^n)$

The properties of these operations have been studied in (Molina, Sánchez, Vila, & Rodríguez-Ariza, 2006).

COMPLEXITY MEASURE

Since our approach is supposedly driven by the desire to reduce the complexity of the obtained results, we therefore need to measure a rule set's complexity in order to compare different results and decide which is the least complex. We follow a similar approach to Atzmueller et al. (Atzmueller, Baumeister, & Puppe, 2004) by considering two factors for the complexity:

- Number of rules: the greater the number of rules in the results, the greater the complexity for the user. The following section will describe a function to measure this factor.
- Complexity of the rule elements: very specific values (e.g. dates) result in more specific information but are more difficult for the user to understand than elements in higher abstraction levels (e.g. months instead of specific dates). Next sections present the functions for measuring the abstraction of a rule and a set of rules.

Number of Rules

As we have already mentioned, a large number of rules will increase the complexity and make the rule set harder to understand. We want to measure the complexity as a value in the [0,1] interval. A rule set with a complexity value which is close to 0 will have very few rules while a value which is close to 1 will correspond to a set with a high cardinality. Under these circumstances, a function can be considered to measure the complexity if it satisfies the following definition:

Definition 19. A function C_{NR} defined as

$$C : N \rightarrow [0,1]$$

is a complexity function based on the number of rules when $C_{NR}(x) \geq C_{NR}(y)$, for all x and y such that $x>y$.

All the functions with this behavior can be used to measure the complexity produced by the number of rules. Nevertheless, this definition does not take into account the size of the problem, i.e. the number of items. If we get a result with 100 rules for a problem that involves relations among 100 items, we can intuitively conclude that this set presents less complexity than another with the same number of rules for a problem with 10 items. This is why we think that the complexity function should also depend on the size of the problem.

Similarly, two result sets for the same problem with either 4000 or 5000 rules will be about as difficult to understand. If, however, the sets have either 10 or 100 rules, although the difference in cardinality is less than in the other case, there will be a greater difference in complexity from the user's point of view. According to this intuitive behavior, the function should not present a linear behavior. Taking this discussion into account, the following function is proposed:

Definition 20. Let N be the number of items in the dimensions of the DataCube C. The complexity of the rule set C_R over the DataCube C is a function $C_{NR}:N \rightarrow [0,1]$ with the value

$$C_{NR}(C_R) = 1 - e^{-\frac{|C_R|}{N}}$$

Figure 4 shows the behavior of the function for three different problem sizes.

Abstraction

The abstraction of an item will depend on the level defined. In a DataCube, elements at higher levels will present a higher abstraction than elements at lower ones, since the first ones group the second ones. Thus, intuitively, an abstraction function would behave in the following way.

Definition 21. Let D be a dimension. A function A defined as

$$A: dom(D) \rightarrow [0, 1]$$

is an abstraction function if it satisfies the following properties:

Figure 4. Complexity function due to number of rules

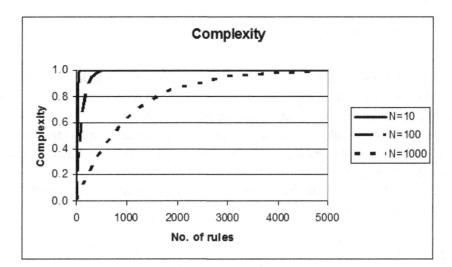

- If $c_i \in l_i \land c_j \in l_j \land l_j \in P_{l_i}$ then $A(cj) \geq A(Ci)$ (the abstraction increases if we go up through the hierarchies defined in the dimension).
- If $c_i \in l\bot$ then $A(c_i)=0$ (all the elements at the most detailed level (the base level of the dimension) have the lowest possible abstraction).
- If for $c_i \in l_i$ we get $\forall c_\bot \in l_\bot$: $\eta_{i\bot}(c_i,c_\bot)=1$ then $A(c_i)=1$ (an element that groups all the elements in the base level has the highest possible abstraction).

In view of the established properties, the abstraction function must take into account the granularity of the elements. One possibility is to define the abstraction according to the levels in the hierarchy. In this case, all the items in a level will share the abstraction value. This situation, however, can present ceratin problems because elements at the same level will not always have the same granularity. For example, if we consider a level to define Legal age, this level has two values: *Yes* and *No*. In Spain, both values will group different numbers of ages (the value No groups the ages *{1,...,17}* and *Yes* the remaining values *{18,...100,....}*) so both have different levels of granularity, and naturally, different levels of (*Yes* abstraction group more values so they appear to present higher abstraction than *No*). Therefore, the proposed abstraction function considers each element independently of its level but measures its granularity. The following definition presents the abstraction function we have chosen.

Definition 22. A is an abstraction function defined as $A:dom(D) \rightarrow [0, 1]$ when for an element $c_i \in l_i$ the value is

$$A(c_i) = \frac{V_{l_i}(c_i)}{|l_\bot|}$$

where $|l\bot|$ represents the number of elements in the base level of the dimension and

$$V_{l_i}(c_i) = \begin{cases} \sum_{\forall c_\perp \in l_\perp} \eta_{i\perp}(c_i, c_\perp) & \text{if } l_i \neq l_\perp \\ 0 & \text{otherwise} \end{cases}$$

It should be noted that we consider the number of elements in the base level grouped by value in order to define the abstraction. This approach is similar to the one proposed by Lui and Chung (Lui & Chung, 2000) but considering fuzzy hierarchical relations.

The abstraction of a rule would depend on the items that appear in the rule. Once we know the abstraction of each of the items, the abstraction of the whole rule is defined as the average abstraction of the items that define the rule.

Definition 23. Let R be a rule with the elements $I_1, ..., I_N$ and $_A$ an abstraction function. The abstraction of the rule is

$$A_R = \frac{\sum_{i=1}^{N} A(I_i)}{N}$$

In order to measure the abstraction of a rule set, we consider the abstraction of each rule that appears in the set. Not all the rules, however, have the same importance and some may be more representative of the data set according to their support. In order to measure the abstraction of the set, we consider the abstraction of each rule weighted by the support of the rule. Under these considerations, the abstraction of a rule set is defined as follows.

Definition 24. Let $C_R = \{R_1, ..., R_N\}$ be a rule set with associated support $sop(R_1), ..., sop(R_N)$ and A be an abstraction function. The abstraction of C_R would be

$$A_{C_R} = \frac{\sum_{i=1}^{N} A_{R_i} sop(R_i)}{\sum_{i=1}^{N} sop(R_i)}$$

Global Measure

In previous sections, we have defined two functions which are useful for measuring the complexity due to the number of rules and to the abstraction of a result rule set. In order to define a global measure, we now need to combine both functions to obtain a value in [0, 1] that represents the complexity of the set according to both factors:

Definition 25. Let $\alpha \in [0, 1]$. We define the global complexity of a rule set CR as

$$C_{global}(C_R) = \alpha \times C_{NR}(C_R) + (1 - \alpha) \times (1 - A_{C_R})$$

Depending on the value of α, the function controls the relative importance of each complexity measure in the final value. The abstraction of the items will help in the comprehension of the rules but the

Table 1. Contingency table with relative values

	Satisfy C	Not satisfy C	
Covered by R	f_{rc}	$f_{r\bar{c}}$	f_r
Not covered by R	$f_{\bar{r}c}$	$f_{\bar{r}\bar{c}}$	$f_{\bar{r}}$
	f_c	$f_{\bar{c}}$	1

number of rules may have a greater influence on the complexity for the final user (intuitively, a low number of rules with concrete values will be easier to understand than a high number of rules defined at high abstraction levels). Therefore, we suggest a value of $\alpha = 0.6$.

QUALITY MEASURES

The method we used is based on the complexity of the result obtained, but controlling the quality loss of the rule set. Thus, the method must use a quality measure. We first describe the measures that are conventionally used. Later, a new way of computing the quality of a rule set based on these measures is introduced.

Classical Measures

In this section, we will present some of the main quality measures used in the literature. We will only introduce the expression and briefly comment on the characteristics of these measures. For a deeper study, the reader can consult comparative studies about the performances of these measures in (An & Cercone, 2004; Dean & Famili, 1997; Pedrycz, 2004; Tan & Kumar, 2000). All the measures can be expressed in terms of relative frequencies. If $R:A \rightarrow C$ is a rule, Table 1 shows the contingency table with relative values.

Consistency is the normal quality measure used in association rule extraction, called in this field the Confidence of the rule. Its aim is to measure specificity, but various problems arise when very frequent items appear.

Coverage measures the extent to which the domain of the consequent is covered by the rule (the maximum value is reached when all the elements that satisfy C are covered by the rule). Both the Confidence and Coverage, measure two important factors for the rule quality, but if we use them separately we can reach bad conclusions (rules that cover few elements in the case of Consistency, or a high number of false positives when using the Coverage). To improve the performance, certain authors have proposed a combination of both measures: Michalski (1990) uses a weighted combination which concedes greater importance to Consistency when it reaches high values, and Brazdil and Torgo (1990) propose a combination that adjusts the Consistency according to the Coverage.

Another classical measure is the Certainty factor, proposed by Shortliffe and Buchanan (1975). This has been used in induction systems and measures both direct relations (antecedent implies the consequent) and indirect relations (when the antecedent appears, it implies no occurrence of the consequent). This measure has also been used in association rules (Delgado, Marin, Sanchez, & Vila, 2003) because it does not present some of the problems of the Confidence.

Agreement measures use the main diagonal of the contingency table, and Cohen and Coleman's measures are defined in this way. Bruha (1996) proposed two measures that attempt to combine the best characteristics of both. Measures from other knowledge fields have also been used to compute the quality of the rules, such as Information Gain, Logical Sufficiency,and Discrimination. In some situations, the measures lack a formal analysis of the dependencies and are empirically defined. An example of these measures is IMAFO (Famili, 1990) which combines two measures for the accuracy and coverage of the rules.

Table 2 gathers the expressions of the measures based on the contingency values.

Quality Measure for a Rule Set

Although all of the previously presented quality measures compute the quality of a given rule, we need to measure the quality of an entire rule set. As we have previously done with abstraction, we now propose a general measure that takes into account the importance of each rule. We propose the use of the weighted arithmetic average. The following definition shows the quality measure for a rule set.

Definition 26. Let $C_R = \{R_1,...,R_N\}$ be a set of rules, $sop(R_i)$ be the support for rule R_i, and Q_R be a quality measure for the rules. The quality of the rule set is defined as

$$Q_{C_R} = \frac{\sum_{i=1}^{|C_R|} Q_R(R_i) \times sop(R_i)}{\sum_{i=1}^{|C_R|} sop(R_i)}$$

COGARE ALGORITHM

As we have already mentioned, one of the main problem of previous rule extraction methods is the complexity of the results. Normally, the number of rules obtained is high and this complicates their interpretation. In addition, if the elements used to define the rules have a high level of detail, they will be even more complex for the user.

In this section, we will describe method to accomplish this task based on fuzzy DataCubes: COGARE (*COmplexity Guided Association Rule Extraction*). This method extracts inter-dimensional association rules and tries to reduce the complexity of the obtained rules using the fuzzy concepts defined in the dimensions and hierarchies. The use of fuzzy logic allows concepts to be defined more naturally from the user's point of view. If the rules are defined using these concepts, they will be more understandable for the user due to the use of concepts nearer to the user's language. The hierarchies are helpful in two ways:

Table 2. Quality measures

Measure	Expression
Consistency	$Cons(R) = \dfrac{f_{rc}}{f_r}$
Coverage	$Cov(R) = \dfrac{f_{rc}}{f_c}$
Michalski	$M(R) = w_1 \times Cons(R) + w_2 \times Conv(R)$ where $w_1 = 0.5 + \dfrac{1}{4} Cons(R)$ and $w_2 = 0.5 - \dfrac{1}{4} Cons(R)$
Brazdil and Torgo	$BT(R) = Cons(R) \times e^{Conv(R)-1}$
Centainty factor	$CF(R) = \begin{cases} \dfrac{Cons(R) - f_c}{1 - f_c} & if \quad Cons(R) > f_c \\ \dfrac{Cons(R) - f_c}{f_c} & if \quad Cons(R) < f_c \\ 0 & otherwise \end{cases}$
Cohen	$Cohen(R) = \dfrac{Cons(R) - f_c}{\frac{1}{2}\left(1 + \dfrac{Cons(R)}{Cov(R)}\right) - f_c}$
Coleman	$Coleman(R) = \dfrac{Cons(R) - f_c}{1 - f_c}$
Bruha	$C1(R) = Coleman(R) \times \dfrac{2 + Cohen(R)}{3}$ $C2(R) = Coleman(R) \times \dfrac{1 + Cov(R)}{2}$
Information gain	$IG(R) = -\log(f_c) + \log\dfrac{f_{rc}}{f_r}$

- Firstly, it is possible that a relation does not appear in a detailed level but can be found at higher detail levels. Thus, by using hierarchies we can extract rules at different abstraction levels and get information that does not appear at lower levels;

Table 2. continued

Measure	Expression
Logical sufficiency	$$LS(R) = \dfrac{\left.f_{rc}\middle/f_c\right.}{\left.f_{r\bar{c}}\middle/f_{\bar{c}}\right.}$$
Discrimination	$$D(R) = \log \dfrac{\left.f_{rc}\middle/f_{\bar{r}c}\right.}{\left.f_{r\bar{c}}\middle/f_{\bar{r}\bar{c}}\right.}$$
IMAFO	$IMAFO(R) = (AC \times E_C) \times 10$ where $AC = f_{rc} + f_{\bar{r}\bar{c}}$ and $$E_C = e^{\frac{f_{rc}}{f_c} - 1}$$

- Secondly, according to the hierarchical relation between elements, the number of rules can be reduced because some rules can be generalized to a single rule using elements which group the elements that appear in the rules we want to reduce.

COGARE is based on these ideas, and two main steps can be identified in the method:

- Rule generation: the extraction begins by obtaining rules at the most detailed possible level. It attempts to calculate the frequent item sets at base levels of the dimensions. If an item set is not frequent at this level, the method generalizes the items using the hierarchies. This process is repeated until the item set is frequent or the elements can no longer be generalized. The rules are generated using these frequent item sets.
- Generalization process: the result of the previous step is then generalized using the hierarchical relations. In this case, the method tries to reduce the complexity of the result, using more abstract elements in the definition of the rules and reducing the cardinality. In this step, the quality loss is also controlled.

Since the method is developed to work over fuzzy DataCubes, COGARE manages fuzzy concepts in both steps. The following sections will explain each phase.

Rule Generation

In this phase, the algorithm extracts association rules between elements at different dimensions and multiple levels. We can differentiate two steps:

- Obtain the frequent item sets.
- Generate rules using the item sets found in the previous step.

COGARE uses an extension of the Apriori algorithm (Agrawal & Sritkant, Fast Algorithms for Mining Association Rules in Large Databases, 1994). Candidates to obtain the frequent 1-itemset (item sets that only have 1 element) are all the elements defined at the base level of all the dimensions:

$$C_1 = \bigcup_{\forall D_i \in C} l_{i\perp}$$

where C is a DataCube. An item set will be frequent if its support is equal to or greater than a given threshold. For the base level, the process uses a value given by the user (*threshold$_{SUP}$*). If the item set is not frequent, then it is generalized, considering all the elements in parent levels that are directly connected and that group the item (Figure 5). The new item sets obtained are considered as candidates. This process is repeated until the item set is accepted as frequent or we can no longer generalize. We follow a similar strategy to Lui and Chung's proposal (Lui & Chung, 2000).

These new item sets are defined using elements at a more abstract level. Each item may group more than one element at the base level. Then, to be considered interesting, the support threshold should be defined according to the abstraction level. All the elements at higher levels may group several values at the base level; the support threshold should therefore be greater than the one established for these. Under these circumstances, the algorithm should use different support thresholds for each abstraction level. Some approaches ask the user for a value for each level (Alhajj & Kaya, 2003). Depending on the number of dimensions and the level, this approach may imply asking the user for an excessive number of values. In order to avoid this problem, we propose that the abstraction of an item set be used in order to define the threshold as follows: for an item set I and an abstraction function A, the support threshold is defined as

$$\text{threshold}_I = \text{threshold}_{SUP} + (1 - \text{threshold}_{SUP}) \times A(I)$$

where:

- *threshold$_{SUP}$* is the support threshold established by the user for the basic levels.

Figure 5. Example of generalization of non frequent 1-itemset

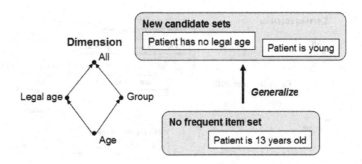

- *A(I)* is the abstraction of the item set I.

Once the process has all the frequent 1-item sets, it applies an Apriori strategy to obtain frequent item sets with more elements: to calculate the frequent k-item sets, it considers as candidates all the k-element sets that can be built using the frequent (k – 1)-item sets, as long as all their subsets are frequent. In our case, the item sets must be defined using elements at different dimensions (we look for inter-dimensional relations).

The candidate k-item sets are considered frequent if their support is greater than the support threshold corresponding to their abstraction (using the previous formulation). As in the 1-item sets case, if a set is not frequent, the algorithm considers as new candidates all the possible generalized item sets defined using elements at parent levels which group the elements of the set (Figure 6). The pseudo-code of the process is shown in Figure 7.

From the frequent item sets, the algorithm builds association rules using the same *Apriori* method (considering a certainty factor threshold *threshold$_{CF}$* instead of a threshold over the rule consistency).

Generalization Process

At the end of the previous phase, the algorithm obtains a rule set, trying to represent as much information as possible about the DataCube. The method then tries to reduce the complexity of this set. The method must deal with the factors we have identified: the number of rules and the abstraction.

The method applies a generalization process to reduce the complexity. This approach works directly on the abstraction and indirectly on the number of rules. We shall explain this by means of an example.

Let us suppose we have the following two rules:

If [Patient is 13 years old] then [Severity is low]
If [Patient is 20 years old] then [Severity is low]

We can generalize both antecedents, replacing 13 years old and 20 years old with the value Young that groups both elements. The abstraction of the rules will increase because new rules are defined using a higher level concept. However, the number of rules also decreases because both rules will be translated into the same one as in the generalization:

Figure 6. Example of generalization of non frequent 2-item set

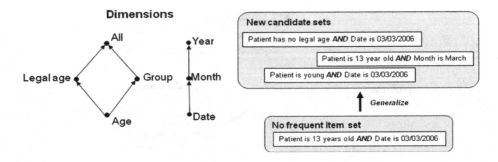

Figure 7. Algorithm to obtain frequent itemsets

Algorithm: $CalculateFrequentItemSets(threshold_{SUP}, C)$

- Input:
  - $threshold_{SUP}$: support threshold to consider an itemset as frequent
  - C: DataCube
- Output:
  - Set of frequent itemsets (C_F)

1) $C_F \leftarrow \emptyset$
2) $k \leftarrow 0$
3) Do
    a) $k \leftarrow k+1$
    b) If $k = 1$ then
        i) $C_1 \leftarrow \bigcup_{\forall D_i \in C} l_{i\perp}$
    c) else
        i) $C_k \leftarrow$ Generate candidates using C_{Fk-1}
    d) $C_{Fk} \leftarrow \emptyset$
    e) While $C_k \neq \emptyset$ do
        i) $I \leftarrow$ First element of C_k
        ii) $C_k \leftarrow C_k - \{I\}$
        iii) $sop_I \leftarrow$ calculate the support of I
        iv) If $sop_I \geq threshold_{SUP} + (1 - threshold_{SUP}) \times A(I)$ then
            A) $C_{Fk} \leftarrow C_{Fk} \bigcup \{I\}$
        v) else
            A) $C_k \leftarrow C_k \bigcup Generalize(I)$
    f) End while
    g) If $k \neq 1$ then
        i) $C_F \leftarrow C_F \bigcup C_{Fk}$
4) While $C_{Fk} \neq \emptyset \wedge k <$ No. of dimensions
5) Return C_F

If [Patient is Young] then [Severity is low]

In view of this, the generalization process is expected to reduce the complexity due to the number of rules and abstraction. This process will be applied until the complexity of the result is below a threshold established by the user (*threshold_{Complexity}*) without disregarding the loss of quality.

The generalization process has two steps. First, it tries to reduce the complexity through generalization but without allowing loss of quality. Then, if the method does not obtain a result set below the threshold, it applies a generalization allowing the decrease of quality.

Loss-Less Generalization

This first approach applies an iterative generalization but only accepts a new rule set if the quality of the new set is greater than or equal to the previous one. The scheme of the process is shown in Figure 8.

The first step in the process is to find the elements that generalize the rule set (C_R). The method looks at each item in each rule and obtains the elements in the DataCube which group them with a kinship relationship which is greater than 0 ($\mu_{ij} > 0$). Under these circumstances, the method only looks for generalization elements at parent levels which are directly connected to the considered item level.

One element must then be chosen to generalize the rule set. In order to select the element, all the items are sorted using a heuristic: an element that generalizes more elements would be better if it is supposed

Figure 8. Generalization process

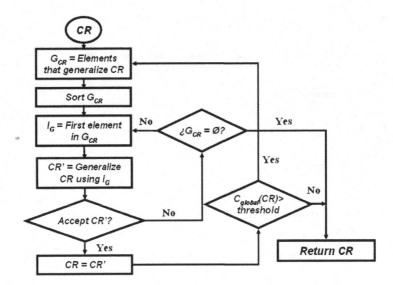

to greatly increase the abstraction of the result. Then, the method selects the first element. If the method generalizes the rule set and obtains a new set with an unacceptable quality (it is lower than the previous one), then it could be very expensive in the sense that the method had to recalculate the quality of all the generalized rules. In order to sort the elements, the method therefore takes into account the number of times an item has been used unsuccessfully in the generalization process.

In this way, the weight of an item I will be calculated as

$$Weight_I = \frac{N_{RG}}{N_F \times \beta + 1}$$

where N_{RG} represents the number of rules that item $_I$ generalizes, N_F the times that I has been used and the result set was not accepted, and $\beta \in [0, \infty)$ measures the penalty for each failed generalization. Taking this into account, the method decreasingly sorts the elements according to their weights. Once we have the generalized rule set (CR'), we accept it if the complexity has decreased and the quality has not decreased:

$$C_{global}(CR') < C_{global}(CR) \wedge Q(CR') \geq Q(CR)$$

If the new set satisfies the condition, this set becomes the new result, and if the complexity is above the threshold, the entire process is repeated. If the set is not accepted, the process takes the next element that generalizes the rule set and the process is repeated.

The process finishes if the obtained rule set satisfies the complexity threshold or there are no elements to generalize. The pseudo-code is shown in Figure 9.

Figure 9. Loss-less generalization algorithm

Algorithm: $Generalize_{WL}(CR, threshold, \beta)$

- Input:
  - CR: Rule set
  - $threshold$: value in [0,1] with the complexity threshold
  - β: value in $[0, +\infty]$ with the penalty for failed generalization elements
- Output:
  - Rule set

1) While $Complexity(CR) > threshold$ do
      a) $G_{CR} \leftarrow$ Set of items than generalize CR order using β
      b) Do
         i) If $G_{CR} \leftarrow \emptyset$ then
            A) Return CR
         ii) $I_G \leftarrow$ first element in G_R
         iii) $G_{CR} \leftarrow G_{CR} - \{I_G\}$
         iv) $CR' \leftarrow$ generalize CR using I_G
      c) While $(Quality(CR') < Quality(CR)) \vee (Complexity(CR') > Complexity(CR))$
      d) $CR \leftarrow CR'$
2) End while
3) Return CR

Lossy Generalization

If the previous process fails to obtain a rule set with a complexity below the threshold, then we apply another generalization process but allowing quality loss. The general process is the same as the one shown in Figure 9, but we change the new set acceptance criteria. In this case, for a new rule set to be accepted, it must satisfy two constraints:

- First, the process compares the reduced complexity and the quality loss to decide if the generalization is good enough to accept the new rule set. The condition can be written as

$$QualityLoss < \gamma \times ComplexityLoss$$

where $\gamma \in [0, +\infty)$ and establishes when the complexity reduction is good enough compared to the quality lost.

- In any case, the generalized rule set will not be accepted if its quality is below a threshold based on the best quality obtained throughout the entire process:

$$Q(CR') \geq \delta \times BestQuality$$

where $\delta \in [0, 1]$. *BestQuality* will be at least the quality of the first rule set generated, but if when applying the loss-less generalization we obtained a higher quality rule set and it is accepted, then this new quality will be used.

If we set $\gamma = 0$ or $\delta = 1$, then quality loss is not allowed, so the process performs in exactly the same way as the lossless generalization. The pseudo-code of the process is presented in Figure 10.

Figure 10. Lossy generalization algorithm

Algorithm: $Generalize_L(CR, threshold, \beta, \delta, \gamma)$

- Input:
  - CR: Rule set to generalize
  - $threshold$: value in [0,1] for the complexity threshold
  - β: value in $[0, +\infty]$ with the penalty for failed generalization elements
  - δ: value in [0,1] with the quality threshold to preserve
  - γ: value in [0,1] indicating the quality loss allowed to accept a new rule set
- Output:
  - Rule set

1) $BestQuality \leftarrow Quality(CR)$
2) While $Complexity(CR) > threshold$ do
   a) $G_{CR} \leftarrow$ Set of item than generalize CR ordered using β
   b) Do
      i) If $G_{CR} \leftarrow \emptyset$ then
         A) Return CR
      ii) $I_G \leftarrow$ first element in G_R
      iii) $G_{CR} \leftarrow G_{CR} - \{I_G\}$
      iv) $CR' \leftarrow$ generalize CR using I_G
      v) $QualityLoss \leftarrow \frac{Quality(CR) - Quality(CR')}{Quality(CR)}$
      vi) $ComplexityLoss \leftarrow \frac{Complexity(CR) - Complexity(CR')}{Complexity(CR)}$
   c) While $(QualityLoss > \gamma \times ComplexityLoss) \vee$
      $(Quality(CR') < \delta \times BestQuality)$
   d) $CR \leftarrow CR'$
   e) $BestQuality \leftarrow max\{BestQuality, Quality(CR)\}$
3) End while
4) Return CR

Algorithm

In Figure 11, the main function of COGARE is presented. Let us comment on all the parameters needed by the method:

Figure 11. COGARE algorithm

Algorithm:
$COGARE(C, threshold_{Complexity}, threshold_{SUP}, threshold_{CF}, \beta, \delta, \gamma)$

- Input:
  - C: DataCube to apply the method
  - $threshold_{Complexity}$: value in [0,1] with the complexity threshold
  - $threshold_{SUP}$: value in [0,1] with the support threshold to accept frequent itemsets
  - $threshold_{CF}$: value in [-1,1] with the threshold to accept a rule
  - β: value in $[0, +\infty)$ with the penalty for failed generalization elements
  - δ: value in [0,1] with the quality threshold to preserve
  - γ: value in $[0, +\infty)$ indicating the quality loss allowed to accept a new rule set
- Output:
  - Rule set

1) $C_F \leftarrow CalculateFrequentItemSets(threshold_{SUP}, C)$
2) $CR \leftarrow AssociationRules(C_F, threshold_{CF})$
3) If $Complexity(CR) > threshold_{Complexity}$ then
   a) $CR \leftarrow Generalize_{WL}(CR, threshold_{Complexity}, \beta)$
4) If $Complexity(CR) > threshold_{Complexity}$ then
   a) $CR \leftarrow Generalize_L(CR, threshold_{Complexity}, \beta, \delta, \gamma)$
5) Return CR

- *C*: DataCube to apply the method.
- *threshold$_{Complexity}$*: value in [0,1] with the complexity threshold.
- *threshold$_{SUP}$*: value in [0,1] with the support threshold to accept frequent itemsets. This value will be used for items at base levels. For items at other levels, the support threshold is calculated according to their abstraction as shown before.
- *threshold$_{CF}$*: value in [-1,1] with the threshold to accept a rule.
- β: value in [0, +∞) with the penalty for failed generalization elements. This value will have more influence on the time taken by the algorithm than on the quality of the results.
- δ: value in [0,1] with the quality threshold to preserve.
- γ: value in [0, +∞) indicating the quality loss allowed in order to accept a new rule set.

EXPERIMENTS

To study the scalability of the algorithm we proposed two different experiments:

- First, study the influence of the density of the datacubes.
- Second, consider the influence of the number of dimensions (structure).

We now present the datacubes and the parameters used and then the experiments and results for each type.

Figure 12. Multidimensional schema over medical data

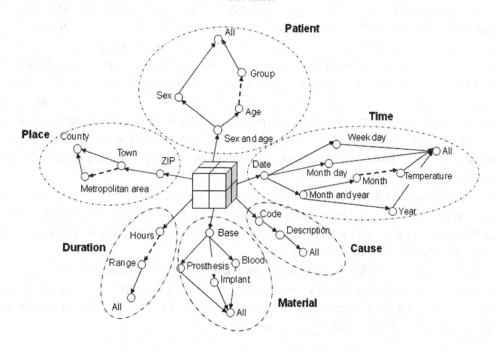

The DataCubes

We have used DataCubes defined over three different domains: medical, financial, and census data. For each domain, we have defined two multidimensional schemata that model the same information from both crisp and fuzzy perspectives. The reason for this choice is to test the influence of using fuzzy logic.

Figure 12, Figure 15, and Figure 18 show the three multidimensional schemata. Fuzzy relations are represented by means of a dotted line connecting two levels. Crisp schemata are defined in the same way, translating the fuzzy relations into crisp ones (an element would be grouped by a value in the parent level -the one with the greatest kinship relationship value in the fuzzy case).

We will briefly explain the structures of the multidimensional schemata below.

$C_{Medical}$

This schema is defined over data collected for non-postponed operations which were carried out in hospitals in Granada between 2002 and 2004. For the facts, we only consider the data when the patients are from Granada. There are 50185 facts with one variable (amount) and 6 dimensions. Let us briefly explain each one.

Dimensions

- *Patient*: in this dimension, we model patient data. The most detailed levels consider the different combinations of sex and age of each patient (the base level therefore has 2 sexes for 101 possible ages, totalling 202 values). Over this level, we group the patients according to their sex (level sex) and age (level age). Over this last one, we group the values more naturally for user (level group), and so we define what we can consider to be young, adult and old patients using linguistic terms over the concrete values. The definition of these terms is the same as that shown in Figure 2. The last level groups all the values so we have called it all with a single value (all). The structure of the dimension is as follows: Patient =({Sex and age, Sex, Age, Group, All},$\leq_{Patient}$,Sex and age,All)
- *Time*: in this dimension we consider the date when the operations took place. Over this level, we have defined a normal hierarchy over dates: weekday, month day, month, month and year, and year. The level Tem-perature represents information about the average temperature of each month in Granada using the values cold, warm and hot to group the values. The relationships between the month and the temperature are not crisp because the user normally considers these concepts with imprecision. The definition of the relationships are shown in Figure 13. The structure of the dimensions is as follows: Time =({Date, Weekday, Month day, month and year, Temperature, Year, All},$\leq_{Time}$,Date,All)
- *Place*: this dimension stores information about where the patients live. Since the definition of the metropolitan area of Granada is not clear, we have used a fuzzy relation to establish the relationship between this level and the towns. The structure of the dimension is: Place =({ZIP, Town, County, Metropolitan area, All},$\leq_{Place}$,ZIP,All)
- *Duration*: we also consider the amount of time each operation lasted. The level Range groups this information according to three categories: normal, long and very long duration. These groups have been defined imprecisely as shown in Figure 14. The structure of the dimension is: Duration=({Hours, Range, All},$\leq_{Duration}$,Hours,All)

Figure 13. Definition of level Temperature in dimension Time for C_{Medical}

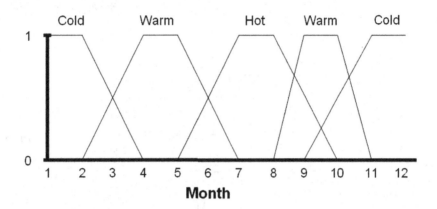

Figure 14. Definition of level Range in dimension Duration for C_{Medical}

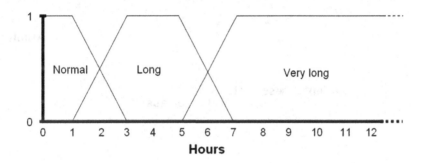

- *Material*: we want to analyze whether any materials were required for the operations, i.e. blood, prothesis, implants. The dimension Material models this information and has the following structure: Material =({Base, Blood, Implant, Prothesis, All},$\leq_{Material}$,Base,All)
- *Cause*: in this dimension we model the causes according to the codes established by the WHO. We consider the 9 main categories as the base level and the description on them. The structure of the dimension is as follows: Cause =({Code, Description, All},$\leq_{Cause}$,Code,All)

Measures

The only measure we consider is the number of operations with exactly the same values for all the dimensions we have built. This measure has been called the amount.

DataCube

The structure of the DataCube modeling the data is as follows:

$$C_{Medical} =(\{Duration, Time, Patient, Material, Place, Cause\}, \{Amount\}\emptyset, \Omega, A)$$

Figure 15. Multidimensional schema over financial data

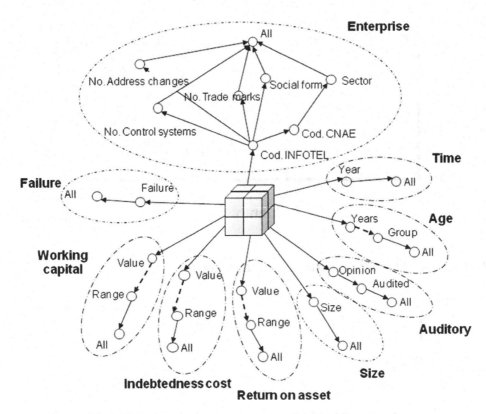

$C_{Financial}$

In this section, we present the structure of the DataCube built using the fuzzy multidimensional model presented. We have built a DataCube using the data obtained from Asexor about 872 companies from three sectors (service, commercial and industrial) using the National Classification of Economic Activities (CNAE). In each sector, we differentiate between failed companies and those which have not in accordance with Spanish Law applied in 2001. We have considered three economic-financial variables: return on asset, working capital, and indebtedness cost, over the years 1998-2000.

Dimensions

We have defined five dimensions. In all of these, we have used the minimum and maximum operator as t-norm and t-conorm when calculating the extended kinship relationship. In the following sections, we will present the structure of each one.

- *Time*: the time dimension in this datacube is defined at a detail level of years. The structure of this dimension is: Time $=(\{Year, All\}, \leq_{Time}, Year, All)$, where $\leq_{Time}$ defines the hierarchical relation as: Year $\leq_{Time}$ Year, Year $\leq_{Time}$ All, All $\leq_{Time}$ All

- *Failure*: we have mentioned that we study the companies differentiating between those which have failed and those which have not. This dimension gives this information. The basic level (*Fail*) only has two values, representing the failure of the company (value *Yes*) or not (value *No*), respectively. The following structure is associated to the dimension: Failure =({Fail, All},$\leq_{Failure}$,Fail,All).

- *Company*: this dimension models information about a company. We have used the INFOTEL code as the base level. Over this, we have defined the CNAE codes to group the companies according to a detail sector classification. Over this, we define the sector level that groups the CNAE codes into service, commercial or industrial companies. The other levels represent the number of control systems used, the number of changes of social address, the number of trademarks obtained by the company and the social form. This hierarchy translated into the fuzzy model proposed corresponds to the following structure: Company =({INFOTEL, CNAE, No. control systems, No. changes, No. marks, social form, sector, all},$\leq_{Company}$,INFOTEL,All), where $\leq_{Company}$ defines the hierarchical relation as shown in the figure.

- *Age*: the base level of this dimension is the number of years that a company has been in operation. Over this level, we define another which groups this value in years to classify the companies depending on whether they are very young, young, mature or very mature. This kind of concept is ill-defined, and they are normally defined using crisp intervals. This is not how people normally use these concepts and the previously mentioned edge problem may arise. The use of fuzzy logic in this situation is useful as it characterizes the concepts in a more intuitive way. The definition we have used is shown in Figure 16. The structure of the dimension Age is: Age =({Years, Group, all},$\leq_{Age}$,Years,All).

Figure 16. Definition of level Group in dimension Age for C$_{Financial}$

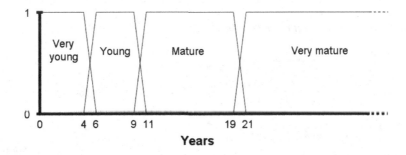

Figure 17. Definition of ranges over the economic-financial variables for C$_{Financial}$

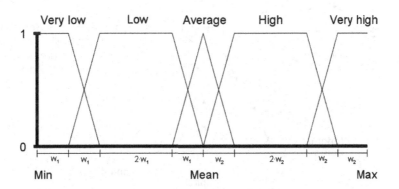

- *Return on asset, Indebtness cost*, and *Working capital*: for the three dimensions over the economic-financial variables we have used the values observed in the data set for these variables to define the base level of the dimensions. Over these levels we have defined another (*Range*) which groups the values into five categories to facilitate the analysis. For the user, the use of categorical values (e.g. average, low, high, etc.) is more intuitive than numeric values (e.g. a 6.51 return on asset). In order to avoid the edge problem, we fuzzify the intervals associated to each category.

We consider five categories according to the distance of the value to the mean of the variable and so we have used the categories very low, low, average, high and very high. The values which are very near to the mean will be in the average category, those not so near will be in the low or high categories if they are lower or higher than the mean, respectively, and so on. We have used the mean, maximum and minimum value of the variable to define the categories. Each interval [minimum, mean]and [mean, maximum] has been divided into five intervals of width w1 for the first, and w2 for the other. The categories have then been defined as shown in Figure 17.

The structures of the three dimensions are therefore very similar:

- *Return on asset = ({Values, Range, All},$\leq_{RoA}$, Values,All)*, where $\leq_{RoA}$ defines the hierarchical relation between the levels.
- *Indebtness cost = ({Values, Range, All},$\leq_{IC}$, Values,All)*,
- *Working capital = ({Values, Range, All},$\leq_{WC}$, Values,All)*.

Figure 18. Multidimensional schema over census data

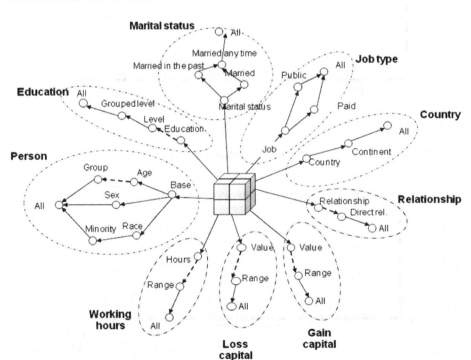

Measures

We have used the return on asset and working capital. Both variables are considered as measures and dimensions because we want to analyze the relation between both (e.g. return on asset according to the working capital or viceversa). All the data is obtained from a reliable source so we assign a value 1 of α to all the facts.

DataCube

Finally, the structure of the DataCube is:

$C_{Financial}$ =({Time, Failure, Company, Return on asset, Working capital},{return on asset, Working capital}$\varnothing,\Omega,A$),

where A is the relation that associates each fact with the corresponding values of the base level of the dimensions.

C_{Census}

This schema has been defined over 34198 facts with one variable (amount) and 9 dimensions using the data from adults in the Census database from the University of California[2].

Dimensions

- *Marital status*: this dimension stores information about the individual's marital status. We consider different aspects about this topic to build the hierarchy as shown. The structure of the dimension is as follows: Marital status =({Marital status, Married, Married in the past, Married at any time, All},$\leq_{MT}$, Marital status,All).
- *Education*: we also consider the level of education. We have grouped the values according to four categories: basic, medium, high, and very high. The relationships are defined imprecisely because we usually manage these concepts with imprecise borders between them. Table 3 collects the values for the relationships. The level *Grouped level* groups these four categories into normal (values basic and medium) and high (high and very high). The dimension has the following structure: Education =({Education, Level, Grouped level, All},$\leq_{Education}$,Education,All).
- *Person*: we consider the combination of the individual's age, sex and race as the base level. Over this level, we group the values according to these three variables. The ages are grouped in the

Table 3. Relationship between Education and Level in C_{Census}

Level	Education
Basics	1/Preschool, 1/1st-4th, 1/5th-6th, 1/7th-8th, 0.8/9th
Medium	0.2/9th, 1/10th, 1/11th, 1/12th, 1/HSgrad, 0.2/Assoc-voc, 0.2/Some-college
High	0.8/Some-college, 0.8/Assoc-voc, 1/Bachelors, 1/Assoc-acdm, 0.2/Profschool
Very high	0.8/Prof-school, 1/Doctorate, 1/Master

Figure 19. Definition of ranges over Hours for C_{Census}

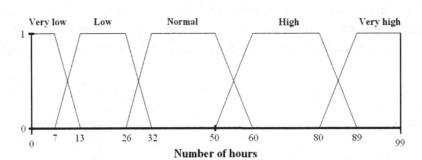

Figure 20. Definition of ranges over Loss capital and Gain capital for C_{Census}

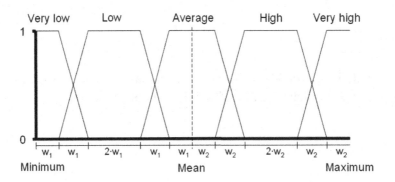

same way as in the medical DataCube. The races have been categorized depending on whether they can be considered as minorities. The black race represents 10% of the population whereas others such as amer-indian-eskimo only 3%, and each of these may be considered a minority at different degrees. Table 4 shows the kinship relationship.

- *Working hours*: we also consider the working hours. The values have been grouped according to how the number is considered as very low, low, normal, high or very high. In order to build this classification, we have used fuzzy intervals because the borders between them are not clear. The Figure 19 shows the structures of the intervals.

- *Loss capital* and *Gain capital*: these two dimensions represent the loss capital and the gain capital. The values have been categorized following a similar approach as for the economic-financial variables in the $C_{Financial}$ DataCube but changing the middle value (Figure 20). The structure is therefore similar to those proposed for these dimensions in $C_{Financial}$.

- *Relationship*: over the values of the base level (*husband, wife, own-child, other-relative,* and *not-in-family*) we have defined a level to classify the values according to the degree of relationship. We have considered the values as direct or not but this classification is not always clear. The Table 5 shows the defined kinship relationship.

- *Country*: another variable to classify the measures is the individual's country. Countries are classified by continent. The dimension has the following structure: Country =({Country, Continent, All},$\leq_{Country}$, Country, All),

Table 4. Kinship relationship between races and yes value in Minority

Race	$\mu_{Yes,Race}$
Amer-Indian-Eskimo	1
Asian-Pac-Islander	0.7
Black	0.5
Other	1
White	0

Table 5. Kinship relationship between relationships and yes value in Direct

Relationship	$\mu_{Yes,Relationship}$
Husband	1
Wife	1
Unmarried	0
Own-child	0.5
Other-relative	0.25
Not-in-family	0

- *Job type*: in this dimension we consider the job type. The values are grouped according to whether the job types are paid (level *Paid*) and if they correspond to the civil service (level Public).

Measures
We only consider the number of transactions with the same values for all the considered dimensions (amount) as measures.

DataCube
Finally, the structure of the DataCube is

C_{Census}=({Marital status, Person, Working hours, Education, Loss capital, Gain capital, Relationship, Country, Job type}, {amount}$\varnothing,\Omega,A$)

Support Calculation

In all of the DataCubes presented, there is a measure that stores the number of elements in the original data sharing the coordinates (e.g. in the medical DataCube, the fact amount represents the number of patients of the same sex and age, with the same ZIP code, undergoing the same operation, lasting the same amount of time on the same date). When calculating the support, we must therefore consider the number of transactions that each fact represents (e.g. in the medical data if a fact amount has the value 5, this means that these coordinates represent 5 operations).

In crisp DataCubes, this only involves changing one aggregation operator: instead of the count operator, we will use the sum aggregation operator. In fuzzy ones, we also have the sum operator, but it returns fuzzy sets as the result (see (Molina, Sánchez, Vila, & Rodríguez-Ariza, 2006) for further details). Concrete values are needed to apply the quality measures and the support. In this case, we will use the same approach proposed in (Delgado, Marin, Sanchez, & Vila, 2003). The authors propose the use of quantified sentences of the type:

"Q of F are G"

where F and G are fuzzy sets and Q is a linguistic quantifier for calculating the support. In order to evaluate the sentence and obtain the support, the GD quantifier (Delgado, Sánchez, & Vila, 1999) is used:

$$GD_Q\left(\frac{G}{F}\right) = \sum_{\alpha_i \in \Delta(G/F)} \left(\alpha_i - \alpha_{i+1}\right) Q\left(\frac{\left|(G \cap F)_{\alpha_i}\right|}{\left|F_{\alpha_i}\right|}\right)$$

where $\Delta(G/F) = \Lambda(G \cap F) \cup \Lambda(F)$, $\Lambda(F)$ is the level set of F, and $\Delta(G/F) = \left\{\alpha_1, ..., \alpha_p\right\}$ with $\alpha_i > \alpha_{i+1}$ for every $i \in \{1, ..., p\}$.

If we consider the quantifier $Q(x) = x$, it can be proved that it behaves coherently in the crisp case (see (Delgado, Marin, Sanchez, & Vila, 2003) for more details). There are two reasons for using this approach:

- The quantifier GD can be adapted to work over the result of the aggregation operators for the fuzzy multidimensional model.
- The support calculation is efficient.

Parameter

We have to establish the rest of the parameters of the method:

- *threshold$_{Complexity}$*: we want the method to tray to reduce the complexity as much as possible, so we use 0 for this parameter.
- *threshold$_{SUP}$*: for each domain we use a different one:
  ○ Medical: 0.1
  ○ Financial: 0.1
  ○ Census: 0.2

These values are relatively low, but we want the method to extract a high number of rules in order to include as much influence of the fuzzy logic calculation as possible.

- *threshold$_{CF}$*: for all the domain we use the value 0.4.
- β: we want a high penalization, so 10 is the value chosen.
- δ: 0.6 so the method will never accept a new rule set if the quality is less tan the 60% of the best quality obtained throughout the process.

- • γ: The user normally prefers to lose quality if the method obtains a good complexity reduction. We propose a value of 1.2.

We now have all the elements needed to do the experiments.

Density

To compare the scalability of both approaches (fuzzy and crisp) we consider three different DataCubes over three domains and execute the COGARE algorithm with different number of facts comparing the time needed. For each domain we consider six different number of facts as 10%, 30%, 50%, 70%, 90%, and 100% of the whole set (Table 6 collects the number of facts on each case). As the selection of the facts may has influence in the number of frequent itemsets, we build five different DataCubes for each size choosing different sets of facts, randomly selected. Over each DataCube we apply the 14 different quality measures to reduce the influence of this parameter in the tests. Regarding this, at the end we will consider the average value of the 14 measures as the time for that size.

This process is applied for crisp and fuzzy approaches, so we have 2520 results to compare: 3 domains, using 2 approaches (fuzzy and crisp), considering 6 different fact sets size, 5 different DataCubes per each size, and with 14 quality measures.

Following sections presents the DataCubes used for the tests. After these sections, we present the parameters used for the COGARE algorithm, and we finish with the results obtained.

Results

Figure 21 shows graphically the data obtained for the experiments. In Table 7 and Table 9 the data to build the graphics is collected.

As you can see, in three domains the behavior of the algorithm is almost lineal and the time for fuzzy and, for Medical and Financial, crisp approach is very similar. To compare the results we use the regression line for these values. In the case that the size of the DataCube is 0 (no records) the method will not be applied because we have no data to work with, so the time spend is zero. Under this fact, we can consider than the lineal functions are of the form $\alpha \times size$, where *size* is the number of facts. Table 8 shows the regression data.

The quality of the regressions is good enough to get significant results when comparing the coefficients. As we can see, in the case of Medical, the slopes of the function in crisp and fuzzy approaches are very similar, so we can conclude that the use of fuzzy logic has no influence on these domains. In Financial one, the slopes are very similar but with a small different (around 5.5%), so fuzzy logic has a very low influence.

Table 6. Number of facts for each domain

	10%	*30%*	*50%*	*70%*	*90%*	*100%*
Medical	5019	15056	25093	35130	45167	50185
Financial	311	934	1556	2178	2801	3112
Census	3420	10259	17099	23239	30778	34198

The census domain is more interesting because we can find significant differences between the values. In the fuzzy case, the coefficient is 33.31% higher than the crisp one. So, in this domain the use of fuzzy logic has a higher influence, but not enough to change the order of the algorithm (in both cases it needs lineal time).

Figure 21. Time and memory result for density test

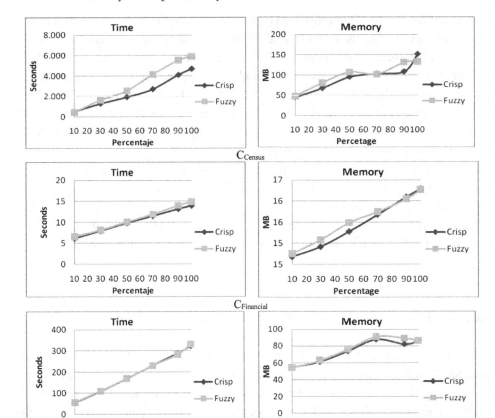

Table 7. Time for density tests

Domain	Approach	Time (seconds)					
		10%	30%	50%	70%	90%	100%
Census	Crisp	517.690	1302.905	1938.571	2701.333	4095.571	4686.214
	Fuzzy	467.476	1643.310	2554.357	4148.357	5522.000	5911.643
Financial	Crisp	6.167	7.952	9.810	11.452	13.142	13.928
	Fuzzy	6.595	8.167	10.095	11.905	14.123	14.929
Medical	Crisp	55.310	109.905	169.357	230.857	288.643	323.642
	Fuzzy	55.929	110.000	169.524	229.667	282.357	331.571

Table 8. Regression lines

Domain	Approach	Expression	R^2
Financial	Crisp	0.00505x size	0.943
	Fuzzy	0.00533x size	0.946
Medical	Crisp	0.00652x size	0.997
	Fuzzy	0.00654x size	0.997
Census	Crisp	0.12882x size	0.994
	Fuzzy	0.17173x size	0.996

Table 9. Memory for density tests

Domain	Approach	Memory (MB)					
		10%	30%	50%	70%	90%	100%
Census	Crisp	45.318	68.039	95.551	103.325	108.576	152.102
	Fuzzy	47.662	80.639	107.230	102.090	131.070	133.073
Financial	Crisp	14.685	14.923	15.283	15.680	16.099	16.296
	Fuzzy	14.759	15.084	15.488	15.744	16.046	15.984
Medical	Crisp	54.510	61.515	74.227	87.939	82.420	86.048
	Fuzzy	54.186	63.096	76.245	91.153	89.289	86.444

Another important factor in the scalability is the space needed for the executions (memory). Table 9 collects the average values for each density for the three domains.

To get the regression models we consider three different functions that may fit the results. Table 10 shows the quality for each approach.

For financial and medical domains the best model is the logarithmic, although the quality for square root is very good too. In census domain the best model is the square root, having the logarithmic approach good quality too. There is no difference between fuzzy and crisp approaches in the order but we have to consider the overload in the first approach. Table 11 collects the regression model to compare the overload.

In census and medical domains the overload is very similar (3.73% and 3.34% respectively) and for financial one the influence is even lower (0.4%). So we can conclude that the influence of using fuzzy logic in the memory needed is not very significative.

Structure

In this section we presents the experiments to test the influence of the structure of the DataCubes (the dimensions) when using fuzzy logic. In that case we will know the influence of the number of dimensions in the time and memory needed. If N is the number of dimensions of a datacube, we build new datacubes from 2 to N-1 dimensions for each one, choosing.20 of each number of dimensions. Then we consider three executions with each quality measure. So we have 2520 executions.

Table 10. Regression quality for memory

Domain	Approach	Regression model		
		Lineal (R^2)	$X^{\frac{1}{2}}$ (R^2)	Logaritmic (R^2)
Census	Crisp	0.9581	**0.9875**	0.9705
	Fuzzy	0.9441	**0.9950**	0.9901
Financial	Crisp	0.8014	0.9243	**0.9716**
	Fuzzy	0.7981	0.9224	**0.9708**
Medical	Crisp	0.8731	0.9729	**0.9947**
	Fuzzy	0.8884	0.9760	**0.9955**

Table 11. Regression models for memory

Domain	Approach	Expression (MB)
Financial	Crisp	$2.710 \; x \; log_2(x)$
	Fuzzy	$2.721 \; x \; log_2(x)$
Medical	Crisp	$13.351 \; x \; log_2(x)$
	Fuzzy	$13.796 \; x \; log_2(x)$
Census	Crisp	$13.163 \; x \; x^{1/2}$
	Fuzzy	$13.654 \; x \; x^{1/2}$

Results

The summary of the results for the experiments are shown in Figure 22 and Table 12 and Table 13.

We first consider the time spent on the executions. As in the previous section we try to get a regression model for the evolution of the time. We consider three possible models: lineal, quadratic and exponential. Table 14 collects the quality of each approach.

For census and medical domains the best results are for exponential regression in crisp and fuzzy approaches, although the quality for medical in the case of quadratic is good too. In the case of financial domain the best model is the quadratic. The first conclusion is that the number of dimensions has a higher influence in the complexity than the density. In Table 15 the regression expression are presented to compare the crisp and fuzzy approach.

Both crisp and fuzzy approaches have the same complexity for all the domains. But there is an overload in the case of fuzzy ones. In financial and medical domains the overload is not very high (17% and 21% respectively) but in census the influence in higher (158%).

The same analysis is carried out for the memory. In Table 16 the quality of the considered model is presented.

As in the time tests, medical and census domains present the same complexity (quadratic in these cases) and financial ales expensive one (lineal). So, although the memory needs are important in these cases, the number of dimensions has more influence in the time needed. In Table 17 the regression expression for memory are shown.

Figure 22. Time and memory results for structure test

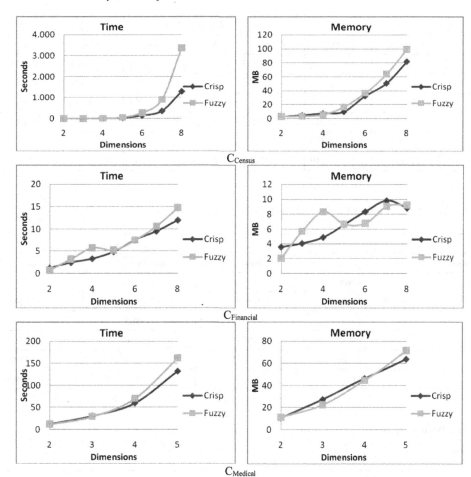

C_{Census}

$C_{Financial}$

$C_{Medical}$

Table 12. Time for structure tests

Domain	Approach	Time (seconds)						
		2 dim.	3 dim.	4 dim.	5 dim.	6 dim.	7 dim.	8 dim
Census	Crisp	2.45	5.3	12.45	32.75	148.7	364.85	1295.06
	Fuzzy	2.3	3.4	13.25	58.1	283.6	911.9	3374.33
Financial	Crisp	1.2	2.45	3.3	4.85	7.5	9.5	12
	Fuzzy	0.75	3.25	5.75	5.25	7.5	10.65	14.778
Medical	Crisp	12.85	30.95	60	132.75			
	Fuzzy	11.85	29.55	70.2	162.333			

Table 13. Memory for structure tests

Domain	Approach	Memory (MB)						
		2 dim.	3 dim.	4 dim.	5 dim.	6 dim.	7 dim.	8 dim
Census	Crisp	3.202	5.029	7.739	10.059	32.646	50.891	81.684
	Fuzzy	2.851	3.235	5.439	16.431	36.630	63.898	99.461
Financial	Crisp	3.573	4.064	4.871	6.585	8.348	9.824	8.829
	Fuzzy	2.041	5.686	8.324	6.656	6.760	9.064	9.246
Medical	Crisp	10.867	27.459	46.313	63.956			
	Fuzzy	11.310	22.574	44.624	71.625			

Table 14. Quality of the regression models for time

Domain	Approach	Regression model		
		Lineal (R^2)	Quadratic (R^2)	Exponential (R^2)
Census	Crisp	0.5296	0.7144	*0.9932*
	Fuzzy	0.5029	0.6885	*0.9891*
Financial	Crisp	0.9615	*0.9965*	0.7370
	Fuzzy	0.9531	*0.9850*	0.7598
Medical	Crisp	0.8661	0.9719	*0.9866*
	Fuzzy	0.8324	0.9560	*0.9951*

Table 15. Regression expressions for time

Domain	Approach	Expression (seconds)
Financial	Crisp	$0.1943 \times N^2$
	Fuzzy	$0.2272 \times N^2$
Medical	Crisp	$0.9304 \times e^N$
	Fuzzy	$1.1233 \times e^N$
Census	Crisp	$0.4209 \times e^N$
	Fuzzy	$1.0881 \times e^N$

Table 16. Regression quality for memory

Domain	Approach	Regression model		
		Lineal (R^2)	Quadratic (R^2)	Exponential (R^2)
Census	Crisp	0.8012	*0.9430*	0.9146
	Fuzzy	0.7886	*0.9399*	0.9184
Financial	Crisp	*0.9872*	0.9009	0.4995
	Fuzzy	*0.9568*	0.8419	0.4678
Medical	Crisp	0.9668	*0.9955*	0.8845
	Fuzzy	0.9382	*0.9988*	0.9366

Table 17. Regression models for memory

Domain	Approach	Expression (MB)
Financial	Crisp	1.287 x N
	Fuzzy	1.309 x N
Medical	Crisp	2.690 x N²
	Fuzzy	2.815 x N²
Census	Crisp	1.064 xN²
	Fuzzy	1.294 x N²

The results are very similar to time models. In all the domains the crisp and fuzzy approaches have the same order but the fuzzy ones introduce an overload. In this case, for medical and financial this overload is not very important (4.7% and 1.7% respectively). In the census domain the influence is higher (21.7%).

CONCLUSION

In this chapter we have compare the performance of an association rule extraction algorithm over fuzzy and crisp DataCubes to test the influence of using fuzzy logic in the model. To achieve this goal we have build DataCubes over three different domains and considering different number of facts, so we can evaluate the scalability of both approaches according to the density of the DataCubes (number of records) and the topology (the dimensions)

As result we have the number of dimensions has a higher influence in the scalability of the algorithm in time and memory. This situation is normal due to the method extract inter-dimensional association so a higher number of dimensions introduce more possible associations. The use of fuzzy logic does not change the order of efficiency of the method but introduce an overload in both cases.

Considering the density the influence in most of the domains is not very important (around 5.5% in time and 3.5% in memory). Only for one domain the time needed have and overload around 33% which may be consider significant.

If we change the topology (dimensions) the influence is higher but this is normal due to the underlying multidimensional model has a more complex structure to model the hierarchy. In that case the influence in the time is near 20% for two domains and 158% for the other. So the fuzzy logic modeling of the hierarchies introduces an important overload but does not change the order of efficiency. The overload in the memory needed is not very significant in two domains to (4.7% and 1.7%) but in the other is higher (21.7%). So we can conclude that the overload depends on the complexity of the domain to model.

Although we would need more experiments to extends the results, the results indicates that, in the case of extracting association rules over DataCubes using COGARE, the fuzzy logic allows to enrich the data representation and, due to this fact, introduces an overload in the process but keeping the scalability (order of efficiency) of the algorithm. As it was expected the influence depends on the complexity of the domain to model.

REFERENCES

Agrawal, R., Gupta, A., & Sarawagi, S. (1995). *Modeling multidimensional databases.* Armonk, NY: IBM.

Agrawal, R., Imielinksi, T., & Swami, A. (1993). Mining Association Rule Between Sets of Items in Large Databases. In *Proceedings of the 1993 ACM SIGMOD international conference on Management of data* (pp. 207-216). New York: ACM.

Agrawal, R., & Sritkant, R. (1994). Fast algorithms for mining association rules in large databases. In *VLDB '94: Proceedings of the 20th International Conference on Very Large Data Bases* (pp. 478-499). San Francisco: Morgan Kaufman.

Alhajj, R., & Kaya, M. (2003). Integrating Fuzziness into OLAP for Multidimensional Fuzzy Association Rules Mining. In *Proceedings of the Third IEEE International Conference on Data Mining* (p. 469). Washington, DC: IEEE Computer Society.

An, A., & Cercone, N. (2004). An Empirical Study on Rule Quality Measures. In *Proceedings of the 7th International Workshop on New Directions in Rough Sets, Data Mining, and Granular-Soft Computing* (LNCS 1711, pp. 482-491). Berlin, Germany: Springer-Verlag.

Angryk, R. A., & Petry, F. E. (2005). Mining Multi-Level Associations with Fuzzy Hierarchies. In *Proceedings of the 14th IEEE International Conference on Fuzzy Systems, 2005, FUZZ '05* (pp. 785-790). Washington, DC: IEEE.

Atzmueller, M., Baumeister, J., & Puppe, F. (2004). Quality measures for semi-automatic learning of Simple diagnostic rule bases. In *Proceedings of the 15th International Conference on Applications of Declarative Programming and Knowledge Management (INAP 2004)* (pp. 65-78).

Brazdil, P., & Torgo, L. (1990). Knowledge adquisition via knowledge integration. In B. Wielinga et al. (Eds.), *Current trends in knowledge acquisition.* Amsterdam: IOS Press.

Brin, S., Motwani, R., Ullman, J. D., & Tsur, S. (1997). Dynamic itemset counting and implication rules for market basket data. In *Proceedings of the 1997 ACM SIGMOD international conference on Management of data* (pp. 255-264). New York: ACM.

Bruha, I. (1996). *Machine learning and statistics.* John Wiley & Sons Inc.

Cabibbo, L., & Torlone, R. (1997). Querying multidimensional databases. In *Proceedings of the 6th International Workshop on Database Programming Languages* (LNCS 1369, pp. 319-335). Berlin, Germany: Springer.

Cabibbo, L., & Torlone, R. (1998). A logical approach to multidimensional databases. In *Proceedings of the Advances in Database Technologies – EDBT '98* (LNCS 1377, pp. 183-197). Berlin, Germany: Springer-Verlag.

Council, O. (n.d.). *The OLAP Council.* Retrieved from http://www.olapcouncil.org

Datta, A., & Thomas, H. (1999). The cube data model: A conceptual model and algebra for on-line analytical processing in data warehouses. *Decision Support Systems, 27*, 289–301. doi:10.1016/S0167-9236(99)00052-4

Dean, P., & Famili, A. (1997). Comparative performance of rule quality measures in an induction system. *Applied Intelligence, 7*, 113–124. doi:10.1023/A:1008293727412

Delgado, M., Marin, N., Sanchez, D., & Vila, M. (2003). Fuzzy association rules: General model and applications. *IEEE transactions on Fuzzy Systems, 11*, 214–225. doi:10.1109/TFUZZ.2003.809896

Delgado, M., Martin-Bautista, M. J., Sanchez, D., & Vila, M. A. (2003). On a characterization of fuzzy bags. In *Proceedings of the Fuzzy Sets and Systems – IFSA 2003* (LNCS 2715, pp. 119-126). Berlin, Germany: Springer.

Delgado, M., Sánchez, D., & Vila, M. (1999). Fuzzy cardinality based evaluation of quantified sentences. *International Journal of Approximate Reasoning, 23*(1), 23–66. doi:10.1016/S0888-613X(99)00031-6

Famili, A. (1990). Integrating learning and decision-making in intelligent manufacturing systems. *Journal of Intelligent & Robotic Systems, 3*, 117–130. doi:10.1007/BF00242160

Fayyad, U. M., Piatetsky-Shapiro, G., Smyth, P., & Uthurusamy, R. (1996). *Advances in knowledge discovery and data mining.* AAAI/MIT Press.

Gorry, G., & Morton, M. S. (1971). A framework for management information systems. *Sloan Management Review, 13*, 50–70.

Gray, J., Chaudhuri, S., Bosworth, A., Layman, A., Reichart, D., & Venkatrao, M. (1997). Data cube: A relational aggregation operator generalizing group-by, cross-tab, and sub-totals. *Data Mining and Knowledge Discovery, 1*, 29–53. doi:10.1023/A:1009726021843

Han, J. (1997). OLAP mining: Integration of OLAP with data mining. In *Proceedings of the 7th IFIP 2.6 Working Conference on Database Semantics* (pp. 1-11).

Han, J., Cai, Y., & Cercone, N. (1993). Data-driven discovery of quantitative rules in relational databases. *IEEE Transactions on Knowledge and Data Engineering, 5*, 29–40. doi:10.1109/69.204089

Han, J., & Fu, Y. (1995). Discovery of multiple-level association rules from large databases. In *Proceedings of the 21st International Conference on Very Large Data Bases* (pp. 420-431). San Francisco: Morgan Kaufman.

Han, J., & Fu, Y. (1999). Discovery of multiple-level association rules from large databases. *IEEE Transactions on Knowledge and Data Engineering, 11*, 798–805. doi:10.1109/69.806937

Han, J., Pei, J., & Yin, Y. (2000). Mining frequent patterns without candidate generation. In *Proceedings of the 2000 ACM SIGMOD international conference on Management of data* (pp. 1-12). New York: ACM.

Jensen, C., Kligys, A., Pedersen, T., & Timko, I. (2004). Multimendional data modeling for location-based services. *The VLDB Journal, 13*, 1–21. doi:10.1007/s00778-003-0091-3

Kamber, M., Han, J., & Chiang, J. (1997). Metarule-guided mining of multi-dimensional association rules using data cubes. In *Proceedings of the KDD* (pp. 207-210).

Kaya, M., & Alhajj, R. (2005). Fuzzy OLAP association rules mining-based modular reinforcement learning approach for multiagent systems. *IEEE Transactions on Systems, Man, and Cybernetics*, *35*, 326–338.

Kimball, R. (1996). *The data warehouse toolkit.* John Wiley & Sons.

Laurent, A. (2002). *Extraction de connaissances pertinentes à partir de baes de données multidimensionnelles.* Laboratoire d'Informatique de Paris 6.

Lee, D. h., & Kim, M. H. (1997). Database sumarization using fuzzy ISA hierarchies. *IEEE Transactions on Systems, Man, and Cybernetics. Part B, Cybernetics*, *27*, 68–78. doi:10.1109/3477.552184

Li, C., & Wang, X. (1996). A data model for supporting on-line analytical processing. In *Proceedings of the fifth international conference on Information and knowledge management* (pp. 81-88). New York: ACM.

Lui, C.-L., & Chung, F.-L. (2000). Discovery of generalized association rules with multiple minimum supports. In *Principles of data mining and knowledge discovery* (LNCS 1910, pp. 510-515). Berlin, Germany: Springer-Verlag.

Michalski, R. (1990). Pattern recognition as rule-guided inductive inference. *IEEE Transactions on Patter Analysis and Machine Learning*, *PAMI-2*(4), 349–361. doi:10.1109/TPAMI.1980.4767034

Molina, C., Sánchez, D., Vila, M. A., & Rodríguez-Ariza, L. (2006). A new fuzzy multidimensional model. *IEEE transactions on Fuzzy Systems*, *14*, 897–912. doi:10.1109/TFUZZ.2006.879984

Muyeba, M. K., & Keane, J. A. (2000). Interestingness in attribute-oriented induction (AOI): Multiple-level rule generation. In *Principles of data mining and knowledge discovery* (LNCS 1910, pp. 542-549). Berlin, Germany: Springer-Verlag.

Park, J. S., Chen, M. S., & Yu, P. S. (1995). An effective hash based algoritm for mining association rules. *SIGMOD Record*, *24*(2), 175–186. doi:10.1145/568271.223813

Pedrycz, W. (2004). Associations and rules in data mining: A link analysis. *International Journal of Intelligent Systems*, *19*, 653–670. doi:10.1002/int.20016

Savasere, A., Omiecinski, E., & Navathe, S. (1995). An efficient algorithm for mining association rules in large databases. In *Proceedings of the 21st International Conference on Very Large Data Bases* (pp. 432-444). San Francisco: Morgan Kaufman.

Shen, L., & Shen, H. (1998). Mining flexible multiple-level association rules in all concept hierarchies (extended abstract). In *Proceedings of the 9th International Conference on Database and Expert Systems Applications* (LNCS 1460, pp. 786-796). Berlin, Germany: Springer.

Shortliffe, E., & Buchanan, B. (1975). A model of inexact reasoning in medicine. *Mathematical Biosciences*, *23*, 351–379. doi:10.1016/0025-5564(75)90047-4

Srikant, R., & Agrawal, R. (1995). Mining generalized association rules. (pp. 407-419). San Francisco: Morgan Kaufmann Publishers Inc.

Tan, P.-N., & Kumar, V. (2000). Interestingness measures for association patterns: A perspective. *Future Generation Computer Systems*, *13*(2-3), 161–180.

Yager, R. R. (1986). On the theory of bags. *International Journal of General Systems*, *13*, 23–37. doi:10.1080/03081078608934952

Yager, R. R. (1994). Aggregation operators and fuzzy systems modeling. *Fuzzy Sets and Systems*, *67*, 129–145. doi:10.1016/0165-0114(94)90082-5

Yen, S.-J. (2000). Mining generalized multiple-level association rules., In *Principles of data mining and knowledge discovery* (LNCS 1910, pp. 679-684). Berlin, Germany: Springer.

Zhu, H. (1998). *On-line analytical mining of association rules*. Simon Fraser University.

ENDNOTES

[1] Corresponding author. E-mail: carlosmo@ujaen.es. Partially supported by research project TIC03175

[2] URL: http://kdd.ics.uci.edu

Chapter 5
Scalable Reasoning with Tractable Fuzzy Ontology Languages

Giorgos Stoilos
National and Technical University of Athens, Greece

Jeff Z. Pan
University of Aberdeen, UK

Giorgos Stamou
National and Technical University of Athens, Greece

ABSTRACT

The last couple of years it is widely acknowledged that uncertainty and fuzzy extensions to ontology languages, like description logics (DLs) and OWL, could play a significant role in the improvement of many Semantic Web (SW) applications like matching, merging and ranking. Unfortunately, existing fuzzy reasoners focus on very expressive fuzzy ontology languages, like OWL, and are thus not able to handle the scale of data that the Web provides. For those reasons much research effort has been focused on providing fuzzy extensions and algorithms for tractable ontology languages. In this chapter, the authors present some recent results about reasoning and fuzzy query answering over tractable/polynomial fuzzy ontology languages namely Fuzzy DL-Lite and Fuzzy EL+. Fuzzy DL-Lite provides scalable algorithms for very expressive (extended) conjunctive queries, while Fuzzy EL+ provides polynomial algorithms for knowledge classification. For the Fuzzy DL-Lite case the authors will also report on an implementation in the ONTOSEARCH2 system and preliminary, but encouraging, benchmarking results.

INTRODUCTION

Nowadays, many applications and domains use some form of knowledge representation language and exploit their inference mechanisms in order to improve their capabilities and simulate intelligent human behavior. Many such examples exist, like knowledge-based multimedia analysis (Neumann & Möller,

DOI: 10.4018/978-1-60566-858-1.ch005

2006; Simou et al., 2008a), bioinformatics (Dameron et al., 2004) and databases (Calvanese et al., 1998) and more. Nevertheless the most prominent example is undoubtedly the World Wide Web aiming for intelligently managing the vast amount of information that lays on the Web. Among several proposals for structuring knowledge in such applications, Description Logic based *ontologies* seem to be an approach that has gained considerable attention. Description Logics (DLs) (Baader et al., 2002) is a modern knowledge representation formalism that is a fragment of First-Order Logic, enjoying well-defined model-theoretic semantics, decidability and practically efficient reasoning systems. Most importantly expressive DLs form the logical underpinnings of the W3C standard language for representing ontologies in the Semantic Web, namely OWL (Bechhofer et al., 2004; Patel-Schneider et al., 2004). Although several successful OWL DL reasoning systems have been developed, like FaCT++[1] and Pellet[2], even very basic and inexpressive DLs come with come with (at least) ExpTime computational complexity. Thus, their ability to scale in large application like the once found on the Web is still an open issue. For those reasons the last years great research effort has been focusing in identifying fragments/clusters of the OWL DL language for which it is known that reasoning is scalable and efficient. This research has led to the development of several languages, but the two most interesting and predominant ones are EL+ (Baader et al.) and DL-Lite (Calvanese et al., 2005; Calavanese et al., 2007). The interesting thing is that these languages will most likely form the logical underpinnings of the OWL 2 EL and OWL 2 QL[3] recommendations which consist of *profiles*/fragments of the upcoming extension of OWL, OWL 2[4].

Although DLs are relatively quite expressive they feature limitations mainly with what can be said about imperfect (uncertain, vague/fuzzy or imprecise) knowledge. Such types of knowledge appears in many domains but also in several Semantic Web tasks, like in the representation of trust, in knowledge fusion, assessing the similarity between resources and many more. For those reasons *fuzzy ontologies* are envisioned to be useful in the Web (Stoilos et al., 2006) and *fuzzy Description Logics (f-DLs)* (Hölldobler et al., 2005; Straccia, 2001; Tresp & Molito, 1998) have been proposed as formalisms capable of capturing and reasoning with such knowledge. Research in f-DLs was mainly focused on providing reasoning support for very expressive fuzzy DLs, like reasoning with the f-DL f_{KD}-SHIN (Stoilos et al., 2007; Stoilos et al. 2005b), reasoning with f_{KD}-SHI (Li et al., 2006), supporting reasoning in f-DLs that allow for general concept inclusion axioms (Li et al., 2006; Stoilos et al., 2006), fuzzy extensions of the OWL language (Stoilos et al., 2005a) supporting expressive datatypes (Wang et al., 2008) or adding more expressive fuzzy features, like *comparison expressions* (Kang et al., 2006; Lu et al., 2008) and *concept modifiers* (Hölldobler et al., 2006; Wang et al., 2006). Interestingly, there also exist two f-DL reasoners, FiRE[5] (Stoilos et al., 2007), which supports f_{KD}-SHIN and the *fuzzyDL*[6] (Straccia, 2008), which supports f_{KD}-SHIf(**D**) and f_L-SHIf(**D**). Unfortunately, like their crisp counterparts, fuzzy-SHIN and fuzzy-SHIf(**D**) come with (at least) ExpTime computational complexity. Additionally, the practical behavior of implementations of such logics would also have to deal with the degrees thus adding more to the practical complexity.

Following current research developments in crisp DLs, there is an effort on developing lightweight fuzzy ontology languages. In particular, today there exist two such languages, namely *fuzzy DL-Lite* (Pan et al., 2008; Straccia, 2006) and *fuzzy EL+* (Stoilos et al., 2008). Like their crisp counterparts, fuzzy DL-Lite is specifically tailored for data intensive applications, offering for efficient instance retrieval services by utilizing datbase technologies, while fuzzy EL+ is especially tailored for applications that require the managements of large concept hierarchies/taxonomies offering for efficient classification services. Even more interestingly, in the fuzzy case fuzzy DL-Lite allows for far more expressive and flexible queries that utilize the power of the fuzzy component. For example, one can issue a query of the form:

get me all e-shops that are popular [with degrees at least 0.8] and sell good books [with degree at least 0.9],

adding threshold criteria in the search, or expressing weight/preferences on query atoms like in the query

get me all cars that are fast and fancy but consider speed more important [with weight 0.7] than design [with weight 0.3].

Similarly important is the fact that in fuzzy EL+ we can support efficient classification over *fuzzy inclusion axioms*. Such axioms can be proven very important is several Semantic Web related tasks like in ontology matching (Ferrara et al., 2008), where algorithms establish fuzzy mappings between ontologies like the following ones:

$onto_1: MobilePhone \xrightarrow{0.7} onto_1: CellularPhone$

$onto_1: DarkGrey \xrightarrow{0.85} onto_2: Black$

which (fuzzy) map concept *MobilePhone* from ontology $onto_1$ and *CellularPhone* from ontology $onto_2$ with a degree 0.7 since an automatic procedure is not possible to assess the semantic correspondence of these two entities. A different problem also arises in the case that there is no actual one-to-one correspondence between all the concepts of two ontologies. For example in the above case one ontology defines the concept *DarkGrey* while the other concept. Still one might want to match these concepts to a certain degree. Similar representation mechanisms have also been used in other contexts and frameworks like for example searching in Semantic Portals (Holi & Hyvonen, 2006), where again fuzzy subsumption was used to define fuzzy mappings between concepts.

The current Chapter has the following two major objectives. On the one hand we want to show that it is possible to provide efficient querying services over fuzzy ontologies, even in the case of using very expressive queries allowing for thresholds, weights or preferences. For our purposes we will use the f-DL-Lite language (Pan et al., 2008; Straccia, 2006). On the other hand we also want to cover the second most important inference problem of (fuzzy) ontologies, that of concept classification. Thus, we will show that indeed there are classes of ontology languages for which such a problem can be decided in an efficient way. In this case we will use the fuzzy EL+ (Stoilos et al., 2008) language. More precisely, the Chapter focuses on the following major issues:

- It overviews some recent work about providing scalable query answering with very expressive extended conjunctive queries over lightweight ontologies created with the fuzzy DL-Lite language. The framework is motivated by the field of fuzzy information retrieval (Cross, 1994) where *weighted Boolean queries* (Waller & Kraft, 1979) have been proposed for retrieving fuzzy information from fuzzy relational databases. Nevertheless, the presented approach is general enough to cover most of the former popular approaches like the fuzzy implication-based approaches (Bookstein, 1980; Bordogna, 1996; Radecki, 1979; Yager, 1987) p-norm's (Salton et al., 1983a), the geometric mean approach (Chen & Chen), weighted min queries (Sanchez, 1989) and fuzzy aggregation type queries (Vojtas, 2001), as well as to extend them by supporting *threshold queries* which are a natural extension of the entailment problem. Thus, the main strength of the general fuzzy query language is the openness on the semantics.

- In order to support queries of the above form in Semantic Web applications it presents a method to extend the SPARQL (a well known Semantic Web query language) syntax for the proposed query languages in the framework. The extension uses specially formatted SPARQL comments, thus the fuzzy queries are still valid SPARQL queries, and it does not affect current SPARQL tools and implementations.

- It presents the very first scalable query engine for fuzzy ontologies, based on the ONTOSEARCH2 system[7] (Pan et al., 2006b), which consists of, among others, a query engine for DL-Lite and one for fuzzy DL-Lite. The ONTOSEARCH2 implementation of f-DL-Lite is known to be able to handle millions of data and its performance has been tested against a benchmark, a fuzzy variant of the Lehigh University Benchmark (LUBM) (Guo et al, 2005), called f-LUBM[8], that has been proposed in the literature (Pan et al., 2008).

- It overviews the syntax and semantics of a fuzzy extension of the lightweight fuzzy ontology language f-EL+ (Stoilos et al., 2008). Additionally, it also overviews the reasoning algorithm proposed for f-EL+ which is able to polynomialy classify a given fuzzy EL+ ontology which additionally allows for fuzzy inclusion axioms (Straccia, 2005).

- It not only presents a detailed reasoning algorithm for classifying fuzzy EL+ ontologies which allow for fuzzy inclusion axioms, but it also provides some necessary refinements for the basic algorithm which are know from the classical EL+ language that greatly increase the performance.

The rest of the paper is organized as follows. First we introduce the reader to the necessary mathematical background of the rest of the Chapter, by briefly introducing Description Logics and fuzzy Description Logics. Then we present fuzzy-DL-Lite and a set of extended weighted query languages that have been proposed in the literature for querying fuzzy-DL-Lite ontologies. We also show how querying can be supported by the SPARQL language as well as a preliminary implementation of the idea. Subsequently, we present a fuzzy extension of the EL+ language providing also a reasoning algorithm for supporting classification over fuzzy EL+ ontologies. We also show how one can obtain a refined classification algorithm which can be the base of an optimized procedure. Finally, we conclude the Chapter.

BACKGROUND

Description Logic Ontologies

Description Logics (DLs) (Baader et al., 2002) are a family of logic-based knowledge representation formalisms designed to represent and reason about the knowledge of an application domain in a structured and well-understood way. They are based on a common family of languages, called description languages, which provide a set of constructors to build *concept* and *role descriptions*. Such descriptions can then be used to define *axioms* and *assertions* of DL knowledge bases and can be reasoned about with respect to DL knowledge bases by DL systems. It is known that DLs consist of an expressive fragment of First-Order Logic and more precisely a fragment that allows only for unary predicates (corresponding to concepts), binary predicates (corresponding to roles), constants (called *individuals*), while addition-

Table 1. Syntax, Semantics and naming of the most popular DL languages

DL Operator	Syntax	Semantics	Language
top concept	⊤	$\top^I = D^I$	
bottom concept	⊥	$\bot^I = \varnothing$	
negation	$\neg C$	$(\neg C)^I = D^I \setminus C^I$	
conjunction	$C \sqcap D$	$(C \sqcap D)^I = C^I \cap D^I$	ALC
disjunction	$C \sqcup D$	$(C \sqcup D)^I = C^I \cup D^I$	
existential restriction	$\exists R.C$	$(\exists R.C)^I = \left\{ a \in \Delta^I \mid \exists b.\langle a,b \rangle \in R^I \wedge b \in C^I \right\}$	
universal restriction	$\forall R.C$	$(\forall R.C)^I = \left\{ a \in \Delta^I \mid \forall b.\langle a,b \rangle \in R^I \rightarrow b \in C^I \right\}$	
transitive role axioms	**Trans(R)**	$\left\{ \langle a,b \rangle, \langle b,c \rangle \right\} \subseteq R^I \rightarrow \langle a,c \rangle \in R^I$	$\mathcal{ALC}_{R^+}$ or S
Role inclusion axioms	$R \subseteq S$	$\langle a,b \rangle \in R^I \rightarrow \langle a,b \rangle \in S^I$	H
nominals	$\{a\}$	$\{a\}^I = \{a^I\}$	O
inverse roles	R^-	$\langle a,b \rangle \in (R^-)^I \rightarrow \langle b,a \rangle \in R^I$	I
at-least restrictions	$\geq nR$	$(\geq nR)^I = \left\{ a \in \Delta^I \mid \left| b \mid \langle a,b \rangle \in R^I \right| \geq n \right\}$	N
at-most restrictions	$\leq nR$	$(\geq nR)^I = \left\{ a \in \Delta^I \mid \left| b \mid \langle a,b \rangle \in R^I \right| \leq n \right\}$	

ally also restricting the use of the connectives thus reducing their interaction and gaining in reasoning efficiency and decidability. The most basic DL language is ALC which is the smallest propositionally closed DL, allowing for negation ($\neg$) conjunction ($\sqcap$), disjunction ($\sqcup$), existential quantification ($\exists$) and universal quantification ($\forall$). Then ALC can be extended by adding more expressive means like for example the ability to state that a role is *transitive* or that a role is a *super-role* of another role, *inverse roles*, singleton concepts (called *nominals*) or by adding *cardinality restrictions*. Table 1 summarizes the most important and common DL constructors. It presents their name, syntax and the naming scheme that is followed in DLs in order to indicate the presence of such operators[9]. Using the expressivity of these DL constructors one can represent the concept of humans who have exactly 3 children specifying the concept

$$Human \sqcap \geq 3\,hasChild \sqcap \leq 3\,hasChild$$

where *Human* is a concept, and *hasChild* is a role, or the concept of faulty machines with the concept

$$Machine \sqcap \exists hasPart.MachinePart \sqcap \forall hasPartFaultyPart$$

or the concept of the days of week, writing

$$\{Sunday\} \sqcup \{Monday\} \sqcup \ldots \sqcup \{Saturday\}$$

where *Sunday, Monday,…, Saturday* are individuals. Such complex concepts are called *concept descriptions*. Moreover, we can state that roles *hasPart* is transitive by the axiom, **Trans**(*hasPart*), that role *hasChild* is a sub-role of role *hasOffspring*, by the axiom *hasChild hasChild* ⊑ *hasOffspring*, or that role *hasParent* is the inverse of role *hasChild*, writing *hasParent* ⊑ *hasChild⁻*. We note here that the set of transitive role and role inclusion axioms is usually referred to as RBox *R*.

Subsequently, one is able to use concept descriptions in order to define new concepts. This is done with the aid of axioms. More formally we have: A SHOIN TBox denoted by T, is a finite set of concept inclusion axioms, also called concept subsumptions of the form $C \subseteq D$, and concept equivalence axioms of the form $C \circ D$ where *C,D* are SHOIN-concepts. With concept one can give names to the created concept descriptions. For example in the above case we could have the concept equivalence:

FaultyMachine ° *Machine* ⊓ ∃*hasPart.MachinePart* ⊓ ∀*hasPartFaultPart*

Finally, DLs allow us to create individual axioms, which intuitively account for instance relations between objects (pairs of objects) and concepts (roles). A SHOIN ABox *A*, is a finite set of assertions of the form *a*: *C*, called *concept assertions*, of the form (*a,b*): *R*, called *role assertions*, or of the form *a* = *b* or *a* ≠ *b*. Using such expressive means we can describe instance relation like for example that John is a parent, by writing *john*: *Parent* or that he has Dora as a child, by (*john, dora*): *hasChild*.

A knowledge base Σ is a triple of the form $\Sigma = \langle T,R,A \rangle$, where *T* is a TBox, *R* an RBox and *A* an ABox.

As a fragment of First-Order Logic Description Logics feature well-defined model theoretic semantics which are defined with the aid of interpretations. An *interpretation* (written as *I*) is a pair of the form $\langle \Delta^I, \cdot^I \rangle$ where D^I is a non-empty set of objects called the *domain of interpretation* while $\cdot^I$ is an *interpretation function* which maps each *individual a* to an element $a^I \in D^I$ each *concept* C to a subset $C^I \subseteq D^I$ and each *role R* to a binary relation $R^I \subseteq D^I \times D^I$. The interpretation function can be extended to give semantics to concept and role description. Table 1 summarizes the semantics of DL constructors. Furthermore, we say an interpretation *I* satisfies an axiom $C \subseteq D$ if $C^I \subseteq D^I$, while it satisfies an axiom $C \circ D$ if $C^I = D^I$. *I* satisfies a TBox *T* if it satisfies every axiom in T. Then we say that *I* is a *model* of *T*. Similarly an interpretation *I* satisfies an assertion *a*: *C* if a^I: C^I, an assertion (*a,b*): *R* if (a^I, b^I): R^I, $a = b$ if $a^I = b^I$ and $a \neq b$ if $a^I \neq b^I$. *I* satisfies a knowledge base Σ if it a model of T, R and A.

Besides their formality knowledge representation languages and DLs also provide a number of inference services, which can be issued over a created knowledge base. The aim of such services is to extract new implied information out of the explicitly stated one. Every knowledge representation language usually offers a different set of inference services. Next we present the most common set of services offered by Description Logics:

- **KB Satisfiability:** A KB Σ is satisfiable if and only if (iff) there exists a model *I* of Σ. Similarly we can define the notion of unsatisfiability.
- **Concept Satisfiability:** A concept *C* is satisfiable with respect to Σ if there exists a model *I* of Σ such that (s.t.) $C^I \neq \varnothing$.
- **Concept Subsumption:** A concept *C* is subsumed by a concept *D* w.r.t. Σ if for every model *I* of Σ it holds that $C^I \subseteq D^I$.
- **ABox Consistency:** An ABox *A* is consistent if there exists a model for *A*.

- **Logical Entailment**: Given a concept or role axiom, or an assertion ϕ, we say that Σ entails ϕ, writing $\Sigma \models \phi$ if for every model I of Σ, I satisfies ϕ.
  - **Conjunctive query answering:** A *conjunctive query (CQ)* q is of the form

$$q(X) \leftarrow \exists Y. conj(X,Y) \tag{1}$$

where $q(X)$ is called the *head*, $conj(X,Y)$ is called the *body*, X is a vector of variables called *distinguished variables*, Y are existentially quantified variables called the *non-distinguished variables*, and $conj(X,Y)$ is a conjunction of atoms of the form $A(u)$, $R(v_1, v_2)$, where A,R are respectively named classes and named properties, v,v_1,v_2 are individuals in X and Y or individuals in Σ. Given an *evaluation* of variables $[X \rightarrow S]$ (where S is a set of individuals), if every model I of Σ satisfies $q_{[X \rightarrow S]}$, we say Σ entails $q_{[X \rightarrow S]}$; in this case, S is called a solution of q. A *disjunctive query (DQ)* is a set of conjunctive queries sharing the same head.

Conjunctive query answering actually consists of a retrieval task. Informally, one can understand a query as "give me all X such as the conjunction of atoms $conj(X,Y)$ holds." Then, S will contain the set of all individuals that substituted in X will make the body true for some other individuals S' substituted for Y. As it is known it consists of a generalization of the entailment task.

Today, there have been developed several reasoning systems that realize most of the above inference problems for SHOIN knowledge bases. The most important and popular ones are FaCT++[1] and Pellet[2] and RacerPro[10]. These tools have shown that although the worst case complexity of reasoning in DLs is exponential they can scale quite good in relatively big knowledge bases in most practical applications. Nevertheless, it is still unknown if they could scale up to the millions or even billion of (Semantic) Web data. Furthermore, regarding conjunctive query answering it is still an open problem if an algorithm for answering queries over SHOIN knowledge bases exists. Even if it does we already know that the complexity of query answering for SHIN is already 2-EXPTIME -hard (Lutz, 2008).

It is well known that expressive Description Logics form the logical underpinnings of the OWL DL ontology language (Horrocks & Patel-Schneider, 2004). OWL is the W3C standard for expressing ontologies in the Semantic Web and is actually an XML like rendering of the constructors of the SHOIN language, while additionally adding several syntactic sugar constructors for assisting inexperienced user of the Web create ontologies. For example, on the one hand it provides the owl:instersectionOf constructor for specifying the conjunction of two concepts while on the other hand it also provides the rdfs:domain constructor for defining the domain of a role (property) which semantically is a combination of the existential constructor and a concept inclusion. For more information about OWL the reader is referred to (Bechhofer et al., 2004; Patel-Schneider et al., 2004) while for its correspondence with expressive DLs to (Horrocks & Patel-Schneider, 2004).

Fuzzy Ontologies

Fuzzy Description Logics (Straccia, 2001) have been proposed as powerful knowledge representation languages capable of capturing vague (fuzzy) knowledge that exists in many applications. The intuition is to interpret (fuzzy) concepts and (roles) not as subsets of D^I and $D^I \times D^I$, respectively, but with the aid of membership function (Zadeh, 1965) giving a fuzzy meaning. Syntactically, one should at least be able to specify degrees of membership for instance relations. Thus, fuzzy DL extensions usually keep the same syntax for concept and role axioms as their crisp (classical) counterpart, while they extend the syntax of concept and role assertions with membership degrees creating *fuzzy assertions* (Hölldobler et al., 2005; Tresp & Molitor 1998; Stoilos et al., 2007; Straccia, 2001). For example, one is able to state that a specific grass is seeing to be green to a degree greater or equal than 0.7, writing (*grass:Green*) $\geq$ 0.7. Hence, fuzziness is added at the instance level. Some notable exceptions found in the literature are *fuzzy subsumption* axioms (Straccia, 2005) and *fuzzy nominals* (Bobillo et al., 2006) which also extend the syntax of concept inclusion axioms and the. Fuzzy subsumption extends classical subsumption with degrees of truth. More formally a fuzzy subsumption is a concept axiom of the form $\langle C \subseteq D, n \rangle$, where $n \in [0,1]$. Note that we will not deal with fuzzy nominals in the current Chapter.

As with classical DLs fuzzy DLs have a formal semantics provided by *fuzzy interpretation*. Intuitively, fuzzy interpretations map concepts to membership functions in order to provide a fuzzy meaning. More formally a fuzzy interpretation consists of a pair $I = \langle \Delta^I, \cdot^I \rangle$ where D^I is as before, while $\cdot^I$ is a *fuzzy interpretation function*, which maps:

- an individual a to an element $a \in D^I$,
- a concept name A to a membership function $A^I : \Delta^I \to [0,1]$, and
- a role name R to a membership function $R^I : \Delta^I \times \Delta^I \to [0,1]$.

Using well known fuzzy set theoretic operations (Klir & Yuan, 1995), like t-norms (t), t-conorms (u), fuzzy complements (c) and fuzzy implications (J), fuzzy interpretations can be extended to interpret f-SHOIN-concepts. Table 2 summarizes the syntax and semantics of concept descriptions, concept axioms, roles axioms and fuzzy assertions for the fuzzy DL f-SHOIN. In Table 2, a is an arbitrary individual of D^I.

Now we can proceed to define the inference services of fuzzy Description Logics.

- **KB Satisfiability:** An f-SHOIN knowledge base Σ is satisfiable (unsatisfiable) iff there exists (does not exist) a fuzzy interpretation I which satisfies all axioms in Σ.
- **Concept n-satisfiabilty:** An f- SHOIN -concept C is n-satisfiable w.r.t. Σ iff there exists a model I of Σ in which there exists some $a \in D^I$ such that $C^I(a) = n$, and $n \in (0,1]$.
- **Concept Subsumption:** An f-SHOIN-concept C is subsumed by D w.r.t. Σ iff in every model I of Σ we have that $\forall a \in \Delta^I, C^I(a) \leq D^I(a)$.
- **ABox Consistency:** An f-SHOIN is consistent (inconsistent) w.r.t. a TBox T and an RBox R if there exists (does not exist) a model I of T and R which satisfies every assertion in A.
- **Entailment:** Given a concept or role axiom or a fuzzy assertion Ψ, we say that Σ entails Ψ, writing $\Sigma \models \Psi$ iff every model I of Σ satisfies Ψ.
- **Greater Lower Bound (glb):** The greatest lower bound of an individual a to a concept C w.r.t. Σ is defined as, $\text{glb}(\Sigma, C, a) = \sup\{n \mid \Sigma \models a : C \geq n\}$ with $\sup\varnothing = 0$.

Similarly to OWL and DLs the fuzzy OWL (Stoilos et al., 2005a) proposal consists of an extension of the OWL standard in order to represent fuzzy knowledge in the Semantic Web. As in the crisp case the logical underpinnings of f-OWL is f-SHOIN, while fuzziness can be captured in the instance level in the form of fuzzy instance relations called *fuzzy facts*. For example, one can have the following f-OWL instance axiom:

Table 2. Semantic of fuzzy SHOIN -concept descriptions and axioms

Syntax	Semantics
$\top$	$\top^I(a) = 1$
$\bot$	$\bot^I(a) = 0$
$\neg C$	$(\neg C)^I(a) = c(C^I(a))$
$C \sqcap D$	$(C \sqcap D)^I(a) = t(C^I(a), D^I(a))$
$C \sqcup D$	$(C \sqcup D)^I(a) = u(C^I(a), D^I(a))$
$\exists R.C$	$\exists R.C^I(a) = \sup_b \left\{ t(R^I(a,b), C^I(b)) \right\}$
$\forall R.C$	$\forall R.C^I(a) = \inf_b \left\{ \mathcal{J}(R^I(a,b), C^I(b)) \right\}$
$\{a\}$	$\{a\}^I(b) = 1$ if $b \in \left\{ a^I \right\}$, $\{a\}^I(b) = 0$ otherwise
R^-	$(R^-)^I(b,a) = R^I(a,b)$
$\geq nR$	$(\geq pR)^I(a) = \sup_{b_1,\ldots,b_n} t(\underset{i=1}{\overset{p}{t}} R^I(a,b_i), \underset{i<j}{t} \left\{ b_i \neq b_j \right\})$
$\leq nR$	$(\leq pR)^I(a) = \sup_{b_1,\ldots,b_{n+1}} \mathcal{J}(\underset{i=1}{\overset{p+1}{t}} R^I(a,b_i), \underset{i<j}{u} \left\{ b_i = b_j \right\})$
Trans(R)	$R^I(a,b) \geq \sup_c \left\{ t(R^I(a,c), R^I(c,b)) \right\}$
$R \sqsubseteq S$	$\forall a,b \in \Delta^I . R^I(a,b) \leq S^I(a,b)$
$C \sqsubseteq D$	$\forall a \in \Delta^I . C^I(a) \leq D^I(a)$
$C \circ D$	$\forall a \in \Delta^I . C^I(a) = D^I(a)$
$(a{:}C) \geq n$	$C^I(a) \geq n$
$(a,b){:} R \geq n$	$R^I(a,b) \geq n$

```
<HotPlace rdf:about="Athens" owlx:ineqType=">=" owlx:degree="0.85">
<closeTo rdf:resource="Larnaca" owlx:ineqType=">=" owlx:degree="0.75"/>
</HotPlace>
```

saying that Athens is a hot place to a degree at least 0.85, while it is close to Larnaca to a degree at least equal to 0.75.

SCALABLE QUERY ANSWERING WITH FUZZY DL-LITE

In the current section we will review some recent developments on the f-DL-Lite language. More precisely we will present a framework of very expressive fuzzy conjunctive query languages over the fuzzy DL-Lite language. We first introduce fuzzy DL-Lite as a restriction of f-SHOIN and we briefly sketch its query answering algorithm. Then we present the syntax and semantics of the expressive weighted query languages. Subsequently, we show how such queries can be supported through SPARQL, a well known query language that will consist of a W3C standard, and finally we present an implementation of the aforementioned framework.

The Fuzzy DL-Lite Language

In order to gain in reasoning efficiency it is obvious that the DL-Lite language (and its fuzzy extension) consists of a restriction of the classical DL constructors.

A DL-Lite ontology (O)[11] is a set of axioms of the following forms[12]:

1. *class inclusion axioms*: $B \subseteq C$ where B is called a *basic concept* defined as:

$B := A \mid \exists R \mid \exists R^-$

and C is called a *general concept* and is defined as

$C := B \mid \neg B \mid C_1 \sqcap C_2$

2. *functional property axioms*: **Func**(R), **Func**(R^-), where R is a role, and
3. *individual axioms*: $B(a) \geq n, R(a,b) \geq n$ where a and b are individuals.

Note that $B(a) \geq n$ is just another syntax for $(a:B) \geq n$. As we can see in DL-Lite besides limiting the number of the available DL constructors one additionally restricts the use of the allowed ones in concept axioms. For example, negation is only allowed in the right-hand side of axioms and only in front of basic concepts. Although DL-Lite is significantly restrictive, compared to OWL DL, it is known that is expressive enough to represent most features of UML class diagrams. Furthermore, this restrictiveness is the reason that DL-Lite provides efficient query answering. More precisely, it is known (and we will briefly sketch below) that after careful rewriting conjunctive query answering over DL-Lite can be reduced to a set of SQL queries over a relational database system. Consequently, the complexity of DL-Lite query answering is LogSpace w.r.t. data, which is obviously far more computationally easy than that of SHIN.

Like in other fuzzy extensions to DLs, fuzzy DL-Lite (Straccia, 2006) (or f-DL-Lite for short), extends DL-Lite with fuzzy assertions, as described in the previous section. The semantics of f-DL-Lite ontologies are again defined in terms of fuzzy interpretations. Since we have already presented the semantics of most of the constructors used by f-DL-Lite we will not repeat them here. We only note that a fuzzy interpretation I satisfies a functional property axiom of the form **Func**(R) if $\forall a \in \Delta^I . \#\{o \mid R^I(a,o) > 0\} = 1$.

Similarly to crisp DL lite, *fuzzy-DL-Lite*, provides means to specify *role-typing* and *participation constraints* but interestingly it assigns fuzzy meaning on them. More precisely, a role-typing assertion of the form $\exists R \subseteq A_1$ (resp. $\exists R^- \subseteq A_2$) states that the first (resp. second) component of a relation $R(a,b)$ belongs to A_1 (resp. A_2) at-least to the membership degree that the relation holds, i.e. $R^I(a^I,b^I) \leq A_1^I(a^I)$ (resp. $(R^-)^I(b^I,a^I) = R^I(a^I,b^I) \leq A_2^I(b^I)$.

Similar to the crisp algorithm, the algorithm for answering conjunctive queries over f-DL-Lite ontologies consists mainly of three steps (Calvanese, 2005; Calavanese et al., 2007; Straccia, 2006), which can be briefly summarized as follows:

1. **Normalization:** During this step, axioms of the form $B \subseteq C_1 \wedge C_2$ are replaced by two axioms of the form $B \subseteq C_1$ and $B \subseteq C_2$, while concept axioms are closed under subsumption ($\subseteq$) and under the rule, if $B_1 \subseteq B_2 \in T$ and $B_3 \subseteq \neg B_2 \in T$, then $T \cup \{B_1 \subseteq \neg B_3\}$. Moreover, the ABox is normalized by adding fuzzy assertions $\exists R(a) \geq n$ and $\exists R^-(b) \geq n$ for each $R(a,b) \geq n \in A$ (Calvanese et al., 2005; Calavanese et al., 2007).

2. **Query reformulation:** In the second step the input query is *reformulated* by a process known as *perfect reformulation* (Calvanese et al., 2005; Calavanese et al., 2007). The idea is to expand the query according to the given concept axioms in order to obtain a set of queries which issued to the ABox discarding the TBox will retrieve all the certain answers of the original query as if it was issued over the overall knowledge base.

3. **Query evaluation:** Finally, the set of conjunctive queries is evaluated over the given ABox.

An important property of the (fuzzy) DL-Lite algorithm is that the ABox can be faithfully stored in a data base. Hence, every step that involves assertions of the ABox, like consistency checking and query evaluation can be performed by applying SQL queries to the data base.

Expressive Query Languages

How one can efficiently and effectively access fuzzy information has been a significant issue in the fuzzy information retrieval community (Cross, 1994). The idea is that fuzziness allows for many new capabilities for accessing information. More precisely, the fuzzy degrees can be used in order to provide rankings of result sets. Furthermore, these degrees can be combined with degrees issued by the user which intuitively represent their preferences about the elements of the query. For example, a user might be more interested in retrieving objects that have a certain property than another, or although he/she would prefer to see objects satisfying specific constraints he/she is also flexible if his/her criteria could not be met to an absolute degree. Thus the results will be ranked according to fuzziness but also according to user data. Consequently, approaches to *weighted conjunctive queries* (Waller & Kraft, 1979) have been proposed and many proposals/strategies for combining the user specified degrees with the fuzzy degrees have been developed (Bookstein, 1980; Bordogna, 1996; Chen & Chen; Radecki, 1979; Salton et al., 1983a; Sanchez, 1989; Yager, 1987).

Pan et al. (2008) were inspired by weighted conjunctive query languages and the work in the field of fuzzy information retrieval and extended the classical conjunctive query language of f-DL-Lite with two very expressive query languages providing algorithms for evaluating such queries. On the one hand they propose new query languages, which generalize the entailment problem, while on the other hand they propose a general framework which encapsulates many of the query languages proposed in the literature for fuzzy information retrieval. Implementation over f-DL-Lite shows that such expressive queries can also be handled in a scalable and efficient way even in fuzzy ontology languages. In the following we first introduce *conjunctive threshold queries* that were proposed in (Pan et al., 2008) and consist of a totally new query language, while later on we introduce *general fuzzy queries*.

Threshold Queries: As it was noted in (Calvanese, 2005; Calavanese et al., 2007) in DL-Lite (and in all DLs) the entailment problem is a special case of conjunctive query answering. Since f_{KD}-DL-Lite allows for fuzzy assertions, it would be reasonable that our query language was an extension of the entailment of fuzzy assertions. This implies that the query language should allow users to write the conjunction of fuzzy assertions. Working that way we can define *conjunctive threshold queries* (*CTQ*) which extend the atoms $A(u), R(v_1, v_2)$ in conjunctive queries of the form (1) to the following form $A(u) \geq t_1, R(v_1, v_2) \geq t_2$, where $t_1, t_2 \in (0,1]$ represent thresholds. As it was proven these queries are very important since they can be used in order to devise a reasoning algorithm for the fuzzy language fuzzy-CARIN (Mailis et al., 2007).

Example. Using threshold queries we can ask a database of human models for all the models of that are tall to a degree no less than 0.7 and light to a degree no less than 0.8 using the following conjunctive threshold query:

$q(x) \leftarrow Model(x) \geq 1 \wedge Tall(x) \geq 0.7 \wedge Light(x) \geq 0.8$

Obviously, CTQs are more flexible than queries of the form (1) since users are allowed to specify for different thresholds to each atom of the query.

Formally, given an f_{KD}-DL-Lite ontology O, a CTQ q_T and an evaluation $[X \mapsto S]$, we say that O entails q_T (writing $O \models q_T$) if every interpretation I of O satisfies the following condition: for every atom $A(u) \geq t_1, R(u_1, u_2) \geq t_2$ of q_T, we have $A^I(u)_{[X \mapsto S]} \geq t_1, R(u_1, u_2)_{[X \mapsto S]} \geq t_2$. Then we say that S is a *solution* of q_T. From the above we note that the solution set of a CTQ is crisp. i.e. a tuple either belongs or not to it. *Disjunctive threshold queries* (*DTQs*) are defined accordingly.

Generalized Fuzzy Queries: Since f_{KD}-DL-Lite allows for fuzzy assertions it would be useful if we could find a way to assess a membership degree of a tuple to the result set of a given query. As we show this is not the case for CTQs where a tuple either belongs or not to the solution set. For that reason we introduce general fuzzy conjunctive queries. Syntactically, a *general fuzzy conjunctive queries* (*GFCQ*) extends the atoms $A(u), R(v_1, v_2)$ of conjunctive queries of the form (1) with those of the form $A(u) : k_1, R(v_1, v_2) : k_2$, where $t_1, t_2 \in (0,1]$ are degrees called *weights*.

This extension of conjunctive query languages was already proposed in (Waller & Kraft, 1979) for fuzzy databases and fuzzy information retrieval. All the approaches that followed argued in favor for specific semantics for such queries (Bookstein, 1980; Chen & Chen; Radecki, 1979; Salton et al., 1983a). Differently, we will try to use generalized fuzzy operators in order to keep the choice of the semantics open. Thus in our case, conjunction of atoms will be performed by a general function denoted by G as well as the degree of each atom with the associated weight will be denoted by a function a. To simplify the presentation we will represent query atoms of GFCQs with $atom_i(\overline{u})$. Given a f_{KD}-DL-Lite ontology O, a fuzzy interpretation I of O, a GFCQ q_F and an evaluation $[X \mapsto S]$, the truth degree of q_F in I for the specific evaluation is given by:

$$d = \sup_{S' \subseteq \Delta^I \times ... \times \Delta^I} G_{i=1}^n a(k_i, atom_i^I(\overline{u})_{[X \mapsto S, Y \mapsto S']})$$

where for $1 \leq I \leq n$, k_i and $atom_i$ are as shown before, G is a function that evaluates conjunctions of atoms and a is a function that evaluates the weight associated atoms. $S:d$ is called a *candidate solution* of q_F. When $d > 0$, then $S:d$ is called a solution of q_F. Additionally, the semantic function must also satisfy the following condition:

If $atom_i^I(\overline{u})_{[X \mapsto S, Y \mapsto S']} = 0$ for every valuation S' and $1 \leq I \leq n$, then $d = 0$. \hfill (2)

General fuzzy disjunctive query (*GFDQ*) is defined as a set of GFCQs that share the same head.

As we noted above Pan et al. (2008) have left the evaluation of conjunctions and degree associated weights open. Consequently, there are many different ways to provide semantics and meaning to our queries. In what follows we will briefly overview several such important choices that have been examined in (Pan et al., 2008).

1. **Fuzzy threshold queries:** As we show the result set of CTQs is always a crisp set. This implies that if we have a fuzzy assertion of the form $(a{:}C) \geq 0.18$ and a CTQ of the form $q_T(x) \leftarrow C(x) \geq 0.2$ then a will not be included in the result set. On the other hand if we choose a t-norm (t) as a function for G and an R-implication as a function for a then we obtain fuzzy threshold queries, in which the truth degree of q_F in I is given by the equation:

$$d = \sup_{S' \subseteq \Delta^I \times \ldots \times \Delta^I} t_{i=1}^n J(k_i, atom_i^I(\overline{u})_{[X \mapsto S, Y \mapsto S']})$$

Given some set S', if for all atoms of the query we have $atom_i^I(\overline{u})_{[X \mapsto S, Y \to S']} \geq k_i$, then $d = 1$. On the other hand, if for some atom it was the case that $atom_i^I(\overline{u})_{[X \mapsto S, Y \to S']} < k_i$ then the R-implication would gradually filter (penalize) the membership degree of the solution to the result set according to weight k_i.

As it was shown by Bordogna (1996) many of the proposed semantic functions found in the literature, like those in (Bookstein, 1980; Buel & Kraft, 1981; Radecki, 1979), can be grouped under the general framework of fuzzy threshold queries. Moreover, Pan et al. (2008) show that the (classical) conjunctive query language used by Straccia (2006), is also a special case of fuzzy threshold queries if we set all weights equal to 1.

2. **Fuzzy aggregation queries:** Another commonly used fuzzy operator in fuzzy set literature that can be used as a semantic function for interpreting general fuzzy queries is that of fuzzy aggregation functions (Klir & Yuan, 1995). For example, if we use the weighted average we will get the semantic function:

$$d = \sup_{S' \subseteq \Delta^I \times \ldots \times \Delta^I} \frac{\sum_{i=1}^n (k_i \times atom_i^I(\overline{u})_{[X \mapsto S, Y \mapsto S']})}{\sum_{i=1}^n k_i}$$

Similarly to fuzzy threshold queries, Pan et al. (2008) show that many proposals for semantics of weighted queries, like the ones of Salton et al. (1983a) and S.-J. Chen and S.-M. Chen (2000), are special cases of the family of fuzzy aggregation queries.

3. **Fuzzy weighted t-norms:** If we use the weighted t-norm operators proposed and studied by Chortaras et al. (2006) as functions for conjunctions and for associated weights, then the truth degree of q_F in I is given by:

$$d = \sup_{S' \subseteq \Delta^I \times \ldots \times \Delta^I} \left\{ \min_{i=1}^n u(\overline{k} - k_i, t(\overline{k}, atom_i^I(\overline{u})_{[X \mapsto S, Y \mapsto S']})) \right\}$$

Table 3. Example Consider the following set of fuzzy assertions

Tall		hasFriend		
Individual	**Degree**	**Individual**	**Individual**	**Degree**
george	0.8	goerge	mary	0.8
tom	0.79	tom	mary	0.9
mary	0.75	mary	tom	0.9

where $\bar{k} = \max_{i=1}^{n} k_i$. For more information about these fuzzy operators the reader is referred to (Chortaras et al., 2006). Once more we can use this generalized class of query languages to show that several approaches, like the one proposed by Yager (1987) and Sanchez (1989), fall into it

It is easily shown that the above fuzzy conjunctive query languages satisfy condition (2).

Table 3 depicts fuzzy assertions with the fuzzy concept Tall, while the second one with the fuzzy relation hasFriend. Consider now the following GFCQ:

$$q(x) \leftarrow Tall(x) : 0.8 \wedge hasFriend(x, y) : 0.6$$

Table 4 summarizes the results of issuing such a query in the above fuzzy knowledge by using several of the semantic functions introduced before.

From the above we see that different choices of semantic functions could lead to different ranking results since the considered semantics are different. The first semantic function teats weight as thresholds, penalizing the individuals that fail to satisfy them, while the second one aggregates all the degrees. The choice of the semantic function is context dependent and as far as we know there are no criteria or methodology found in the literature for choosing among them.

Supporting Querying with SPARQL

After presenting the abstract syntax and semantics of our proposed languages, and important issue is to how such queries can be represented using Semantic Web standards. In the following we show how to extend the syntax of SPARQL (Prud'hommeaux & Seaborne, 2006), a well known Semantic Web query language, for the proposed languages. We call our extension f-SPARQL. SPARQL is a query language (candidate recommendation from the W3C Data Access Working Group[13]) for getting information from RDF graphs. SPARQL allows for a query to constitute of triple patterns, conjunctions, disjunctions and optional patterns. A SPARQL query is a quadruple $Q = (V,P,DS,SM)$, where V is a *result form*, P is a *graph pattern*, DS a *data set* and *SM* a set of solution modifiers. Among others, SPARQL allows for select queries, formed in a SELECT-FROM-WHERE manner. The result form represents the set of variables appearing in the SELECT, the dataset forms the FROM part, constituted by a set of IRIs of RDF documents, while the graph pattern forms the WHERE part which is constituted by a set of RDF triples.

In order to maintain backward compatibility with existing SPARQL tools, we propose to use specially formatted SPARQL comments to specify extra information needed in our proposed languages (see Table 5). Firstly, one should declare the query type before a select query. For example, #TQ# declares a threshold query, while #GFCQ:SEM=FUZZY THRESHOLD# declares a general fuzzy query, with the fuzzy threshold semantic functions. Secondly, following each triple in the WHERE clause, one can

Table 4.

Fuzzy Threshold Queries with the Lukasiewicz operators $t(a,b) = \mathbf{max}(0,a+b-1)$ $J(a,b) = \mathbf{min}(1,1-a+b)$		Fuzzy Aggregation Queries using weighted average	
x	d	x	d
george	1	tom	0.837
tom	0.99	mary	0.81
mary	0.95	george	0.8

use #TH# (resp. #DG#) to specify a threshold in a threshold query (resp. a degree in a general fuzzy query). For instance, the threshold query presented in a previous Example can be represented by the following f-SPARQL query:

```
#TQ#
SELECT ?x WHERE {
?x rdf:type Model . #TH# 1.0
?x rdf:type Tall . #TH# 0.7
?x rdf:type Light . #TH# 0.8
}
```

In the case of general fuzzy queries, one must specify the semantic functions (i.e. *a* and *G*). Below is an example fuzzy threshold query.

```
#GFCQ:SEM=FUZZYTHRESHOLD#
SELECT ?x WHERE {
?x rdf:type Model . #DG# 1.0
?x rdf:type Tall . #DG# 0.7
?x rdf:type Light . #DG# 0.8
}
```

Table 5 presents the f-SPARQL syntax. f-SPARQL extends two of SPARQL's elements, namely the "Query" and the "TriplesBlock" element. As illustrated above, each select query is extended with

Table 5. Syntax of Fuzzy SPARQL

Query	:= Prologue (*QueryType* SelectQuery | ConstructQuery| DescribeQuery | AskQuery)
QueryType	::= '#TQ# \n' | '#GFCQ:SEM=' *FuzzySemantics* '# \n'
FuzzySemantics	::= 'AGGREGATION' | 'FUZZYTHRESHOLD' | 'FUZZYTHRESHOLD-1' | 'FUZZYWEIGHTEDNORMS'
TriplesBlock	:= TriplesSameSubject ('.' *TripleWeight Degree* TriplesBlock?)?
TripleWeight	:= '#TH#' | '#DG#'
Degree	:= real-number-between-0-and-1-upper-inclusive

the element *QueryType*. In particular, for general fuzzy queries, the declaration `#GFCQ:SEM=' is followed by the element *FuzzySemantics*, which is used to specify the semantic functions, such as the ones we presented in the previous section. More precisely, we use the keywords `FUZZYTHRESHOLD', `FUZZYTHRESHOLD-1', `AGGREGATION' and `FUZZYWEIGHTEDNORMS' to indicate the four fuzzy general queries we introduced in Section 3.1.2. When one uses `FUZZYTHRESHOLD-1', the fuzzy threshold is set as 1, and the values specified by the #TH# comments are ignored. Finally, the `"TriplesBlock" element is extended with the elements *TripleWeight* and *Degree*, which are used to associated a threshold or weight with each triple of the SPARQL query.

The ONTOSEARCH2 System

Our implementation is based on the ONTOSEARCH2 system (Pan et al., 2006b; Thomas et al., 2007), which is an infrastructure for supporting ontology searching and query answering. The f-DL-Lite query engine is implemented as an extension of the crisp DL-Lite query engine in ONTOSEARCH2[7] (Pan & Thomas, 2007), so as to support threshold queries and general fuzzy queries. The core part of the f-DL-Lite query engine includes implementations of algorithms that realize the expressive conjunctive queries we have presented in the previous section over fuzzy DL-Lite (Pan et al., 2008). The system was written in Java 5 and uses PostgreSQL 8.1 RDBMS for the repository storage. PostgreSQL was setup with default installation, no additional configuration was performed.

Users of the f-DL-Lite query engine can submit f-DL-Lite ontologies via the Web interface of ONTOSEARCH2, and then submit f-SPARQL queries against their target ontologies. Figure 1 depicts the web interface of ONTOSEARCH2.

The fuzzy query engine operates in two modes: TQ mode (for threshold queries) and GFCQ mode (for general fuzzy queries). When users submit an f-SPARQL query, the fuzzy query engine parses it, so as to determine the query type (whether the query is a threshold query or a general fuzzy query), as well as the thresholds (for threshold queries) or degrees (for general fuzzy queries), depending on the query types. The implementation over ONTOSEARCH2 has been evaluated against a fuzzy variant of the Lehigh University Benchmark (Pan et al., 2008). In brief, the LUBM benchmark has been enriched with two fuzzy concepts, that of a "Busy" and a "Famous" for which fuzzy assertions are created. The system has been shown to be highly scalable, being able to answer threshold queries and general fuzzy queries over about 7,000,000 individuals in a matter of a few seconds, comparable to the query answering time of classical DL-Lite.

Besides the DL-Lite and the f-DL-Lite query engine, the ONTOSEARCH2 system consists of other components, such as the ontology search engine. According to this functionality the implementation has been tested with a realistic Semantic Web scenario, which we briefly sketch below.

One of the major limitations of existing ontology search engines is that searching is *only* based on keywords and metadata information of ontologies, rather than semantic entailments of ontologies (e.g., one wants to search for ontologies in which Bass Clarinet is a sub-class of Woodwind). On the other hand, searching only based on semantic entailments might not be ideal either, as synonyms appearing in the metadata could not be exploited.

By making use of the f-DL-Lite query engine, our ontology search engine supports keyword-plus-entailment searches, such as *searching for ontologies in which class X is a sub-class of class Y, and class X is associated with the keywords "Bass" and "Clarinet", while class Y is associated with the keyword "Woodwind"*. The search could be represented as the following threshold query:

Figure 1. The ONTOSEARCH2 Web Interface

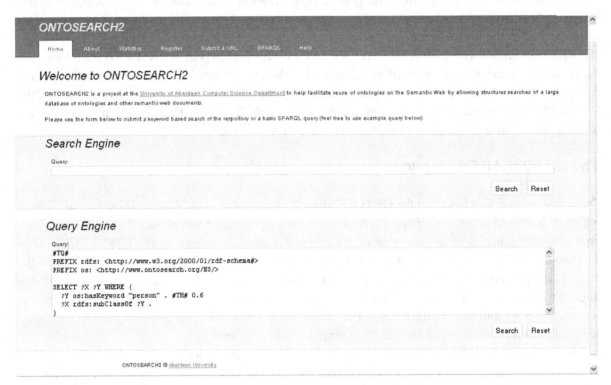

```
#TQ#
SELECT ?x WHERE {
?x hasKeyword i-bass . #TH# 0.6
?x hasKeyword i-clarinet . #TH# 0.6
?x rdfs:subClassOf ?y .
?y hasKeyword i-woodwind . #TH# 0.7
}
```

where i-bass, i-clarinet and i-woodwind are representative individuals for keywords "Bass", "Clarinet" and "Woodwind", resp. The thresholds 0.6 and 0.7 can be specified by users.

In order to support keyword-plus-entailment searches, our ontology search engine, for each indexed ontology, stores its semantic approximation (in DL-Lite) (Pan & Thomas, 2007) and accompanies each ontology in its repository with an f-DL-Lite *meta-ontology*, which (i) materialises all TBox reasoning based on the semantic approximation and, most importantly, (ii) uses fuzzy assertions to represent associations of each class (property) and keywords[14] appearing in the metadata of the ontology, with some degrees. Keywords appearing in the ontology metadata are associated with scores based on ranking factors[15]. We use these scores to calculate the *tf · idf* (Salton & McGill, 2983b) for each keyword, and normalise them using a sigmoid function such as the one shown in the following to a degree between 0 and 1.

$$w(n) = \frac{2}{1.2^{-n} + 1} - 1$$

Hence, the ontology search engine can use the f-DL-Lite query engine to query across all the meta-ontologies in its repository, so as to support keyword-plus-entailment searches. Further discussions of this use case go beyond the scope of this paper.

Concluding our presentation in expressive querying over f-DL-Lite ontologies, we would like to point out that the respective querying framework is not specifically tailored for f-DL-Lite ontologies. This framework has also been implemented in the FiRE[5] fuzzy DL reasoner and queries are realized through the Sesame RDF triple store[16]. More precisely, expressive reasoning is firstly applied in order to extract new implied information from the facts and axioms, then the knowledge base is stored in a proper form in Sesame and finally FiRE uses SPARQL queries to Sesame in order to implement expressive weighted queries (Simou et al., 2008b). The respective implementation has been evaluated against an industrial strength scenario about casting actors for TV spots and commercials and its performance has been assessed.

SCALABLE KNOWLEDGE CLASSIFICATION WITH FUZZY EL+

In the current section we will present a fuzzy extension of the EL+ language. EL+ (Baader et al.) is another very famous tractable Description Logic that has been proposed in the literature. It actually consists of one member of the EL family of languages consisting of EL, EL+ and EL++ (Baader et al., 2005). The EL family has been developed by an effort to identify the fragment of Description Logics that is usually used in creating medical ontologies, like the SNOMED[17] (Systematized Nomenclature of Medicine) and the Galen[18] ontologies. It was only later proved that the used fragment enjoys polynomial algorithms for concept classification. This was a very important feature since concept classification is a very important (if not the most important) reasoning problem in medical applications, where the classification of medical terms within the ontologies is required, rather than performing retrieval tasks, as is the case for DL-Lite. Thus, differently than DL-Lite, EL+ offers for more expressive means of representing knowledge (see next section), but still no more than is required to allow for polynomial concept classification. Regarding, query answering it has been later shown that conjunctive query answering over EL+ ontologies is undecidable (Rosati, 2007), which also justifies the fact that EL+ is not tailored for query answering tasks.

In the following we present the fuzzy EL+ language. First we introduce the syntax and semantics, while later we focus in providing an algorithm that computes the concept hierarchy of f-EL+ ontologies. The interesting feature is that the algorithm manages to classify f-EL+ ontologies that allow for fuzzy subsumption. Finally, we present some refinements of the algorithm that can be the base for an optimized implementation, as in the crisp case.

The Fuzzy EL+ Language

In this section we introduce a fuzzy extension to the EL+ DL. Our semantics will be tailored for the operators of the Gödel logic we call our language $f_G - EL+$.

As is the case with DL-Lite, the high efficiency of EL+ is attributed to the restriction of the available set of constructors. More precisely, $f_G - EL+$ only allows for the top concept ($\top$), for full existential restrictions ($\exists R.C$) and conjunction ($C \sqcap D$). We note that unlike DL-Lite the use of these constructors in EL+ concept axioms is unrestricted. Furthermore, in comparison with DL-Lite, EL+ allows for *full* existential quantification, thus significantly more complex concepts can be defiled. We clarify here that since EL+ is more expressive w.r.t. what can be said about concepts, f-DL-Lite classification is also tractable (polynomial), but due to the very restricted constructors, not of great interest.

An f_G – EL+ *ontology* consists of a finite set of *concept* and *role axioms*. Differently, than f-DL-Lite we allow for *fuzzy general concept inclusions (f-GCIs)* of the form $\langle C \subseteq D, n \rangle$, where $n \in [0,1]$. Intuitively, these axioms say that the degree of subsethood of C to D is at-least equal to n. In contrast to what we have seen until now EL+ allows for what is called complex role inclusion axioms (RIAs) of the form $R_1 \circ ... \circ R_n \subseteq S$, where $\circ$ denotes the composition of two roles. Again, we note that EL+ allows for operators over roles, and more precisely for role composition which is a significant expressive constructor. With RIAs one is able to state that a role R is transitive, by $R \circ R \subseteq R$ or express right- and left-identity rules, which are very important in medical application, by axioms of the form $R \circ S \subseteq R$.

The semantics of f_G – EL+ are again provided by the aid of fuzzy interpretations. Again using fuzzy set theoretic operators we are able to interpret complex f_G – EL concepts. Table 6 summarizes the semantics. Most of them have already been presented in previous sections. Nevertheless the semantics of fuzzy inclusion axioms and complex role inclusion axioms are new. In Table 6 $\circ^t$ denotes the sup-t composition of two fuzzy roles (Klir & Yuan, 1995). Given an interpretation I we say that I is a *model* of an f_G – EL+ *ontology* if for each f-GCI and RIA, the conditions in this table are satisfied. For example, a fuzzy interpretation I satisfies $\langle C \subseteq D, n \rangle$ if $\inf_a \mathcal{J}(C^I(a), D^I(a)) \geq n$, where J is a fuzzy implication.

The basic inference problem of f_G – EL+ is fuzzy concept subsumption: A concept C is fuzzy subsumed by a concept D to a degree $n \in [0,1]$ w.r.t. an f_G – EL+ ontology O, written $\langle C \subseteq_O D, n \rangle$ if $\inf_a \mathcal{J}(C^I(a), D^I(a)) \geq n$ for every model I of O. Moreover we are also interested in the problem of *classifying* an f_G – EL+ ontology which contains fuzzy-GCIs, i.e. compute all fuzzy subsumptions between concepts of the ontology.

As we see, we interpret fuzzy GCIs with the aid of R-implications. This semantics is derived by translating $C \subseteq D$ into the First-Order formula $\forall x. C(x) \rightarrow D(x)$ and then interpreting $\rightarrow$ with an R-implication and $\forall$ with inf (Straccia, 2005). Although fuzzy subsumption for fuzzy DLs was first proposed by Straccia, several works in the fuzzy set literature regarding this issue already existed. The first idea was presented by Bandler and Kohout (1980). Similarly to Straccia, Bandler and Kohout used fuzzy implications to give semantics to fuzzy set inclusion. The first attempt to provide axioms that characterize the operators used to interpret fuzzy subsumption was presented by Sinha and Dougherty (1993). Many of these axioms are satisfied by R-implications, but only the Lukasiewicz implication satisfies all of them. A different set of axioms was proposed by Young (1996). Again R-implications are quite

Table 6. Semantics of f-EL+

Constructor	DL Syntax	Semantics
top concept	$\top$	$\top^I(a) = 1$
conjunction	$C \sqcap D$	$(C \sqcap D)^I(a) = t(C^I(a), D^I(a))$
existential restriction	$\exists R.C$	$\exists R.C^I(a) = \sup_b \{t(R^I(a,b), C^I(b))\}$
Fuzzy GCIs	$\langle C \subseteq D, n \rangle$	$\inf_a \mathcal{J}(C^I(a), D^I(a)) \geq n$
RIAs	$R_1 \circ ... \circ R_n \subseteq S$	$R_1^I \circ^t ... \circ^t R_n^I(a,b) \subseteq S^I(a,b)$

close to satisfying all proposed axioms. Thus, we see that each author provided different set of axioms according to the specific problem they wanted to tackle. Sinha and Dougherty (1993) wanted to define new mathematical morphology operators, while Young (1993) was studying fuzzy entropy. We conclude that R-implications generally provide a good intuition for semantics of fuzzy subsumption.

The use of fuzzy inclusion axioms in fuzzy EL+ was motivated by the field of ontology matching and ontology alignment. Ontology matching consists of the process of identifying semantic similarities between heterogeneous ontologies. More precisely, an ontology alignment algorithm is never capable of assessing the similarity of two entities with 100% confidence. What is more likely is to have degrees of confidence for each mapping. For example, in a realistic ontology alignment example and for two relatively simple ontologies, o_1 and o_2, about mobile phones an algorithm can produce the following (fuzzy) mappings:

map(o_1: MobileDevice, o_2: ElectronicDevice, 0.7)

map(o_1: MobilePhone, o_2: Phone, 0.6)

map(o_1: MobilePhone, o_2: CablePhone, 0.4)

map(o_1: MobilePhone, o_2: CellularPhone, 1.0)

Ferrara et al. (2008) have already proposed the use of fuzzy inclusion axioms of fuzzy DLs in order to provide formal semantics to such fuzzy mappings and interpret them. For example, the first mapping could be represented by the following fuzzy inclusion axiom . Ferrara et al. (2008) then use the semantics of such axioms together with standard fuzzy reasoning services in order to perform fuzzy validation, i.e. to refine or remove a mapping according to whether it causes inconsistencies of the fuzzy knowledge base. Although, they did not use fuzzy classification services, it is quite evident that if such services could be supported then new (inferred) mappings between the two ontologies could be identified. Furthermore, Holi & Hyvonen (2006) have also proposed the use of fuzzy inclusion axioms for representing fuzzy mappings between search views in Semantic Portals. Again no reasoning over fuzzy subsumption was performed. Consequently, from both applications we can note that the use of fuzzy inclusion axioms with f-EL+ (that allows for efficient classification) is of great interest.

Classifying Knowledge with Fuzzy EL+

In the current section we will provide a detailed presentation of the algorithm for classifying fuzzy subsumption in f-EL+ ontologies. As we will see in the following the algorithm for $f_G - EL+$ is quite similar to the algorithm for classical EL+ modulo the degrees of fuzzy-GCIs. This is to some extent expected since on the one hand fuzzy logics are generalization of classical logics which is different compared to uncertainty handling logics (probabilistic, possibilistic), thus at the extremes of 0 and 1 they provide the same results. On the other hand EL+ is already a sub-boolean logic (it is not propositionally closed under negation) so the logical differences with $f_G - EL+$ cannot be revealed. Nevertheless, discovering the degrees of membership in the inference rules (see Table 8) and generalizing the algorithm was extremely difficult and involved deep investigation of the properties of fuzzy operators.

Before applying the polynomial algorithm for classification a $f_G - EL+$ ontology needs to be normalized (Baader et al.). Given an ontology O, we write CN_O^U and CN_O to denote the set of concept names with and without the top concept ($\top$), respectively. Then, an $f_G - EL+$ ontology O is in *normal form* if

1.   all fuzzy GCIs in O have one of the following forms, where $A_i \in CN_O^U$ and $B \in CN_O$:

$\langle A_1 \sqcap ... \sqcap \subseteq B, n \rangle\, A_k$

$\langle A_1 \subseteq \exists R.A_2, n \rangle$

$\langle \exists R.A_1 \subseteq B, n \rangle$

2.   all role inclusions are of the form $R \subseteq S$ or $R_1 \circ R_2 \subseteq S$.

As shown in (Baader et al.) every EL+ ontology O can be turned into a normalized one O' by exhaustively applying proper normalization rules, which introduce new concept and role names in the ontology. The complete set of normalization rules for $f_G - EL$ is described in Table 7. where $\overline{C}, \overline{D} \notin CN_O^U, C_i, C, D$ are arbitrary concepts, $B \in CN_O^U$, P denotes a new role and A denotes a new concept name.

Lemma. An $f_G - EL$ ontology O is satisfiable iff the normalized one O' is satisfiable.

Theorem. Subsumption w.r.t. $f_G - EL$ ontologies can be reduced in linear time to subsumption w.r.t. normalized ontologies in $f_G - EL$.

In the following we assume that an input ontology O is in normal form.

Let O be an $f_G - EL$ ontology in normal form. Our subsumption algorithm for normalized $f_G - EL$ ontologies can be restricted to subsumption checking between concept names. More precisely, $\langle C \sqsubseteq_O D, n \rangle$ iff $\langle A \sqsubseteq_{O'} B, n \rangle$, where $O' = O \cup \{ \langle A \subseteq C, n \rangle, \langle D \subseteq B, n \rangle \}$ and A, B are new concept names.

Let RN_O be the set of all role names occurring in O. The algorithm computes:

•   A mapping S assigning to each concept name of CN_O a subset $S(A)$ of $CN_O^U \times [0,1]$, and
•   A mapping r assigning to each role name R of RN_O a ternary relation $r(R)$ which is a subset of $CN_O^U \times CN_O^U \times [0,1]$.

Table 7. Normalization rules for $f_G - EL$

NF1	$R_1 \circ ... \circ R_n \subseteq S$	→	$R_1 \circ ... \circ R_{n-1} \subseteq P,\, P \circ R_n \subseteq S$
NF2	$\langle C_1 \sqcap ... \sqcap \overline{C} \sqcap ... \sqcap C_k \subseteq D, n \rangle$	→	$\langle \overline{C} \subseteq A, n \rangle, \langle C_1 \sqcap ... \sqcap \overline{A} \sqcap ... \sqcap C_k \subseteq D, n \rangle$
NF3	$\langle \exists R.\overline{C} \subseteq D, n \rangle$	→	$\langle \overline{C} \subseteq A, n \rangle, \langle \exists R.A \subseteq D, n \rangle$
NF4	$\langle \overline{C} \subseteq \overline{D}, n \rangle$	→	$\langle \overline{C} \subseteq A, n \rangle, \langle A \subseteq \overline{D}, n \rangle$
NF5	$\langle B \subseteq \exists R.\overline{C}, n \rangle$	→	$\langle B \subseteq \exists R.A, n \rangle, \langle A \subseteq \overline{C}, n \rangle$
NF6	$\langle B \subseteq C \sqcap D, n \rangle$	→	$\langle B \subseteq C, n \rangle, \langle B \subseteq D, n \rangle$

Table 8. Completion rules for $f_G - EL+$

Rule	Description
R1	If $\langle A_1, n_1 \rangle \in S(X), \ldots, \langle A_l, n_l \rangle \in S(X), \langle A_1 \sqcap \ldots \sqcap A_l \sqsubseteq B, k \rangle \in O$ and $\langle B, m \rangle \notin S(X)$, where $m = \min(n_1, \ldots, n_l, k)$ then $S(X) := S(X) \cup \{\langle B, m \rangle\}$ where $m = \min(n_1, \ldots, n_l, k)$
R2	If $\langle A, n \rangle \in S(X), \langle A \sqsubseteq \exists R.B, k \rangle \in O$ and $\langle X, B, m \rangle \notin r(R)$, where $m = \min(n, k)$ then $r(R) := r(R) \cup \{\langle X, B, m \rangle\}$, where $m = \min(n, k)$
R3	If $\langle X, Y, n_1 \rangle \in r(R), \langle A, n_2 \rangle \in S(Y), \langle \exists R.A \sqsubseteq .B, n_3 \rangle \in O$ and $\langle B, m \rangle \notin S(X)$, where $m = \min(n_1, n_2, n_3)$ then $S(X) := S(X) \cup \{\langle B, m \rangle\}$, where $m = \min(n_1, n_2, n_3)$
R4	If $\langle X, Y, n \rangle \in r(R), R \sqsubseteq S \in O$, and $\langle X, Y, n \rangle \notin r(S)$ then $r(S) := r(S) \cup \{\langle X, Y, n \rangle\}$
R5	If $\langle X, Y, n_1 \rangle \in r(R), \langle Y, Z, n_2 \rangle \in r(S), R \circ S \sqsubseteq F \in O$ and $\langle X, Z, m \rangle \notin r(F)$, where $m = \min(n_1, n_2)$ then $r(F) := r(F) \cup \{\langle X, Z, m \rangle\}$ where $m = \min(n_1, n_2)$

As we can see, due to the presence of fuzzy subsumptions we have extended the mappings $S(A)$, $r(R)$ to range over subsets of $CN_O^U \times [0,1]$ and $CN_O^U \times CN_O^U \times [0,1]$, respectively. As with crisp EL+ intuitively, these mappings make implicit fuzzy subsumption relationships explicit in the sense that

- $\langle B, n \rangle \in S(A)$ implies $\langle A \sqsubseteq B, n \rangle$ and
- $\langle A, B, n \rangle \in r(R)$ implies $\langle A \sqsubseteq \exists R.B, n \rangle$.

The mappings are initialized as follows:

- $S(A) = \{\langle A, 1 \rangle, \langle \top, 1 \rangle\}$, for each $A \in CN_O$
- $r(R) = \varnothing$, for each $R \in RN_O$

Then, the sets $S(A)$ and $r(R)$ are extended by applying the completion rules shown in Table 8 until no more rules are applied.

Theorem. The algorithm runs in polynomial time and it is sound and complete, i.e. after it terminates on input O, we have for all $A, B \in CN_O^U$, $n \in (0,1]$, $\langle A \sqsubseteq_O B, n \rangle$ iff $\langle B, n' \rangle \in S(A)$, for some $n' \in (0,1]$, with $n' \geq n$.

A Refined and Optimised Algorithm

As it was pointed in (Baader et al.) although EL+ is a tractable DL, in practice the above algorithm might fail to provide truly tractable, scalable and efficient reasoning. This is due to the fact that the application of rules is performed using a naïve brute-force search. This effect is remedied by proposing a refined algorithm which is shown to provide truly scalable practical reasoning. The algorithm is realized by introducing a set of queues, one for each concept name, which intuitively guide the application of the expansion rules. In the following we sketch the necessary modifications to the EL+ refined algorithm in order to also provide optimisations for the $f_G - EL$ algorithm. Our entries of the queues are of the form:

$B_1, \ldots, B_m \rightarrow \langle B', n' \rangle$ and $\langle \exists R.B, n \rangle$

with $B_1,...,B_m$ and B' concept names, R role name, $m \geq 0$ and $n' \in (0,1]$. For $m = 0$ we simply write $\langle B', n' \rangle$. Intuitively,

- an entry $B_1,...,B_m \rightarrow \langle B', n' \rangle \in queue(A)$ means that $\langle B', k \rangle$, with $k = \min(n', n_1,...,n_m)$ has to be added in $S(A)$ if $S(A)$ already contains information for $B_1,...,B_m$, i.e. entries $\langle B_1, n_1 \rangle,...,\langle B_m, n_m \rangle$, and
- $\langle \exists R.B, n \rangle \in queue(A)$ means that $\langle A, B, n \rangle$ has to be added to $r(R)$.

Similarly to the optimised algorithm of EL+ we use the mapping $\hat{O}$ from concepts to sets of queue entries as follows:

For each concept name $A \in CN_O^U$, $\hat{A}$ is the minimal set of queue entries such that:

- if $\langle A_1 \sqcap ... \sqcap A_m \sqsubseteq B, n \rangle \in O$ and $A = A_i$, then

$$A_1,...,A_{i-1}, A_{i+1},...,A_m \rightarrow \langle B, n \rangle \in \hat{O}(A) \text{ and}$$

- if $\langle A \sqsubseteq \exists R.B, n \rangle \in O$, then $\langle \exists R.B, n \rangle \in \hat{O}(A)$.

Similarly, for each concept $\exists R.A$, $\hat{O}(\exists R.A)$ is the minimal set of queue entries such that, if $\exists R.A \sqsubseteq B \in O$, then $\langle B, n \rangle \in \hat{O}(\exists R.A)$.

Using the above changes the refined algorithm of EL+ can be changed accordingly in order to also take into account fuzziness in subsumption axioms and provide an algorithm for processing the queue entries.

Theorem. The refined algorithm runs in polynomial time and it is sound and complete, i.e. after it terminates on input O, we have for all $A, B \in CN_O^U$, $n \in (0,1]$ that $\langle A \sqsubseteq_O B, n \rangle$ iff $\langle B, n' \rangle \in S(A)$, for some degree $n' \in (0,1]$, with $n' \geq n$.

DISCUSSION AND FUTURE WORK

How to apply Description Logic based ontologies in the Web has been a pressing issue for the Semantic Web community (Mika, 2005). On the one hand (Semantic) Web applications would require ontologies to be able to handle hundreds of thousands of data in reasonable amount of time in order to deliver services to end users, while on the other hand they should be able to deal with fuzzy and imprecise data which emerge from automated procedures or are inseparable part of every-day, common, human reasoning. Our current Chapter tries to provide the state-of-the-art of works tackling such a problem. On the one hand we want to show that handling fuzziness in Semantic Web applications is feasible and we have presented a number of fuzzy extensions of popular ontology languages. Nevertheless, our main aim is to show that handling vagueness although it adds more expressivity over the crisp (classical) approaches can still be done very efficiently and in a way that can scale up to millions of data. Hence, for a certain class of fuzzy ontology languages fuzziness and scalability are not antagonistic concepts.

The contribution of the Chapter is divided in two major parts.

- On the first part we present a fuzzy extension of the DL-Lite language that has been proposed in the literature (Straccia, 2006). The DL-Lite language is particularly interesting since it can provide efficient query answering services and can scale over millions of data. The power of DL-Lite lies in the fact that its constructors have been carefully selected such that after careful rewriting queries over DL-Lite ontologies can be reformulated and issued over a relational database. Thus one can exploit the vast amount of research and optimizations that have been developed in this field for many years. After reviewing its syntax and semantics we take the fuzzy-DL-Lite proposal one step further and present a proposal for performing very expressive weighted/fuzzy conjunctive queries over fuzzy-DL-Lite ontologies (Pan et al, 2008). Many of these languages have been proposed many years ago in the field of fuzzy information retrieval and querying over fuzzy databases (Cross, 1994). Taking these approaches even further we have shown that these can be represented under a general framework and the semantic possibilities are merely endless adding more, like conjunctive threshold queries which have been proven very important (Mailis et al., 2007). Overall, we have shown that evaluating very expressive extended queries over fuzzy ontologies are not antagonistic concepts and can be done in a very efficient and scalable way for the fuzzy-DL-Lite language.

- On the second part of the Chapter we have focused on the second most important inference service of (fuzzy) ontology languages, that of concept (class) classification (i.e. computing the implied concept hierarchy). To this extend we focused on the EL+ language, which is known to be able to solve such a problem in a very efficient way (Baader et al). Consequently, we present the fuzzy EL+ language (Stoilos et al., 2008). Besides the syntax and semantics we also focus in providing a classification algorithm for fuzzy EL+ ontologies in order to realize such a problem in the fuzzy case. The interesting part in this approach is that fuzzy EL+ ontologies are extended to allow for fuzzy subsumption, that is important in several Semantic Web tasks like ontology matching (Ferrara et al., 2008) and semantic portals (Holi & Hyvonen, 2006). Furthermore, we have presented the refinements/optimizations that have been proposed for the classification of the fuzzy EL+ algorithm (Stoilos et al., 2008) and can be the base for an efficient implementation. Hence, again in this case we have shown that there exist fuzzy ontology languages which can support concept classification over fuzzy subsumption in a scalable manner.

In conclusion we have shown that scalability and reasoning over fuzzy ontologies are two concepts that can indeed live together. Both of the aforementioned fuzzy ontology languages provide ways to solve efficiently the two most important inference problems of ontology languages and Description Logics, namely, query answering and entailment and classification.

The main aspect of future work is to investigate how the aforementioned languages and algorithms can be extended in order to support in a scalable and efficient way more expressive ontology languages. Regarding fuzzy-DL-Lite, scalable querying services for more expressive fuzzy ontology languages, such as fuzzy-OWL (Stoilos et al., 2005a), can be performed along the lines of semantic approximation (Pan & Thomas, 2007), which is a technique to reduce query answering over OWL DL ontologies to query answering over DL-Lite. Regarding fuzzy EL+ an obvious way would be to extend the algorithm for supporting classification over fuzzy EL++, which is a fuzzy extension of the well known extension of EL+, EL++ (Baader et al., 2005). Although such a fuzzy extension exists in the literature (Mailis et al., 2008) it is well known that the reasoning algorithm of (fuzzy) EL++ does not usually scale in practical settings due to the lack of refinements (Baader et al.). Investigating such refinements is still an open problem even for the classical EL++ language.

REFERENCES

Baader, B., McGuiness, D. L., Nardi, D., & Patel-Schneider, P. (Eds.). (2002). *Description logic handbook: Theory, implementation and applications*. Cambridge, UK: Cambridge University Press.

Baader, F., Brandt, S., & Lutz, C. (2005). Pushing the EL envelope. In *Proceedings of the International Joint Conference on Artificial Intelligence (IJCAI 05)*.

Baader, F., Lutz, C., & Suntisrivaraporn, B. (in press). Is tractable reasoning in extensions of the description logic EL useful in practice? *Journal of Logic, Language and Information, Special Issue on Method for Modality (M4M)*.

Bandler, W., & Kohout, L. (1980). Fuzzy power sets and fuzzy implication operators. *Fuzzy Sets and Systems*, *4*, 13–30. doi:10.1016/0165-0114(80)90060-3

Bechhofer, S., van Harmelen, F., Hendler, J., Horrocks, I., McGuinness, D.L., Patel-Schneider, P. F., & Stein, L. A. (2004). OWL Web ontology language reference. *W3C Recommendation*.

Bobillo, F., Delgado, M., & Gomez-Romero, J. (2006). A crisp representation for fuzzy SHOIN with fuzzy nominals and general concept inclusions. In *Proc. of the 2nd International Workshop on Uncertainty Reasoning for the Semantic Web (URSW 06)*.

Bookstein, A. (1980). Fuzzy requests: An approach to weighted Boolean searches. *Journal of the Americal Society for Information Science*, *31*, 240–247. doi:10.1002/asi.4630310403

Bordogna, G., Bosc, P., & Pasi, G. (1996). Fuzzy inclusion in database and information retrieval query interpretation. In *Proceedings of the 1996 ACM symposium on Applied Computing* (pp. 547-551).

Buell, D. A., & Kraft, D. H. (1981). Threshold values and Boolean retrieval systems. *Journal of Information Processing and Management*, *17*, 127–136. doi:10.1016/S0306-4573(81)80004-0

Calvanese, D., De Giacomo, G., Lembo, D., Lenzerini, M., & Rosati, R. (2005). DL-Lite: Tractable description logics for ontologies. In *Proc. of the AAAI*.

Calvanese, D., De Giacomo, G., Lembo, D., Lenzerini, M., & Rosati, R. (2007). Tractable reasoning and efficient query answering in description logics: The DL-Lite family. *Journal of Automated Reasoning*, *39*(3), 385–429. doi:10.1007/s10817-007-9078-x

Calvanese, D., De Giacomo, G., Lenzerini, M., Nardi, D., & Rosati, R. (1998). Description logic framework for information integration. In *Proc. of the 6th Int. Conf. on the Principles of Knowledge Representation and Reasoning (KR'98)*.

Chen, S. J., & Chen, S. M. (2000). A new method for fuzzy information retrieval based on geometric-mean averaging operators. In *Proceedings of the Workshop on Artificial Intelligence*, 2000.

Chortaras, A., Stamou, G., & Stafylopatis, A. (2006). Adaptation of weighted fuzzy programs. In *Proc. of the International Conference on Artificial Neural Networks (ICANN 2006)* (pp. 45-54).

Cross, V. (1994). Fuzzy information retrieval. *Journal of Intelligent Information Systems, 3*, 29–56. doi:10.1007/BF01014019

Dameron, O., Gibaud, B., & Musen, M. (2004). Using semantic dependencies for consistency management of an ontology of brain-cortex anatomy. In *Proceedings of the First International Workshop on Formal Biomedical Knowledge Representation KRMED04* (pp. 30-38).

Ferrara, A., Lorusso, D., Stamou, G., Stoilos, G., Tzouvaras, V., & Venetis, T. (2008). Resolution of conflicts among ontology mappings: A fuzzy approach. In *Proceedings of the International Workshop on Ontology Matching (OM2008)*, Karlsruhe.

Guo, Y., Pan, Z., & Heflin, J. (2005). LUBM: A benchmark for OWL knowledge base systems. *Journal of Web Semantics, 3*(2), 158–182. doi:10.1016/j.websem.2005.06.005

Holi, M., & Hyvonen, E. (2006). Fuzzy view-based semantic search. In *Proceedings of the Asian Semantic Web Conference*.

Hölldobler, S., Nga, N. H., & Khang, T. D. (2005). The fuzzy description logic ALC_{FLH}. In *Proceedings of the International workshop on Description Logics*.

Horrocks, I., & Patel-Schneider, P. (2004). Reducing OWL entailment to description logic satisfiability. *Journal of Web Semantics*, 345–357. doi:10.1016/j.websem.2004.06.003

Kang, D., Xu, B., Lu, J., & Li, Y. (2006). Reasoning for fuzzy description logic with comparison expressions. In *Proceedings of the International Workshop on Description Logics (DL 06)*, Lake District, UK.

Klir, G. J., & Yuan, B. (1995). *Fuzzy sets and fuzzy logic: Theory and applications*. Upper Saddle River, NJ: Prentice-Hall.

Li, Y., Xu, B., Lu, J., & Kang, D. (2006). Discrete tableau algorithms for FSHI. In *Proceedings of the International Workshop on Description Logics (DL 2006)*, Lake District, UK.

Lu, J., Kang, D., Zhang, Y., Li, Y., & Zhou, B. (2008). A family of fuzzy description logics with comparison expressions. In *Proceedings of the Third International Conference, Rough Sets and Knowledge Technology (RSKT 08)*.

Lutz, C. (2008). Two upper bounds for conjunctive query answering in SHIQ. In *Proceedings of the 21st International Workshop on Description Logics (DL 2009)*.

Mailis, T., Stoilos, G., Simou, N., & Stamou, G. (2008). Tractable reasoning based on the fuzzy-EL++ algorithm. In *Proc. of the 4th International Workshop on Uncertainty Reasoning for the Semantic Web (URSW 08)*.

Mailis, T., Stoilos, G., & Stamou, G. (2007). Expressive reasoning with horn rules and fuzzy description logics. In *Proceedings of the first international conference on web reasoning and rule systems (RR-07)*.

Mika, P. (2005). Ontologies are us: A unified model of social networks and semantics. In *Proceedings of the 4th International Semantic Web Conference (ISWC 2005)*.

Neumann, B., & Möller, R. (2006). On scene interpretation with description logics. In H.I. Christensen & H.-H. Nagel (Eds.), *Cognitive vision systems: Sampling the spectrum of approaches* (pp. 247-278). Berlin, Germany: Springer.

Pan, J. Z., Stamou, G., Stoilos, G., & Thomas, E. (2008). Scalable querying services over fuzzy ontologies. In *Proceedings of the International World Wide Web Conference (WWW 2008)*, Beijing.

Pan, J. Z., Stoilos, G., Stamou, G., Tzouvaras, V., & Horrocks, I. (2006a). f-SWRL: A fuzzy extension of SWRL. *Journal on Data Semantics, 4090*, 28–46. doi:10.1007/11803034_2

Pan, J. Z., & Thomas, E. (2007) Approximating OWL-DL ontologies. In *Proc. of the 22nd National Conference on Artificial Intelligence (AAAI-07)*.

Pan, J. Z., Thomas, E., & Sleeman, D. (2006b). ONTOSEARCH2: Searching and querying Web ontologies. In *Proc. of WWW/Internet* (pp. 211-218).

Patel-Schneider, P. F., Hayes, P., & Horrocks, I. (2004). OWL Web ontology language semantics and abstract syntax. *W3C Recommendation*.

Prud'hommeaux, E., & Seaborne, A. (2006). *SPARQL query language for RDF* (W3C Working Draft). Retrieved from http://www.w3.org/TR/rdf-sparql-query/

Radecki, T. (1979). Fuzzy set theoretical approach to document retrieval. *Journal of Information Processing and Management, 15*, 235–245. doi:10.1016/0306-4573(79)90030-X

Rosati, R. (2007). On conjunctive query answering in EL. In *Proceedings of the 2007 International Workshop on Description Logic (DL 2007)*.

Salton, G., Fox, E. A., & Wu, H. (1983a). Extended Boolean information retrieval. *Journal of Communications of ACM, 26*, 1022–1036. doi:10.1145/182.358466

Salton, G., & McGill, M. J. (1983b). *Introduction to modern information retrieval*. New York: McGraw-Hill.

Sanchez, E. (1989). Importance in knowledge systems. *Information Systems, 14*(6), 455–464. doi:10.1016/0306-4379(89)90013-6

Simou, N., Athanasiadis, Th., Stoilos, G., & Kollias, S. (2008a). image indexing and retrieval using expressive fuzzy description logics. *Signal . Image and Video Processing, 2*, 321–335. doi:10.1007/s11760-008-0084-1

Simou, N., Stoilos, G., Tzouvaras, V., Stamou, G., & Kollias, S. (2008b). Storing and querying fuzzy knowledge in the Semantic Web. In *Proceedings of the 7th International Workshop on Uncertainty Reasoning For the Semantic Web*, Karlsruhe, Germany.

Sinha, D., & Dougherty, E. R. (1993). Fuzzification of set inclusion: Theory and applications. *Fuzzy Sets and Systems, 55*, 15–42. doi:10.1016/0165-0114(93)90299-W

Stoilos, G., Simou, N., Stamou, G., & Kollias, S. (2006). Uncertainty and the Semantic Web. *IEEE Intelligent Systems, 21*(5), 84–87. doi:10.1109/MIS.2006.105

Stoilos, G., Stamou, G., & Pan, J. Z. (2008). Classifying fuzzy subsumption in Fuzzy-EL+. In *Proceedings of the 21st International Workshop on Description Logics (DL 08)*, Dresden, Germany.

Stoilos, G., Stamou, G., Pan, J. Z., Tzouvaras, V., & Horrocks, I. (2007). Reasoning with very expressive fuzzy description logics. *Journal of Artificial Intelligence Research, 30*(5), 273–320.

Stoilos, G., Stamou, G., Tzouvaras, V., Pan, J. Z., & Horrocks, I. (2005a). Fuzzy OWL: Uncertainty and the Semantic Web. In *Proceedings of the International Workshop on OWL: Experiences and Directions*.

Stoilos, G., Stamou, G., Tzouvaras, V., Pan, J. Z., & Horrocks, I. (2005b). The fuzzy description logic f-SHIN. In *Proc. of the International Workshop on Uncertainty Reasoning for the Semantic Web* (pp. 67-76).

Stoilos, G., Straccia, U., Stamou, G., & Pan, J. Z. (2006). General concept inclusions in fuzzy description logics. In *Proceedings of the 17th European Conference on Artificial Intelligence (ECAI 06)*, Riva del Garda, Italy.

Straccia, U. (2001). Reasoning within fuzzy description logics. *Journal of Artificial Intelligence Research, 14*, 137–166.

Straccia, U. (2005). Towards a fuzzy description logic for the Semantic Web. In *Proceedings of the 2nd European Semantic Web Conference*.

Straccia, U. (2006). Answering vague queries in fuzzy DL-Lite. In *Proceedings of the 11th International Conference on Information Processing and Management of Uncertainty in Knowledge-Based Systems (IPMU-06)* (pp. 2238-2245).

Straccia, U. (2008), *fuzzyDL*: An expressive fuzzy description logic reasoner. In *Proceedings of the International Conference on Fuzzy Systems (Fuzz-IEEE 08)*.

Thomas, E., Pan, J. Z., & Sleeman, D. (2007). ONTOSEARCH2: Searching ontologies semantically. In *Proceedings of OWL Experience Workshop*.

Tresp, C., & Molitor, R. (1998). A description logic for vague knowledge. In *Proc of the 13th European Conf. on Artificial Intelligence (ECAI-98)*.

Vojtas, P. (2001). Fuzzy logic programming. *Fuzzy Sets and Systems, 124*, 361–370. doi:10.1016/S0165-0114(01)00106-3

Waller, W. G., & Kraft, D. H. (1979). A mathematical model of a weighted Boolean retrieval system. *Journal of Information Processing and Management, 15*, 247–260. doi:10.1016/0306-4573(79)90031-1

Wang, H., Ma, Z. M., Yan, L., & Cheng, J. (2008). A fuzzy description logic with fuzzy data type group. In *Proceedings of the International Fuzz-IEEE Conference*, Hong Kong.

Wang, H., Ma, Z. M., Yan, L., & Zhang, G. (2006). A fuzzy extension of ALC with fuzzy modifiers. In *Proceedings of the Knowledge-Based Intelligent Information and Engineering Systems*.

Yager, R. R. (1987). A note on weighted queries in information retrieval systems. *Journal of the Americal Society for Information Science, 38*, 23–24. doi:10.1002/(SICI)1097-4571(198701)38:1<23::AID-ASI4>3.0.CO;2-3

Young, V. R. (1996). Fuzzy subsethood. *Fuzzy Sets and Systems, 77*, 371–384. doi:10.1016/0165-0114(95)00045-3

Zadeh, L. A. (1965). Fuzzy sets. *Information and Control, 8*, 338–353. doi:10.1016/S0019-9958(65)90241-X

ENDNOTES

1   http://owl.man.ac.uk/factplusplus/
2   http://pellet.owldl.com/
3   http://www.w3.org/TR/owl2-profiles/
4   http://www.w3.org/2007/OWL/wiki/OWL_Working_Group
5   http://www.image.ece.ntua.gr/~nsimou
6   http://gaia.isti.cnr.it/~straccia
7   http://www.ontosearch.org/
8   http://www.csd.abdn.ac.uk/~sttaylor/f-LUBM.zip
9   The "semantics" column will be discussed later.
10   http://www.racer-systems.com/
11   The term ontology is just another name for the term knowledge base. In the following we will use both.
12   DL-Lite actually consists of a family of languages, like DL-Lite$_R$, DL-Lite$_F$ and DL-Lite$_A$ (Calvanes et al., 2007). Here we will present DL-Lite$_R$ and will refer to it as DL-Lite.
13   http://www.w3.org/2001/sw/DataAccess/
14   As mentioned above, keywords are represented by representative individuals.
15   http://www.seomoz.org/article/search-ranking-factors
16   http://www.openrdf.org/
17   http://www.ihtsdo.org/snomed-ct/
18   http://www.opengalen.org/

Chapter 6

A Random Set and Prototype Theory Model of Linguistic Query Evaluation

Jonathan Lawry
University of Bristol, UK

Yongchuan Tang
Zhejiang University, PR China

ABSTRACT

This chapter proposes a new interpretation of quantified linguistic queries based on a combination of random set theory and prototype theory and which is consistent with the label semantics framework. In this approach concepts are defined by random set neighbourhoods of a set of prototypes and quantifiers are similarly defined by random set constraints on ratios or absolute values. The authors then propose a computationally feasible method for evaluating quantified statement describing the elements of a database.

INTRODUCTION

The term *computing with words* was introduced by Zadeh (Zadeh 1996), (Zadeh 2002) to refer to computation involving natural language expression and queries. Such an approach allows for a high-level and intuitive representation of information which is vital for the development of transparent human-understandable decision making software tools. Zadeh proposed a methodology for computing with words incorporating fuzzy set theory and fuzzy quantifiers. *Label semantics* (Lawry 2004), (Lawry 2006) is an alternative framework for linguistic modeling based on random set theory and where emphasis is given to decisions concerning the appropriateness of labels to describe a particular instance or object. Recent work has demonstrated a clear and natural link between label semantics and the prototype theory of concepts. In this paper we will propose a new methodology for evaluating queries about a database which involve both linguistic expressions and generalized (linguistic) quantifiers. This approach will be based on the combination of prototype theory and random set theory underlying the interpretation of

DOI: 10.4018/978-1-60566-858-1.ch006

label semantics proposed in (Lawry & Tang 2008), (Lawry & Tang 2009). Furthermore, we will show that, given certain assumptions, the evaluation of appropriateness measures for quantified statements is computationally tractable. This suggests that the proposed approach has practical potential as a means of linguistic query evaluation in information retrieval.

An outline of the paper is as follows: An introduction to label semantics is given, with a brief discussion of the underlying philosophy together with basic definitions including appropriateness measures and mass functions. In the next section we describe the prototype theory of label semantics whereby a label L is deemed appropriate to describe an instance x, provided x is sufficiently close to the prototypes of L. In this interpretation linguistic descriptions are represented by random set neighborhoods of a set of prototypes. Following this we then propose a random set, prototype theory interpretation of quantified linguistic expressions and define measures of the appropriateness of such expressions to describe a given set of data elements. We show that such measures can be evaluated using a simple computational procedure. Finally, we present conclusions and indicate possible directions for future research.

LABEL SEMANTICS

In contrast to fuzzy set theory, *label semantics* encodes the meaning of linguistic labels according to how they are used by a population of communicating agents to convey information. From this perspective, the focus is on the decision making process an intelligent agent must go through in order to identify which labels or expressions can actually be used to describe an object or value. In other words, in order to make an assertion describing an object in terms of some set of linguistic labels, an agent must first identify which of these labels are appropriate or assertible in this context. Given the way that individuals learn language through an ongoing process of interaction with the other communicating agents and with the environment, then we can expect there to be considerable uncertainty associated with any decisions of this kind. Furthermore, there is a subtle assumption central to the label semantic model, that such decisions regarding appropriateness or assertibility are meaningful. For instance, the fuzzy logic view is that vague descriptions like 'John is *tall*' are generally only partially true and hence it is not meaningful to consider which of a set of given labels can truthfully be used to described John's height. However, we contest that the efficacy of natural language as a means of conveying information between members of a population lies in shared conventions governing the appropriate use of words which are, at least loosely, adhere to by individuals within the population.

It cannot be denied that in their use of linguistic labels human's posses a mechanism for deciding whether or not to make assertions (e.g. 'John is *tall*') or to agree to a classification (e.g. 'Yes, that is *a tree*'). Further, although the concepts concerned are vague this underlying decision process is fundamentally crisp (bivalent). For instance, you are either willing to assert that '*x* is *a tree*' given your current knowledge, or you are not. In other words, either tree is an appropriate label to describe *x* or it is not. As humans we are continually faced with making such crisp decisions regarding vague concepts as part of our every day use of language. Of course, we may be uncertain about labels and even express these doubts (e.g. 'I'm not sure whether you would call that a tree or a bush, or both') but the underlying decision is crisp.

Given this decision problem, we suggest that it is useful for agents to adopt what might be called an *epistemic stance* as follows:

Each individual agent in the population assumes the existence of a set of labeling conventions, valid across the whole population, governing what linguistic labels and expression can be appropriately used to describe particular instances.

Of course, such linguistic conventions do not need to be imposed by some outside authority, but instead would emerge as a result of interactions between agents each adopting the epistemic stance. Hence, label semantics does not attempt to link label symbols to fuzzy set concept definitions but rather to quantify an agent's subjective belief that a label L is appropriate to describe an object x and hence whether or not it is reasonable to assert that 'x is L'. Further discussion of the epistemic stance and the philosophical underpinnings of label semantics can be found in (Lawry 2008).

Label semantics proposes two fundamental and inter-related measures of the appropriateness of labels as descriptions of an object or value. Given a finite set of labels LA, a set of compound expressions LE can be generated through recursive application of logical connectives. The labels $L_i \in LA$ are intended to represent words such as adjectives and nouns which describe the underlying universe Ω. In other words, L_i corresponds to a description label for which the expression 'x is L_i' is meaningful for any element $x \in \Omega$. The measure of appropriateness of an expression $\theta \in LE$ as a description of the element x is denoted by $\mu_\theta(x)$ and quantifies the agent's subjective belief that θ can be used to describe x based on his/her partial knowledge of the current labeling conventions of the population. From an alternative perspective, when faced with an example to describe, an agent may consider each label in LA and attempt to identify the subset of labels which are appropriate to use. Let this set be denoted by D_x. In the face of their uncertainty regarding labeling conventions the agent will also be uncertain as to the composition of D_x, and in label semantics this is quantified by a mass function $m_x : 2^{LA} \to [0,1]$ on subsets of labels. The relationship between these two measures is described below.

Definition 1. *Label Expressions.*

Given a finite set of labels LA the corresponding set of label expressions LE is defined recursively as follows:

- If $L \in LA$ then $L \in LE$
- If $\theta, \phi \in LE$ then $\neg\theta, \theta \wedge \phi, \theta \vee \phi \in LE$

The mass function m_x on sets of labels then quantifies the agent's belief that any particular subset of labels contains all and only the labels with which it is appropriate to describe x.

Definition 2. *Mass Function on Labels.*

$\forall x \in \Omega$ a mass function on labels is a function $m_x : 2^{LA} \to [0,1]$ such that $\sum_{F \subseteq LA} m_x(F) = 1$ and where for $F \subseteq LA$, $m_x(F)$ is the belief that $D_x = F$.

The appropriateness measure, $\mu_\theta(x)$, and the mass function m_x are then related to each other on the basis that asserting 'x is θ' provides direct constraints on D_x. For example, asserting 'x is $L_1 \wedge L_2$', for labels $L_1, L_2 \in LA$ is taken as conveying t:he information that both L_1 and L_2 are appropriate to describe x, so that $\{L_1, L_2\} \subseteq D_x$. Similarly, '$x$ is $\neg L$' implies that L is not appropriate to describe x, so that

$L \notin D_x$. In general, we can recursively define a mapping $\lambda : LE \to 2^{2^{LA}}$ from expression to sets of subsets of labels, such that the assertion 'x is θ' directly implies the constraint $D_x \in \lambda(\theta)$ where $\lambda(\theta)$ is dependent on the logical structure of θ.

Definition 3. λ-*mapping.*

$\lambda : LE \to 2^{2^{LA}}$ is defined recursively as follows: $\forall \theta, \phi \in LE$

- $\forall L_i \in LA \ \lambda\left(L_i\right) = \left\{ F \subseteq LA : L_i \in F \right\}$
- $\lambda\left(\theta \wedge \phi\right) = \lambda\left(\theta\right) \cap \lambda\left(\phi\right)$
- $\lambda\left(\theta \vee \phi\right) = \lambda\left(\theta\right) \cup \lambda\left(\phi\right)$
- $\lambda\left(\neg\theta\right) = \lambda\left(\theta\right)^c$

Based on the λ-mapping we then define the appropriateness measure $\mu_\theta(x)$ as the sum of m_x over those sets of labels in $\lambda(\theta)$.

Definition 4. *Appropriateness Measure.*

The appropriateness measure defined by the mass function m_x is a function $\mu : LA \times \Omega \to [0,1]$ satisfying:

$$\forall \theta \in LE, \forall x \in \Omega \ \mu_\theta\left(x\right) = \sum_{F \in \lambda(\theta)} m_x\left(F\right)$$

and where $\mu_\theta(x)$ is used as shorthand for $\mu(\theta, x)$.

Note that in label semantics there is no requirement for the mass associated with the empty set to be zero. Instead, $m_x(\varnothing)$ quantifies the agent's belief that none of the labels are appropriate to describe x. We might observe that this phenomenon occurs frequently in natural language, especially when labeling perceptions generated along some continuum. For example, we occasionally encounter colours for which none of our available colour descriptors seem appropriate. Hence, $m_x(\varnothing)$ is an indicator of the describability of x in terms of the labels in LA.

A PROTOTYPE THEORY INTERPRETATION OF LABEL SEMANTICS

Prototype theory was proposed by Rosch (Rosch 1973) as a means of defining concepts in terms of similarity to prototypical cases. A prototype theory interpretation of label semantics has been proposed (Lawry & Tang 2008), (Lawry & Tang 2009) in which the basic labels LA correspond to natural categories each with an associated set of prototypes. A label L is then deemed to be an appropriate description of an element $x \in \Omega$ provided x is *sufficiently similar* to the prototypes for L. The requirement of being 'sufficiently similar' is clearly imprecise and is modeled here by introducing an uncertain threshold on distance from prototypes. In keeping with the epistemic stance this uncertainty is assumed to be

Figure 1. with prototypes $P_1, ..., P_7$ D_x^ε as ε varies is defined as follows: For ε_1, ε_2 and ε_3 shown in the diagram we have that $D_x^{\varepsilon_1} = \varnothing$, $D_x^{\varepsilon_2} = \{L_1, L_2\}$ and $D_x^{\varepsilon_3} = \{L_1, L_2, L_3, L_4\}$

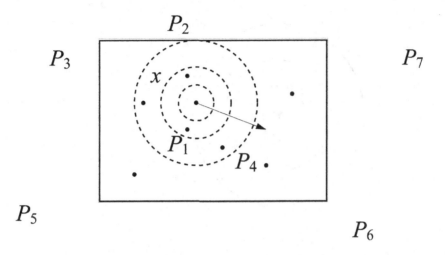

probabilistic in nature. In other words, an agent believes that there is some optimal threshold of this kind according to which he or she is best able to abide by the conventions of language when judging the appropriateness of labels. However, the agent is uncertain as to exactly what this threshold should be and instead defines a probability distribution on potential threshold values.

A distance function d is defined on Ω such that $d : \Omega^2 \rightarrow [0, \infty)$ and satisfies $d(x,x) = 0$ and $d(x,y) = d(y,x)$ for all elements $x, y \in \Omega$. This function is then extended to sets of elements such that for $S, T \subseteq \Omega$, $d(S, T) = \inf\{d(x,y) : x \in S, y \in T\}$. For each label $L_i \in LA$ let there be a set $P_i \subseteq \Omega$ corresponding to prototypical elements for which L_i is certainly an appropriate description. Within this framework L_i is deemed to be appropriate to describe $x \in \Omega$ provided x is sufficiently close or similar to a prototypical element in P_i. This is formalized by the requirement that x is within a maximal distance threshold ε of P_i i.e. L_i is appropriate to describe x if $d(x, P_i) \leq \varepsilon$ where $\varepsilon \geq 0$. From this perspective an agent's uncertainty regarding the appropriateness of a label to describe a value x is characterized by his or her uncertainty regarding the distance threshold ε. Here we assume that ε is a random variable and that the uncertainty is represented by a probability density function δ for ε defined on $[0,\infty)$. Within this interpretation a natural definition of the complete description of an element D_x and the associated mass function m_x can be given as follows:

Definition 5. *Prototype Interpretations of D_x and m_x.*

For $\varepsilon \in [0, \infty)$, $x \in \Omega$ let $D_x^\varepsilon = \{L_i \in LA : d(x, P_i) \leq \varepsilon\}$ and $m_x(F) = \delta(\{\varepsilon : D_x^\varepsilon = F\})$ (see figure 1)

Appropriateness measures can then be evaluated according to definition 4. Alternatively we can define a random set neighborhood for each expression $\theta \in LE$ corresponding to those element of Ω which can be appropriately described as θ, and then define $\mu_\theta(x)$ as the single point coverage function of this random set as follows:

Figure 2. Random set neighborhood $N_{L_i}^{\varepsilon}$ *as ε varies:* $N_{L_i}^{\varepsilon_1} \subseteq N_{L_i}^{\varepsilon_2} \subseteq N_{L_i}^{\varepsilon_3}$

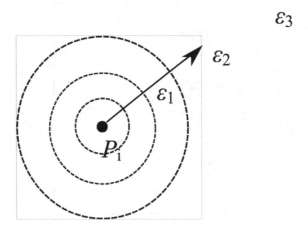

Definition 6. *Random Set Neighborhood of an Expression.*

For $\theta \in LE$ and $\varepsilon \in [0,\infty)$ $N_{\theta}^{\varepsilon} \subseteq \Omega$ is defined recursively as follows: $\forall \theta, \phi \in LE$, $\forall \varepsilon \in [0,\infty)$

- $\forall L_i \in LA$, $N_{L_i}^{\varepsilon} = \left\{ x \in \Omega : d\left(x, P_i\right) \leq \varepsilon \right\}$ (figure 2)
- $N_{\theta \wedge \phi}^{\varepsilon} = N_{\theta}^{\varepsilon} \cap N_{\phi}^{\varepsilon}$
- $N_{\theta \vee \phi}^{\varepsilon} = N_{\theta}^{\varepsilon} \cup N_{\phi}^{\varepsilon}$
- $N_{\neg \theta}^{\varepsilon} = \left(N_{\theta}^{c}\right)^{c}$

Theorem 1. *Random Neighborhood Representation Theorem* (Lawry & Tang 2009).

$$\forall \theta \in LE, \forall x \in \Omega, \mu_{\theta}\left(x\right) = \delta\left(\left\{\varepsilon : x \in N_{\theta}^{\varepsilon}\right\}\right)^{1}$$

Clearly D_x^{ε} and N_{θ}^{ε} are both random sets (i.e. set valued variables), the former taking sets of labels as values and the latter taking subsets of N_{θ}^{ε} as values. Theorem 1 shows that appropriateness measures can be interpreted as single point coverage functions of the random set N_{θ}^{ε}. This links label semantics with the random set interpretation of fuzzy sets proposed by Goodman and Nguyen (Goodman 1982), (Goodman & Nguyen 1985) and (Nguyen 1984) in which membership functions are interpreted as single point coverage functions.

QUANTIFIED STATEMENTS AND QUERY EVALUATION

The use of quantifiers significantly enhances the expressive power of natural language allowing for the representation of statements identifying general facts and rules. Linguistic statements can include a wide variety of quantifiers, in fact many more that standard universal and existential quantifiers of classical logic. Furthermore, general quantifiers can apply to imprecise expressions and can also be themselves imprecisely defined. For example, statements such as *most men are tall*, and *about 30% blonde men are tall*, involve imprecise quantifiers *most* and *about 30%* as well as imprecise labels *tall* and *blonde*. The idea of introducing general quantifiers into formal languages as a means of enhancing their knowledge representation capabilities dates back to Barwise and Cooper (Barwise & Cooper 1981). Following Zadeh's original proposal (Zadeh 1983), fuzzy logic has been widely applied to model vague quantifiers such as *most, few many* etc. See (Liu & Kerre 1998) for an overview of different fuzzy logic based interpretations of quantifiers. Indeed, information processing involving fuzzy quantified expressions is central to Zadeh's original formulation of computing with words (Zadeh 1996). However, the methods outlined in (Liu & Kerre 1998) do not tend to be based on a clear operational interpretation of fuzzy sets, but rather take membership values as primitives. This makes it difficult to assess the validity of definitions from a semantic perspective. Dubois and Prade (Dubois & Prade 1997) identify three potential semantics for fuzzy sets as being likelihood, similarity and random sets. In the following we propose a concrete model of quantified linguistic queries motivated by and based on a combination of the similarity and the random set view. This provides a clear interpretation of such queries from the perspective of the epistemic stance as discussed in a previous section.

Information retrieval and database querying are significant application areas for linguistic quantifiers (see for example (Bosc, Lietard & Pivert 1995) and (Losada et. al. 2004)). A formal framework for representing quantified linguistic statements can allow us to define measures of the applicability of such statements to a particular database. This can in turn allow users the flexibility to formulate and evaluate intuitive natural language queries. In recent work Diaz-Hermida etal (Diaz-Hermida et. al. 2005) have proposed a probabilistic approach to fuzzy quantifiers. In this section we propose a new model of linguistic quantified expressions based on the prototype theory interpretation of label semantics described in previously. In particular, we introduce measures of the appropriateness of quantified linguistic statement for describing a data set where both quantifiers and basic labels are defined in terms of random set neighborhoods.

Suppose we are given a database $DB \subseteq \Omega$ corresponding to a finite sample of elements from Ω. For $S \subseteq \Omega$ let $|S|_{DB} = |S \cap DB|$ denote the number of elements from DB contained in S. As in earlier sections we assume that the elements of Ω are described in terms of a set of labels LA and where for each label $L_i \in \Omega$ there are a set of prototypical cases P_i. We now consider the application of classical universal and existential quantifiers to expressions in LE. For $\theta \in LE$ consider the statement 'All elements of DB are θ'. Given the random neighborhood representation of the meaning of θ, according to which θ identifies the set $N_\theta^\varepsilon \subseteq \Omega$ (definition 6), then a natural interpretation of this quantified statement would be that every element in DB is contained in N_θ^ε i.e. $DB \subseteq N_\theta^\varepsilon$. Hence, the appropriateness of a universally quantified statement of this kind would depend on the probability of the similarity threshold ε being such that $DB \subseteq N_\theta^\varepsilon$. Similarly, we propose to interpret existentially quantified statements of the form 'Some element of DB are θ' as meaning that $DB \cap N_\theta^\varepsilon \neq \varnothing$.

Definition 7. *Classical Quantifiers.*

- For $\theta \in LE$ let $\left(\forall\right)_{DB} \theta$ denote the statement 'All elements of DB are θ'. The appropriateness of this statement to describe DB is given by: $\mu_{(\forall)\theta}\left(DB\right) = \delta\left(\left\{\varepsilon : DB \subseteq N_\theta^\varepsilon\right\}\right)$

- For $\theta \in LE$ let $(\exists)_{DB} \theta$ denote the statement 'Some elements of DB are θ'. The appropriateness of this statement to describe DB is given by: $\mu_{(\exists)\theta}(DB) = \delta\left(\left\{\varepsilon : DB \cap N_\theta^\varepsilon \neq \varnothing\right\}\right)$

We now introduce quantifiers describing the proportion of a database which can be described by a given expression θ e.g. at least 50% of the men in DB are *tall*. In fact, this paper focuses entirely on proportional quantifiers and their generalizations and does not consider absolute quantifiers e.g. less than 10 men in DB are *tall*. Random set definitions of absolute quantifiers can be given but these lie beyond the scope of the current study.

Definition 8. *Proportional Quantifiers.*

- For $\alpha \in [0,1]$, $\theta \in LE$ let $(\alpha)_{DB}\theta$ denote the statement 'The proportion DB which are θ is (exactly) α'. The appropriateness of this expression to describe DB is given by:

$$\mu_{(\alpha)\theta}(DB) = \delta\left(\left\{\varepsilon : \frac{\left|N_\theta^\varepsilon\right|_{DB}}{|DB|} = \alpha\right\}\right)$$

- For $\alpha \in [0,1]$, $\theta \in LE$ let $(\geq \alpha)_{DB}\theta$ denote the statement 'The proportion DB which are θ is at least α'. The appropriateness of this expression to describe DB is given by:

$$\mu_{(\geq \alpha)\theta}(DB) = \delta\left(\left\{\varepsilon : \frac{\left|N_\theta^\varepsilon\right|_{DB}}{|DB|} \geq \alpha\right\}\right)$$

- For $I \subseteq [0,1]$, $\theta \in LE$ let $(I)_{DB}\theta$ denote the statement 'The proportion DB which are θ is in I'. The appropriateness of this expression to describe DB is given by:

$$\mu_{(I)\theta}(DB) = \delta\left(\left\{\varepsilon : \frac{\left|N_\theta^\varepsilon\right|_{DB}}{|DB|} \in I\right\}\right)$$

Relative quantifiers describe the proportion of the database which given it is describable using one expression is also describable by a second expression e.g. At least 80% of *Swedes* in DB are *tall*.

Definition 9. *Relative Quantifiers.*

- For $\theta, \phi \in LE$, let $(\forall)_{DB}(\phi|\theta)$ denote the statement 'All elements in DB describable as θ, are also describable as ϕ' The appropriateness of this expression to describe DB is given by:
  $\mu_{(\forall)(\phi|\theta)}(DB) = \delta\left(\left\{\varepsilon : N_{\theta \wedge \phi}^\varepsilon = N_\theta^\varepsilon\right\}\right)$

- For $\theta, \phi \in LE$, let $\left(\exists\right)_{DB}\left(\phi|\theta\right)$ denote the statement 'Some elements in DB describable as θ, are also describable as ϕ' The appropriateness of this expression to describe DB is given by:

$$\mu_{(\exists)(\phi|\theta)}\left(DB\right) = \delta\left(\left\{\varepsilon : N^{\varepsilon}_{\theta\wedge\phi} \neq \varnothing\right\}\right)$$

- For $\alpha \in [0,1]$, $\theta, \phi \in LE$, let $\left(\alpha\right)_{DB}\left(\phi|\theta\right)$ denote the statement 'The proportion of elements in DB describable as θ, which are also describable as ϕ is exactly α'. The appropriateness of this expression to describe DB is given by:

$$\mu_{(\alpha)(\phi|\theta)}\left(DB\right) = \delta\left(\left\{\varepsilon : \left[\frac{\left|N^{\varepsilon}_{\theta\wedge\phi}\right|_{DB}}{\left|N^{\varepsilon}_{\theta}\right|_{DB}} = \alpha\right]\right\}\right)$$

- For $\alpha \in [0,1]$, $\theta, \phi \in LE$, let $\left(\geq\alpha\right)_{DB}\left(\phi|\theta\right)$ denote the statement 'The proportion of elements in DB describable as θ, which are also describable as ϕ is at least α'. The appropriateness of this expression to describe DB is given by:

$$\mu_{(\geq\alpha)(\phi|\theta)}\left(DB\right) = \delta\left(\left\{\varepsilon : \left[\frac{\left|N^{\varepsilon}_{\theta\wedge\phi}\right|_{DB}}{\left|N^{\varepsilon}_{\theta}\right|_{DB}} \geq \alpha\right]\right\}\right)$$

- For $I \subseteq [0,1]$, $\theta, \phi \in LE$, let $\left(I\right)_{DB}\left(\phi|\theta\right)$ denote the statement 'The proportion of elements in DB describable as θ, which are also describable as ϕ is in I'. The appropriateness of this expression to describe DB is given by:

$$\mu_{(I)(\phi|\theta)}\left(DB\right) = \delta\left(\left\{\varepsilon : \left[\frac{\left|N^{\varepsilon}_{\theta\wedge\phi}\right|_{DB}}{\left|N^{\varepsilon}_{\theta}\right|_{DB}} \in I\right]\right\}\right)$$

The following theorem shows that, using the combined random set and prototype theory approach, certain natural properties of quantifiers are preserved from classical logic.

Theorem 2.

1. If $\models\theta$ (i.e. θ is a tautology in Boolean logic) then $\mu_{(\forall)\theta}\left(DB\right) = 1$
2. If $\models\neg\theta$ (i.e. θ is a contradiction in Boolean logic) $\mu_{(\exists)\theta}\left(DB\right) = 0$
3. For all $\theta \in LE$ $\mu_{(\forall)(\theta|\theta)}\left(DB\right) = 1$
4. For all $\theta \in LE$ $\mu_{(\exists)(\theta|\neg\theta)}\left(DB\right) = 0$
5. If $\theta \models \phi$ then $\forall\alpha \in [0,1]$ $\mu_{(\geq\alpha)(\theta)}\left(DB\right) \leq \mu_{(\geq\alpha)(\phi)}\left(DB\right)$

Proof.

From (Lawry & Tang 2008) and (Lawry & Tang 2009) we have that:

1. If $\models \theta$ then $\forall \varepsilon \geq 0$ $N_\theta^\varepsilon = \Omega$ and hence $DB \subseteq N_\theta^\varepsilon$

2. If If $\models \neg\theta$ then $\forall \varepsilon \geq 0$ $N_\theta^\varepsilon = \varnothing$ and hence $N_\theta^\varepsilon \cap DB = \varnothing$

3. $\forall \theta \in LE, \forall \varepsilon \geq 0$ $N_{\theta \wedge \theta}^\varepsilon = N_\theta^\varepsilon$

4. $\forall \theta \in LE, \forall \varepsilon \geq 0$ $N_{\theta \wedge \neg\theta}^\varepsilon = \varnothing$

In the following definition we introduce linguistic quantifiers in the form of labels describing proportion of the database e.g. *about 50%* of men in *DB* are *tall* or *Most Swedes* in *DB* are *tall*.

Definition 10. *Linguistic Quantifiers.*

Let $LR = \{R_1,\ldots,R_m\}$ be a set of labels for proportions from the universe $[0,1]$, where label R_i has prototypes PR_i. Let d': $[0,1]^2 \to [0,1]$ be a distance function defined on $[0,1]$ and let ε' be the threshold random variable for d' with density δ'.

*   Let $\left(R_i\right)_{DB} \theta$ denote the statement 'R_i of *DB* are θ' or more precisely 'the proportion of *DB* which is θ can be described as R_i'. The appropriateness of this expression to describe *DB* is given by

$$\mu_{(R_i)\theta}\left(DB\right) = \delta \times \delta'\left(\left\{(\varepsilon,\varepsilon') : \frac{\left|N_\theta^\varepsilon\right|_{DB}}{|DB|} \in N_{R_i}^{\varepsilon'}\right\}\right) = \int_0^1 \delta'\left(\varepsilon'\right)\delta\left(\left\{\varepsilon : \frac{\left|N_\theta^\varepsilon\right|_{DB}}{|DB|} \in N_{R_i}^{\varepsilon'}\right\}\right)d\varepsilon'$$

*   Let $\left(R_i\right)_{DB}\left(\phi|\theta\right)$ denote the statement 'R_i of *DB* which are θ are also ϕ'. The appropriateness of this expression to describe *DB* is given by

$$\mu_{(R_i)(\phi|\theta)}\left(DB\right) = \int_0^1 \delta'\left(\varepsilon'\right)\delta\left(\left\{\varepsilon : \frac{\left|N_{\theta \wedge \phi}^\varepsilon\right|_{DB}}{\left|N_\theta^\varepsilon\right|_{DB}} \in N_{R_i}^{\varepsilon'}\right\}\right)d\varepsilon'$$

Note that definition 10 makes an assumption of independence between the threshold variables ε and ε'. This would see justifiable here, since we would expect labeling decisions concerning individual elements of *DB* and overall proportions to be taken independently.

When evaluating statements involving proportional quantifiers it is necessary only to consider the relevant proportion values within the range of the quantifier, defined as follows:

Definition 11. *Relevant Proportions.*

- $$PP_{\theta} = \left\{ \frac{\left| N_{\theta}^{\varepsilon} \right|}{\left| DB \right|} : \varepsilon \geq 0 \right\}$$

- $$PP_{(\phi|\theta)} = \left\{ \frac{\left| N_{\theta \wedge \phi}^{\varepsilon} \right|}{\left| N_{\theta}^{\varepsilon} \right|} : \varepsilon \geq 0 \right\}$$

Theorem 3.

For $I \subseteq \Omega$ and $\theta, \phi \in LE$

- $$\mu_{(I)\theta}(DB) = \sum_{\beta \in PP_{\theta} \cap I} \mu_{(\beta)\theta}(DB)$$

- $$\mu_{(I)(\phi|\theta)}(DB) = \sum_{\beta \in PP_{(\phi|\theta)} \cap I} \mu_{(\beta)(\phi|\theta)}(DB)$$

Proof

- $$\mu_{(I)\theta}(DB) = \delta\left(\left\{ \varepsilon : \frac{\left| N_{\theta}^{\varepsilon} \right|_{DB}}{\left| DB \right|} \in I \right\} \right) = \sum_{\beta \in PP_{\theta} \cap I} \delta\left(\left\{ \varepsilon : \frac{\left| N_{\theta}^{\varepsilon} \right|_{DB}}{\left| DB \right|} = \beta \right\} \right) = \sum_{\beta \in PP_{\theta} \cap I} \mu_{(\beta)\theta}(DB)$$

- Similarly replacing PP_{θ} with $PP_{(\phi|\theta)}$ $\square$

Theorem 4.

For $R_i \in LR$ and $\theta \in LE$, let $PP_{\theta} = \left\{ \beta_1, \cdots, \beta_t \right\}$ ordered such that $d'\left(\beta_j, PR_i \right) \leq d'\left(\beta_{j+1}, PR_i \right)$ then

$$\mu_{(R_i)\theta}(DB) = a_1 \int_{y_1}^{y_2} \delta'(\varepsilon') d\varepsilon' + \ldots + a_{t-1} \int_{y_{t-1}}^{y_t} \delta'(\varepsilon') d\varepsilon' + a_t \int_{y_t}^{1} \delta'(\varepsilon') d\varepsilon'$$

where $a_j = \sum_{i=1}^{j} \mu_{(\beta_i)\theta}(DB)$ and $y_j = d'\left(\beta_j, PR_i \right)$

Proof.

Since R_i is a basic label we have that:

$$N_{R_i}^{\varepsilon'} \cap PP_\theta = \begin{cases} \varnothing : \varepsilon' < d'(\beta_1, PR_i) \\ \{\beta_1\} : \varepsilon' \in \left[d'(\beta_1, PR_i), d'(\beta_2, PR_i)\right) \\ \{\beta_1, \beta_2\} : \varepsilon' \in \left[d'(\beta_2, PR_i), d'(\beta_3, PR_i)\right) \\ \vdots \\ \{\beta_1, \ldots, \beta_t\} : \varepsilon' \in \left[d'(\beta_t, PR_i), 1\right] \end{cases}$$

Hence by theorem 3 we have that

$$\delta\left(\left\{\varepsilon : \frac{\left|N_\theta^\varepsilon\right|_{DB}}{|DB|} \in N_{R_i}^{\varepsilon'}\right\}\right) = \begin{cases} 0 : \varepsilon' < d'(\beta_1, PR_i) \\ \mu_{(\beta_1)\theta}(DB) : \varepsilon' \in \left[d'(\beta_1, PR_i), d'(\beta_2, PR_i)\right) \\ \mu_{(\beta_1)\theta}(DB) + \mu_{(\beta_2)\theta}(DB) : \varepsilon' \in \left[d'(\beta_2, PR_i), d'(\beta_3, PR_i)\right) \\ \vdots \\ \sum_{i=1}^{t} \mu_{(\beta_i)\theta}(DB) : \varepsilon' \in \left[d'(\beta_t, PR_i), 1\right] \end{cases}$$

$$= \begin{cases} 0 : \varepsilon' < y_1 \\ a_1 : \varepsilon' \in [y_1, y_2) \\ a_2 : \varepsilon' \in [y_2, y_3) \\ \vdots \\ a_t : \varepsilon' \in [y_t, 1] \end{cases}$$

Therefore

$$\mu_{(R_i)\theta}(DB) = \int_0^1 \delta'(\varepsilon') \delta\left(\left\{\varepsilon : \frac{\left|N_\theta^\varepsilon\right|_{DB}}{|DB|} \in N_{R_i}^{\varepsilon'}\right\}\right) d\varepsilon'$$

$$= a_1 \int_{y_1}^{y_2} \delta'(\varepsilon') d\varepsilon' + \ldots + a_{t-1} \int_{y_{t-1}}^{y_t} \delta'(\varepsilon') d\varepsilon' + a_t \int_{y_t}^{1} \delta'(\varepsilon') d\varepsilon'$$

Corollary 1.

If $\mu_{(R_i)\theta}(DB) = 1$ then $\mu_{(\beta_1)\theta}(DB) = 1$ where $\beta_1 = \arg\min\left\{d'(\beta, PR_i) : \beta \in PP_\theta\right\}$

Proof.

By theorem 4 we have that:

$$\mu_{(R_i)\theta}\left(DB\right) = a_1 \int_{y_1}^{y_2} \delta'\left(\varepsilon'\right)d\varepsilon' + \ldots + a_{t-1}\int_{y_{t-1}}^{y_t}\delta'\left(\varepsilon'\right)d\varepsilon' + a_t\int_{y_t}^{1}\delta'\left(\varepsilon'\right)d\varepsilon'$$

$$\leq \int_{y_1}^{y_2}\delta'\left(\varepsilon'\right)d\varepsilon' + \ldots + \int_{y_{t-1}}^{1}\delta'\left(\varepsilon'\right)d\varepsilon' + \int_{y_t}^{1}\delta'\left(\varepsilon'\right)d\varepsilon' = \int_{y_1}^{1}\delta'\left(\varepsilon'\right)d\varepsilon' \leq 1$$

and hence $\int^{1}\delta'\left(\varepsilon'\right)d\varepsilon' = 1$

Also $\mu_{R_i}^{y_1}\left(\beta_1\right) = \delta'\left(\left[d'\left(\beta_1, PR_i\right), \infty\right)\right) = \int_{y_1}^{1}\delta'\left(\varepsilon'\right)d\varepsilon' = 1$ as required. $\square$

The following theorem show that an imprecisely quantified expression $(R_i)\theta$ is certainly appropriate to describe DB exactly when an associated (simpler) expression $(I)\theta$ is certainly appropriate, where I is the set of proportions in PP_θ which can certainly be described by R_i.

Theorem 5.

$\mu_{(R_i)\theta}\left(DB\right) = 1$ iff $\mu_{(I)\theta}\left(DB\right) = 1$ where $I = \left\{\beta \in PP_\theta : \mu_{R_i}\left(\beta\right) = 1\right\}$

Proof.

Clearly, if $I \neq \varnothing$ then $I = \{\beta_1, \ldots, \beta_k\}$ where $\beta_k = \arg\max\left\{d'\left(\beta, PR_i\right) : \beta \in I\right\}$. In this case, $\mu_{R_i}\left(\beta_k\right) = 1$ implies that $\delta'\left(\left[d'\left(\beta_k, PR_i\right), \infty\right)\right) = \int_{y_k}^{1}\delta'\left(\varepsilon'\right)d\varepsilon' = 1$ which implies that $\int_0^{y_k}\delta'\left(\varepsilon'\right)d\varepsilon' = 0$. Hence,

$$\mu_{(R_i)\theta}\left(DB\right) = a_k\int_{y_k}^{y_{k+1}}\delta'\left(\varepsilon'\right)d\varepsilon' + \ldots + a_t\int_{y_1}^{1}\delta'\left(\varepsilon'\right)d\varepsilon'$$

$(\Rightarrow)$ Suppose $\mu_{(R_i)\theta}\left(DB\right) = 1$ then $I \neq \varnothing$ since if $I = \varnothing$ then $\mu_{R_i}\left(\beta_1\right) < 1$ which is a contradiction by corollary 1. Hence,

$$a_k\int_{y_k}^{y_{k+1}}\delta'\left(\varepsilon'\right)d\varepsilon' + \ldots + a_t\int_{y_1}^{1}\delta'\left(\varepsilon'\right)d\varepsilon' = 1$$

Also, since $\mu_{R_i}\left(\beta_{k+1}\right) < 1$ then $\int_{y_k}^{y_{k+1}}\delta'\left(\varepsilon'\right)d\varepsilon' > 0$ and hence $a_k = 1$ since otherwise $\mu_{(R_i)\theta}\left(DB\right) < \int_{y_k}^{1}\delta'\left(\varepsilon'\right)d\varepsilon' \leq 1$. Hence

$$\mu_{(I)\theta}\left(DB\right) = \sum_{j=1}^{k}\mu_{(\beta_j)\theta}\left(DB\right) = a_k = 1$$

as required.

$(\Leftarrow)$ Suppose $\mu_{(I)\theta}\left(DB\right) = 1$ then clearly $I \neq \varnothing$. Hence, $a_k = 1$ and since $a_j \geq a_k$ for $j \geq k$ then $a_j = 1$ for $j \geq k$. Therefore,

$$\mu_{(R_i)\theta}\left(DB\right) = \int\limits_{y_k}^{1} \delta'\left(\varepsilon'\right)d\varepsilon' = \mu_{R_i}\left(\beta_k\right) = 1$$

as required.

Example 1.

Let $\Omega = [0,10]$, $d(x,y) = \|x - y\|$ and $\delta(\varepsilon) = \begin{cases} 1 : \varepsilon \in [0,1] \\ 0 : \varepsilon > 1 \end{cases}$. Let *high* $\in LA$ be a label describing elements of Ω such that $P_{high} = [7,8]$.

Now consider the queries $(\forall)_{DB}$ *high* and $(\exists)_{DB}$ *high* for the following database:

DB={0.1795, 1.051, 1.075, 7.367, 7.5, 7.57, 7.66, 7.86, 8.06, 8.61}

Now $N_{high}^{\varepsilon} = [7 - \varepsilon, 8 + \varepsilon]$ so that $DB \subseteq N_{high}^{\varepsilon}$ iff $7 - \varepsilon \leq 0.1795$ iff $\varepsilon \geq 6.8205$. Therefore,

$$\mu_{(\forall)high}\left(DB\right) = \int\limits_{6.8205}^{\infty} \delta\left(\varepsilon\right)d\varepsilon = 0.$$

Also, $DB \cap P_{high} = \left\{7.367, 7.5, 7.56, 7.66, 7.86\right\} \neq \varnothing$ and hence $N_{high}^{\varepsilon} \cap DB \neq \varnothing$ for all $\varepsilon \geq 0$. Therefore, $\mu_{(\exists)high}\left(DB\right) = \int\limits_{0}^{\infty} \delta\left(\varepsilon\right)d\varepsilon = 1.$

Let *most* $\in LR$ where $P_{most} = [0.6, 0.8]$. Also let $d'(x,y) = \|x - y\|$ and $\delta'\left(\varepsilon'\right) = \begin{cases} 10 : \varepsilon' \in [0,0.1] \\ 0 : \varepsilon' > 0.1 \end{cases}$. (see figure 3)

Now consider the query $(most)_{DB}$ *high*

Figure 3. Appropriateness measures for high together with DB (top) and most (bottom) together with PP_{most} as defined in example 1

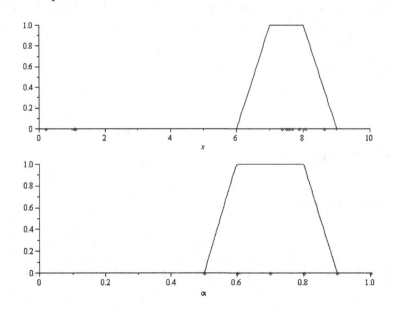

Now $PP_{high} = \left\{\dfrac{5}{10}, \dfrac{6}{10}, \dfrac{7}{10}, \dfrac{8}{10}, \dfrac{9}{10}, 1\right\}$ and $d'(1, P_{most}) = 0.2$, $d'\left(\dfrac{9}{10}, P_{most}\right) = 0.1$, $d'\left(\dfrac{8}{10}, P_{most}\right) = 0$, $d'\left(\dfrac{7}{10}, P_{most}\right) = 0$, $d'\left(\dfrac{6}{10}, P_{most}\right) = 0$, $d'\left(\dfrac{5}{10}, P_{most}\right) = 0.1$. Hence, we let

$$\beta_1 = \frac{8}{10}, \ \beta_2 = \frac{7}{10}, \ \beta_3 = \frac{6}{10}, \ \beta_4 = \frac{9}{10}, \ \beta_5 = \frac{5}{10}, \ \beta_6 = 1 \text{ and}$$

$$y_1 = 0, \ y_2 = 0, \ y_3 = 0, \ y_4 = 0.1, \ y_5 = 0.1, \ y_6 = 0.2$$

Therefore, from theorem 4

$$\mu_{(most)high}(DB) = a_3 \int_0^{0.1} \delta'(\varepsilon')d\varepsilon' + a_4 \int_{0.1}^{0.2} \delta'(\varepsilon')d\varepsilon' + a_5 \int_{0.2}^{1} \delta'(\varepsilon')d\varepsilon' = a_3$$

where $a_3 = \mu_{\left(\frac{8}{10}\right)high}(DB) + \mu_{\left(\frac{7}{10}\right)high}(DB) + \mu_{\left(\frac{6}{10}\right)high}(DB)$

Now $\dfrac{\left|N^\varepsilon_{high}\right|_{DB}}{|DB|} = \dfrac{8}{10}$ if $7 - \varepsilon \le 1.075$ and $7 - \varepsilon > 1.051$ if $5.925 \le \varepsilon < 5.949$. Hence,

$$\mu_{\left(\frac{8}{10}\right)most}(DB) = \int_{5.925}^{5.949} \delta(\varepsilon)d\varepsilon = 0$$

$\dfrac{\left|N^\varepsilon_{high}\right|_{DB}}{|DB|} = \dfrac{7}{10}$ if $8 + \varepsilon \ge 8.61$ if $\varepsilon \ge 0.61$. Hence,

$$\mu_{\left(\frac{7}{10}\right)most}(DB) = \int_{0.61}^{\infty} \delta(\varepsilon)d\varepsilon = \int_{0.61}^{1} d\varepsilon = 0.39$$

$\dfrac{\left|N^\varepsilon_{high}\right|_{DB}}{|DB|} = \dfrac{6}{10}$ if $8 + \varepsilon \ge 8.06$ and $8 + \varepsilon > 8.61$ if $0.06 \le \varepsilon < 0.61$. Hence

$$\mu_{\left(\frac{6}{10}\right)most}(DB) = \int_{0.06}^{0.61} \delta(\varepsilon)d\varepsilon = \int_{0.06}^{0.61} d\varepsilon = 0.55. \text{ Hence}$$

$$\mu_{(most)high}(DB) = a_3 = 0.55 + 0.39 = 0.94$$

Let the label *very low* be defined by the prototypes $P_{very\ low} = [0,1]$. Consider the query $(\ge 0.5)_{DB}$ (*very low|¬high*) (i.e. *At least 50% of the not high elements in DB are very low*). Now $N^\varepsilon_{very\ low} = [0, 1 + \varepsilon]$ and $N^\varepsilon_{\neg high} = [0, 7 - \varepsilon] \cup (8 + \varepsilon, 10]$ and for $\varepsilon \le 3$ $N^\varepsilon_{very\ low \wedge \neg high} = N^\varepsilon_{very\ low} \cap N^\varepsilon_{\neg high} = [0, 1 + \varepsilon]$. Therefore,

$$\frac{\left|N^\varepsilon_{very\ low \wedge \neg high}\right|_{DB}}{\left|N^\varepsilon_{\neg high}\right|_{DB}} = \frac{\left\|[0, 1 + \varepsilon]\right\|_{DB}}{\left\|[0, 7 - \varepsilon]\right\|_{DB} + \left\|(8 + \varepsilon, 10]\right\|_{DB}} \text{ so that}$$

$$\frac{\left|N^{\varepsilon}_{very\ low \wedge \neg high}\right|_{DB}}{\left|N^{\varepsilon}_{\neg high}\right|_{DB}} = \begin{cases} 0.25 : \varepsilon < 0.051 \\ 0.5 : 0.051 \leq \varepsilon < 0.06 \\ 0.4 : 0.06 \leq \varepsilon < 0.075 \\ 0.75 : 0.075 \leq \varepsilon < 0.61 \\ 0.6 : \varepsilon \geq 0.61 \end{cases}$$

From this we have that $PP_{very\ low|\neg high} = \{0.25, 0.4, 0.5, 0.6, 0.75\}$ and from theorem 3 it follows that:

$$\mu_{(\geq 0.5)(very\ low|\neg high)}\left(DB\right) = \mu_{(0.5)(very\ low|\neg high)}\left(DB\right) + \mu_{(0.6)(very\ low|\neg high)}\left(DB\right) + \mu_{(0.75)(very\ low|\neg high)}\left(DB\right)$$

where

$$\mu_{(0.5)(very\ low|\neg high)}\left(DB\right) = \int_{0.051}^{0.06} d\varepsilon = 0.009 \quad \mu_{(0.6)(very\ low|\neg high)}\left(DB\right) = \int_{0.61}^{1} d\varepsilon = 0.39 \quad \text{and}$$

$$\mu_{(0.75)(very\ low|\neg high)}\left(DB\right) = \int_{0.075}^{0.61} d\varepsilon = 0.535$$

Hence, $\mu_{(\geq 0.5)(very\ low|\neg high)}\left(DB\right) = 0.009 + 0.39 + 0.535 = 0.934$

Versions of theorems 4 and 5 can be proved for the case of relative quantifiers by replacing P_{θ} with $P_{(\phi|\theta)}$. Hence we also have the following results:

Theorem 6.

For $R_i \in LR$ and $\phi, \theta \in LE$, let $P_{(\phi|\theta)} = \{\beta_1, ..., \beta_t\}$ ordered such that $d'\left(\beta_j, PR_i\right) \leq d'\left(\beta_{j+1}, PR_i\right)$ then

$$\mu_{(R_i)(\phi|\theta)}\left(DB\right) = a_1 \int_{y_1}^{y_2} \delta'\left(\varepsilon'\right)d\varepsilon' + ... + a_{t-1} \int_{y_{t-1}}^{y_t} \delta'\left(\varepsilon'\right)d\varepsilon' + a_t \int_{y_t}^{1} \delta'\left(\varepsilon'\right)d\varepsilon'$$

where $a_j = \sum_{i=1}^{j} \mu_{(\beta_i)(\phi|\theta)}\left(DB\right)$ and $y_j = d'\left(\beta_j, PR_i\right)$

Theorem 7.

$$\mu_{(R_i)(\phi|\theta)}\left(DB\right) = 1 \text{ iff } \mu_{(I)(\phi|\theta)}\left(DB\right) = 1 \text{ where } I = \left\{\beta \in PP_{(\phi|\theta)} : \mu_{R_i}\left(\beta\right) = 1\right\}$$

A SCALEABLE ALGORITHM FOR EVALUATING SIMPLE LINGUISTIC QUERIES

In this section we propose an algorithm for evaluating linguistic queries on a database which only involve basic labels. By considering the computational complexity of this algorithm we show that, for simple linguistic queries of this kind, the approach is scaleable to databases with a large number of elements.

Consider a basic label $L_i \in LA$ with prototypes P_i. Also consider a database DB of N elements ordered such that $DB = \left\{ x_{i,j} : j = 1, \cdots, N \right\}$ where $d\left(x_{i,j}, P_i\right) \leq d\left(x_{i,j+1}, P_i\right)$. In this case, denoting $d\left(x_{i,j}, P_i\right) = d_{i,j}$, we clearly have that:

$$N^{\varepsilon}_{L_i} = \begin{cases} \varnothing : \varepsilon < d_{i,1} \\ \left\{ x_{i,1} \right\} : d_{i,1} \leq \varepsilon < d_{i,2} \\ \quad \vdots \\ \left\{ x_{i,1}, \cdots, x_{i,j} \right\} : d_{i,j} \leq \varepsilon < d_{i,j+1} \\ \quad \vdots \\ \left\{ x_{i,1}, \cdots, x_{i,N} \right\} : d_{i,N} \leq \varepsilon \end{cases}$$

From this the set of relevant proportions for L_i in DB (definition 11) is then given directly by:

$$PP_{L_i} = \left\{ \frac{j}{N} : d_{i,j} < d_{i,j+1} \right\}$$

Now consider the computational complexity of this algorithm to determine the relevant proportions PP_{L_i}. Initially, the elements of DB must be sorted on the basis of their distance from P_i. Using the quicksort algorithm this has average computational cost $O(N \log (N))$. Determining PP_{L_i} then requires only N checks for $d_{i,j} \leq d_{i,j+1}$ with cost $O(N)$. Hence, the overall computational cost of determining PP_{L_i} is $O\left(N \log (N) + N \right) = O\left(N \log (N) \right)$.

Given PP_{L_i} we know from an earlier section that the evaluation of quantified queries is straightforward. For example, for $\frac{j}{N} \in PP_{L_i}$ we have that:

$$\mu_{\left(\frac{j}{N}\right)L_i} (DB) = \int_{d_{i,j}}^{d_{i,j+1}} \delta(\varepsilon) d\varepsilon$$

Now assuming that, for a well behaved density function δ, integrals of the above form can be effectively evaluated in one computational step then for any $I \subseteq [0,1]$ the computational cost of evaluating $\mu_{(I)L_i} (DB)$ is at worst $O(N)$. To see this, recall from theorem 3 that:

$$\mu_{(I)L_i} (DB) = \sum_{\beta \in PP_{L_i} \cap I} \mu_{(\beta)L_i} (DB)$$

The cost of this calculation is then bounded by $\left| PP_{L_i} \right| \leq N$.

To evaluate linguistically quantified theory of the form $\mu_{(R_j)L_i} (DB)$, we see from theorem 4 that this only requires us to evaluate $\mu_{\left(\frac{j}{N}\right)L_i} (DB)$ for each $\frac{j}{N} \in PP_{L_i}$ with the additional computational cost of sorting the elements of PP_{L_i} relative to their distance from PR_j (the prototypes of R_j). Again by using quicksort the average computational cost of this operation is $O(N \log N)$.

We now consider the evaluation of relative quantifier queries involving basic labels. Let $L_r \in LA$ be a second label with prototypes P_r. As before order the elements of the database in terms of their distance from P_r so that $DB = \left\{ x_{r,k} : k = 1, \cdots, N \right\}$ where $d_{r,k} = d\left(x_{r,k}, P_r\right) \leq d\left(x_{r,k+1}, P_r\right) = d_{r,k+1}$. In this case:

$$N^\varepsilon_{L_i \wedge L_r} = \left\{ x_{i,1}, \cdots, x_{i,j} \right\} \cap \left\{ x_{r,1}, \cdots, x_{r,k} \right\} \text{ if } \max\left(d_{i,j}, d_{r,k} \right) \leq \varepsilon \leq \min\left(d_{i,j+1}, d_{r,k+1} \right)$$

Hence,

$$PP_{\left(L_i | L_r \right)} = \left\{ \frac{b_{j,k}}{k} : d_{i,j} < d_{i,j+1}, d_{r,k} < d_{r,k+1}, \min\left(d_{i,j}, d_{r,k} \right) \leq \max\left(d_{i,j+1}, d_{r,k+1} \right) \right\}$$

where $b_{j,k} = \left| \left\{ x_{i,1}, \cdots, x_{i,j} \right\} \cap \left\{ x_{r,1}, \cdots, x_{r,k+1} \right\} \right|$

From this we see that the computational cost of determining $PP_{\left(L_i | L_r \right)}$ is as follows: The elements DB must be sorted twice, once with respect to distance from P_i and once with respect to distance from P_r. Using quicksort the combined cost of this repeated operation is still $O(N \log (N))$. $b_{j,k}$ must then be calculated and distances compared for each pair j,k with cost $O(N^2)$. Consequently the overall computational cost of calculating $PP_{\left(L_i | L_r \right)}$ is $O(N^2)$.

Given $PP_{\left(L_i | L_r \right)}$ the appropriateness of a simple query such as $(I)(L_i | L_j)$ is then determined by:

$$\mu_{(I)\left(L_i | L_r \right)}(DB) = \sum_{j,k: \frac{b_{j,k}}{k} \in I} \int_{\max\left(d_{i,j}, d_{r,k} \right)}^{\min\left(d_{i,j+1}, d_{r,k+1} \right)} \delta(\varepsilon) d\varepsilon$$

This requires at most a further $\left| PP_{\left(L_i | L_r \right)} \right| \leq N^2$ calculations and consequently the entire cost of evaluating such queries from DB, including determining $PP_{\left(L_i | L_r \right)}$, is $O(N^2)$.

CONCLUSION

In this paper we have introduced a new model of linguistic quantified statements based on a combination of random set theory and prototype theory. The theory is a generalization of Lawry's label semantic framework. We have shown that the proposed model is computationally feasible and hence potentially has practical applications in information retrieval.

Overall the proposed model makes a number of simplification assumptions. For instance, we have only investigated a limited range of quantifiers essentially based on proportions. In future work a thorough study of a wide range of quantifiers should be carried out. Furthermore, we have assumed that the appropriateness of labels to describe an example in the database is always judged on the basis of the same shared characteristics. In other words, there is one single distance function for comparing elements to prototypes for every single label. In many cases the applicability of different labels may be judged on the basis of different distance functions defined on different sets of attributes. Future work will investigate extending the proposed methods to the multi-criterion case and consider the impact of this generalization on computational costs.

ACKNOWLEDGMENT

Yongchuan Tang is funded by the National Natural Science Foundation of China (NSFC) under Grant 60604034, the joint funding of NSFC and MSRA under Grant 60776798, and the Science and Technology Program of Zhejiang Province under Grant 2007C223061

REFERENCES

Barwise, J., & Cooper, R. (1981). Generalized quantifiers in natural language. *Linguistics and Philosophy, 4*(2), 159–219. doi:10.1007/BF00350139

Bosc, P., Lietard, L., & Pivert, O. (1995). Quantified statements and database fuzzy querying. In P. Bosc & J. Kacprzyk (Eds.), *Fuzziness in database management systems, studies in fuzziness* (pp. 275-308). Heidelberg, Germany: Physica-Verlag.

Diaz-Hermida, F., Losada, D. E., Bugarin, A., & Barro, S. (2005). A probabilistic quantifier fuzzification mechanism: The model and its evaluation for information retrieval. *IEEE transactions on Fuzzy Systems, 13*(5), 688–700. doi:10.1109/TFUZZ.2005.856557

Dubois, D., & Prade, H. (1997). The three semantics of fuzzy sets. *Fuzzy Sets and Systems, 90,* 141–150. doi:10.1016/S0165-0114(97)00080-8

Goodman, I. R. (1982). Fuzzy sets as equivalence classes of random sets. In R. Yager (Ed.), *Fuzzy set and possibility theory* (pp. 327-342). New York: Pergamon.

Goodman, I. R., & Nguyen, H. T. (1985). *Uncertainty models for knowledge based systems: A unified approach to the measurement of uncertainty.* New York: Elsevier.

Lawry, J. (2004). A framework for linguistic modelling. *Artificial Intelligence, 155,* 1–39. doi:10.1016/j.artint.2003.10.001

Lawry, J. (2006). *Modelling and reasoning with vague concepts.* Berlin, Germany: Springer.

Lawry, J. (2008). Appropriateness measures: An uncertainty model for vague concepts. *Synthese, 161*(2), 255–269. doi:10.1007/s11229-007-9158-9

Lawry, J., & Tang, Y. (2008). Relating prototype theory and label semantics. In D. Dubois, M. A. Lubiano, H. Prade, M. A. Gil, P. Grzegorzweski, & O. Hryniewicz (Eds.), *Soft methods for handling variability and imprecision* (pp. 35-42). Berlin, Germany: Springer.

Lawry, J., & Tang, Y. (2009). Uncertainty modelling for vague concepts: A prototype theory approach. *Submitted.*

Liu, Y., & Kerre, E. E. (1998). An overview of fuzzy quantifiers. (I). Interpretations. *Fuzzy Sets and Systems, 95,* 1–21. doi:10.1016/S0165-0114(97)00254-6

Losada, D. E., Diaz-Hermida, R., Bugarin, A., & Barro, S. (2004). Experiments on using fuzzy quantified sentences in adhoc retrieval. In *Proceedings ACM Symposium on Applied Computing* (pp. 1059-1066).

Nguyen, H. T. (1984). On modelling of linguistic information using random sets. *Information Science*, *34*, 265–274. doi:10.1016/0020-0255(84)90052-5

Rosch, E. (1973). Natural categories. *Cognitive Psychology*, *4*, 328–350. doi:10.1016/0010-0285(73)90017-0

Zadeh, L. A. (1983). A computational approach to fuzzy quantifiers in natural languages. *Natural Languages*. *Computers & Mathematics with Applications (Oxford, England)*, *8*, 149–184. doi:10.1016/0898-1221(83)90013-5

Zadeh, L. A. (1996). Fuzzy logic = computing with words. *IEEE transactions on Fuzzy Systems*, *4*, 103–111. doi:10.1109/91.493904

Zadeh, L. A. (2002). From computing with numbers to computing with words – from manipulation of measurements to manipulation of perceptions. *Int. J. Appl. Math. Comput. Sci.*, *12*(3), 307–324.

ENDNOTE

[1]   Here we also use δ to denote the probability measure generated by the density δ i.e. for $I \subseteq [o, \infty)$

$$\delta(I) = \int_I \delta(\varepsilon) d\varepsilon$$

Chapter 7
A Flexible Language for Exploring Clustered Search Results

Gloria Bordogna
CNR IDPA, Italy

Alessandro Campi
Politecnico di Milano, Italy

Stefania Ronchi
Politecnico di Milano, Italy

Giuseppe Psaila
Università di Bergamo, Italy

ABSTRACT

In this chapter the authors consider the problem of defining a flexible approach for exploring huge amounts of results retrieved by several Internet search services (like search engines). The goal is to offer users a way to discover relevant hidden relationships between documents. The proposal is motivated by the observation that visualization paradigms, based on either the ranked list or clustered results, do not allow users to fully appreciate and understand the retrieved contents. In the case of long ranked lists, the user generally analyzes only the first few pages. On the other side, in the case the documents are clustered, to understand their contents the user does not have other means that looking at the cluster labels. When the same query is submitted to distinct search services, they may produce partially overlapped clustered results, where clusters identified by distinct labels collect some common documents. Moreover, clusters with similar labels, but containing distinct documents, may be produced as well. In such a situation, it may be useful to compare, combine and rank the cluster contents, to filter out relevant documents. In this chapter the authors present a novel manipulation language, in which several operators (inspired by relational algebra) and distinct ranking methods can be exploited to analyze the clusters' contents. New clusters can be generated and ranked based on distinct criteria, by combining (i.e., overlapping, refining and intersecting) clusters in a set oriented fashion. Specifically, the chapter is focused on the ranking methods defined for each operator of the language.

DOI: 10.4018/978-1-60566-858-1.ch007

INTRODUCTION

Retrieving useful and relevant information over the Internet is not an easy task by using current search engines. Too often, the relevant documents are merged and hidden in the long ranked list of retrieved documents. The list can span over hundreds of web pages, each one containing just few retrieved items.

To discover the relevant documents, users have to browse the titles of the documents, but generally only the first two or three web pages are analyzed, while the content of the successive ones is missed. Thus, if users do not find what they are looking for in the first pages, they reformulate a new query trying to capture what they are looking for in the top ranked items.

Some users turned to using meta-search engines, such as *mamma*, *dogpile*, *Metacrawler* etc., in an attempt to optimize their search effort. The assumption is that, if one regards a search engine as an expert in finding information, by using several experts together one should achieve better results. However this is not generally true, since meta-search engines fuse the individual ranked lists of documents retrieved by each underlying system by applying rigid and static fusion functions, applying criteria that are not transparent to the user. The side effect of list merging is to augment the number of retrieved documents, leaving the user skeptics as far as the actual correspondence of the ranking to her/his relevance judgments is concerned. Furthermore, the retrieved documents besides the first page will be hardly analyzed by users; thus, this makes much of the meta search engine's effort useless.

To overcome this problem, some search services such as *vivisimo, Snaket, Ask.com, MS AdCenter Labs Search Result Clustering* etc., have shifted from the usual ranked list to the clustered results paradigm. This consists in organizing the documents retrieved by a query into containers (i.e., clusters), possibly semantically homogeneous with respect to their contents, and in presenting them labeled, so as to synthesize their main content focus (Osinski, 2003).

Clustering is often proposed as a viable way of narrowing a search into a more specific query, like in Ask.com (Chen &Dumais, 2000; Zamir & Etzioni, 1999; Coates et al., 2001).

On the other side, one problem users encounter with such clustered results, is the inability of fully understanding and appreciating the contents of the clusters. This is mainly due to the short and sometimes bad quality of the labels of the clusters, which generally consist of a few terms, or individual short phrases, which are automatically extracted from the documents of the cluster based on statistics and co-occurrence analysis. Often, several clusters have similar labels that differ just for a single term. To effectively explore the cluster contents, users have no other means than clicking on the cluster labels and browsing the clusters themselves.

This problem is much more apparent when submitting the same request to distinct search engines, each one producing a group of clustered results reflecting distinct criteria. For example, the *Gigabits* search engine clusters retrieved documents by their freshness dating (Last Day, Last Week, Last Month, Last Year, etc.), the *vivisimo* search service presents clustered documents. In such a situation, one may want to explore if a given cluster contains documents that are fresh or not; this necessity may occur quite frequently in analyzing news streams (RSS) to find out the frequency of a given news story reported by media as a function of time.

When the groups of clusters are generated by distinct search services, users may be faced with distinct clusters, possibly with the same labels. In this situation, it becomes necessary to explore the relationships between the contents of these clusters to identify common and distinct documents, and re-rank the contents of the clusters based on distinct criteria. This may require the application of several manipulation operations, such as the intersection and join of clusters, as well as their union and re-clustering, and so on; the different ranking options for these operations are an important feature, to re-rank the content of clusters, and the clusters themselves, so as to make new documents and clusters emerge in top positions, depending on distinct criteria. But, currently, there is no means to carry out this exploratory activity. This exploratory activity can be useful also in the case in which one formulates distinct queries (expressing the same information needs) to the same search engine and wants to explore the contents of the retrieved ranked lists.

These considerations motivate our proposal of defining and implementing an interaction framework based on a flexible exploratory language for carrying out manipulation operations of groups of clustered results, retrieved by one or several search services (basically search engines) over the internet, correlated with several ranking functions that can be explicitly specified by users.

It is an exploratory language, since the richness of operators and ranking functions makes it possible to either reveal common and implicit contents of the clusters, and implicit relationships between clusters, such as similarity and inclusion (i.e., similar, more specific or more general contents).

The language is also flexible, since it allows the application of several ranking criteria to re-organize the documents inside each cluster, and the clusters inside each group of retrieved clusters, reflecting a distinct semantics, such as content relevance, exhaustiveness of retrieval, novelty of the new cluster with respect to the original ones. For example, one can apply a ranking that favors the exhaustivity of the clusters' contents, i.e., the number of documents they group. Another choice could be to rank first the clusters obtained by a join of two original clusters, which have a high degree of correlation; conversely, one could rank first the clusters exhibiting a greater degree of novelty with respect to the common contents of the original clusters. The application of different ranking functions when applying a combination operation between clusters allows one to highlight different elements in the top position in a controlled manner, reflecting different properties of the clusters.

The formalization of ranking criteria is consistent with the basic operations of intersection and union of fuzzy sets, since we regard each cluster as a fuzzy set of documents, and each group, as a fuzzy set of clusters (Zadeh, 1965).

Since manipulation operations may require the reuse of intermediate results several times, we have conceived the storing of the intermediate results into a database as an essential phase for successive manipulation. Furthermore, the local manipulation of results avoids useless network and search services overloading; in fact, in current practice, several modified queries are submitted to the search engines, trying to capture relevant documents in the first positions of the ranked list, documents that were already retrieved by the previous queries, although hidden to the user since they did not occurred in the first positions.

In our view, the usual ranked list, produced by search engines is regarded as a group consisting of a single cluster that has the query itself as label. Thus, our language can be used to compare the results of any search service producing ranked lists too.

While, in (Bordogna, Campi, Psaila, & Ronchi, 2008a) we first proposed the data model and the operators of the language, in this chapter we recall the language and focus on the semantics of the distinct ranking methods.

In the next paragraph the background literature related to the proposal is reviewed. Further, a use case is introduced to exemplify the usefulness of the language. The successive paragraph defines the language, in terms of basic operations, group operators, ranking methods, and group functions, and we report about the experimental evaluation about scalability of the algorithms. Finally, the conclusions summarize the main achievements.

BACKGROUND OF THE PROPOSED LANGUAGE

In this paragraph, we review works that are somehow related to our proposal, although they have been conceived either with a different purpose than the analysis of web documents retrieved by search services, or with distinct functionalities. In fact, to the best of our knowledge, there is not a language similar to our proposal.

In conceiving our approach we started from the consideration that "many IR problems are, by nature, ranking problems". This is the starting point also of the approaches known as "*to learn how to rank documents*" presented within the ACM SIGIR 2008 Workshop "Learning to rank for information retrieval" (Li, Liu, Zhai, 2008), that propose to use learning methods to adapt the ranking of retrieved results in order to enhance effectiveness of IR.

Our proposal also shares the idea of the works presented within the ACM SIGIR 2008 Workshop "Aggregated search" (Lalmas, Murdock, 2008) that pursue the task of searching and assembling information from a variety of sources, placing it in a single interface to improve the effectiveness of retrieval. In (White et al., 2008) they propose a metasearch framework directing the search to the engine that yields the best results for the current query.

Our solution however is different, since it does not exploit the strict ranking of documents, but it exploits the application of clustering techniques to group documents that are homogeneous as far as their contents are concerned, and furthermore we propose the use of a manipulation language of group of clusters, to re-rank the documents within the clusters based on personal preferences of the user.

A motivation of the utility of our proposal can be found in (Leouski & Croft, 1996). In this pioneer work, the authors advocate the need of tools for giving the user more immediate control over the clusters of retrieved web documents; such tools should serve as means for exploring the similarity among documents and clusters. They also consider giving the user some means to correct, or even completely change, the classification structure. To support the manipulation of clusters, they suggest the development of graphic user interfaces.

Indeed, the literature on visual paradigms for the presentation of textual search results is too extensive to review; for a survey, the reader can see (Card, Mackinlay, & Shneiderman, 1999; Staley, & Twidale, 2000). One goal of these approaches is to perform some kind of text mining based on conceptual maps visualization (Chung, Chen, Nunamaker, 2003; Kampanya, Shen, Kim, North, & Fox, 2004).

Nevertheless, our proposal is different, since we do not exploit a graphical representation of relationships between documents at this level, but we provide a language for flexibly exploring the hidden relationships. The work presenting the NIRVE prototype (Sebrechts, Cugini, Laskowski, Vasilakis, & Miller, 1999) evaluates and compares several graphical interfaces for showing the retrieved results of NIST's PRISE search engine. In the conclusions, it states that "a good visualization of search results depends on a good structure and what often happens is that developers perform a deeper analysis of results in order to generate that structure".

In this respect, we envisage that our proposed language could be employed for the purpose of exploring and finding a good structure of results that can then be presented by taking advantages of the proposed graphic visualization techniques.

Personalization is a distinctive characteristic of our approach, since the manipulation of the clustered documents, possibly retrieved by multiple search services, is demanded to the user, who can perform distinct kinds of combinations by means of the operators of the language. In this sense, we can regard the application of the operators on the retrieved results as a kind of a personal information filter defined by the user or, in other words, the manipulation language can be seeing as a means to define personalized information filters (Agichtein, Brill, Dumais, 2006).

An approach that shares some similarity of intent to our proposal is the Scatter/Gather algorithm (Hearst & Pederson, 1996), in that it allows doing dynamic clustering and refinement of search results. Its distinctive feature is the way it allows clusters to be selected, recombined (gathered) and re-clustered (scattered) by the user. However, the user has to decide which clusters have a relevant theme based solely on keywords and titles. No functionality is available to detect the degree of sharing between clusters. Furthermore, since new clusters are generated based on re-clustering, the generation criteria remain implicit and unknown to the user. On the contrary, in our approach, the user is perfectly aware of the criteria that generated the new clusters, since they depend on the applied group operator and the specified ranking method. Moreover, the intersection and union operations between cluster representatives generate the label of the resulting cluster through the processing of its items (titles and snippets), so as to reveal and synthesize its hidden semantics. In facts, the label conveys new information previously not known on the common contents of the documents in the cluster.

We can also find some similarity of our approach with respect to clustering ensemble techniques, that have been defined to compare either the results obtained by the application of distinct clustering algorithms on the same set of items, or to compare distinct partitions of the same set of items obtained based on distinct views (representations) of the items (Punch, Jain, & Topchy, 2005; Strehl & Ghosh, 2002; Pagani, Bordogna, & Valle, 2007). The main goal of these techniques is to achieve a robust and consensual clustering of the items. Robust clustering is achieved by combining data partitions (forming a clustering ensemble) produced by multiple clustering. The approaches are defined within an information-theoretical framework; in fact, mutual information is the underlying concept used in the definition of quantitative measures of agreement or consistency between data partitions. The group intersection operator of our language takes inspiration from these ideas, since its goal is, given two distinct partitions (i.e., groups of clusters), to identify the common partitions, i.e., those sharing the same sets of documents. If we iteratively apply the intersection operator to a set of groups, we thus find the consensual partitions among these groups. As far as the join operator is concerned, it can be regarded as the generation of a new partition (group) containing only the unions of the original clusters that have a non-empty intersection. Its meaning is that of expanding the result of the intersection operator between groups, so as to consider indirect correlations among the items of the original clusters.

As a means for exploring the set of retrieved documents, also the ranking methods have a central role: they allow rearranging the ordering of clusters within groups by highlighting either some inner property of the clusters themselves, e.g., their exhaustivity in terms of cluster cardinality, or their reliability/quality in satisfying the search needs of the user, or even their degree of novelty or specificity. To define the ranking methods, we based on the literature regarding information retrieval with query weights, and flexible querying in fuzzy databases (Buell, & Kraft, 1981; Bosc & Prade, 1997; Galindo, 2008). The relative importance semantics for query term weights in extended Boolean information retrieval is here revisited for specifying the relative importance of clusters for computing weighted rankings (Bookstein, 1980; Yager, 1987).

Figure 1. Clusters examples. The first rows report the group's identifiers, the search service name and the query text that is the group label; the other rows report a cluster identifier within the group, and the label of the cluster.

g1: Google – "Napa Valley"
cl.1: Wine Wineries
cl.2: Hotels Amp Spa
cl.3: Opera House
cl.4: Travel Guide
cl.5: Napa Valley Reservation
cl.6: Wine Tasting
cl.7: Country Club
cl.8: Destinations
cl.9: Napa Valley Redwood Inn
cl.10: Napa Valley Marathon
cl.11: Symphony

g2: Yahoo! – "Napa Valley"
cl.1: Wine tasting and Wineries
cl.2: Tours in Napa
cl.3: Plan Your Travel Vacation
cl.4: Napa Valley Spas Amp
cl.5: Wine Country
cl.6: Map
cl.7: Recreational Sports in Napa
cl.8: Napa Valley California
cl.9: Bed and Breakfast
cl.10: Wikipedia the Free Encyclopedia
cl.11: Wine Train

g3: MSN Live Search – "Napa Valley"
cl.1: Wine Wineries
cl.2: Napa Valley Email
cl.3: Napa Valley Clickable Map
cl.4: Napa Valley Hotel
cl.5: Beautiful
cl.6: Napa Valley Regions
cl.7: Napa Valley Symphony
cl.8: Visitors

PRACTICAL UTILITY OF THE EXPLORATORY LANGUAGE: A USE CASE EXAMPLE

In order to give a practical idea of the kind of exploratory tasks that can be performed by means of the proposed language, in this paragraph we introduce a use case.

Let us suppose we want to go on a tour in Napa Valley; to plan the trip, we need to collect information concerning wineries, sites to visit, close cities to reach, e.g., by car, as well as hotels and restaurants. The search services provide a large set of documents concerning Napa Valley, so it becomes a hard task to find, among them, the most relevant ones for our goal. Consequently, it can be convenient to semantically characterize them, by organizing them in groups of semantically homogeneous documents (clusters), and then to perform a kind of exploratory task, in which we try to combine the results of queries submitted to search services, in order to filter out useful documents. This novel practice can be carried out locally, thus minimizing the need of new remote searches, as it generally happens with current search services. The results obtained by analyzing and combining previously submitted queries could also inspire new and more focused queries.

Hereafter, we start a use case example that we will use throughout the chapter to clarify our approach and to explain the proposed language.

Example 1: To start our search of information to organize the tour to Napa Valley, we submit the query *"Napa Valley"* to the search services Google, Yahoo! and MSN Live Search.

To have a rapid glance at the main topics retrieved, the documents returned by each service are clustered. This is done on the basis of the documents' snippets (brief piece of content) shown in the results pages. The labels of the obtained clusters are represented in Figure 1.

On the basis of these results, it could be interesting to apply some manipulations on the groups, in order to filter out in the top positions results that are most relevant to the user's needs. For example, it may be interesting to keep, in the groups, only the *most relevant* clusters concerning some particular contents (identified through the clusters' label): this way we reduce the whole set of documents to only those that are deemed relevant, and that really cover the desired aspects, thus saving time for their inspection. To this aim one can use the **cluster selection operation** of the proposed manipulation language, to select only desired clusters in a group.

Alternatively, it may be interesting to obtain new groups in which clusters are composed of the most *authoritative and reliable* documents concerning a specific desired topics only, such as *Hotel* or *Hotel and Travel Guide* that are deemed relevant by all the search services. In this case we can assume that documents recommended by all the search services are the most reliable and authoritative ones; thus we want to obtain highly specific clusters containing documents recommended by all the search services. To this aim one can use the **group intersection** operator of the proposed language that allows maintaining only the documents that are contained within all the groups.

Another possibility could be to have an overview of the main general topics represented by a combination of the retrieved clusters. To this end one can specify the **group union** operator to generate a single group by uniting two groups, and then the **group coalescing** operator to fuse all the clusters within a group into a single labeled cluster, expressing by its label the main retrieved contents.

Another case is when we want to generate clusters by the union of clusters that have some correlated contents. The **group join** operator can perform this task.

A final example could be to obtain new groups from the results of previous searches, in such a way specific topics, hidden within the retrieved documents, are identified. This can be performed by filtering sets of already retrieved documents, based on a more specific request, through the **group refinement** operator.

We may also be interested in re-ordering the new clusters in the resulting group, based on some property of clusters and documents, that may differ from the default one, i.e., the initial ranking provided by the search service that first retrieved the document.

For example, one could be interested in performing a survey on a topic and be interested in achieving exhaustive results: in this case, he/she could prefer to rank first the relevant clusters with greatest cardinality. To this aim one can apply the **group union** operator with the **cardinality rank** method.

An alternative could be to perform an exploratory analysis of the main general topics dealt with in the whole set of retrieved documents: in this case, one could prefer to rank first the clusters with greatest novelty with respect to the clusters from which they originated. To this aim one can apply the **group join** operator with the **expansion rank** method. Conversely, one could be interested in exploring the most exhaustive results retrieved by a previous search on specific topics; in this case, one could prefer to rank first the clusters obtained by joining original clusters with greatest correlation. This is achieved by applying the **group join** operator with the **correlation rank** method.

THE FLEXIBLE EXPLORATORY LANGUAGE

In this paragraph we introduce the ingredients of the proposed language. First we define the data model, then we introduce the basic operations between clusters derived from fuzzy set operations of union, intersection and complement; finally we define the main group operators of the language by discussing, for each of them, an application in the context of the use case. Along with the group operators, we also define their ranking methods by discussing their semantics.

We recall that the proposed language offers a means that users, performing web searches by possibly multiple search services, can exploit to filter relevant documents already retrieved, but hidden to them within the huge amount of retrieved results. The specification of the operators of the language for manipulating groups of clustered documents can serve to distinct purposes, as it will be discussed along with the introduction of the operators. It is worth pointing out that the applicability of the operators of the language can be far more general than the combination of clustered results obtained by distinct search services. One could apply the operators also to explore the results retrieved by distinct queries submitted to the same search engine. In fact it is not necessary that the results are clustered, they can be organized as the usual ranked list retrieved by search engines, since the operators regard the ranked list as a group, containing one single cluster labeled by the terms of the query that retrieved the list.

The Data Model

Consider a *query q* submitted to a search engine; the query result is a ranked list of documents, that we call *ranked items*.

Definition 1: Ranked Item

A *ranked item r* represents a document retrieved by a web search. It is defined as a tuple:

r:(uri, title, snippet, irank)

where: *uri* is the Uniform Resource Identifier of the ranked web document; *title* is the document title and *snippet* is an excerpt of the document, made by a set of sentences that may contain the keywords of the query; *irank* is a score (in the range [0,1]) that expresses the estimated relevance of the retrieved document with respect to the query. Distinct items in distinct results lists may represent the same document. In facts, we assume that a document is uniquely identified by its *uri* (Coates et al., 2001) (near duplicates are not detected), while it may have distinct *snippets* and *irank* when retrieved by different search services. We assume that *irank* is a function of the position of the item in the query result list.

Definition 2: Cluster

A *cluster* representative *c* is a set of ranked items, having itself a rank. It is defined as a tuple:

c:(label, crank, items)

where: *label* is a set of terms that semantically synthesizes the cluster's content; *crank* is a score (in the range [0,1]) depending on the ranks of the items belonging to the cluster; *items* is the set of *ranked items* constituting the cluster.

With $|c|$ we denote the *cardinality* of the cluster representative, that is defined as $|c| \equiv |c.items|$. A cluster label *c.label* is generally automatically generated by a function *SynthLabel(c.items)*. Function *SynthLabel (R)* generates a representative label from the set of ranked items *R* (or ranked clusters *C* in the case of a group), by extracting the most meaningful non-stopwords terms from within *titles* and *snippets* associated with items in *R*. The significance of a term is determined based on the occurrences of the terms. The labeling algorithm is described in subparagraph "*Labeling Algorithm*" .

The default value of *crank* of a cluster is defined as its natural rank (see Definition 7). When a cluster belongs to a group generated by one operator of the language, its *crank* can assume a different semantics corresponding to the ranking method that the operator supports, and that has been applied to produce the cluster.

For the sake of simplicity, in the remainder of the chapter, we use the term *cluster* to intend *cluster representative*.

Definition 3: Group

A *group g* is a not empty and ordered set of clusters. It is the main element of the data model and it is defined as a pair:

$$g: (l; <c_1; \dots ; c_n>)$$

in which *l* is the label of the group, automatically generated by function *SynthLabel*, and with $<c_1; \dots ; c_n>$ we denote the list of clusters. A special kind of group is the empty group, that is defined as $g_0 := (l; \varnothing)$. This group can be explicitly generated by the user through the function *EmptyGroup* (see Definition 26).

A group *g* can contain a single cluster. Observe that a particular kind of cluster is the one that represents the ranked list obtained as the result of a query *q*; in this case, *c:label= q*.

The procedure that generates a group is initially activated by a search operator, named *CQuery*, that allows users to query a search service (e.g., *Google*, *Yahoo!*, *MSN Search*) and to cluster the results. We assume that a search service retrieves a maximum of *N* documents: in particular, in the case of *Yahoo! Search API*, *N* is upper limited to 100, while in the case of *MSN Live Search API*, *N* is upper limited to 50.

On this basis, for each retrieved document, the operator builds an item *r*, whose *irank* value depends on the position of the document in the result list: $r.irank=(N-Pos(d)+1)/N$, where $Pos(d)$ is the position of the document in the query result list. In this way, a document in the first positions has a rank *r.irank* very close to 1.

The ranked list obtained as a result by the search operator, is then clustered by applying the *Lingo* algorithm (Osinsli, 2003). Lingo is used to perform a flat crisp clustering of the query results on the basis of their snippets and titles. Once clusters are obtained, they are labeled. Finally also the groups are labeled to synthesize the most central contents retrieved by all their clusters. The labeling algorithm is hereafter described.

Labeling Algorithm

When a new cluster or a new group is generated, it is fundamental to be able to synthesize its main contents through a label. To this end, we designed and implemented a labeling algorithm that exploits the representation of documents in a vector space. The label of both a cluster and a group is built by function *SynthLabel* starting from the documents within. This guarantees that the associative property of the operators of the language generating groups and clusters is satisfied. In particular, the labeling algorithm performs the following steps.

- Extraction of the *M* most frequent terms from *title* and *snippet* of each document (*M* is an empirical value chosen to minimize the selection of terms with a low frequency, e.g., equal to one); filtering of terms that appeared in at least more than one document, and creation of the base of terms. In particular, title and snippet for documents are tokenized, deprived of stop-words and finally stemmed. Then, from the totality of the resulting terms, the first N terms with greatest frequency are extracted. The set of all extracted terms, excluding duplicates and those appearing in several documents, originates the complete base of terms where the vectors are represented.

- Definition of the documents vectors with respect to the base of terms. Each vector is defined by n components, where n is the term space size. The value of each vector component is the number of occurrences of the corresponding term within the *title* plus *snippet*.
- Identification of the *centroid* vector of the cluster, also called the *average vector of the set of documents*. The centroid vector, defined as the average of all the vectors of the documents belonging to the cluster or group, identifies the typical concepts of the cluster (or group); for this reason, it can be used as a prototype vector to identify a meaningful label.
- Identification of the vector associated with the document (or a cluster) closest to the centroid vector, using the cosine similarity measure.

For each document (cluster) vector, the value of cosine similarity with respect to the centroid vector is evaluated. The vector obtaining the greatest value of similarity will be the candidate for the definition of the label. In fact, the label is defined as the corresponding document title (resp. cluster label).

Basic Operations

In order to define the operators and the functions that constitute the proposed language, it is necessary to define some basic operations on sets of ranked items and on cluster labels.

The basic operations that we are going to define work on two input sets of ranked items R_1 and R_2 and generate a new set of ranked items R'.

Definition 4: Ranked Intersection

The operation *RIntersect*, denoted as $\cap^R$, performs the intersection of two sets of ranked items. R' contains all ranked items r' such that there are two ranked items $r_1 \in R_1$ and $r_2 \in R_2$ which refer to the same *uri*. The *irank* of r' is defined as the minimum *irank* value of r_1 and r_2.

Formally: $r' \in R'$, if and only if there exists $r_1 \in R_1$ and $r_2 \in R_2$ such that:

$r'.uri = r_1.uri = r_2.uri$ then

$r'.title = Comb(r_1.title, r_2.title, r_1.irank, r_2.irank, \cap^R)$;

$r'.snippet = Comb(r_1.snippet, r_2.snippet, r_1.irank, r_2.irank, \cap^R)$;

$r'.irank = min(r_1.irank, r_2.irank)$.

$r'.irank$ is the common level of relevance of both the retrieved items in the web searches from which R_1 and R_2 are obtained. This choice is in accordance with the interpretation of the sets of ranked items R_1 and R_2 as fuzzy sets of items, in which the *irank* of an item is its membership degree. The intersection of two fuzzy sets generates a fuzzy set in which the membership degree of an item is the minimum of the original membership degrees $r_1.irank$ and $r_2.irank$ (Dubois and Prade, 1988). In the case of $\cap^R$, function

Comb selects between the two input strings, the one with lowest *irank* value.

Definition 5: Ranked Union

The operation *RUnion*, denoted as $\cup^R$, performs the union of two sets of ranked items. R' contains all ranked items r' such that there is a ranked item $r_1 \in R_1$ (resp. $r_2 \in R_2$) such that r_1 (resp. r_2) refers to the same *uri*.

Formally: $r' \in R'$, if and only if one of the two following situations occurs.

1) If there exists $r_1 \in R_1$ (respectively exists $r_2 \in R_2$) with $r'.uri = r_1.uri$ ($r'.uri = r_2.uri$), and there not exists $r_2 \in R_2$ (respectively there not exists $r_1 \in R_1$) with $r'.uri = r_2.uri$ ($r'.uri = r_1.uri$), then $r' = r_1$ ($r' = r_2$ in the dual case).

2) If there exist $r_1 \in R_1$ and $r_2 \in R_2$ such that: $r'.uri = r_1.uri = r_2.uri$ then

$r'.title = Comb(r_1.title, r_2.title, r_1.irank, r_2.irank, \cup^R);$

$r'.snippet = Comb(r_1.snippet, r_2.snippet, r_1.irank, r_2.irank, \cup^R);$

$r'.irank = max(r_1.irank, r_2.irank).$

Differently from the case of $\cap^R$, the *irank* of a ranked item r' in the result of $\cup^R$ is the maximum of *irank* values of items $r_1 \in R_1$ 1 and $r_2 \in R_2$, because it represents the best level of relevance obtained by the retrieved items in both the web searches. This is also consistent with the definition of union of fuzzy sets by interpreting the *irank* as the membership degree (Dubois and Prade, 1988). Consistently with this fuzzy set interpretation, in this case function *Comb* selects between the two input strings, the one with greatest *irank* value.

Notice that it may occur that several ranked items get the same *irank* value in the generated cluster. This is not regarded as a problem since this situation indicates that the corresponding items belong to the cluster with the same degree.

Properties. The *associative, commutative, monotonicity and idempotency* properties hold for ranked intersection and ranked union, since they are the intersection and union operations between fuzzy sets based on the min and the max.

The cluster label is generated by function *SynthLabel(c.items)* described above.

Group Operators

In this paragraph, we define the algebra for groups of clusters by defining the group operators.

The first operation that a user may wish to perform is to search information by submitting a query to one or more search engines. To this end the following operator is provided.

Definition 6: CQuery

The *CQuery* operator allows to submit a query to a given search service and cluster the results. It is responsible for the start up of the process supported by the proposed language. It is defined as

Figure 2. Clusters selection

g1: Google – "Napa Valley"
cl.1: Wine Wineries
cl.2: Travel Guide

g2: Yahoo! – "Napa Valley"
cl.1: Wine tasting and Wineries
cl.3: Plan Your Travel Vacation

g3: MSN Live Search – "Napa Valley"
cl.1: Wine Wineries
cl.4: Napa Valley Hotel

$$CQuery: G \times S \times \{0,1\} \to G \quad CQuery(g, s, b) \to g'$$

where G is the set of groups, S is the set of names of available services, s is the service that evaluates the query $q=g.l$, b is a Boolean value, while g' is the resulting group of clusters whose label $g'.l=g.l$.

When the user wants to submit a query to a service for the first time (when no groups are available), the input group is an empty group generated by the function *EmptyGroup* (see paragraph "Functions on Groups").

In order to allow the user to submit a query to a search service without clustering the ranked list of documents, she/he can specify the value $b=0$ in input. In this case the resulting group g contains one single cluster, i.e., the trivial cluster that contains an item for each document retrieved by the search service. When $b=1$ the results are clustered and labeled by function *SynthLabel*.

Definition 7: Natural Rank

Each set of items R (and consequently, each cluster c) has a *Natural Rank* (denoted as $NRank(R)$) that is the average of ranks of items in the set. Formally

$$NRank(R) = (\sum_{r \in R} r.irank)/|R|$$

If we refer to a cluster c, the natural rank of c, that we denote simply by $NRank(c)$, is the natural rank of its items (i.e., $NRank(c.items)$).

Figure 3. Expanded clusters. Each cluster is expanded with the items in it; for each item, we report its uri, its rank r and (posQ: n) that is its position in the original ranked list retrieved by the query through the search service in the corresponding column.

g1: Google – "Napa Valley"
cl.1: Wine Wineries (0.9575)
u.1 (r: 1 – posQ: 1)
u.1 (r: 0.99 – posQ: 2)
u.1 (r: 0.94 – posQ: 7)
u.1 (r: 0.9 – posQ: 11)
cl.2: Travel Guide (0.945)
u.1 (r: 0.98 – posQ: 3)
u.1 (r: 0.97 – posQ: 4)
u.1 (r: 0.94 – posQ: 7)
u.1 (r: 0.89 – posQ: 12)

g2: Yahoo! – "Napa Valley"
cl.1: Wine tasting and Wineries (0.975)
u.1 (r: 1 – posQ: 1)
u.3 (r: 0.99 – posQ: 2)
u.10 (r: 0.96 – posQ: 5)
u.11 (r: 0.95 – posQ: 6)
cl.3: Plan Your Travel Vacation (0.925)
u.4 (r: 0.97 – posQ: 4)
u.15 (r: 0.94 – posQ: 7)
u.13 (r: 0.91 – posQ: 10)
u.14 (r: 0.88 – posQ: 13)

g3: MSN Live Search – "Napa Valley"
cl.1: Wine Wineries (0.94)
u.1 (r: 0.99 – posQ: 2)
u.1 (r: 0.98 – posQ: 3)
u.1 (r: 0.94 – posQ: 7)
u.1 (r: 0.91 – posQ: 10)
u.1 (r: 0.88 – posQ: 13)
cl.4: Napa Valley Hotel (0.92)
u.1 (r: 0.97 – posQ: 4)
u.1 (r: 0.93 – posQ: 8)
u.1 (r: 0.86 – posQ: 15)

This ranking method is the default one, that reflects the ordering of the items retrieved by the search services belonging to the cluster.

Example 2: let us observe the labels of the clusters in Figure 1, and let us assume that we want to plan a tour. We can easily identify which of them are most closely related to our needs for planning a tour. To this aim, we may want to select a subset of clusters. Therefore we introduce the following operator.

Definition 8: Cluster Selection

The *Cluster Selection* operator σ allows selecting the clusters in a group.

It is defined as:

$$\sigma \, (g, P) \rightarrow g'$$

where g is the group whose clusters must be selected, and P is a predicate on positions of clusters in the group, or on cluster labels; the selected clusters maintain the original order.

Returning to Example 2 and assuming that we are planning a wine-tour, the clusters about gastronomy, wine and touristic topics are the most interesting ones. The reduced set of clusters on which we focus is depicted in Figure 2. In Figure 3 we show the selected clusters with their contents.

On the other side, one may wish to cancel some retrieved clusters about uninteresting topics. To this end we introduce the following operator.

Definition 9: Cluster Deletion

The *Cluster Deletion* operator defined as:

$$\delta \, (g, P) \rightarrow g'$$

deletes clusters in a group g that satisfy predicate P. (thus, g' contains all clusters in g that do not satisfy P).

Since a group is an ordered list of clusters, one may desire to see the clusters in it ordered with respect to their *crank*, or may desire to change the default ordering by specifying preferences for a different ranking method. To this aim we provide the following operator.

Definition 10: Group Sorting

Since a group is an ordered list of clusters, group sorting operators must be provided. Shortly, operator $S(g;L) \rightarrow g'$ sorts clusters in g based on the ordered list of positions L; operator $\hat{S}(g) \rightarrow g'$ sorts clusters in g with respect to their *crank* in decreasing order.

The list of simple operators might be longer; however, they are not essential in this chapter, and for the sake of space we do not further discuss this topic.

Example 3: let us suppose that we want to filter out the most reliable documents within the clusters in Figure 3, we could identify the common documents retrieved by all the three search engines. To this aim we introduce the following operator.

Definition 11: Group Intersection

The first complex operator we introduce is the *Group Intersection*. Intuitively, it is a quite straightforward wish of users to intersect clusters in two groups, to find more specific clusters. The assumption is that the more search services retrieve a document, the more the document content is worth analyzing.

The *Group Intersection* operator $\cap$ is defined as:

$$\cap: G \times G \times T_\cap \rightarrow G \quad \cap(g_1, g_2, t) \rightarrow g'$$

where g_1 and g_2 are the groups of clusters to intersect, g' is the resulting group, t is the ranking method adopted to evaluate the *crank* of clusters in g'.

$t \in T_\cap = \{Natural, WNatural, Cardinality, Weighted\}$.

For each pair of clusters $c_1 \in g_1$, $c_2 \in g_2$, such that their intersection is not empty (i.e., $|c_1.items \cap^R c_2.items)| \neq 0$), there is a cluster $c' \in g'$. c' is defined as follows:

$c'.items = c_1.items \cap^R c_2.items$,

$c'.label = SynthLabel(c'.items)$.

If t is *Natural*, the *crank* value is obtained as:

$c'crank = NRank(c'.items)$.

If t is *WNatural*, the *crank* value is obtained as:

$c'crank = WNRank(c'.items, c_1.crank, c_2crank, g_1, g_2)$.

If t is *Cardinality*, the *crank* value of each resulting cluster is defined as: $c'crank = CardRank(c',g')$.
If t is *Weighted*, the *crank* value is obtained as:

$c'.crank = WminRank(c_1.items, c_1.crank, c_2.items, c_2crank, c'.items)$.

$g'.l = SynthLabel(C)$ with C the set of ranked clusters in g'.

The operator provides four distinct methods to compute the ranking of resulting clusters, each one reflecting a distinct semantics.

If t is *Natural*, the *crank* value of a cluster is obtained by computing its *Natural Rank* as defined in Definition 7. In this way, the relevance of a cluster is defined by the average of the ranks of the items common to both intersected clusters. Thus, this ranking criterion *reflects the relevance judgments of the search services* that first retrieved the items, and is independent of the properties of the original clusters to which they belong. Instead, if t is *WNatural*, the *crank* value of each resulting cluster is obtained by means of function *WNRank*, defined by the following definition.

Definition 12: Weighted Natural Rank

Each set of items R (and consequently, each cluster c) has a *Weighted Natural Rank* (denoted as $WNRank(R, C_1, C_2, g_1, g_2)$) that is the weighted average of ranks of items in the cluster, with weights C_1 and C_2 of *the original clusters*. Formally:

$$WNrank(R, C_1, C_2, g_1, g_2) = C_1 {}^*C_2\, NRank(R)/(MaxRank(g_1) * MaxRank(g_2))$$

where function *MaxRank* is defined as $MaxRank(g) = max\ \{c.crank \mid c \in g\}$

This ranking method reflects the ordering of the items retrieved by the search services belonging to the cluster by also taking into account the relevance, i.e., quality or reliability, of the cluster determined by a previous search.

Instead, if t is *Cardinality*, the *crank* value of each resulting cluster is obtained by means of function *CardRank*, defined by the following definition.

Definition 13: Cardinality Rank

Given the group g' obtained by intersecting two groups, the *Cardinality Rank* of each cluster c' is the ratio between the cardinality of c' and the maximum cardinality of the clusters in g':

$$CardRank(c',g')=|c'.items|/max_{c \in g'}|c|.$$

The *cardinality rank* determines the relevance of clusters, locally within the group: the largest cluster has *crank* equals to 1, while the others have a smaller value: it determines the rank of the cluster in the group based on its cardinality, i.e., the number of items it contains. This can be useful when one is interested in analyzing first big sets of documents about a relevant topic, giving higher importance to clusters that are larger than the others in the same group. The semantics of this ranking criterion is to favor, in the first positions of the generated group, the most exhaustive clusters, i.e., the most populous ones, which are likely to bear much information. This ranking can be useful in the case of a surveyor, who wants to retrieve as much as possible information on the interesting contents, and that is, at the same time, recommended by all the search services, i.e., anything that is worth analyzing. The focus of the use of the group intersection operator with the cardinality rank option is to perform a *quality survey* on a topic.

Finally, if t is *Weighted*, the *crank* value is obtained by means of function *WMinRank*, defined in the following definition.

Definition 14: Weighted Minimum Rank

Given a set of items R', obtained combining sets R_1 and R_2 of ranked items belonging to clusters with *crank* C_1 and C_2 respectively, its *Weighted Minimum Rank* (denoted as *WMinRank*) is the average of the *iranks* of items in R', weighted with respect to the *crank* of C_1 and C_2. Formally:

$$WMinRank(R_1,C_1,R_2,C_2,R')= \frac{\sum_{r\in R'} \min(\max((1-C_1),r_1.irank),\max((1-C_2),r_2.irank))}{|R'|}$$

Where $r_1 \in R_1$ and $r_2 \in R_2$ are the original items describing the same document represented by r' with $r'.uri= r_1.uri=r_2.uri$). We assume $r_1.rank$=0 ($r_2.rank$=0) if there is not an item $=r_1\in R_1$ ($r_2\in R_2$) with $r'.uri = r_1.uri$ ($r'.uri= r_2.uri$).

By choosing this ranking method, one is willing to apply a *weighted ranking method* that reflects a twofold criteria: it determines the rank not only based on the natural ranks of items, but also on the basis of the *cranks* C_1 and C_2 of the incoming clusters. This way, one wants to take into account the search engines votes of the items, and at the same time wants to weight these contributions with respect to the relevance of the original clusters to which they belong. This means that one is willing to consider, as indications of relevance of the cluster contents (that can be interpreted as either reliability or quality), the ranking C_1 and C_2 determined by the application of the combination operations that produced the clusters c_1 and c_2. The final rank reflects the semantics of the intersection between fuzzy sets of items r with membership degrees $r.irank$ having distinct priorities (C_1 and C_2) (Yager, 1987)

In fact, the reader can notice that the *irank* value of the two input items is weighted with the one complement of the *crank* value of the cluster. Consequently, the *irank* of items in the cluster with greatest priority, i.e., with greatest ranked cluster (cluster in the top position of the group) are more likely to contribute to the weighted rank of the intersection. This definition is in accordance with the goal of being cautious in determining the rank of an item common to the original clusters since we favor the minimum *irank* of the most relevant, i.e., reliable or authoritative, cluster.

Properties. The *associative* property holds for the *Group Intersection Operator*, provided that the same ranking method is chosen for all the occurrences of the group intersection operator in the expression. The *commutative* property holds as well, since, it holds for ranked intersection.

Returning to the example 3, in order to filter out the most reliable documents by all the three search engines in Figure 3 we apply the operators reported in the headings of groups depicted in Figure 4. Consider groups g_4 and g_5: first of all, we intersect g_1 and g_2, obtaining group g_4; then, we further intersect g_4 with g_3, obtaining group g_5. The obtained clusters in g_5 are the intersection of c_1=*Wine Wineries* and c_4=*Travel Guide* from g_1, of c_1=*Wine Tasting and Wineries* and c_3=*Plan your Travel Vacation* from g_2, of c_1=*Wine Wineries* and c_4=*Napa Valley Hotel* from g_3. Since the intersection is an associative operation, we can write the expression to obtain g_5 in a different way. This is done to obtain groups g_6 and g_7, depicted in Figure 4. Looking at groups g_5 and g_7, the reader can see that they are identical, apart for the expressions that generated them. For this reason, cluster cl.1 in g_5 and cluster cl.1 in g_7 have the same label $label_{5,1}$.

After having generated several groups of results, one may desire to explore their implicit correlations, and unify those clusters that share some common documents in order to reduce the redundancy of having the same documents in distinct clusters, and at the same time to eliminate the clusters that do not share anything with other clusters, i.e., that are uncorrelated. To this aim the following operator can be applied.

Definition 15: Group Join

The second complex operator we introduce is the *Group Join* operator.

Figure 4. Group Intersection. In the expressions, t denotes a generic ranking method

g_4: $\cap(g_1, g_2, t)$
cl.1: label $_{4,1}$ (NRank= 0.995; WMinRank = 0.977; CardRank=1)   u.1 (r:1); u3 (r:0.99)
cl.2: label $_{4,2}$ (NRank= 0.9; WMinRank = 0.872; CardRank=0.5)   u.4 (r:0.9)

g_5: $\cap(g_4, g_3, t)$ = ($\cap$ ($\cap(g_1, g_2, t)$, g_3, t)
cl.1: label $_{5,1}$ (NRank= 0.985; WMinRank = 0.930; CardRank=1)   u.1 (r:0.98); u3 (r:0.99)

g_6: $\cap(g_2, g_3, t)$
cl.1: label $_{6,1}$ (NRank= 0.985; WMinRank = 0.950; CardRank=1)   u.1 (r:0.98); u3 (r:0.99)
cl.2: label $_{6,2}$ (NRank= 0.86; WMinRank = 0.811; CardRank=0.5)   u.10 (r:0.86)

g_7: $\cap(g_1, g_6, t)$ = $\cap($ g_1,$\cap(g_2, g_3, t)$, t)
cl.1: label $_{5,1}$ (NRank= 0.985; WMinRank = 0.930; CardRank=1)   u.1 (r:0.98); u3 (r:0.99)

The *Group Join* operator $\triangleright\triangleleft$ is defined as:

$$\triangleright\triangleleft: \quad G\times \quad G\times \quad T_{\triangleright\triangleleft} \quad \to G \qquad \triangleright\triangleleft (g_1, g_2, t) \to g'$$

where g_1 and g_2 are the groups of clusters to join, g' is the resulting group. t is the ranking method adopted to evaluate the *crank* of clusters in g'.

$t\in T\triangleright\triangleleft$ = {*Natural, WNatural, Cardinality, Weighted, Correlation, Expansion, Weighted-Correlation, Weighted-Expansion*}.

For each pair of clusters $c_1 \in g_1$, $c_2 \in g_2$, such that their intersection is not empty (i.e., $|c_1.items \cap^R c_2.items)|\neq0$), there is a cluster $c'\in g'$ defined as follows:

$c'.items = c_1.items \cup^R c_2.items$,

$c'.label=SynthLabel(c'.items)$.

If t is *Natural, WNatural* or *Weighted,* or *Correlation,* or *Expansion,* or *Weighted-Correlation,* or *Weighted-Expansion, c'.crank* is respectively obtained as:

$c'.crank=NRank(c'.items)$,

$c'.crank=WNRank(c'.itemsm\ c_1.crank\ c_2.crank,\ g_1,\ g_2)$,

$c'.crank= WMaxRank(c_1.items,\ c_1.crank,\ c_2.items,\ c_2.crank,\ c'.items)$

$c'.crank = CRank(c_1.items,\ c_2.items)$

$c'.crank = ERank(c_1.items,\ c_2.items)$

c'.crank = *WCRank(c$_1$.items, c$_1$.crank, c$_2$.items, c$_2$.crank)*

c'.crank = *WERank(c$_1$.items, c$_1$.crank, c$_2$.items, c$_2$.crank)*

Finally, *g'.l* = *SynthLabel(C)* with C set of ranked clusters in *g'*.

The Group Join operator can be used to explicit indirect correlations between the topics represented by the clusters in the two groups. The basic idea underlying its definition is that if two clusters overlap, i.e., have some common items, it means that the contents of these items are related with both topics represented by the clusters. This may hint the existence of an implicit relationship between the two topics. By assuming that topics can be organized into a hierarchy, by grouping the two overlapping clusters into a single one, *we may reveal the more general topic representing the whole content of the new cluster*, which subsumes, as most specific topics, those of the original clusters.

As for group intersection, the natural rank is the basic rank value of a cluster. An alternative is to compute the rank in a weighted way; in this case we define the *WmaxRank* criterion, since we want to give more chance in determining the final rank to the items belonging to the highest weighted cluster.

Definition 16: Weighted Maximum Rank

Given a cluster *c'*, obtained by combining clusters c_1 and c_2, its *Weighted Maximum Rank* is defined as

$$WMaxRank(R_1,C_1,R_2,C_2, R') = \frac{\left(\sum_{r \in R'} \frac{\max(C_1 * r_1.irank, C_2 * r_2.irank)}{\max(C_1,C_2)} \right)}{|R'|}$$

where $r_1 \in R_1$ and $r_2 \in R_2$ are ranked items of clusters c_1 and c_2, respectively.

By choosing this ranking method one is willing to apply a *weighted ranking method* that reflects a twofold criteria: it determines the rank not only based on the natural ranks of items, but also on the basis of the ranks C_1 and C_2 of the incoming clusters, i.e, their assumed reliability or quality. This way, one wants to take into account the search engines votes of the items, and at the same time wants to weight these contributions with respect to the relevance C_1 and C_2, of the original clusters to which they belong. The final rank reflects the semantics of the union of fuzzy sets of items *r* with membership degrees *r.irank*, having distinct priorities (C_1 and C_2) (Bookstein, 1980). In fact, the reader can notice that the *irank* value of the two input items is weighted with the *crank* value of the cluster. Consequently, the *irank* of items in the cluster with greatest priority, i.e., with greatest ranked cluster (cluster in the top position of the group) are more likely to contribute to the weighted rank of the union. This definition is in accordance with the goal of being optimistic in determining the rank of an item belonging at least to one of the original clusters, since we favor the maximum *irank* of the most relevant (i.e., reliable or authoritative) cluster.

A third alternative to compute the ranking of clusters after a join is the *Correlation Rank*, that estimates the degree of correlation of the two incoming clusters.

Definition 17: Correlation Rank

Given two sets of ranked items R_1 and R_2 of clusters c_1 and c_2, their *Correlation Rank* (shortly, *CRank*) is the overlapping value between R_1 and R_2. Formally, we define the *CRank* as the fuzzy Jaccard coefficient (Dubois & Prade, 1982) between two clusters c_1 and c_2, regarded as fuzzy sets of items, with *irank* their membership values:

$$CRank(R_1, R_2) = \frac{\left|R_1 \cap^R R_2\right|}{\left|R_1 \cup^R R_2\right|} = \frac{\sum_{r_1,r_2 \in I, r_1.uri = r_2.uri} \min(r_1.irank, r_2.irank)}{\sum_{r_1,r_2 \in U} \max(r_1.irank, r_2.irank)}$$

where $I = R_1 \cap^R R_2$ and $U = R_1 \cup^R R_2$, $r_1 \in R_1$ and $r_2 \in R_2$; the items $r_1 \in R_1$ and $r_2 \in R_2$ belonging to I with $r_1.uri = r_2.uri$ describe the same document; we assume $r_1.irank = 0$ ($r_2.irank = 0$) if there is not an item $r_1 \in R_1$ ($r_2 \in R_2$). Note that the membership degree, i.e., *irank*, of an item r belonging to the intersection $R_1 \cap^R R_2$ is computed as the minimum between the *irank* values of the document and the two clusters of belonging, respectively, while that of the union $R_1 \cup^R R_2$ is the maximum.

This ranking method computes a degree of overlapping of the clusters c_1 and c_2, that is interpreted as a correlation measure of the contents of the two clusters. The properties of this measure allow deriving some interesting properties of the relationships between the two clusters and the generated cluster:

- the greater is the membership value *irank* of an item to a cluster, the more is the contribution of the item to determine the degree of overlapping.
- since the overlapping measure is symmetric, it establishes a bi-directional relationships between the topics of the clusters;
- *CRank* assumes the maximum value of one only when R_1 and R_2 contain exactly the same items, with the same *irank* values; this allows to state than when $CRank(R_1,R_2)=1$ the two clusters c_1 and c_2 deal with the same topic;
- *CRank* assumes the minimum value of zero only when R_1 and R_2 do not share any items; in this case when $CRank(R_1,R_2)=0$ the two clusters c_1 and c_2 deal with distinct topics;
- finally, the more the clusters are overlapped, the more they share some contents, i.e., the more related they are. If $CRank(R_1,R_2)>0.5$ it means that they share more with respect to what they do not share, and vice versa. We can assume that the topics of the two clusters c_1 and c_2 are strictly related if their $CRank(R_1,R_2) > 0.5$, while they are weakly related when $0<CRank(R_1,R_2)\leq0.5$. In the case in which $CRank(R_1,R_2)>0.5$, by joining the two clusters c_1 and c_2 to generate a cluster c' we can guess that two specific and related topics are subsumed into a more general topic, that is still specific. In particular, the degree of specificity of the topic of c' is likely to increase with the increase of $CRank(R_1,R_2)$ to one. In this case, we can expect that the shared items of c_1 and c_2 will prevalently determine the label of the generated cluster c'. Thus the generated label should not convey much novelty with respect to the labels of c_1 and c_2. On the other side, when $0<CRank(R_1,R_2)\leq0.5$, by joining the two clusters c_1 and c_2 we generate a cluster c' representing a very broad topic, since in this case the not shared items prevail over the shared ones. In this case, we can expect that the label of c' is more heavily determined by the non-common items; consequently, the new label should convey much novelty with respect to the original labels of c_1 and c_2.

A fourth alternative to compute the ranking of a cluster after a join, is the *Expansion Rank*.

Definition 18: Expansion Rank

Given two sets of ranked items R_1 and R_2, their *Expansion Rank* (shortly, *ERank*) is the complementary value of their *CRank*. Formally:

$$ERank(R_1, R_2) = 1 - \frac{\left| R_1 \cap^R R_2 \right|}{\left| R_1 \cup^R R_2 \right|} = 1 - \frac{\sum\limits_{r_1, r_2 \in I, r_1.uri = r_2.uri} \min(r_1.irank, r_2.irank)}{\sum\limits_{r_1, r_2 \in U} \max(r_1.irank, r_2.irank)}$$

By specifying this ranking option, one wants to favor, in the top positions, the generated clusters c' that convey much novelty with respect to the original weakly related clusters c_1 and c_2. The lesser the two topics (represented by the original clusters) are related, the greater the novelty of joined cluster. This hints to the fact that the cluster with high novelty rank can represent a very general topic.

Another alternative to compute the ranking of clusters after a join is to weight the correlation rank.

Definition 19: Weighted Correlation Rank

Given two sets of ranked items R_1 and R_2, their *Weighted-Correlation Rank* (shortly, *WCRank*) is defined as the weighted *CRank* of the two fuzzy sets R_1 and R_2.

Formally:

$$WCRank(R_1, C_1, R_2, C_2) = \frac{\sum\limits_{r_1.uri = r_2.uri, r_1, r_2 \in I} \min(C_1 * r_1.irank, C_2 * r_2.irank)}{\sum\limits_{r_1, r_2 \in U} \max(C_1 * r_1.irank, C_2 * r_2.irank)} =$$

where $I = R_1 \cap^R R_2$ and $U = R_1 \cup^R R_2$, $r_1 \in R_1$, $r_2 \in R_2$ and C_1 and C_2 are the *crank* of the clusters c_1 and c_2, respectively; the items $r_1 \in R_1$ and $r_2 \in R_2$ belonging to I with $r_1.uri = r_2.uri$ describe the same document; we assume $r_1.irank = 0$ ($r_2.irank = 0$) if there is not an item $r_1 \in R_1$ ($r_2 \in R_2$).

With this ranking criterion, we want to penalize more heavily the contributions of the items belonging to the least relevant clusters. The idea is that the relevance of clusters, intended as either reliability or quality, is propagated to their items when computing their overlapping degree. The *crank* of the clusters are used to decrease the membership degrees of the items so that the lower the *crank* the greater the reduction that is applied to the membership value of the item. This way, the overlapping degree is more heavily determined by the items belonging to the most relevant clusters. By applying this ranking method, one expects to rank, in top positions, clusters c' derived by the joining of relevant and highly correlated original clusters c_1 and c_2.

Finally, it is possible to choose the *Weighted Expansion Rank*.

Definition 20: Weighted Expansion Rank

Given two sets of ranked items R_1 and R_2, their *Weighted Expansion Rank* (shortly *WERank*) is the complement of the weighted correlation rank.

$$WERank(R_1, C_1, R_2, C_2) = 1 - \frac{\sum\limits_{r_1.uri=r_2.uri, r_1, r_2 \in I} \min((1 - C_1) * r_1.irank, (1 - C_2) * r_2.irank)}{\sum\limits_{r_1, r_2 \in U} \max((1 - C_1) * r_1.irank, (1 - C_2) * r_2.irank)}$$

Its semantics is that of the expansion rank in which we take into account that the contributions of the items (i.e., their ranking values) to the overlapping degree is modified by the relevance of the cluster they come from. By applying this ranking method, one expects to rank, in top positions, clusters c' obtained by joining relevant and weakly correlated clusters c_1 and c_2. In this case, the contributions of the items to the overlapping degree are more penalized if they belong to the most relevant clusters. Thus, the most relevant clusters contribute more heavily to determine the novelty *WErank* of the generated cluster.

Properties. The *associative* property holds for the *Group Join Operator*, provided that the same ranking method is chosen for all the occurrences of the group join operator in the expression. The *commutative* property holds as well, since, it holds for ranked union.

Example 4: The application of the group join operator to our running example is shown in Figure 5. The unified clusters that group documents common to the original clusters are about both topics (such as *Wine Wineries* and *Wine Tasting and Wineries*), and at the same time, include also not common documents, which are apparently unrelated. This is the case of clusters *Plan your Travel vacation* and *Wine Wineries* which both contain some documents, such as *Featured Wineries in Napa Valley - Plan your Wine Tasting Room Tour*. By joining these two clusters together, we generate a more populous cluster in which information about wineries and travel vacations are included. At this point, we could also sort the resulting clusters with respect to the degree of correlation (i.e., overlapping) between the two original clusters, to identify the most correlated topics. In this example, in the same result cluster there are docu-

Figure 5. Group Join. In the expressions, t denotes a generic ranking method

g_8: (g_1, g_2, t)
cl.1: label $_{8,1}$ (NRank= 0.968; WMaxRank = 0.965; Crank= 0.333; ERank= 0.667; WCRank=0.112; WERank=0.887; CardRank=0.857) u.1 (r: 1); u2 (r: 0.94); u3 (r: 0.99); u4 (r: 0.97) ; u10 (r: 0.96); u11 (r: 0.95)
cl.1: label $_{8,2}$ (NRank= 0.947; WMaxRank = 0.951; Crank= 0.143; ERank= 0.857; WCRank=0.019; WERank=0.981; CardRank=1) u.1 (r: 1); u2 (r: 0.94); u3 (r: 0.99); u4 (r: 0.97) ; u13 (r: 0.91); u14 (r: 0.88); u15(r: 0.94)

g_9: (g_8, g_3, t)
cl.1: label $_{9,1}$ (NRank= 0.96; WMaxRank = 0.941; Crank= 0.37; ERank= 0.62; WCRank=0.141; WERank=0.859; CardRank=1) u.1 (r: 1); u2 (r: 0.94); u3 (r: 0.99); u4 (r: 0.97) ; u6 (r: 0.97); u7 (r: 0.94); u10 (r: 0.96); u11 (r: 0.95)
cl.1: label $_{9,2}$ (NRank= 0.947; WMaxRank = 0.951; Crank= 0.143; ERank= 0.857; WCRank=0.019; WERank=0.981; CardRank=1) u.1 (r: 1); u2 (r: 0.94); u3 (r: 0.99); u4 (r: 0.97) ; u5 (r: 0.98); u8 (r: 0.93); u10 (r: 0.96); u11 (r: 0.95)

ments both concerning only *Wineries* or only *Travel Vacation,* and containing both. We can so expand the intersection between the two original clusters with documents correlated with them.

Observing the various ranks reported in Figure 5 for clusters, it is possible to see that different ranking methods give a different relevance to clusters.

For example, in group g_8, the weighted rank is similar for both the clusters, but the correlation rank is quite different: in fact, cluster cl.1 has *CRank*=0.333, while cluster cl.2 has *CRank*=0.143; this means that clusters joined together to obtain cl.2 were less correlated than the ones joined to form cl.1. This result is coherent with the expansion rank: *ERank*=0.857 for cluster cl.2, that is much higher than the expansion rank for cluster cl.1.

If we observe the basic weighted rank (*WMaxRank*), it is evident that its values are coherent with respect to the correlation rank; however, the distance between the two values is much smaller than the distance between the values of the correlation rank; this is due to the fact that the *crank* values of original clusters influence the final rank.

Finally, we can notice that sorting clusters in g_8 based on cardinality ranking and (weighted) expansion ranking, results in clusters sorted in a different order than the one depicted in the figure.

Now, let us consider the need to refine the clusters in a group on the basis of the clusters belonging to another reference group. This my be useful in the case in which one has retrieved information about a topic and wants to refine this, on the basis of the results retrieved with respect to another topic. For example, one has retrieved the keynote comments on *Napa Valley Wineries* and wants to refine the results of *Napa Valley Restaurants*. To this aim one can use the following operator.

Definition 21: Group Refinement

The *Group Refinement* operator $\triangleright$ is defined as:

$$\triangleright: G \times G \times T_{\triangleright} \to G \qquad \triangleright (g_1, g_2, t) \to g'$$

where g_1 is the group to refine on the basis of g_2, g' is the resulting group. t is the ranking method adopted to evaluate the *crank* of clusters in g'.

$$t \in T_{\triangleright} = \{ \text{Natural, WNatural, } Cardinality, Refinement\}$$

The use of this operator is to refine the clusters in a group, based on clusters in another group.

For each cluster $c_k \in g_1$, for each cluster $c_i \in g_2$, $I_i = c_k.items \cap^R \overline{c_i.items}$.
If at least one $I_i \neq \varnothing$, there is a cluster $c' \in g'$ defined as follows:

$$c'.items = \bigcup^R_{i=1,G} I_i$$

$c'.label=SynthLabel(c'.items)$, where $G = |g_2|$.

While the *group join* operator generates a cluster representing a more general topic than the topics in both the original clusters, the *refinement operator* can be regarded as generating clusters specializing the topics of the clusters in the first group on the basis of the topics of any cluster in the second group. The idea underlying this operator is that we want to collect, in a unique cluster, the items that belong to both a cluster $c_k \in g_1$ and any of the clusters in the second group g_2. This way, by eliminating some items from c_k we generate a cluster representing a more specific topic with respect to c_k, but not necessarily more specific with respect to the clusters of the second group. The clusters of the second group act then as a filter on the contents of each cluster in the first group.

If *t* is *Natural or WNatural* the *crank* value is obtained by applying Definitions 7 and 8:

If *t* is *Cardinality*, the *crank* value of each resulting cluster (called *Cardinality Rank*). is defined as in Definition 13.

Definition 22: Refinement Rank

If *t* is *Refinement*, the *crank* value of a cluster *c'*, generated from a cluster $c_k \in g_1$ (called *Refinement Ranking*) and the clusters in the second group g_2 is obtained as:

$$c'.crank = \frac{|c'.items|}{|c_k.items|}.$$

This is indeed an inclusion degree of the cluster c_k in the resulting cluster *c'*, i.e., in any of the clusters of g_2. and it expresses how much original contents of c_k is kept in the refinement based on g_2.

When using this ranking method, one is willing to favor, in top positions, the clusters *c'* generated by a cluster c_k of g_1 that has maintained in *c'* as much as possible all its original items. This ranking method satisfies some interesting properties:

When *c'.crank*=1 it means that the whole content of c_k is kept in the resulting cluster *c'*.

When *c'.crank*=0 it means that the result is empty, then no item of c_k is contained in any cluster of g_2. Intermediate values of *c'.crank* mean that only some items of c_k are present in *c'*. Notice that the contrary is not generally true since this measure is not symmetric.

Example 5: Suppose that, by analyzing the results in Figure 5, we discover that no cluster has been retrieved concerning restaurants (i.e., with the word *Restaurant* in the label). We could take a remedy by submitting the new query "Napa Valley Restaurants" to *Yahoo!*; the resulting clusters shown in Figure 6 (strongly focused on restaurants) are used to filter out sub-clusters of documents concerning restaurants from within clusters in the previous lists (we *refine* clusters in the first list).

During a search session in which the user has submitted several queries to the search services and has applied several operators to manipulate the retrieved results, one may have generated too many groups and too many clusters, and may wish to reduce their number. To this aim the following two operators can be applied.

Definition 23: Group Union

The *group union* operator $c_1 \cup c_2 = c'$ generates *c'* in such a way it contains all clusters in c_1 and all clusters in c_2. This operator can be useful during long interactive search and processing sessions, when too many groups have been generated. It makes it possible to collect together two or more groups in a single group.

Figure 6. Group Refinement. In the expression labeling the group on the right, t denotes a generic ranking method

g_{10}: Yahoo! – "Napa Valley Restaurants"
cl.1: Restaurants Visitors Info (0.955)
u.16 (r: 1 – posQ: 1)
u.17 (r: 0.97 – posQ: 4)
u.18 (r: 0.95 – posQ: 6)
u.4 (r: 0.9 – posQ: 11)
cl.2: Travel Guide (0.95)
u.19 (r: 0.98 – posQ: 3)
u.1 (r: 0.96 – posQ: 5)
u.7 (r: 0.91 – posQ: 10)
cl.3: Seafood Resaurants in Napa Valley (0.913)
u.21 (r: 0.99 – posQ: 2)
u.22 (r: 0.93 – posQ: 8)
u.23 (r: 0.89 – posQ: 12)
u.24 (r: 0.84 – posQ: 17)

g_{11}: g_9 g_{10}
cl.1: label $_{11,1}$ (NRank= 0.97; RefRank = 0.375; CardRank=1)   u.1 (r: 1); u4 (r: 0.97) ; u7 (r: 0.94)
cl.3: label $_{11,2}$ (NRank= 0.985; RefRank = 0.25; CardRank=0.667)   u.1 (r: 1); u4 (r: 0.97)

Definition 24: Group Coalescing

The *group coalescing* operator $\oplus(c)=c'$ generates c' in such a way that c' contains only one cluster, obtained by applying the ranked union operation to all clusters in c.

This operator may be necessary in long interactive processing sessions, when too many clusters have been generated in a group. It makes it possible to fuse all clusters in a group into one global cluster.

After complex transformations, it might be necessary to reapply the clustering method to a group. In fact, re-clustering documents in a group may let new and unexpected semantic information emerge.

Definition 25: Reclustering

The *Reclustering* Operator *Cluster*$(c)=c'$ performs the ranked union of all clusters in c, and generates c' in such a way that it contains all the clusters obtained by clustering all ranked documents.

Closure Property of Group Operators: The data model and the group operators were designed in such a way the *Closure Property* holds: operators are defined on groups and generate groups.

Functions on Groups

The group operators so far described allows to conduct a powerful exploratory activity: by combining groups, the user can discover useful information and may be inspired for new searches; the results of these new searches might be combined with previously computed groups, and so on. The distinct ranking methods let users re-arrange the contents of the groups so as to make more evident some properties of the clusters that can be of interest for a search.

However, being an exploratory activity, it might be useful to evaluate the results of group operations without actually building and storing a new group. If the user were provided with functions that returns a quantitative summary of what would be obtained by applying an operator on already computed groups, the user could decide whether to actually apply a group operator to obtain a new group.

For this reason, the proposed language provides some useful evaluation functions that we introduce in this sub-paragraph.

Definition 26: *EmptyGroup* Function

The first function that we need to define is the *EmptyGroup* function, that makes it possible to generate an empty group with a desired label *l*. It is defined as:

$EmptyGroup(l) \rightarrow g_0$ where $g_0 = (l, \varnothing)$

This function is necessary to generate the input group for the *CQuery* operator when the user wants to submit a query for the first time. This allows to archive the closure of the whole set of group operators.

Definition 27: Selection Function

Selection function, σ_ε, evaluates the effect of a cluster selection. It is defined as:

$\sigma_\varepsilon, (g, P) \rightarrow (nc, mincard, maxcard, mincrank, maxcrank)$

where *g* is the group to which to apply the selection, and *P* is the selection predicate. The function produces a 5-tuple with the following fields: *nc* is the number of clusters that would be selected, *mincard* and *maxcard* are, respectively, the minimum and maximum cardinality of clusters that would be selected, while *mincrank* and *maxcrank* are, respectively, their minimum and maximum *crank* values.

Definition 28: Intersection, Join and Refinement functions

Three functions are defined, corresponding to the main group operators: $\cap_\varepsilon$ evaluates intersection, $\bowtie_\varepsilon$ evaluates join, $\rhd_\varepsilon$ evaluates refinement.

$\cap_\varepsilon (g_1, g_2, t) \rightarrow (nc, mincard, maxcard, mincrank, maxcrank)$

$\bowtie_\varepsilon (g_1, g_2, t) \rightarrow (nc, mincard, maxcard, mincrank, maxcrank)$

$\rhd_\varepsilon (g_1, g_2, t) \rightarrow (nc, mincard, maxcard, mincrank, maxcrank)$

where g_1 and g_2 are the groups of clusters to intersect (resp. join or refine). *t* is the ranking method adopted to evaluate the *crank* of clusters that would be produced: for $\cap_\varepsilon$ it is chosen among the methods *Natural, WNatural, Weighted* and *Cardinality*; for $\bowtie_\varepsilon$, it is chosen among the methods *Natural, WNatural, Weighted, Correlation, Expansion, Weighted-Correlation, Weighted-Expansion* and *Cardinality*; for $\rhd_\varepsilon$, it is chosen among the methods *Natural, WNatural, Refinement* and *Cardinality*.

As for selection evaluation, the functions produces a 5-tuple with the previously defined fields.

Example 6: An example of application of these functions could be proposed on each of the operators previously described. For the group intersection, for example, whose results are represented in Figure

4, we may want to know if it is convenient (in terms of obtained results) to execute the operation g_4: $g_1 \cap g_2$. To this aim, we can compute $\cap_\varepsilon(g_1, g_2, t)$ that will return, as a result,

(nc=2, mincard=1, maxcard=2, mincrank=0.8723, maxcrank=0.9771)=(2,1,2,0.8723,0.9771)

On the basis of this information, the user can see that only two clusters are retrieved containing a total of three documents with high minimum and maximum rank (in the range [0,1]). Thus it can be worth executing the intersection operator.

SCALABILITY ISSUES

In this paragraph we analyze the complexity of the operators of the proposed language and run some experiments in which we apply the operators to combine groups containing increasing number of clusters so as to evaluate the efficiency of the approach.

Computational Complexity

The operators previously defined are applied to pairs of groups and are executed in several subsequent steps. Thus, in order to study the computational complexity of the operators, it is necessary to study the computational complexity of the basic steps.

First of all, let us consider the ranked intersection and ranked union of two clusters c_1 and c_2. These operations can be implemented in a very efficient way. In fact, if we maintain the list of documents in a cluster ordered by document *uri*, ranked intersection and ranked union can be implemented on the basis of a merge operation, whose complexity is $O(|c_1|+|c_2|)$.

Let us consider now operators such as group intersections, group join and group refinement. These are binary operators that explore combinations of each cluster in the first operand with each cluster in the second operand. Thus, if with N_1 and N_2 we denote the number of clusters in the first and second group operand, respectively, the complexity of such operators is $O(N_1 \cdot N_2)$.

Consequently, if we denote with c the maximum cardinality of clusters and with $N=\max(N_1, N_2)$ the maximum number of clusters in the input groups, the final complexity of the main algorithm (intersection, join, refinement) is $O(c \cdot N^2)$.

Another step is the labeling algorithm applied to generate the clusters' and the groups' labels. We recall that the cluster labels are generated based on the snippets and the titles of their ranked items, i.e., short pieces of text, while the labels of the groups are generated from the analysis of the cluster labels. If we indicate by c the number of the items (i.e, either the number of ranked items in a cluster, or the number of clusters in a group), and with k the maximum number of the single terms either within the snippets plus titles, or within the cluster labels, the complexity of this labeling algorithm is determined by the following steps.

First we need to rank, in decreasing frequency, the $c \cdot k$ terms to select the m most frequent ones. This is performed in $O(c \cdot k \log (c \cdot k))$. Then, the vector base of the m dimensional space is built in which the ranked items (clusters) vectors are mapped: this has a complexity $O(c \cdot m \log (c \cdot m))$. Finally, the centroid vector is computed in $O(c \cdot m)$, and the title (or label) of closest element is chosen with a complexity $O(c)$.

The reader can assume that the labeling task is computationally expensive. Nevertheless this phase is not critical, as each element contains a limited number of words, since we consider titles and snippets, not the entire documents. Further the labeling is performed only for the generated clusters that do not grow quadratically. Consequently, as the reader can see in the experiments reported hereafter, the critical phase is the execution of the main algorithm (intersection, join).

Experiments

In order to evaluate the scalability of our proposal, we conducted a set of experiments. The experiments were performed on a PC powered by an Intel Pentium 4 641 3.2 GHZ processor, equipped with 1 GByte RAM (of type DDR2 PC2-4200 SYNCH DRAM NON-ECC), a 256 GByte Hard Disk (Serial ATA II). The installed operating system is Linux Fedora 6 Core Distribution (kernel version 2.6.20-1.2952.fc6). Java classes were compiled with JDK version 1.6.0 03. Classes were executed using the Java Runtime Environment JRE1.6.0 03.

We ran separately experiments on the intersection and join operators. We considered two sets of source groups, reported in Figure 7 and Figure 10. The first set is obtained by performing the following queries: "*London*" to Google, "*London*" to Yahoo, "*New York*" to Goggle, "*New York*" to Yahoo, "*Los Angeles*" to Yahoo. For each query, the first 100 ranked items are considered, and the clustering algorithm is applied. Finally, five groups are obtained: group g_1 contains clusters resulting from the first query; group g_3 unites clusters obtained by the first and the second query; group g_5 unites clusters obtained by the first, the second and the third query; group g_7 unites clusters obtained by all queries except the last one; group g_9 unites all clusters obtained by all the queries.

The groups reported in Figure 10 are obtained in the same way: groups g_2, g_4 g_6, g_8 and g_{10} unites the clusters obtained by queries "*London Hotels*" to Google, "*London Hotels*" to Yahoo, "*New York Hotels*" to Google, "*New York Hotels*" to Yahoo and "*Los Angeles Hotels*" to Yahoo.

Figure 8 reports the results of the first set of experiments. Each group reported in Figure 7 was intersected with itself. This way, it is possible to obtain a large number of clusters in the resulting groups. The table reports the execution times for the five experiments. In particular, we separately consider the *Data Loading* time, the time needed by the *main algorithm* (in this case, the intersection algorithm), the time needed for *labelling the group* (that analyzes all documents in the resulting clusters), the time for *sorting the group* and finally the time needed to *write the resulting XML document* that describes the

Figure 7. First set of input groups for operators. With (query, engine) we denote that the specified query is submitted to the specified engine, taking the first 100 documents. Groups from g3 to g9 are obtained by uniting the clusters obtained for each single query.

Group	Query	# Documents	# Clusters
g_1	London (Google)	100	23
g_3	(London, Google) + (London, Yahho)	200	44
g_5	(London, Google) + (London, Yahho) + (New York, Google)	300	67
g_7	(London, Google) + (London, Yahho) + (New York, Google) + (New York, Yahho)	400	89
g_9	(London, Google) + (London, Yahho) + (New York, Google) + (New York, Yahho) + (Los Angeles, Yahoo)	500	112

Figure 8. First experiments of application of the group intersection operator. Execution times are in milliseconds

	$g_1 \cap g_1$	$g_3 \cap g_3$	$g_5 \cap g_5$	$g_7 \cap g_7$	$g_9 \cap g_9$
Input Documents	100x 00	200x200	300x300	400x400	500x500
Input Clusters	23x23	44x44	67x67	89x89	112x112
Output Clusters	98	210	329	485	580
Data Loading	214	463	765	1131	1325
Main Algorithm	2093	7421	14455	28814	38527
Group Labeling	961	4313	13754	29424	43797
Group Sorting	326	732	1339	2324	2964
Writing XML File	146	349	543	1020	1100
Overall Process	3740	13278	30856	62713	87713

Figure 9. Chart of the experiments reported in Figure 8 of application of the group intersection. Execution times are in milliseconds

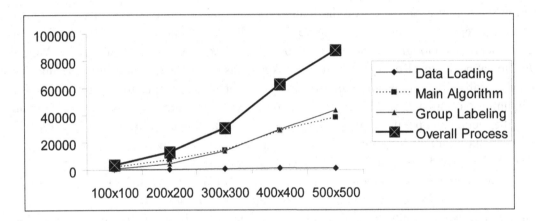

resulting group. Figure 9 shows a chart with the *overall execution time*, the *Data Loading* time, the *Main Algorithm* time and the *Group Labelling* time (the other items are negligible, in comparison).

Notice that, while the data loading time grows linearly, the other components of the implementation behaves in a quadratic way, thus meeting the considerations about complexity previously reported.

The reader can also observe that the overall execution time in the last case is still limited to one minute and a half, even though the large number of resulting clusters.

In the second sets of experiments performed on the intersection operator, groups g_1 were intersected with group g_2, group g_3 with group g_4, group g_5 with group g_6, group g_7 with group g_8 and group g_9 with group g_{10}. For each pair, groups are rather heterogeneous, so that the number of intersecting clusters is small, as the reader can see in Figure 10. Similarly to the previous experiment, Figure 12 shows the chart of the execution times reported in Figure 11.

The reader can see the behavior of the algorithm is still quadratic.

However, we must point out that the number of clusters actually intersecting, and thus generating a new cluster, are far less than the potential number indicated on the x-axis: in the case indicated by 500x500 documents on the x-axis which are grouped in 112 x 98 clusters, only 101 clusters are generated, and in the case of 400x400 documents partitioned into 89 x 76 clusters only 95 clusters are generated

Figure 10. Second set of input groups. With the pair (query, engine) we denote that the specified query is submitted to the specified engine, taking the first 100 documents. Groups from g43 to g10 are obtained by uniting the clusters obtained for each single query.

Group	Query	# Documents	# Clusters
g_2	(London Hotels,Google)	100	17
g_4	(London Hotels, Google) + (London Hotels, Yahho)	200	34
g_6	(London Hotels, Google) + (London Hotels, Yahho) + (New York Hotels, Google)	300	55
g_8	(London Hotels, Google) + (London Hotels, Yahho) + (New York Hotels, Google) + (New York Hotels, Yahho)	400	76
g_{10}	(London Hotels, Google) + (London Hotels, Yahho) + (New York Hotels, Google) + (New York Hotels, Yahho) + (Los Angeles Hotels, Yahoo)	500	98

Figure 11. Second experiments on application of the group intersection operator. Execution times are in milliseconds

	$g_1 \cap g_2$	$g_3 \cap g_4$	$g_5 \cap g_6$	$g_7 \cap g_8$	$g_9 \cap g_{10}$
Input Documents	100x 00	200x200	300x300	400x400	500x500
Input Clusters	23x17	44x34	67x55	89x76	112x98
Output Clusters	1	17	54	95	101
Data Loading	315	612	901	1259	1484
Main Algorithm	1029	4051	8530	16407	21181
Group Labeling	5	111	158	400	451
Group Sorting	12	732	117	217	216
Writing XML File	6	349	68	118	119
Overall Process	1367	5855	9774	18401	23451

Figure 12. Chart of the experiments of application of the group intersection operator reported in Figure 11. Execution times are in milliseconds

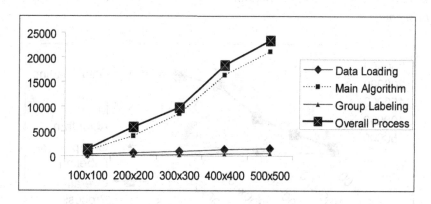

containing only a subset of the items in the original clusters. So, we can observe that the efforts needed to manage the generated clusters is not very significant, since the steps Group Labeling, Group Sorting and Writing XML File are applied only to the actual generated clusters containing few ranked items. To conclude, most of the effort of the algorithm implementing the group intersection operator is due to the need of checking each cluster in the first operand with each cluster in the second, to determine if they intersect, and this heavily affects the execution times.

We repeated the same experiments by applying the join operator to the same sets of source groups. Recall from the definition of the operators that the group join operator produces the same number of clusters than the group intersection; however, the resulting clusters are larger, since they contain all the documents in both the intersecting source clusters. Consequently, this set of experiments is useful to understand the impact of data structures necessary to manage the resulting clusters before writing the final XML document to disk.

The reader can easily see from Figure 13, Figure 14, Figure 15, Figure 16 that the behavior of the operator is still quadratic. However, the time needed to manage the data structure is significant: in the case denoted 500x500, the join algorithm needed 192167msec, while the intersection algorithm needed 38527msec; the consequence is that the main algorithm dominates the execution times, and in charts

Figure 13. First experiments of application of the join operator. Execution times are in milliseconds

	$g_1 \bowtie g_1$	$g_3 \bowtie g_3$	$g_5 \bowtie g_5$	$g_7 \bowtie g_7$	$g_9 \bowtie g_9$
Input Documents	100x 00	200x200	300x300	400x400	500x500
Input Clusters	23x23	44x44	67x67	89x89	112x112
Output Clusters	98	210	329	485	580
Data Loading	214	460	751	1135	1268
Main Algorithm	14564	53067	91258	170809	192177
Group Labeling	566	2426	7405	15628	24137
Group Sorting	855	2280	3902	6884	8129
Writing XML File	521	1390	2300	3967	4519
Overall Process	16720	59623	105616	198423	230230

Figure 14. Chart of the experiments of application of the join operator reported in Figure 13. Execution times are in milliseconds

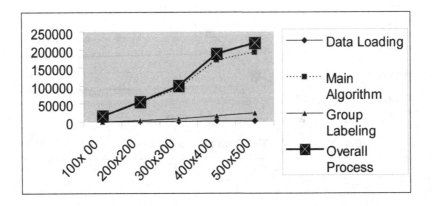

reported in Figure 14 and Figure 16 the dashed line corresponding to the main algorithm is substantially overlapped with the thick line corresponding to the overall process.

CONCLUSION

In this chapter, we addressed the problem of defining a language for manipulating huge amounts of results provided by search services over the Internet. The work is motivated by the need to better exploit, in an integrated way, the results obtained by different search services like, e.g., web search engines, that generally produced long ranked lists. The large number of documents retrieved by such services constitute a serious obstacle for users, that are not able to extract a semantic summarization of the results. The language can be useful also to explore the results obtained by submitting distinct queries to the same search service, to filter out redundant documents, to reveal implicit correlations, and to overview the main retrieved contents.

The proposed language provides operators to manipulate, in a complex and controlled way, groups of ranked clusters of retrieved documents.

Further, each operator can be specified with distinct ranking methods to favor, in top positions, clusters having distinct properties. The richness of the proposed language allows users to integrate the

Figure 15.Second experiments of application of the join operator. Execution times are in milliseconds

	$g_1 \cap g_2$	$g_3 \cap g_4$	$g_5 \cap g_6$	$g_7 \cap g_8$	$g_9 \cap g_{10}$
Input Documents	100x 00	200x200	300x300	400x400	500x500
Input Clusters	23x17	44x34	67x55	89x76	112x98
Output Clusters	1	17	54	95	101
Data Loading	313	645	869	1327	1558
Main Algorithm	3295	29305	37734	73371	816121
Group Labeling	6	144	252	532	652
Group Sorting	87	759	1030	1927	1940
Writing XML File	55	540	650	1236	1241
Overall Process	3756	31393	40535	78393	821512

Figure 16. Chart of the experiments of application of the join operator reported in Figure 15. Execution times are in milliseconds

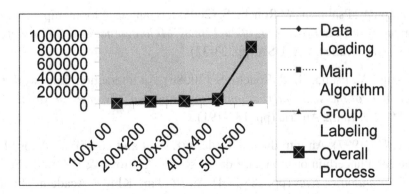

results of different search services in several ways, then revealing more general or more specific topics than those carried by the single documents.

We have developed a software prototype, named *Matrioshka*, that supports the proposed language. Based on a Service Oriented Architecture, it provides a web service interface, that can be exploited to develop multi-channel applications (http://matrioshka.unibg.it) (Bordogna, Campi, Psaila, & Ronchi, 2008b)

The Matrioshka system is based on a client-server architecture. It is constituted by three main parts: the Client Side Components handle the user interaction; the Server Side Component interfaces the search engines and executes the clustering operations; finally, the Communication Layer dispatches the messages between client and server.

Along with the core capabilities of Matrioshka, we have also developed a comprehensive infrastructure with the twofold purpose of supporting the user in editing queries, executing them and analyzing the results, so that the process can be fully tracked.

Consequently, Matrioshka is an interaction framework, in which the client provides a query editor for the user, the server either executes the queries and builds the groups containing clusters, or executes the operations on previously generated groups.

ACKNOWLEDGMENT

This work was supported in part by the EU, within the 7FP project, under grant agreement 216483 "*PrimeLife*".

REFERENCES

Agichtein, E., Brill, E., & Dumais, S. (2006). Improving Web search ranking by incorporating user behavior information. In *Proceeding of the 29th Annual International ACM Conference on Research and Development in Information Retrieval* (*SIGIR '06*), Seattle, Washington, USA (pp. 19-26). New York: ACM.

Bookstein, A. (1980). Fuzzy requests: An approach to weighted Boolean searches. *Journal of the American Society for Information Science American Society for Information Science, 31*(4), 240–247. doi:10.1002/asi.4630310403

Bordogna, G., Campi, A., Psaila, G., & Ronchi, S. (2008a). A language for manipulating groups of clustered Web documents results. In *Proceeding of the 17th ACM Conference on Information and Knowledge Mining (CIKM08)*, Napa Valley, CA, USA,(pp. 23-32).

Bordogna, G., Campi, A., Psaila, G., & Ronchi, S. (2008b). An interaction framework for mobile Web search. In *Proceedings of the sixth International Conference on Advances in Mobile Computing and Multimedia (MoMM08)*, Lintz, Austria (pp. 183-191).

Bosc, P., & Prade, H. (1997). An introduction to the fuzzy set and possibility theory-based treatment of flexible queries and uncertain or imprecise databases. In A. Motro & P. Smets (Eds.), *Uncertainty management in information systems* (pp. 285-324). Amsterdam: Kluwer Academic Publishers.

Buell, D., & Kraft, D. H. (1981). A model for a weighted retrieval system. *Journal of the American Society for Information Science American Society for Information Science, 32*, 211–216. doi:10.1002/asi.4630320307

Card, S. K., Mackinlay, J. D., & Shneiderman, B. (2000). *Readings in information visualization: Using vision to think.* San Francisco, CA: Morgan Kaufmann Publishers Inc.

Chen, H., & Dumais, S. (2009). Bringing order to the Web: Automatically categorizing search results. In *Proceedings of the SIGCHI Conference on Human factors in computing systems* (pp. 145-152).

Chung, W., Chen, H., & Nunamaker, J. J. (2003). Business intelligence explorer: A knowledge map framework for discovering business intelligence on the Web. In *Proceedings of the 36th Annual Hawaii International Conference on System Sciences* (pp. 10-18).

Coates, T., Connolly, D., Dack, D., Daigle, L., Denenberg, R., Durst, M., et al. (2001). *URIs, URLs, and URNs: Clarifications and recommendations, 1.0* (Tech. Rep. WWW Consortium, URI Planning Interest Group). Retrieved from http://www.w3.org/TR/2001/NOTE-uri-clarification-20010921/

Dubois, D., & Prade, H. (1982). A unifying view of comparison indices a fuzzy set-theoretic framework. In R. R. Yager (Ed.), *Recent development in fuzzy set and possibility theory* (pp. 3-13). New York: Pergamon Press.

Dubois, D., & Prade, H. (1988). *Possibility theory: An approach to computerized processing of uncertainty.* New York: Plenum Press.

Fred, A. L. N., & Jain, A. K. (2003). Robust data clustering. In *Proceedings of the IEEE Computer Society Conference on Computer Vision and Pattern Recognition (CVPR '03)* (pp. 2-128).

Galindo, J. (Ed.). (2008). *Handbook of research on fuzzy information processing in databases.* Hershey, PA: Information Science Reference.

Hearst, M. A., & Pederson, J. O. (1996). Re-examining the cluster hypothesis: Scatter/gather on retrieval results. In *Proceedings of the 19th Annual International ACM SIGIR Conference* (pp. 76-84).

Kampanya, N., Shen, R., Kim, S., North, C., & Fox, E. A. (2004). Citiviz: A visual user interface to the citidel system. In *Research and advanced technology for digital libraries* (LNCS 3232, pp. 122-133). Berlin, Germany: Springer.

Lalmas, M., & Murdock, V. (2008). Workshop on aggregated search. In *Proceedings of the ACM SIGIR 2008.* Retrieved from http://www.yr-bcn.es/sigir08

Leouski, A. V., & Croft, W. B. (1996). *An evaluation of techniques for clustering search results* (Tech. Rep. IR-76). Department of Computer Science, University of Massachusetts at Amherst.

Li, H., Liu, T. Y., & Zhai, C. X. (2008). Workshop on learning to rank for information retrieval. In *Proceedings of the Annual International ACM Conference on Research and Development in Information Retrieval (SIGIR2008).* Retrieved from http://research.microsoft.com/en-us/um/beijing/events/LR4IR-2008/

Osinski, S. (2003). *An algorithm for clustering of Web search results*. Unpublished master's thesis, Department of Computing Science, Poznan' University of Technology. Retrieved from http://project. carrot2.org/publications/osinski-2003-lingo.pdf

Pagani, M., Bordogna, G., & Valle, M. (2007). G. Mining multidimensional data using clustering techniques. In . *Proceedings of the DEXA Workshop, FLEXDBIST-07, 382–386.*

Punch, W., Jain, A. K., & Topchy, A. (2005). Clustering ensembles: Models of consensus and weak partitions. *IEEE Transactions on Pattern Analysis and Machine Intelligence, 27*(12), 1866–1881. doi:10.1109/TPAMI.2005.237

Sebrechts, M. M., Cugini, J. V., Laskowski, S. J., Vasilakis, J., & Miller, M. S. (1999). Visualization of search results: A comparative evaluation of text, 2D, and 3D interfaces. In *Proceedings of the 22nd annual international ACM SIGIR conference on Research and development in information retrieval* (pp. 3-10).

Staley, E., & Twidale, M. (2000). *Graphical interfaces to support information search* (Tech. Rep.). Graduate School of Library and Information Science, University of Illinois. Retrieved from http://people. lis.uiuc.edu/~twidale/irinterfaces/bib-main.html

Strehl, A., & Ghosh, J. (2002). Cluster ensembles – a knowledge reuse framework for combining partitionings. *Journal of Machine Learning Research, 3*, 583–617. doi:10.1162/153244303321897735

White, R. W., Richardson, M., Bilenko, M., & Heath, A. P. (2008). Enhancing Web search by promoting multiple search engine use. In *Proceedings of the 31st Annual international ACM Conference on Research and Development in information Retrieval* (SIGIR '08), Singapore (pp. 43-50). New York: ACM.

Yager, R. R. (1987). A note on weighted queries in information retrieval systems. *Journal of the American Society for Information Science American Society for Information Science, 38*(1), 23–24. doi:10.1002/ (SICI)1097-4571(198701)38:1<23::AID-ASI4>3.0.CO;2-3

Zadeh, L. (1965). Fuzzy sets. *Information and control, 8*, 338-353.

Zamir, O., & Etzioni, O. (1999). Grouper: A dynamic clustering interface to Web search results. In *Proceedings of the 8th International World Wide Web Conference* (pp. 1361-1374).

Section 3
Summarization

Chapter 8
Linguistic Data Summarization:
A High Scalability through the Use of Natural Language?

Janusz Kacprzyk
Polish Academy of Sciences, Poland

Sławomir Zadrożny
Polish Academy of Sciences, Poland

ABSTRACT

The authors discuss aspects related to the scalability of data mining tools meant in a different way than whether a data mining tool retains its intended functionality as the problem size increases. They introduce a new concept of a cognitive (perceptual) scalability meant as whether as the problem size increases the method remains fully functional in the sense of being able to provide intuitively appealing and comprehensible results to the human user. The authors argue that the use of natural language in the linguistic data summaries provides a high cognitive (perceptional) scalability because natural language is the only fully natural means of human communication and provides a common language for individuals and groups of different backgrounds, skills, knowledge. They show that the use of Zadeh's protoform as general representations of linguistic data summaries, proposed by Kacprzyk and Zadrożny (2002; 2005a; 2005b), amplify this advantage leading to an ultimate cognitive (perceptual) scalability.

INTRODUCTION

The purpose of this paper is to present a novel, different argument for the usefulness and power of linguistic data(base) summarization the essence of which was proposed by Yager (1982), and an extended, implementable version was shown by Kacprzyk & Yager (2001) and Kacprzyk, Yager & Zadrożny (2000).

We consider our further developments of the basic solutions presented in those papers which are relevant for our discussion, notably:

DOI: 10.4018/978-1-60566-858-1.ch008

- a close relation between the linguistic data summarization and fuzzy database querying, to be more specific using fuzzy queries with linguistic quantifiers proposed by us (Kacprzyk & Ziółkowski, 1986) and in a much more extended form in (Kacprzyk, Zadrożny & Ziółkowski, 1989), and even more so in FQUERY for Access (Kacprzyk & Zadrożny, 2001b),
- our general approach to linguistic data summarization viewed as an interactive process in which fuzzy querying makes possible the articulation of the user's intentions, interests and information needs proposed by Kacprzyk & Zadrożny (1998; 2001a), and
- our formulation of linguistic data summarization in terms not only of the calculus of linguistically quantified proposition but in terms of Zadeh's protoforms (cf. (Kacprzyk & Zadrożny, 2002; 2005a; 2005b)) which can provide an extraordinary transparency, versatility and generality.

Our purpose in this paper will not be, however, a traditional exposition of the essence of those ideas which have been presented in our papers as referred to above, and which have proved to be very effective and efficient. We will discuss these tools and techniques from the perspective of this volume, that is, from the perspective of *scalability* of data mining (knowledge discovery) tools and techniques. In the case of linguistic data(base) summarization this will have a couple of aspects exemplified by both more technical computation time and memory related aspects of the scalability of databases and querying, and more conceptual aspects of what might be called a *cognitive* or *perceptional scalability* of tools from the point of view of human facilities and capabilities. Ultimately, we will argue that linguistic data summarization may be viewed from some points of view, notably with respect to the cognitive and perceptual scalability, as an ultimately scalable (in the cognitive or perceptual sense) tool for data mining and knowledge discovery.

BACKGROUND

The first question we should ask is: What is actually meant by *scalability*, in particular in the context of broadly perceived information technology? Usually, *scalability* is meant in two basic ways. First, it is understood as the ability of a computer application or system (i.e. hardware and/or software) to continue to function when the size of the problem in question (e.g. the size of a computer network, number of clients, size of data sets, etc.) changes, usually grows up. In our context of a broadly perceived data analysis, in this paper the scalability will be meant in the upward sense. Second, in a modern view, scalability is meant as the ability of a computer application and/or system not only to function as the size of the problem and/or context increases (or decreases but this case will not be considered) but to even take advantage of that increase in size and volume, for instance to provide more adequate results because of a larger basic data set, or an ability to more adequately grasp the very essence of a larger data set. Needless to say that scalability is a desirable property of any application or system, and virtually all nontrivial applications and systems are designed and implemented with scalability in mind.

As one can expect, though scalability is easily intuitively comprehensible, it is difficult to define, and may mean different things to different people, in particular when they come from different areas. What is relevant to us, a scalable online transaction processing system or database management system is the one that can be upgraded to process more transactions by adding new processors, devices and storage, and which can be upgraded easily and transparently. This is one of the reasons that we concern the scalability in the sense of what happens when the size and volume of data increase.

Scalability is a multidimensional concept. For instance, people often confuse *performance* and *scalability*. As pointed out by Haines (2006): "The terms "performance" and "scalability" are commonly used interchangeably but the two are distinct: performance measures the speed with which a single request can be executed, while scalability measures the ability of a request to maintain its performance under increasing size and volume. For example, the performance of a request may be said to generate a valid response within three seconds, but the scalability of the request concerns the ability to maintain that three-second response time as the user load increases" (p. 224). This distinction has a great impact for our discussion, and will be dealt with later.

Viewed simplistically, scalability is about "doing more of something" like responding to more user requests, executing more work or handling more data. Traditionally, this is done by either increasing the sheer computing power and/or data handling power exemplified by using parallel computation, grid computing, etc.

In this context a popular belief is that databases do not scale up well, i.e. that it is difficult to keep growing the size of a database, or too hard to handle the load of an increasing number of concurrent users. In other words, it is often believed that systems that are database centric are fundamentally incapable of efficiently coping with the (growing) demands of high performance distributed computing. This may be true to some extent even in view of a growing storage capacity at a diminishing cost, parallelization of processing, new software developments, etc. One can easily reach limits of the same inherent nature as those characteristic for even the best, most advances and densely packed traditional silicon integrated circuits: sooner or later, a new type of processors (biological?) will be needed.

This example of an unavoidable necessity of a technological change in processors can be rephrased in the context of the scaling up of database centric systems and applications which is what our work is concerned with.

Now, let us present the basic context we will be operating in, and issues related to scalability. We are concerned with data summarization which is one of basic capabilities of any "intelligent" system, and since for the human being the only fully natural means of communication is natural language, a linguistic summarization would be very desirable, exemplified by, for a data set on employees, a statement (linguistic summary) "almost all young and well qualified employees are well paid".

Unfortunately, data summarization is still in general unsolved a problem. Very many techniques are available but they are not "intelligent enough", and not human-consistent, partly due to a limited use of natural language (cf. Lesh & Mitzenmacher, 2004).

We deal with a conceptually simple approach to the linguistic database summaries introduced by Yager (1982; 1991; 1996), and then considerably advanced by Kacprzyk (2000), Kacprzyk & Yager (2001), and Kacprzyk, Yager & Zadrożny (2000; 2001), Zadrożny and Kacprzyk (1999), and implemented in Kacprzyk and Zadrożny (2000a-d; 2001a-e; 2002; 2003; 2005b). In this approach linguistic data summaries are derived as linguistically quantified propositions as, e.g., "most of the employees are young and well paid", with a degree of truth (validity), possibly extended with other measures.

For an effective and efficient derivation of linguistic summaries, we employ Kacprzyk and Zadrożny's (1998; 2000a-d; 2001a) interactive approach to linguistic summaries in which the determination of a class of summaries of interest is done via Kacprzyk and Zadrożny's (1994; 1995a-b; 2001b) FQUERY for Access, a fuzzy querying add-in to Microsoft Access, extended to the querying over the Internet in Kacprzyk and Zadrożny (2000b). Since a fully automatic generation of linguistic summaries is not feasible at present, mainly because it is difficult if not impossible at all to automatically reveal the user's real intentions, interests and information needs, an interaction with the user is assumed for the determination of a class of summaries of interest, and this is done via the above fuzzy querying add-in.

Extending Kacprzyk & Zadrożny (2002; 2005a; 2005b), we show that by relating various types of linguistic summaries to fuzzy queries, with various known and sought elements, we can arrive at a hierarchy of prototypical forms, or – in Zadeh's (2002) terminology – protoforms, of linguistic data summaries. This seems to be a very powerful conceptual idea because it provides a simple structural expression, with a comprehensible semantics, of even the most complicated linguistic summaries.

Notice that, first, through the use of natural language to present (verbalize) the very essence and contents of data with respect to an aspect in question we certainly attain a high, maybe even the best scalability. First, natural language can express that information in a fully comprehensible way no matter how large the data set is. Second, such simple linguistically quantified propositions with which data summaries are equated may semantically be adequate as representations of data sets of any size as they represent some highly abstracted linguistic statements, of a simple syntax and of what might be described as a "commonsense based" semantics. Third, protoforms of linguistic summaries provide a uniform, easily comprehensible form of linguistic summaries for any size of data sets, and virtually all intentions and information needs of the user. Finally, natural language summaries are comprehensible to individuals, small and larger groups, people from different backgrounds, people coming from various geographic locations, sexes, age groups, etc. Clearly, an obvious condition of an agreed upon semantics of language used should be assumed but this is a prerequisite of any human communication, and any implementation of a computer system to be employed by various human users.

A natural question is: what is the relation of the approach and view presented in this paper to the problem of natural language generation (NLG), and in particular to the scalability of natural language generation. We will not deal in more detail with these important issues. For an analysis of relations between the linguistic data summaries used in this paper, and in all our previous works, and some extension of the template based approach to natural language generation we refer the reader to Kacprzyk & Zadrożny (2009). Moreover, for very interesting remarks and their justification that natural language generation itself can be viewed as a very effective and efficient, yet conceptually simple and natural, and extremely human consistent way to improve the scalability of a dialog system, we refer the reader to Reiter (1995).

For more detail on the issue of scalable natural language generation we refer the reader to, for instance, Klarner (2004). Basically, in those works scalability of the natural language generation is also considered in the context of dialog systems, i.e. slightly more general than in our context of just the linguistic summarization of numerical sets of data, but concerns many aspects that are relevant for us too. Basically, scalability for (spoken) dialog systems is meant as the ability to:

- enlarge the domain content by modifying and extending its thematic orientation,
- refine the domain language to extend the linguistic coverage and expressibility of the domain,
- change the application domain which usually concerns the two above ones and can lead to completely new requirements for a dialog system and its parts,
- change the discourse domain which may alter the discourse type within the same domain.

As it can clearly be seen there are strong, intrinsic relations between our concept of a linguistic data summary, and its protoform based representation, and various concepts of scalability both in a general context of systems and applications in information technology, database related technology, and – finally – natural language generation (NLG).

It should be noted that our approach to scalability is different than that of most researchers who practically equate the property of scalability with whether, and how well, a given approach, tool, technique, … can retain its functionality, effectiveness and efficiency when the size of the problem is growing, i.e. in our case the size of a data set is growing. This is upward scalability. Sometimes very relevant is downward scalability when the size of the problem is diminishing. A trivial example is that (many if not all) statistical methods are not downward scalable in this sense because they do not work properly for small problems (samples). The downward scalability is in general difficult to deal with.

Most works on the (upward) scalability concern the efficiency of search for a solution, here for a best linguistic summary, which may be called a *technical scalability*. In this work we are basically concerned with a much more general and foundational type of scalability, which might be called a *conceptual* or *perceptional scalability* which has to do with a fundamental question: will our tools remain conceptually or perceptually appropriate (human consistent) when our problem will greatly increase? We will advocate that due to the use of natural language we obtain an ultimate conceptual or perceptional scalability because a natural language statement will always be comprehensible to the human being(s) no matter what size of the data set it is meant to represent. We will also give some remarks on technical scalability by, first, reviewing some approaches that make possible the generation of linguistic summaries for large data sets. We will not, however, mention our approach based on a relation between the generation of linguistic data summaries and association rules which was originally proposed by Kacprzyk & Zadrożny (2001d; 2003). This approach shows a different perspective and its role in the context of scalability, both technical and cognitive (perceptual), of linguistic data summaries needs a different exposition which will be presented in a next paper.

We will present now in more detail an implementation of our interactive approach to the derivation of linguistic summaries, and while discussing particular elements we will indicate relations to those scalability issues and aspects mentioned above. We hope that this will provide another justification to the power of both linguistic data summaries in the simple sense assumed here, and the power of Zadeh's protoforms, and maybe even – more generally – the power of Zadeh's computing with words and perceptions paradigm (cf. Zadeh & Kacprzyk, 1999). All this will be presented in a novel, not yet explored perspective of a conceptual (perceptional) scalability.

LINGUISTIC DATA(BASE) SUMMARIES

Data summarization is one of basic capabilities now needed by any "intelligent" system that is meant to operate in real life situations. Basically, due to the availability of relatively cheap and efficient hardware and software tools, we usually face an abundance of data that is beyond human cognitive, perceptional and comprehension skills.

Since for the human being the only fully natural means of communication is natural language, a linguistic (say, by a sentence or a small number of sentences in a natural language) summarization of a set of data would be very desirable and human consistent. For instance, having a data set on employees, a statement (linguistic summary) like "almost all younger and well qualified employees are well paid" would be useful and human consistent in many cases.

Unfortunately, data summarization is still in general unsolved a problem in spite of vast research efforts. Very many techniques are available but they are not "intelligent enough", and not human consistent, partly due to a little use of natural language. This concerns, e.g., summarizing statistics, exemplified by the average, median, minimum, maximum, α-percentile, etc. which – in spite of recent efforts to soften them – are still far from being able to reflect a real human perception of their essence.

Linguistic Data Summarization: The Basic Case

In this paper we will use a simple yet effective and efficient approach to the linguistic summarization of data sets (databases) proposed by Yager (1982), and then presented in a more advanced, and implementable form by Kacprzyk & Yager (2001), and Kacprzyk, Yager & Zadrożny (2000). This will provide a point of departure for our further analysis of more complicated and realistic summaries.

In Yager's (1982) approach, we have (we use here the author's terminology):

- V is a quality (attribute) of interest, e.g. salary in a database of workers,
- $Y = \{y_1, \dots, y_n\}$ is a set of objects (records) that manifest quality V, e.g. the set of workers; hence $V(y_i)$ are values of quality V for object $y_i \in Y$;
- $D = \{V(y_1), \dots, V(y_n)\}$ is a set of data (the "database" on question)

A *linguisticsummary* of a data set consists of:

- a summarizer S (e.g. young),
- a quantity in agreement Q (e.g. most),
- truth T - e.g. 0.7,

as, e.g., "$T(most$ of employees are $young)=0.7$". The truth T may be meant in a more general sense, e.g. as validity or, even more generally, as some quality or goodness of a linguistic summary.

Basically, given a set of data D, we can hypothetize any appropriate summarizer S and any quantity in agreement Q, and the assumed measure of truth will indicate the truth of the statement that Q data items satisfy the statement (summarizer) S.

Notice that we consider here some specific, basic form of a linguistic summary. We do not consider other forms of summaries exemplified by "over 70% of employees are under 35 years of age" that may be viewed to provide similar information as "most of employees are young" because the latter are clearly outside of the class of linguistic summaries considered. Notice also that we discuss here the linguistic summarization of sets of numeric values only. One can clearly imagine the linguistic summarization of symbolic attributes but this relevant problem is outside of the scope of this paper. We do not consider here the linguistic summarization of textual information.

We should also note that we do not consider in this paper some other approaches to the linguistic summarization of databases (data sets) that are based on a different philosophy, exemplified by works by Bosc et al. (2002), Dubois & Prade (1992), Raschia & Mouaddib (2002) or Rasmussen & Yager (1996; 1997a; 1997b; 1999). Basically, one can very briefly summarize the approaches employed as follows. First, Bosc et al. (1992) use a gradual rule view of linguistic summaries, which has been proposed by Dubois & Prade (1992) and use linguistic quantifiers as tools for the aggregation. Rasmussen & Yager

(1999) consider both the traditional Yager summaries and a type of Dubois & Prade's gradual rules showing that they can be obtained (or, more precisely, verified) via some extension of SQL. Raschia & Mouaddib (2002) propose, and develop in a series of papers, a different approach based on hierarchical summaries, their tree representations, and relations to OLAP based techniques. Summaries are here meant as aggregated ("generalized") tuples which cover parts of the database at different levels of abstraction.

We will not consider some other related techniques exemplified by the mining of fuzzy association rules (cf. (Chen, Liu & Li, 2001; Chen & Wei, 2002; Chen, Wei & Kerre; 2000; Hu, Chen & Tzeng, 2002; Lee & Lee-Kwang, 1997)), even in the context of linguistic summaries (cf. (Kacprzyk and Zadrożny, 2001d; 2003)). These approaches reflect a different perspective and, as already mentioned, will be a subject of a next paper which will consider scalability of linguistic data summaries in a comprehensive way, as a confluence of the technical and conceptual (perceptional) scalability.

First, we should consider the forms of the particular elements of a linguistic summary in our sense. Since we use natural language throughout our analysis, as it is the only fully natural and human consistent means of communication for the humans, we assume the summarizer S to be a linguistic expression semantically represented by a fuzzy set like, for instance "young" would be represented as a fuzzy set in the universe of discourse as, e.g., {1, 2, ..., 90}, i.e. containing possible values of the human age, and "young" could be given as, e.g., a fuzzy set with a non-increasing membership function in that universe such that, in a simple case of a piecewise linear membership function, the age up to 35 years is for sure "young", i.e. the grade of membership is equal to 1, the age over 50 years is for sure "not young", i.e. the grade of membership is equal to 0, and for the ages between 35 and 50 years the grades of membership are between 1 and 0, the higher the age the lower its corresponding grade of membership. A simple one-attribute-related summarizer exemplified by "young" can clearly be extended to some confluence of attribute values as, e.g., "*young* and *well paid*".

Clearly, in the context of linguistic summarization of data, the most interesting are more sophisticated, *human-consistent* summarizers (concepts) as, e.g.:

* productive workers,
* stimulating work environment,
* difficult orders, etc.

whose definition involves complicated *combinations of attributes*, e.g.: a hierarchy (not all attributes are of the same importance), the attribute values are ANDed and/or ORed, k out of n, *most*, etc. of them should be accounted for, etc. The definition, processing and generation of such non-trivial summarizers needs some specific tools and techniques to be discussed later.

The quantity in agreement, Q, is an indication of the extent to which the data satisfy the summary. Once again, a precise indication is not human consistent, and a linguistic term represented by a fuzzy set is employed. Basically, two types of such a linguistic quantity in agreement can be used:

* absolute as, e.g., "about 5", "more or less 100", "several", and
* relative as, e.g., "a few", "more or less a half", "most", almost all"etc.

Notice that the above linguistic expressions are the so-called fuzzy linguistic quantifiers (cf. Zadeh, 1983) that can be handled by fuzzy logic.

Similarly as for the fuzzy summarizer, the form (basically, the definition of a fuzzy linguistic quantifier) of a fuzzy quantity in agreement is also subjective, and can be either predefined or elicited from the user.

The calculation of the truth (or, more generally, validity) of the linguistic summary considered above is equivalent to the calculation of the truth value (from the unit interval) of a linguistically quantified statement (e.g., "*most* of the employees are *young*"). This can be calculated by using two most relevant techniques: Zadeh's (1983) calculus of linguistically quantified statements (cf. (Zadeh & Kacprzyk, 1999) or Yager's (1988) OWA operators (cf. (Yager & Kacprzyk, 1997)). Since these calculi are well known and are widely used in many works involving linguistic quantifier based aggregation of partial scores, we will discuss them only briefly in what follows and will refer the reader to, for instance, Zadeh's (1983; 1985) or Yager's (1988) source papers for more details.

A linguistically quantified proposition, exemplified by "most experts are convinced", is written as "Qy's are F" where Q is a linguistic quantifier (e.g., most), $Y = \{y\}$ is a set of objects (e.g., experts), and F is a property (e.g., convinced). Importance B may be added yielding "QBy's are F", e.g., "most (Q) of the important (B) experts (y's) are convinced (F)". The problem is to find $\mathrm{truth}(Qy$'s are $F)$ or $\mathrm{truth}(QBy$'s are $F)$ respectively, knowing $\mathrm{truth}(y$ is $F), \forall y \in Y$ which is done here using Zadeh's (1983; 1985) fuzzy logic based calculus of linguistically quantified propositions.

Property F and importance B are fuzzy sets in Y, and a (proportional, nondecreasing) linguistic quantifier Q is assumed to be a fuzzy set in $[0,1]$ as, e.g.

$$\mu_Q(x) = \begin{cases} 1 & \text{for } x \geq 0.8 \\ 2x - 0.6 & \text{for } 0.3 < x < 0.8 \\ 0 & \text{for } x \leq 0.3 \end{cases}$$

(1)

Then, due to Zadeh (1983)

$$\mathrm{truth}(Qy\text{'s are } F) = \mu_Q[\tfrac{1}{n}\sum_{i=1}^{n}\mu_F(y_i)]$$

(2)

$$\mathrm{truth}(QBy\text{'s are } F) = \mu_Q[\sum_{i=1}^{n}(\mu_B(y_i) \wedge \mu_F(y_i)) / \sum_{i=1}^{n}\mu_B(y_i)]$$

(3)

These formulas are clearly based on the non-fuzzy cardinalities of the respective fuzzy sets, the so-called Σ-Counts (cf. Zadeh, 1983).

An OWA operator (Yager, 1988; Yager & Kacprzyk, 1997) of dimension p is a mapping $F : [0,1]^p \to [0,1]$ if associated with F is a weighting vector $W = [w_1,...,w_p]^T$, $w_i \in [0,1]$, $w_1 + \cdots + w_p = 1$, and

$$F(x_1,...,x_p) = w_1 b_1 + \cdots w_p b_p = W^T B$$

(4)

where b_i is the i-th largest element among $x_1,...,x_p$, $B = [b_1,...,b_p]$.

The OWA weights may be found from the membership function of Q due to (cf. Yager, 1988):

$$w_i = \begin{cases} \mu_Q(i) - \mu_Q(i-1) & \text{for } i = 1, \ldots, p \\ \mu_Q(0) & \text{for } i = 0 \end{cases} \tag{5}$$

The OWA operators can model a wide array of aggregation operators (including linguistic quantifiers), from $w_1 = \ldots = w_{p-1} = 0$ and $w_p = 1$ which corresponds to "all", to $w_1 = 1$ and $w_2 = \ldots = w_p = 0$ which corresponds to " at least one", through all intermediate situations, and that is why they are widely employed.

An important case is when with the OWA operator importance qualification of the particular pieces of data is associated. Suppose that with the data $A = [a_1, \ldots, a_p]$, a vector of importances $V = [v_1, \ldots, v_p]$, such that $v_i \in [0,1]$ is the importance of $a_i, i = 1, \ldots, p$, $v_1 + \cdots v_p = 1$, is associated. Then, for an *ordered weighted averaging operator with importance qualification* based on a linguistic quantifier Q, denoted OWA_Q, Yager (1988) proposed that, first, some redefinition of the OWA's weights w_i's into $\bar{w}_i$'s is performed, and (4) becomes

$$F_I(x_1, \ldots, x_p) = \bar{w}_1 b_1 + \cdots \bar{w}_p b_p = \bar{W}^T B \tag{6}$$

where

$$\bar{w}_j = \mu_Q \left(\frac{\sum_{k=1}^{j} u_k}{\sum_{k=1}^{p} u_k} \right) - \mu_Q \left(\frac{\sum_{k=1}^{j-1} u_k}{\sum_{k=1}^{p} u_k} \right) \tag{7}$$

where u_k is the importance of b_k, i.e. the k-largest element of A.

Some Other Validity Measures of Linguistic Summaries

The basic validity criterion, i.e. the truth of a linguistically quantified statement given by (2) and (3), is certainly the most natural and important but it does not grasp all aspects of a linguistic summary. We will present here some other quality (validity) criteria, notably those proposed by Kacprzyk & Yager (2001), and Kacprzyk, Yager & Zadrożny (2000).

First, Yager (1982) proposed a measure of informativeness whose essence is: suppose that we have a data set, whose elements are from a space X. One can view the data set itself as its own most informative description, and any other summary implies a loss of information, and therefore informativeness comes into play

The degree of truth is unfortunately not a good measure of informativeness (cf. Yager, 1982; 1991). Let the summary be characterized by the triple (S, Q, T), and let a related summary be characterized by the triple (S^c, Q^c, T) such that S^c is the negation of S, i.e. $\mu_S^c(.) = 1 - \mu_S(.)$, and similarly $\mu_Q^c(.) = 1 - \mu_Q(.)$. Then, Yager (1982; 1991) proposed the following measure of informativeness of a summary

$$I = [T \cdot SP(Q) \cdot SP(S)] \vee [(1 - T) \cdot Sp(Q^c) Sp(S^c)] \tag{8}$$

where $SP(Q)$ is the specificity of Q given as

$$SP(Q) = \int_0^1 \frac{1}{\mathrm{card}\, Q_\alpha} d_\alpha \tag{9}$$

where Q_α is the α-cut of Q and card(.) is the "cardinality" (in fact, the area) of the respective set; and similarly for Q^c, S, S^c. Notice that in (8) we also have the specificity of S/S^c, $SP(S/S^c)$, which is meant similarly.

The rationale behind this measure of informativeness differs from that of, e.g., Chen, Liu & Li (2001). Unfortunately, this measure of informativeness is by no means a definite solution. First, let us briefly mention George and Srikanth's (1996a; 1996b) proposal. Suppose that a linguistic summary of interest involves more than 1 attribute (e.g., "age", "salary" and "seniority" in the case of employees). Basically, for the same set of data, two summaries are generated:

- a constraint descriptor which is the most specific description (summary) that fits the largest number of tuples in the relation (database) involving the attributes in question,
- a constituent descriptor which is the description (summary) that fits the largest subset of tuples with the condition that each tuple attribute value takes on at least a threshold value of membership.

George and Srikanth (1996a; 1996b) use these two summaries to derive a fitness function (goodness of a summary) that is later used for deriving a solution (a best summary) via a genetic algorithm they employ. This fitness function represents a compromise between the most specific summary (corresponding to the constraint descriptor) and the most general summary (corresponding to the constituent descriptor).

Then, some additional measures have been developed by Kacprzyk & Yager (2001) and Kacprzyk, Yager & Zadrożny (2000). Let us briefly repeat some basic notation. We have a data set (database) D that concerns some objects (e.g. employees) $Y = \{y_1, ..., y_n\}$ described by some attribute V (e.g. age) taking on values in a set $X = \{x_1, x_2, ...\}$ exemplified by $\{20, 21, ..., 100\}$ or even $\{$very young, young, ..., old, very old$\}$ though this case will not be considered here. Let $d_i = V(y_i)$ denote the value of attribute V for object y_i. Therefore, the data set to be summarized is given as a table

$$D = [d_1,...,d_n] = [V(y_1), V(y_2), ..., V(y_n)] \tag{10}$$

In a more realistic case the data set is described by more than one attribute. Let $V = \{V_1, V_2,..., V_m\}$ be a set of such attributes taking values in X_i, $i = 1, ..., m$; $V_j(y_i)$ denotes the value of attribute V_j for object y_i, and attribute V_j takes on its values from a set X_j.

The data set to be summarized is therefore:

$$D = \{[V_1(y_1), V_2(y_1),..., V_m(y_1)], [V_1(y_2), V_2(y_2),..., V_m(y_2)], ..., [V_1(y_n), V_2(y_n),..., V_m(y_n)]\} \tag{11}$$

In case of multiple (m) attributes the description (summarizer) S is assumed as a family of fuzzy sets $S = \{S_1, S_2,... S_m\}$ where $S_i \in S$ is a fuzzy set in X_i, $i = 1,...,m$. Then, $\mu_S(y_i)$, $i = 1,2,..., n$, may be defined as:

$$\mu_S(y_i) = \min_{j \in \{1,2,...,m\}} [\mu_{Sj} (V_j(v_i))] \tag{12}$$

and

$$r = \frac{\sum_{i=1}^{n} \mu_S(y_i)}{n} \tag{13}$$

and $T = \mu_Q(r)$.

So, having S, we can calculate the truth value T of a summary for any quantity in agreement. To find a best (optimal) summary, we should calculate T for each possible summarizer, and for each record in the database in question which may be computationally prohibitive for virtually all non-trivial databases and number of attributes. Therefore, from the point of view of scalability, this suggests that the process of finding an optimal linguistic summary is not *technically scalable*.

A natural line of reasoning would be to either limit the number of attributes of interest or to limit the class of possible summaries by setting a more specific description (e.g. very young, young and well paid, etc. employees). This will limit the search space, and may help attain an acceptable technical scalability.

We will deal now with the second option. The user can limit the scope of a linguistic summary to, for instance, those for which the "age" takes on the value "young" only, i.e. to fix the summarizer related to that attribute. This would correspond to the searching of the database using the query w_g equated with the fuzzy set in X_g corresponding to "young" related to attribute V_g (i.e. age), i.e. characterized by $\mu_{w_g}(.)$. In such a case, $\mu_S(y_i)$ given by (12) becomes

$$\mu_S(y_i) = \min_{j \in \{1,2,...,m\}} [\mu_{Sj} (V_j(v_i)) \wedge \mu_{w_g} (V_g(y_i)], i=1, ..., n \tag{14}$$

where "$\wedge$" is the minimum (or, more generally, a t-norm), and then

$$r = \frac{\sum_{i=1}^{n} \mu_S(y_i)}{\sum_{i=1}^{n} \mu_{w_g} (V_g(y_i))} \tag{15}$$

and $T = \mu_Q(r)$. This is clearly related to how Zadeh's calculus of linguistically quantified propositions works.

Now, we will briefly mention the 5 quality measures of linguistic database summaries, in particular four additional ones as introduced in Kacprzyk & Yager (2001), and Kacprzyk, Yager & Zadrożny (2000):

- a truth value [which basically corresponds to the degree of truth of a linguistically quantified proposition representing the summary given by, say, (2) or (3)],

- a degree of imprecision,
- a degree of covering,
- a degree of appropriateness,
- a length of a summary.

For notational simplicity later on, let us rewrite (12) and (1) as:

$$\mu_S(d_i) = \min_{j \in \{1,2,...,m\}} [(\mu_{S_j}(V_j(y_i))], i=1, ..., n \tag{16}$$

and

$$r = \frac{\sum_{i=1}^{n} [\mu_S(V_g(y_i)) \wedge \mu_{w_g}(V_g(y_i))]}{\sum_{i=1}^{n} \mu_{w_g}(V_g(y_i))} \tag{17}$$

where, clearly, (16) and (17) are equivalent to (12) and (15) though rewritten in the form more suitable for our present discussion.

The **degree of truth**, T_1, is the basic validity criterion introduced in the source Yager's (1982) work and commonly employed. It is clearly equal to

$$T_1 = \mu_Q(r) \tag{18}$$

which results directly from Zadeh's (1983; 1985) calculus of linguistically quantified propositions.

The **degree of imprecision** is an obvious and important validity criterion. Basically, a very imprecise linguistic summary (e.g. on almost all winter days the temperature is rather cold) has a very high degree of truth yet it is not useful.

Suppose that description (summarizer) S is given as a family of fuzzy sets $S=\{S_1, S_2, ... S_m\}$. For a fuzzy set $S_j, j=1, ..., m$, we can define its degree of fuzziness as, e.g.:

$$in(S_j) = \frac{\text{card } \{x \in X_j : \mu_{S_j}(x) > 0 \}}{\text{card } X_j} \tag{19}$$

where card denotes the cardinality of the corresponding (nonfuzzy) set and the domains X_j are all assumed to be finite (what is reasonable from the practical point of view). That is, the "flatter" the fuzzy set S_j the higher the value of $in(S_j)$.

The degree of imprecision, T_2, of the summary – or, in fact, of S – is then defined as:

$$T_2 = 1 - \sqrt[m]{\prod_{j=1,...,m} in(S_j)} \tag{20}$$

Notice that the degree of imprecision T_2 depends on the form of the summary only and not on the database, that is its calculation does not require the searching of the database (all its records) which is very important.

The **degree of covering**, T_3, is defined as

$$T_3 = \frac{\sum_{i=1}^{n} t_i}{\sum_{i=1}^{n} h_i}$$

(21)

where:

$$t_i = \begin{cases} 1 & \text{if } \mu_S(y_i) > 0 \quad \text{and} \quad \mu_{w_g}(V_g(y_i)) > 0 \\ 0 & \text{otherwise} \end{cases}$$

$$h_i = \begin{cases} 1 & \text{if } \mu_{w_g}(V_g(y_i)) > 0 \\ 0 & \text{otherwise} \end{cases}$$

and the denominator of (21) is assumed to be different from 0 - otherwise T_3 is defined to be equal 0.

The degree of covering says how many objects in the data set corresponding to the query w_g are "covered" by the particular summary. Its interpretation is simple as, e.g., if it is equal to 0.15, then this means that 15% of the objects are consistent with the summary in question. The value of this degree depends clearly on the contents of the database.

The **degree of appropriateness** is probably the most relevant measure. Suppose that the summary containing the description (fuzzy sets) $S = (S_1, S_2, ..., S_m)$ is partitioned into m partial summaries each of which encompasses the particular attributes $V_1, V_2, ..., V_m$, such that each partial summary corresponds to one fuzzy set only, then if we denote:

$$S_j(y_i) = \mu_{S_j}(V_j(y_i))$$

(23)

then

$$r_j = \frac{\sum_{i=1}^{n} h_i}{n}, j = 1, ..., n$$

where, $h_i = \begin{cases} 1 & \text{if } S_j(y_i) > 0 \\ 0 & \text{otherwise} \end{cases}$, and the degree of appropriateness, T_4, is defined as:

$$T_4 = \text{abs}(\prod_{j=1,...,m} r_j - T_3)$$

(24)

The degree of appropriateness means that, for a database concerning the employees, if – for instance – 50% of them are less than 25 years old and 50% are highly qualified, then we may expect that 25% of the employees would be less than 25 years old and highly qualified; this would correspond to a typical, fully expected situation. However, if the degree of appropriateness is, e.g., 0.39 (i.e. 39% are less than 25 years old and highly qualified), then the summary found reflects an interesting, not fully expected relation in our data. This degree describes therefore how characteristic for the particular database the summary found is. T_4 is very important because a trivial summary like, for instance, "100% of employees is of some age" has truth equal 1 but its degree of appropriateness is clearly equal 0.

The **length** of a summary is relevant because a long summary is not easily comprehensible by the human user. This length, T_5, may be defined in various ways, and the below form has proven to be useful:

$$T_5 = 2\,(0.5^{\text{card}S}) \tag{25}$$

Now, the (total) degree of validity, T, of a particular linguistic summary is defined as the weighted average of the above 5 degrees of validity, i.e.:

$$T = T(T_1, T_2, T_3, T_4, T_5; w_1, w_2, w_3, w_4, w_5) = \sum_{i=1,2,\ldots,5} w_i T_i \tag{26}$$

and the problem is to find an optimal summary, $S^* \in \{S\}$, such that

$$S^* = \arg\max_S \sum_{i=1,2,\ldots,5} w_i T \tag{27}$$

where: $w_1,\ldots,w_5$ are weights assigned to the particular degrees of validity, with values from the unit interval, the higher, the more important such that $\sum_{i=1,2,\ldots,5} w_i = 1$.

The definition of weights, $w_1,\ldots,w_5$, is a problem in itself, and will not be dealt with in more detail. The weights can be predefined or elicited from the user.

As we have already mentioned, the linguistic summarization meant in terms of (27) is clearly not technically scalable, even if some more sophisticated search techniques are used which limit the size of the problem as exemplified by George & Srikanth's (1996a; 1996b) use of a genetic algorithm. However, let us notice that the situation is completely different when cognitive (perceptional) scalability is accounted for. It is clear that the very concept of linguistic data summary as presented above is what might be said totally cognitively (perceptionally) scalable because it is comprehensible to a human being, either an individual or a group of individuals, no matter what size of the data set is, and also to a large extent independently of the background, sex, age, etc. of the individuals. This is a direct result of, on the one hand, the use of natural language, which is the only fully natural means of articulation and communication of a human being, and – on the other hand – of a simple and intuitively appealing form of a linguistic summary which basically says what most of the data exhibit, i.e. what *usually happens* (holds). This is in fact what is looked for and found by all data analysis tools and techniques.

PRACTICAL DETERMINATION OF LINGUISTIC DATA SUMMARIES

One can clearly notice that a fully automatic determination of a best linguistic summary, i.e. the solution of (26) may be infeasible in practice due to a high number of possible summaries. In (Kacprzyk &

Zadrożny, 1998; 2001a) an *interactive approach* was proposed with a *user assistance* in the definition of summarizers, by the indication of attributes and their combinations of interest. This proceeds via a user interface of a fuzzy querying add-on. Basically, the queries (referring to summarizers) allowed are:

- *simple* as, e.g., "salary is *high*"
- *compound* as, e.g., "salary is *low* AND age is *old*"
- *compound (with quantifier)*, as, e.g., "*most* of {salary is *high*, age is *young*, ..., training is *well above average*}.

We will also use "natural" linguistic terms, i.e. (7±2!) exemplified by: *very low, low, medium, high, very high*, and also "comprehensible" fuzzy linguistic quantifiers as: *most, almost all*, ..., etc.

In (Kacprzyk &Zadrożny, 1994; 1995a; 1995b; 2001b), a conventional DBMS is used, and a fuzzy querying tool is developed to allow for queries with fuzzy (linguistic) elements of the "simple", "compound" and "compound with quantifier" types. This fuzzy querying system (add in) has been developed for Microsoft Access® but its concept is clearly applicable to any DBMS. The main problems to be solved are here: (1) how to extend the syntax and semantics of the query, and (2) how to provide an easy way of eliciting and manipulating those terms by the user.

We will now briefly describe the very essence of FQUERY for Access, emphasizing those aspects which are relevant for the purposes of this paper. One should notice that we will use here terms, exemplified by "attributes", "fields", etc. as used in our source papers on FQUERY for Access, which should help the interested readers follow more specialized discussions concerning FUERY for Access given in these papers. These insignificant terminological differences should not lead to any confusion or misunderstanding. It should be noted that a slightly different approach to the use of linguistic quantifiers in fuzzy queries has been proposed – cf. Bosc, Lietard & Pivert (1995) – but it will not be used here.

FQUERY for Access is embedded in the native Access's environment as an add-in. All the code and data is put into a database file, a *library*, installed by the user. Definitions of attributes, fuzzy values etc. are maintained in a dictionary (a set of regular tables), and a mechanism for putting them into the Query-By-Example (QBE) sheet (grid) is provided. Linguistic terms are represented within a query as parameters, and a query transformation is performed to provide for their proper interpretation during the query execution.

FQUERY for Access is an add-in that makes it possible to use fuzzy terms in queries. Briefly speaking, the following types of fuzzy terms are available:

- fuzzy values, exemplified by *low* in "profitability is *low*",
- fuzzy relations, exemplified by *much greater than* in "income is *much greater than* spending", and
- linguistic quantifiers, exemplified by *most* in "*most* conditions have to be met".

The elements of the first two types are elementary building blocks of fuzzy queries in FQUERY for Access. They are meaningful in the context of numerical fields only. There are also other fuzzy constructs allowed which may be used with scalar fields.

If a field is to be used in a query in connection with a fuzzy value, it has to be defined as an *attribute*. The definition of an attribute consists of two numbers: the attribute's values lower (LL) and upper (UL) limit. They set the interval which the field's values are assumed to belong to, according to the user. This interval depends on the meaning of the given field. For example, for *age* (of a person), the reasonable interval would be, e.g., [18,65], in a particular context, i.e. for a specific group. Such a concept of an attribute makes it possible to universally define fuzzy values.

Fuzzy values are defined as fuzzy sets on [-10, +10]. Then, *the matching degree md(·,·)* of a simple condition referring to attribute AT and fuzzy value FV against a record R is calculated by:

$$md(\text{AT}=\text{FV},\text{R})=\mu_{\text{FV}}(\tau(\text{R}(\text{AT})))$$

where: R(AT) is the value of attribute AT in record R, μ_{FV} is the membership function of fuzzy value FV, τ: $[\text{LL}_{\text{AT}},\text{UL}_{\text{AT}}]\rightarrow[-10,10]$ is the mapping from the interval defining AT onto [-10,10] so that we may use the same fuzzy values for different fields. A meaningful interpretation is secured by τ which makes it possible to treat all fields domains as ranging over the unified interval [-10,10]. For simplicity, it is assumed that the membership functions of fuzzy values are trapezoidal.

Linguistic quantifiers provide for a flexible aggregation of simple conditions. In FQUERY for Access the fuzzy linguistic quantifiers are defined in Zadeh's (1983; 1985) sense, as fuzzy set on [0, 10] interval instead of the original [0, 1] – cf. *most* given as (1). They may be interpreted either using original Zadeh's (1983) approach or via the OWA operators (cf. (Yager, 1988) or (Yager & Kacprzyk, 1997)); Zadeh's interpretation will be considered in what follows. The membership functions of fuzzy linguistic quantifiers are assumed piece-wise linear, hence two numbers from [0,10] are needed. Again, a mapping from [0, *N*], where *N* is the number of conditions aggregated, to [0,10] is employed to calculate the matching degree of a query. More precisely, the matching degree, *md(·,·)*, for the *query "Q of N conditions are satisfied"* for record R is equal to

$$md(Q, \text{condition}_{\text{i}},\text{R})=\mu_{\text{Q}}[\tau(\sum_i md(\text{condition}_{\text{i}},\text{R}))]$$

and we can also assign different importance degrees for particular conditions. Then, the aggregation formula is equivalent to (3). The importance is identified with a fuzzy set on [0,1], and then treated as property *B* in (3).

Before a fuzzy term may be used in a query, it has to be defined using the toolbar provided by FQUERY for Access and stored internally. This feature, i.e. maintenance of dictionaries of fuzzy terms defined by users, strongly supports our approach to data summarization discussed in this paper. In fact, the package comes with a set of predefined fuzzy terms but the user may enrich the dictionary too.

When the user initiates the execution of a query it is automatically transformed by appropriate FQUERY for Access's routines and then run as a native query of Access. The transformation consists primarily in the replacement of parameters referring to fuzzy terms by calls to functions implemented by the package which secure a proper interpretation of these fuzzy terms. Then, the query is run by Access as usually. Details can be found in Kacprzyk & Zadrożny (1994 – 1995b).

It is obvious that fuzzy queries directly correspond to summarizers in linguistic summaries. Thus, the derivation of a linguistic summary may proceed in an interactive (user assisted) way as follows:

- the user formulates a set of linguistic summaries of interest (relevance) using the fuzzy querying add in,

- the system retrieves records from the database and calculates the validity of each summary adopted, and
- a best (most appropriate) linguistic summary is chosen.

The use of fuzzy querying is very relevant because we can restate the summarization in the fuzzy querying context. First, (2) may be interpreted as:

"Most records match query S" (28)

where S replaces F in (2) since we refer here directly to the concept of a summarizer (of course, S is in fact the whole condition, e.g., price = *high*, while F is just the fuzzy value, i.e. *high* in this condition; this should not lead to confusion).

Similarly, (3) may be interpreted as:

"Most records meeting conditions B match query S" (29)

Thus, (29) says something only about a subset of records specified by (28). In database terminology, B corresponds to a *filter* and (29) claims that *most* records passing through B match query S. Moreover, since the filter may be fuzzy, a record may pass through it to a degree from $[0,1]$.

And, again, one can argue for a very high conceptual (perceptional) scalability of linguistic data summaries because their determination boils down to a well known process of database querying which virtually all users of computer systems, even novice users, are accustomed to.

Looking at the form of (28) and (29), which specify the user's interest and intent as to linguistic data summaries put in the context of database querying, it was proposed by Kacprzyk & Zadrożny (2002; 2005b) that the concept of a *protoform* in the sense of Zadeh (2002; 2006) is highly relevant. A protoform is defined as an abstract prototype, that is, in our context, for the query (summary) given by (28) and (29) as follows, respectively:

"*Most R's are S*" (30)

and

"*Most BR's are S*" (31)

where R means "records", B is a filter, and S is a query.

Since protoforms can obviously form a hierarchy, we can define higher level (more abstract) protoforms, for instance replacing *most* by a generic linguistic quantifier Q, we obtain, respectively:

"*QR's are S*" (32)

and

"*QBR's are S*" (33)

Obviously, the more abstract protoforms correspond to cases in which we assume less about summaries sought. There are two limit cases, where we: (1) assume totally abstract protoform or (2) assume all elements of a protoform are given as specific linguistic terms. In case 1 data summarization will be extremely time consuming, as the search space may be enormous, but may produce interesting, unexpected views on data. In case 2 the user has to guess a good candidate formula for summarization but the evaluation is fairly simple, just equivalent to the answering of a (fuzzy) query. Thus, the second case refers to the summarization known as *ad hoc queries*.

Then, going further along this line, we can show in Table 1 a classification of linguistic summaries into 5 basic types corresponding to protoforms of a more and more abstracted form.where $S^{structure}$ denotes that attributes and their connection in a summary are known, while S^{value} denotes a summarizer sought.

Type 1 may be easily produced by a simple extension of fuzzy querying as in Kacprzyk & Zadrożny's (2001b) FQUERY for Access. Basically, the user has to construct a query – a candidate summary, and it has to be determined what is the fraction of rows matching this query and what linguistic quantifier best denotes this fraction. A Type 2 summary is a straightforward extension of Type 1 by adding a fuzzy filter. Type 3 summaries require much more effort. Their primary goal is to determine typical (exceptional) values of an attribute. So, query S consists of only one simple condition built of the attribute whose typical (exceptional) value is sought, the "=" relational operator and a placeholder for the value sought. For example, using the following summary in the context of personal data: $Q =$ *"most"* and $S =$ "age=?" (here "?" denotes a placeholder mentioned above) we look for a typical value of age. A Type 4 summary may produce typical (exceptional) values for some, possibly fuzzy, subset of rows. From the computational point of view Type 5 summaries represent the most general form considered here: fuzzy rules describing dependencies between specific values of particular attributes. Here the use of B is essential, while previously it was optional. The summaries of Type 1 and 3 have been implemented as an extension to Kacprzyk & Zadrożny's (1994; 1995a-b; 2001b) FQUERY for Access. Two approaches to Type 5 summaries have been proposed. Firstly, a subset of such summaries may be produced by exploiting similarities with the *association rules* concept (Agrawal & Srikant, 1994) and employing their efficient algorithms. Second, genetic algorithm may be employed to search the summaries' space as initiated by George & Srikanth (1996a; 1996b). We will not consider these issues because they refer more to technical scalability and are dealt with in a different perspective than the one assumed in this paper.

Clearly, the protoforms are a powerful conceptual tool because we can formulate many different types of linguistic summaries in a uniform way, and devise a uniform and universal way to handle different linguistic summaries. Therefore, Kacprzyk & Zadrożny (2002; 2005) have certainly confirmed frequent claims by Zadeh and other researchers that protoforms are powerful indeed.

Notice, that all our previous statements about a very high conceptual (perceptional) scalability of linguistic data summaries in the form considered here are valid to an even higher extent when protoforms

Table 1. Classification of linguistic summaries

Type	Given	Sought	Remarks
1	S	Q	Simple summaries through ad-hoc queries
2	$S\,B$	Q	Conditional summaries through ad-hoc queries
3	$Q\,S^{structure}$	S^{value}	Simple value oriented summaries
4	$Q\,S^{structure}\,B$	S^{value}	Conditional value oriented summaries
5	Nothing	$S\,B\,Q$	General fuzy rules

are involved. Namely, the simplicity and intuitive appeal of the protoforms used in the context of linguistic data summaries make them applicable to data sets of any size. Even if the size of a data set increases, the very essence of a particular protoform just catches the contents of the data set in a user comprehensible form. And, by imposing a general template on the form of a summary, a protoform would presumably make the transition to the analysis of data sets of a larger size much smoother because no new general pattern of expected results would be necessary. That is why one can argue that our approach of using linguistic data summaries for data mining (knowledge discovery) can be viewed as a significant step towards the ultimate scalability of data mining (knowledge discovery) tools and techniques in all cases when the human user plays a significant role.

SOME FUTURE RESEARCH DIRECTIONS

Among many possible future works related to the concept of a cognitive (perceptional) scalability of data mining tools and techniques via linguistic data summaries, the following ones seem important and viable. First, the issue of a "comprehensive" scalability of linguistic data summaries can be considered in the sense that both the traditionally meant scalability (i.e. the retaining of functionality as the problem size, for instance the size of a database, increases) and the cognitive (perceptional) scalability proposed are combined. This has to do with many aspects including the development of more effective and efficient fuzzy querying tools, and of generation methods of linguistic data summaries, for instance using some more advanced evolutionary tools than in George & Srikanth (1996b).

An interesting future research direction would be to extend the arguments of this paper to cover another relevant approach to linguistic data summaries, namely through the use of gradual rules introduced by Dubois & Prade (1992). Similarly, an interesting issue would be to analyze yet another, different approach to linguistic summarization by Raschia & Mouaddib (2002), maybe even more so by considering their later papers in which a relation to OLAP has been indicated. The use of another approach to the introduction of quantified statements into fuzzy queries due to Bosc, Lietard and Pivert (1995) and their later works can be interesting.

Finally, one can also consider in the perspective of cognitive (perceptional) scalability the use of various protoforms extending our works Kacprzyk & Zadrożny (2005a; 2005b), in which an approach has also been proposed relating the generation of linguistic data summaries to some ways of generating some fuzzy association rules so that quite effective and efficient (though maybe not fully scalable) algorithms for association rule mining can be employed.

CONCLUDING REMARKS

We have discussed some aspects related to a crucial issue of scalability of data mining (knowledge discovery) tools and techniques by considering some special modern approach in that area, the so called linguistic data summaries.

We have argued first that the scalability should be meant in a more sophisticated way than just in terms of whether a particular tool and/or technique can retain its intended functionality, effectiveness and efficiency as the size of the problem (here the size and volume of data) increases.

We have introduced a new concept of a cognitive (perceptional) scalability whose essence is whether as the size of the problem increases a particular method will be fully functional, effective and efficient, but in the sense of being able to provide intuitively appealing and comprehensible results. We have argued that the use of natural language in the linguistic summaries provides a high cognitive (perceptual) scalability because natural language is the only fully natural means of articulation and communication of a human being, and also the use of natural language provides a common language for both the individuals and groups of different background, technical skills, knowledge, etc. No other communication means, as numbers or graphics, exhibit this property to the same extent.

Then, going even further in this direction, we have shown that Zadeh's protoform as general representations of linguistic data summaries, as proposed by Kacprzyk and Zadrożny (2002; 2005a; 2005b) amplify even more this advantage leading to what might be called an ultimate cognitive (perceptual) scalability.

REFERENCES

Agrawal, R., & Srikant, R. (1994). Fast algorithms for mining association rules. In J. B. Bocca, M. Jarke, & C. Zaniolo (Eds.), *Proceedings of the 20th International Conference on Very Large Databases,* Santiago de Chile, Chile (pp. 487-499). San Francisco, CA, USA: Morgan Kaufmann Publishers Inc.

Bosc, P., Dubois, D., Pivert, O., Prade, H., & de Calmes, M. (2002). Fuzzy summarization of data using fuzzy cardinalities. In *Proceedings of the 9th International Conference Information Processing and Management of Uncertainty in Knowledge-Based Systems (IPMU 2002),* Annecy, France (pp. 1553-1559).

Bosc, P., Lietard, L., & Pivert, O. (1995). Quantified statements and database fuzzy querying. In P. Bosc & J. Kacprzyk (Eds.), *Fuzziness in database management systems* (pp. 275-308). Heidelberg, Germany: Physica-Verlag.

Chen, G., Liu, D., & Li, J. (2001). Influence and conditional influence – new interestingness measures in association rule mining. In Proceedings of the *IEEE International Conference on Fuzzy Systems (FUZZ-IEEE'2001),* Vancouver, Canada (pp. 1440-1443).

Chen, G., & Wei, Q. (2002). Fuzzy association rules and the extended mining algorithm. *Information Sciences, 147,* 201–228. doi:10.1016/S0020-0255(02)00264-5

Chen, G., Wei, Q., & Kerre, E. E. (2000). Fuzzy data mining: Discovery of fuzzy generalized association rules. In G. Bordogna & G. Pasi (Eds.), *Recent research issues on fuzzy databases* (pp. 45-66). New York: Springer-Verlag.

Dubois, D., & Prade, H. (1992). Gradual rules in approximate reasoning. *Information Sciences, 61,* 103–122. doi:10.1016/0020-0255(92)90035-7

George, R., & Srikanth, R. (1996a). A soft computing approach to intensional answering in databases. *Information Sciences, 92,* 313–328. doi:10.1016/0020-0255(96)00049-7

George, R., & Srikanth, R. (1996b). Data summarization using genetic algorithms and fuzzy logic. In F. Herrera & J.L. Verdegay (Eds.), *Genetic algorithms and soft computing* (pp. 599-611). Heidelberg, Germany: Physica-Verlag.

Haines, S. (2006). *Pro Java EE 5 performance management and optimization.* Berkeley, CA: Apress.

Hu, Y.-Ch., Chen, R.-Sh., & Tzeng, G.-H. (2002). Mining fuzzy association rules for classification problems. *Computers & Industrial Engineering, 43,* 735–750. doi:10.1016/S0360-8352(02)00136-5

Kacprzyk, J. (2000). Intelligent data analysis via linguistic data summaries: A fuzzy logic approach. In R. Decker & W. Gaul (Eds.), *Classification and information processing at the turn of the millennium* (pp. 153-161). New York: Springer-Verlag.

Kacprzyk, J., & Yager, R. R. (2001). Linguistic summaries of data using fuzzy logic. *International Journal of General Systems, 30,* 133–154. doi:10.1080/03081070108960702

Kacprzyk, J., Yager, R. R., & Zadrożny, S. (2000). A fuzzy logic based approach to linguistic summaries of databases. *International Journal of Applied Mathematics and Computer Science, 10,* 813–834.

Kacprzyk, J., Yager, R. R., & Zadrożny, S. (2001). Fuzzy linguistic summaries of databases for an efficient business data analysis and decision support. In W. Abramowicz & J. Żurada (Eds.), *Knowledge discovery for business information systems* (pp. 129-152). Boston: Kluwer.

Kacprzyk, J., & Zadrożny, S. (1994). Fuzzy querying for Microsoft Access. In *Proceedings of the IEEE International Conference on Fuzzy Systems (FUZZ-IEEE'94) vol. 1,* Orlando, USA (pp. 167-171).

Kacprzyk, J., & Zadrożny, S. (1995a). Fuzzy queries in Microsoft Access v. 2. In *Proceedings of the IEEE International Conference on Fuzzy Systems (FUZZ-IEEE'95), Workshop on Fuzzy Database Systems and Information Retrieval,* Yokohama, Japan (pp. 61-66).

Kacprzyk, J., & Zadrożny, S. (1995b). FQUERY for Access: Fuzzy querying for a Windows-based DBMS. In P. Bosc & J. Kacprzyk (Eds.), *Fuzziness in database management systems* (pp. 415-433). Heidelberg, Germany: Physica-Verlag.

Kacprzyk, J., & Zadrożny, S. (1998). Data mining via linguistic summaries of data: An interactive approach. In T. Yamakawa & G. Matsumoto (Eds.), *Methodologies for the Conception, Design and Application of Soft Computing - Proceedings of IIZUKA'98,* Iizuka, Japan (pp. 668-671).

Kacprzyk, J., & Zadrożny, S. (2000a). On combining intelligent querying and data mining using fuzzy logic concepts. In G. Bordogna & G. Pasi (Eds.), *Recent research issues on the management of fuzziness in databases* (pp. 67-81). New York: Physica-Verlag.

Kacprzyk, J., & Zadrożny, S. (2000b). Data mining via fuzzy querying over the Internet. In O. Pons, M.A. Vila, & J. Kacprzyk (Eds.), *Knowledge management in fuzzy databases* (pp. 211-233). New York: Physica-Verlag.

Kacprzyk, J., & Zadrożny, S. (2000c). On a fuzzy querying and data mining interface. *Kybernetika, 36,* 657–670.

Kacprzyk, J., & Zadrożny, S. (2000d). Computing with words: Towards a new generation of linguistic querying and summarization of databases. In P. Sinčak & J. Vaščak (Eds.), *Quo vadis computational intelligence?* (pp. 144-175). New York: Springer-Verlag.

Kacprzyk, J., & Zadrożny, S. (2001a). Data mining via linguistic summaries of databases: An interactive approach. In L. Ding (Ed.), *A new paradigm of knowledge engineering by soft computing* (pp. 325-345). Singapore: World Scientific.

Kacprzyk, J., & Zadrożny, S. (2001b). Computing with words in intelligent database querying: Standalone and Internet-based applications. *Information Sciences, 34*, 71–109. doi:10.1016/S0020-0255(01)00093-7

Kacprzyk, J., & Zadrożny, S. (2001c). On linguistic approaches in flexible querying and mining of association rules. In H.L. Larsen, J. Kacprzyk, S. Zadrożny, T. Andreasen, & H. Christiansen (Eds.), *Flexible query answering systems. Recent advances* (pp. 475-484). New York: Springer-Verlag.

Kacprzyk, J., & Zadrożny, S. (2001d). Fuzzy linguistic summaries via association rules. In A. Kandel, M. Last, & H. Bunke (Eds.), *Data mining and computational intelligence* (pp. 115-139). New York: Physica-Verlag.

Kacprzyk, J., & Zadrożny, S. (2001e). Using fuzzy querying over the Internet to browse through information resources. In B. Reusch & K.-H. Temme (Eds.), *Computational intelligence in theory and practice* (pp. 235-262). New York: Physica-Verlag.

Kacprzyk, J., & Zadrożny, S. (2002). Protoforms of linguistic data summaries: Towards more general natural-language-based data mining tools. In A. Abraham, J. Ruiz del Solar, & M. Koeppen (Eds.), *Soft computing systems* (pp. 417-425). Amsterdam: IOS Press.

Kacprzyk, J., & Zadrożny, S. (2003). Linguistic summarization of data sets using association rules. In *Proceedings of the IEEE International Conference on Fuzzy Systems (FUZZ-IEEE'03),* St. Louis, USA (pp. 702-707).

Kacprzyk, J., & Zadrożny, S. (2005a). Protoforms of linguistic database summaries as a tool for human-consistent data mining. In *Proceedings of the 14th Annual IEEE International Conference on Fuzzy Systems (FUZZ-IEEE 2005)* (pp. 591-596). Reno, NV, USA: IEEE.

Kacprzyk, J., & Zadrożny, S. (2005b). Linguistic database summaries and their protoforms: Towards natural language based knowledge discovery tools. *Information Sciences, 173*, 281–304. doi:10.1016/j.ins.2005.03.002

Kacprzyk, J., & Zadrożny, S. (2009). Protoforms of linguistic database summaries as a human consistent tool for using natural language in data mining. *International Journal of Software Science and Computational Intelligence, 1*, 100–111.

Kacprzyk, J., Zadrożny, S., & Ziółkowski, A. (1989). FQUERY III+: a 'human-consistent' database querying system based on fuzzy logic with linguistic quantifiers. *Information Systems, 14*, 443–453. doi:10.1016/0306-4379(89)90012-4

Kacprzyk, J., & Ziółkowski, A. (1986). Database queries with fuzzy linguistic quantifiers. *IEEE Transactions on Systems . Man and Cybernetics SMC, 16*, 474–479. doi:10.1109/TSMC.1986.4308982

Klarner, M. (2004). Hyperbug - a scalable natural language generation approach. In R. Portzel (Ed.), *Proceedings of the 2nd International Workshop on Scalable Natural Language Understanding (ScaNa-Lu-2004)* (pp. 65-71). Boston, MA, USA: Association for Computational Linguistics.

Lee, J.-H., & Lee-Kwang, H. (1997). An extension of association rules using fuzzy sets. In *Proceedings of the 7th IFSA World Congress,* Prague, Czech Republic (pp. 399-402).

Lesh, N., & Mitzenmacher, M. (2004). Interactive data summarization: An example application. In *Proceedings of the Working Conference on Advanced Visual Interfaces (AVI '04),* Gallipoli, Italy (pp.183-187). New York: ACM.

Raschia, G., & Mouaddib, N. (2002). SAINTETIQ: A fuzzy set-based approach to database summarization. *Fuzzy Sets and Systems, 129,* 137–162. doi:10.1016/S0165-0114(01)00197-X

Rasmussen, D., & Yager, R. R. (1999). Finding fuzzy and gradual functional dependencies with summarySQL. *Fuzzy Sets and Systems, 106,* 131–142. doi:10.1016/S0165-0114(97)00268-6

Reiter, E. (1995). Building natural language generation systems. In A. Cawsey (Ed.), *Proceedings of the AI and Patient Education Workshop.* Glasgow, UK: University of Glasgow.

Yager, R. R. (1982). A new approach to the summarization of data. *Information Sciences, 28,* 69–86. doi:10.1016/0020-0255(82)90033-0

Yager, R. R. (1988). On ordered weighted averaging operators in multicriteria decision making. *IEEE Transactions on Systems, Man, and Cybernetics, SMC–18,* 183–190. doi:10.1109/21.87068

Yager, R. R. (1991). On linguistic summaries of data. In G. Piatetsky-Shapiro, & W.J. Frawley (Eds.), *Knowledge discovery in databases* (pp. 347-363). Menlo Park: AAAI Press/The MIT Press.

Yager, R. R. (1996). Database discovery using fuzzy sets. *International Journal of Intelligent Systems, 11,* 691–712. doi:10.1002/(SICI)1098-111X(199609)11:9<691::AID-INT7>3.0.CO;2-F

Yager, R. R., & Kacprzyk, J. (1997). *The ordered weighted averaging operators: Theory and applications.* Boston: Kluwer.

Zadeh, L., & Kacprzyk, J. (Eds.). (1999). *Computing with words in information/intelligent systems, 1. Foundations, 2. Applications.* New York: Physica-Verlag.

Zadeh, L. A. (1983). A computational approach to fuzzy quantifiers in natural languages. *Computers & Mathematics with Applications (Oxford, England), 9,* 149–184. doi:10.1016/0898-1221(83)90013-5

Zadeh, L. A. (1985). Syllogistic reasoning in fuzzy logic and its application to usuality and reasoning with dispositions. *IEEE Transactions on Systems, Man, and Cybernetics, SMC-15,* 754–763.

Zadeh, L. A. (2002). A prototype-centered approach to adding deduction capabilities to search engines – the concept of a protoform. In *Proceedings of the BISC Seminar, 2002.* Berkeley: University of California.

Zadeh, L. A. (2006). From search engines to question answering systems - the problems of world knowledge relevance deduction and precisiation. In E. Sanchez (Ed.), *Fuzzy logic and the Semantic Web* (pp. 163-210). Amsterdam: Elsevier.

Zadrożny, S., & Kacprzyk, J. (1999). On database summarization using a fuzzy querying interface. In *Proceedings of the IFSA'99 World Congress,* Taipei, Taiwan R.O.C. (pp. 39-43).

ADDITIONAL READING

Anwar, T. M., Beck, H. W., & Navathe, S. B. (1992). Knowledge mining by imprecise querying: A classification based system. In *Proceedings of the International Conference on Data Engineering,* Tampa, USA (pp. 622-630).

Bosc, P., & Kacprzyk, J. (Eds.). (1995). *Fuzziness in database management systems.* Heidelberg, Germany: Physica-Verlag.

Bosc, P., & Pivert, O. (1992). Fuzzy querying in conventional databases. In L.A. Zadeh & J. Kacprzyk (Eds.), *Fuzzy logic for the management of uncertainty* (pp. 645-671). New York: Wiley.

Kacprzyk, J., Pasi, G., Vojtaš, P., & Zadrożny, S. (2000). Fuzzy querying: issues and perspective. *Kybernetika, 36,* 605–616.

Kacprzyk, J., & Zadrożny, S. (1999). The paradigm of computing with words in intelligent database querying. In L.A. Zadeh & J. Kacprzyk (Eds.), *Computing with words in information/intelligent systems. Part 2. Foundations* (pp. 382-398). New York: Springer-Verlag.

Petry, F. E. (1996). *Fuzzy databases: Principles and applications.* Boston: Kluwer.

Rasmussen, D., & Yager, R. R. (1996). Using SummarySQL as a tool for finding fuzzy and gradual functional dependencies. In *Proceedings of the 6th International Conference Information Processing and Management of Uncertainty in Knowledge-Based Systems (IPMU'96),* Granada, Spain (pp. 275-280).

Rasmussen, D., & Yager, R. R. (1997a). Fuzzy query language for hypothesis evaluation. In T. Andreasen, H. Christiansen, & H. L. Larsen (Eds.), *Flexible query answering systems* (pp. 23-43). Boston: Kluwer.

Rasmussen, D., & Yager, R. R. (1997b). A fuzzy SQL summary language for data discovery. In D. Dubois, H. Prade, & R.R. Yager (Eds.), *Fuzzy information engineering: A guided tour of applications* (pp. 253-264). New York: Wiley.

Rasmussen, D., & Yager, R. R. (1999). Finding fuzzy and gradual functional dependencies with SummarySQL. *Fuzzy Sets and Systems, 106,* 131–142. doi:10.1016/S0165-0114(97)00268-6

Yager, R. R., & Kacprzyk, J. (1999). Linguistic data summaries: A perspective. In *Proceedings of the IFSA'99 Congress,* Taipei, Taiwan R.O.C. (pp. 44-48).

Zadeh, L. A., & Kacprzyk, J. (Eds.). (1992). *Fuzzy logic for the management of uncertainty.* New York: Wiley.

Zadrożny, S., Kacprzyk, J., & Gola, M. (2005). Towards human friendly data mining: Linguistic data summaries and their protoforms. In *Proceedings of the Artificial Neural Networks: Formal Models and their Applications – ICANN 2005* (LNCS 3697, pp. 697-702). Berlin, Germany: Springer.

Chapter 9
Human Focused Summarizing Statistics Using OWA Operators

Ronald R. Yager
Iona College, USA

ABSTRACT

The ordered weighted averaging (OWA) operator is introduced and the author discusses how it can provide a basis for generating summarizing statistics over large data sets. The author further notes how different forms of OWA operators, and hence different summarizing statistics, can be induced using weight-generating functions. The author shows how these weight-generating functions can provide a vehicle with which a data analyst can express desired summarizing statistics. Modern data analysis requires the use of more human focused summarizing statistics then those classically used. The author's goal here is to develop to ideas to enable a human focused approach to summarizing statistics. Using these ideas we can envision a computer aided construction of the weight generating functions based upon a combination of graphical and linguistic specifications provided by a data analyst describing his desired summarization.

INTRODUCTION

While many applications make use of the **O**rdered **W**eighted **A**veraging (OWA) operator (Yager, 1988) one under-explored application has been in summarizing data sets. We note that formally the OWA operator can be used to model different types of summarizing statistics depending on the choice of OWA weighting vector. Summarizing statistics are of particular importance in the field of data management and analysis and data mining (Tan, Steinbach & Kumar, 2006; Bouchon-Meunier, Rifqi & Lesot, 2008). Among the most well known summarizing statistics are the average, median and mode. While these have been extremely useful they don't completely enable the kinds of sophisticated analysis desired by modern

DOI: 10.4018/978-1-60566-858-1.ch009

data analysts. Intelligent data analysis requires the use of concepts appropriate for understanding by human cognition, which are often expressed in linguistic terms. With the availability of modern computing technology allowing rapid processing of vast amounts of data the only thing keeping us from providing this capability, is the availability of computable representations of human focused cognitive concepts. In this work we take a step in this direction. Our human focused approach to developing summarizing statistics makes use of two fundamental developments in computational intelligence. The first is ability to specify different OWA weighting vectors in terms of functions called weight-generating functions. The second is the ability to represent, with the aid of fuzzy sets, many linguistic and cognitive concepts in terms of functions. Here then a data analyst can input a function corresponding to some cognitive concept to induce the type of summary statistic they are interested in. Using these ideas we can envision a computer aided construction of the weight generating functions based upon a combination of graphical and linguistic specifications provided by a data analyst. The important point here is that now we have the framework to begin to develop a tools allowing both natural language and graphical input for aiding a data analyst in describing to the machine the types of intelligent summaries that may be desired.

Aspects and concerns with issues related to scalability are implicit in the approach discussed here. The use of summarization provides an important historically well established means of addressing large amounts of data by reducing it to a small number of characterizing statistics that can easily be comprehended by human decision makers and analysts (Stigler, 2002). Here we advance this approach by introducing methods for user-customizable summarizing statistics. In addition, the formal computational methodology used, based on the OWA operator, is computational inexpensive in terms of time as it only involves ordering and linear aggregation.

From a more general perspective, concerns about scalability can, in addition to being related to managing large amounts of data, can also be concerned with issues involving the description and modeling of complex concepts. By using linguistic terms and simple graphical constructs in coordination with the OWA operator we are providing a simple scalable methodology for modeling complex cognitive concepts. It is here that the work presented here is suggesting a new direction, cognitive scalability. An important benefit of the human use of categorization and concept formation in language is to provide a means to simplify the complex environment in which they must function. The approach presented here can be seen as part an agenda of bringing this scalability implicit in language to computational machines. It is a kind of computing with words.

OWA OPERATORS

The **O**rdered **W**eighted **A**veraging (OWA) operator of dimension n is a mapping $F: R^n \to R$ such that $F(a_1, ..., a_n) = \sum_{j=1}^{n} w_j b_j$ where b_j is the jth**largest** of the a_i. The w_j are weights such that $w_j \in [0, 1]$ and $\sum_{j=1}^{n} w_j = 1$. An alternative representation of the OWA operator can be had by letting d_j be the jth**smallest** of the arguments, $d_j = b_{n+1-j}$. Using this we get $F(a_1, ..., a_n) = \sum_{j=1}^{n} w_j b_j = \sum_{j=1}^{n} w_{n+1-j} d_j$. Letting $v_j = w_{n+1-j}$ we can express $F(a_1, ..., a_n) = \sum_{j=1}^{n} v_j d_j$. Here v_j is the weight associated with j^{th} smallest of the arguments.

We shall find it intuitively more satisfying to use this representation of the OWA operator. Collectively we can represent the v_j by an n-dimension vector **V** called the weighting vector. In this vector the weights associated with the smaller arguments are at the top. A further notational convenience can be had if we let **D** be the n–dimensional vector whose components are the d_j, we call **D** the ordered argument vector. Using this we get $F(a_1, ..., a_n) = \mathbf{V}^T\mathbf{D}$.

If *index* is a mapping such that index(j) is the index of the jth smallest of the arguments then $d_j = a_{index(j)}$, using this we get $F(a_1, ..., a_n) = \sum_j v_j a_{index(j)}$.

The OWA operator is characterized by its weighting vector **V**. By selecting different **V** we obtain different types of aggregations. Yager (1996) suggested an approach for obtaining the weights using a functional characterization. Let f: $[0, 1] \rightarrow [0, 1]$ satisfy: **1.** $f(0) = 0$, **2.** $f(1) = 1$ and **3.** $f(x) \geq f(y)$ if x > y. Using this function we specify the weights for j = 1 to n as

$$v_j = f(\frac{j}{n}) - f(\frac{j-1}{n}).$$

We call f the **weight-generating function** (wg function).

Using the weight generating function to generate the weights has a number of useful features. One property is that we can use a weight generating function to specify weights in a consistent manner for aggregations of different cardinalities. Secondly, particularly in the case of large *n*, a functional specification is often simpler than direct specification of the weights. Thirdly the use of a visual (graphical) characterization of the weight generating function can be helpful in understanding the performance and properties of the resulting aggregations. Another benefit is the availability of parameterization. We can easily modify the performance of the aggregation by changing the parameters in the function. For example the function $f(x) = x^r$ provides a valid weight generator function for all $r \in [0, \infty]$. However vastly different performances are obtained as we modify r.

Another important benefit is the possibility of associating the function f with some linguistic or cognitive concept. This feature is based upon the ability of fuzzy subsets to provide a representation of cognitive and linguistic concepts using membership grades in the unit interval (Zadeh, 1983). Here then one can linguistically specify some aggregation imperative, which can then be modeled as a fuzzy subset. This fuzzy subset can be used to denote a related weight generating function f.

We now provide some definitions and properties associated with these wg functions. First we can express the OWA aggregation directly in terms of the wg function

$$F(a_1, ..., a_n) = \sum_{j=1}^{n} (f(\frac{j}{n}) - f(\frac{j-1}{n})) d_j = d_n + \sum_{j=1}^{n-1} f(\frac{j}{n})(d_j - d_{j-1}) = d_n - \sum_{j=1}^{n-1} f(\frac{j}{n})(d_{j+1} - d_j).$$

If f_1 and f_2 are two wg functions we denote $f_1 \leq f_2$ if $f_1(x) \leq f_2(x)$ for all x and we say f_2 is **more rapid**. From the above we observe the more rapid the weight generating function the smaller the aggregation, if $f_2 \geq f_1$ then for all arguments $f_2(a_1, ..., a_n) \leq f_1(a_1, ..., a_n)$.

We now introduce some characterizing features associated with a wg function. Consider the three weighting vectors shown below:

$$\mathbf{V}_1 = \begin{bmatrix} 0.8 \\ 0.2 \\ 0 \\ 0 \\ 0 \end{bmatrix} \quad \mathbf{V}_2 = \begin{bmatrix} 0 \\ 0 \\ 0 \\ 0.2 \\ 0.8 \end{bmatrix} \quad \mathbf{V}_3 = \begin{bmatrix} 0 \\ 1/3 \\ 1/3 \\ 1/3 \\ 0 \end{bmatrix}$$

These are clearly distinguished from each other by the fact that the first gives preference to the lower values in the aggregation, the second gives preference to the higher values and the third makes no distinction in this respect, it is neutral or unbiased. In the following we introduce a measure that characterizes a weight generating function with respect to this feature. If f is a weight generating function we define $\text{Bias}(f) = 1 - \int_0^1 f(x)dx$. We note that $0 \le \text{Bias}(f) \le 1$ and if $f_1 \le f_2$ then $\text{Bias}(f_2) \le \text{Bias}(f_1)$. This characterizes any OWA aggregation based on the wg functions bias with respect to giving more weight to larger or smaller argument values. In particular those f's with lower values of bias below 0.5, have a tendency to give more weight to the smaller arguments in the aggregation while those with higher values of Bias given preference to the bigger values in the aggregation. An f with $\text{Bias}(f) = 0.5$ is neutral or unbiased in its preference, it give equal consideration to high and low values. We note that $\int_0^1 f(x)dx$ is the area under the curve f(x) thus $\text{Bias}(f) = 1 - \text{Area}(f)$.

Consider now the two weighting vectors: **I.** $v_1 = v_2 = v_3 = v_4 = v_5 = 0.2$ **II.** $v_1 = v_2 = v_4 = v_5 = 0$ and $v_3 = 1$. While they are both unbiased with respect to their handling large and small values they are clearly different in terms of their distribution of the weights. In the first case all arguments are treated the same while in the second case we only use one argument to determine the aggregated value. Yager (1988) suggested an entropy-like measure to capture this feature. If **V** is an n-dimensional weighting vector with components v_j then $\text{Disp}(\mathbf{V}) = -\sum_{j=1}^n v_j \ln\left[v_j\right]$ is called the **disparity** of **V**. The characterization a wg function f with respect to its disparity is $\text{Disp}(f) = \int_0^1 \frac{df}{dx} \ln\left[\frac{df}{dx}\right] dx$. We call $\text{Disp}(f)$ the disparity of f. For the types of wg functions of interest here we have $\text{Disp}(f) \ge 0$.

The smaller $\text{Disp}(f)$ the more uniformly the weights are distributed. The case when $\text{Disp}(f) = 0$ corresponds to the case where all weights are the same. As $\text{Disp}(f)$ gets larger, the less this equality in the weights. In the most disparate case, when all the weight is focused on one data element, we get $\text{Disp}(f) = \infty$.

MODELING BASIC STATISTICS WITH OWA OPERATORS

Here we begin to consider the role of OWA operators in providing summarizing statistics. We shall let $A = \langle a_1, ..., a_n \rangle$ and refer to this as our data set. Formally A is a bag (Yager, 1986). We recall a bag is a collection of elements, which like a set is indifferent to the ordering of its members but unlike a set allows duplication. We shall let F(A) indicate the OWA aggregation of the elements in the data set A, $F(A) = \mathbf{V}^T\mathbf{D} = \sum_j v_j d_j$ where $d_j = a_{\text{index}(j)}$. By appropriately selecting the weighting vector **V** be can provide many different summarizing statistics.

If **V** is selected such that $v_j = 1/n$ for all n then $F(a_1, ..., a_n) = 1/n \sum_j a_j$, this is the average. The median can also be modeled. If n is odd we let $v_q = 1$, where $q = (n+1)/2$ and $v_j = 0$ for all other j. If n is even we let $v_q = 0.5$ and $v_{q+1} = 0.5$ where $q = n/2$.

If **V** is such that $v_1 = 1$ and $v_j = 0$ for all $j \neq 1$ then $\mathbf{V^T D} = \text{Min}_j[a_j]$, thus we get the minimal element in the data set. We shall denote this vector as $\mathbf{V}_\wedge$. If **V** is such that $v_n = 1$ and $v_j = 0$ for all $j \neq n$ then $\mathbf{V^T D} = \text{Max}_j[a_j]$, we get the maximal value in the data set. We shall denote this vector as $\mathbf{V}_\vee$. More generally we can consider the kth representative value. If **V** is such that $v_k = 1$ and $v_j = 0$ for all $j \neq k$ and then $\mathbf{V^T D} = a_{index(k)}$ it selects the kth smallest element in the data set.

A large body of established and as well as new summarizing statistics can be obtained if we begin to consider the use of weight generating (wg) functions of the type discussed earlier. We recall with a wg function f we have $v_j = f(\frac{j}{n}) - f(\frac{j-1}{n})$. The average is obtained when $f(x) = x$. The Min is obtained if f is $f_\wedge$ where $f_\wedge(0) = 0$ and $f_\wedge(x) = 1$ for all $x \neq 0$. Thus using $f_\wedge$ we get $\mathbf{V}_\wedge$. The Max summarizing statistics is obtained if f is $f_\vee$ where $f_\vee(x) = 0$ for $x \neq 1$ and $f_\vee(1) = 1$. Using $f_\vee$ we get $\mathbf{V}_\vee$. For any wg function $f_\wedge(x) \leq f(x) \leq f_\vee(x)$ for all x,. This implies that for any data set A and any weight generating function f we have $F_\wedge(A) \leq F(A) \leq F_\vee(A)$ where F is the OWA aggregation generated by f. This of supports the property that $\text{Min}(A) \leq F(A) \leq \text{Max}(A)$.

An often-used summarizing statistic is the α percentile. We recall that if A is our data set the αth percentile is an element contained in A such that approximately α % of the elements in A are less then it and (100 - α) % are more then it. This statistic can easily be modeled with the OWA operator. Consider the function shown in figure 1 where $f(x) = 0$ if $x < \alpha$ and $f(x) = 1$ if $x \geq \alpha$. For this function we get that $v_q = 1$, for q such that $(q-1)/n \leq \alpha \leq q/n$ and $v_j = 0$ for all other j. If we let $q = \text{Int}(n\alpha)$, the integer portion of nα.we get $F(A) = d_q = a_{index(q)}$. It evaluates to the qth smallest element in A. In particular α portion of the arguments are smaller than $a_{index(q)}$ and $(1-\alpha)$ portion are bigger. Thus we see that this weight generating function provides the α percentile element of the data set. We note that the median is a special case of the preceding where $\alpha = 0.5$. The 25% percentile occurs when $\alpha = 0.25$ and 75% requires $\alpha = 0.75$. We also note that Max and Min are also special cases of this class. For the Max, $\alpha = 1$ and for the Min, $\alpha = 0$.

For this class $\text{Bias}(f) = \alpha$. This class of summarizers is the most disparate, it only users one element in the aggregation, hence $\text{Disp}(f) = \infty$

The mean where all weights are 1/n is obtained using the wg function $f(x) = x$. For this function the $\text{Bias}(f) = 1 - \int_0^1 x \, dx = 0.5$, it is unbiased with respect to high and low values. In addition we have

Figure 1. Percentile function

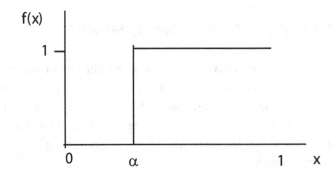

Disp(f) = 0. This is consistent with the fact that the smallest disparity occurs when we equally allocate the weights among all the data set elements.

We have shown that the mean, median, the Max, and Min and all percentile summarizing statistics can be expressed using this OWA formulation. Let us now look beyond these classical summarizing statistics and try to provide some new ones to aid in obtaining more intuitive summaries.

A CLASS OF LINEAR STATISTICS

Consider the summarizing statistic associated with the function shown in figure 2. For this function we have $f(x) = 0$ for $x \le \rho$, $f(x) = \dfrac{x - p}{1 - 2p}$ for $\rho < x < 1$ -ρ and $f(x) = 1$ for $x \ge \rho$.

This can be seen as a summarizing statistic that discounts the upper and lower ρ portion of the data set. It can be seen as a kind of outlier discounting aggregation. If n is the cardinality of our data set and $n\rho$ is an integer then: $v_j = 0$ for j = 1 **to** $n\rho$, $v_j = \dfrac{1}{n} \dfrac{1}{(1 - 2p)}$ for j = $n\rho$ + 1 **to** n - $n\rho$ and $v_j = 0$ for j = n - $n\rho$

+ 1 **to** n. This gives us $F(A) = \dfrac{1}{n} \dfrac{1}{(1 - 2p)} \displaystyle\sum_{j=n\rho+1}^{n(1-p)} d_j$

If np is not an integer we get a slight modification. In the following we let Int(np) denote the integer portion of np. If $n\rho \ne \text{Int}(n\rho)$ and $\Delta = n\rho - \text{Int}(n\rho)$ then we get

$v_j = 0$ for j = 1 **to** Int($n\rho$)

$v_j = \dfrac{1}{n} \dfrac{1}{(1 - 2p)}$ (1 - Δ) for j = Int($n\rho$) + 1

$v_j = \dfrac{1}{n} \dfrac{1}{(1 - 2p)}$ for j = Int($n\rho$)+ 2 **to** n - Int($n\rho$) - 1

$v_j = \dfrac{1}{n} \dfrac{1}{(1 - 2p)}$ (1 - Δ) for j = n - Int($n\rho$) - 1

Figure 2. Discounting type weight function

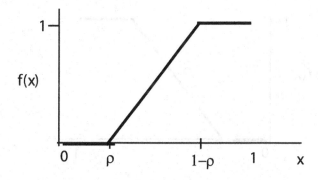

$v_j = 0$ for $j = n - \text{Int}(n\rho) + 1$ **to** n

We see that only a slight modification has occurred in two weights. In the following we shall assume, unless it hides a substantial issue, that we always have an integer when we perform operations like $n\rho$. In real application with large data a small change in ρ can always assure this.

Essentially here the data in the middle are averaged using weights $1/n *$ Slope where $1/(1-2\rho)$ is the Slope. For this wg function Bias(f) = 0.5 for all ρ. This is a neutral type aggregation with respect to its bias. It can also be shown that Disp(f) = -ln[1 - 2ρ]. We see the disparity is dependent upon ρ, as ρ decreases the disparity decreases. As ρ increases the disparity increases because more elements are being eliminated from the summarization process and more of the weight is being focused on the remaining elements. We note that since $1/(1-2\rho)$ is the slope we have Disp(f) = - ln(1 - 2ρ) = ln(Slope), it is the log of the slope.

While the preceding statistic can be viewed as an outlier discounting type of statistic we note that as ρ increases and approaches its largest allowable value, $\rho = 0.5$ we obtain the median statistic. Thus we see that this provides a family of unbiased statistics running between the simple average and the median. The difference being the number of data elements discounted. The median discounts all except the middle one. It is the most disparate member of this family. We see that for median with $\rho = 0.5$ we have Disp(f) = ∞ .

Essentially with this wg function, assuming $n\rho$ is an integer, we average the middle elements with weight $\dfrac{1}{n} * \dfrac{1}{1-2p}$ where $\dfrac{1}{1-2p}$ is the slope. We can express this as

$$\text{Mid}_\rho(A) = \frac{1}{n}\frac{1}{(1-2p)} \sum_{j=np+1}^{n(1-p)} d_j$$

If $\rho = 0$ we get the mean and if $\rho = 0.5$ we get the median

In figure 3 we show a slightly more general class of weight generating functions.

Here $f(x) = 0$ for $0 \le x \le a$, $f(x) = \dfrac{x-a}{b-a}$ for $a \le x \le b$ and $f(x) = 1$ for $x \ge b$. This wg function generates an unbalanced discounting. Assuming integers for na and nb we get: $v_j = 0$ for $j = 1$ to na, $v_j = \dfrac{1}{n}\dfrac{1}{b-a}$ for $j = na + 1$ to nb and $v_j = 0$ for $j = nb + 1$ to n. In this case our statistic is $F(A) = \dfrac{1}{n}\dfrac{1}{b-a}\sum_{j=na+1}^{nb} d_j$.

Figure 3. Unbalanced Discounting

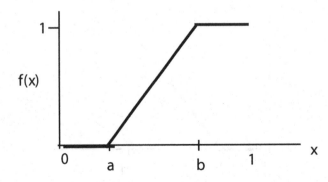

Figure 4. Lower ρ percent

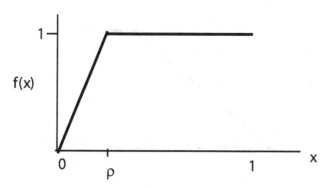

Here $\text{Bias}(f) = \dfrac{1}{2}\,(b+a)$ and $\text{Disp}(f) = -\ln(b-a)$. Again we see $\text{Disp}(f) = \ln(\text{Slope})$. The steeper the slope the more the disparity. We note that if we define $\text{Sum}(i, k) = \displaystyle\sum_{j=1}^{k} d_j$ then we see this statistic is $F(A) = \dfrac{1}{(k-1+1)}\,\text{Sum}(i, k)$. It is a linear statistic.

Let us look at some specific examples of summarizing statistics of the class corresponding to those in figure 3. We call these linear type summaries. Consider the summary based upon the weight generating function shown in figure 4 where $a = 0$ and $b = \rho$. This corresponds to a summary which takes the average of lowest ρ % of data values. Here $v_j = \dfrac{1}{np}$ for $j = 1$ to np and $v_j = 0$ for all others. This has a bias of $\dfrac{1}{2}\,\rho$ and disparity of $-\ln(\rho)$.

A closely related summarizing statistic is captured using the wg function shown in figure 5. This has $a = 1 - \rho$ and $b = 1$. This can be seen as corresponding to a statistic that takes the average of the ρ percent of the largest data values. Here our weight is $v_j = 1/(np)$ for the bigger values and zero for the others. It has a bias of $1 - 0.5\,\rho$, the complement of the preceding wg function. Its disparity is the same as the preceding $-\ln(\rho)$.

An interesting example of summarizing statistic is shown in figure 6. Here we are discounting the upper ρ portion in calculating the average. This can have particular usefulness in situations in which we

Figure 5. Upper ρ percent

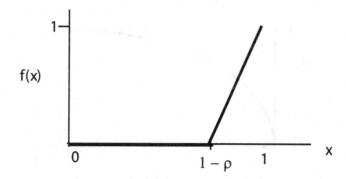

Figure 6. Discounting top ρ portion

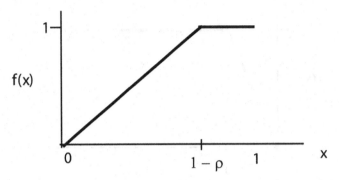

are trying to obtain the average of some non-negative quantity such as salary or gross income. In these situations it is often the case, especially in financial type data, that there exists a small portion of people whose incomes are so astronomical that including them in a summary calculation greatly distorts the statistic. The use of a statistic such as that shown in Figure 6 provides for a discounting of these outliers. For example, if the government is interested in summarizing the effects of some policy on salary or income it may find this a useful statistic.

A GENERAL OWA APPROACH TO SUMMARIZING STATISTICS

More generally we can use the connection between a wg function and the resulting summarizing statistic to allow a user to express there desired statistic in terms of a function f. We note that visual or graphical descriptions are particularly appropriate here. In support of this type of approach let us describe some features of the wg function and relate them to the properties of the resulting summarizing statistic. As we have indicated a wg function must be a mapping from the unit interval into the unit interval. It must be monotonic and satisfy $f(0) = 0$ and $f(1) = 1$. Figure 7 generically represents such a function.

A correspondence holds between the abscissa, x axis, and the ordered position of the data. In particular low x's correspond to the smaller data values in the data set and higher x's correspond to the bigger data values in the data set. The form of f for the low values of x describe how we are going to handle the smaller data set values while the form of f for high values of x describe how we handle the larger data

Figure 7. Generic Weight generating function

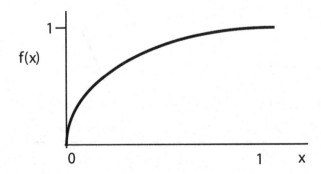

Figure 8. Illustrative weight generating function

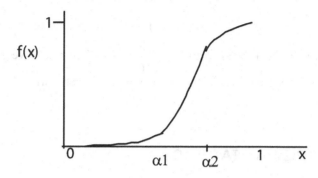

values. More specifically the change in ordinate values, the derivative of f(x), tells us how we allocate the weight. Thus if $[x_1, x_2]$ is a range on the x scale the difference $f(x_2) - f(x_1)$ indicates what portion of the total weight of one will be assigned to the data set elements falling between the nx_1 and nx_2 smallest. If $x_1 n = k_1$ and $x_2 n = k_2$ then $\sum_{j=k_1}^{k_2} v_j = f(x_2) - f(x_1)$. In particular we see that flat sections of f correspond to ranges of data elements contributing little to summary, while steep portions of f correspond to ranges getting much of the weight.

Using figure 8 as an illustration we see that much of the weight would be allocated to data elements d_j where j lies between $n\alpha_1$ and $n\alpha_2$. Since f(x) is relatively flat in the range for x = 0 to α_1 little of the weights would be assigned to the data elements d_j where j lies between 1 and $n\alpha_1$ and similarly the flatness of f(x) in the interval of α_2 to 1 would result in little of the weight being assigned to the d_j when j is in the range $n\alpha_2$ to n.

Using these ideas we can envision a computer aided construction of the weight generating function based upon a combination of graphical and linguistic specifications provided by a data analyst. Here then an analyst can input the specifications of a wg function which can induce the type of summary they are interested in. Once having obtained a formulation for f we use these to obtain the weights. The important point here being that we now have the understanding to begin to develop a graphical language for aiding a data analyst in describing to the machine various sophisticated types of summaries that may be desired

Actually once having formulated f it may be more useful to try to best match this f with a wg function from a set of available well defined functional forms. This makes it easily to actually generate the weights. Following we shall describe some useful classes of nonlinear wg functions.

Consider the class of functions $f(x) = x^r$ for $r \in [0, \infty]$. This has three special cases: when $r \to 0$ we get $f(x) \to f_\wedge(x)$ the Min statistic, when r = 1 we get that f(x) = x the average and when $r \to \infty$ we get $f(x) \to f_\vee(x)$ the Max statistic. The essential feature of this class of wg functions is that for r < 1 we allocate more of the weights to the smaller valued data elements while for r > 1, we allocate more of the weights to the larger valued elements in the data set. As r goes to its extremes of 0 and ∞ the allocation becomes more disparate ending in the Min when r = 0 and the Max when $r \to \infty$.

For this class of wg functions $v_j = (\frac{j}{n})^r - (\frac{j-1}{n})^r = \frac{j^r - (j-1)^r}{n^r}$. The Bias of this wg function is $\mathrm{Bias}(f) = r/(r+1)$ and $\mathrm{Disp}(f) = \log(r) + \frac{r-1}{r}$.

This class of wg functions can be further generalized if we consider the wg functions defined by: f(x) = 0 for $0 \leq x \leq a$, f(x) = $(\dfrac{x-a}{b-a})^r$ for $a \leq x \leq b$ and f(x) = 1 for $b \leq x \leq 1$ Here we have three parameters: a, b, and r. When r = 1 we get the a linear form f(x) = $\dfrac{x-a}{b-a}$. When r → 0 we get the *a* percentile, f(x) = 0 for x < a and f(x) = 1 for x ≥ a while for r → ∞ we get the b percentile, f(x) = 0 for x < b and f(x) = 1 for x ≥ b.

WEIGHTED SUMMARIZING STATISTICS

In (Yager, 1998) we discussed importance weighted OWA aggregations denoted WOWA aggregation. Here we shall consider their use in the construction of weighted summarizing statistics. Let A = (a_1, ..., a_n) be a data set and let $u_i \geq 0$ be the importance associated with the data point a_i. Let f be a weight generating function guiding the aggregation. Again we let index(i) be the index of the ith smallest data value. We denote T(j) = $\sum_{i=1}^{j} u_{index(i)}$, the sum of the importances of the j smallest data points. We denote T = T(n), it is the sum of all the importance weights. By default we let T(0) = 0. We now let z_j = f($\dfrac{T(j)}{T}$) - f($\dfrac{T(j-1)}{T}$) and define the WOWA aggregation as

$$F_f((u_i, a_i)) = \sum_{j=1}^{n} z_j\, a_{index(j)}.$$

We can use an alternative notation. Let $u_j = \dfrac{u_j}{T}$ and $S_j = \dfrac{T_j}{T} = \dfrac{1}{T}\sum_{i-1}^{j} u_{index(i)} = \sum_{i=1}^{j} u_{index(i)}$. Using this we have z_j = f(S_j) - f(S_{j-1}).

In the case where f(x) = x we have f(S_j) = S_j and z_j = S_j - S_{j-1} = â$_{index(j)}$ thus $F_f(u_i, a_i)$ = $\sum_{j=1}^{n} u_{index(j)} a_{index(j)} = \sum_{i-1}^{n} u_i a_i$. This is the ordinary weighted average.

Interesting uses of this WOWA aggregation can be made in data analysis. Assume we have a collection of data about a group of people containing their salary and age. Assume we want to calculate the average salary of the young people. Here we can define the concept young as a fuzzy subset, *young*. We can then calculate for each person the degree to which they are young and use these as our importance in the WOWA summarization. Thus if (age$_i$, salary$_i$) is the information available about the ith person then u_i = *young*(age$_i$), the membership grade of age$_i$ in *young*. We then can use $\sum_{i=1}^{n} u_i\, salary_i$ to give us the average salary of the young people.

A more sophisticated statistic associated with this data set is the following. Assume we want to calculate "the average salary of the ρ portion of the young people with the lowest salary". To obtain this we use the wg function f shown in figure 4. Here f(x) = $\dfrac{1}{\rho}$ x for $0 \leq x \leq \rho$ and f(x) = 1 for x > ρ. Our weights for the WOWA aggregation are obtained from $\hat{z}_j$ = f(S_j) - f(S_{j-1}). Without loss of generality we assume there is a q such that $S_q = \sum_{i=1}^{q} u_{index(x)} = \rho$ hence $\dfrac{1}{\rho} S_q = 1$. In this case a$_{index(i)}$ for i = 1 to q constitute the smallest data points with ρ portion of the importance weight. Here we get $z_j = \dfrac{1}{\rho} \, \hat{u}_{index(j)}$ for $j = 1$ to q and $z_j = 0$ for $j > q$. Using this we get the desired summary as $F_f((u_i, a_i)) = \displaystyle\sum_{j=1}^{n} z_i \, a_{index(j)} = \dfrac{1}{\rho}\sum_{j=1}^{q} u_{index(j)} a_{index(j)}$.

In the preceding we have considered the situation in which the weights are obtained as a result of the satisfaction of some condition by the object. Thus the WOWA provided some kind of conditioned aggregation. We have looked at the asituation in which the property on which we are conditioning is different from the actual value being aggregated. Some interesting statistics can be obtained if we allow the weight to be related to the value being aggregated. Let us look at some of these.

Assume we have a data set $A = \{a_1, ..., a_n\}$ of salaries. Assume we desire to calculate the average of the salaries over the value **b**. In this case we can assign weights such that $u_i = 0$ if $a_i \le b$ and $u_i = 1$ if $a_i > b$ and then use a WOWA aggregation. If we want to calculate the average of the salaries greater than 50% of the maximum we let $a^* = \mathrm{Max}_j[a_j]$ and then define $u_j = 0$ if $a_j \le 0.5\,a^*$ and $u_j = 1$ if $a_j > 0.5\,a^*$.

Another example is to obtain *the average salary of the people with high salaries*. Here we would define a fuzzy subset **H** corresponding to the concept high salary and the let u_i be the membership degree of a_i in H, $u_i = H(a_i)$. Furthermore we note the concept "high salary" can be absolute or relative. That is, H can be defined based upon some independent idea of what we mean by high salary or it can be dependent upon the set A.

MODELING THE MODE

We recall the mode corresponds to the value with the most replications in a data set. Here we provide a OWA representation of the mode as well as some generalizations of it. In order to capture the mode we must describe the Induced OWA (IOWA) operator (Yager & Filev, 1999) and the concept of similarity. We note the power average introduced in Yager (2001) provides a data aggregation that manifests features of average and the mode.

The IOWA operator is an extension of the OWA that operates on pairs. Assume (a_i, h_i) are a collection of n data point and let **V** be an n-dimensional OWA vector, $v_j \in [0, 1]$ and $\sum_j v_j = 1$. Let h–index be an index function such that h–index(j) is the index of the jth smallest of the h_i. We now define the h Induced OWA aggregation as $I\text{--}F((a_i, h_i)) = \sum_j v\, a_{h\text{--}index(j)}$. Thus in the OWA operator while we aggregator the a_i we order them by their h value. In the light of this for the pair (a_i, h_i) we call a_i the argument or data variable and h_i the order inducing value.

We define similarity as a function that takes any pair of data points into the unit interval, $\mathrm{Sim}(a_i, a_j) \in [0, 1]$. The larger $\mathrm{Sim}(a_i, a_j)$ the more similar the data points. While the definition of similarity is generally context dependent we require some properties on Sim. First it must be commutative $\mathrm{Sim}(a_i, a_j) = \mathrm{Sim}(a_j, a_i)$. Secondly it must be reflexive $\mathrm{Sim}(a_i, a_j) = 1$ if $a_i = a_j$. However, we don't require that $a_i = a_j$ for $\mathrm{Sim}(a_i, a_j) = 1$, two elements can be maximally similar even if they are not equal. We also require that if $a_1 > a_2 > a_3$ then $\mathrm{Sim}(a_1, a_2) \ge \mathrm{Sim}(a_1, a_3)$, this is a kind of transitivity. There is an inverse relationship between similarity and the distance metric, $\mathrm{Dist}(a, b) = a\text{-}b$. In particular the preceding is equivalent to requiring if $\mathrm{Dist}(a, b) \ge \mathrm{Dist}(a, c)$ then $\mathrm{Sim}(a, c) \ge \mathrm{Sim}(a, b)$. However we are **not** necessarily requiring $\mathrm{Dist}(a, b) \ge \mathrm{Dist}(c, d) \Rightarrow \mathrm{Sim}(a, b) \le \mathrm{Sim}(c, d)$. The lack of this condition allows us, for some purposes, to consider salaries of \$10 million or \$10.5 million to be more similar then salaries of \$10,000 and \$100,000.

We now introduce some prototypical similarity relations. A prototypical binary similarity relation is defined by Sim(a, b) = 1 if a-b $\leq \Delta$ and Sim(a, b) = 0 if a-b $> \Delta$. We note that when Δ = 0 we get S(a, b) = 1 if a = b and S(a, b) = 0 if a $\neq$ b, we denote this relation, as SIM*. SIM* is the most strict in the sense that if Sim is any similarity relation then Sim(x, y) $\geq$ SIM*(x, y). Another useful similarity relation is Sim(a, b) = $e^{-\frac{(a-b)^2}{\mu^2}}$ Here μ is a parameter such that the larger μ the more generous the similarity measure. In the special case when our data points are restricted to the unit interval we can use Sim(a, b) = 1 - a-b.

We shall now introduce a new class of summarizing statistics based upon the idea of similarity and the IOWA aggregation operator. Assume we have a data set A= {a_1, ..., a_n} and let Sim be a similarity relation on A. Let $S(a_i) = \sum_{j=1}^{n} Sim(a_i, a_j)$ be the total of the similarities for data point a_i. We call this the **similarity score** of a_i.

To obtain our new class of summarizing statistics we use the collection of pairs (a_i, h_i) where a_i is a data point and $h_i = S(a_i)$ is its similarity score. Consider the IOWA aggregation F((a_i, h_i)) where a_i is the argument value and h_i is the order inducing value and **V** is an OWA weighting vector. In this case F((a_i, h_i)) = $\sum_{j=1}^{n} v_j a_{s-index(j)}$ where s-index(j) is the index of the data point with the jth smallest similarity. So here we are ordering the data by their similarity score and then combining the data values using the vector **V**. Here F((a_i, h_i)) is going to be our summarizing statistic.

Let us now look at some special cases of this aggregation and see what kinds of summarizing statistics we get. We note that in formulating this summarizing statistic we have two degrees of freedom, the weighting vector **V** and the similarity measure. By appropriately selecting these we can get different summarizing statistics.

Initially we use the strict binary measure, SIM*. In this case we shall denote the similarity score as of a_i as S*. Choosing **V** such that v_n = 1 and v_j = 0 for all j $\neq$ n we get â = $\sum_{j=1}^{n} v_j a_{s^*-index(j)} = a_{s^*-index(n)}$. Here we get the data point with the largest similarity score. However since we are using SIM* this is the data value which has the most number of replications, it is the mode. Thus using this choice of Sim and **V** we have obtained a representation of the mode.

Let us now take advantage of the generality of this formulation and consider another example of weighting vector **V**. Consider the vector **V** where v_1 = 1 and v_j = 0 for j $\neq$ n. In this case â = $a_{s^*-index(1)}$. Here we get the data point with the smallest similarity score. From our definition of SIM* we see that $a_{s^*-index(1)}$ is the data value having the least number of replications. Thus whereas the mode, $a_{s^*-index(n)}$, can be seen being a kind of most typical value, this new statistic, $a_{s^*-index(1)}$, can be seen as a most **atypical** or **unusual** value in the data set.

We have seen that by selecting **V** we are able to get significant extreme elements from the data set. By selecting **V** using $f_\wedge$ gives us the most typical element in the set while selecting **V** using $f_\vee$ gives us the most atypical element in the data set. We note that in the case of the ordinary OWA aggregation, where we are just aggregating the data points without the order inducing variable, using the weighting vectors generated from $f_\wedge$ and $f_\vee$ also gives us extreme elements from the data set; however, the diversity is based of the value, we get the largest and smallest valued elements in the data set. Here our diversity is with respect to being the most typical and least typical. Thus we see that the use of similarity along

Figure 9. ρ Elimination

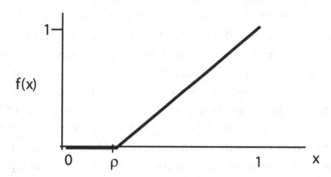

with the IOWA aggregation can provide us with tools which can help us understand a data set along another dimension.

We can consider the use of other weight vectors or wg functions f with the similarity inducing ordering. If we use $f(x) = x$ we get **V** such that $v_j = 1/n$. In this case our statistic is $F((a_i, h_i)) =$

$$\sum_{j=1}^{n} v_j \, a_{s^*-index(j)} = \frac{1}{n} \sum_{i=1}^{n} a_i \,,$$ the ordinary average.

Consider now using the wg function f shown in figure 9 in the aggregation $F((a_i, h_i))$. For small ρ we can be seen to be removing the ρn most **atypical** values from the aggregation. So here we are taking an average that eliminates the atypical values. This can be seen as eliminating "outliers", where the idea of outlier is not based on the value but is based on the number of replications. The less they're replicated the more they are outliers or atypical. On the other hand if ρ is big, close to one, then we see that we essentially obtain an average of the most typical values in the data set.

Consider the wg function shown in figure 4 in the aggregation $F((a_i, h_i))$. Here, for small ρ, we are taking an average of the atypical values. On the other hand as ρ increases we are taking an average which eliminates the most typical elements. This may be an interesting statistic.

Consider now using the wg function shown in figure 1 in the aggregation This generates a statistic, normally a hard one, which calculates the data point for which α portion of the data points are less typical, more unique, while 1 - α portion of the data have values that are more typical . For α = 0.5 we find the data value that lies in the middle with respect to its typicality –atypicality.

Figure 10. Histogram of Data Set

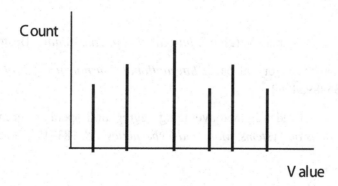

An understanding of the approaches developed and the role of the wg function f can be had if we consider the histogram representation of a data set depicted in figure 10. In this figure the abscissa axis corresponds to the data point values and the ordinate axis corresponds to the count of points having that value. In our original OWA method, $F((a_i))$, we take an aggregation of the data values in which the OWA weights are determined by the wg $f(x)$ so that the form of $f(x)$ in the low range of x determines the weights for the **smaller data values** and the form of $f(x)$ in the high range of x determines the weights for the **bigger data values**. In the case where we use the similarity and the induced OWA, $F((a_i, h_i))$, while we are still taking aggregation of the data values the role of the wg function is different. Here the OWA weights are determined by the wg $f(x)$ so that the form of $f(x)$ in the low range of x determines the weights for the data values with the **smaller count** and the form of $f(x)$ in the high range of x determines the weights for the data values with the **larger counts**. With this understanding we can construct the wg function to generate desired summarizing statistics. In addition we note that the importance weight u_i associated with a data point can be seen as affecting the count. Instead of counting a data value as one we count it by its importance weight.

CONCLUSION

In the preceding we have investigated the use of the OWA operator as a basis for providing summarizing statistics. We showed the centrality of the weight generating function in inducing the various statistics and begun to get an understanding of the relationship between the wg functions and the resulting statistic. We envision the use of fuzzy methods to enrich the capability of this approach. Specifically we see fuzzy logic as providing a bridge for translating linguistically expressed requirements for data summarizing into mathematical functional forms which can then be used as weight generating functions. We feel this work is an early step to the development of tools enabling the kind of man-machine cooperation enabling the human focused summarizing statistics.

REFERENCES

Bouchon-Meunier, B., Rifqi, M., & Lesot, M. J. (2008). Similarities in fuzzy data mining: From a cognitive view to real -world applications. In J. M. Zurada, G. G. Yen, & J. Wang (Eds.), *Computational intelligence: Research frontiers* (pp. 349-367). Berlin, Germany: Springer.

Stigler, S. M. (2002). *Statistics on the table: The history of statistical concepts and methods*. Boston: Harvard University Press.

Tan, P. N., Steinbach, M., & Kumar, V. (2006). *Introduction to data mining*. Boston: Addison Wesley.

Yager, R. R. (1986). On the theory of bags. *International Journal of General Systems, 13*, 23–37. doi:10.1080/03081078608934952

Yager, R. R. (1988). On ordered weighted averaging aggregation operators in multi-criteria decision making. *IEEE Transactions on Systems, Man, and Cybernetics, 18*, 183–190. doi:10.1109/21.87068

Yager, R. R. (1996). Quantifier guided aggregation using OWA operators. *International Journal of Intelligent Systems, 11,* 49–73. doi:10.1002/(SICI)1098-111X(199601)11:1<49::AID-INT3>3.0.CO;2-Z

Yager, R. R. (1998). Including importances in OWA aggregations using fuzzy systems modeling. *IEEE transactions on Fuzzy Systems, 6,* 286–294. doi:10.1109/91.669028

Yager, R. R. (2001). The power average operator. *IEEE Transactions on Systems . Man and Cybernetics Part A, 31,* 722–730.

Yager, R. R., & Filev, D. P. (1999). Induced ordered weighted averaging operators. *IEEE Transactions on Systems, Man, and Cybernetics, 29,* 141–150. doi:10.1109/3477.752789

Zadeh, L. A. (1983). A computational approach to fuzzy quantifiers in natural languages. *Computers & Mathematics with Applications (Oxford, England), 9,* 149–184. doi:10.1016/0898-1221(83)90013-5

Chapter 10
(Approximate) Frequent Item Set Mining Made Simple with a Split and Merge Algorithm

Christian Borgelt
European Center for Soft Computing, Spain

Xiaomeng Wang
Otto-von-Guericke University of Magdeburg, Germany

ABSTRACT

In this chapter the authors introduce SaM, a split and merge algorithm for frequent item set mining. Its core advantages are its extremely simple data structure and processing scheme, which not only make it very easy to implement, but also fairly easy to execute on external storage, thus rendering it a highly useful method if the data to mine cannot be loaded into main memory. Furthermore, the authors present extensions of this algorithm, which allow for approximate or "fuzzy" frequent item set mining in the sense that missing items can be inserted into transactions with a user-specified penalty. Finally, they present experiments comparing their new method with classical frequent item set mining algorithms (like Apriori, Eclat and FP-growth) and with the approximate frequent item set mining version of RElim (an algorithm the authors proposed in an earlier paper and improved in the meantime).

INTRODUCTION

It may not even be an exaggeration to say that the tasks of frequent item set mining and association rule induction started the popular research area of data mining. At least, however, these tasks have a strong and long-standing tradition in data mining and knowledge discovery in databases and account for a huge number of publications in data mining conferences and journals. The enormous research efforts devoted to these tasks have led to a variety of sophisticated and efficient algorithms to find frequent item sets. Among the best-known are Apriori (Agrawal and Srikant 1994, Agrawal et al. 1996), Eclat (Zaki et al. 1997) and FP-growth (Han et al. 2000).

DOI: 10.4018/978-1-60566-858-1.ch010

Nevertheless, there is still room for improvement: while Eclat, which is the simplest of the mentioned algorithms, can be fairly slow on some data sets (compared to other algorithms), FP-growth, which is usually the fastest algorithm, employs a sophisticated data structure and requires to load the transaction data to mine into main memory. Hence a simpler processing scheme, which still maintains efficiency, is desirable. Other lines of improvement include filtering the found frequent item sets and association rules (see, for example, [Webb and Zhang 2005, Webb 2007]), identifying temporal changes in discovered patterns (see, for example, [Böttcher et al. 2005, Böttcher et al. 2007]), and discovering fault-tolerant or approximate frequent item sets (see, for example, [Cheng et al. 2001, Pei et al. 2001, Wang et al. 2005]).

In this paper we introduce SaM, a split and merge algorithm for frequent item set mining. Its core advantages are its extremely simple data structure and processing scheme, which not only make it very easy to implement, but also fairly easy to execute on external storage, thus rendering it a highly useful method if the data to mine cannot be loaded into main memory. Furthermore, we present extensions of this algorithm, which allow for approximate or "fuzzy" frequent item set mining in the sense that missing items can be inserted into transactions with a user-specified penalty. We developed this algorithm as a simplification of the (already very simple) RElim algorithm (Borgelt 2005b), which we improved in the meantime.

The rest of this paper is structured as follows: first we briefly review the fundamentals of frequent item set mining, and especially the basic divide-and-conquer scheme underlying many frequent item set mining algorithms. Secondly, we present our SaM (Split and Merge) algorithm for exact frequent item set mining and compare it experimentally to classic frequent item set mining algorithms like Apriori, Eclat, and FP-growth, but also our own RElim algorithm (Borgelt 2005b). In the next step we review approximate or "fuzzy" frequent item set mining in the sense that missing items can be inserted into transactions with a user-specified penalty. Based on this review we present two extensions of our SaM algorithm that allow to perform such approximate frequent item set mining with unlimited and limited item insertions, respectively. These extensions are then experimentally compared to the corresponding extensions of the RElim algorithm (Wang et al 2005). Finally, we draw conclusions from our discussion and experiments.

FREQUENT ITEM SET MINING

Frequent item set mining is a data analysis method that was originally developed for market basket analysis. It aims at finding regularities in the shopping behavior of the customers of supermarkets, mail-order companies and online shops. In particular, it tries to identify sets of products that are frequently bought together. Once identified, such sets of associated products may be exploited to optimize the organization of the products on the shelves of a supermarket or on the pages of a mail-order catalog or web shop, may be used to suggest other products a customer could be interested in, or may give hints which products may conveniently be bundled.

Formally, the task of frequent item set mining can be described as follows: we are given a set B of items, called the item base, and a database T of transactions. Each item represents a product, and the item base represents the set of all products offered by a store. The term item set refers to any subset of the item base B. Each transaction is an item set and represents a set of products that has been bought by an actual customer. Since two or even more customers may have bought the exact same set of products, the total of all transactions must be represented as a vector, a bag or a multiset[1], since in a simple set each transaction could occur at most once. Note that the item base B is usually not given explicitly, but only implicitly as the union of all transactions.

The support sT(I) of an item set I ⊆ B is the number of transactions in the database T it is contained in. Given a user-specified minimum support smin ∈ IN (an integer number), an item set I is called frequent in T iff sT(I) ≥ smin. The goal of frequent item set mining is to identify all item sets I ⊆ B that are frequent in a given transaction database T. Note that the task of frequent item set mining may also be defined with a relative minimum support (a number in the real interval [0,1]), which is the fraction of transactions in T that must contain an item set I in order to make I frequent. However, this alternative definition is obviously equivalent.

A standard approach to find all frequent item sets w.r.t. a given database T and support threshold smin, which is adopted by basically all frequent item set mining algorithms (except those of the Apriori family), is a depth-first search in the subset lattice of the item base B. Viewed properly, this approach can be interpreted as a simple divide-and-conquer scheme. For some chosen item i, the problem to find all frequent item sets is split into two subproblems: (1) find all frequent item sets containing the item i and (2) find all frequent item sets not containing the item i. Each subproblem is then further divided based on another item j: find all frequent item sets containing (1.1) both items i and j, (1.2) item i, but not j, (2.1) item j, but not i, (2.2) neither item i nor j etc. In this way all possible item sets are eventually considered.

All subproblems that occur in this divide-and-conquer recursion can be defined by a conditional transaction database and a prefix. The prefix is a set of items that has to be added to all frequent item sets that are discovered in the conditional database. Formally, all subproblems are tuples $S = (C, P)$, where C is a conditional database and $P ⊆ B$ is a prefix. The initial problem, with which the recursion is started, is $S = (T, ∅)$, where T is the given transaction database to mine and the prefix is empty. A subproblem $S0 = (C0, P0)$ is processed as follows: Choose an item $i ∈ B0$, where B0 is the set of items occurring in C0. This choice is arbitrary, but usually follows some predefined order of the items. If $s_{C_0}(i) ≥ s_{min}$, then report the item set $P0 ∪ \{i\}$ as frequent with the support $s_{C_0}(i)$, and form the subproblem $S1 = (C1, P1)$ with $P1 = P0 ∪ \{i\}$. The conditional database C1 comprises all transactions in C0 that contain the item i, but with the item i removed. This also implies that transactions that contain no other item than i are entirely removed: no empty transactions are ever kept. If C1 is not empty, S1 is processed recursively. In any case (that is, regardless of whether $s_{C_0}(i) ≥ s_{min}$ or not), form the subproblem $S2 = (C2, P2)$, where P2 = P0 and the conditional database C2 comprises all transactions in C0 (including those that do not contain the item i), but again with the item i removed. If C2 is not empty, S2 is processed recursively.

Eclat, FP-growth, RElim and several other frequent item set mining algorithms all follow this basic recursive processing scheme. They differ mainly in how they represent the conditional transaction databases and thus in how they do the support counting. There are basically two fundamental approaches, namely horizontal and vertical representations. In a horizontal representation, the database is stored as a list (or array) of transactions, each of which is a list (or array) of the items contained in it. In a vertical representation, a database is represented by first referring with a list (or array) to the different items. For each item a list of transaction identifiers is stored, which indicate the transactions that contain the item.

However, this distinction is not pure, since there are many algorithms that use a combination of the two forms of representing a database. For example, while Eclat uses a purely vertical representation,

FP-growth combines in its FP-tree structure a vertical representation (links between branches) and a (compressed) horizontal representation (prefix tree of transactions). RElim uses basically a horizontal representation, but groups transactions w.r.t. their leading item, which is, at least partially, a vertical representation. The SaM algorithm presented below is, to the best of our knowledge, the first frequent item set mining algorithm that is based on the general processing scheme outlined above and uses a purely horizontal representation.[2]

The basic processing scheme can easily be improved with so-called perfect extension pruning, which relies on the following idea: given an item set I, an item $i \notin I$ is called a perfect extension of I if I and $I \cup \{i\}$ have the same support, that is, if i is contained in all transactions containing I. Perfect extensions have the following properties: (1) if the item i is a perfect extension of an item set I, then it is also a perfect extension of any item set $I \subseteq J$ as long as $i \notin J$ and (2) if I is a frequent item set and K is the set of all perfect extensions of I, then all sets $I \cup J$ with $J \in 2K$ (where 2K denotes the power set of K) are also frequent and have the same support as I.

These properties can be exploited by collecting in the recursion not only prefix items, but also, in a third element of a subproblem description, perfect extension items. Once identified, perfect extension items are no longer processed in the recursion, but are only used to generate all supersets of the prefix that have the same support. Depending on the data set, this can lead to a considerable acceleration. It should be clear that this optimization can, in principle, be applied in all frequent item set mining algorithms.[3]

A SIMPLE SPLIT AND MERGE ALGORITHM

The SaM (Split and Merge) algorithm presented in this paper can be seen as a simplification of the already fairly simple RElim (Recursive Elimination) algorithm, which we proposed in (Borgelt 2005b) and extended to approximate or "fuzzy" frequent item set mining in (Wang et al. 2005). While RElim represents a (conditional) database by storing one transaction list for each item, the split and merge algorithm presented here uses only a single transaction list, stored as an array. This array is processed with a simple split and merge scheme, which computes a conditional database, processes this conditional database recursively, and eliminates the split item from the original (conditional) database.

SaM preprocesses a given transaction database in a way that is very similar to the preprocessing used by many other frequent item set mining algorithms. The steps are illustrated in Figure 1 for a simple example transaction database. Step 1 shows the transaction database in its original form. In step 2 the frequencies of individual items are determined from this input in order to be able to discard infrequent items immediately. If we assume a minimum support of three transactions for our example, there are no infrequent items, so all items are kept. In step 3 the (frequent) items in each transaction are sorted according to their frequency in the transaction database, since it is well known that processing the items in the order of increasing frequency usually leads to the shortest execution times. In step 4 the transactions are sorted lexicographically into descending order, with item comparisons again being decided by the item frequencies, although here the item with the higher frequency precedes the item with the lower frequency. (This order, which may appear strange at first sight, is chosen to take care of the fact that in a lexicographic order a word is preceded by any of its prefixes.) In step 5 the data structure on which SaM operates is built by combining equal transactions and setting up an array, in which each element consists of two fields: an occurrence counter and a pointer to the sorted transaction. This data structure is then processed recursively to find the frequent item sets.

Figure 1. The example database: original form (1), item frequencies (2), transactions with sorted items (3), lexicographically sorted transactions (4), and the used data structure (5)

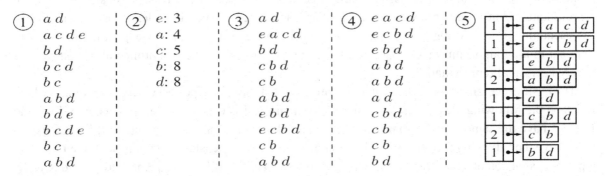

The basic operations of the recursive processing, which follows the general depth-first/divide-and-conquer scheme reviewed above, are illustrated in Figure 2. In the split step (see the left part of Figure 2) the given array is split w.r.t. the leading item of the first transaction (item e in our example): all array elements referring to transactions starting with this item are transferred to a new array. In this process the pointer (in)to the transaction is advanced by one item, so that the common leading item is "removed" from all transactions. Obviously, this new array represents the conditional database of the first subproblem (see the description of the general depth-first/ divide-and-conquer scheme), which is then processed recursively to find all frequent items sets containing the split item (provided this item is frequent – otherwise the recursion is skipped as it cannot yield any frequent item sets).

The conditional database for frequent item sets not containing this item (needed for the second sub-problem – see the description of the general depth-first/divide-and-conquer scheme) is obtained with a simple merge step (see the right part of Figure 2). The created new array and the rest of the original array (which refers to all transactions starting with a different item) are combined with a procedure that is almost identical to one phase of the well-known mergesort algorithm. Since both arrays are obviously lexicographically sorted, one merging traversal suffices to create a lexicographically sorted merged array.

Figure 2. The basic operations of the SaM algorithm: split (left) and merge (right)

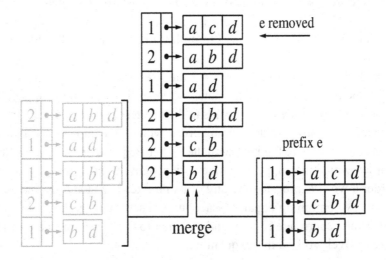

The only difference to a mergesort phase is that equal transactions (or transaction suffixes) are combined. That is, there is always just one instance of each transaction (suffix), while its number of occurrences is kept in the occurrence counter. In our example this results in the merged array having two elements less than the input arrays together: the transaction (suffixes) c b d and b d, which occur in both arrays, are combined and their occurrence counters are increased to 2.

Note that in both the split and the merge step only the array elements (that is, the occurrence counter and the (advanced) transaction pointer) are copied to a new array. There is no need to copy the transactions themselves (that is, the item arrays), since no changes are ever made to them. (In the split step the leading item is not actually removed, but only skipped by advancing the pointer (in)to the transaction.) Hence it suffices to have one global copy of all transactions, which is merely referred to in different ways from different arrays used in the processing.

Note also that the merge result may be created in the array that represented the original (conditional) database, since its front elements have been cleared in the split step. In addition, the array for the split database can be reused after the recursion for the split w.r.t. the next item. As a consequence, each recursion step, which expands the prefix of the conditional database, only needs to allocate one new array, with a size that is limited to the size of the input array of that recursion step. This makes the algorithm not only simple in structure, but also very efficient in terms of memory consumption.

Finally, note that the fact that only a simple array is used as the underlying data structure, the algorithm can fairly easily be implemented to work on external storage or a (relational) database system. There is, in principle, no need to load the transactions into main memory and even the array may easily be stored as a simple (relational) table. The split operation can then be implemented as an SQL select statement. The merge operation is very similar to a join, even though it may require a more sophisticated comparison of transactions (depending on how the transactions are actually stored).

Pseudo-code of the recursive procedure is shown in Figure 3. As can be seen, a single page of code is sufficient to describe the whole recursion in detail. The actual C code we developed is even shorter than this pseudo-code, despite the fact that the C code contains additional functionality (like, for example, perfect extension pruning – see the general description of frequent pattern mining), because certain operations needed in this algorithm can be written very concisely in C (especially when using pointer arithmetic to process arrays).

EXACT FREQUENT ITEM SET MINING EXPERIMENTS

In order to evaluate the proposed SaM algorithm, we ran it against our own implementations of Apriori (Borgelt 2003), Eclat (Borgelt 2003), FP-growth (Borgelt 2005a), and RElim (Borgelt 2005b), all of which rely on the same code to read the transaction database and to report found frequent item sets. Of course, using our own implementations has the disadvantage that not all of these implementations reach the speed of the fastest known implementations.[4] However, it has the important advantage that any differences in execution time can only be attributed to differences in the actual processing scheme, as all other parts of the programs are identical (loading transactions, reporting item sets). Therefore we believe that the measured execution times are still reasonably expressive and allow us to compare the different approaches in a reliable manner.

We ran experiments on five data sets, which were also used in (Borgelt 2003, Borgelt 2005a, Borgelt 2005b). As they exhibit different characteristics, the advantages and disadvantages of the different

Figure 3. Pseudo-code of the SaM algorithm. The actual C code is even shorter than this description, despite the fact that it contains additional functionality (like perfect extension pruning), because certain operations that are needed in this algorithm can be written very concisely in C (using pointer arithmetic to process arrays).

```
function SaM (a: array of transactions,        (* conditional database to process *)
              p: set of items,                 (* prefix of the conditional database a *)
              s_min: int) : int                (* minimum support of an item set *)
var i: item;                                   (* buffer for the split item *)
    s: int;                                    (* support of the current split item *)
    n: int;                                    (* number of found frequent item sets *)
    b, c, d: array of transactions;            (* split result and merged database *)
begin                                          (* – split and merge recursion – *)
    n := 0;                                     (* initialize the number of found item sets *)
    while a is not empty do                     (* while conditional database is not empty *)
        b := empty; s := 0;                     (* initialize split result and item support *)
        i := a[0].items[0];                     (* get leading item of the first transaction *)
        while a is not empty and a[0].items[0] = i do  (* and split database w.r.t. this item *)
            s := s + a[0].wgt;                  (* sum the occurrences (compute support) *)
            remove i from a[0].items;           (* remove the split item from the transaction *)
            if      a[0].items is not empty      (* if the transaction has not become empty *)
            then remove a[0] from a and append it to b;  (* move it to the conditional database, *)
            else remove a[0] from a; end;        (* otherwise simply remove it *)
        end;
        c := b; d := empty;                      (* initialize the output array *)
        while a and b are both not empty do      (* merge split result and rest of database *)
            if      a[0].items > b[0].items       (* if trans. in a is lexicographically smaller, *)
            then remove a[0] from a and append it to d;  (* copy it to the output array d *)
            else if a[0].items < b[0].items       (* if trans. in b is lexicographically smaller, *)
            then remove b[0] from b and append it to d;  (* copy it to the output array d *)
                b[0].wgt := b[0].wgt + a[0].wgt;  (* sum the occurrence counters/weights *)
                remove b[0] from b and append it to d;  (* move combined transaction and *)
                remove a[0] from a;               (* delete the other, equal transaction: *)
            end;                                  (* keep only one instance per transaction *)
        end;
        while a is not empty do                   (* copy the rest of the transactions in a *)
            remove a[0] from a and append it to d; end;
        while b is not empty do                   (* copy the rest of the transactions in b *)
            remove b[0] from b and append it to d; end;
        a := d;                                   (* second recursion is executed by the loop *)
        if s ≥ s_min then                          (* if the split item is frequent: *)
            p := p ∪ {i};                          (* extend the prefix item set and *)
            report p with support s;               (* report the found frequent item set *)
            n := n + 1 + SaM(c, p, s_min);         (* process the conditional database recursively *)
            p := p − {i};                          (* and sum the found frequent item sets, *)
        end;                                       (* then restore the original item set prefix *)
    end;
    return n;                                      (* return the number of frequent item sets *)
end;   (* function SaM() *)
```

algorithms can be observed well. These data sets are: census (a data set derived from an extract of the US census bureau data of 1994, which was preprocessed by discretizing numeric attributes), chess (a data set listing chess end game positions for king vs. king and rook), mushroom (a data set describing poisonous and edible mushrooms by different attributes), BMS-Webview-1 (a web click stream from a leg-care company that no longer exists, which has been used in the KDD cup 2000 [Kohavi et al. 2000]), and T10I4D100K (an artificial data set generated with IBM's well-known data generator). The first three data sets are available from the UCI machine learning repository (Blake and Merz 1998). The shell script used to discretize the numeric attributes of the census data set can be found at the URL mentioned below.

The first three data sets can be characterized as "dense", meaning that on average a rather high fraction of all items is present in each transaction (the average transaction length divided by the number of different items is 0.1, 0.5, and 0.2, respectively, for these data sets), while the last two are rather "sparse" (the average transaction length divided by the number of different items is 0.01 and 0.005, respectively, for these data sets).[5]

For the experiments we used an Intel Core 2 Quad Q9300 machine with 3 GB of main memory running openSuSE Linux 11.0 (32 bit) and gcc version 4.3.1. The results for these data sets are shown in Figure 4. Each diagram in this figure refers to one data set and shows the decimal logarithm of the execution time in seconds (excluding the time to load the transaction database) over the minimum support (stated as the number of transactions that must contain an item set in order to render it frequent).

These results show a fairly clear picture: SaM performs extremely well on dense data sets. It is the fastest algorithm for the census data set and (though only by a very small margin) on the chess data set. On the mushroom data set it performs on par with FP-growth and Relim, while it is faster than Eclat and Apriori. On "sparse" data sets, however, SaM struggles. On the artificial data set T10I4D100K it performs particularly badly and catches up with the performance of other algorithms only at the lowest support levels.[6] On BMS-Webview-1 it performs somewhat better, but again reaches the performance of other algorithms only for fairly low support values.

Given SaM's processing scheme, the cause of this behavior is easily found: it is clearly the merge operation. Such a merge operation is most efficient if the two lists to merge do not differ too much in length. Because of this, the recursive procedure of the mergesort algorithm splits its input into two lists of roughly equal length. If, to consider an extreme case, it would always merge single elements with the (recursively sorted) rest of the list, its time complexity would deteriorate from $O(n \log n)$ to $O(n2)$. The same applies to SaM: in a dense data set it is more likely that the two transaction lists do not differ too much in length, while in a sparse data set it can rather be expected that the list containing the split item will be rather short compared to the rest. As a consequence, SaM performs well on dense data sets, but poorly on sparse ones.

The main reason for the merge operation is to keep the list sorted, so that (1) all transactions with the same leading item are grouped together and (2) equal transactions (or transaction suffixes) can be combined, thus reducing the number of objects to process. The obvious alternative to achieve (1), namely to set up a separate list for each item, is employed by the RElim algorithm, which, as these experiments show, performs considerably better on sparse data sets. On T10I4D100K it even outperforms all other algorithms by a clear margin if the list for the next item to be processed is not sorted in order to combine duplicate entries (grey curve in Figure 4). The reason is that the sorting, which in RElim only serves the purpose to eliminate possible duplicates, causes higher costs than the gains resulting from having fewer transactions to process. On all other data sets sorting the list (and thus removing duplicates) speeds up the processing, thus providing another piece of evidence why SaM performs badly on T10I4100K.

These insights lead, of course, to several ideas how SaM could be improved. However, we do not explore these possibilities in this paper, but leave them for future work.

APPROXIMATE FREQUENT ITEM SET MINING

In many applications of frequent item set mining the considered transactions do not contain all items that are actually present. However, all of the algorithms mentioned so far seek to discover frequent item sets based on exact matching and thus are not equipped to meet the needs arising in these applications.

Figure 4. Experimental results on five different data sets. Each diagram shows the minimum support (as the minimum number of transactions that contain an item set) on the horizontal axis and the decimal logarithm of the execution time in seconds on the vertical axis. The data sets underlying the diagrams on the left are rather dense; those underlying the diagrams on the right are rather sparse.

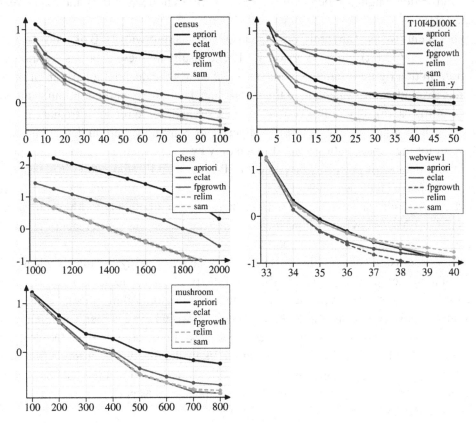

An example is the analysis of alarm sequences in telecommunication networks. A core task of analyzing alarm sequences is to find collections of alarms occurring frequently together – so-called episodes. In (Mannila et al. 1997) a time window was introduced that moves along the alarm sequence to build a sequence of partially overlapping windows. Each window captures a specific slice of the alarm sequence. In this way the problem of finding frequent episodes is transformed into the problem of finding frequent item sets in a database of transactions, where each alarm can be treated as an item, the alarms in a time window as a transaction, and the support of an episode is the number of windows in which the episode occurred. Unfortunately, alarms often get delayed, lost, or repeated due to noise, transmission errors, failing links etc. If alarms do not get through or are delayed, they can be missing from the transaction (time window) its associated items (alarms) occur in. If we required exact containment of an item set in this case, the support of some item sets, which could be frequent if the items did not get lost, may be smaller than the user-specified minimum. This leads to a possible loss of potentially interesting frequent item sets and to possibly distorted support values.

To cope with such missing information, we introduce the notion of an approximate or "fuzzy" frequent item set. In contrast to research on fuzzy association rules (see, for example, [Kuok et al. 1998]), where a fuzzy approach is used to handle quantitative items, we use the term "fuzzy" to refer to an item set that may not be found exactly in all supporting transactions, but only approximately. Related work in this direction includes (Cheng et al. 2001, Pei et al. 2001), where Apriori-like algorithms were introduced and mining with approximate matching was performed by counting the number of different items in the two item sets to be compared. In this paper, however, we adopt a more general scheme, based on an approximate matching approach, which exhibits a much higher flexibility. Our approach employs two core ingredients: edit costs and transaction weights (Wang et al. 2005).

Edit costs: The distance between two item sets can conveniently be defined as the costs of the cheapest sequence of edit operations needed to transform one item set into the other (Moen 2000).

Here we consider only insertions, since they are very easy to implement with our algorithm.[7] With the help of an "insertion cost" or "insertion penalty" a flexible and general framework for modeling approximate matching between two item sets can be established. The interpretation of such costs or penalties depends, of course, on the application. In addition, different items can be associated with different insertion costs. For example, in telecommunication networks different alarms can have a different probability of getting lost: usually alarms originating in lower levels of the module hierarchy get lost more easily than alarms originating in higher levels. Therefore the former can be associated with lower insertion costs than the latter. The insertion of a certain item may also be completely inhibited by assigning a very high insertion cost.

Transaction weights: Each transaction t in the original database T is associated with a weight $w(t)$. The initial weight of each transaction is 1. When inserting an item i into a transaction t, its weight is "penalized" with a cost $c(i)$ associated with the item. Formally, this can be described by a combination function: the new weight of the transaction t after inserting an item $i \notin t$ is $w\{i\} = f(w(t), c(i))$ where f is a function that combines the weight $w(t)$ before editing and the insertion cost $c(i)$. There is, of course, a wide variety of possible combination functions. For example, any t-norm may be used. For simplicity, we use multiplication here, that is, $w\{i\} = w(t) c(i)$, but this is a more or less arbitrary choice. Note, however, that with this choice lower values of $c(i)$ mean higher costs as they penalize the weight more, but it has the advantage that it is easily extended to an insertion of multiple items: $w_{\{i_1,...,i_m\}}(t) = w(t) \cdot \prod_{k=1}^{m} c(i_k)$. It should be clear that it is $w\emptyset(t) = 1$ due to the initial weighting $w(t) = 1$.

How many insertions into a transaction are allowed may be limited by a user-specified lower bound wmin for the transaction weight. If the weight of a transaction falls below this threshold, it is not considered in further mining steps and thus no further items may be inserted into it. Of course, this weight may also be set to zero (unlimited insertions). As a consequence, the fuzzy support of an item set I w.r.t. a transaction database T can be defined as $s_T^{(\text{fuzzy})} = \sum_{t \in T} \tau(w_{I-t}(t) \geq w_{\min}) \, w_{I-t}(t)$, where $\tau(\varphi)$ is a kind of "truth function", which is 1 if φ is true and 0 otherwise.

Note that SaM is particularly well suited to handle this scheme of item insertions, because it relies on a horizontal transaction representation, which makes it very simple to incorporate transaction weights into the mining process. With other algorithms (with the exception of RElim, which also uses a basically horizontal representation), more effort is usually needed in order to extend them to approximate frequent item set mining.

For the implementation of the approximate frequent item set mining scheme outlined above, it is important to distinguish between unlimited item insertions (that is, wmin = 0) and limited item insertions (that is, wmin > 0). The reason is that with wmin = 0 a transaction always contributes to the support of any item set (because, in principle, all items of the item set could be inserted), while with wmin > 0 a transaction only contributes to those item sets which it can be made to contain by inserting items without reducing the transaction weight below the threshold wmin .

As a consequence it is possible to combine equal transactions (or transaction suffixes) without restriction if wmin = 0: if we have two equal transactions (or transactions suffixes) t1 and t2 with weights w1 and w2, respectively, we can combine t1 and t2 into one transaction (suffix) t with weight w1 + w2 even if w1 ≠ w2. If another item i needs to be inserted into t1 and t2 in order to make them contain a given item set I, the distributive law (that is, the fact that w1 c(i) + w2 c(i) = (w1 + w2) c(i)) ensures that we still compute the correct support for the item set I in this case.

If, however, we have wmin > 0 and, say, w1 > w2, then using (w1 + w2) c(i) as the support contributed by the combined transaction t to the support of the item set I may be wrong, since it may be that w1 c(i) > wmin, but w2 c(i) < wmin. In this case the support contributed by the two transactions t1 and t2 would rather be w1 c(i). Effectively, transaction t2 does not contribute, since its weight would fall below the minimum transaction weight threshold by inserting the item i. Hence, under these circumstances, we can combine equal transactions (or transaction suffixes) only if they have the same weight (that is, only if w1 = w2).

UNLIMITED ITEM INSERTIONS

If unlimited item insertions are possible (wmin = 0), only a minor change has to be made to the data structure: instead of an integer occurrence counter for the transactions (or transaction suffixes), we need a real-valued transaction weight. In the processing, the split step stays the same (see Figure 5 on the left). However, now it only yields an intermediate database, into which all transactions (or transaction suffixes) have been transferred that actually contain the split item under consideration (item e in the example).

In order to build the full conditional database, we have to add those transactions that do not contain the split item, but can be made to contain it by inserting it. This is achieved in the merge step, in which two parallel merge operations are carried out now (see Figure 5 on the right). The first part (shown in black) is the merge that yields (as in the basic algorithm) the conditional database for frequent item sets not containing the split item. The second part (shown in blue) adds those transactions that do not contain the split item, weighted down with the insertion penalty, to the intermediate database created in the split step. Of course, this second part of the merge operation is only carried out, if c(i) > 0, where i is the split item, because otherwise no support would be contributed by the transactions not containing the item i and hence it would not be necessary to add them. In such a case the result of the split step would already yield the conditional database for frequent item sets containing the split item.

Note that in both parts of the merge operation equal transactions (or transaction suffixes) can be combined regardless of their weight. As a consequence we have in Figure 5 entries like for the transaction (suffix) c b d, with a weight of 1.2, which stands for one occurrence with weight 1 and one occurrence with weight 0.2 (due to the penalty factor 0.2, needed to account for the insertion of item e). As an additional illustration, Figure 6 shows the split and merge operations for the second recursion level (which work on the conditional database for the prefix e constructed on the first level).

Figure 5. The extended operations: unlimited item insertions, first recursion level

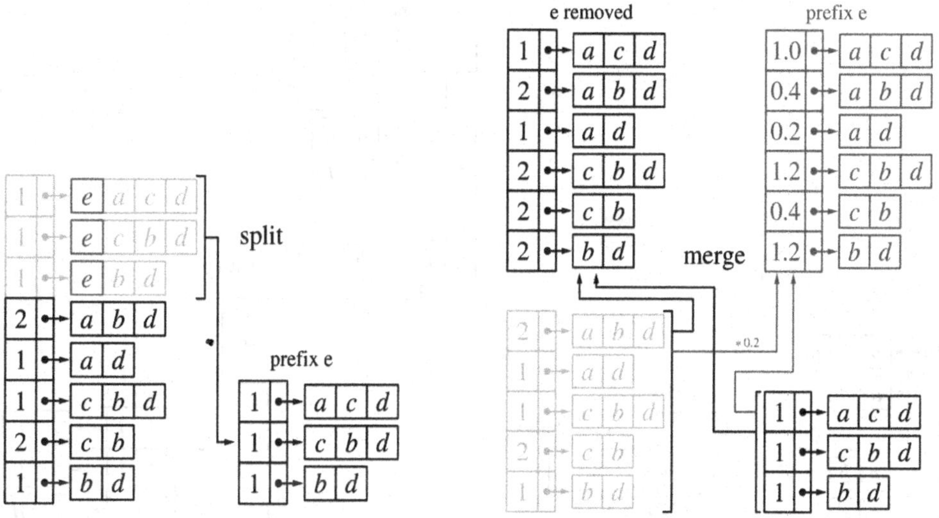

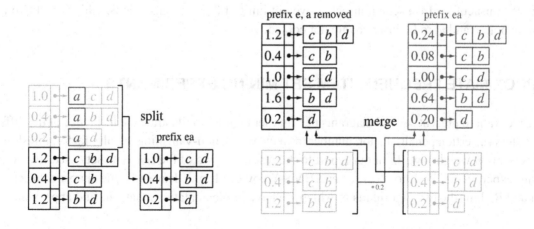

LIMITED ITEM INSERTIONS

If item insertions are limited by a threshold for the transaction weight (wmin > 0), we have to represent the transaction weight explicitly and keep it separate from the number of occurrences of the transaction. Therefore the data structure must be extended to comprise, per transaction (suffix), (1) a pointer to the item array, (2) an integer occurrence counter, and (3) a real-valued transaction weight. The last field will be subject to a thresholding operation by wmin and no transactions with this field lower than wmin will ever be kept. In addition, there may now be array elements that refer to the same transaction (suffix) – that is, the same list of items – and which differ only in the transaction weight (and maybe, of course, at the same time in the occurrence counter).

Figure 6. The extended operations: unlimited item insertions, second recursion level

Figure 7. The extended operations: limited item insertions, first recursion level

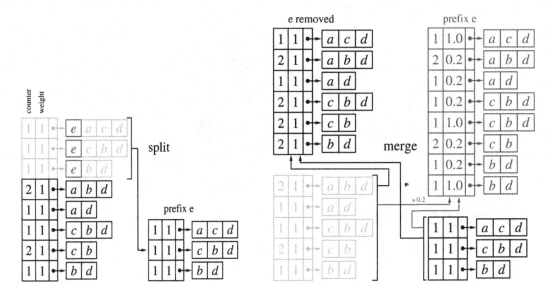

The processing scheme is illustrated in Figure 7 with the same example as before. The split step is still essentially the same and only the merge step is modified. The difference consists, as already pointed out, in the fact that equal transactions (or transaction suffixes) can no longer be combined if they differ in weight. As a consequence, there are now, in the result of the second part of the merge operation (shown in blue) two array elements for c b d and two for b d, which carry a different weight (one has a weight of 1, the other a weight of 0.2). As already explained above, this is necessary, because two transactions with different weight may reach, due to item insertions, the transaction weight threshold at different times and thus cannot be combined.

Of course, it rarely happens on the first level of the recursion that transactions are discarded due to the weight threshold. This can only occur on the first level, if the insertion penalty factor of the split item is already smaller than the transaction weight threshold, which is equivalent to inhibiting insertions of the split item altogether. Therefore, in order to illustrate this aspect of the processing scheme, Figure 8 shows the operations on the second recursion level, where the conditional database with prefix e (that is, for frequent item sets containing item e) is processed. Here the second part of the merge process actually discards transactions if we set a transaction weight limit of 0.1: all transactions, which need two items (namely both e and a) to be inserted, are not copied.

APPROXIMATE FREQUENT ITEM SET MINING EXPERIMENTS

Since we want to present several diagrams per data set in order to illustrate the influence of the different parameters (insertion penalty factor, number of items with a non-vanishing penalty factor, threshold for the transaction weight), we limit our report to the results on two of the five data sets used for the exact mining experiments. We chose census and BMS-Webview-1, one dense and one sparse data set, since SaM and RElim (the two algorithms of which we have implementations that can find approximate fre-

Figure 8. The extended operations: limited item insertions, second recursion level

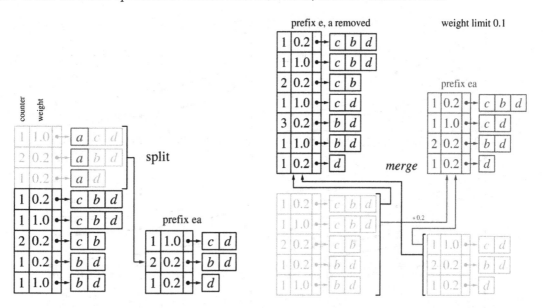

quent item sets) exhibit a significantly different behavior on dense and sparse data sets (as can already be seen from the exact mining results).

The results are shown in Figure 9 for the census data set and in Figure 10 for the BMS-Webview-1 data set. In both figures the diagrams on the left show the decimal logarithm of the number of found frequent item sets, while the diagrams on the right show the decimal logarithm of the execution times (in seconds) for our implementations of SaM and RElim. The different parameters we tested in our experiments are: insertion penalty factors of $1/8 = 0.125$, $1/16 = 0.0625$, and $1/32 = 0.03125$, non-vanishing insertion penalty factors for 10, 20, and 40 items, and transaction weight thresholds that allowed for 1, 2 or an unlimited number of item insertions.[8]

As can be seen from the diagrams on the left of each figure, the two data sets react very differently to the possibility of inserting items into transactions. While the number of found frequent item sets rises steeply with all parameters for the census data set, it rises only very moderately for the BMS-Webview-1 data set, with the factor even leveling off for lower support values. As it seems, this effect is due, to a large degree, to the sparseness of the BMS-Webview-1 data set (this needs closer examination, though, and provides a direction for future work).

As could be expected from the results of the basic algorithms on the five data sets used for the exact mining experiments, SaM fares better on the dense data set (census), beating RElim by basically the same margin (factor) in all parameter settings, while SaM is clearly outperformed by RElim on the sparse data set (BMS-Webview-1), even though the two algorithms were on par without item insertion. On both data sets, the number of insertions that are allowed has, not surprisingly, the strongest influence: with two insertions about an order of magnitude larger times result than with only one insertion. However, the possibility to combine equal transactions with different weights still seems to keep the execution times for unlimited insertions within limits.

The number of items with a non-vanishing penalty factor and the value of the penalty factor itself seem to have a similar influence: doubling the number of items leads to roughly the same effect as keeping

Figure 9. Experimental results on census data; left: frequent item sets, right: execution times

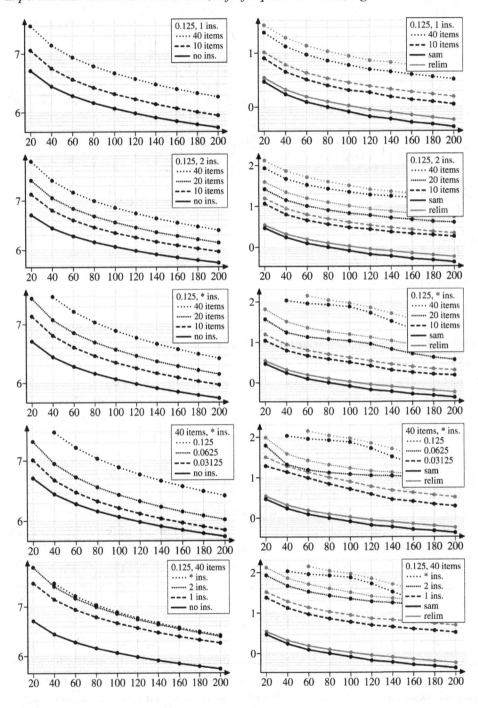

the number the same and doubling the penalty factor. This is plausible, since there should not be much difference in having the possibility to insert twice the number items or preserving twice the transaction weight per item insertion. Note, however, that doubling the penalty factor from 1/32 to 1/16 has only a comparatively small effect on the BMS-Webview-1 data set compared to doubling from 1/16 to 1/8. On the census data set the effects are a bit more in line.

Figure 10. Experimental results on webview1; left: frequent item sets, right: execution times

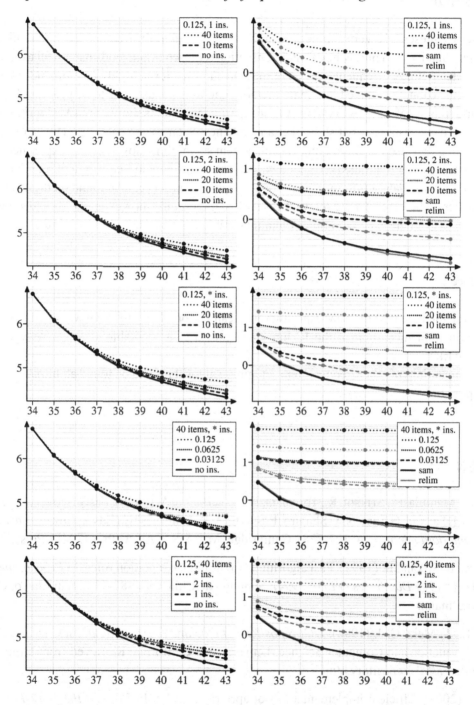

Overall it should be noted that the execution times, though considerably increased over those obtained without item insertions, still remain within acceptable limits. Even with 40 items having an insertion penalty factor of 1/8 and unlimited insertions, few execution times exceed 180 seconds (log(180) ≈ 2.25). In addition, we can observe the interesting effect on the BMS-Webview-1 data set that at the highest parameter settings the execution times become almost independent of the minimum support threshold.

CONCLUSION

In this paper we presented a very simple split and merge algorithm for frequent item set mining, which, due to the fact that it uses a purely horizontal transaction representation, lends itself well to an extension to approximate or "fuzzy" frequent item set mining. In addition, it is a highly recommendable method if the data to mine cannot be loaded into main memory and thus the data has to be processed on external storage or in a (relational) database system. As our experimental results show, our SaM algorithm performs excellently on dense data sets, but shows certain weaknesses on sparse data sets. This applies not only for exact mining, but also for approximate frequent item set mining. However, our experiments provide some evidence (to be substantiated on other data sets) that approximate frequent item set mining is much more useful for dense data sets as more additional frequent item sets can be found on these. Hence SaM performs better in the (likely) more relevant case. Most importantly, however, one should note that with both SaM and RElim the execution times remain bearable (in the order of a few minutes).

SOFTWARE

- An implementation of the SaM algorithm in C can be found at: http://www.borgelt.net/sam.html
- while an implementation of the RElim algorithm in C is available at: http://www.borgelt.net/relim.html
- Implementations of other frequent item set mining algorithms can be found at: http://www.borgelt.net/fpm.html

REFERENCES

Agrawal, R., Mannila, H., Srikant, R., Toivonen, H., & Verkamo, A. (1996). Fast discovery of association rules. In U. M. Fayyad, G. Piatetsky-Shapiro, P. Smyth, & R. Uthurusamy (Eds.), *Advances in knowledge discovery and data mining* (pp. 307-328). Cambridge, MA, USA: AAAI Press / MIT Press.

Agrawal, R., & Srikant, R. (1994). Fast algorithms for mining association rules. In *Proc. of the 20th Int. Conf. on Very Large Databases (VLDB 1994),* Santiago de Chile (pp. 487-499). San Mateo, CA, USA: Morgan Kaufmann.

Blake, C. L., & Merz, C. J. (1998). *UCI repository of machine learning databases*. Irvine, CA, USA: Dept. of Information and Computer Science, University of California. Retrieved from http://www.ics.uci.edu/~mlearn/MLRepository.html

Borgelt, C. (2003). Efficient implementations of apriori and eclat. In *Proc. of the Workshop Frequent Item Set Mining Implementations (FIMI 2003, Melbourne, FL, USA), CEUR Workshop Proceedings 90.* Aachen, Germany: Sun SITE Central Europe / University of Aachen. Retrieved from http://www.ceur-ws.org/Vol-90/

Borgelt, C. (2005a). An implementation of the FP-growth algorithm. In *Proc. of the Workshop Open Software for Data Mining (OSDM'05 at KDD'05)* Chicago, IL (pp. 1-5). New York, NY, USA: ACM Press.

Borgelt, C. (2005b). Keeping things simple: Finding frequent item sets by recursive elimination. In *Proc. of the Workshop Open Software for Data Mining (OSDM'05 at KDD'05)*, Chicago, IL (pp. 66-70). New York, NY, USA: ACM Press.

Böttcher, M., Spott, M., & Nauck, D. (2005). Detecting temporally redundant association rules. In *Proc. of the 4th Int. Conf. on Machine Learning and Applications (ICMLA 2005)*, Los Angeles, CA (pp. 397-403). Piscataway, NJ, USA: IEEE Press.

Böttcher, M., Spott, M., & Nauck, D. (2007). Framework for discovering and analyzing changing customer segments. In *Advances in data mining - theoretical aspects and applications* (LNCS 4597, pp. 255-268). Berlin, Germany: Springer.

Cheng, Y., Fayyad, U., & Bradley, P. S. (2001). Efficient discovery of error-tolerant frequent itemsets in high dimensions. In *Proc. of the 7th Int. Conf. on Knowledge Discovery and Data Mining (KDD'01)*, San Francisco, CA (pp. 194-203). New York, NY, USA: ACM Press.

Han, J., Pei, H., & Yin, Y. (2000). Mining frequent patterns without candidate generation. In *Proc. of the Conf. on the Management of Data (SIGMOD'00)*, Dallas, TX (pp. 1-12). New York, NY, USA: ACM Press.

Kohavi, R., Bradley, C. E., Frasca, B., Mason, L., & Zheng, Z. (2000). KDD-Cup 2000 organizers' report: Peeling the onion. *SIGKDD Exploration, 2*(2), 86–93. doi:10.1145/380995.381033

Kuok, C., Fu, A., & Wong, M. (1998). Mining fuzzy association rules in databases. [New York, NY, USA: ACM Press.]. *SIGMOD Record, 27*(1), 41–46. doi:10.1145/273244.273257

Moen, P. (2000). *Attribute, event sequence, and event type similarity notions for data mining.* Unpublished doctoral dissertation (Report A-2000-1), Helsinki, Finland: Department of Computer Science, University of Helsinki.

Pei, J., Han, J., Mortazavi-Asl, B., & Zhu, H. (2000). Mining access patterns efficiently from Web logs. In *Proc. of the Pacific-Asia Conf. on Knowledge Discovery and Data Mining (PAKDD'00)*, Kyoto, Japan (pp. 396-407). New York, NY, USA: Springer.

Pei, J., Tung, A. K. H., & Han, J. (2001). Fault-tolerant frequent pattern mining: Problems and challenges. In *Proc. of the ACM SIGMOD Workshop on Research Issues in Data Mining and Knowledge Discovery (DMK'01)*, Santa Babara, CA (pp. 7-12). New York, NY, USA: ACM Press.

Rász, B. (2004). nonordfp: An FP-growth variation without rebuilding the FP-Tree. In *Proc. of the Workshop Frequent Item Set Mining Implementations (FIMI 2004), Brighton, UK, CEUR Workshop Proceedings 126.* Aachen, Germany: Sun SITE Central Europe / University of Aachen. Retrieved from http://www.ceur-ws.org/Vol-126/

Rász, B., Bodon, F., & Schmidt-Thieme, L. (2005). On benchmarking frequent itemset mining algorithms. In *Proc. of the Workshop Open Software for Data Mining (OSDM'05 at KDD'05),* Chicago, IL (pp. 36-45). New York, NY, USA: ACM Press.

Wang, X., Borgelt, C., & Kruse, R. (2005). Mining fuzzy frequent item sets. In *Proc. of the 11th Int. Fuzzy Systems Association World Congress (IFSA'05),* Beijing, China (pp. 528-533). Beijing, China: Tsinghua University Press.

Webb, G. I. (2007). Discovering significant patterns. *Machine Learning, 68*(1), 1–33. doi:10.1007/s10994-007-5006-x

Webb, G. I., & Zhang, S. (2005). *k*-Optimal-rule-discovery. *Data Mining and Knowledge Discovery, 10*(1), 39–79. doi:10.1007/s10618-005-0255-4

Zaki, M., Parthasarathy, S., Ogihara, M., & Li, W. (1997). New algorithms for fast discovery of association rules. In *Proc. of the 3rd Int. Conf. on Knowledge Discovery and Data Mining (KDD'97),* Newport Beach, CA (pp. 283-296). Menlo Park, CA, USA: AAAI Press. Mannila, H., Toivonen, H., & Verkamo, A.I. (1997). *Discovery of frequent episodes in event sequences* (Report C-1997-15). Helsinki, Finland: Department of Computer Science, University of Helsinki.

ENDNOTES

[1]   Alternatively, each transaction may be enhanced by a unique transaction identifier, and these enhanced transactions may then be combined in a simple set.

[2]   Note that Apriori, which also uses a purely horizontal representation, relies on a different processing scheme, since it traverses the subset lattice level-wise rather than depth-first.

[3]   Note that exploiting perfect extensions in the search for frequent item sets and restricting this search to so-called *closed item sets* are not equivalent, even though a closed item set can be defined as an item set that does not possess any perfect extensions. The reason is that in the search, due to the guidance by a global order of the items, not all possible extensions are considered and thus an item set may be non-closed even though none of the *considered* extensions is perfect.

[4]   In particular, in [Rasz 2004] an FP-growth implementation was presented, which is highly optimized to how modern processor access their main memory [Rasz et al. 2005].

[5]   Note that the density defined in this way is equivalent to the fraction of ones in a bit matrix representation of the transaction database, which may be the more common form in which this measure can be defined.

[6]   It should be noted, though, that SaM's execution times on T10I4D100K are always around 5 seconds on this data set and thus not unbearable.

[7]   Note that deletions are implicit in the mining process anyway (as we search for *subsets* of the transactions). Only replacements are an additional case we do not consider here.

[8]   Since we used the same insertion penalty factor $c(i)$ for all items having $c(i) > 0$, the transaction weight threshold effectively limits the number of insertions regardless of which items are inserted. Hence this description is more expressive than stating the actual values w_{min} used.

Chapter 11
Fuzzy Association Rules to Summarise Multiple Taxonomies in Large Databases

Trevor Martin
University of Bristol, UK; Intelligent Systems Research Centre, BT Innovate, UK

Yun Shen
University of Bristol, UK

ABSTRACT

When working with large datasets, a natural approach is to group similar items into categories (or sets) and summarise the data in terms of such categories. Fuzzy set theory allows us to represent and reason about sets of objects without providing crisp definitions for each group, an approach that often reflects the human interpretation of categories. Given two or more hierarchical sets of categories, our aim is to determine the correspondence between categories (e.g., approximate equivalence). Association rules are a useful tool in knowledge discovery from databases but are normally defined in terms of crisp rather than fuzzy categories. In this chapter, the authors describe a new method for calculating a fuzzy confidence value for association rules between fuzzy categories, using a novel approach based on mass assignment theory.

INTRODUCTION

A key feature of human intelligence is our ability to categorise and summarise large quantities of data, whether this data arises from sensory input or from other sources. The ability to group multiple entities together into an (approximately) uniform whole allows us to efficiently represent a whole group as a single concept, enabling us to reason, and to derive knowledge, about groups of entities. A simple form of derived knowledge is *association* - essentially, that the extensions of two concepts overlap significantly. One of the fundamental tenets underlying fuzzy set theory (Zadeh, 1965) is the idea that humans work with groups of entities (or conceptual categories) that are loosely defined, able to admit elements according to some scale of membership rather than according to an absolute yes/no test. This

DOI: 10.4018/978-1-60566-858-1.ch011

is particularly true where the knowledge and/or reasoning uses natural language - humans can communicate quickly and efficiently with an informal shared understanding of the vocabulary. Although different individuals may have slightly different interpretations of terms, meaning can still be conveyed sufficiently accurately in almost all cases.

A further step in the idea of grouping entities together leads us to the notion of a taxonomy, i.e. a hierarchical series of progressively more refined categories. This enables us to represent / reason about problems at the appropriate level of granularity, and the use of taxonomic hierarchies to organise information and sets of objects into manageable chunks (granules) is widespread. For example, taxonomies serve as the main organisational principle for the grouping of species, for systems of government (national - regional - local), for corporate and command structures, for libraries, for document repositories and very many other applications.

Granules were informally defined by (Zadeh, 1997) as a way of decomposing a whole into parts, generally in a hierarchical way using fuzzy representations. Although in principle a taxonomic hierarchy is crisply defined, in practice there is often a degree of arbitrariness in its definition. For example, we might divide the countries of the world by continent at the top level of a taxonomic hierarchy. However, continents do not have crisp definitions - Europe contains some definite members (e.g. France, Germany) but at the Eastern and South-Eastern border, the question of which countries belong / do not belong is less clear. Iceland is generally included in Europe despite being physically closer to Greenland (part of North America). Thus although the word "Europe" denotes a set of countries (i.e. it is a granule) and can be used as the basis for communication between humans, it does not have an unambiguous definition in terms of the elements that belong to the set. Different "authorities" adopt different definitions - the set of countries eligible to enter European football competitions differs from the set of countries eligible to enter the Eurovision song contest, for example.

Of course, mathematical and some legal taxonomic structures can be very precisely defined - in plane geometry, the class of polyhedra further subdivides into triangles, quadrilaterals, etc and triangles may be subdivided into equilateral, isosceles etc. Such definitions admit no uncertainty. Most information systems model the world in some way, and need to represent categories which correspond to the loosely defined classes used by humans in natural language. For example, a company may wish to divide adults into customers and non-customers, and then sub-divide these into high-value customers, dissatisfied customers, potential customers, etc. Such categories are not necessarily distinct (i.e. they may be a covering rather than a partition) but more importantly, membership in these categories is graded - customer X may be highly dissatisfied and about to find a new supplier whilst customer Y is only mildly dissatisfied. We argue that most hierarchical taxonomies involve graded or loosely defined categories, but the nature of computerised information systems means that a more-or-less arbitrary decision has to be made on borderline cases, giving the taxonomy the appearance of a crisp, well-defined hierarchy. This may not be a problem as long as a rigorous and consistent criterion for membership is used (e.g. a dissatisfied customer is defined as one who has made at least two calls complaining about service), but the lack of subjectivity in a definition is rare. The use of graded membership (fuzziness) in categories enhances their expressive power and usefulness.

There is rarely a unique way of splitting data into conceptual categories, and numerous methodologies exist to aid with design of databases and similar information systems. Our previous work *"Smart Queries and Adaptive Data"* (*SQuAD*) project is concerned with adding structure to data (i.e. moving up the metadata scale) and refining approximate knowledge (in the form of fuzzy association rules) from this data (see (Martin *et al.*, 2008b) (Martin & Azvine, 2003, 2005; Martin *et al.*, 2007b)). The aim is to assist in the creation of useful information from diverse sources of semi-structured data - allowing extraction and integration from multiple sources of information and re-organisation based on an individual's personal categories. The final stage is to look for strong associations between different (fuzzy) categories. This is the main point of the work reported here - given two different conceptual categorisation hierarchies, how can we find correspondences (e.g. approximate equivalence) between classes?

Association rules (in their crisp form) are a well-established technique for knowledge discovery in databases, enabling "interesting" relations to be discovered. There have been a number of proposals to develop fuzzy association rules, that is to discover the degree of association between fuzzy categories. Some of our recent work has used mass assignment theory (Baldwin, 1992; 1994; Baldwin *et al.*, 1995) to develop a novel approach able to find a point valued association strength between fuzzy categories (Martin *et al.*, 2007a) and an interval-valued version (Martin & Shen, 2008).

In common with other work on fuzzy association rules, this work assumes there is a crisp value for the rule confidence. We note that much of the power of fuzzy approaches arises from the ability to produce fuzzy results, i.e. to effectively postpone the decision on whether a given element "belongs" to a set or not. For example, if a cooling fan is controlled by the control rules

- if temperature is *a little high*, increase fan speed *slightly*
- if temperature is *a little low*, decrease fan speed *slightly*

then a traditional approach requires us to specify precise limits for the intervals "*a little high*" and "*a little low*", and precise single values for a "*slight*" increase or decrease in speed. In contrast, a fuzzy control approach allows us to return the fuzzy definitions and propagate them through the inference process, only converting to a crisp value at the final stage when a decision must be made to change the fan speed. In a similar vein, we argue that, in looking for association strengths between fuzzy categories, it is better to propagate the fuzziness through the calculation and produce a fuzzy value rather than a single value to represent the association strength. Our mantra is *fuzzy in, fuzzy out*.

In this paper we describe a new method for calculating a fuzzy confidence for association rules between normal fuzzy categories (or granules), to be used in finding correspondences between fuzzy taxonomies. We briefly summarise previous discussion of the semantics of fuzzy sets when used to describe granules, and problems that arise from fuzzy association rule approaches based on crisp cardinalities of fuzzy sets. Some difficulties with our previous interval-based confidence measure are also outlined.

The main contribution of this paper is a novel mass assignment-based method for calculating a fuzzy confidence in associations between fuzzy categories. It relies on a new method of converting fuzzy relations to mass assignments and a definition of membership in the fuzzy confidence values related to the movement of mass needed to produce that association confidence value, relative to the confidence value derived from a least prejudiced mass assignment. We show that minimum and maximum values for the confidence can be found quickly, and memberships calculated based on the corresponding mass assignments. A "conceptual" algorithm is presented, although the actual implementation is considerably more efficient. Finally, some results are presented showing that the algorithm can scale to large calculations and comparing results to our previous implementation.

FUZZY SETS IN INFORMATION SYSTEMS

Many authors (e.g. (Bosc & Bouchon-Meunier, 1994)) have proposed the use of fuzzy sets to model uncertain values in databases and other knowledge based applications. The standard interpretation of a fuzzy set in this context is as a possibility distribution - that is to say it represents a single valued attribute which is not known exactly. For example we might use the fuzzy set *tall* to represent the height of a specific person or *low* to represent the value shown on a dice. The fuzzy sets *tall* and *low* admit a range of values, to a greater or lesser degree; the actual value is taken from the range. Knowing that a dice value *val* is *even* restricts the possible values to *val*=2 XOR *val*=4 XOR *val*=6 (where XOR is an exclusive or). If a fuzzy set on the same universe is defined as *low* = {1/1, 2/1, 3/0.4} then knowing the value *val* is *low* restricts the possible values to *val*=1 XOR *val*=2 XOR *val*=3 with corresponding memberships.

The conjunctive interpretation of a fuzzy set occurs when the attribute can have multiple values. For example, a person may be able to speak several languages; we could model this as a fuzzy set of languages, where membership would depend on the degree of fluency. This is formally a relation rather than a function on the underlying sets. Our position is to make a distinction between the conjunctive interpretation - modelled by a monadic fuzzy relation – and the disjunctive interpretation – modelled by a possibility distribution. To emphasise the distinction, we use the notation

$$F(a) = \{x/\mu(x) \mid x \in U\}$$

to denote a single valued attribute F of some object a (i.e. a possibility distribution over a universe U) and

$$R(a) = [x/\chi(x) \mid x \in U]$$

to denote a multi-valued attribute (relation). Fuzzy categories (granules) represent the latter case, since we have multiple values that satisfy the predicate to a greater or lesser degree.

EXTENDING ASSOCIATION RULES TO FUZZY CATEGORIES

In creating association rules within transaction databases (e.g. (Agrawal & Srikant, 1994), see also (Dubois *et al.*, 2006) for a clear overview), the standard approach is to consider a table in which columns correspond to items and each row is a transaction. A column contains 1 if the item was bought, and 0 otherwise. The aim of association rule mining is to determine whether or not there are links between two disjoint subsets of items – for example, do customers generally buy biscuits and cheese when beer, lager and wine are bought? These disjoint subsets can represent categories, as described earlier.

Let I denote the set of items, so that any transaction can be represented as $tr \subseteq I$, and consider X, the set of all transactions (strictly speaking, X is a multi-set but can be made into a set by adding a unique identifier to each transaction). We must also specify two categories (or itemsets) s and t, which are non-empty, non-overlapping subsets of I,

$$t \subset I$$

$s \subset I$

$s \cap t = \varnothing$

and the sets of transactions containing s and t

$$S = \left\{ x \,\middle|\, x \in X \wedge s \subseteq x \right\}$$
$$T = \left\{ x \,\middle|\, x \in X \wedge t \subseteq x \right\}$$

An association rule is of the form $s => t$ and is interpreted as stating that when the items in s appear in a transaction, it is likely that the items in t will also appear i.e. it is not an implication in the formal logical sense. A slight abuse of notation allows us to use $S => T$ or $s => t$ as the rule.

Most authors use two measures to assess the significance of association rules. The support of a rule $s => t$ is the number (or relative number) of transactions in which both s and t appear, and the confidence of the rule is an estimate (based on the samples) of the conditional probability of t being contained in a transaction given that it contains s

$$\text{Support(s, t)} = |S \cap T| \tag{1}$$

and

$$Conf\left(s, t\right) = \frac{|S \cap T|}{|S|} \tag{2}$$

Typically a threshold is chosen for the support, so that only frequently occurring sets of items s and t are considered; a second threshold filters out rules of low confidence.

For example, consider a database of sales employees, salaries and sales figures. A mining task might be to find out whether the good sales figures are achieved by the highly paid employees. Given the database table in Figure 1, we can obtain rule confidences ranging from 1/3 up to 1 by different crisp definitions of *"good sales"* and *"high salary"*, as shown on the right of Figure 1. Although this is a contrived example, such sensitivity to the cut-off points adopted for crisp definitions is a good indication that a fuzzy approach is more in line with human understanding of the categories.

Figure 1. A simple database of names (a, b, c, d), sales and salary figures (left) and (right) the confidences for an association rule good sales => high salary arising from different crisp definitions of the terms good sales and high salary.

name	sales	salary	good sales	high salary	confidence
a	100	1000	sales≥80	high≥400	1
b	80	400	sales≥50	high≥500	0.667
c	50	800	sales>50	high>500	0.5
d	20	700	sales≥50	high>800	0.333

Various approaches to fuzzifying association rules have been proposed e.g. (Bosc & Pivert, 2001; Dubois et al., 2006; Kacprzyk & Zadrozny, 2003). The standard extension to the fuzzy case is to treat the (multi-) sets S, T as fuzzy and find the intersection and cardinality using a t-norm and sigma-count respectively.

$$Conf\left(S,T\right) = \frac{\sum_{x \in X} \mu_{S \cap T}\left(x\right)}{\sum_{x \in X} \mu_S\left(x\right)}$$

(3)

In the example of Figure 1, a fuzzy approach would categorise employees according to whether their salaries are *high*, (or *medium* or *low*) and also according to whether their sales figures are *good, moderate* or *poor*. Taking a simple linear membership function from 0 to the maximum value in *goodSales* and *highSalary* leads to

S = [*a/1, b/0.8, c/0.5, d/0.2*]

and

T = [*a/1, b/0.4, c/0.8, d/0.7*]

which gives a confidence of 0.84 for the association S=>T using eq. (3). NB this example is used throughout the paper.

As pointed out by (Dubois et al., 2006), using min and the sigma count for cardinality can be unsatisfactory because it does not distinguish between several tuples with low memberships and few tuples with high memberships - for example,

$$S = \left[x_1/1\right]$$
$$T = \left[x_2/1\right]$$

leads to *Conf(S, T) = 0* but

$$S = \left[x_1/1, x_2/0.01, x_3/0.01, \ldots, x_{1000}/0.01\right]$$
$$T = \left[x_1/0.01, x_2/1, x_3/0.01, \ldots, x_{1000}/0.01\right]$$

leads to

$$Conf\left(S,T\right) = \frac{1000 \times 0.01}{1 + 999 \times 0.01} \approx 0.91$$

which is extremely high for two almost disjoint sets (this example originally appeared in (Martin-Bautista *et al.*, 2000)). Using a fuzzy cardinality (i.e. a fuzzy set over the possible cardinality values) is also potentially problematic since the result is a possibility distribution over rational numbers, and the extension principle (Zadeh, 1975) gives a wider bound than it should, due to neglect of interactions between the numerator and denominator in this expression. For example, given

$S = [x_1/1, x_2/0.8]$

$T = [x_1/1, x_2/0.4].$

the fuzzy cardinalities are

$|S \cap T| = \{1/1, 2/0.4\},$

$|S| = \{1/1, 2/0.8\}$

leading (by the extension principle) to a confidence of $\{0.5/0.8, 1/1, 2/0.4\}$ which is clearly incorrect as the confidence cannot be greater than 1. We conclude that neither the crisp nor the fuzzy cardinality method is satisfactory. In addition to the problems outlined above, any attempt to derive a crisp association confidence from fuzzy categories is hiding the uncertainty - as is well known from fuzzy control, an output is generally at least as fuzzy as the inputs. Whilst it is possible to defuzzify to an approximate crisp value, this should only be done when necessary.

A number of approaches to association rules have been proposed - for example (Delgado *et al.*, 2003), where the fuzzy association rule is interpreted as a quantified sentence. The confidence of the fuzzy association rule $S \Rightarrow T$ in the set of fuzzy transactions X is the evaluation of the quantified sentence "*Q of Xs are Xt* " where Q is a fuzzy quantifier and Xs (resp Xt) is the (fuzzy) subset of transactions containing s (resp t)

Our previous work (Martin *et al.*, 2008a; Martin & Shen, 2008) started from the fact that a relation represents a conjunctive set of ordered n-tuples i.e. a conjunction of n ground clauses, and used mass assignment theory (Baldwin *et al* 1995; Baldwin 1992; Baldwin 1994) as representation. For example, if U is the set of dice values then we could define a (crisp) predicate *differBy4or5* on $U \times U$ as the set of pairs

$[(1,6), (1,5), (2,6), (5,1), (6,1), (6, 2)]$

This is a conjunctive set, in that each pair satisfies the predicate. In a similar way, a fuzzy relation represents a set of n-tuples that satisfy a predicate to some degree. Thus *differByLargeAmount* could be represented by

$[(1,6)/1, (1,5)/0.6, (2,6)/0.6, (5,1)/0.6, (6,1)/1, (6,2)/0.6]$

The interpretation is not that a single pair satisfies this predicate, but that one set of pairs satisfies it (out of several possible sets of pairs). Thus we represent it as a mass assignment on possible *relations*:

$$R_1 = \left[(1,6),(6,1)\right]$$
$$R_2 = \left[(1,6),(1,5),(2,6),(5,1),(6,1),(6,2)\right]$$
$$m = \left\{\left\{R_1\right\}:0.4,\left\{R_1,R_2\right\}:0.6\right\}$$

This is equivalent to treating the fuzzy relation as a fuzzy set of crisp relations:

differ by large amount={R1/1,R2/0.6}

Similarly, a monadic fuzzy predicate *largeValue* defines a set of 1-tuples such as [6/1, 5/0.8, 4/0.3] which is written as a fuzzy set of crisp relations:

large value={[6]/1,[6,5]/0.8,[6,5,4]/0.3}

and has the mass assignment

$m_{large\,value}$={{[6]}:0.2,{[6],[6,5]}:0.5,{[6],[6,5,4]}:0.3}

Our subsequent studies show that this approach can sometimes overestimate the difference between full and nearly-full membership, which can lead to unreasonably large intervals calculated for the confidence of association rules. For example, under this interpretation, the monadic fuzzy relation $S = [a/1\ b/0.98]$ has the mass assignment

m_S={{[a]}:0.02, {[a], [a,b]}:0.98}

The normal mass assignment interpretation allows us to redistribute the mass on *{[a], [a,b]}* to either of the relations *[a]* or *[a,b]* which leads to the family of distributions:

S = [a]: 1-x, [a,b]: x where $0 \leq x \leq 0.98$

This flexibility in re-assigning mass means that for a source relation $S = [a/1\ b/0.98]$ and a target relation $T = [a/1\ b/0.98\ c/0.02]$ we get an interval [0.51, 1] which is surprisingly wide considering the two relations are so similar. We emphasise that this behaviour arises mostly in contrived cases and that smaller intervals are calculated in the vast majority of "real" association rules that have been considered in our experimental studies such as (Martin & Shen, 2008). Nevertheless, our opinion is that further study is justified.

ALTERNATIVE INTERPRETATION OF RELATIONS AS MASS ASSIGNMENTS

This section outlines our new interpretation of fuzzy relations as mass assignments. As in previous work, we assume that the fuzzy relations are normalised. The approach discussed above, which we will refer to as an open world approach, treats partial membership of a tuple x in a relation R (i.e. $0 < \chi_R(x) < 1$) as an upper bound for the mass that can be assigned to any set of tuples including x. This leads to a wide range of mass distributions that can be derived from the fuzzy relation R.

In the open world approach, for any tuple x such that $\chi_R(x) < 1$, the total mass that can be assigned to relations containing x is given by

$$0 \le \sum_{\substack{t=[x1,...,xn] \\ x \in t}} m(t) \le \chi_R(x)$$

(4)

In the *largeValue* example above, consider the element $x=5$, which has $\chi_R(x) = 0.8$; the relations containing 5 are [5, 6] and [4, 5, 6] and we have

$$0 \le m_{largeValue}([5,6]) + m_{largeValue}([4,5,6]) \le 0.8$$

This gives a considerable degree of flexibility in assigning mass.

Our alternative interpretation - the closed world approach - regards partial membership of a tuple x in a relation R (i.e. $0 < \chi_R(x) < 1$) as strictly equal to the total mass assigned to the sets of tuples which include x, i.e.

$$\sum_{\substack{t=[x1,...,xn] \\ x \in t}} m(t) = \chi_R(x)$$

(5)

This means there is no flexibility in the range of mass distributions that can be derived from the fuzzy relation R. However, there is flexibility in the mass assignments when R is combined with an assignment corresponding to another relation, for example in calculating association confidences as described later.

Under this interpretation, the monadic fuzzy relation *largeValue* discussed above has

$$m_{largeValue}=\{[6]:0.2,\ [6,5]:0.5,\ [6,5,4]:0.3\}$$

and clearly

$$m_{largeValue}([5,6]) + m_{largeValue}([4,5,6]) = 0.8$$

CLOSED WORLD MASS-BASED ASSOCIATION RULES

For a source category

$$S = \left[x_{1/} x_s(x_1),\ x_2\ /\ x_s(x_2),...,x_{|s|}\ /\ x_s(x_{|s|}) \right]$$

and a target category

$$T = \left[x_{1/} x_T(x_1),\ x_2\ /\ x_T(x_2),...,x_{|T|}\ /\ x_T(x_{|T|}) \right]$$

we can define the corresponding mass assignments as follows. Let the set of distinct memberships in S be

$$\wedge_S = \left\{ x_S^{(1)}, x_S^{(2)}, ..., x_S^{(n_s)} \right\}$$

where

$$x_S^{(1)} > x_S^{(2)} > ... > x_S^{(n_s)}$$

and $n_S \leq |S|$. Let

$$S_i = \left\{ \left[x \mid \chi_S\left(x\right) \geq \chi_S^{(i)} \right] \right\}$$

Then the mass assignment corresponding to S is $\left\{ S_i : m_s(S_i) \right\}, 1\pi \leq i \leq n_s$ where

$$m_s\left(S_k\right) = x_S^{(k)} - x_S^{(k+1)} \tag{6}$$

and we define

$$x_S^{(i)} = 0 \; if \; i > n_s$$

For example, the fuzzy category

S = [a/1, b/0.8, c/0.5, d/0.2]

has the corresponding mass assignment

$$M_S = \left\{ [a] : 0.2, \quad [a,b] : 0.3, \quad [a,b,c] : 0.3, \quad [a,b,c,d] : 0.2 \right\}$$

We can calculate the confidence in the association between the categories S and T using mass assignment theory. In general, this will be an interval as we are free to move mass (consistently) between the cells corresponding to S_i and T_j for each i, j.

For two mass assignments

$$M_S = \left\{ S_i : m_S\left(S_i\right) \right\}, \quad 1 \leq i \leq n_S$$
$$M_T = \left\{ T_j : m_T\left(T_j\right) \right\}, \quad 1 \leq j \leq n_T$$

the composite mass assignment is

$$M = M_S \oplus M_T$$
$$= \left\{ X : m\left(X\right) \right\}$$

where *m* is specified by the composite mass allocation function, subject to

$$\sum_{j=1}^{n_T} m_{ij} = m_S\left(S_i\right)$$

$$\sum_{i=1}^{n_S} m_{ij} = m_T\left(T_j\right)$$

This can be visualised using a mass tableau (see (Baldwin, 1992)) as shown in Figure 2. Each row (column) represents a relation of the source (target) mass assignment,. The mass associated with a row (column) can be distributed amongst the cells provided row and column constraints are satisfied. We label the rows S_1, S_2, ... S_{nS} and columns T_1, T_2, ... T_{nT}, and assign mass m_{ij} to cell *(i, j)* subject to row and column constraints. The confidence in the association rule is given by

$$conf\left(M\right) = \frac{\sum_{i,j}\left(m_{ij} \times \left|S_i \cap T_j\right|\right)}{\sum_{i=1}^{n_S}\left(\sum_{j}^{n_T} m_{ij} \times \left|S_i\right|\right)} = \frac{n}{d}$$

$$where \quad n = \sum_{i,j}\left(m_{ij} \times \left|S_i \cap T_j\right|\right)$$

$$d = \sum_{i=1}^{n_S}\left(\sum_{j}^{n_T} m_{ij} \times \left|S_i\right|\right)$$

$$= \sum_{i=1}^{n_S}\left|S_i\right| \times m_S^{(i)} \tag{7}$$

Clearly $n \geq 0$, $d > 0$ and *d* is a constant for a given source relation *S*, irrespective of *M*. For example consider the fuzzy categories

$S = [a/1, b/0.8, c/0.5, d/0.2]$

Figure 2. The mass tableau, showing intersections $S_i \cap T_j$ and the least prejudiced mass distribution. The corresponding point valued rule confidence is 1.86 / 2.5 = 0.744

		0.2 [a]	0.1 [ac]	0.3 [acd]	0.4 [abcd]
0.2	[a]	[a] 0.04	[a] 0.02	[a] 0.06	[a] 0.08
0.3	[ab]	[a] 0.06	[a] 0.03	[a] 0.09	[ab] 0.12
0.3	[abc]	[a] 0.06	[ac] 0.03	[ac] 0.09	[abc] 0.12
0.2	[abcd]	[a] 0.04	[ac] 0.02	[acd] 0.06	[abcd] 0.08

and

$T = [a/1, b/0.4, c/0.8, d/0.7]$

Clearly the mass can be allocated in many ways, subject to row and column constraints. One notable assignment is the least prejudiced distribution, obtained by taking the product of source and target masses for each cell as shown in figure 2. This corresponds to the minimum entropy combination of the source and target mass assignments. Different assignments lead to the minimum and maximum confidences.

In the next section, we analyse the effect of moving mass between cells on the confidence and show how the maximum and minimum confidence values can be found quickly.

FAST CALCULATION OF FUZZY CONFIDENCE INTERVAL

We take an arbitrary mass assignment M, and consider the change in confidence when we move mass to create another assignment M^*.

In order to conform to row and column constraints, the net transfer of mass within any row or column is zero. Thus the simplest transfer of mass involves four cells, as shown in figure 3. We refer to this as an *elementary* mass transfer, denoted

$$E\left(x, (i_1, j_1), (i_2, j_2)\right)$$

and write

$$M^* = M + E(x, (i_1, j_1), (i_2 j_2))$$

where $E\left(x, (i_1, j_1), (i_2, j_2)\right)$ indicates that mass x is moved into cells *(i1, j1)* and *(i2, j2)* from cells *(i1, j2)* and *(i2, j1)* and we assume *i1 < i2* and *j1 < j2*

For example, consider the tableau shown in Figure 2. We can move a mass of 0.04 from the top right hand corner to the top left; in order to satisfy row and column constraints, we must also move 0.04 from the bottom left to bottom right, yielding the tableau shown in Figure 4.

Figure 3. An elementary mass transfer. If x > 0 then it is termed a positive elementary mass transfer; if x < 0 it is termed a negative elementary mass transfer

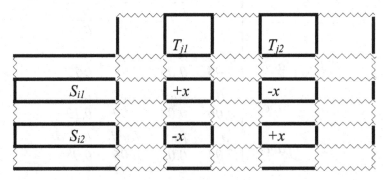

Theorem 1.

Let M^{init} and M^{final} be different allocations of mass to cells in a tableau, both conforming to row and column constraints. Then we can convert M^{init} to M^{final} by a finite sequence of p elementary mass transfers $E1+E2 + ... +Ep$.

Proof.

Define

$$\Delta M = M^{final} - M^{init}$$
$$ie \; \Delta M_{ij} = M_{ij}^{final} - M_{ij}^{init}$$

(where addition and subtraction are defined in the obvious way) and consider the sums of positive and negative elements of ΔM

$$pos(\Delta M) = \sum_{\substack{i,j \\ \Delta M_{ij} < 0}}^{n} \Delta M_{ij}$$
$$neg(\Delta M) = - \sum_{\substack{i,j \\ \Delta M_{ij} < 0}}^{n} \Delta M_{ij}$$

Clearly $pos(\Delta M) = neg(\Delta M)$ and both are zero if the assignments M^{init} and M^{final} are the same.

If they are greater than zero, we construct an elementary mass transfer as follows:

Choose a positive element in ΔM, say at row $r1$ and column $c1$. Choose a negative element in the same row $(r1, c2)$ and a second negative element in the same column $(r2, c1)$ where clearly $r1 \neq r2$ and $c1 \neq c2$. Since rows and columns in ΔM sum to zero, these elements must exist. The elementary transfer is $E \ (x, (i1, j1), (i2, j2))$ where

$i1 = min(r1, r2) \ i2 = max(r1, r2) \ j1=min(c1, c2) \ j2 = max(c1, c2)$

Figure 4. The mass tableau, from Figure 2 after an elementary mass transfer E(0.04, (1,1), (4,4))

		0.2 [a]	0.1 [ac]	0.3 [acd]	0.4 [abcd]
0.2	[a]	[a] 0.08	[a] 0.02	[a] 0.06	[a] 0.04
0.3	[ab]	[a] 0.06	[a] 0.03	[a] 0.09	[ab] 0.12
0.3	[abc]	[a] 0.06	[ac] 0.03	[ac] 0.09	[abc] 0.12
0.2	[abcd]	[a] 0	[ac] 0.02	[acd] 0.06	[abcd] 0.12

The sign of x depends on the relative values of $r1$, $r2$, $c1$, $c2$ and the absolute value of x depends on the value of $\Delta M_{r2\,c2}$ (and the other affected elements of ΔM)

There are two possibilities for the value of $\Delta M_{r2\,c2}$

(i) $\Delta M_{r2\,c2} = 0$. In this case, $|x|$ is the smallest absolute value of $\Delta M_{r1\,c1}$, $\Delta M_{r1\,c2}$ and $\Delta M_{r2\,c1}$

(ii) $\Delta M_{r2\,c2} \neq 0$. We choose $|x|$ to be the smallest absolute value of $\Delta M_{r1\,c1}$, $\Delta M_{r1\,c2}$, $\Delta M_{r2\,c1}$ and $\Delta M_{r2\,c2}$

x is positive if $r1 < r2$ and $c1 < c2$, or if $r2 < r1$ and $c2 < c1$; otherwise it is negative.

Writing

$$M^* = M + E(x,(i_1,j_1),(i_2,j_2))$$
$$and\ \Delta M^* = M^* - M^{final}$$

it is clear that

$$\Delta M^* = \Delta M - E\left(x,(i_1,j_1),(i_2,j_2)\right)$$
$$\Delta M^*_{i1j1} = \Delta M_{i1j1} - x$$
$$\Delta M^*_{i1j2} = \Delta M_{i1j2} + x$$
$$\Delta M^*_{i2j1} = \Delta M_{i2j1} + x$$
$$\Delta M^*_{i2j2} = \Delta M_{i2j2} + x$$

where at least one of ΔM^*_{i1j1}, $\Delta M_{i1j2}, \Delta M_{i2j1} \Delta M_{i2j2}$ is zero, and every other element of ΔM^* is the same as the corresponding element in ΔM.

Because x is chosen as the smallest absolute value, each of the four changed cells in ΔM^* is either zero or has the same sign as the corresponding cell in ΔM

If $\Delta M_{r2c2} < 0$, then $\Delta M^*_{r2c2} \leq 0$ and

$$pos\left(\Delta M^*\right) = pos\left(\Delta M\right) - \left|2x\right|$$
$$neg\left(\Delta M^*\right) = neg\left(\Delta M\right) - \left|2x\right|$$

If $\Delta M_{r2c2} \geq 0$, then $\Delta M^*_{r2c2} > 0$ and

$$pos\left(\Delta M^*\right) = pos\left(\Delta M\right) - \left|x\right|$$
$$neg\left(\Delta M^*\right) = neg\left(\Delta M\right) - \left|x\right|$$

Clearly in either case the sum of positive elements (equivalently, the sum of negative elements) decreases after the elementary mass transfer. Furthermore, $|x|$ is a combination (using addition and subtraction only) of the values in the original ΔM, in which each value can be used at most once. Hence after repeating this process a finite number of times, we will reach the situation in which

$$pos(\Delta M^{*}) = neg(\Delta M^{*}) = 0$$

and the sequence of elementary mass transfers will be those required to convert M^{init} into M^{final}

Example.

Consider converting the assignment (Table 1), into Table 2, the initial difference is

$$\Delta M = \begin{matrix} 0.2 & 0 & 0 & -0.2 \\ -0.2 & 0 & 0 & 0.2 \\ 0 & 0 & -0.1 & 0.1 \\ 0 & 0 & 0.1 & -0.1 \end{matrix}$$

which has *pos(ΔM) = 0.6* i.e. the total mass to be moved is 0.6

Choosing *r1=1, c1=1, r2=2, c2=4* and *x=0.2* yields the positive elementary mass transfer *E(0.2, (1,1), (2, 4))* so that

M1 = M^{init} + E(0.2, (1,1), (2, 4))

and M1 is given by Table 3.

A second (negative) elementary mass transfer *E(-0.1, (3,3), (4, 4))* yields the desired result.

M^{final} = M^{init} + E(0.2, (1,1), (2, 4)) + E(-0.1, (3,3), (4,4))

The change in confidence arising from the elementary transfer

$$E(x, (i_1, j_1), (i_2, j_2))$$

Table 1.

M^{init}	0.2	0.1	0.3	0.4
0.2	0	0	0	0.2
0.3	0.2	0	0	0.1
0.3	0	0	0.3	0
0.2	0	0.1	0	0.1

Table 2.

M^{final}	0.2	0.1	0.3	0.4
0.2	0.2	0	0	0
0.3	0	0	0	0.3
0.3	0	0	0.2	0.1
0.2	0	0.1	0.1	0

Table 3.

M1	0.2	0.1	0.3	0.4
0.2	0.2	0	0	0
0.3	0	0	0	0.3
0.3	0	0	0.3	0
0.2	0	0.1	0	0.1

is given by

$$\Delta conf\left((i_1, j_1),(i_2, j_2)\right) = conf\left(M^*\right) - conf\left(M\right)$$
$$= \frac{x\left(\left|S_{i1} \cap T_{j1}\right| - \left|S_{i1} \cap T_{j2}\right| - \left|S_{i2} \cap T_{j1}\right| + \left|S_{i2} \cap T_{j2}\right|\right)}{d} \tag{8}$$

since the denominator and other terms in the numerator are not changed. The denominator d is defined in eq 7.

Theorem 2.

If x is positive in an elementary mass transfer, i.e. we move mass to the left within a higher row and to the right within the lower row, then either the confidence increases or is left unchanged.

Proof.

Since $i2 > i1$ and $j2 > j1$ we have

$$S_{i1} \subseteq S_{i2} \; and \; T_{j1} \subseteq T_{j2}$$

The sets $S_{i2} \; and \; T_{j2}$ can be partitioned as follows

$$S_{i2} = S_{i1} \cup \left(S_{i2} - S_{i1}\right)$$
$$T_{j2} = T_{j1} \cup \left(T_{j2} - T_{j1}\right)$$

so that

$$\left|S_{i2} \cap T_{j1}\right| = \left|S_{i1} \cap T_{j1}\right| + \left|(S_{i2} - S_{i1}) \cap T_{j1}\right|$$
$$\left|S_{i1} \cap T_{j2}\right| = \left|S_{i1} \cap T_{j1}\right| + \left|S_{i1} \cap (T_{j2} - T_{j1})\right|$$
$$\left|S_{i2} \cap T_{j2}\right| = \left|S_{i1} \cap T_{j1}\right| + \left|S_{i1} \cap (T_{j2} - T_{j1})\right| + \left|(S_{i2} - S_{i1}) \cap T_{j1}\right| + \left|(S_{i2} - S_{i1}) \cap (T_{j2} - T_{j1})\right|$$

and we can simplify eq (8) to

$$\Delta conf((i_1, j_2), (i_2, j_2)) = \frac{x \times \left|(S_{i2} - S_{i1}) \cap (T_{j2} - T_{j1})\right|}{d}$$

Clearly for positive x this is zero or positive, so the confidence will either increase or be unchanged.

Corollary 2.1.

If x is negative (i.e. we move mass to the right within the higher row and to the left within the lower row) then the confidence will either be unchanged or will decrease.

By Theorem 1, any compound transfer of mass may be re-written as a sequence of elementary mass transfers. The effect of a compound mass transfer on the rule confidence is dependent on the sets involved in the elementary mass transfers.

In Figure 5, the change in confidence is

$$\Delta conf\left(\Delta M\right) = \Delta conf\left(E1\right) + \Delta conf\left(E2\right)$$
$$= \frac{-x\left(\left\|(S_2 - S_1) \cap (T_2 - T_1)\right\|\right)}{d} + \frac{x\left(\left\|(S_3 - S_2) \cap (T_3 - T_2)\right\|\right)}{d}$$

which can clearly be positive, negative or zero depending on the sets *S1, S2, S3* and *T1, T2, T3*.

On the other hand, the compound transfer in Figure 6 has a change of confidence

$$\Delta conf\left(\Delta M\right) = \Delta conf\left(E1\right) + \Delta conf\left(E2\right)$$

$$= \frac{x\left(\left\|(S_3 - S_1) \cap (T_3 - T_1)\right\|\right)}{d} - \frac{x\left(\left\|(S_3 - S_2) \cap (T_3 - T_2)\right\|\right)}{d}$$

$$= \frac{x\left(\left\|(S_3 - S_2) \cap (T_2 - T_1)\right| + \left|(S_2 - S_1) \cap (T_3 - T_2)\right| + \left|(S_2 - S_1) \cap (T_2 - T_1)\right\|\right)}{d}$$

Figure 5. Combination of a positive and negative elementary mass transfer. Unless we know the sets Si and Tj it is not possible to predict whether the overall result leads to an increase or decrease in confidence

	T1	T2	T3			T1	T2	T3			T1	T2	T3
S1	-x	+x			S1	-x	+x			S1			
S2	+x		-x	=	S2	+x	-x		+	S2		+x	-x
S3		-x	+x		S3					S3		-x	+x

	ΔM		=		E1	+	E2

Figure 6. Combination of a positive and negative elementary mass transfer which must lead to an increase in confidence

	T1	T2	T3			T1	T2	T3				T1	T2	T3
S1	+x		-x		S1	+x		-x			S1			
S2	-x	+x		=	S2				+	S2	-x	+x	
S3		-x	+x		S3	-x		+x			S3	+x	-x	

$$\Delta M \qquad = \qquad E1 \qquad + \qquad E2$$

which is clearly always positive (for positive *x*).

Corollary 2.2.

From eq 8 and the example in Figure 6, we can see that that for any assignment, the maximum increase in confidence will be obtained by moving as much mass as possible to the top left corner of the tableau. The increase in confidence in this case is

$$\Delta conf\left(E\left(x,\ \left(1,1\right),\left(n_S,n_T\right)\right)\right) = \frac{x\left(\left\|\left(S_{n_S} - S_1\right) \cap \left(T_{n_T} - T_1\right)\right\|\right)}{d}$$

which is larger than any other increase obtained by an elementary mass transfer of *x* since the cardinality of the intersection is the maximum possible in the tableau.

Theorem 3.

The mass assignment leading to maximum association confidence is

$$M\left(i,j\right) = min\left(m_S^{(i)},\ m_T^{(j)}, max\left(0, min\left(m_S^{(i)} - \left(\chi_S^{(i)} - \chi_T^{(j)}\right), m_T^{(j)} - \left(\chi_T^{(j)} - \chi_S^{(i)}\right)\right)\right)\right) \qquad (9)$$

Proof.

For an assignment that maximises rule confidence, it must be impossible to choose *i1 < i2, j1 < j2* such that there is a positive elementary mass transfer *E(x, (i1, j1), (i2, j2)*, i.e. it must be impossible to add mass *x* to *(i1, j1)* and *(i2, j2)* and subtract mass *x* from *(i1, j2)* and *(i2, j1)* whilst maintaining row and column constraints.

This is guaranteed if it is impossible for any cell *(i, j)* in the maximum assignment to be at the top left or bottom right corner of a positive elementary mass transfer – i.e.

EITHER **(condition 1a)** all cells to the right of *(i, j)* in row *i* (i.e. cells *(i, j+1)* to *(i, n_T)*) contain zero mass OR **(condition 1b)** all cells below *(i, j)* in column *j* (i.e. cells *(i+1, j)* to *(n_S, j)*) contain zero mass

Figure 7. One possible sequential numbering of the mass tableau such that the index for cell (i, j) is larger than the indices of cells (i-1, j), (i-1, j-1) and (i, j-1)

1	2	$\cdots$	n_T
n_T+1	n_S+2	$\cdots$	$2n_T$
$\cdots$	$\cdots$	$\cdots$	$\cdots$
$(n_S-1)\times n_T+1$	$(n_S-1)\times n_T+2$	$\cdots$	$n_S \times n_T$

Figure 8. Diagrammatic representation of case 1 – equal mass in rows above and columns to the left of(i, j) is allocated to give maximum confidence

AND
EITHER **(condition 2a)** all cells to the left of *(i, j)* in row *i* (i.e. cells *(i, 1)* to *(i, j-1)*) contain zero mass
OR **(condition 2b)** all cells above *(i, j)* in column *j* (i.e. cells *(1, j)* to *(i-1, j)*) contain zero mass.

Lemma 3.1.

Clearly if $M(i, j) = m_s^{(i)}$ then all mass available in the row is in cell *(i, j)* and there is no further mass anywhere in row *i*, satisfying (1a) and (2a). Hence *(i, j)* cannot be the top left or bottom right corner of a positive elementary mass transfer.

Lemma 3.2.

Similarly if $M(i, j) = m_T^{(j)}$ there is no further mass anywhere in column j, satisfying (1b) and (2b) and *(i, j)* cannot be the top left or bottom right corner of a positive elementary mass transfer.

We proceed by strong induction. It is possible to index cells in the tableau such that the index for cell *(i, j)* is larger than the indices of cells *(i-1, j)*, *(i-1, j-1)* and *(i, j-1)*. For example, one can start at the top left corner and number cells sequentially across the first row, then across the second row etc as shown in figure 7. Strong induction allows us to show that the mass in cell *(i, j)* leads to maximum confidence assuming that the masses in all cells with lower index - specifically, cells in the blocks from *(1, 1)* to *(i-1, j-1)*, *(1, 1)* to *(i, j-1)* and *(1, 1)* to *(i-1, j)* - are allocated in a way that leads to maximum confidence.

Clearly for the first cell, (1, 1), equation 9 reduces to

$$M\left(i,j\right) = min\left(m_S^{(i)},\ m_T^{(j)}\right)$$

and by lemma 3.1 or 3.2, this corresponds to the maximum assignment.

For an arbitrary cell *(i, j)*, the sum of mass in the rows 1 to *i-1* is given by

$$\sum_{k=1}^{i-1} m_S^{(k)} = 1 - x_S^{(i)}$$

and the sum of mass in the columns from 1 to *j-1* is

$$\sum_{k=1}^{j-1} m_T^{(k)} = 1 - x_T^{(j)}$$

By the inductive hypothesis, the mass in cells (1, 1) to (*i-1, j-1*) is allocated in a way that leads to maximum confidence, i.e.

$$\sum_{p=1}^{i-1}\sum_{q=1}^{j-1} M\left(p,q\right) = \min\left(1 - x_S^{(i)}, 1 - x_T^{(j)}\right)$$

We must consider five possible cases, labelled 1, 2(i), 2(ii), 3(i), 3(ii) in Figures 9 and 10.

Case 1.

If

$$1 - x_S^{(i)} = 1 - x_T^{(j)}$$

then equation 9 reduces to

Figure 9. Diagrammatic representation of case 2 (i) – mass in rows above i and columns including and to the left of j is allocated to give maximum confidence; no mass in column j is available for cell (i, j)

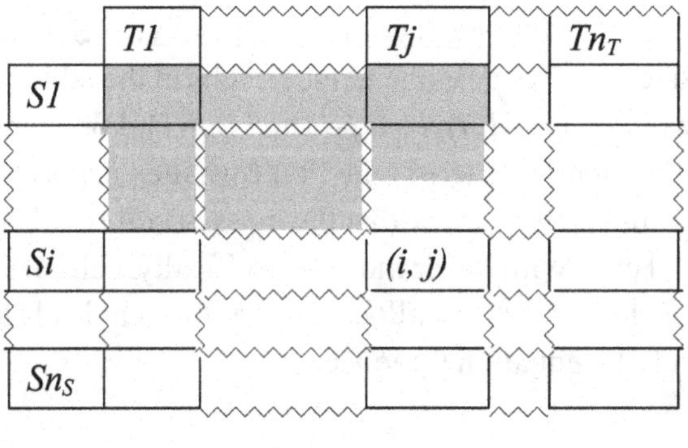

$$M(1,1) = \min\left(m_S^{(1)}, m_T^{(1)}\right)$$

and by lemma 3.1 or 3.2, this corresponds to the maximum assignment.

Case 2. If

$$1 = x_s^{(i)} > 1 - x_T^{(j)}$$

then all mass in columns 1 to *j-1* will be allocated in cells (1, 1) to (*i-1, j-1*) and there will be no mass in cells (*i,* 1) to (*i, j-1*), i.e. condition 2a is satisfied

By the inductive hypothesis, we assume that mass in cells (1, 1) to (*i-1, j*) is allocated in a way that that leads to maximum confidence. The total mass in these cells is

$$\min(1 - x_S^{(i)}, m_T^{(j)} + 1 - x_S^{(j)})$$

so that (**case 2(i)**) if

$$1 - x_S^{(i)} \geq m_T^{(j)} + 1 - x_T^{(j)}$$

then all mass in column *j* will be allocated in some or all of cells (*1, j*) to (*1, j-1*) and there will be no mass in cell (*i, j*) or in any cell below it in column *j*, satisfying condition (1b). Since conditions (2a) and (1b) are satisfied, this allocation leads to maximum confidence. Alternatively (**case 2(ii)**) if

$$1 - x_S^{(i)} < m_T^{(j)} + 1 - x_T^{(j)}$$

then mass will be allocated in all cells from (*1, j*) to (*1, j-1*) and there will be non-zero mass in cell (*i, j*). Eq 9 reduces to

Figure 10. Diagrammatic representation of case 2 (ii) – mass in rows above i and columns including and to the left of j is allocated to give maximum confidence; mass in column j is available for cell (i, j) and possibly cells lower in the column.

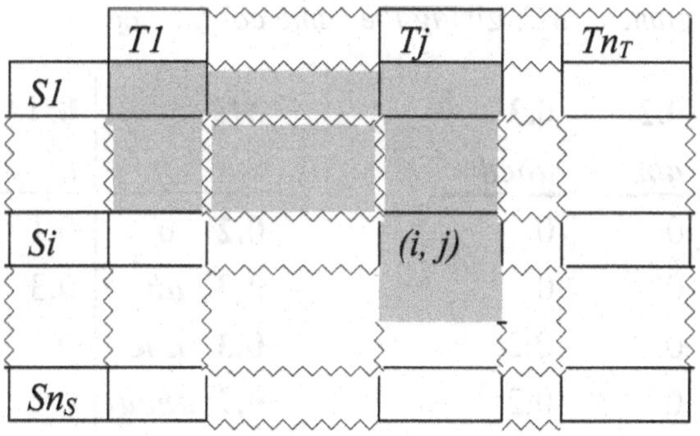

$$M(i, j) = \min\left(m_S^{(i)}, x_T^{(j)} - \left(x_T^{(j)} - x_S^{(i)}\right)\right)$$

Clearly if

$$M(i, j) = m_S^{(i)}$$

then the allocation to cell (i, j) satisfies conditions (1a) and (2a) by lemma 3.1. Alternatively if

$$M(i, j) = m_T^{(j)} - (x_T^{(j)} - x_S^{(i)})$$

then this completes the allocation of mass in column j and there will be no further mass in cells $(i+1, j)$ to (n_S, j) satisfying condition (1b)

In a similar manner (**case 3**) if

$$1 = x_S^{(i)} < 1 - x_T^{(j)}$$

then all mass in rows 1 to i-1 will be allocated in cells $(1, 1)$ to $(i$-$1, j$-$1)$ and there will be no mass in cells $(1, j)$ to $(i$-$1, j)$, i.e. condition 2b is satisfied. We must consider case 3(i)

$$1 - x_T^{(j)} \geq m_S^{(i)} + 1 - x_S^{(i)}$$

which satisfies condition 1a and case 3(ii)

$$1 - x_T^{(j)} \geq m_S^{(i)} + 1 - x_S^{(i)}$$

which also satisfies condition 1b

Hence, for all i and j, if the composite mass assignment obeys eq 9, it is impossible to increase rule confidence by an elementary mass transfer involving cell (i, j).

NB eq 9 leads to a maximal assignment - there may be other assignments leading to the same confidence, as illustrated by the example in figure 11 which shows the assignment using eq 9 leading to maximum confidence 0.68, and a second assignment leading to the same confidence. In this case,

Figure 11. (i) left - assignment M^max produced by eq 9, leading to the maximum confidence of 0.68 (ii) on the right, a different assignment, M2, giving the same confidence

M^{max}		0.4	0.1	0.2	0.3		$M2$		0.4	0.1	0.2	0.3
		c	ac	abc	abcd				c	ac	abc	abcd
0.2	*a*	0.2	0	0	0		0.2	*a*	0.1	0.1	0	0
0.3	*ab*	0.2	0.1	0	0		0.3	*ab*	0.3	0	0	0
0.3	*abc*	0	0	0.2	0.2		0.3	*abc*	0	0	0.2	0.2
0.2	*abcd*	0	0	0	0.2		0.2	*abcd*	0	0	0	0.2

$M^{max} = M2 + E(0.1, (1,1), (2,2))$

where the elementary mass transfer leads to no change in the confidence.

Theorem 4.

The allocation leading to minimum association confidence is

$$M(i,j) = min\left[m_S^{(i)},\ m_T^{(j)}, max\left(0, min\left(m_S^{(i)} - \left(\left(1 - \chi_T^{(j)}\right) - \left(\chi_S^{(i)} - m_S^{(i)}\right)\right),\ m_T^{(j)} - \left(\left(\chi_S^{(i)} - m_S^{(i)}\right) - \left(1 - \chi_T^{(j)}\right)\right)\right)\right)\right]$$

$$= min\left[m_S^{(i)},\ m_T^{(j)}, max\left(0, min\left(\chi_S^{(i)} + \chi_T^{(j)} - 1,\ m_T^{(j)} + m_S^{(i)} - \left(\chi_S^{(i)} + \chi_T^{(j)} - 1\right)\right)\right)\right]$$

$$(10)$$

Proof.

Similar to the proof of theorem 3. For the induction, cells are indexed from the bottom left corner; the total mass in rows $i+1$ to n_S is given by

$$\sum_{k=i+1}^{n_S} m_S^{(k)} = x_S^{(i)} - m_S^{(i)}$$

Membership Function for Fuzzy Confidence

We define the membership function in terms of the quantity of mass which must be moved (relative to the least prejudiced distribution). This can be justified by reference to the Hartley measure or Shannon entropy, and will be covered more fully in a future paper.

The least prejudiced distribution is our reference point, and the resultant confidence is taken to have membership = 1. Any other assignment of mass requires one or more elementary mass transfers relative to the LPD, and we are particularly interested in the mass assignments corresponding to minimum and maximum confidence, M^{MIN} and M^{MAX}. We define a fuzzy interval C representing the confidence such that

$$\mu_C\left(conf\left(M\right)\right) = 1 - \frac{pos\left(M^{LPD} - M\right)}{N}$$

where

Because the membership function varies linearly with the amount of mass moved, it is triangular and can be calculated quickly by considering the end points. We note that it is possible for the membership function to be discontinuous at one end (i.e. to drop abruptly to zero).

Algorithms and Complexity

We outline the conceptual algorithm needed to calculate the fuzzy intervals. Inputs are assumed to be in the appropriate order as described in the section "Closed World Mass-based Association Rules".

The algorithm calculates minimum, expected and maximum values of the cardinality of the intersection between two fuzzy categories using a mass assignment representation. It is thus also suitable for calculating supports for association rules. The quantity can be calculated once and stored, so that a single pass through a database is adequate - this is an important feature when treating very large relations.

Functions *mmax* and *mmin* return the values specified by eqs 10 and 9 respectively, and *intCard* returns the cardinality of the intersection

Calculation of fuzzy confidence interval

```
Inputs: MS[1.....NS],  MT[1.....NT] source, target mass assignments
S[1 … NS], T[1 … NT], source, target level sets
LS[1 … NS], LT[1 … NT], sets of distinct memberships in source, target
Output: a triangular fuzzy number < v1/m1, v2/m2, v3/m3>
lpdConf = 0                  // stores the point value association confidence
minConf = 0                  // stores the minimum value of association confidence
maxConf=0                    // stores the  maximum value of association confidence
minDiff = 0                  // stores pos (M^min - M^lpd)maxDiff = 0                   //
stores pos (M^max - M^lpd)
FOR (i = 1 to NS)
    FOR (j = 1 to NT)
        lpdConf = lpdConf + MS[i] * MS[j] * intCard(S[i], T[j])
        minConf = minConf + mmin(MS[i], LS[i], MT[j], LT[j])* intCard(S[i], T[j]
        maxConf = maxConf + mmax(MS[i], LS[i], MT[j], LT[j])* intCard(S[i], T[j]
        IF    mmin(MS[i], LS[i], MT[j], LT[j])  > MS[i] * MS[j]
        THEN   minDiff = minDiff + mmin(MS[i], LS[i], MT[j], LT[j])  - MS[i] * MS[j]
        ENDIF
        IF    mmax(MS[i], LS[i], MT[j], LT[j])  > MS[i] * MS[j]
        THEN   maxDiff = maxDiff + mmax(MS[i], LS[i], MT[j], LT[j])  - MS[i] * MS[j]
        ENDIF
    ENDFOR
ENDFOR
IF maxDiff > minDiff
THEN norm = 1-maxDiff
ELSE   norm = 1-minDiff
ENDIF
RETURN (< minConf/(1-minDiff/norm), lpdConf / 1, maxConf/(1-maxDiff/norm) >)
```

Note that by making use of the nested structure of the sets, it is not necessary to calculate the intersection at every step as is suggested by the algorithm above. Furthermore, the algorithm can be re-written so that there is a single iteration over elements of the intersection, instead of two iterations over source and target sets. This leads to an overall complexity of $O((n+m) \log (n+m))$. Further details of the algorithm and the more efficient implementation will be discussed in a future paper.

EXPERIMENTS

The algorithm has been implemented in Java and its performance has been investigated using a macbook pro running JDK 6 and Mac OS X 10.5.5. The precise timings are not important, but are intended to give an idea of the scaling behaviour.

The first experiment takes source and target sets defined over a universe of N elements and compares the execution time (y axis) as N increases (x axis) to the theoretically predicted behaviour. As shown by Figure 12, good agreement is obtained, with a constant execution overhead.

The second experiment shows that the fuzzy interval calculation is well-behaved in cases where our earlier algorithm gave very wide intervals.

Taking $S = [x1/1, x2/0.9, x3/0.9, ... x_N/0.9]$ and $T= [x1/0.9, x2/1, x3/0.9, ... x_N/0.9]$, where all intermediate elements also have membership 0.9, and varying N leads to the results shown in Figure 13. Clearly the method returns reasonable results in these cases - note that the point value is very close to the lower limit of the confidence, so that the triangular membership function is truncated at its lower limit.

Figure 12. Scaling behaviour of the algorithm, showing how execution time (y axis) increases as the size of the universe(x axis) increases. The lower line shows theoretical behaviour, the upper line is the actual behaviour. Log scales are used.

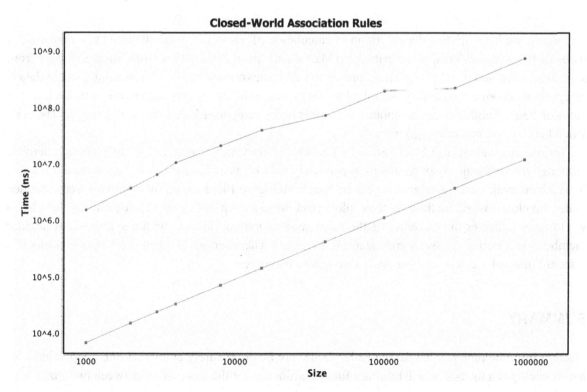

Figure 13. Confidence intervals and point values for nearly identical source and target sets

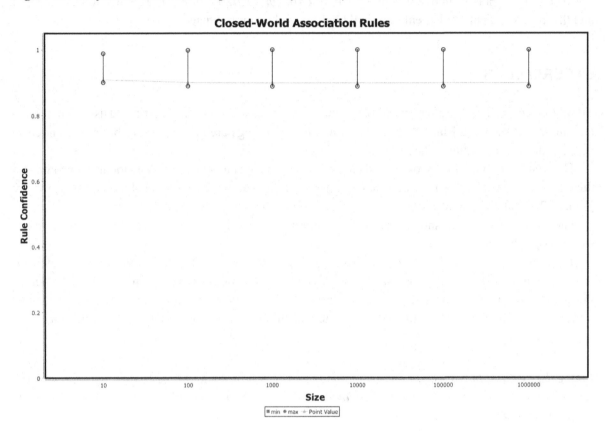

Finally, we have applied the algorithm to calculation of associations in integrated taxonomic databases of terrorist incidents, as described in (Martin and Shen, 2008). This work integrated data from several sources, and recategorised it according to various taxonomic views. For example, where data is categorised according to country, we might prefer to look at fuzzy regions such as the "Middle East" or "in/near Iraq". Another fuzzy taxonomic view uses fuzzy categories based on the casualty levels, classified here as *low, medium, high, very-high*.

Various associations can be extracted by consideration of fuzzy categories in different taxonomies. Although the vast majority of results from that study led to reasonable intervals, there were a few cases in which intervals were quite large. As can be seen from Figure 14, much smaller intervals were obtained under the closed world method. In these plots (and those shown in Figure 13), the interval for closed world rules indicates the extremes of the fuzzy association confidence, with a symmetric triangular membership function (possibly truncated on one side). The interval for open world calculations is a standard interval, i.e. has membership 1 throughout its range.

SUMMARY

Starting from the premise that fuzzy results should not be prematurely converted into crisp values, we have developed a method which returns a fuzzy confidence for the association between two fuzzy sets,

Figure 14. Confidence intervals and point values for associations between the fuzzy categories in/near Iraq and Low casualty levels (top) and Medium casualty levels (bottom). The fuzzy confidence (closed world plots, right hand side) gives a much tighter interval than the open world calculations (left hand side).

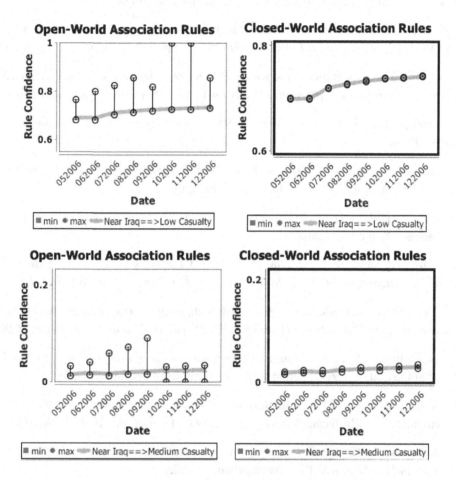

interpreted conjunctively. To our knowledge, this is the only method that generates a fuzzy confidence value for association rules. The method was developed in the context of hierarchical analysis but is suitable to calculate the fuzzy association between *any* pair of fuzzy sets.

It has been implemented using an algorithm having logarithmic complexity in the number of elements in the fuzzy sets, and experiments show that the implementation scales as expected. In particular, it is practical for use on very large fuzzy sets and relations.

ACKNOWLEDGMENT

This work was partly funded by BT and the Defence Technology Centre for Data and Information Fusion.

REFERENCES

Agrawal, R., & Srikant, R. (1994, Sep). *Fast algorithms for mining association rules in large databases.* Paper presented at the 20th Int Conf on Very Large Databases, Santiago.

Baldwin, J. F. (1992). The management of fuzzy and probabilistic uncertainties for knowledge based systems. In S. A. Shapiro (Ed.), *Encyclopedia of AI* (2nd ed., pp. 528-537). New York: John Wiley.

Baldwin, J. F. (1994). Mass assignments and fuzzy sets for fuzzy databases. In M. Fedrizzi, J. Kacprzyk, & R. R. Yager (Eds.), *Advances in the shafer dempster theory of evidence*. New York: John Wiley.

Baldwin, J. F., Martin, T. P., & Pilsworth, B. W. (1995). *Fril - fuzzy and evidential reasoning in AI.* UK: Research Studies Press.

Bosc, P., & Bouchon-Meunier, B. (1994). Databases and fuzziness - introduction. *International Journal of Intelligent Systems, 9*(5), 419. doi:10.1002/int.4550090502

Bosc, P., & Pivert, O. (2001, Jul). *On some fuzzy extensions of association rules.* Paper presented at the IFSA world congress, Vancouver, Canada.

Delgado, M., Marin, N., Sanchez, D., & Vila, M. A. (2003). Fuzzy association rules: General model and applications. *IEEE transactions on Fuzzy Systems, 11*(2), 214–225. doi:10.1109/TFUZZ.2003.809896

Dubois, D., Hullermeier, E., & Prade, H. (2006). A systematic approach to the assessment of fuzzy association rules. *Data Mining and Knowledge Discovery, 13*(2), 167–192. doi:10.1007/s10618-005-0032-4

Kacprzyk, J., & Zadrozny, S. (2003). *Linguistic summarization of data sets using association rules.* Paper presented at the 2003 Fuzzy systems; Exploring new frontiers, St Louis, MO.

Martin, T. P., & Azvine, B. (2003). Acquisition of soft taxonomies for intelligent personal hierarchies and the soft Semantic Web. *BT Technology Journal, 21*(4), 113–122. doi:10.1023/A:1027391706414

Martin, T. P., & Azvine, B. (2005). Soft integration of information with semantic gaps. In E. Sanchez (Ed.), *Fuzzy logic and the Semantic Web*. Amsterdam: Elsevier.

Martin, T. P., Azvine, B., & Shen, Y. (2007a). *Finding soft relations in granular information hierarchies.* Paper presented at the 2007 IEEE International Conference on Granular Computing Fremont, CA, USA.

Martin, T. P., Azvine, B., & Shen, Y. (2007b). Intelligent hierarchy mapping: A soft computing approach. In *Information technology and intelligent computing*.

Martin, T. P., Azvine, B., & Shen, Y. (2008a). Granular association rules for multiple taxonomies: A mass assignment approach to. In M. Nickles (Ed.), *Uncertain reasoning in the Semantic Web*. Berlin, Germany: Springer.

Martin, T. P., & Shen, Y. (2008). Track - time-varying relations in approximately categorised knowledge. *International Journal of Computational Intelligence Research, 4*, 300–313.

Martin, T. P., Shen, Y., & Azvine, B. (2008b). Incremental evolution of fuzzy grammar fragments to enhance instance matching and text mining. *IEEE transactions on Fuzzy Systems, 16*, 1425–1438. doi:10.1109/TFUZZ.2008.925920

Martin-Bautista, M. J., Vila, M. A., Larsen, H. L., & Sanchez, D. (2000). *Measuring effectiveness in fuzzy information retrieval.* Paper presented at the Flexible Query Answering Systems (FQAS).

Zadeh, L. A. (1965). Fuzzy sets. *Information and Control, 8*, 338–353. doi:10.1016/S0019-9958(65)90241-X

Zadeh, L. A. (1975). The concept of a linguistic variable and its application to approximate reasoning (part 1). *Information Sciences, 8*, 199–249. doi:10.1016/0020-0255(75)90036-5

Zadeh, L. A. (1997). Toward a theory of fuzzy information granulation and its centrality in human reasoning and fuzzy logic. *Fuzzy Sets and Systems, 90*(2), 111–127. doi:10.1016/S0165-0114(97)00077-8

Chapter 12
Fuzzy Cluster Analysis of Larger Data Sets

Roland Winkler
German Aerospace Center Braunschweig, Germany

Frank Klawonn
University of Applied Sciences Braunschweig/Wolfenbüttel, Germany

Frank Höppner
University of Applied Sciences Braunschweig/Wolfenbüttel, Germany

Rudolf Kruse
Otto-von-Guericke University Magdeburg, Germany

ABSTRACT

The application of fuzzy cluster analysis to larger data sets can cause runtime and memory overflow problems. While deterministic or hard clustering assigns a data object to a unique cluster, fuzzy clustering distributes the membership of a data object over different clusters. In standard fuzzy clustering, membership degrees will (almost) never become zero, so that all data objects are assigned to – even with very small membership degrees – all clusters. As a consequence, this does not only demand higher computational and memory power, it also leads to the undesired effect that all data objects will always influence all clusters, no matter how far away they are from a cluster. New approaches, modifying the idea of the fuzzifier, have been developed to avoid the problem of nonzero membership degrees for all data and clusters. In this chapter, these ideas will be combined with concepts of speeding up fuzzy clustering by a suitable data organization, so that fuzzy clustering can be applied more efficiently to larger data sets.

INTRODUCTION

Scalability refers to different facets of an algorithm. For data analyzing tools, there are two main interests: first, runtime or storage scalability and second, result quality scalability. Scalability in result quality is of interest i.e. for an algorithm that analyses continuous systems that need to be discretised. Another

DOI: 10.4018/978-1-60566-858-1.ch012

example would be an iterative algorithm to find an approximate solution because the addressed problem is too complex to solve it correctly. Runtime and storage scalability in contrast is an expression for the use of resources (like computation time and local memory) necessary to perform the algorithm. Often it is possible to increase the speed of an algorithm using more storage space and vice versa. If both resources are limited and crucial to an application, a trade-off between both is not sufficient.

As for prototype-based clustering, the above mentioned scalability in accuracy of the result depends on the definition of the term 'cluster'. In this paper, a cluster is defined as a group of data objects in a continuous feature space. The data objects of one group are supposed to be as similar as possible and the data objects of different groups should be as different as possible. If this holds, a group of data objects is called a cluster. The standard Fuzzy c-Means algorithm (FcM) (Bezdek, 1981) may fail to meet these requirements if there are groups of data objects in close proximity, that differ in the density of their data objects. This lack of quality is a result of the fact that the Fuzzy c-Means algorithm tends to calculate a partition of data objects with equal number of data points. The reason for this is that each data point influences all prototypes. Dense groups of data points attract all prototypes, regardless whether there is a prototype in the centre of this dense cluster or not. Klawonn and Höppner (2003a) showed that this effect occurs due to the calculation of fuzzy membership values. An alternative fuzzifier function which explicitly allows membership values of 0 or 1 provides an update scheme which localizes the influence of prototypes and provides a better way of expressing the original idea of clusters. This idea is presented in Section 4.

The two above mentioned modifications to improve the quality of the clustering result and speeding up the calculation process lead to an interesting combination. Since an alternative fuzzifier function includes areas where the membership value of all data objects is 0 for a prototype, neighbourhood information can be used to save computation time. The combination of these two ideas will be presented in this chapter. The first section contains a short introduction to the well known Fuzzy c-Means algorithm, mainly to clarify the notation and to found a good basis for the following sections. Section 4 is dedicated to the changed fuzzifier function and in Section 5, the hierarchical data structure that contains the neighbourhood information is presented. In Section 6, this information is used to calculate membership values for sets of data objects. We finish the chapter with some experimental results and close it with the conclusions in Section 8.

RELATED WORK

This work is related to two major fields of fuzzy clustering. In the first field, the concern is to increase the clustering quality or to adapt FcM to a specific problem because FcM does not generate the desired results. The first approach by Ruspini (1969) of Fuzzy c-Means only considered a fuzzifier value of 2. This approach was extended by Dunn (1973) to an adjustable value which influences the softness of the fuzzy approach. Later, several approaches were made to change the behaviour of FcM by changing the fuzzifier function i.e. (Klawonn & Höppner, 2003a; Klawonn & Höppner, 2003b).

The second large field this work is related to is the concern how to apply an FcM algorithm on very large data sets especially if only limited calculation resources are available. In the past, this was a much more important issue than it is today. For this work, we consider that the data set can be loaded fully into the local memory of the computer which provides random access to the data. Our main concern will be to adapt FcM in a way that reduces the runtime of the algorithm.

Since Fuzzy c-Means is an iterative algorithm, there are in principle three ways to reduce the runtime complexity: a reduction of the data set size via sampling (Cheng, Goldgof & Hall, 1995; Hathaway & Bezdek, 2006; Eschrich, Ke, Hall & Goldgof, 2003; Shankar & Pal, 1994) a reduction of the number of iteration steps (Hershfinkel & Dinstein, 1996), and a faster calculation for each single step (Cannon, Dave & Bezdek, 1986). Höppner (2002) presented a way of reducing the complexity of one iteration step for large sets of data objects by calculating the membership value for sets of data objects that are close together. This is based on a data structure which contains neighbourhood information which we will present in Section 5. A similar approaches are presented by in (Pelleg & Moore, 1999) and (Smellie, 2004) for Hard c-Means. A more geometric approach is used in (Elkan, 2003) also for Hard c-Means. These three approaches benefit directly from the fact, that only the closest prototype to a data object needs to be considered for the clustering process. In a sense, we do something similar in our approach, the difference is, that we consider a set of closest prototypes.

FUZZY C-MEANS ALGORITHM (FCM)

FcM is an algorithm to cluster data sets in a real feature space. The goal is, to find (fuzzy) clusters. In this section, a brief mathematical description of FcM is presented.

Definition 1 (Fuzzy Set). Let M be a set and $\mu : M \to [0,1]$ be a continuous function, then μ is called *fuzzy set on M* and for $x \in M$ is $\mu(x)$ referred as the *membership degree of x to μ.*

Definition 2 (Data). A normed vector space $(V, \|\cdot\|)$ is called **feature space** and a finite, non-empty set $X = \{x_1, \ldots, x_n\} \subset V$ is called **data set** in V with $n \geq 1, n \in \mathbb{N}$ data objects. A subset $W \subset X$ is called a cloud of data objects, if all objects in W are considered to belong together.

It is not really necessary that X is a set i.e. that X consists of n different data objects. In our notation, we will always use X is an indexed set and we allow objects with different indices to be equal.

Definition 3 (Fuzzy Cluster). Let V be a vector space and $X \subset V$ a data set in V with n data objects. A fuzzy set $\mu : X \to [0,1]$ is called *fuzzy cluster*, if μ is defined by an algorithm. A finite, not empty set of fuzzy clusters $\Gamma = \{\mu_1, \ldots, \mu_c : X \to [0,1]\}$ is called *fuzzy partition of X*, iff for $j = 1, \ldots, n$ holds:

$$1 = \sum_{i=1}^{c} \mu_i(x_j).$$

The difference between a cloud and a cluster is the entity which defines it. A cloud is specified by a human while a cluster is defined by an algorithm. While it is relatively easy for a human to find clouds in data sets with up to 3 dimensions, it is almost impossible for higher dimensions because it is harder to visualize. For a computer, the dimension is less important and it can in principle process data of arbitrary dimension. When designing clustering algorithms, the goal is to achieve a match between the clusters derived by the algorithm and the clouds defined by a human. The point here is that the shape of clouds that ought to be found by the algorithm influences the type of algorithm that needs to be used. FcM belongs to the family of prototype based clustering algorithms. That means clouds have a convex form and can be represented by a vector that is called prototype.

Definition 4 (Prototype). Let V be a vector space and $X \subset V$ be a data set and $\mu : X \to [0,1]$ be a fuzzy cluster. A vector $p \in V$ is called *prototype of μ*, if p captures the main characteristics of μ.

For FcM, clouds are considered to be shaped like hyper spheres with the highest density in the middle of a cloud and hence the clusters are defined accordingly: the prototype of a cluster is the centre of the hyper sphere. In the Fuzzy c-Means algorithm itself, the prototypes are used to calculate the fuzzy sets of data objects. The goal of Fuzzy c-Means is to find a fuzzy partition of a data set X into c fuzzy clusters so that the prototypes represent the data objects as well as possible.

Definition 5 (Fuzzy c-Means Clustering (FcM)). *Let* $(V, \|\cdot\|)$ *be a normed vector space,* $X = \{x_1, \ldots, x_n\} \subset V$ *a data set,* $\Gamma = \{\mu_1, \ldots, \mu_c\}$ *a fuzzy partitioning with the corresponding prototypes* $P = \{p_1, \ldots, p_c\} \subset V$ *and the membership matrix* $U \in [0,1]^{c \times n} : u_{ij} = \mu_i(x_j)$ $i = 1..c$, $j = 1..n$. *Let* $\omega \in \mathsf{R}$, $\omega > 1$ *be the fuzzifier,* $\Lambda = \{\lambda_1, \ldots, \lambda_n\} \subset \mathsf{R}$ *some variables. Finally, let* $d_{ij} = \|p_i - x_j\|$, $i = 1..c$, $j = 1..n$ *denote the distance of prototype i to data object j.*

The **objective function** $\mathbf{J}(X, U, P)$ is to be minimized under the constraint $\sum_{i=1}^{c} u_{ij} = 1, j = 1..n$ which is expressed with a Lagrange extension $l(U, \Lambda)$ of **J**:

$$L(X, U, P, \Lambda) = \sum_{i=1}^{c} \sum_{j=1}^{n} u_{ij}^{\omega} d_{ij}^2 + \sum_{j=1}^{n} \lambda_j \left(1 - \sum_{i=1}^{c} u_{ij} \right) \tag{1}$$

A *Fuzzy c-Means clustering* is the fuzzy partition Γ in a (local) minimum of U and P.

If a (local) minimum in U and P is reached, the partial derivatives in all variables of U and P vanish. This leads to an iterative update scheme for the objective function **J** which is based on the idea of gradient descent. We assume in this paper, that the Euclidean distance is used for the function d. All algorithms will be applicable as well for a different (global) distance function. Let $t \in \mathsf{N}$ be a counter for the iteration step, then the variables are updated as follows:

$$u_{ij}^{t+1} = \frac{(d_{ij}^t)^{\frac{2}{1-\omega}}}{\sum_{k=1}^{c} (u_{kj}^t)^{\frac{2}{1-\omega}}} \tag{2}$$

$$p_i^{t+1} = \frac{\sum_{j=1}^{n} (u_{ij}^t)^{\omega} \cdot x_j}{\sum_{j=1}^{n} (u_{ij}^t)^{\omega}} \tag{3}$$

This update scheme is not applicable if one data object is identical to at least one prototype. In the unlikely event that such a situation occurs, the update for u_{ij} is changed to:

$$u_{ij}^{t+1} = \begin{cases} \dfrac{1}{|I_j|} & , \quad i \in I_j \\ 0 & , \quad else \end{cases}$$

Figure 1. Example of a data set with 2 clusters. The Prototypes are represented as filled circles

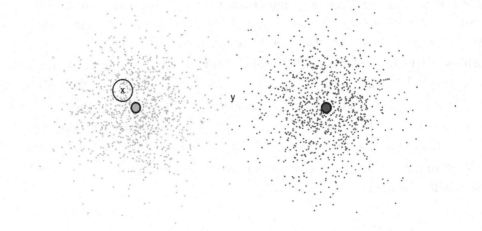

with $I_j = \{k \in \mathbb{N} : x_j = p_k\}$. For the sake of simplicity, it is assumed that such a situation does not appear.

The iteration process is started by some sort of initialization for the prototypes, which can be done by using a random process or a more sophisticated method. The iteration is stopped when the sequence of membership values converges, i.e. $\left\| U^{t+1} - U^t \right\|_M < \varepsilon$ for some $\varepsilon > 0$ and $\|\cdot\|_M$ is the maximum norm for matrices. For further information on the family of fuzzy clustering algorithms we refer the reader to (Bezdek, Keller, Krishnapuram & Pal, 1999; Höppner, Klawonn, Kruse & Runkler, 1999).

ALTERNATIVE FUZZIFIER FUNCTION

The idea of using fuzzy clustering instead of crisp clustering is that it might not be possible to clearly decide whether a data object belongs to just one cluster. For data objects that have no clear nearest prototype, a degree of membership is very useful to express that the clustering algorithm is unsure to which prototype the data object belongs. Consider the classical example in Figure 1. In a crisp clustering i.e. Hard c-Means, the data object *y* would be assigned uniquely to one of the two clusters. Fuzzy c-Means solves that problem by assigning a data object only to a specific degree to a cluster, so that *y* would be assigned by around 0.5 to both clusters.

As plausible as the concept of a fuzzy cluster is for data objects that can not be assigned uniquely, as implausible it is for data objects that are very close to one prototype. Assuming that no data object matches exactly a prototype, all data objects belong to some degree to every cluster. Consider for example data object *x* in Figure 1, no matter how close it is to the left prototype, it will always have a strictly larger than 0 membership value to the right prototype. In other words, all data objects influence all prototypes, so that all prototypes are drawn slightly to the centre of gravity of all data objects, which is not very plausible. The effect increases with the number of dimensions of the data set.

Hard c-Means clustering is plausible for data objects that are very near to exactly one prototype and FcM is plausible for data objects that are between at least two prototypes. The question is, why is FcM not plausible for data objects that are very near exactly one prototype?

Understanding the Fuzzifier

Klawonn and Höppner (2003a) answered the above formulated question by examining a different objective function which depends on a continuous, strictly increasing function $h : [0,1] \rightarrow [0,1]$ with $h(0) = 0$ and $h(1) = 1$ instead of simply a fuzzifier value:

$$\mathbf{J}_h(X, U, P) = \sum_{i=1}^{c} \sum_{j=1}^{n} h(u_{ij}) d_{ij}^2$$

Hard clustering can now be expressed by defining h as identity or FcM by using an exponential function $h(u) = u^\omega$, $\omega > 1$. Consider the special case of two clusters like in Figure 1. $\mathbf{J}_h$ must be minimized for every data object and for x_j in particular, so that the term

$$\begin{aligned} J_{min}(x_j, u_{1j}) &= h(u_{1j}) d_{1j}^2 + h(u_{2j}) d_{2j}^2 \\ &= h(u_{1j}) d_{1j}^2 + h(1 - u_{1j}) d_{2j}^2 \end{aligned}$$

must be a minimum. A necessary condition for a minimum is that the derivative of $\dfrac{\partial}{\partial u_{u1j}} J_{min}$ is zero:

$$\begin{aligned} 0 &= h'(u_{1j}) d_{1j}^2 - h'(1 - u_{1j}) d_{2j}^2 \\ &= h'(u_{1j}) d_{1j}^2 - h'(u_{2j}) d_{2j}^2 , \end{aligned}$$

with h' is the derivation of h. That leads to

$$\frac{h'(u_{1j})}{h'(u_{2j})} = \frac{d_{2j}^2}{d_{1j}^2} .$$

(4)

This means, the ratio of the (transformed) membership value gradients must correspond to the ratio of the squared distances. In the case of $h(u) = u^\omega$, the derivative of h vanishes if the membership value is zero $u_{min} = 0$: $h'(0) = 0$. On the other hand, the derivative for $u_{max} = 1$ is always larger than zero: $h'(1) = \omega \cdot 1^{\omega-1} = \omega > 0$. Because the ratio of Equation (4) still holds, there are no corresponding distances that could cause a crisp membership assignment for the FcM algorithm. For this reason, every data object influences all prototypes as long as it is not identical to one of the prototypes.

Crisp c-Means has a different problem, in this case h is the identity: $h(u) = u$ which leads to a derivative of $h'(u) = 1$, $\forall u$. This is not applicable on the update scheme of FcM, since Equation (4) only holds, if the distances are equal. So the update function cannot be applied in the above specified way. Still the goal is to minimize **J** and since only membership values of 0 and 1 are allowed, the membership corresponding to the closest prototype is set to 1 and 0 otherwise. Obviously, there are no fuzzy membership values, even if the data objects have almost identical distance to all prototypes.

To solve both problems, the fuzzifier function h must be chosen in a way that $h'(0) > 0$ and $h'(u_1) < h'(u_2)$ for all $0 \leq u_1 < u_2 \leq 1$. The function family of $h(u) = \alpha u^2 + (1 - \alpha)u$, $\alpha \in [0.1]$ satisfies this property. The lower bound of the ratio of the membership value gradients is

$$\frac{h'(0)}{h'(1)} = \frac{1-\alpha}{2\alpha + (1-\alpha)} = \frac{1-\alpha}{1+\alpha} .$$

This means, that the ratio of squared distances must exceed this value or the membership values are set to their limits of 0 or 1 respectively. So this fuzzifier function behaves like Hard c-Means if the ratio of squared distances is below $\frac{1-\alpha}{1+\alpha}$ and like FcM with a changed fuzzifier function otherwise. Because this is a very intuitive property, h is parameterized by using $\beta = \frac{1-\alpha}{1+\alpha}$ from which follows:

$$\alpha = \frac{1-\beta}{1+\beta}$$

$$h(u) = \frac{1-\beta}{1+\beta} u^2 + \frac{2\beta}{1+\beta} u .$$

Fuzzy Clustering with Polynomial Fuzzifier Function

Based on the idea above, the update process for fuzzy clustering must be adapted.

Definition 6 (FcM with Polynomial Fuzzifier Function). Let $(V, \|\cdot\|)$ be a normed vector space, $X = \{x_1, \ldots, x_n\} \subset V$ a data set, $\Gamma = \{\mu_1, \ldots, \mu_c\}$ a fuzzy partitioning with the corresponding prototypes $P = \{p_1, \ldots, p_c\} \subset V$ and the membership matrix $U \in [0,1]^{c \times n}$: $u_{ij} = \mu_i(x_j)$ $i = 1..c, j = 1..n$. Let $h : [0,1] \rightarrow [0,1]$ with $h(u) = \frac{1-\beta}{1+\beta} u^2 + \frac{2\beta}{1+\beta} u$, $\beta \in [0,1]$ be the polynomial fuzzifier function, $\Lambda = \{\lambda_1, \ldots, \lambda_n\} \subset \mathsf{R}$ some variables and $d_{ij} = \|p_i - x_j\|$, $i = 1..c, j = 1..n$ denotes the distance of prototype i to data object j.

The objective function $\mathbf{J}_h(X, U, P)$ is to be minimized under the constraint $\sum_{i=1}^{c} u_{ij} = 1$, $j = 1..n$ which is expressed by a Lagrange extension $l(U, \Lambda)$ of $\mathbf{J}_h$:

$$\mathbf{L}(X, U, P, \Lambda) = \sum_{i=1}^{c} \sum_{j=1}^{n} h(u_{ij}) d_{ij}^2 + \sum_{j=1}^{n} \lambda_j \left(1 - \sum_{i=1}^{c} u_{ij} \right)$$

$$= \underbrace{\sum_{i=1}^{c} \sum_{j=1}^{n} \left(\frac{1-\beta}{1+\beta} u_{ij}^2 + \frac{2\beta}{1+\beta} u_{ij} \right) d_{ij}^2}_{=\mathbf{J}_h(X,U,P)} + \underbrace{\sum_{j=1}^{n} \lambda_j \left(1 - \sum_{i=1}^{c} u_{ij} \right)}_{=l(U,\Lambda)}$$

(5)

As before, for all valid solutions, the Lagrange extension $l(U, \Lambda)$ is equal to zero. As for FcM, **L** is w.r.t. u_{ij} and p_i are computed to obtain the update formula:

$$\frac{\partial \mathbf{L}}{\partial u_{ij}} = \left(2 \frac{1-\beta}{1+\beta} u_{ij} + \frac{2\beta}{1+\beta} \right) d_{ij}^2 - \lambda_j \overset{!}{=} 0$$

$$\Rightarrow \quad u_{ij} = \frac{1}{1-\beta} \left[\frac{(1+\beta)\lambda_j}{2d_{ij}^2} - \beta \right]$$

$$(6)$$

The parameter λ_j can be calculated, by using the constraint, $1 = \sum_{i=1}^{c} u_{ij}$. Mathematically, the Lagrange extension transfers the optimization problem into a higher dimensional space and restricts it there to a hyper plane of valid solutions. Additionally, if Equation (6) is used without taking into account that $u_{ij} \in [0,1]$, it will produce membership values that are not restricted to [0,1]. Because the sum of all membership values is fixed at 1, it is enough to ensure that no membership value is strictly less than zero. In other words, the membership values that are strictly less than zero are set to zero and the remaining membership values are reweighted to gain a sum of membership values of 1. Suppose it is known for which membership values Equation (6) gives values greater than zero and that the number of this membership values is $\hat{c}$:

$$1 = \sum_{\substack{k=1 \\ u_{kj} \geq 0}}^{c} u_{kj} = \sum_{\substack{k=1 \\ u_{kj} \geq 0}}^{c} \frac{1}{1-\beta} \left(\frac{(1+\beta)\lambda_j}{2d_{kj}^2} - \beta \right)$$

$$\Rightarrow \quad \lambda_j = \frac{2(1+(\hat{c}-1)\beta)}{(1+\beta) \displaystyle\sum_{\substack{k=1 \\ u_{kj} \geq 0}}^{c} \frac{1}{d_{kj}^2}}$$

which leads to the final equation for u_{ij}:

$$u_{ij} = \frac{1}{1-\beta} \left(\frac{1+(\hat{c}-1)\beta}{\displaystyle\sum_{\substack{k=1 \\ u_{kj} \geq 0}}^{c} \frac{d_{ij}^2}{d_{kj}^2}} - \beta \right)$$

$$(7)$$

At the first glance, this seems to be circular reasoning. And indeed, it is necessary to know for which prototypes the membership value is larger than zero to calculate the membership values. But there is a possibility to solve this problem using the result in Lemma 7 and a sequence of tests.

Lemma 7 (Monotonicity of Membership Values). Let the $V, X, P, U, \Lambda, h, \beta$ and d_{ij} like in Definition 6, then for each data object $x_j, j = 1..n$ and pair of prototypes p_i and p_k, $1 \leq i, k \leq c$, it holds:

$$0 \neq u_{ij} \geq u_{kj} \Rightarrow d_{ij} \leq d_{kj} \tag{8}$$

$$d_{ij} \leq d_{kj} \Rightarrow u_{ij} \geq u_{kj} \tag{9}$$

Proof. Because the membership values of the data objects do not depend on each other, it is enough to consider just one data object x_j. Also consider for a moment that the membership values are not restricted to the interval [0,1]. Then Equation (6) holds for all prototypes. Since λ_j and β are constants, it is easy to see that the membership values are monotonous in the distance values. Because of the restriction to the [0,1]-interval, all prototypes with potential membership values less than 0 are excluded from the calculation process and their membership value is set to 0. That means, the clustering process is done with less prototypes than it would be possible. But because their membership value is set to 0, they have no influence on the value of the objective function **J**. Due to the monotonicity of Equation (6), that means that prototypes with a membership value larger than 0 are closer to x_j than all others. The same holds for a membership value of 1: If there is a prototype to which x_j has a membership of 1, all other membership values are 0, hence they are further away.

For the first statement, there are two cases:

- If $u_{ij} > u_{kj} = 0$: Then p_k is excluded from the calculation and since p_i is not excluded, it follows $d_{ij} < d_{kj}$.

- If $1 > u_{ij} \geq u_{kj} > 0$: In this case, (6) holds for both values and due to its monotony, it follows $d_{ij} \leq d_{kj}$.

The second statement holds, independently of the excluding process. If p_i is excluded, so is p_k and both membership values are set to 0. If only p_k is excluded, $u_{ij} > u_{kj}$ by construction. And if none of them is excluded, Equation (6) holds for both prototypes.

From this lemma, it can be concluded that if Equation (6) for a prototype holds, then it holds for all prototypes that are closer to the data object. Even more importantly, it means: if there is one prototype for which (6) does not hold, then for all prototypes further away, it does not hold either.

To break the circular reasoning in Equation (7), it is necessary to know the set of prototypes that are involved in the calculation of the membership value. With Lemma 7, it is already known that the set of prototypes can be split into two subsets, according to their distance to x_j, hence the first step is, to sort the prototypes w.r.t. the distance to the considered data object. The second step is to find that prototype for which Equation (7) still holds, but no prototype further away can be added to the selection. Let ϕ be a permutation of $(1 \ldots c)$ so that $d_{\phi(i)j} \leq \ldots \leq d_{\phi(c)j}$ holds. Due to Lemma 7 all membership values to the prototypes $p_{\phi(1)}, \ldots, p_{\phi(\hat{c}-1)}$ with $d_{\phi(i)j} < d_{\phi(\hat{c})j}$ are greater than 0. Hence, it is sufficient to test whether $u_{\phi(\hat{c})j}$ is greater than 0:

$$
0 \quad \le \quad \frac{1}{1-\beta}\left(\frac{1+(\tilde{c}-1)\beta}{\displaystyle\sum_{k=1}^{\tilde{c}}\frac{d^2_{\phi(\tilde{c})j}}{d^2_{\phi(k)j}}}-\beta\right)
$$

$$
\Leftrightarrow \quad \sum_{k=1}^{\tilde{c}}\frac{d^2_{\phi(\tilde{c})j}}{d^2_{\phi(k)j}} \quad \le \quad \frac{1}{\beta}+\tilde{c}-1
$$

$$
\Leftrightarrow \quad d^2_{\phi(\tilde{c})j}\left(\sum_{k=1}^{\tilde{c}-1}\frac{1}{d^2_{\phi(k)j}}\right)-\tilde{c} \quad \le \quad \frac{1}{\beta}-2
$$

The test can be done by successively increasing $\tilde{c}$ until the test fails. Let $\hat{c}$ be the highest index for which the test was successful. Note that $\hat{c}$ has to be calculated for each data object individually, hence it might be helpful to consider $\hat{c}$ as indexed variable $\hat{c}_j$. Furthermore, it needs to be recalculated in each iteration, so that an iteration variable $t \in \mathsf{N}$ is useful:

$$
\hat{c}^t_j = \max\left\{\tilde{c}\in\mathsf{N}\,\middle|\,\tilde{c}\le c,\sum_{k=1}^{\tilde{c}}\frac{(d^t_{\phi(\tilde{c})j})^2}{(d^t_{\phi(k)j})^2}\le\frac{1}{\beta}+\tilde{c}-1\right\}
$$

for $j = 1..n$.

Finally, Equation (7) is slightly modified and extended by an iteration variable $t \in \mathsf{N}$:

$$
u^{t+1}_{ij} = \begin{cases} \dfrac{1}{1-\beta}\left(\dfrac{1+(\hat{c}^t_j-1)\beta}{\displaystyle\sum_{k=1}^{\hat{c}^t_j}\frac{(d^t_{ij})^2}{(d^t_{\phi(k)j})^2}}-\beta\right) & \text{iff} \quad \phi(i)\le\hat{c}^t_j \\ \\ 0 \quad \text{otherwise} \end{cases}
$$

$$(10)$$

The update function for the prototypes does not change much to the one in FcM:

$$
p^{t+1}_i = \frac{\displaystyle\sum_{j=1}^{n}h(u^t_{ij})\cdot x_j}{\displaystyle\sum_{j=1}^{n}h(u^t_{ij})}
$$

$$(11)$$

Figure 2 illustrates the effect of the polynomial fuzzifier function. As it can be seen, the clusters are detected very well and data objects very close to a prototype are assigned with membership degree of 1. Data objects with no clear nearest prototype are clustered softly. It is worth to point out, that the prototype positions are almost identical to the ones from FcM on the left hand side picture. The polynomial fuzzifier function can be of great use if there are different dense clusters or clusters of different number of data objects. For more detailed analyses of clustering with polynomial fuzzifier function, see for example (Borgelt, 2005; Klawonn & Höppner, 2003a).

NEIGHBOURHOOD REPRESENTATION OF DATA

The approach of Höppner (2002) reveals that it is not necessary to calculate the membership value for each pair of data object and prototype separately, because the membership values of close data objects might not differ significantly.

Consider the example from the beginning, Figure 1 with normal FcM again. The data objects near the left prototype do not have significant influence on the position of the right prototype. In fact, their exact position is not of much interest for calculating their membership value to the right prototype. FcM is an iterative algorithm, which means, it has a termination test. This test might be $\left\| U^{t+1} - U^t \right\|_M < \varepsilon$ for some $\varepsilon > 0$ and $\left\| \cdot \right\|_M$ the maximum norm for matrices as described in Section 3. The value of the maximum norm $\left\| U^{t+1} - U^t \right\|_M = \max_{i=1..c, j=1..n}(| u_{ij}^{t+1} - u_{ij}^t |)$ is the largest difference of all membership values between two iteration steps. Since the algorithm terminates if the largest difference in membership values is below ε, no difference in membership values smaller than ε is of interest to the calculation process of FcM. Using this tolerance, it is possible to consider groups of close data objects as if they all are located at the same position.

Again, consider example 1. The circle around x denotes the space in which x can be moved so that the difference in membership values to the right prototype is below ε. This means, all data objects within the circle can be considered to be located at position of x and for none would be the difference in membership values towards the right prototype above ε. This gives a basic idea, how to save computation time

Figure 2. The same data set, clustered with FcM (left) and with polynomial fuzzifier function (right). The 'tails' of the prototypes represent the path they took during the clustering process and the large enclosed areas on the right hand side are the convex hulls of all data objects with a membership value of 1. The fuzzifier on the left hand side is $\omega = 2$ and the β-parameter on the right hand side is $\beta = 0.5$.

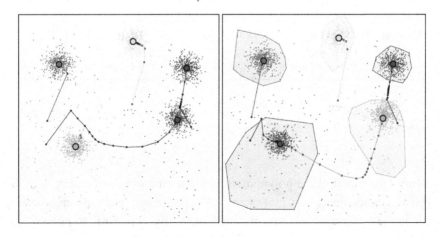

here. But to use this property effectively, the data objects have to be stored in a way that neighbourhood information is available. The data structure is organized as a tree and constructed before starting the clustering process.

Definition 8 (Neighbourhood Tree). Let V be a normed vector space, $X \subset V$ be a data set and $\delta : \mathbf{R}^+ \to \mathbf{R}^+$ a function with $\delta(r) < r, r > 0$. Let $\mathbf{T}$ be a tree and $N = (x \in X, \mathbf{C}, r \in \mathbf{R}^+)$ a node with $\mathbf{C}$ is the set of child nodes. $\mathbf{T}$ is called *neighbourhood tree, if it holds:*

- $succ(N) \subset B_r(x)$
- For all child nodes $N_1 = (x_1, \mathbf{C}_1, r_1) \in \mathbf{C}$ holds: $r_1 \le \delta(r)$
- For all pairs $N_1 = (x_1, \mathbf{C}_1, r_1), N_2 = (x_2, \mathbf{C}_2, r_2) \in \mathbf{C}, N_1 \ne N_2$ holds: $\left\| x_1 - x_2 \right\| > \delta(r)$

with $succ(N) = \{x\} \cup \bigcup_{N' \in \mathbf{C}} succ(N')$ is the set of all successor elements and $B_r(x) \subset V$ is the hyper sphere around x with radius r. The neighbourhood tree T of a data set X is the tree that is associated with the root node $N_{root} = (x \in X, \mathbf{C}_{root}, r_{max})$ so that $succ(N_{root}) = X$, x a random element in X and $r_{max} = \max \left\{ \left\| y - x \right\| : y \in X \setminus \{x\} \right\}$.

A node $N = (x, \mathbf{C}, r)$ can be seen as a representative of its successor elements $succ(N)$. In this matter, a child node $N_1 = (x_1, C_1, d_1)$ of N represents a subset of the data objects $succ(N_1) \subset succ(N)$ which are located in the corresponding hyper sphere $succ(N_1) \subset B_{r_1}(x_1)$. Each data object $y \in succ(N) \setminus \{x\}$ is associated to exactly one of its child nodes. If y is located in the overlap of the hyper spheres of at least two child nodes $N_1, N_2 \in \mathbf{C} : y \in B_{r_1}(x_1) \cap B_{r_2}(x_2)$, there is no clear regulation to which child node y belongs. It is possible to apply an ordering over the child nodes to associate y to the first child node in this ordering, but this is a rather arbitrary regulation. Instead, the neighbourhood tree is extended so that y is associated with the closest child node which leads to the definition of a strict neighbourhood tree:

Definition 9 (Strict Neighbourhood Tree). Let V, X, δ and T be like in Definition 8 above. T is called *strict*, if one more restriction is applied on the child nodes of $N = (x, \mathbf{C}, r)$:

- for all pairs $N_1 = (x_1, \mathbf{C}_1, r_1), N_2 = (x_2, \mathbf{C}_2, r_2) \in \mathbf{C}$ holds:

$$\forall y_1 \in succ(N_1) : \left\| y_1 - x_1 \right\| \le \left\| y_1 - x_2 \right\|$$

A strict neighbourhood tree guarantees that a data object belongs to that child, which is closest to it. In the unlikely event that a data object has exactly the same distance to several child nodes, the data object is associated due to an arbitrary ordering on the child nodes. The following algorithm constructs a strict neighbourhood tree from a set of data objects X and the contraction function δ.

Algorithm 10 (Construct a Strict Neighbourhood Tree).

```
INPUT: Data set X, function δ : R⁺ → R⁺
OUTPUT: A strict neighbourhood tree T = (x ∈ X, C, r_max)
1. x ← randomElement(X), Y ← X \ {x}
```

2. $N_{root} \leftarrow (x, \varnothing, \max\{\|y - x\| : y \in Y\})$

3. $insert(N_{root}, Y)$

4. **end.**

5. **function** $insert(N = (x, \mathbf{C} = \varnothing, r), Y)$

6. $\mathbf{Z} \leftarrow \varnothing$, $\hat{Y} \leftarrow \varnothing$, $i \leftarrow 1$

7.   **for** $y \in Y$ **do**

8.   **if** $\exists (x', \varnothing, r') \in \mathbf{C} : y \in B_{r'}(x')$ **do**

9. $\hat{Y} \leftarrow \hat{Y} \cup \{y\}$

10.   **else**

11. $C_i \leftarrow (y, \varnothing, \delta(r))$, $\mathbf{C} \leftarrow \mathbf{C} \cup \{C_i\}$

12. $Z_i \leftarrow \varnothing$, $\mathbf{Z} \leftarrow \mathbf{Z} \cup \{Z_i\}$

13. $i \leftarrow i + 1$

14.   **end if**

15.   **end for** y

16.   **for** $\hat{y} \in \hat{Y}$ **do**

17. $k_{best} \leftarrow \min_{1 \leq k \leq |\mathbf{C}|} \{\|x_k - \hat{y}\| : (x_k, \varnothing, r_k) \in \mathbf{C}\}$

18. $Z_{k_{best}} \leftarrow Z_{k_{best}} \cup \{\hat{y}\}$

19.   **end for** $\hat{y}$

20.   **for** $k \leftarrow 1$ **to** $|\mathbf{C}|$ **do**

21. $(x_k, \varnothing, r_k) = N_k \leftarrow (x_k, \varnothing, \max\{\|z - x_k\| : z \in Z_k\})$

22.   **if** $|Z_k| > 0$ **do** $insert(N_k, Z_k)$ **end if**

23.   **end for** k

24.   **end function**

The algorithm constructs a strict neighbourhood tree. A random element is selected to generate the root node while the tree is build recursively using the function insert. The first step generates a covering for all the represented data objects, Lines 7 until 15. The set $\hat{Y} \subset X$ contains the data objects that are not used as centres for the child nodes. The covering is generated by testing for each data object $x \in X$, if it can be associated to an already existing child node and if not, a new child node is generated. Due to simplicity, it is assumed that the data is indexed to avoid problems with the definition of mathematical sets. The remaining data objects in $\hat{Y}$ that are not used for child construction are subdivided into the sets $Z_1, \ldots, Z_{|C|}$ according to their closest child node, Line 16 until 19. The recursion is done for each child node if at least one additional data object is associated to it (Line 22).

It is desired to not have only few child node's per node, the function δ must be chosen accordingly, for example $\delta(r) = r \cdot (\frac{(dim(V))}{1 + dim(V)})$. A nodes maximal number of child nodes is a constant K which depends on the dimensions of the underlying vector space V and the function δ. Due to the strict property of the neighbourhood tree, it is likely that a nodes centre object is located in the middle of its represented data objects. Furthermore, because of the shrinking of the distances in Line 21, it is likely that a node has more than one child node, if it represents at least three data objects (The data object contained in the node it self and two more). However, the tree is not constructed to be balanced. It is possible, that the data set is corrupted in a way, that the algorithm would produce a list-like tree. But such situation is more of academic nature because the data set would not be considered for clustering. So in future, it is assumed that the data set is not corrupted in such matter, hence the depth of the tree is logarithmic in the number of data objects. In Figure 3, 4 levels of a strict neighbourhood tree are shown.

If the data set is not corrupted, the runtime complexity of the algorithm is in $O(nlog(n))$. All data objects, associated to a node $N = (x,\mathbf{C},r)$ are contained in the hyper sphere $B_r(x)$. In this hyper sphere, fit at most $K \in \mathbb{N}$ hyper spheres of radius $\delta(r)$, so that no centre of one hyper sphere is contained in any other. Therefore, the computation time of the loops starting in Lines 7 and 16 have both a complexity of $O(K \cdot succ(N))$. The set of all represented data objects of the nodes in one level of the tree, at most the full set of data objects, hence one level of the tree is constructed in $O(2 \cdot K \cdot n)$. The height of the tree is logarithmic in the number of data objects, so that the construction complexity is in $O(2 \cdot K \cdot n)$. During the construction process, it is also possible to store the number of successors $|succ(N)|$ of a node N. This

Figure 3. These four figures represent 4 succeeding levels in a strict neighbourhood tree. The cross symbols represent the centre of gravity of the corresponding data objects

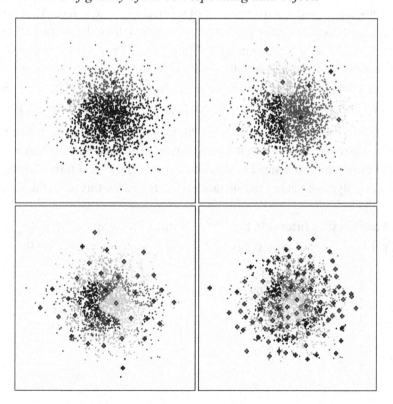

is important for applying the clustering algorithm later. The storage complexity for the neighbourhood tree and its construction is in $O(n)$ because each node stores one data object.

FUZZY CLUSTERING USING NEIGHBOURHOOD INFORMATION

The motivation of constructing the neighbourhood tree is that it is not necessary to calculate the exact membership value for each data object, if the difference between the estimated and the real membership value is below the termination threshold $\forall 1 \leq i \leq c, 1 \leq j \leq n : | u_{ij}^{t} - u_{ij}^{t+1} | < \varepsilon$ of the clustering algorithm. Furthermore, due to the polynomial fuzzifier function, introduced in Section 4 there might be vast areas in which the membership values of data objects to one prototype might be 1 or 0. Obviously, the membership values for these data objects need not be calculated for each data object individually.

Membership Value Interval

Suppose it is desired to calculate the membership value of data object x_j to the prototype p_i. Given a node $N = (x_j, \mathbf{C}, r)$ in the neighbourhood tree guarantees that all data objects $succ(N)$ are in a hyper sphere $B_r(x_j)$. So the location of the data objects do not vary more than a distance r to the data object x_j. Therefore, the distances of the data objects $y \in succ(N)$ to a prototype p_i must be in the interval

$$[d_{ij}^{-}, d_{ij}^{+}] = [\max\{0, \|p_i - x_j\| - r\}, \|p_i - x_j\| + r] \,.$$

Consider the hypothetical case that the distance of the data object $x_k \in succ(N)$ $(k \neq j)$ to the prototype p_i is reduced, but the distance to all other prototypes is constant, then due to Lemma 7 the membership value u_{ik} is *higher* than u_{ij}. Again from Lemma 7 follows that if x_k is closer to prototype p_l $(l \neq i)$, but keeps all other distances fixed, the membership value u_{kj} is *lower* than u_{ij}. So the minimal hypothetical membership value of a data object $x_k \in succ(N)$ towards prototype p_i would be, if x_k reduces its distance to all prototypes but p_i by r and increases its distance to p_i by r. Since the norm $\|\cdot\|$ is symmetric, it does not matter if a data object changes its location or the prototype. According to Equation (10), not the actual position of the prototypes is relevant for calculating the membership value, only its distances to the data object is important. So instead of considering the data object move inside the hyper sphere $B_r(x_j)$, consider the prototypes change their distance to x_j. Based on this idea, the following theorem is formulated:

Theorem 11 (Membership Interval). Let V be a normed vector space, $X = \{x_1, \ldots, x_n\} \subset V$ a data set, $P = \{p_1, \ldots, p_c\} \subset V$ a set of prototypes, $x_j \in X$ and $p_i \in P$ and $r \in \mathsf{R}, r > 0$.

$$\forall x_k \in B_r(x_j) : u_{ik} \in I_i = \left[I_i^{-}, I_i^{+} \right]$$

with

$$
I_i^- = \begin{cases} \dfrac{1}{1-\beta}\left(\dfrac{1+(\hat{c}_i^- - 1)\beta}{1+\displaystyle\sum_{\substack{l=1 \\ \phi_i^-(l)\neq i}}^{\hat{c}_i^-} \dfrac{(d_{ij}^+)^2}{(d_{\phi_i^-(l)j}^-)^2}}\right) & ,\ \phi_i^-(i) \leq \hat{c}_i^- \\[4ex] 0 & ,\ \text{otherwise} \end{cases}
$$

$$
I_i^+ = \begin{cases} \dfrac{1}{1-\beta}\left(\dfrac{1+(\hat{c}_i^+ - 1)\beta}{1+\displaystyle\sum_{\substack{l=1 \\ \phi_i^+(l)\neq i}}^{\hat{c}_i^+} \dfrac{(d_{ij}^-)^2}{(d_{\phi_i^+(l)j}^+)^2}}\right) & ,\ \phi_i^+(i) \leq \hat{c}_i^+ \\[4ex] 0 & ,\ \text{otherwise} \end{cases}
$$

with $d_{ij}^- = \max\{0, \|p_i - x_j\| - r\}$ and $d_{ij}^+ = \|p_i - x_j\| + r$ are the minimal (maximal) hypothetical distances of the data object x_j in the hyper sphere $B_r(x_j)$ to the prototype p_i. $\hat{c}_i^-$ and $\hat{c}_i^+$ denotes the number of relevant prototypes and ϕ_i^- (ϕ_i^+) denote a new ordering of prototypes w.r.t. to the changed distances.

Before proving the statement, please note that the formula for the interval borders is slightly changed to Equation (10). This derives from the fact that the sum in the denominator of the fraction in (10) contains the term $\dfrac{d_{ij}}{d_{\phi(l)j}}$ with $i = \phi(l)$. With changed distances, this would result in $\dfrac{d_{ij}^+}{d_{ij}^-}$ (or $\dfrac{d_{ij}^-}{d_{ij}^+}$) which is not plausible because the distance of the data object x_j to the prototype p_i cannot increase and decrease at the same time. Therefore, this term is excluded from the sum. This change makes it possible to separate the distance change of p_i to the other prototypes $p_{\phi(l)}$, $\phi(l) \neq i$, $l = 1 \ldots \hat{c}$.

The distance of p_i is changed contrary to the other prototype distances. Therefore, position of p_i might change in the distance ordering of prototypes. The new ordering must be calculated individually for both interval borders of each prototype. Let ϕ_i^+ be the permutation for the upper bound of the membership interval of p_i and ϕ_i^- the permutation for the lower bound respectively. Due to the changed distances, it is possible that the number of relevant prototypes changes $\hat{c}_i^\pm \neq \hat{c}$. So this number has to be recalculated for each interval as well.

Proof. From Lemma 7, we know, that the membership values change monotonously. In case the number of relevant prototypes $\hat{c}_i^\pm = \hat{c}_i$ does not change, the result follows directly from Lemma 7. Not clear is, what happens if $\hat{c}_i^\pm \neq \hat{c}$. So the proof shows, that the membership value of x_j towards p_i does not change, if an other prototype p_l is added to the set of relevant prototypes exactly at a distance, where Equation (10) produces a membership value of zero $u_{lj} = 0$. So in other words, the membership values change continuously in the distances towards the prototypes even if the number of relevant prototypes changes. With this result and the monotony from Lemma 7, the above theorem is proven.

Without loss of generality, suppose the prototypes are sorted according to their distance, so we do not need to consider the permutation. To introduce an additional prototype $p_{\hat{c}+1}$ to Equation (7) such that its membership value is zero $u_{(\hat{c}+1)j} = 0$, its distance $d_{(\hat{c}+1)j}$ must follow the following condition:

$$0 \quad = \quad u_{(\hat{c}+1)j} = \frac{1}{1-\beta}\left(\frac{1+((\hat{c}+1)-1)\beta}{\sum\limits_{k=1}^{\hat{c}+1} \frac{d^2_{(\hat{c}+1)j}}{d^2_{kj}}} - \beta \right)$$

$$\Leftrightarrow \quad d^2_{(\hat{c}+1)j} \quad = \quad \frac{1+(\hat{c}-1)\beta}{\beta\sum\limits_{k+1}^{\hat{c}} \frac{1}{d^2_{kj}}}$$

If Equation (7) is now evaluated for u_{ij} adding the additional prototype from the previous calculation, we obtain:

$$u_{ij} = \frac{1}{1-\beta}\left(\frac{1+(\hat{c}+1-1)\beta}{\sum\limits_{k=1}^{\hat{c}} \frac{d^2_{ij}}{d^2_{kj}} + \frac{d^2_{ij}}{d^2_{(\hat{c}+1)j}}} - \beta \right)$$

$$= \frac{1}{1-\beta}\left(\frac{1+\hat{c}\beta}{\sum\limits_{k=1}^{\hat{c}} \frac{d^2_{ij}}{d^2_{kj}} + \frac{\beta\sum\limits_{k=1}^{\hat{c}} \frac{d^2_{ij}}{d^2_{kj}}}{1+(\hat{c}-1)\beta}} - \beta \right)$$

$$= \frac{1}{1-\beta}\left(\frac{1+(\hat{c}-1)\beta}{\sum\limits_{k=1}^{\hat{c}} \frac{d^2_{ij}}{d^2_{kj}}} - \beta \right)$$

This means, the membership value u_{ij} does not change by introducing the additional prototype. Now it is possible to consider (7) as a continuous function in the distance variables, even if the number of involved prototypes $\hat{c}$ changes. The only condition up to this point is, that the ordering of the prototypes stays the same.

Therefore it follows with Lemma 7, Equation (7) is a continuous, decreasing function in distances d_{lj} with $l \neq i$ and increasing in d_{ij}. If there is a $x_k \in X$ with $u_{ik} \notin I_i = [u_{ij}^-, u_{ij}^+]$, there are two cases left to consider:

- $u_{ik} < u_{ij}^-$. Since (7) is continuous and monotonous, it means that $d_{ik} > d_{ij}^+$ and/or $\exists l \neq i : d_{lk} < d_{ij}^-$.

- $u_{ik} > u_{ij}^+$. With the same argument, it follows that $d_{ik} < d_{ij}^-$ and/or $\exists l \neq i : d_{lk} > d_{ij}^+$.

In both cases, $x_k \notin B_d(x_i)$. That means, when ever $x_k \in B_d(x_j)$, $u_{ik} \in I_i$.

Consider a node of the neighbourhood tree: $N = (x_i, \mathbf{C}, r)$ let its membership interval with distance r be $I_i \subset [u_{ij} - \varepsilon, u_{ij} + \varepsilon]$, then all successors $succ(N)$ can be treated exactly like x_j hence, their membership value towards prototype p_i does not need to be calculated individually.

Note that the membership value interval is a very pessimistic estimation, since it is assumed that the distances to all prototypes become worst case. In practise, such situation nearly never occurs and in most cases, the real range of membership values is far smaller than the calculated interval. A much better estimation for the membership interval would arise from the following formula:

$$u_{ij}^- = \inf_{y \in B_d(x_j)} \left(\left| \frac{1}{1-\beta} \left| \frac{1 + (\hat{c}_y - 1)\beta}{\sum_{k=1}^{\hat{c}_y} \frac{\|y - p_i\|^2}{\|y - p_k\|^2}} - \beta \right| \right| \right)$$

To give a general case solution for this problem is not trivial and might be even impossible. This question is subject to further research.

Alternative Fuzzy c-Means

In this subsection, we introduce the Fuzzy-c Means algorithm using a polynomial fuzzifier and the strict neighbourhood tree. There are two versions for this algorithm, one with more memory consumption and the other which uses a different termination rule. At first, the version which uses more memory is presented, because it needs one less user defined parameter and is more consistent with the motivation of using neighbourhood information. The other version of the algorithm is presented in the next subsection.

Algorithm 12 (Modified FcM). INPUT: *Data set X*, function $\delta : \mathsf{R}^+ \rightarrow \mathsf{R}^+$, number of prototypes *c*, termination threshold $\varepsilon > 0$, a parameter $\beta \in [0,1]$

```
OUTPUT: A fuzzy partition U
```

1. $N_{root} \leftarrow neighbourhoodTree(X, \delta)$

2. $P \leftarrow initialize(\{p_1, \ldots, p_c\})$

3. $U \leftarrow [0]_{(c,n)}$, $\quad U' \leftarrow [1]_{(c,n)}$

4. **while** $\exists 1 \leq i \leq c, 1 \leq j \leq n : |u_{ij} - u_{ij}'| > \varepsilon$ **do**

5. $\quad U \leftarrow U'$

6. $\quad P' \leftarrow \{p_1' \leftarrow 0, \ldots, p_c' \leftarrow 0\}$

7. $\quad T \leftarrow \{t_1 \leftarrow 0, \ldots, t_c \leftarrow 0\}$, $\quad Z \leftarrow \{z_1 \leftarrow -1, \ldots, z_c \leftarrow -1\}$

8. $\quad update(N_{root}, Z)$

9. $\quad$ **for** $i = 1$ **to** c **do** $p_i \leftarrow \dfrac{p_{i'}}{t_i}$ **end for**

10. **end while**

11. **end.**

12.

13. $\quad$ **function** $update(N = (x_j, \mathbf{C}, r), Z)$

14. $\quad\quad D \leftarrow \{\|x_j - p_1\|^2, \ldots, \|x_j - p_c\|^2\}$

15. $\quad\quad \phi \leftarrow prototypePermutation(x_j, D)$

16. $\quad\quad \hat{c} \leftarrow validPrototypes(x_j, D, \phi)$

17. $\quad\quad$ **for** $i \leftarrow 1$ **to** c **do**

18. $\quad\quad\quad$ **if** $z_i < 0$ **do**

19. $\quad\quad\quad\quad u_{ij}' \leftarrow membershipValue(x_j, D, i, \hat{c}, \phi, \beta)$

20. $\quad\quad\quad\quad (u^-, u^+) \leftarrow membershipInterval(x_j, r, D, i, \phi, \beta)$

21. $\quad\quad\quad\quad$ **if** $u^+ - u_{ij}' < \varepsilon$ **and** $u_{ij}' - u^- < \varepsilon$ **do**

22. $\quad\quad\quad\quad\quad z_i \leftarrow u_{ij}'$

23. $\quad\quad\quad\quad$ **end if**

24. $\quad\quad\quad$ **else**

25. $\quad\quad\quad\quad u_{ij}' \leftarrow z_i$

26. $\quad\quad\quad$ **end if**

27. $\quad\quad\quad p_i' \leftarrow p_i' + h(u_{ij}') \cdot x_j$

28. $\quad\quad\quad t_i \leftarrow t_i + h(u_{ij}')$

29. $\quad\quad$ **end for** i

30. $\quad\quad$ **for** $N' \in \mathbf{C}$ **do** $update(N', copy(Z))$ **end for**

31. $\quad$ **end function** $update$

The first part is quite self explaining. The variables P' and T represent global variables (they are also valid in the function *update*) that are used to calculate the new prototype positions. The recursive update function is evoked as long as at least one membership value changes more than ε. The update function itself is a little more complicated. Basically, it traverses the neighbourhood tree in depth first ordering by recursively evoking itself. The parameters in Z contains the information whether a set of data objects need further calculation and if not, the membership value is stored in Z for the corresponding prototype.

In Line 14, the distances from x_j to all prototypes are stored in D because these values are used quite often(complexity $O(c)$). In the next step, the prototypes are sorted according to their distance (complexity $O(c \cdot log(c))$). In Line 16, the number of prototypes with larger than 0 membership function is calculated (complexity: $O(c)$). Then, for each prototype, the new membership value is calculated. In case $z_i < 0$, it means the membership interval was not narrow enough, which means the membership value for x_j must be calculated. This is done in Line 19 with $O(1)$ complexity because $\sum_{k=1}^{\hat{c}} \dfrac{1}{d^2_{\phi(k)j}}$ can be calculated once before the loop is started. Calculating the membership interval however (Line 20), has a complexity of $O(c)$, since $\hat{c}_i^{\pm}$ and the above mentioned sum has to be recalculated with the changed distances for each prototype individually. If the resulting membership interval is narrow enough, all subsequent data objects are associated with the same membership value for prototype p_i. This information is stored in r_i for use in the next recursions.

In Line 27, the factors for the new prototype position are calculated. Finally, the recursion is performed in Line 30 for all child nodes of N with a copy of the values of Z because they might be changed differently in the subsequent branches of the neighbourhood tree. So the overall runtime complexity for one iteration step is in

$$O(\underbrace{(c + c \cdot log(c) + c^2)}_{\text{calculation for one node}} \cdot \underbrace{n}_{\text{n nodes}} + \underbrace{c \cdot n}_{\text{termination test}}) \subset O(c^2 \cdot n).$$

This implementation of the modified FcM is exactly the implementation of the mathematical definition. Unfortunately, it is not feasible for really many data objects, since the membership matrix U has to be stored. This is necessary because the very essence of the algorithm is the use of ε for optimizations. Hence the storage complexity of the algorithm is in $O(n \cdot c)$ which might be too much in storage critical applications.

For means of termination, it is not necessary to store the membership matrix. It would be equally accurate, to test the convergence of FcM using the distance, prototypes move between two iteration steps. It is easy to show that the convergence in membership values is equivalent to the convergence in prototype position. However, if there is a threshold defined for convergence in prototype positions, it is not trivial to calculate a corresponding threshold for convergence in membership values. In a too harsh estimation, the membership interval that is used to optimize the clustering process would become extremely small. Therefore, these two parameters must be chosen separately by the user. The membership value interval can be based on an accuracy parameter ε_m while the convergence test is done with the threshold ε_p.

With using a convergence in prototype positions, it is possible to cease storing the membership matrix during the calculation process. This gives room for even more optimization because it would not be necessary to traverse the entire neighbourhood tree. However, a few technical modifications to the neighbourhood tree are required. It is necessary to store the number of successors $s \mid succ(N) \mid$ of a node N and the centre of gravity of all succeeding data objects: $\nu = \dfrac{1}{s} \sum_{y \in succ(N)} y$. Both can be easily calculated during the construction process of the neighbourhood tree, so that a node is expanded to

$N = (x_j, \mathbf{C}, r, s, \nu)$.

Algorithm 13 (2. Modified FcM). INPUT: *Data set X*, function $\delta : \mathsf{R}^+ \rightarrow \mathsf{R}^+$, number of prototypes c, termination threshold $\varepsilon_p > 0$, membership value calculation accuracy $\varepsilon_m > 0$, a parameter $\beta \in [0,1]$.

```
OUTPUT: The set of Prototypes P
```

1. $N_{root} \leftarrow extNeighbourhoodTree(X, \delta)$

2. $P \leftarrow \{p_1 \leftarrow 0, \ldots, p_c \leftarrow 0\}$

3. $P' \leftarrow initialize(\{p_1', \ldots, p_c'\})$

4. **while** $\exists 1 \leq i \leq c : | p_i - p_{i'} | > \varepsilon_p$ **do**

5.   **for** $i = 1$ **to** c **do** $p_i \leftarrow p_{i'}$ **end for**

6. $P' \leftarrow \{p_1' \leftarrow 0, \ldots, p_c' \leftarrow 0\}$

7. $T \leftarrow \{t_1 \leftarrow 0, \ldots, t_c \leftarrow 0\}, \quad Z \leftarrow \{1, \ldots, c\}$

8. $update2(N_{root}, Z)$

9.   **for** $i = 1$ **to** c **do** $p_{i'} \leftarrow \dfrac{p_{i'}}{t_i}$ **end for**

10.   **end while**

11.   **end.**

12.

13.   **function** $update2(N = (x_j, \mathbf{C}, r, s, \nu), Z)$

14. $D \leftarrow \{\|x_j - p_1\|^2, \ldots, \|x_j - p_c\|^2\}$

15. $\phi \leftarrow prototypePermutation(D)$

16. $\hat{c} \leftarrow validPrototypes(x_j, D, \phi)$

17.   **for** $i \in R$ **do**

18. $(u^-, u^+) \leftarrow membershipInterval(\nu, r, D, i, \phi, \beta)$

19.   **if** $u^+ - u^- < \varepsilon_m$ **do**

20. $u \leftarrow membershipValue(\nu, D, i, \hat{c}, \phi, \beta)$

21. $Z \leftarrow Z \setminus \{i\}$

22. $p_i' \leftarrow p_i' + s \cdot h(u) \cdot \nu$

23. $t_i \leftarrow t_i + s$

24.   **else**

25. $u \leftarrow membershipValue(x_j, D, i, \hat{c}, \phi, \beta)$

26. $p_i' \leftarrow p_i' + h(u) \cdot x_j$

27. $t_i \leftarrow t_i + h(u)$

```
28.                    end if
29.              end for i
30.              if |Z| > 0 do
31.                    for N' ∈ C do update2(N', copy(Z)) end for
32.              end if
33.        end function update2
```

This second algorithm has several advantages over the first version. The storage complexity is in $O(c + n)$ rather than $O(c \cdot n)$. Also the calculation can be simplified by using the centre of gravity of a node's successors. This was not possible in the first version, because all membership values had to be computed to fill the matrix at all positions, so that the traversing of the neighbourhood tree had to be carried out completely.

In detail, the variables P' and T have the same meaning as in Algorithm 12, they are used to calculate the new locations of the prototypes. The variable Z holds now the indices of the prototypes for which a membership value needs to be calculated. However, the main difference to the first version of this algorithm is in Line 4 where the iteration process is stopped when the difference in prototype position converges. All changes in *update2* are a possible due to this change. The function *update2* differs mainly in its behaviour to previously calculated membership values. In its first version, the entire neighbourhood tree is traversed. In this version, only for a subset of all prototypes, the calculation is performed which is defined by Z in Line 17. So, if the membership value for the prototype i is not already known, it is calculated in Lines 17 until 29.

If the calculated membership value interval is narrow enough, the change in location of prototype i is calculated using the with s times the centre of gravity of the subtree and i is removed from Z to prevent any further calculation in the subtree. For all prototypes the membership interval is not narrow enough, the calculation is done solely for x_j. The recursion in Line 31 is done only if there are prototype indices left in Z.

The drawback of the optimized Algorithm 13 is that the usage of the neighbourhood tree loses its justification provided by the termination threshold. On the other hand, this gives the user the advantage to manage calculation precision and termination threshold independently. Consider the example presented in Figure 4. The same data set is clustered with 4 different algorithms. The upper two examples are the FcM algorithm with the normal fuzzifier function, once in standard form (left) and once using neighbourhood information (right). For the other two examples, the polynomial fuzzifier function was used, again once in normal form (left) and once using neighbourhood information (right). As it can be seen, the clustering result is almost not influenced by using neighbourhood information. The tails of the prototypes show that even the clustering process is almost identical (the difference is not visible in the pictures, but the paths differ slightly due to the approximation of using neighbourhood information.) even if the membership interval of $\varepsilon_m = 0.1$ is rather large compared to the calculation accuracy.

Figure 4. The same data set, clustered with FcM (upper left), FcM using neighbourhood information (upper right), FcM with Polynomial fuzzifier function (lower left) and FcM with polynomial fuzzifier function and using neighbourhood information (lower right). In the two right hand side examples, the maximal membership interval length was set to $\varepsilon_m = 0.1$, in the two above examples, the fuzzifier value is set to $\omega = 2$ and in the two lower examples, the fuzziness parameter was set to $\beta = 0.3$.

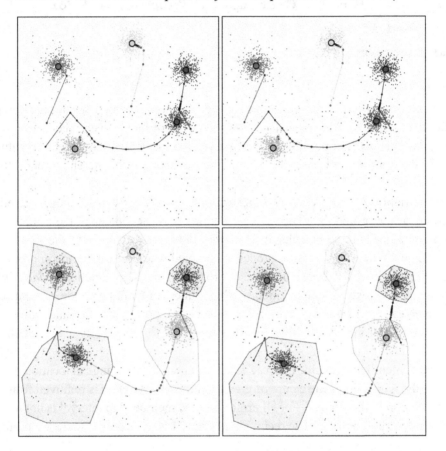

EXPERIMENTAL RESULTS

The four algorithms standard FcM, FcM using Neighbourhood Information(**NFcM**), FcM with Polynomial Fuzzifier Function(**PFcM**) and FcM with Polynomial Fuzzifier Function and using Neighbourhood Information(**NPFcM**), compared in this section, differ in their property of scaling. Runtime tests for these algorithms regarding the number of data objects and the number of prototypes are presented. The values of the parameter β, had no, or only very little influence on the runtime of PFcM and NPFcM.

Figure 5. Two examples for the test data sets: uniform distributed data (left) and Gaussian distributed data objects in randomly positioned clusters

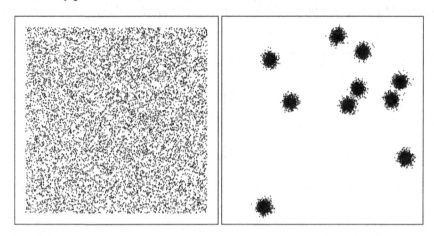

In all cases, the tests are performed using 2, 5 and 10 dimensional artificial data. It was not focused on the algorithm convergence properties because the convergence of the algorithms using neighbourhood information does not differ distinctly from those without. The average Euclidean distance (in one experiment) in prototype positions is almost always below 0.001. Still, it is useful to compare FcM with and without polynomial fuzzifier functions.

Two different artificially created test environments are used, a hypercube with an edge length of 1, filled with uniformly distributed data objects (Figure 5) and randomly placed cluster centres with normally distributed data objects (Figure 5 right). In the second case, there are always as many clusters in the data set as there are prototypes, the number of data objects in the data set is not affected by the number of prototypes. In each test, the algorithms perform 100 iterations, which is usually enough for convergence.

Since NFcM is already well discussed in (Höppner, 2002), we do not discuss runtime differences due to the fuzzifier, a constant value of $\omega = 2$ is used in all cases. This value was chosen, because the polynomial fuzzifier function of PNcM and NPFcM is a Linear combination of crisp clustering and fuzzy clustering with a fuzzifier of $\omega = 2$. Our tests have shown that even a relatively large maximal membership value interval of $\varepsilon_m = 0.1$ is usable for NFcM and NPFcM. The parameter β was set to 0.5. The data set and initialization of the prototypes were identical for all clustering algorithms. The generation of the data, the calculation of the neighbourhood tree as well as the initialization of the prototypes was not taken into account.

In Figures 6 and 7, we present our test results. Always on the left hand side, we present the results of the test environment with uniformly distributed data objects while on the right side the environment with Gaussian clusters is shown. The discussion regarding the algorithms properties is done below.

Figure 6. Runtime experiments for 2, 5 and 10 dimensions with variations in the number of data objects (x-axis, in 1000 data objects). The remaining parameters are: 5 prototypes, ω = 2, β = 0.5, maximal membership interval length 0.1, 100 iterations, and no termination due to converging prototype positions.

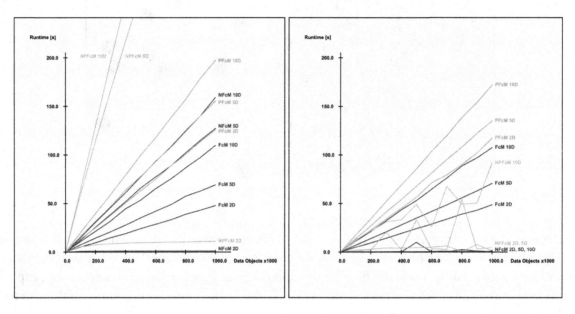

Figure 7. Runtime experiments for 2, 5 and 10 dimensions with variations in the number of prototypes (x-axis). The remaining parameters are: 50000 data objects, ω = 2, β = 0.5, maximal membership interval length 0.1, 100 iterations, and no termination due to converging prototype positions.

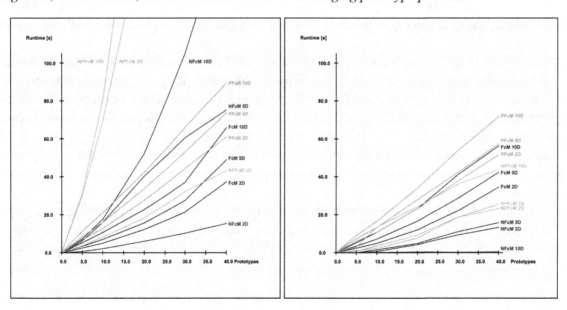

Standard FcM

Not surprisingly, standard FcM has Linear complexity in the number of data objects, number of prototypes and number of dimensions in all examples. The shape of data sets does not affect the runtime of the algorithm.

FcM using Neighbourhood Information

The behaviour of NFcM is quite interesting and shows the potential of the optimization process and some problems in FcM with high dimensional data (> 5 dimensions). The potential is well visible in the 2-dimensional data sets. If the data reaches a certain density, the runtime of this algorithm does not increase because only groups of data objects are used for calculation. This effect is well visible in Figures 6, graph 'NFcM 2D'. Even though, the algorithm is linear in the number of prototypes, a higher number of prototypes lead to smaller sets of data objects during the calculation (Figure 7).

In higher dimensions, the density of the data object decreases considerably in Figure 6 left, graphs NFcM 5D and 10D, if the data objects are uniformly distributed. The result is a huge increase of the runtime pruning of the neighbourhood tree works not as good as in 2D. In case of several Gaussian distributed clusters (Figure 6 right), the density of the data objects is still high enough for the pruning due to neighbourhood information. As it is said before, higher dimensional data leads to a reduced density and more prototypes leads to smaller sets of data objects during the calculation process. In combination, the both effects cause a huge increase in runtime which is even worse than standard Fuzzy c-Means because the membership interval still has to be calculated for every data object (Figure 7 left), graphs NFcM 5D and 10D.

Very surprisingly is the runtime graph in Figure 7 right for NFcM 10D. The source for this effect is that FcM does not work for higher dimensions. In Figure 8, a 2D projection of a 10 dimensional data

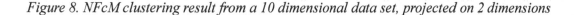

Figure 8. NFcM clustering result from a 10 dimensional data set, projected on 2 dimensions

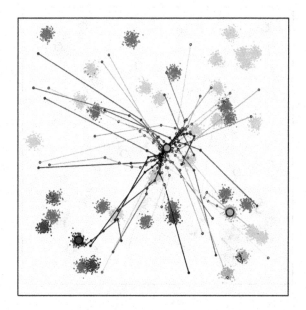

set is shown. All prototypes go to the centre of gravity of the complete data set, hence the membership values of all data objects are almost identical for all prototypes. This leads to huge sets of data objects that can be treated identical, hence the optimization is very effective. Unfortunately, the clustering result is completely useless.

It is also worth mentioning again that the difference of the clustering result compared to standard FcM is almost identical. In data sets with maximal 5 dimensions or in data sets where the majority of the data objects is located in high density areas, this algorithm is almost independent to the number of data objects. Hence it is highly scalable in data size if the prototypes are well separated from each other.

FcM with Polynomial Fuzzifier Function

The runtime of this algorithm is no surprise, since it works basically the same way as standard FcM. The higher runtime is a result of the increased calculation complexity of the membership value. The prototypes have to be sorted and a subset has to be calculated for each data object. Therefore, the algorithm has a runtime complexity of $O(c \cdot log(c))$ for each data object. This makes it even less scalable in the number of prototypes than FcM.

Also for this algorithm, the clustering result in higher dimensions is questionable at best. But in contrast to Fuzzy c-Means, it is not completely useless. Figure 9 shows a 2-dimensional projection of the same 10 dimensional data set as in Figure 8, but this time clustered with PFcM.

FcM with Polynomial Fuzzifier Function and using Neighbourhood Information

Finally, this algorithm is a combination of the last two, it uses neighbourhood information as NFcM and has a fuzzifier function like PFcM. This combination has several advantages and some disadvantages.

Figure 9. PFcM clustering result from a 10 dimensional data set, projected on 2 dimensions

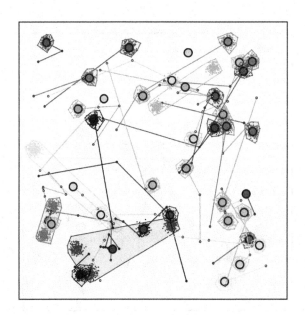

Due to the polynomial fuzzifier function, data objects in the surrounding area of a prototype have a membership value of 1. Hence the membership value to all other prototypes is 0 which leads to very large sets of data object with a membership interval of 0 length. This can speed up the calculation process considerably in comparison to the other algorithms. The drawback, however, is that the prototypes have to be sorted for the membership value interval of each prototype. Because only one prototype is changed every time, this sorting process has a complexity of $O(c)$. But this must be done for each prototype, hence the calculation complexity for each data object is in $O(c^2)$.

The algorithm has the same problems with low density data sets as NFcM and which are enforced by the much higher runtime complexity. In data sets with well separated high density areas, the algorithm is faster, compared to PFcM. This contrast is well visible in Figure 7. In the low density case of uniform distributed data, the algorithm is much slower than all others. Only in the 2 dimensional case, the density is high enough so that the neighbourhood information can reduce the runtime complexity considerably. Like NFcM, NPFcM is highly scalable in data object size if the density areas are well separated and found by prototypes. That this is not always the case is shown in Figure 7 right. For each combination of parameter, only one runtime test is performed. Depending on the initialization, the algorithm separates the data well or less well which has a high impact on the runtime. If there are no high density areas, the algorithm has a very bad runtime performance, as can be seen in Figure 6 left and Figure 7 left.

The polynomial fuzzifier function prevents that the clustering result in higher dimensions is completely useless which makes it possible that the algorithm can use neighbourhood information which makes it faster than PFcM.

CONCLUSION

We presented and compared four prototype based algorithms and tested them on two families of artificial data sets. We showed that using sets of data object that are located close to each other can make FcM almost independent of the number of data objects and we have shown that a polynomial fuzzifier function can be used to make a FcM-based algorithm more useful for high dimensional data sets. The combination of both approaches can be fast, but its performance degrades rapidly if the data set is unsuited for clustering, that is, it has no dense areas. Approaches that analyse the clustering tendency of a dataset beforehand may be applied to circumvent such situations.

ACKNOWLEDGMENT

This work was done at the DLR in Braunschweig in cooperation with the University of Applied Sciences Braunschweig/Wolfenbüttel and the Otto-von-Guericke University of Magdeburg, Germany. We want to thank especially the kind reviewer who helped to increase the quality of this work with a lot of constructive comments.

REFERENCES

Bezdek, J. C. (1981). *Pattern recognition with fuzzy objective function algorithms*. Norwell, MA, USA: Kluwer Academic Publishers.

Bezdek, J. C., Keller, J. M., Krishnapuram, R., & Pal, N. R. (1999). *Fuzzy models and algorithms for pattern recognition and image processing*. Boston, USA: Kluwer Academic Publishers.

Borgel, C. (2005). *Prototype-based classification and clustering (Habilitationsschrift)*. Unpublished habilitation, Otto-von-Guericke-University of Magdeburg, Germany.

Cannon, R. L., Dave, J. V., & Bezdek, J. C. (1986). Efficient implementation of the fuzzy c-means clustering algorithms. *IEEE Transactions on Pattern Analysis and Machine Intelligence, 8*(2), 248–255. doi:10.1109/TPAMI.1986.4767778

Cheng, T. W., Goldgof, D. B., & Hall, L. O. (1995). Fast clustering with application to fuzzy rule generation. In *Proceedings of the 4th IEEE International Conference on Fuzzy Systems*, Yokohama, Japan (pp 2289-2295). Piscataway, NJ: IEEE Press.

Dunn, J.C. (1973). A fuzzy relative of the ISODATA process and its use in detecting compact well-separated clusters. *Journal of Cybernetics*, (3), 32-57.

Elkan, C. (2003). Using the triangle inequality to accelerate k-means. In *Proceedings of the Int. Conf. Machine Learning* (pp. 147-153).

Enrique, H. R. (1969). A new approach to clustering. *Information and Control, 15*(1), 22–32. doi:10.1016/S0019-9958(69)90591-9

Eschrich, S., Ke, J., Hall, L. O., & Goldgof, D. B. (2003). Fast accurate fuzzy clustering through data reduction. *IEEE transactions on Fuzzy Systems, 11*(2), 262–270. doi:10.1109/TFUZZ.2003.809902

Hathaway, R. J., & Bezdek, J. C. (2006). Extending fuzzy and probabilistic clustering to very large data sets. *Computational Statistics & Data Analysis, 51*(1), 215–234. doi:10.1016/j.csda.2006.02.008

Hershfinkel, D., & Dinstein, I. (1996). Accelerated fuzzy c-means clustering algorithm. In *Proceedings SPIE Applications of Fuzzy Logic Technology III* (pp. 41-52).

Höppner, F. (2002). Speeding up fuzzy c-means: Using a hierarchical data organisation to control the precision of membership calculation. *Fuzzy Sets and Systems, 128*(3), 365–376. doi:10.1016/S0165-0114(01)00204-4

Höppner, F., Klawonn, F., Kruse, R., & Runkler, T. (1999). *Fuzzy cluster analysis*. Chichester, England: John Wiley & Sons.

Klawonn, F., & Höppner, F. (2003a). What is fuzzy about fuzzy clustering? Understanding and improving the concept of the fuzzifier. In *Advances in intelligent data analysis* (LNCS 2779, pp. 254-264). Berlin, Germany: Springer.

Klawonn, F., & Höppner, F. (2003b). An alternative approach to the fuzzifier in fuzzy clustering to obtain better clustering. In *Proceedings of the EUSFLAT Conf.* (pp. 730-734).

Pelleg, D., & Moore, A. (1999). Accelerating exact k-means algorithms with geometric reasoning. In *KDD '99: Proceedings of the fifth ACM SIGKDD international conference on Knowledge discovery and data mining*, New York, USA (pp. 277-281).

Shankar, B. U., & Pal, N. R. (1994). FFCM: An effective approach for large data sets. In *Proceedings of the 3rd International Conference on Fuzzy Logic, Neural Nets and Soft Computing*, Iizuka, Japan (pp. 331-332).

Smellie, A. (2004). Accelerated k-means clustering in metric spaces. *Journal of Chemical Information and Modeling, 44*(6), 1929–1935. doi:10.1021/ci0499222

Chapter 13
Fuzzy Clustering with Repulsive Prototypes

Frank Rehm
German Aerospace Center, Germany

Roland Winkler
German Aerospace Center, Germany

Rudolf Kruse
Otto-von-Guericke University Magdeburg, Germany

ABSTRACT

A well known issue with prototype-based clustering is the user's obligation to know the right number of clusters in a dataset in advance or to determine it as a part of the data analysis process. There are different approaches to cope with this non-trivial problem. This chapter follows the approach to address this problem as an integrated part of the clustering process. An extension to repulsive fuzzy c-means clustering is proposed equipping non-Euclidean prototypes with repulsive properties. Experimental results are presented that demonstrate the feasibility of the authors' technique.

INTRODUCTION

Clustering has become a very popular technique to discover interesting patterns in complex data. Due to its clear output, results are easily interpretable by all audience. It is thus not surprising that clustering is applied in various domains, e.g. the analysis of gene expression data, customer behavior, air traffic management and many more (Raytchev and Murase, 2001, Frigui and Krishnapuram, 1999; Ressom et al., 2003; Rehm and Klawonn, 2005). The purpose of clustering is to divide a dataset into different groups or clusters such that elements of the same cluster are as similar as possible and elements of different clusters are as dissimilar as possible (Duda and Hart, 1973; Bezdek, 1981). It is generally applied to data where no class labels are assigned to the single entities. In fact, the intention of using clustering is to gain this class information as a result of the clustering process. It is therefore known as unsupervised classification.

DOI: 10.4018/978-1-60566-858-1.ch013

Most clustering algorithms can be categorized into hierarchical clustering and partitional clustering. Hierarchical clustering groups data over a variety of scales by constructing a cluster tree. This tree represents a multilevel hierarchy, where clusters at one level are joined as clusters at the next level (Duda and Hart, 1973). This allows to decide the scale of clustering that is most appropriate for the respective application. Hierarchical clustering either builds a hierarchy of clusters bottom-up (agglomerative), starting with each sample as a cluster and forming a sequence by successively merging clusters, or splits clusters top-down (divisive), starting with all samples in on cluster and successively separating the data and forming a sequence of partitions (Duda and Hart, 1973). Partitional clustering attempts to directly decompose the dataset into a set of disjoint clusters that ideally comply with the natural grouping present in the data.

Prototype-based clustering algorithms represent the most popular class of partitional clustering techniques. The nature of prototype-based clustering is that, as a result, some representatives, the so-called prototypes, typify a subset of data objects by its position in the center of the respective data cluster. Typically, the number of data clusters is not known in advance but must be specified when applying prototype-based clustering algorithms. In fact, the determination of the exact number of clusters is a difficult problem. Most clustering algorithms can partition a dataset into any specified number of clusters even if the data contain no cluster structure (Jain and Moreau, 1987). Numerous cluster validity measures, procedures for determining the number of clusters, have been proposed. Global cluster validity measures mostly utilize a kind of square error criterion and condense the clustering result to a scalar value after the clustering process which is associated with a huge loss of information. Local cluster validity measures try to estimate the optimal number of clusters as an integrated part the clustering process. These techniques mostly over specify the number of clusters for the initial partition and the final one has the optimal number of clusters (Timm et al., 2001; Krishnapuram and Freg, 1992; Xiong et al., 2004). Another approach to assess cluster validity is to visualize the resulting cluster partition and inspect it visually (Hathaway and Bezdek, 2003; Hathaway et al., 2006; Havens et al., 2008; Klawonn et al., 2003; Rehm et al., 2006). Mostly, several runs with various parameter sets must be performed in order to find a suitable solution. Besides that, initialization may have a considerable impact on the clustering result. Unfortunately, no holistic solution for these problems can be provided until now. However, if certain knowledge about the data is available, e.g. what will be the approximate size of the clusters and how far are they separated, clustering algorithms can use these information to reduce user load doing expert working, e.g. in finding parameters, and finally improve clustering results.

Prototype-based clustering techniques can be distinguished into hard (crisp) clustering and soft (fuzzy) clustering. Hard clustering techniques assign each element to exactly one cluster. Since most of these algorithms are highly sensitive to noise they are favorably applied on data where clusters are well separated. Experiments have demonstrated that fuzzy clustering is more robust against outliers or noise. Apart from this, a major advantage of fuzzy clustering over crisp clustering is the ability to express ambiguity in the assignment of objects to clusters (Klawonn, 2004; Klawonn, 2006).

Moreover, fuzzy clustering can be subclassified into probabilistic clustering and possibilistic clustering. Probabilistic approaches generate partitions, where the total membership degree that is equal for each data object, is assigned to all clusters gradually. Possibilistic algorithms assign data objects to the clusters independently, i.e. the membership value of a data object represents the typicality of the point in the cluster or the possibility of the data object belonging to the cluster (Krishnapuram and Keller, 1993; Lesot and Kruse, 2006; Pal et al., 2005).

Noise clustering is another approach that can handle the problem of noise or outliers. The idea of noise clustering is based on the introduction of a virtual cluster that is supposed to contain all outliers. Feature vectors that are about a certain noise distance or further away from any regular cluster get high membership degrees to this noise cluster. The regular prototypes can thus better match the regular clusters (Dave, 1991; Dave and Krishnapuram, 1997; Wu and Zhou, 2006).

Repulsive clustering makes use of additional knowledge about the expected cluster structure (Winkler et al., 2009; Cheng and Wang, 2003; Timm et al., 2001). A recent approach allows to widely over-specify the number of clusters for a given dataset (Winkler et al., 2009). A repulsive component that is associated to each prototype assures that data clusters will be represented by one single prototype only. Redundant prototypes will be pushed away to where they have no or only little impact on regular prototypes. Finally they can be detected and eliminated, such that only meaningful prototypes remain. In this paper we propose an extension to repulsive clustering, equipping non-Euclidean fuzzy prototypes, as they are used with Gustafson-Kessel and alike fuzzy clustering algorithms, with repulsive properties (Gustafson and Kessel, 1979).

The rest of the paper is organized as follows. The next section gives a brief overview of related work. Then we describe fuzzy clustering and repulsive clustering followed by an introduction of a new extension that provides non-Euclidean distance measures to repulsive clustering. Results on demonstrative examples will be provided before we finally conclude with the last section.

BACKGROUND

(Timm et al., 2001) proposed an approach that combines the partitioning property of probabilistic clustering with the robust noise insensibility of possibilistic clustering (Wachs et al., 2006; Qin and Suganthan, 2004). A modification of the objective function that integrates both, the probabilistic approach and the possibilistic approach, and the introduction of a repulsion term provide prototypes with repulsive characteristics.

(Cheng and Wang, 2003) introduced a repulsive clustering algorithm that makes no use of prototypes. Instead, the idea of this approach is that pairs of data objects repulse each other if their distance exceeds a predefined threshold. Pairs of data objects that are closer to each other than this distance attract each other. This rule is iterated with an appropriate learning rate avoiding widely jumping data points. The algorithm converges after some iterations resulting in a layout that accentuates the inherent cluster structure.

Clustering with attraction and repulsion (CAR) is an algorithm described in (Raytchev and Murase, 2001). Two types of opposing forces, attraction and repulsion, operate across in order to autonomously organize a dataset. This technique has been successfully applied in the field of image analysis coping with the problem of unknown number of clusters and clusters that differ in shape and size.

FUZZY CLUSTERING

Cluster analysis divides data into groups (clusters) such that similar data objects belong to the same cluster and dissimilar data objects to different clusters. The resulting data partition improves data understanding and reveals internal data structures. Partitional clustering algorithms provide representatives (prototypes) that indicate the center of each cluster.

Fuzzy c-Means Clustering

Fuzzy clustering algorithms aim at minimizing an objective function that describes the sum of weighted distances d_{ij} between c prototype vectors v_i and n feature vectors x_j of the feature space $\mathbb{R}^p$:

$$J = \sum_{i=1}^{c}\sum_{j=1}^{n}(u_{ij})^m d_{ij}.$$

(1)

With the fuzzifier $m \in (1,\infty]$ one can determine how much the clusters overlap. While high values for m lead to widely overlapping clustering solutions, small values, m tending to 1, lead to rather crisp partitions. In order to avoid the trivial solution assigning no data to any cluster by setting all u_{ij} to zero and avoiding empty clusters, the following constraints are required:

$$u_{ij} \in [0,1] \quad 1 \le i \le c, \quad 1 \le j \le n$$

(2)

$$\sum_{i=1}^{c}u_{ij} = 1 \quad 1 \le j \le n$$

(3)

$$0 < \sum_{j=1}^{n}u_{ij} < n \quad 1 \le i \le c.$$

(4)

When the squared Euclidian norm

$$d_{ij} = d^2(v_i, x_j) = (x_j - v_i)^T(x_j - v_i)$$

(5)

is used as distance measure for distances between prototype vectors v_i and feature vectors x_j, the fuzzy clustering algorithm is called *fuzzy c-means algorithm* (FCM). With the Euclidian distance measure FCM searches equally sized (hyper)-spherical clusters.

The minimization of the function (1) represents a nonlinear optimization problem that is usually solved by means of Lagrange multipliers, applying an alternating optimization scheme (Bezdek, 1980). This optimization scheme considers alternatingly one of the parameter sets, either the prototypes

$$v_i = \frac{\sum_{j=1}^{n}(u_{ij})^m x_j}{\sum_{j=1}^{n}(u_{ij})^m}$$

(6)

or the membership degrees

$$u_{ij} = \frac{1}{\sum_{k=1}^{c} \left(\frac{d_{ij}}{d_{kj}} \right)^{\frac{1}{m-1}}}$$

(7)

as fixed, while the other parameter set is optimized according to equations (6) and (7), respectively, until the algorithm finally converges.

There are some reasons why FCM should be run several times. First of all, no guarantee can be given that the optimal solution can be found, since the alternating optimization scheme can lead to a local optimum. Initialization of the prototypes may impact the final result. Secondly, the exact number of clusters is not known in advance in most use cases. In order to determine this parameter, a series of runs with different number of prototypes need to be conducted. Cluster validity measures may give hints towards the right solution (Bezdek and Pal, 1998; Davies and Bouldin, 1979; Dunn, 1974; Höppner et al., 1999; Wu and Yang, 2005). Repulsive clustering provides an alternative approach to obtain an estimate of the number of clusters as an integral part of the clustering process.

Repulsive Fuzzy-c Means Clustering

Repulsive clustering is an extension to conventional clustering (Winkler et al., 2009). It makes use of additional knowledge about the expected cluster structure and allows to widely overestimate the number of clusters for a given dataset. A repulsive component that is associated to each prototype assures that data clusters, for which the assumptions are correct, will be represented by one single prototype only. Redundant prototypes will be pushed away to where they have no, or only little, impact on regular prototypes. Finally they can be detected and eliminated such that only meaningful prototypes remain.

Equipping FCM-prototypes with repulsive characteristics can be done by a simple modification of the update equation (6) for the prototypes:

$$v_i^{(t)} = \underbrace{\frac{\sum_{j=1}^{n} \left(u_{ij} \right)^m \cdot x_j}{\sum_{j=1}^{n} \left(u_{ij} \right)^m}}_{A} + \omega \cdot \sum_{k \neq i} \left(\underbrace{\frac{v_i^{(t-1)} - v_k^{(t-1)}}{\left\| v_i^{(t-1)} - v_k^{(t-1)} \right\|}}_{B} \cdot \underbrace{\frac{\sum_{j=1}^{n} u_{kj}}{\sum_{j=1}^{n} \left(u_{ij} + u_{kj} \right)}}_{C} \cdot \underbrace{\frac{\phi \left(\left\| v_i^{(t-1)} - v_k^{(t-1)} \right\| \right)}{D}} \right)$$

(8)

Term A is the same as for conventional FCM-clustering. The repulsion of prototypes is calculated pairwise for each pair of prototypes based on the relative position of the prototypes (term B), the different weight of the prototypes (term C) and the distance between the respective prototypes (term D). The parameter t is introduced to distinguish prototypes of succeeding iterations. Thus, the positions of the prototypes of the preceding iteration ($t - 1$) are employed to compute the prototypes of the tth iteration. Parameter ω handles the balance between the attracting force of the data and the repulsion between prototypes. If the dataset is standardized, ω can be set to 1. Term B is a unified vector describing the direction of the repulsion that exerts prototype v_k towards v_i. Term C assures that prototypes representing more data repulse prototypes representing less data with greater force. This is important since otherwise two prototypes could push each other out of a cluster without leaving one inside. The amount of data that is represented by one prototype can be expressed by the sum of membership degrees to the respective prototype. Finally, term D takes the distance between prototypes into account. The repulsion should decrease with increasing distance between two prototypes. Any monotonously falling and contiuous function $\phi : \mathsf{R} \to [0,1]$ can be used. The following logistic function has proven to work well in practice:

$$\phi(x) = \frac{1}{1 + e^{a(x-\sigma)}}$$ (9)

with

$$a = \frac{\ln(\frac{1}{\alpha} - 1)}{\gamma - \sigma}.$$ (10)

The parameter a describes the gradient of ϕ at the point σ. Figure 1 shows the repulsion funtion ϕ for different parameter sets. In this example α and σ are fixed while γ varies. The value σ is the distance at which the function ϕ has the value 0.5, thus, where the strength of repulsion is halve. γ denotes the distance at which the repulsion has almost no effect. Mathematically, *almost no effect* is described by α that should be chosen out of the interval (0,0.5). Usually α is set to 0.05, restricting the repulsion to only 0.05 times its maximal strength.

After running repulsive clustering with an overestimated number of prototypes, a simple test $T : \mathsf{B} \to \{1,0\}$ can be used to determine whether a prototype is inside a data cluster or not

$$T(v_i) = \begin{cases} 1 & , \quad \sum_{j=1}^{n} u_{ij} > u_{min} \\ 0 & , \quad \text{otherwise.} \end{cases}$$

T is 1 if the sum of membership degrees for the respective prototype exceeds a user-defined minimum u_{min} that usually depends on the number of data objects. Finally, the position of all positively tested prototypes can be used to initialize another prototype-based clustering algorithm, e.g. FCM.

Repulsive clustering has been successfully applied in practical applications where mainly spherical clusters can be found (Winkler et al., 2009). Due to the underlying FCM-model that focuses on that kind of data, repulsive clustering cannot be applied to data sets comprising ellipsoidal clusters without a suitable adaptation of the repulsion process. Since ellipsoidal clusters may overlap and thus prototypes of ellipsoidal clusters can be arbitrary close without representing identical data, the repulsion process need to be redesigned accordingly. After a brief revision of Gustafson-Kessel clustering, a modification of FCM that allows to find ellipsoidal clusters, we will address the problem of cluster repulsion in the Gustafson-Kessel clustering environment.

Figure 1. The repulsion function ϕ for different parameter sets

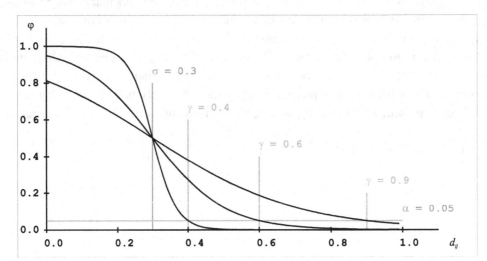

Gustafson-Kessel Clustering

Modifications of the fuzzy c-means algorithm by means of the distance measure allow the algorithm to adapt to different cluster shapes. A common representative applying such a modification is the algorithm of Gustafson-Kessel (GK) (Gustafson and Kessel, 1979).

Whereas FCM makes the implicit hypothesis that clusters are spherical, GK associates each prototype with a fuzzy covariance matrix and thus removes this constraint. This enables GK to find ellipsoidal clusters of arbitrary orientations. The fuzzy covariance matrix is defined as the fuzzy equivalent of the classic covariance:

$$C_i = \frac{1}{\displaystyle\sum_{j=1}^{n} u_{ij}^m} \sum_{j=1}^{n} u_{ij}^m (x_j - v_i)(x_j - v_i)^T$$

(11)

Instead of using the Euclidean distance measure, the Mahalanobis distance is applied (Mahalanobis, 1936):

$$d_{ij} = d^2(v_i, x_j) = (\det C_i)^{\frac{1}{p}}(x_j - v_i)^T C_i^{-1}(x_j - v_i).$$

(12)

Avoiding J in equation (1) to get minimal, by simply making C_i less positive definite, C_i is constrained to the determinant $|C_i|$, limiting GK to find ellipsoidal clusters of approximately the same size only.

REPULSIVE GUSTAFSON-KESSEL CLUSTERING

Since GK-prototypes may represent ellipsoidal cluster of different directions it may occur - quite contrary to fuzzy c-means prototypes - that some prototypes have very close (or even equal) positions while representing completely different data clusters. Therefore, using the pairwise prototype distance, see term D in equation (8), as the driving parameter to control the repulsion process does not lead to the desired result. It is neither feasible to simply use the Mahalanobis distance in term D in equation (8) since the covariance matrices are derived from the relation of the prototype to the respective data cluster and do not correlate to the prototype's position to other prototypes (see Figure 2).

The above discussion explains that repulsion of prototypes GK-prototypes is fairly different to the repulsion of FCM-prototypes. The inverse case - namely the merging of compatible clusters - has been solved successfully already. Compatible Cluster Merging (CCM) was proposed as a kind of local clustering validity measure for 2D and 3D-datasets (Krishnapuram and Freg, 1992). CCM explores the feature space with an overspecified number of GK-prototypes and tries to merge prototypes that seem to represent the same data cluster. The merging process is controlled by means of a compatibility relation that indicates the compatibility of two prototypes if they have the same main orientation, they are adjacent to each other and if there is no gap between.

A similar compatibility relation can be used to repulse two prototypes v_i and v_k that represent one cluster redundantly:

$$v_i \doteq v_k \Leftrightarrow \left| e_i^T \cdot e_k \right| \geq \gamma_1 \tag{13}$$

$$\wedge \left| \frac{(e_i + e_k)^T}{\|e_i + e_k\|} \cdot \frac{v_i - v_k}{\|v_i - v_k\|} \right| \geq \gamma_2 \tag{14}$$

Figure 2. Algorithm 1. Repulsive GK-Clustering

```
1:  Given a dataset X = {x₁,x₂,…,xₙ} ⊂ ℝᵖ
2:  Set number of prototypes c ∈ {2,…,n−1}
3:  Set fuzzifier m
4:  Set maximum number of iterations t_max
5:  Initialize partition matrix U
6:  t = 0
7:  Initialize prototypes vᵢ⁽ᵗ⁾
8:  repeat
9:      Compute fuzzy covariance matrices Cᵢ
10:     Compute repulsion weighting parameters wᵢₖ,   i,k = 1,…,c
11:     Compute prototypes vᵢ⁽ᵗ⁾
12:     Update partition matrix U⁽ᵗ⁾
13:     t = t + 1
14: until ‖U⁽ᵗ⁾ − U⁽ᵗ⁻¹⁾‖ ≤ E or t ≥ t_max
15: Output partition maxtrix U
16: Output prototypes vᵢ
```

$$\wedge \left\| v_i - v_k \right\| \leq \gamma_3 \left(\sqrt{\lambda_i} + \sqrt{\lambda_k} \right). \tag{15}$$

e_i and e_k are the eigenvectors that are associated with the largest eigenvalues λ_i and λ_k of the respective matrices C_i and C_k. The scalar product in equation (13) is near 1 if the clusters are parallel and 0 for orthogonal clusters. The desired degree of parallelism for compatible clusters can be controlled by means of γ_1. Equation (14) is fulfilled for λ_2 near 1 if two prototypes are adjacent along their principle eigenvectors. This guarantees that prototypes that represent orthogonally translated clusters will not be repulsed. Finally, equation (15) takes the extent of influence of the two prototypes in form of the eigenvectors into account. Prototypes that overlap according to this criteria should be repulsed.

It is not advisable to activate the repulsion process only if the above similarity relation indicates the compatibility of two prototypes. This would lead to abrupt changes in the membership degrees and the prototype positions from one iteration to another and could prevent the algorithms' convergence. Instead, the degree of compatibility should be considered continuously and can be used to weight the repulsion intensity. This can be expressed by the product of the parallelism and the orthogonal translation of two prototypes. The distance between prototypes needs not to be considered explicitly since the repulsion function, equation (9), makes use of this information already. The weighting parameter $w_{ik} = [0,1] \in \mathsf{R}$ for the repulsion of GK-prototypes

$$w_{ik} = \left| e_i^T \cdot e_k \right| \cdot \left| \frac{(e_i + e_k)^T}{\left\| e_i + e_k \right\|} \cdot \frac{v_i - v_k}{\left\| v_i - v_k \right\|} \right|^{\delta} \cdot \frac{1}{n} \sum_{j=1}^{n} u_{kj} \tag{16}$$

tends 1, allowing the repulsion to be maximal, if two prototypes v_i and v_k represent parts of the same data cluster. If w is near 0 the repulsion has no effect and conventional GK-clustering is done. By means of $\delta \in \mathsf{R}^+$ one can tune the repulsion process. Small $\delta = [0,1]$ favor conventional repulsion disregarding the prototype influence direction. Larger $\delta > 1$ require the prototypes to have very similar influence directions in order to activate the repulsion.

So far, the repulsion function takes only relative differences in prototype weight into account. In unfavorable circumstances this can lead to the setting that a weak prototype, a prototype that represents only few data, repulses another weak prototype disproportionally far away. The sum of the membership degrees divided by the number of data, so to speak the absolute weight of prototype v_k, addresses that issue assuring weak prototypes not repulse others significantly.

For repulsive GK-clustering we can adopt update equation (8) by slight changes

$$v_i^{(t)} = \underbrace{\frac{\sum_{j=1}^{n} \left(u_{ij} \right)^m \cdot x_j}{\sum_{j=1}^{n} \left(u_{ij} \right)^m}}_{A} + \omega \cdot \sum_{k \neq i} \left(w_{ik} \cdot \underbrace{\frac{v_i^{(t-1)} - v_k^{(t-1)}}{\left\| v_i^{(t-1)} - v_k^{(t-1)} \right\|}}_{B} \cdot \underbrace{\left(\frac{\sum_{j=1}^{n} u_{kj}}{\sum_{j=1}^{n} \left(u_{ij} + u_{kj} \right)} \right)^{\beta}}_{C} \cdot \underbrace{\frac{\phi\left(\left\| v_i^{(t-1)} - v_k^{(t-1)} \right\| \right)}{D}}_{} \right). \tag{17}$$

Figure 3. Clustering of the Gustafson cross using ten prototypes. Two prototypes represent the overlapping clusters. The remaining prototypes are intentionally repulsed

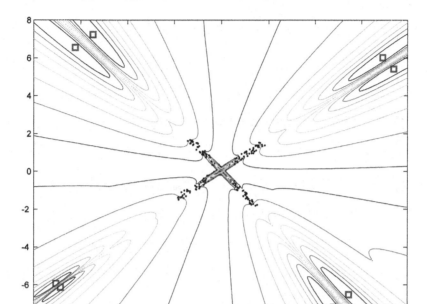

Besides parameter w, that allows weighting of the repulsion, exponent $\beta \in R^+$ can be used to accentuate the different weight of two competing prototypes. A prototype cannot be pushed out of a cluster by one prototype that represents less data. However, larger $\beta > 1$ ensure that a prototype will not be pushed out of a cluster by numerous weaker prototypes.

In the standard GK clustering numerical problems occur frequently when the number of data samples in some clusters is small or when the data within a cluster are nearly linearly correlated. In such a case the respective covariance matrix becomes singular and cannot be inverted. The improvements that have been proposed in this regard in (Babuka et al., 2002) have been applied to repulsive GK clustering to avoid these problems.

Conventional fuzzy clustering mainly scales in the number of data objects, the dimensionality of the feature space and the number of prototypes. However, scalability can be interpreted in many ways. As this term it is typically used describe the ability of an algorithm to handle growing amounts of work in a graceful manner it also concerns the means of generality. For a specific problem, it is feasible to design a narrow algorithm. On the other hand, an abstract problem requires a general algorithm. In the case of fuzzy c-means (or related algorithms), the parameter c describes the number of clusters that are expected in a dataset. If this information is not available, the problem becomes more general. If then information about the separation of clusters is available, it can be used to specify the problem statement accordingly. Due to its integrated mechanism to cope with an unknown number of clusters repulsive clustering provides scalability to conventional clustering.

Figure 4. Artificial data set showing four ellipsoidal clusters. Each of the clusters is represented by one prototype. The remaining prototypes are intentionally repulsed

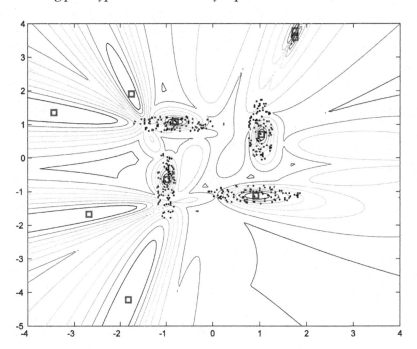

EXPERIMENTAL RESULTS

Figure 3 and Figure 4 show some experimental results on artificial data. The first figure shows two overlapping clusters similar to the Gustafson cross (Gustafson and Kessel, 1979). By means of this data one can exemplarily demonstrate the particular characteristic of the GK-algorithm. Due to its capability to locally estimate the covariance matrix for each cluster, prototypes can be arbitrarily close, as long as they represent different data. Thus, it is very important that this property will be preserved for the repulsive GK model, too. As Figure 3 shows, also repulsive GK locates both clusters correctly. Equation (16) prevents the mutual repulsion of the two prototypes. The redundant prototypes, however, are repulsed intentionally such that the data is partitioned in a proper style. Figure 4 depicts an artificial dataset comprising four ellipsoidal clusters. As for the first example, ten prototypes were used to explore the feature space. While four prototypes find the center of gravity of the regular data clusters correctly, the remaining six prototypes are repulsed from the data.

These two examples demonstrate the principle of repulsive GK-clustering. Although, the final partitioning result of repulsive GK remains stable across the iterations, it may occur that the prototypes slightly move due to oppositional attraction and repulsion by data and other prototypes, respectively. The discontinue in change of the membership degrees may serve as a feasible termination criterion for the repulsive clustering algorithm instead of the prototypes position.

CONCLUSION

In this paper we have presented a practical extension to repulsive clustering. The proposed technique allows to equip GK-prototypes with repulsive properties. The repulsion process is balanced as a function of prototype weight, pair-wise prototype distance and cluster orientation. Due to its relatedness to compatible cluster merging and due to the known constraints of GK, the application of repulsive GK is limited to low-dimensional datasets in this stage. However, results on demonstrative examples are promising and encourage further research on this topic.

REFERENCES

Babuka, R., van der Veen, P., & Kaymak, U. (2002). Improved covariance estimation for Gustafson-Kessel clustering. In *Proceedings of the FUZZ-IEEE Conference on Fuzzy Systems*, Honolulu, HI, USA (pp. 1081-1085).

Bezdek, J. C. (1980). A convergence theorem for the fuzzy isodata clustering algorithms. *IEEE Transactions on Pattern Analysis and Machine Intelligence, 2*, 1–8. doi:10.1109/TPAMI.1980.4766964

Bezdek, J. C. (1981). *Pattern recognition with fuzzy objective function algorithms* (2nd ed.). New York: Plenum Press.

Bezdek, J. C., & Pal, N. (1998). Some new indexes of cluster validity. *IEEE Transactions on Systems, Man, and Cybernetics, 28*(3), 301–315. doi:10.1109/3477.678624

Cheng, C.-S., & Wang, S.-S. (2003). A repulsive clustering algorithm for gene expression data. In *Proceedings of the IEEE International Symposium on Bioinformatic and Bioengineering* (pp. 407-412).

Dave, R. (1991). Characterization and detection of noise in clustering. *Pattern Recognition Letters, 12*(11), 657–664. doi:10.1016/0167-8655(91)90002-4

Dave, R., & Krishnapuram, R. (1997). Robust clustering methods: A unified view. *IEEE transactions on Fuzzy Systems, 5*(2), 270–293. doi:10.1109/91.580801

Davies, D., & Bouldin, D. (1979). A cluster separation measure. *IEEE Transactions on Pattern Analysis and Machine Intelligence, 1*(2), 224–227. doi:10.1109/TPAMI.1979.4766909

Duda, R., & Hart, P. (1973). *Pattern classification and scene analysis*. New York: John Wiley.

Dunn, J. (1974). Well-separated clusters and optimal fuzzy partitions. *Cybernetics and Systems, 4*(1), 95–104. doi:10.1080/01969727408546059

Frigui, H., & Krishnapuram, R. (1999). A robust competitive clustering algorithm with applications in computer vision. *IEEE Transactions on Pattern Analysis and Machine Intelligence, 21*(5), 450–465. doi:10.1109/34.765656

Gustafson, D., & Kessel, W. (1979). Fuzzy clustering with a fuzzy covariance matrix. In *Proceedings of the IEEE Conference on Decision and Control*, San Diego, CA (pp. 761-766).

Hathaway, R. J., & Bezdek, J. C. (2003). Visual cluster validity for prototype generator clustering models. *Pattern Recognition Letters, 24*(9–10), 1563–1569. doi:10.1016/S0167-8655(02)00395-1

Hathaway, R. J., Bezdek, J. C., & Huband, J. M. (2006). Scalable visual assessment of cluster tendency for large data sets. *Pattern Recognition, 39*(7), 1315–1324. doi:10.1016/j.patcog.2006.02.011

Havens, T., Bezdek, J., Keller, J., & Popescu, M. (2008). Dunn's cluster validity index as a contrast measure of vat images. In *Proceedings of the 19th International Conference on Pattern Recognition (ICPR)* (pp. 1-4).

Höppner, F., Klawonn, F., Kruse, R., & Runkler, T. A. (1999). *Fuzzy cluster analysis*. Chichester, UK: John Wiley & Sons.

Jain, A. K., & Moreau, J. V. (1987). Bootstrap technique in cluster analysis. *Pattern Recognition, 20*(5), 547–568. doi:10.1016/0031-3203(87)90081-1

Klawonn, F. (2004). Fuzzy clustering: insights and a new approach. *Mathware & soft computing, 11*(2-3).

Klawonn, F. (2006). Understanding and controlling the membership degrees in fuzzy clustering. In *From data and information analysis to knowledge engineering* (pp. 446-453).

Klawonn, F., Chekhtman, V., & Janz, E. (2003). Visual inspection of fuzzy clustering results. In J. Benitez, O. Cordon, F. Hoffmann, & R. Roy (Eds.), *Advances in soft computing - engineering, design and manufacturing* (pp. 65-76). London: Springer.

Krishnapuram, R., & Freg, C.-P. (1992). Fitting an unknown number of lines and planes to image data through compatible cluster merging. *Pattern Recognition, 25*(4), 385–400. doi:10.1016/0031-3203(92)90087-Y

Krishnapuram, R., & Keller, J. (1993). A possibilistic approach to clustering. *IEEE transactions on Fuzzy Systems, 1*(2), 98–110. doi:10.1109/91.227387

Lesot, M.-J., & Kruse, R. (2006). Data summarisation by typicality-based clustering for vectorial and non vectorial data. In *Proceedings of the IEEE International Conference on Fuzzy Systems* (pp. 547-554).

Mahalanobis, P. (1936). On the generalized distance in statistics. In *Proceedings of the National Institute of Science of India* (pp. 49-55).

Pal, N., Pal, K., Keller, J., & Bezdek, J. (2005). A possibilistic fuzzy c-means clustering algorithm. *IEEE transactions on Fuzzy Systems, 13*(4), 517–530. doi:10.1109/TFUZZ.2004.840099

Qin, A., & Suganthan, P. (2004). Robust growing neural gas algorithm with application in cluster analysis. *Neural Networks, 17*(8-9), 1135–1148. doi:10.1016/S0893-6080(04)00166-2

Raytchev, B., & Murase, H. (2001). Unsupervised face recognition from image sequences based on clustering with attraction and repulsion. In *Proceedings of the 2001 IEEE Computer Society Conference on Computer Vision and Pattern Recognition (CVPR 2001), Vol. 2* (pp. II–25-II–30).

Rehm, F., & Klawonn, F. (2005). Learning methods for air traffic management. In L. Godo (Ed.), *Symbolic and quantitative approaches to reasoning with uncertainty*. Berlin, Germany: Springer.

Rehm, F., Klawonn, F., & Kruse, R. (2006). Visualization of single clusters. In L. Rutkowski, R. Tadeusiewicz, L. Zadeh, & J. Zurada (Eds.), *Proceedings of the Artificial Intelligence and Soft Computing - ICAISC 2006*. Berlin, Germany: Springer.

Ressom, H. W., Wang, D., & Natarajan, P. (2003). Adaptive double self-organizing maps for clustering gene expression profiles. *Neural Networks, 16*(5-6), 633–640. doi:10.1016/S0893-6080(03)00102-3

Timm, H., Borgelt, C., Döring, C., & Kruse, R. (2001). Fuzzy cluster analysis with cluster repulsion. In *Proceedings of the European Symposium on Intelligent Technologies, Hybrid Systems and their implementation on Smart Adaptive Systems*.

Wachs, J., Shapira, O., & Stern, H. (2006). A method to enhance the possibilistic c-means with repulsion algorithm based on cluster validity index. In A. Abraham, B. D. Baets, M. Köppen, & B. Nickolay (Eds.), *Applied soft computing technologies: The challenge of complexity*. Berlin, Germany: Springer.

Winkler, R., Rehm, F., & Kruse, R. (2009). Clustering with repulsive prototypes. In *Studies in classification, data analysis, and knowledge organization*. Berlin, Germany: Springer.

Wu, K., & Yang, M. (2005). A cluster validity index for fuzzy clustering. *Pattern Recognition Letters, 26*, 1275–1291. doi:10.1016/j.patrec.2004.11.022

Wu, X.-H., & Zhou, J.-J. (2006). Noise clustering using a new distance. In *Proceedings of the 2nd International Conference on Information and Communication Technologies (ICTTA)* (pp. 1938-1943).

Xiong, X., Chan, K. L., & Tan, K. L. (2004). Similarity-driven cluster merging method for unsupervised fuzzy clustering. In *Proceedings of the 20th conference on uncertainty in artificial intelligence* (pp. 611-618). AUAI Press.

Section 4
Real–World Challenges

Chapter 14
Early Warning from Car Warranty Data using a Fuzzy Logic Technique

Mark Last
Ben-Gurion University of the Negev, Israel

Yael Mendelson
Formerly of Ben-Gurion University of the Negev, Israel

Sugato Chakrabarty
India Science Lab, GM Technical Center, India

Karishma Batra
Formerly of India Science Lab, GM Technical Center, India

ABSTRACT

Car manufacturers are interested to detect evolving problems in a car fleet as early as possible so they can take preventive actions and deal with the problems before they become widespread. The vast amount of warranty claims recorded by the car dealers makes the manual process of analyzing this data hardly feasible. This chapter describes a fuzzy-based methodology for automated detection of evolving maintenance problems in massive streams of car warranty data. The empirical distributions of time-to-failure and mileage-to-failure are monitored over time using the advanced, fuzzy approach to comparison of frequency distributions. The authors' fuzzy-based early warning tool builds upon an automated interpretation of the differences between consecutive histogram plots using a cognitive model of human perception rather than "crisp" statistical models. They demonstrate the effectiveness and the efficiency of the proposed tool on warranty data that is very similar to the actual data gathered from a database within General Motors.

INTRODUCTION

Car manufacturers are responsible for the vehicle maintenance during the entire warranty period. Consequently, the warranty data is being continuously reported by the manufacturer dealers to a central

DOI: 10.4018/978-1-60566-858-1.ch014

database. The warranty database is expected to include the following information for each customer complaint: dealer location, car model, car manufacturing and selling dates, claim date, mileage to date, complaint code, labor code, etc. The taxonomy of labor codes is usually available in a hierarchical form corresponding to car systems and sub-systems.

The central warranty database can be used to continuously monitor the empirical distributions of time and mileage to failure for various problem types in each new car model. In this chapter, the empirical distributions in consecutive time windows are compared to each other using the advanced, fuzzy approach to comparison of frequency distributions (Last & Kandel, 2002a, 2002b) developed within the framework of *automated perceptions* (Last and Kandel, 1999). This novel monitoring method provides an automated interpretation of the differences between histogram plots using a cognitive model of human perception rather than rigid statistical models. It is able to discover a positive or a negative shift in the histogram of the target distribution, based upon the apparent shift in the central tendency, the sample size, and the available domain knowledge. The proposed fuzzy-based method is implemented by the Early Warning Tool, which issues a warning about a *negative shift* whenever the values of the new histogram are shifted to the left more than a pre-defined Alarm Threshold and a *positive shift* whenever the values of the new histogram are shifted to the right more than the same threshold. A car manufacturer would be particularly interested in timely discovery of negative shifts, which indicate an increase in the probability of a certain problem type after a lower mileage or a shorter amount of time elapsed since the car left the factory or since the previous visit to the dealer. Identifying the most common labor codes ("root causes") associated with negative and positive shifts is another important objective. Fuzzy shifts across multiple consecutive periods can be aggregated to compute a long-term trend of the warranty data. The proposed Early Warning Tool has also to be highly scalable in the size of the warranty database that is updated with thousands of new warranty claims on a daily basis.

This chapter is organized as follows. The next section provides the necessary background on emerging issues analysis in a car fleet. Then we proceed with describing the steps needed for selecting and preparing the warranty data for the early warning purposes. Fuzzy shift and fuzzy trend calculation along with the root cause analysis are presented next. The proposed fuzzy-based methodology is then demonstrated on warranty data that is very similar to the actual data gathered from a database within a major car manufacturer (General Motors). Finally we outline the future research directions and provide some concluding remarks.

BACKGROUND

Tracking of warranty trend of a particular product based on the claim distribution over time is an important problem of any company and industry. Most companies maintain warranty databases for purposes of financial reporting and warranty expense forecasting. Such warranty field data is largely extensive and messy, and hence special tools and algorithms are needed to extract useful information. In some cases, there are attempts to extract engineering information from such databases. Another important application is to use warranty data to detect potentially serious field reliability problems known as *emerging issues*, as early as possible. With detection of sudden emerging issues it is also important to track the other trends such as "bygone problem" (the failure rate has decreased back to normal), "emerging issue under control" and "emerging issue came gradually over a passage of time". This is because after some action was taken by the manufacturing process or a precautionary measure taken by dealers through service enhancement it is important to study the behavior of the trends i.e. after process rectification whether the previous emerging issues trends for a group of failure components now changed to the "under control" or "bygone" trends.

In describing the use of warranty data a number of papers and books have been written. Blischke and Murthy (1994, 1996) covered a wide range of topics related to warranty issues. General reviews of statistical methods for warranty data were provided by Robinson and McDonald (1991), Lawless and Kalbfleisch (1992), and Lawless (1998). Specific technical methods for dealing with problems arising in field and warranty data (reporting delays, censoring, truncation, and sparsity) were provided, for example by Suzuki (2001a, b), Kalbfleisch and Lawless (1988), Lawless, Hu, and Cao (1995), Hu, Lawless and Suzuki (1998), Karim, Yamamoto, and Suzuki (2001 a) and Wang and Suzuki (2001 a, b). Kalbfleisch, Lawless and Robinson (1991) described prediction methods. Karim, Yamamoto and Suzuki (2001b) provided methods for detecting a change point from marginal count warranty data that arise when one cannot identify the date of manufacture of units that are serviced under warranty. A generalization of the Shewhart process monitoring scheme for early detection of reliability problems was provided by Wu and Meeker (2002).

Quite a few statistical algorithms are currently being used for early detection of potential problems. However, there are many limitations associated with these methods. Parametric assumptions significantly contribute in giving incorrect results as the actual field data rarely follows any of the rigid statistical models. Also, the control limits used as thresholds in the control chart technique are static as they are based on the previously collected data. Moreover, missing data between the time points is linearly interpolated which may cause overestimation and underestimation problems. Another important point to be noted is that most of these methods take into account only the number of claims related to a particular failure component. It is to be noted that the number of claims may not be a good indicator for tracking a true warranty trend, since the number of claims is affected primarily by the number of sold vehicles, whereas we are interested in the distribution of time and mileage between failures *per vehicle*, disregarding the total number of new vehicles on the road. In addition to this, the estimation procedures heavily depend on the sample size. If the sample size is low the statistical estimations are considered unreliable disregarding any available expert knowledge. In general, most of the statistical algorithms are complex in nature and not easily comprehensible. As shown in Last & Kandel (2002a), the fuzzy methods of data analysis are more intuitive and their settings can be modified to represent the user prior knowledge.

Detection of emerging trends is important in many different areas beyond product maintenance. Thus, Koenigstein *et al.* (2008) investigate the popularity of new artists according to their local popularity as reflected in a file sharing network. Their detection algorithm is able to identify emerging artists based on specific patterns of weekly popularity increase, with a 15-30% prediction success. They predict the artist success probability using the Kullback-Leibler Divergence for the difference between the actual geographical distributions of the weekly downloads and the uniform distribution.

Similar problems of tracking trends and frequency distributions over time arise in mining large amounts of *sensor data* (Cohen *et al*, 2008). Sensor networks provide a new source of massive, continuous streams of information that can be used by automated systems like temperature monitoring, precision agriculture, and urban traffic control. One of the main difficulties in mining non-stationary continuous data streams is to cope with the changing data concept. The fundamental processes generating most real-time data streams may change over years, months and even seconds, at times drastically. This change, also known as *concept drift*, causes the data-mining model generated from past data, to become less accurate in the classification of new data. According to Zeira *et al.* (2004), possible causes for significant changes in the performance of a data-mining classification model include changes in the distributions of one or several predictive features as well as a change in the distribution of the target (predicted) attribute.

FUZZY-BASED MONITORING OF WARRANTY DATA

This section describes the warranty data monitoring with the Early Warning Tool built upon an automated interpretation of differences between consecutive histograms. The trend detection and tracking process includes the following stages: data selection and preparation, computing fuzzy shifts between distributions, exploring the root causes of significant shifts, and fuzzy trend detection. Each stage is covered in a separate sub-section.

Data Selection and Preparation

The tool Main Screen displays the filtering criteria that can be used for selecting the analyzed data:

- **Vehicle selection**:
  ○ Make (e.g., Buick or Chevy)
  ○ Line Series (e.g., Impala)
  ○ Platform (e.g., engine used by several line series).
- **Period selection** (given as a range of dates):
  ○ Model Build Dates: only cars manufactured between these dates will be included in the analysis.
  ○ Delivery Dates: only cars delivered between these dates will be included in the analysis.
  ○ Claim Dates: the histograms will be based only on claims submitted between these dates. This defines the monitoring period (one month, two months, one year, etc.).
- **Months in Service (MIS)**: car age (in months) calculated as the difference between the Claim Date and the Delivery Date (given as a range of values)
- **Geographical region** (e.g., Midwest)
- **Labor code**: the histograms can be based on a single labor code, a list of labor codes, a single Bill of Materials category, a single Vehicle Subsystem category or just all claims satisfying the other selection criteria. We assume here that each labor code is a part of a pre-defined taxonomy, where it is associated with a specific BOM code and its respective Vehicle Subsystem code. For example, the "Replace Battery" Labor Code belongs to the "Battery" BOM Category, which is part of the Electrical Subsystem.
- **Histogram Selection**. The user can choose one of the following variables for creating the histograms:
  ○ *TTF (Time to Failure)*: the software will build histograms for the Time to Failure elapsed since the previous claim having *any* labor code. If there is no previous claim for a car, the Time to Failure will be calculated since the Delivery Date.
  ○ *TTF same Vehicle Subsystem*: the software will build histograms for Time to Failure elapsed since the previous claim having the same Vehicle Subsystem or since the Delivery Date (if there is no previous claim).
  ○ *MTF (Mileage to Failure)*: the software will build histograms for Mileage to Failure elapsed since the previous claim of any labor code or for the total car mileage (if this is the first claim).
  ○ *MTF same Vehicle Subsystem*: the software will build histograms for Mileage to Failure elapsed since the previous claim having the same Vehicle Subsystem or for the total car mileage (if this is the first claim).

○   *Max TTF/MTF*: the software will ignore claims with Time to Failure or Mileage to Failure higher than this threshold (empty: no threshold).

- **Time Unit**. The monitoring period is divided into time units and the histograms of consecutive time units within the monitoring period are compared to each other in order to compute fuzzy shifts and trends. The available time units include one week (7 days), two weeks (15 days), and one month (30 days). For example, dividing the monitoring period between May 1 and June 30 into 15-day time units will result in four histograms for the following sub-periods: May 1 – May 15, May 16 – May 31, June 1 – June 15, and June 16 – June 30.
- **Claim Selection**. The following types of claims can be selected for monitoring:
  ○   *First Claims*: the histograms will be based on the first vehicle claims only. This implies that all TTF / MTF values will be calculated since the Delivery Date.
  ○   *Others*: the histograms will be based on non-first warranty claims only. This implies that all TTF / MTF values will be calculated since the date of the previous claim, which does not need to be in the selected monitoring period.
  ○   *Both*: the histograms will be based on all claims. TTF / MTF values will be calculated since the Delivery Date for the first claims or since the date of the previous claim for all other claims.

The Main Screen is also used for choosing the number and the boundaries of bins in the histograms constructed for every time unit. The histogram bins can be defined either manually or automatically. In case of manual selection, the user should specify the upper boundary of each bin except for the last one, for which the upper boundary is equal to the maximum value in the monitoring period. The software verifies that the upper boundary of each bin is higher than the boundary of the previous one.

In case of automatic bin selection, the user enters the total number of bins, whereas their boundaries are determined using equal-frequency discretization over all claims selected during the monitoring period. The bin boundaries are found by a single scan of selected claims sorted in the ascending order of their TTF / MTF values. The target number of claims in each bin is calculated as the ratio between the total number of selected claims and the user-specified number of bins. The upper boundary index of each bin, except for the last one, is set to this target number plus the upper boundary index of the previous bin. In case of a tie (several claims sharing the same value across the calculated boundary), the upper boundary index is changed to the index of a threshold value closest to the calculated boundary in terms of the number of claims. Finding the best number of bins automatically is a subject of our future research.

Computing Fuzzy Shifts between Distributions

The Cognitive Process of Shift Detection

The simplest way to detect positive and negative shifts between empirical distributions is by visually comparing the distribution histograms. Three simulated examples of histograms representing mileage-to-failure distributions in a pair of consecutive bi-weekly time units are given in Figure 1, Figure 2, and Figure 3. The original mileage-to-failure values have been discretized to 10 bins of equal frequency over the entire monitoring period. The curves in the figures show the proportions (relative frequencies) of claims in each bin out of the total number of claims in the corresponding time unit. A human observer can easily distinguish between the following cases represented by these three figures:

Figure 1. Distribution Histograms: Time Unit T3 vs. Time Unit T4

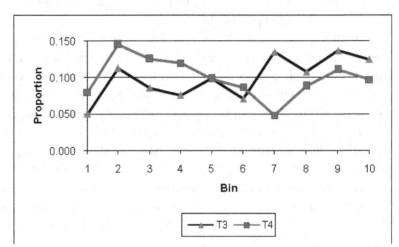

- **Negative** ("emerging") shift between distributions (Figure 1).
  - Most proportions in the first six bins are *bigger* in the second time unit (T4) than in the first one (T3). On the other hand, all proportions of T3 are bigger than the proportions of T4 in last four bins.
- **Positive** ("decreasing") shift between distributions (Figure 2).
  - Most proportions in the first four bins are *smaller* in the second time unit (T6) than in the first time unit (T5). On the other hand, all proportions of T6 are bigger than or equal to the proportions of T5 in the last six bins
- **No shift** between distributions (Figure 3).
  - No clear shift between the distributions in time units T6 and T7 can be detected. The two curves cross each other at least five times.

The cognitive process of comparing two different histograms, shown on the same chart, can be summarized as follows (based on Last & Kandel, 2002a):

Step 1 – If in most bins there is no significant difference between the proportions, conclude that there is no change in the central tendency of parameter values (see an example in Figure 3). Otherwise, go to Step 2.

Step 2 – Find an imaginary point between the bins, such that before that "threshold" point, most proportions of one distribution are significantly higher (lower) than the proportions of the other one and vice versa. In Figure 1, we can locate such a point between bins 6 and 7. The claims in the first time unit (T3) have mostly lower frequencies in the bins 1-6 than in the bins 7-10. The opposite is true about the values of the second time unit (T4). The resulting picture is that the first distribution (T3) is shifted to the right vs. the second distribution (T4).

Step 3 – Make the final conclusion about a positive or a negative shift in the target distribution, based upon the apparent shift in the histogram, the sample size, and some tuning parameters that are explained below.

This cognitive process is not based on any statistical assumptions about the behavior of the underlying distributions. In fact, it is hard to identify any standard distribution representing the mileage histograms

Figure 2. Distribution Histograms: Time Unit T5 vs. Time Unit T6

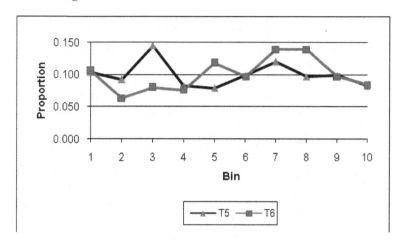

in Figures 2-4. Still, the human perception can be very efficient when dealing with the uncertainty of visual representations. The human observations tend to bear some amount of vagueness and are much easier to be described by words (e.g., "most", "significantly", etc.), than by some crisp mathematical terms. Thus, the shift detection can be seen as a particular case of *Approximate* (or *Fuzzy*) *Reasoning* (see Kandel et al., 1996). Consequently, the Fuzzy Set theory can be used to model the shift detection process.

The histogram construction procedure involves two computationally intensive parts: computing time-to-failure (TTF) or mileage-to-failure (MTF) values for each warranty claim and sorting the selected claims in the ascending order of these values. The TTF/MTF calculation requires finding the previous claim for each claim. Thus, its run time complexity is $O(n^2)$, where n is the number of recorded claims. The computational complexity of sorting n values representing TTF/MTF of n claims is not worse than $O(n^2)$ (e.g., using the QuickSort algorithm). Once the histograms are built, the complexity of the fuzzy shift computation does not depend on the number of underlying claims. Thus, we can say that the proposed approach is relatively scalable, since it is only quadratic in the number of claims.

Figure 3. Distribution Histograms: Time Unit T6 vs. Time Unit T7

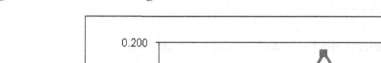

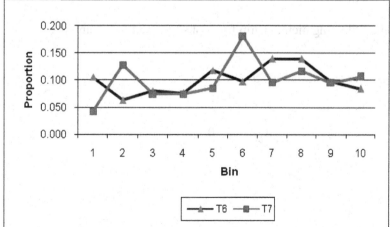

Figure 4. Example of a Decreasing Shift

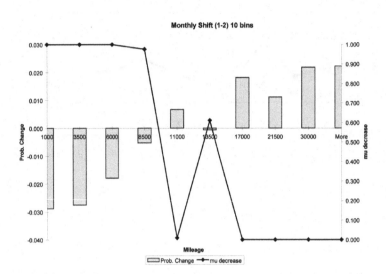

Pairwise Comparison of Histogram Bins

Based on (Last & Kandel, 2002a), we assume here that the linguistic variable *proportion change* (denoted by *d*) can take the following two linguistic values: *bigger* and *smaller*, each being a fuzzy set. The membership function μ_B associated with the fuzzy set *bigger* should have the following properties:

- Being close to zero, when *d* is close to *–1*.
- Being low for *d = 0*.
- Being close to *1*, when *d* is close to *1.*

Similarly, the membership function μ_S (*smaller*) should satisfy the following:

- Being close to 1, when d is close to –1.
- Being low for d = 0.
- Being close to 0, when d is close to 1.

In our model, the following membership functions are used for μ_S and μ_B:

$$\mu_S(d) = \frac{1}{1 + e^{\beta(d + \alpha_S)}}, \; d \in [-1, 1], \; \alpha_S, \beta \geq 0 \tag{1}$$

$$\mu_B(d) = \frac{1}{1 + e^{-\beta(d - \alpha_B)}}, \; d \in [-1, 1], \; \alpha_B, \beta \geq 0 \tag{2}$$

where:

- d is the difference between measured proportions (relative frequencies) of the same bin in compared distributions;

- α_S, α_B are the scale factors, which determine the scale of the membership functions. More specifically, these parameters determine the point of these functions intersection with the Y-axis, or the degrees of *bigger* and *smaller* for $d = 0$. Last and Kandel (2002a) have proposed the guidelines for choosing α_S and α_B based on the concept of a *Type-2 Fuzzy Logic System* (Karnik *et al.*, 1999) and the user prior knowledge about emerging or decreasing trends in the data.

- β is the shape factor, which can change the shape of the membership function from a constant value of 0.5 ($\beta = 0$) to a step function, which takes the value of 1.0 for nearly any $|d| > 0$ ($\beta \rightarrow \infty$). We associate β with the sample size used for building the histograms. The expression for calculating β is:

$$\beta = \gamma\, n_{min} \tag{3}$$

where n_{min} is the minimum number of examples in one of the two compared histograms and γ is a linear coefficient expressing the user confidence in a sample of a given size.

Detecting Emerging and Decreasing Shifts between Histograms

After calculating the membership grades of each proportion change in the "smaller" and the "bigger" fuzzy sets, we can evaluate the *fuzzyshift* between the compared distributions.

According to the above definition of the threshold point, the number of candidate thresholds is $D - 1$, where D is the number of bins in the histogram of the attribute in question. Each candidate threshold $T \in D$ separates between the bins $i = 1, ..., T$ and $i = T+1, ..., D$. We calculate the *net shift* for a candidate threshold T by the following expression:

$$NS(T) = \sum_{i=1}^{T} [\mu_S(d_i) - \mu_B(d_i)] + \sum_{i=T+1}^{D} [\mu_B(d_i) - \mu_S(d_i)] \tag{4}$$

where d_i is the proportion change for the bin i.

Both sum terms of the above expression should be positive if there is a positive shift in the distribution and negative in the opposite case. When there is no shift, both terms will be close to zero.

The automated process of detecting emerging and decreasing shifts during the monitored period includes the following steps:

Step 1: Build Mileage-to-Failure or Time-to-Failure histograms for all time units in the monitored period (e.g., build 12 monthly histograms for a one-year period). As indicated above, the histogram bins can be selected either manually or automatically

Step 2: For each pair of consecutive time units, Do:

Step 2.1: Use Eq. (4) to calculate the fuzzy shift between distributions *NS (T)* with respect to each interval bin $T = 1, ..., D-1$ and find the minimal and the maximal values of the net shift.

Step 2.2: Find the threshold T^* providing the maximal *absolute* value of the net shift:

$$T^* = \arg \max_T |NS\,(T)| \tag{5}$$

Step 2.3: Normalize the net shift *NS (T*)* w. r. t. the number of histogram bins *D*:

$$NS_{Norm} = NS\,(T^*)\,/\,D \tag{6}$$

Step 3: During the monitored period, find the pairs of consecutive time units having absolute fuzzy shifts, which exceed a pre-defined Alarm Threshold. Flag those time unit pairs and notify the user of a positive (decreasing) or a negative (emerging) shift, according to the sign of NS_{Norm}.

The selection of the threshold for the maximal absolute value of the net shift depends on the amount of early warnings expected from the algorithmic tool. In the extreme case of Alarm Threshold = 0, all positive and negative shifts will be presented to the user.

Exploring the Root Causes of Significant Shifts

Emerging and decreasing shifts between mileage and time to failure distributions, which are computed using the procedure described above, represent the overall behavior of *all* claims recorded during each time unit. However, many high positive and low negative shifts in mileage to failure histograms are caused by *specific* failure types, which tend to occur at lower or higher mileage, respectively. In case of time to failure histograms, certain failures may occur later, if the shift is positive, or earlier, if the shift is negative. Identifying the most frequent failures associated with a positive and, more importantly, with a negative shift is a primary interest of a car manufacturer, since they may lead to the root causes of those shifts. The proposed process of root cause exploration implemented by the Early Warning Tool includes the following steps:

Step 1 - In case of a positive shift, find the intervals (bins) with the highest fuzzy grade of probability decrease (representing failures that became less frequent). In case of the negative shift, find the intervals with the highest fuzzy grade of probability increase (representing failures that became more frequent). In both cases, the corresponding time or mileage threshold *T** can be found automatically using Eq. (5). Thus, Figure 4 shows that in the case of a positive shift between months 1 and 2, the interval with the highest fuzzy grade of probability decrease (above 0.9) represents mileage to failure of 8,500 and less. Respectively, Figure 5 shows that in the case of a negative shift between months 8 and 9, the interval with the highest fuzzy grade of probability increase (above 0.9) represents mileage to failure of 13,500 and less.

Step 2 - Retrieve all claims from the time units with the flagged absolute shifts w.r.t. the previous time unit such that the claim mileage or time to failure belongs to the bins with the highest fuzzy grade of probability change identified in the previous step.

Step 3 - Find the most frequent labor codes in the claims retrieved in the previous step and present them to the user. The number of the most frequent labor codes to be presented to the user is one of the configurable parameters in the Early Warning Tool. The analysis of these codes can reveal the most common causes for the flagged probability shifts (positive and negative) during the monitored period. For example, if there is a positive or negative trend persistent over multiple time units, a set of the most frequent labor codes recurring in nearly every fuzzy shift may indicate a common *root cause* of the overall trend.

Figure 5. Example of an Emerging Shift

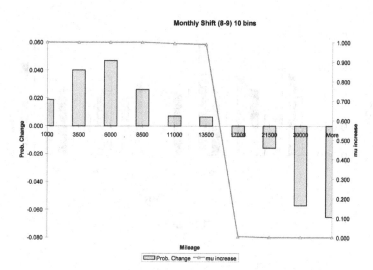

FROM FUZZY SHIFTS TO FUZZY TRENDS

Shifts between mileage and time to failure distributions may persist over multiple time units. Such shifts are particularly important to detect, since they may represent long-term trends in the car maintenance data. Figure 6 shows example of an apparently emerging trend across four consecutive time units in a given monitoring period. Here we can see a continuous increase in the probability of the three lowest bins (1 - 3) and a continuous decrease in the probability of the next five bins (4 – 8). Thus, we can suspect that the overall trend of this distribution is "emerging", which means that in each time unit more cars have failures earlier than in the preceding time unit. To quantify a long-term trend in a given distribution, we suggest computing the *average fuzzy shift* during the entire monitored period, which starts with time unit t_1 and ends at time unit t_2, using the following expression:

$$Trend(t_1; t_2) = \frac{\sum_{t=t_1+1}^{t=t_2} NS_{Norm}(t)}{t_2 - t_1}$$

(7)

Where $NS_{Norm}(t)$ is the normalized net shift between the time units t and $t-1$ computed using Equation (6). In case of Figure 6, $t_2 = 4$, $t_1 = 1$, and, consequently, the overall trend is calculated as an average of three fuzzy shifts. In addition to strong trends, Equation (7) is also able to identify weak trends that persist over most time units of the monitored period.

CASE STUDY

Our simulated case study is based on claims submitted during a monitored period partitioned into four time units of equal duration. This could be a four-month period partitioned into four one-month units

Figure 6. Example of an Emerging Trend

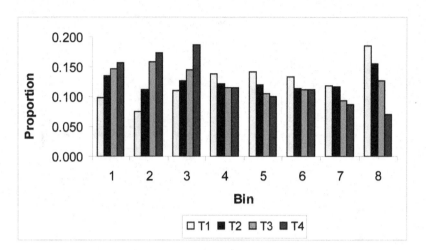

or a two-month period partitioned into four units of 15 days each. We assume that the original mileage-to-failure values of each claim have been discretized to eight bins of equal frequency over the entire monitored period. The four histograms representing the mileage-to-failure distributions in each time unit are superimposed and shown in Figure 6 and the actual histogram proportions are given in Table 1. The number of claims in each 15-day time unit has been 637, 386, 429, and 288, respectively. Thus, about 3,027,600 (the square of the total number of claims) join operations are needed to compute the mileage-to-failure value of each claim. On a standard desktop computer (such as Pentium 4 with 3GHz CPU and 1GB of RAM), this does not take more than a few seconds of the CPU time using the MS-AccessTM software.

As indicated above, the membership functions used for μ_S ("smaller") and μ_B ("bigger") are affected by the scale factors α_S and α_B, respectively. In Figure 7, we analyze the effect of α_B on the corresponding membership function μ_B applied to the differences between the first and the second time unit proportions. When the value of α_B is increased from 0 to 0.1, its impact decreases dramatically and the μ_B membership function becomes very close to zero even for relatively large absolute differences of 0.03 and higher (bins 1 and 8). If the user is not interested to miss even minor proportion differences of 0.02, he can

Table 1. Case Study - Histogram Proportions

Bin	T1	T2	T3	T4
1	0.099	0.135	0.147	0.156
2	0.075	0.111	0.159	0.174
3	0.110	0.127	0.145	0.188
4	0.138	0.122	0.114	0.115
5	0.141	0.119	0.105	0.101
6	0.133	0.114	0.112	0.111
7	0.118	0.117	0.093	0.087
8	0.185	0.155	0.126	0.069

Figure 7. Case Study - The effect of the scale factor

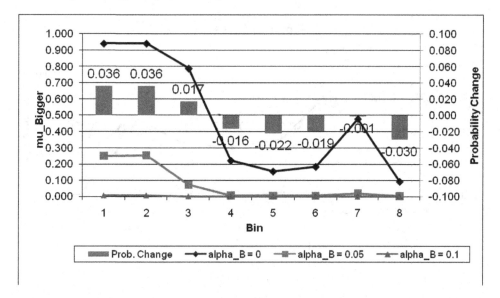

keep both scale factors equal to zero. Otherwise, the scale factors can be increased beyond 0.1 causing all differences between the periods T1 and T2 to be completely ignored.

The effect of the shape factor γ on the μ_B ("bigger") membership function is analyzed in Figure 8 for $\alpha_B = 0$. Given a fixed amount of observations (claims) in each histogram, increasing the shape factor magnifies the "bigger" grades of positive differences and shrinks the "bigger" grades of negative differences. This means that the user is more confident about both positive and negative differences between bin proportions. The same effect will be observed if we increase the amount of observations without changing the value of γ. In the case of comparison between time units T1 and T2, the minimum number of observations (386) produces relatively high values of μ_B even for $\gamma = 0.1$.

As indicated by Last & Kandel (2002a), both scale factors α_S and α_B can be modified to represent the user prior knowledge about the difference between bin proportions. The three possible cases of that prior knowledge are:

- The distributions are nearly the same (no significant difference between proportions is expected). In that case, both scale factors should have positive and equal values (e.g., 0.20).
- The distributions are different (high absolute differences between proportions are expected). This implies that one of the factors should be negative and the other one – positive or vice versa (e.g., $\alpha_B = -0.20$, $\alpha_S = 0.20$ or $\alpha_B = 0.20$, $\alpha_S = -0.20$).
- No prior knowledge on the distributions is available. Then we can use $\alpha_S = \alpha_B = 0$.

The last case of no prior knowledge is represented by the leftmost point on Figure 9, where $\alpha_S = \alpha_B = 0$ produces a negative shift of -0.637 between the time units T1 and T2. Once we increase the values of both scale factors (assuming that no shift is expected), the absolute fuzzy shift decreases rapidly to 0.124 for $\alpha_S = \alpha_B = 0.05$ and to 0.003 for $\alpha_S = \alpha_B = 0.10$.

Figure 10 represents the second case, where we do expect a shift between proportions. Here we set the value of α_B to -0.2 and vary α_S between 0 and 0.20. Consequently, the absolute fuzzy shift goes up

Figure 8. Case Study - The effect of the shape factor

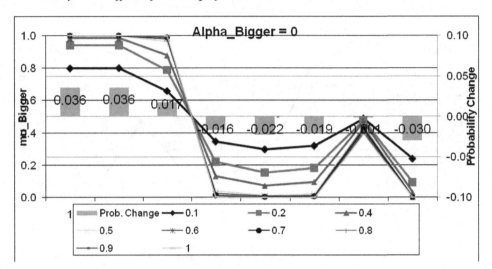

from 0.452 to 0.750 starting with $\alpha_S = 0.10$. This value is higher than the absolute shift of 0.637 based on no prior knowledge at all.

Table 2 shows the number of discovered significant shifts during the monitored period as a function of the scale and shape parameters. We use here the alarm threshold of 0.5, i.e., only positive shifts above 0.5 and negative shifts below -0.5 are counted. The table confirms our earlier expectation that more shifts are considered significant when the scale parameter values are higher and different in their sign from each other. Also, an increase in the shape parameter value causes more shifts to become significant. However, for relatively large (0.05 and higher) and identical values of the scale parameters, no shifts are considered significant, since as indicated above, these parameter values express our disbelief in any difference between the distributions.

Figure 9. Normalized Net Shift as a function of $\alpha_S = \alpha_B$

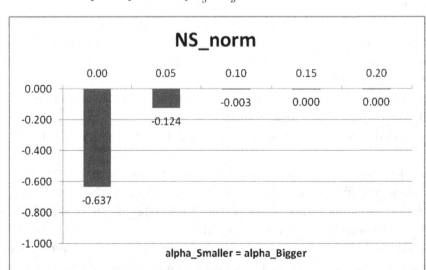

Figure 10. Normalized Net Shift as a function of α_S (α_B = -0.2)

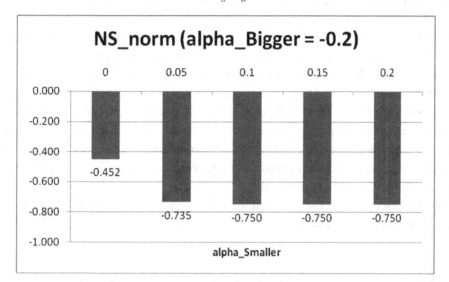

The average trend over the entire monitored period (T1 – T4) exhibits a similar behavior as a function of the scale factors. When the values of both factors are equal and positive, the average trend goes down -0.510 to 0.0 as we increase α_S and α_B from 0 to 0.15. Keeping α_B at the level of -0.2 while increasing α_S from 0 to 0.15 results in an increase of the average trend up to 0.750.

Due to the confidentiality of the actual claims data, we cannot provide here any identifying information about the most frequent labor codes found as potential root causes in similar case studies. Still, without revealing any sensitive information, we can refer to a specific case of two-month data, which included a large cluster of labor codes. The data was partitioned into four 15-day time units and the fuzzy shifts between consecutive units were computed using $\alpha_S = \alpha_B = 0$ and $\gamma = 0.2$. The shift was found positive between T1 and T2 and negative between T2 and T3 and between T3 and T4. The root cause analysis has revealed a single labor code responsible for more than 20% of all claims causing the positive shift in the second time unit. Interestingly enough, the same labor code caused more than 25% of all claims between the next two time units, where a negative shift was observed. The same negative trend continued into the fourth time unit resulting in an increase of the frequency of *the same* labor code (from 26% to 36%) *along with* 28% of additional claims, where *similar* labor codes have been involved. Thus, a timely fuzzy-based analysis of car warranty data would produce an early warning of an emerging trend in *certain* failure types apparently resulting from *the same* root cause.

Table 2. Case Study - Number of Discovered Shifts

α_S	0.01	0.01	0.05	-0.05	0.1	-0.1
α_B	0.01	-0.01	0.05	0.05	0.1	0.1
$\gamma = 0.1$	0	0	0	2	0	3
$\gamma = 0.2$	2	1	0	3	0	3
$\gamma = 0.5$	2	3	0	3	0	3

FUTURE RESEARCH DIRECTIONS

Fuzzy-based analysis of warranty data for various manufacturing industries can be extended in many directions. One important issue is finding the optimal number of histogram bins as a function of the number of claims in each time unit and in the entire monitored period. Currently, we assume that the user finds this number manually and then applies equal-frequency discretization to the data. Completely automating the entire discretization process should provide a significant benefit to the system users.

Automatic determination of the algorithm settings (namely, the values of the shape and the scale factors) is another important research question. In a future extension of the algorithm, the best settings will be selected based on the algorithm ability to predict future shifts and long-term trends as well as its potential contribution to the root cause analysis.

We also intend to compare the fuzzy algorithm performance to some basic statistical techniques for time-series analysis and trend detection.

CONCLUSION

In this chapter, we have presented a novel, fuzzy-based method for automated detection of evolving maintenance problems in massive streams of warranty data. The method provides an automated comparison of frequency histograms, based on a cognitive model of human perception rather than "crisp" statistical models. The method has been implemented in the Early Warning Tool, which has been applied to empirical distributions of time-to-failure and mileage-to-failure of warranty claims of a major car manufacturer (GM). The results have revealed significant emerging and decreasing trends in the car warranty data. Important clues for the root causes of the discovered trends have also been provided. The method can be further enhanced in several directions.

ACKNOWLEDGMENT

This work was supported in part by the General Motors Research & Development – India Science Lab.

REFERENCES

Blischke, W. R., & Murthy, D. N. P. (1994). *Warranty cost analysis*. New York: Marcel Dekker.

Blischke, W. R., & Murthy, D. N. P. (1996). *Product warranty handbook*. New York. Marcel Dekker.

Cohen, L., Avrahami-Bakish, G., Last, M., Kandel, A., & Kipersztok, O. (2008). Real-time data mining of non-stationary data streams from sensor networks. *Information Fusion*, *9*(3), 344–353. doi:10.1016/j.inffus.2005.05.005

Hu, X. J., Lawless, J. F., & Suzuki, K. (1998). Nonparametric estimation of a lifetime distribution when censoring times are missing. *Technometrics*, *40*, 3–13. doi:10.2307/1271388

Kalbfleisch, J. D., & Lawless, J. F. (1988). Estimation of reliability in field-performance studies. *Technometrics, 30*, 365–388. doi:10.2307/1269797

Kalbfleisch, J. D., Lawless, J. F., & Robinson, J. A. (1991). Methods for the analysis and prediction of warranty claims. *Tecnometrics, 33*, 273–285. doi:10.2307/1268780

Kandel, A., Pacheco, R., Martins, A., & Khator, S. (1996). The foundations of rule-based computations in fuzzy models. In W. Pedrycz (Ed.), *Fuzzy modelling, paradigms and practice* (pp. 231-263). Boston: Kluwer.

Karim, M. R., Yamamoto, W., & Suzuki, K. (2001a). Statistical analysis of marginal count failure data. *Lifetime Data Analysis, 7*, 173–186. doi:10.1023/A:1011300907152

Karim, M. R., Yamamoto, W., & Suzuki, K. (2001b). Change-point detection from marginal count failure data. *Journal of the Japanese Society for Quality Control, 31*, 318–338.

Karnik, N. N., Mendel, J. M., & Liang, Q. (1999). Type-2 fuzzy logic systems. *IEEE transactions on Fuzzy Systems, 7*(6), 643–658. doi:10.1109/91.811231

Koenigstein, N., Shavitt, Y., & Tankel, T. (2008). Spotting out emerging artists using geo-aware analysis of P2P query strings. In *Proceeding of the 14th ACM SIGKDD international Conference on Knowledge Discovery and Data Mining. KDD '08* (pp. 937-945). New York: ACM.

Last, M., & Kandel, A. (1999). Automated perceptions in data mining. In *1999 IEEE International Fuzzy Systems Conference Proceedings* (Part I, pp. 19-197).

Last, M., & Kandel, A. (2002a). Perception-based analysis of engineering experiments in semiconductor industry. *International Journal of Image and Graphics, 2*(1), 107–126. doi:10.1142/S0219467802000512

Last, M., & Kandel, A. (2002b). Fuzzy comparison of frequency distributions. In P. Grzegorzewski *et al.* (Eds.), *Soft methods in probability, statistics, and data analysis* (pp. 219-227). Heidelberg, Germany: Physica-Verlag.

Lawless, F. (1998). Statistical analysis of product warranty data. *International Statistical Review, 66*, 227–240.

Lawless, J. F., Hu, J., & Cao, J. (1995). Methods for the estimation of failure distributions and rates from automobile warranty data. *Lifetime Data Analysis, 1*, 227–240. doi:10.1007/BF00985758

Lawless, J. F., & Kalbfleisch, J. D. (1992). Some issues in the collection and analysis of field reliability data. In J.P. Klein & P.K.Goel (Eds.), *Survival analysis: State of the art* (pp. 141-152). Amesterdam: Kluwer.

Robinson, J. A., & McDonald, G. C. (1991). Issues related to field relibility and warranty data. In G.E. Liepins & V.R.R. Uppuluri (Eds.), *Data quality control: Theory and pragmatics* (pp. 69-89). New York: Marcel Dekker.

Suzuki, K. (1985a). Estimation of lifetime parameters from incomplete field data. *Technometrics, 27*, 263–272. doi:10.2307/1269707

Suzuki, K. (1985b). Nonparametric estimation of lifetime distributions from a record of failures and follow-ups. *Journal of the American Statistical Association, 80*, 68–72. doi:10.2307/2288041

Wang, L., & Suzuki, K. (2001a). Nonparametrc estimation of lifetime distribution from warranty data without monthly unit sales information. *The Journal of Reliability Engineering Association Japan, 23*, 14–154.

Wang, L., & Suzuki, K. (2001b). Lifetime estimation on warranty data without date-of-sale information-case where usage time distributions are unknown. *Journal of the Japanese Society for Quality Control, 31*, 148–167.

Wu, H., & Meeker, W. Q. (2002). Early detection of reliability problems using information from warranty databases. *Technometrics, 44*, 120–133. doi:10.1198/004017002317375073

Zeira, G., Maimon, O., Last, M., & Rokach, L. (2004). Change detection in classification models induced from time series data. In M. Last, A. Kandel, & H. Bunke (Eds.), *Data mining in time series databases* (pp. 101-125). Singapore: World Scientific.

Chapter 15
High Scale Fuzzy Video Mining

Christophe Marsala
Université Pierre et Marie Curie Paris6, France

Marcin Detyniecki
Université Pierre et Marie Curie Paris6, France

ABSTRACT

In this chapter, the authors focus on the use of forests of fuzzy decision trees (FFDT) in a video mining application. They discuss how to learn from a high scale video data sets and how to use the trained FFDTs to detect concepts in a high number of video shots. Moreover, the authors study the effect of the size of the forest on the performance; and of the use of fuzzy logic during the classification process. The experiments are performed on a well-know non-video dataset and on a real TV quality video benchmark.

INTRODUCTION

Nowadays, the amount of recorded video is continually increasing leading to a growing need to find a way to handle it automatically. One of the main issues is to be able to index these data with high-level semantic concepts (or features) such as "indoor/outdoor", "people", "maps", "military staff", etc.

Video indexing aims at analyzing a video, to find its seminal content, and to associate concepts to any of its part. Today effective video indexing is done manually, by a human operator, who associates concepts to parts of a video. However, due to the growth of recorded video, the introduction of automatic approaches, as data-mining-based ones, is a promising perspective.

Video mining is typically an inductive machine learning approach. It has as starting point a set of correctly labeled examples used to train or to build a model. Later, the model is used to perform an automatic classification of any of the forthcoming examples, even if they have not been met before. Video mining is becoming a very active domain today and several conferences take into account this domain in their topics (for instance, the workshop on Video Mining of last IEEE International Conference on

DOI: 10.4018/978-1-60566-858-1.ch015

Data Mining, or ACM Multimedia conferences, etc.). Some works related to video mining can be cited: (Pan, J.-Y., & Faloutsos, C., 2002), (Rosenfeld, A. et al.; 2003), (Zhu, X., et al. 2005), the proceedings of the TRECVid challenge organized by the US institute NIST.

Inductive machine learning is a well-known research topic with a large set of methods, one of the most commonly used approaches being the decision tree approach (DT). However, robustness and threshold problems appear when considering classical DTs to handle numerical or imprecisely defined data. The introduction of fuzzy set theory, that leads to the construction of fuzzy decision trees (FDT) able to smooth out these negative effects.

In the 2005 TRECVID competition, we studied the use of Fuzzy Decision Trees for this kind of applications (Marsala, C., & Detyniecki, M., 2005). The approach, based on single FDTs (one per concept), provided as result a set of classification rules, which were in the one hand, human understandable, thus allowing further human development; but in the other hand, this first series of tests enables us to discover that, when addressing large, unbalanced, multiclass datasets, a single classifier is not sufficient for direct automatic exploitation. Thus, based on these observations, in (Marsala, C., & Detyniecki, M., 2006) forests of FDT were introduced to cover better the whole input space. The use of forests of decision trees is well-known in classical machine learning, see for instance (Breiman, L., 2001). In fuzzy machine learning, forests of fuzzy decision trees have been introduced some years ago and are becoming more popular nowadays (Bonissone, P.P. et al., 2008), (Crockett, K., et al. (2001), (Janikow, C. Z., & Faifer, M., 2000), (Marsala, C., & Bouchon-Meunier, B., 1997). These approaches differ by the way the FDT are multiplied to grow the forest.

In this chapter, we show that this kind of approach is very useful for high scale challenge. First, we present how the video is pre-processed in order to obtain a set of descriptors to feed a video mining algorithm. Afterwards, we explain how Forest of Fuzzy Decision Trees are built and consecutively used to detect concepts in video shots.

In the experimental part of the chapter, we first study on a well-studied dataset both the influence of the size of the forest (in terms of number of trees), and the influence of using the FDTs in a fuzzy manner or not. Afterward, the proposed approach is confronted to a real world video dataset. The performance of FFDTs with respect to other approaches is explored. And the observations obtained on the previous dataset are confronted.

FROM VIDEO TO TRAINING SETS

From a video, a sequence of steps, such as the extraction of basic descriptors is necessary to feed the video mining algorithm.

First of all, the video is automatically segmented into temporal shots. Here, a *shot* is a sequence of the video with a more or less constant content. The content of a shot is considered to have the same "meaning". Generally, all the frames that compose a shot are very similar visually and differ only slightly. A shot can be very short (less than 1 second), for instance in action sequences of a video, or it can be very long, for instance if the sequence in the video shows only a still host talking to the camera. A shot can be associated with a set of representative images, called *frames*. The number of frames can vary from at least 1 to more than 10 frames, depending on the complexity of its contents.

Secondly, two kinds of descriptors are extracted from each frame: *Visual Information Descriptors* and *Video Information Descriptors*. Moreover, frames from the video training set are also associated with a set of *Class Label* obtained through a manual indexation of the videos.

Figure 1. Spatial segmentation of a frame

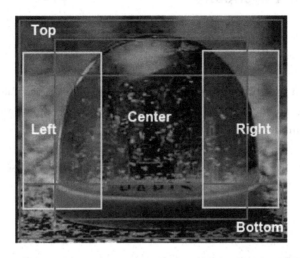

Visual Information Descriptors

The *Visual Information Descriptors* are obtained directly and exclusively from the frames. In order to obtain spatial-related information, each frame is segmented into five overlapping regions (see Figure 1).

Each of them corresponds to a spatial part of the frame: top, bottom, left, right, and middle. The five regions have not the same size to reflect the importance of the contained information based on its position. Moreover, regions overlap in order to introduce a dependency between them.

For each region the associated histogram in Hue-Saturation-Value (HSV) space is computed. The number of bins of the histogram follows the importance of the region by being valued in a more or less precise way: 6x3x3 or 8x3x3.

At the end of these steps, a set of Visual Information Descriptors characterizing each frame is provided. This set is composed of values ranging from *0* to *1*. Each value represents the frequency of a color in the HSV space for the corresponding region it is associated with.

For instance, if the number of bins in the HSV space is 8x3x3 for the "Center" region, and if the number of bins is 6x3x3 for the four other regions, the Visual Information Descriptors of a frame is composed of 288 numerical values from [0,1].

The main interest in choosing overlapping regions in the frame is to create a link between the regions. This link is defined by the fact that their HSV histograms are valued on a same subset of pixels. The aim here is to alleviate a drawback of the attribute oriented inductive learning where attributes are usually considered as independent. Thus, creating a link between them will enable the learning model to take into account information about the color in the frame as a whole.

Here, the use of fuzzy histograms (histograms defined by means of a fuzzy definition of colors) can be a very interesting improvement of our approach and deserves further research.

Temporal Information Descriptors

The *Temporal Information Descriptors* are information related to the position of the frames, and of the shots, in the video. For every shot, we extract:

- the temporal position (time code of the beginning) of the shot and of the frame itself,
- the duration of the shot containing the frame and the duration of the original shot if the shot results from a merging of smaller shots.

At the end of this step, the Temporal Information Descriptors, a second set of numerical values that characterize a shot and its frames is obtained.

Class Label

The *Class Label* is the result of a human indexation of the video. It corresponds to the *correct* high-level concept(s) (features) to be detected on a given shot.

A concept is associated to each *frame* of the video through a human indexation process. Thus, the shots are described by the concepts appearing in at least one of its frames. Furthermore, a frame can be associated with more than one class descriptor.

Building a Training Set

In order to use the Fuzzy Decision Trees (FDT) learning method, we must have a training set in which there are cases *with* the concept to be recognized and examples that do *not* possess that concept. Moreover, the decision tree construction methods are based on the hypothesis that the value for the class is equally distributed. Thus, we have to balance the number of frames of each class by (randomly) selecting a subset of the whole development dataset. Each of such a subset must contain an equal number of cases in each class.

LEARNING AND DETECTING HIGH LEVEL CONCEPTS

In the particular context of large datasets, as for instance for video indexing, we can focus our attention on the elements (here shots) that are classified with a high degree of confidence. In fact, it may be sufficient and more interesting to have some good examples rather than an average classification overall. Thus, often in video indexing the classified shots are ranked based on the credibility on the fact that the shot contains the concepts or not.

FFDT can be easily used to provide a ranking of shots for a given concept. First, a classification of frames is done by means of each tree of the FFDT. Secondly, an aggregation of the results leads to the classification of the shot. Finally, the shots are ranked based on the aggregated value, which corresponds to credibility that the concepts appear in it.

First of all, we briefly recall how the training enables us to obtain a classifier (FFDT) that will be used later to classify and rank the test frames. For more technical details on this method, please refer to (Marsala, C., & Detyniecki, M., 2006).

Fuzzy Decision Trees

Inductive learning raises from the *particular* to the *general*. A tree is built, from the root to the leaves, by successively partitioning the training set into subsets. Each partition is done by means of a test on an attribute and leads to the definition of a node of the tree (for more details, please, refer to Marsala, C., & Bouchon-Meunier, B., 1999).

When mining numerical data, with a *Fuzzy* Decision Tree, a definition of fuzzy values of attributes is necessary. In the case of high scale mining, an automatic method is necessary. We build a fuzzy partition on the set of values of the numerical descriptors.

Finally, in order to address high scale datasets, the FDT has to be built efficiently and the use of the Salammbô software has been introduced in this step. This software has been introduced in (Marsala, C., & Bouchon-Meunier, B., 1999). It enables the construction and the use of fuzzy decision trees. A lot of parameters can be set (measure of discrimination, family of t-norms, parameters to build fuzzy partitions, etc.) in this software to build the FDT. Moreover, it has been written in C that enables it to handle very efficiently training sets with a very high number of examples.

Classifying Frames with a Fuzzy Decision Tree

The process of a frame classification (*i.e.* detecting whether a concept is present), using a *single* Fuzzy Decision Tree is straightforward (Marsala, C., & Detyniecki, M., 2005). From each image-frame low-level features (in the same description space as for the training) are extracted. Based on this description, starting from the top of the tree, decisions are successively performed. The decisions can be made either in a *classical* or in a *fuzzy* manner as it is explained in the following.

When doing it classically, the decision is to follow one and only one of the branches. Technically the decision is done using the 0.5 alpha-cut degree of the fuzzy values. At the end, when a leaf is reached, the FDT outputs a single class with a full membership, either "has the class" or "has not the class", for each tested example.

When doing it in a fuzzy manner, if the decision is not crisp, for instance if the case to classify is close to the boundaries of the decision frontier, several branches can be followed. At the end the FDT's output is a degree of membership (ranging from 0 to 1) of the example observing the class. In order to compute these degrees, the trees are considered as a set of rules. All possible top-to-leaf paths are considered as a disjunctive set of rules and each individual path is considered as a conjunction of decisions. Based on this logical representation, the final degree can be computed using standard fuzzy logic operators. In this chapter, we consider Zadeh's family (maximum and minimum) and the Lukasiewicz one (bounded sum and its dual)[1].

These two families of t-norms have been chosen because their behavior is very different. However, any other family of t-norms could be used in this process and it deserves further research. For more details on the use of FDTs in fuzzy manner please refer to (Marsala, C., & Bouchon-Meunier, B., 1999).

Forests of Fuzzy Decision Trees

One way to address high scale datasets is to reduce the size of the problem. We propose to create, by sampling the large dataset, several smaller ones. Then we train one classifier on each of the size reduced sets. As a result we obtain a set of classifiers, which decisions have to be combined at the decision stage. An ensemble of decision tree classifiers is a so-called forest of decision trees.

This approach produces global classifiers that are not only robust, but having their score more reliable. Moreover, this technique allows to address another problem often observed in high scale-datasets: the balance of positive versus negative examples. In fact, even there is a lot of positive examples, the number of negative (or not labeled) examples is quickly overwhelming. If we sample several times asymmetrically, so that we obtain balanced smaller training sets, we not only solve the balance problem, but we also cover better the larger negative examples space.

A question remains the number of decision trees of need. Later in this chapter we study the influence, in terms of performance (error rate), of the number of Decision Trees used in a forest.

In the particular case of video mining, we construct a forest of FDTs for each high-level concept to be detected. A FFDT is composed of *n* Fuzzy Decision Trees. Each FDT *Fi* of the forest is constructed based on the training set *Ti*, each training set *Ti* being a balanced random sample of the whole training set, as described previously.

Classifying Frames with a Forest of Decision Trees

The classification using a forest of *n* FDTs, is reduced to an aggregation problem. In fact, for a single concept, the classification of a frame *k* is carried out in two steps:

1. Classification of the frame by means of the *n* FDTs of the forest: each frame *k* is classified by means of each FDT *Fi* in order to obtain a degree $d_i(k) \in [0, 1]$ of having the concept. Thus, *n* degrees $d_i(k)$, *i=1...n* are obtained, from the forest, for each *k*.
2. Aggregation of the $d_i(k)$ (*i=1...n*) degrees, into a single value *d(k)*, which corresponds to the degree in which the forest believes that the keyframe *k* contains the concept.

Two kinds of aggregating methods to compute the degree *d(k)* were tested:

1. *Simple vote*: This basic aggregation corresponds to the sum of all the degrees:

$$d(k) = \sum_{i=1}^{n} d_i(k)$$

2. *Weighted vote*: Aggregation can also be weighted by taking into account the training accuracy of the FDT. Thus, the sum of the degrees becomes

$$d(k) = \sum_{i=1}^{n} w_i d_i(k)$$

where w_i from [0, 1] corresponds to the accuracy of the corresponding FDT *Fi* valued on the training set.

Other aggregating methods could be used here and the choice of a convenient operator deserves further research. Moreover, a more complex aggregator could be used here in this step. For instance, a model could be tuned on the training data and a machine learning tool could be very useful to improve this aggregation.

Detecting a Concept in a Shot

The degrees of all the frames $d(k)$ of *one* shot are aggregated to obtain a global degree $D(S)$. Since it is sufficient that at least one frame in the shot presents the concept to be able to state that the shot contains the concept, the degree $D(S)$ for the shot S containing the concept is obtained as

$$D(S) = \max_{\{k \in S\}} d(k)$$

Here, the choice of another aggregating operator (as the sum for instance) could also be done and it deserves further research in order to study whether it could improve the approach.

So, after this aggregation, for every shot, a degree is obtained. The higher $D(S)$ is, the higher it is believed that the shot S contains the corresponding concept.

NUMBER OF DECISION TREES FOR HIGH SCALE MINING

As stated before, in order to cover high scale datasets it is suitable to sample the problem into several reduced sets of data and go from fuzzy decision trees (FDT) to forests of FDTs.

What is not clear is what is the precise effect, in terms of performance, on the number of trees that are used. The performance is measured by the error rate (*i.e.* the ratio of wrong classifications to the total number of classification evaluated). Thus, the error rate ranges from 0 ("no wrong classification") to 1 ("no correct classification").

Waveform Datasets

In order to avoid any particularities of a video data set, we study the influences of the size of the forest and of the choice of the aggregation operators on the well-known Waveform dataset (Breiman, L. et al., 1984), from the UCI repository (Asuncion, A., & Newman, D., 2007). This dataset is often used in the machine learning community and a lot of algorithms have been evaluated on it. For instance, in (Breiman, L., 2001) or in (Geurts, P., et al. 2006), some results with this dataset can be found for algorithms combining decision trees (Adaboost, Random Forests, ...).

The Waveform dataset has the following interesting properties. There are 3 (symbolic) classes to recognize, and 21 real-valued attributes. Data can be noised (as in real-world problems). The dataset is composed of a total of 5000 instances and the proportion of positive and negative examples is balanced. This dataset comes from an artificial problem where three different triangular functions (named either 1, 2, or 3) are defined by means of 21 real-valued attributes. For more detail on this dataset, please, refer to (Breiman, L. et al., 1984).

Figure 2. Influence of the size of the forest on the error rate

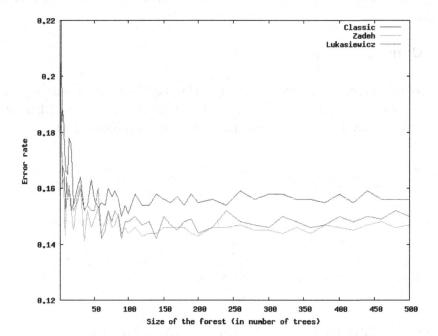

Experiments

In order to correctly measure the error rate, the dataset is decomposed into two subsets: the training set composed of 3500 examples, and the test set composed of 1500 examples.

Using the training set Forest of FDTs of different sizes (ranging from 1 to 500 FDTs) are built using a similar protocol as the one used for the video indexing application:

- *step 1*: a class c is chosen from the set of classes
- *step 2*: the training set is sampled by taking all the examples associated with the class c, and a random sample of examples of the other classes (i.e. negative examples). The idea here is to build a set of examples where there is the same number of examples of the class c, than examples of another class.
- *step 3*: from this sampling, a FDT is constructed using the Salammbô software (Marsala, C., & Bouchon-Meunier, B., 1999).

This process is repeated for each of the three classes in order to obtain three FDT, each one enabling the classification of an example with regards to a given class.

In the evaluation step, for each class, each example from the test set was classified by each of the FDTs. The classification was repeated three times, each time using the decision in a different manner: classical, fuzzy using the Zadeh operators and fuzzy using the Lukasiewicz ones. The individual tree classification degrees were then aggregated using a simple vote approach, to determine the final class of the example.

In Figure 2, we present the variation of the error rate when classifying the test set for various sizes of FFDT (in terms of number of trees). We notice that no matter how we use the FDTs (i.e. classically or fuzzy) the error rate decreases with the size of the forest.

Moreover, we notice that the error rate has great variations for small sized forests and stabilizes for larger ones. There seems to be a boundary error rate of around 0.15 (15% examples are badly classified). These results confirm the intuition: the more the number of trees is the lower the error rate. However, we remark that there is a limit to this approach. In fact, after a certain number of trees the results do not improve and we can even notice a slight worsening. It is also remarkable that a relatively small number of trees (for this problem around 100) is needed to get the limit performance.

Now, when comparing the classical use of the FDTs (curve labeled "classical) with the fuzzy-logic-based use of the same FDTs (curves labeled Zadeh and Lukasiewicz), it becomes clear that the use of the fuzzy set theory reduces the error rate for this problem, and this no matter the size of the forest. When comparing the fuzzy approaches we notice slight advantage for Zadeh's logic.

The complexity and runtime of the whole process is relatively low. In fact, the total runtime of all the experiment described here, composed of the construction of 500 FDT, the classification of the test set by each of these FDT and with each of the presented operators (Classic, Zadeh, and Lukasiewicz), is around 7350 seconds on a multiprocessor computer (10 core 2.93 Ghz, 64 Gb RAM, with GNU/Linux 2.6). This can be explained by the fact that the construction of a FDT was optimized in previous works and here the construction of the Forest of FDTs is just related to the number of trees built and, thus, is relatively low (taking into account the small number of trees needed to obtain a small error rate).

High Scale Mining on TV Video Data

In order to compare our approach to others high scale approaches in a real-world framework, we participated to the high-level feature extraction task, at the TRECVid 2007 Challenge (Over, P., et al., 2007). Here, we only report the results obtained with our submission (Marsala, C., et al., 2007), the interested reader could refer to the proceedings of the TRECVid 2007 Challenge to have a good overview of the results of the whole participating teams.

The video corpus was composed of 109 videos (around 30 minutes length each) and 18142 reference shots (shots were provided by (Petersohn, C., 2004)). The challenge addressed 39 concepts: sports (1), weather (3), office (5), meeting (6), desert (10), mountain (12), waterscape-waterfront (17), police security (23), military staff (24), animal (26), computer TV screen (27), US flag (28), airplane (29), car (30), truck (32), boat or ship (33), walking or running (34), people marching (35), explosion fire (36), maps (38), and charts (39).

The evaluation process was independently conducted by the NIST institute. Since TRECVid is information retrieval oriented, and given the size of the test set, each participating team had to propose, for each high-level concept, a ranking of at most 2000 video shots from the test set, that contain each of the concepts.

Due to the high size of the test corpus, it is impossible to manually annotate all examples for each concept. Thus, the TRECVid evaluators propose to evaluate a sample of the selected (by the submissions) shots and based on that infer the average precision. Thus, official metric (NIST, 2006) used to evaluate the runs was the *Inferred Average Precision*. Evaluating methods by means of an inferred value is a well-known approach whenever the size of the corpus is too large to be fully handled.

TRECVid Experiments

Several kinds and sizes of forests were studied (and submitted). Here, we focus on two sizes of forests (25 FDTs and 35 FDTs) and on the use of fuzzy logic in the classification step (classical use versus Zadeh and Lukasiewicz uses). More precisely, four approaches are compared: results obtained by means of a forest of 25 FDTs used classically ("F25_Classic"), results of a forest of 25 FDTs used with the Zadeh's t-norms ("F25_Zadeh"), results of a forest of 35 FDTs used with the Zadeh's t-norms ("F35_Zadeh"), and the median of the results for all the participating teams (to TRECVID 2007).

In Figure 3, variations of the *Inferred Average Precision* (Inf. AP.) are presented. The *average precision* combines the ideas behind both precision and recall by considering the precision at different depths of a list. It gives a paramount importance to the first shots returned, but also considers the total number of correct shots returned. It can be observed that the FFDT performance highly depends on the kind of concepts to be recognize. It is greatly linked to the low level descriptors used to represent the shots. Some concepts are simple to learn (not only for the FFDTs): waterscape-waterfront (17), animal (26), computer TV screen (27), US flag (28), airplane (29), car (30), boat or ship (33). However, concepts, such as weather (3), desert (10), US flag (28), people marching (35), need better (specialized) descriptors in order to allow the FFDT to perform better.

In average the FFDTs ranked among the first half of all the approaches that participated to the challenge. When compared to the median FFDTs perform for some concepts and less good for other and this independently of its "difficulty" to be learned. FFDTs outperform for the complex concepts: police security (23), military personnel (24), explosion fire (36); and for the simpler ones: TV screen (27), airplane (29).

As shown on the Waveform dataset, the increase of number of trees in the forest improves the results. Here the Inf. AP. (Inferred Average Precision) of forests of 35 fuzzy trees outperforms forests of 25 fuzzy trees, for almost all concepts.

Figure 3. Global Inf. Avg. Precision

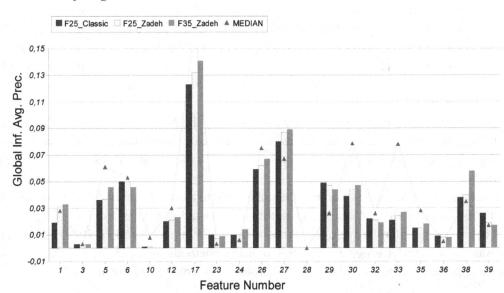

In Figure 4, Figure 5, and Figure 6, the number of correct classified shots (hits), for each concept, is presented when considering the first 100, 1000 and 2000 shots of the list, respectively. By considering the hits we do not take into account the order of the results. These 3 values, for each concept, are part of the evaluation metrics available at the TRECVid Challenge.

When considering the number of hits in 100, 1000 and 2000 first shots for the FFDTs compared to the median (seen here as a reference point), we observe that the FFDT performs relatively better when considering most of the list. We claim that the main reason lies in the fact that the FFDT is a classi-

Figure 4. Good Hits in the 100 firsts

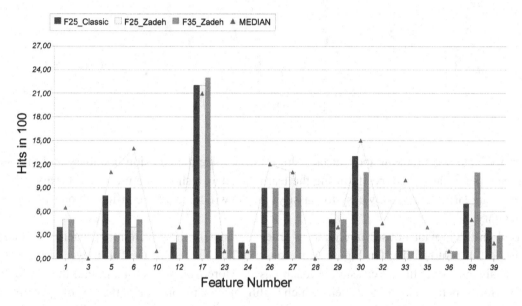

Figure 5. Good Hits in the 1000 firsts

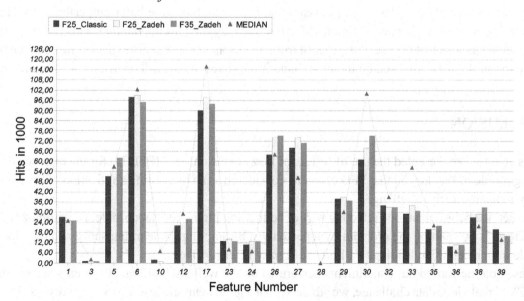

Figure 6. Good Hits in the 2000 firsts

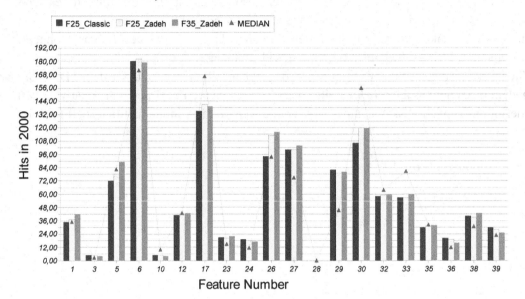

fication tool and not a ranking tool. In fact, the DTs optimize the decision boundary and the distance of the example to the boundary. If, during the learning stage, a shot is naturally put far away from the decision boundary (*i.e.* it is very easy to classify) then it will have a little influence on the selection of the boundary.

Based on the previous observation and in order to compare the different approaches it is better to choose the full returned list. On Figure 6, we observe that the use of the full power of the fuzzy set theory is always better than a classic-approach based. Moreover, we see again that the "F35_Zadeh" FFDT performs better than "F25_Zadeh" which highlights the importance of the size of the forest in this application too. Thus, confirming the results observed on the Waveform dataset. If we now focus our attention on the number of hits at 100 (Figure 4) and we compare the use of Fuzzy Logic ("F25_Zadeh") to the classical use ("F25_Classic"), it appears that in several times the latter outperforms the former. In other words, fuzzy logic is good for classification but it aggravates the ranking. This behavior can be explained by the fact that the use of degrees of truth on the one hand scrambles the strong decision (good for the top of the list), however, on the other hand it improves the overall decision (i.e. classification).

CONCLUSION

In this chapter, we presented the use of forests of fuzzy decision trees (FFDTs) for the high scale video mining problem. We showed that FFDTs can be considered as an interesting application of the fuzzy set theory to handle such a challenge.

In fact, we believe that, one effective way of addressing high scale data problems, with Fuzzy Decision Trees, is by splitting the problem by repeatedly sub-sampling the learning space and then for each sample train a classifier, leading to a Forest of Fuzzy Decision Trees.

Based on the carried out experiments performed on the well-studied Waveform data set and on the TRECVId real video data challenge, we advocate that a good heuristic leading to better results is to have as many FDT as possible. Moreover, we observed that the fuzzy of FFDTs outperforms the classical approach in a high scale classification problem.

The results on real world data (TV quality videos) from the TRECVid challenge highlight that this approach is already competitive with respect to others'. We show that FFDTs are good at detecting high-level concepts in shots (classification), but do not optimize the rank of the results.

In this real-world application that took place in a highly competitive context (the TRECVid Challenge that involved not only academic teams but also industrial teams) the tools from the fuzzy set theory have been proven to be a very sizeable and tractable approach. Moreover, the robustness of these tools when handling real-world measures enables the improvement of a classical data mining tools to construct fuzzy decision trees and build forests that benefit from the fuzzy degrees offer as output of the trees.

Several future works should be done in order to improve and to study better the proposed approach. For instance, the study of other kinds of descriptors to encode the video shots will be conducted in order to improve the results for other kinds of high-level concepts. Fuzzy descriptors could be introduced here (for instance, to build histograms defined on fuzzy colors, to define the boundaries of a shot, or to handle better the temporal measures related to the video) to take into account better this real-world data.

Moreover, several parameters that are used during the construction of the fuzzy decision trees, and the ones that are used to set the size of the forest deserve a deeper study. The study and the choice of the aggregation operators involved in various step of the use of the FFDT will also be studied deeper in order to be optimized for a given domain of application. The influence of the number of the FDTs to build a forest deserves also a deeper study that could brought out a better understanding of how to set a convenient size for such an ensemble of classifier.

REFERENCES

Asuncion, A., & Newman, D. (2007). *UCI machine learning repository – University of California, Irvine, School of Information and Computer Sciences*. Retrieved from http://www.ics.uci.edu/~mlearn/MLRepository.html

Bonissone, P. P., Cadenas, J. M., Garrido, M. C., & Diaz-Valladares, R. A. (2008). A fuzzy random forest: Fundamental for design and construction. In *Proceedings of the 12th International Conference on Information Processing and Management of Uncertainty in Knowledge-Based Systems (IPMU'08)*, Malaga, Spain (pp. 1231-1238).

Breiman, L. (2001). Random forests. *Machine Learning, 45*, 5–32. doi:10.1023/A:1010933404324

Breiman, L., Friedman, J., Olshen, R., & Stone, C. (1984). *Classification and regression trees*. New York: Chapman and Hall.

Crockett, K., Bandar, Z., & McLean, D. (2001). Growing a fuzzy decision forest. In *Proceedings of the 10th IEEE International Conference on Fuzzy Systems*, Melbourne, Australia (pp. 614-617).

Geurts, P., Ernst, D., & Wehenkel, L. (2006). Extremely randomized trees. *Machine Learning, 63*(1), 3–42. doi:10.1007/s10994-006-6226-1

Janikow, C. Z., & Faifer, M. (2000). Fuzzy decision forest. In *Proceedings of the 19th International Conference of the North American Fuzzy Information Processing Society (NAFIPS'00)* (pp. 218-221).

Marsala, C., & Bouchon-Meunier, B. (1997). Forest of fuzzy decision trees. In M. Mares, R. Mesiar, V. Novak, J. Ramik, & A. Stupnanova (Eds.), *Proceedings of the Seventh International Fuzzy Systems Association World Congress, volume 1,* Prague, Czech Republic (pp. 369-374).

Marsala, C., & Bouchon-Meunier, B. (1999). An adaptable system to construct fuzzy decision trees. In *Proc. of the NAFIPS'99 (North American Fuzzy Information Processing Society),* New York, USA (pp. 223-227).

Marsala, C., & Detyniecki, M. (2005). University of Paris 6 at TRECVID 2005: High-level feature extraction. In *TREC Video Retrieval Evaluation Online Proceedings*. Retrieved from http://www-nlpir. nist.gov/projects/tvpubs/tv.pubs.org.html

Marsala, C., & Detyniecki, M. (2006). University of Paris 6 at TRECVID 2006: Forests of fuzzy decision trees for high-level feature extraction. In *TREC Video Retrieval Evaluation Online Proceedings*. Retrieved from http://wwwnlpir.nist.gov/projects/tvpubs/tv.pubs.org.html

Marsala, C., Detyniecki, M., Usunier, N., & Amini, M.-R. (2007). High-level feature detection with forests of fuzzy decision trees combined with the rankboost algorithm. In *TREC Video Retrieval Evaluation Online Proceedings*. Retrieved from http://www-nlpir.nist.gov/projects/tvpubs/tv.pubs.org.html

NIST. (2006). *Guidelines for the TRECVID 2006 evaluation, National Institute of Standards and Technology*. Retrieved from http://www-nlpir.nist.gov/projects/tv2006/tv2006.html

Over, P., Kraaij, W., & Smeaton, A. F. (2007). *Guidelines for the TRECVID 2007 evaluation*. National Institute of Standards and Technology. Retrieved from http://www-nlpir.nist.gov/projects/tv2007/tv2007. html

Pan, J.-Y., & Faloutsos, C. (2002). VideoCube: A novel tool for video mining and classification. In *Proceedings of the International Conference on Asian Digital Libraries* (LNCS 2555, pp. 194-205). Berlin, Germany: Springer.

Petersohn, C. (2004). Fraunhofer HHI at TRECVID 2004: Shot boundary detection system.(Tech. Rep.). In *TREC Video Retrieval Evaluation Online Proceedings, TRECVID*. Retrieved from http://www-nlpir. nist.gov/projects/tvpubs/tvpapers04/fraunhofer.pdf

Rosenfeld, C., Doerman, D., & DeMenthon, D. (2003). *Video mining*. Amsterdam: Kluwer Academic Publishers.

Zhu, X., Wu, X., Elmagarmid, A. K., Feng, Z., & Wu, L. (2005). Video data mining: Semantic indexing and event detection form the association perspective. *IEEE Transactions on Knowledge and Data Engineering, 17*(5), 665–677. doi:10.1109/TKDE.2005.83

ENDNOTE

[1] We recall briefly that, given two values *x* and *y* from [0,1], the aggregation by means of the *Lukasiewicz t-norm* is valued as T*(x,y)= max(x+y-1,0)* and the aggregation by means of the *Lukasiewicz t-conorm* is valued as ⊥*(x,y)=min(x+y,1)*.

Chapter 16
Fuzzy Clustering of Large Relational Bioinformatics Datasets

Mihail Popescu
University of Missouri, USA

ABSTRACT

In this chapter the author presents a fuzzy clustering methodology that can be employed for large relational datasets. Relational data is an N×N matrix that consists of pair-wise dissimilarities among N objects. Large relational datasets are encountered in many domains such as psychology or medical informatics, but they are abundant in bioinformatics where gene products are compared to each other based on various characteristics such as DNA or amino acid sequence. The fuzzy clustering methodology is exemplified on a set of about 30,000 human gene products.

INTRODUCTION

Bioinformatics is, arguably, the application domain where large relational datasets are most abundant. There are two main reasons for this abundance. First, numerous genome projects completed in the last 10 years have generated a large amount of sequence data. For example, the RefSeq database (http://www. ncbi.nlm.nih.gov/RefSeq/) contains, as of September, 2008, about 5,400 genomes with a total of about 5.6 million identified protein sequences. At the same time, the total number of sequences deposited in another sequence database GenBank, http://www.ncbi.nlm.nih.gov/Genbank (Pruitt, Tatusova & Maglott, 2007), is close to 85 million. The difference between the numbers of sequences in the two databases is represented, in part, by sequences with unknown function. Even for the case of the human genome, only about 21,000 genes have been annotated from an estimated total of 30,000. Second, functional annotation is a tedious process that is mainly accomplished by comparing the sequence of an unknown protein to the sequence of a protein with known functions. The sequence comparison is often performed

DOI: 10.4018/978-1-60566-858-1.ch016

with BLAST (Altshul et al., 1990), one of the most used tool in bioinformatics. When performed on an entire genome, this method produces large matrices (relational data) of gene sequence similarity values. There are other applications beside sequence comparison where large relational datasets are generated, such as gene comparison based on Gene Ontology annotations or microarray expression (Havens et al. 2008), and document comparison based on *Medical Subject Headings* (MeSH) annotations.

Clustering plays an important role in genome annotation process. In the first phase of the process, after the hypothetical gene boundaries are determined, the gene products are annotated based on their sequence similarity to gene products in related species that are well studied. Next, all the gene products in a given genome are clustered based on their sequence similarity in order to find proteins with similar functions (Enright, Van Dongen & Ouzounis, 2002). Most of the time, gene products with high sequence similarity have similar functions. However, there are gene products with similar functions with less than 30% sequence similarity. The well characterized proteins from the same cluster can then be used to determine the functions of the unknown members of the group, a strategy often called "guilt by association". The most used annotation type is based on Gene Ontology terms. For example, if an annotated gene A clusters together with an annotated gene B due to a high sequence similarity (e.g. computed with BLAST) or due to a high similarity of their expression profiles (computed based on microarray data), we have reason to believe that B shares all/some of the annotations (functions) of A. The most popular clustering algorithms for relational datasets in bioinformatics are hierarchical clustering and Markov clustering (Enright, Van Dongen & Ouzounis, 2002). A scalable version of the hierarchical clustering algorithm, CURE, has been proposed (Guha et al., 1998), but we are not aware of its application to bioinformatics. An implementation of Markov clustering, TRIBE-MCL, has reportedly grouped about 80,000 sequences in 8,000 clusters in approximately 5 minutes on a Sun Ultra 10 workstation. However, both previous clustering approaches are crisp, that is, they assign each sequence to a unique cluster. Because many proteins have multiple sequence domains that correspond to various functions, it is more natural to allow each sequence to belong to multiple clusters (Xu et al., 2008). By employing fuzzy clustering, an unknown gene product can be assigned to more than one group, receiving in this fashion putative annotations from multiple gene families (Popescu et al., 2004). For example, if the unknown gene B has a 0.5 membership in A's cluster and, at the same time, has a 0.5 membership in another cluster where gene C is representative, then we have 50% confidence that B shares both A's and C's annotations. More applications of the fuzzy clustering in bioinformatics, such as gene product summarization and microarray processing, are presented in (Xu et al., 2008).

A relational fuzzy clustering algorithm for very large databases, eNERF, has been recently introduced by Bezdek et al. (Bezdek et al., 2006, Wang et al., 2008). However, eNERF was not applied to any large bioinformatics data sets. In this paper we intend to employ eNERF to fuzzy cluster the human genome sequences available in the RefSeq database. We will concentrate on the process of assigning fuzzy memberships to gene products and not on the annotation process itself. For a review of the automatic gene annotation methods we refer the reader to (Ouzounis and Karp, 2002) and (Stothard and Wishart, 2006). We will analyze eNERF behavior both in scalability (speed and memory requirements) and cluster coherence. We will also describe eCCV, an extension of the CCV cluster validation algorithm described in (Popescu et al., 2008).

The organization of this chapter is as follows: in the first section we describe eNERF, in the second one we present eCCV, in the third section we describe the RefSeq human gene product dataset, in the next one we show the results obtained on RefSeq data using the presented methodology, and in the last section we summarize our experiments.

EXTENDED NON-EUCLIDEAN RELATIONAL FUZZY C-MEANS (ENERF)

The meaning of the term "large datasets" is elusive due to its relation to available computing resources, such as processor speed and memory. Two decades ago, a 500 KB dataset was considered large; now the processing limit is in the gigabyte range. Specifically, for relational algorithms that deal with distances between objects, the main limitation is the amount of computer memory available. For example, a PC with 2GB of memory can directly handle a square distance matrix between about 16,000 objects, number that can go up to ~45,000 if the internal memory increases to 16 GB. For comparison, as of February 2008, GenBank (Benson et al., 2008) contains about 82 million sequences from about 260,000 different organisms. Even employing various strategies to increase storage, such as sparse matrices and parallel processing, a gap of several orders of magnitude still exists between the number of the possible objects (sequences) to compare and the storage capability. This gap needs to be bridged by using modified algorithms able to integrate information obtained from various parts of the data.

Aside of the internal memory availability problem, there are other difficulties in handling large relational datasets that new algorithms have to address, such as processing speed and numerical stability. One possible approach to modifying existent algorithms for handling large relational datasets can be summarized as sample-process-extend (SPE); that is, the regular algorithm application is preceded by a sampling scheme and followed by an extension procedure. Among the clustering algorithms developed based on the SPE framework, we mention bigVAT (Huband et al., 2005), sVAT (Hathaway et al., 2006), geFFCM (Bezdek et al, 2006a) and eNERF (Bezdek et al., 2006, Wang et al., 2008). In what follows, we discuss eNERF in more detail.

Relational clustering can be defined as a method for assigning C labels to a set of N objects O = {o_1, ..., o_N} using the dissimilarity between them. Based on the type of labeling, we distinguish two classes of relational clustering algorithms: hard and fuzzy (or soft). Hard clustering algorithms are those in which an object can have only one label at a time, or, in other words, any given object belongs to only one group. On the other hand, fuzzy relational clustering algorithms may label an object with multiple labels, i.e., they allow the object memberships in multiple groups. The outcome of the hard labeling may be represented as a list L, L = {l_1, ...,l_N}, where l_j ∈ [1,C] is the label assigned to object o_j. However, this type of representation does not easily extend to the fuzzy clustering case. To allow for the extension, we represent the outcome of the hard clustering as a C × N matrix, U, called membership matrix, in which the l_j^{th} element of jth column is 1 if object o_j belongs to cluster l_j and all the other elements of the column are 0. We can easily see that, by using the membership matrix, we are able to represent multiple cluster membership degrees by assigning numbers in the [0,1] interval to other elements from the jth column.

eNERF is a relational clustering algorithm that compute fuzzy memberships, U={u_{ij}} $_{i∈[1,C],j∈[1,N]}$, U∈M_{fCN}, in C clusters for a set of N objects O={o_1, ..., o_N}, given the dissimilarity matrix between the objects D_N={d_{ij}}$_{i,j∈[1,N]}$. The elements of the membership matrix U, u_{ij}, are subjected to two conditions: 1) the sum of the memberships of any object j∈[1,N] in all clusters has to sum to 1, and 2) any cluster i∈[1,C] has to have some objects assigned to it. Formally, we can define the set of fuzzy partition matrices of size C×N, M_{fCN}, as:

$$M_{fCN} = \left\{ U_{C \times N} \Big| u_{ij} \in \left[0,1\right], \sum_{i=1}^{C} u_{ij} = 1, \forall j \in \left[1.N\right]; \sum_{j=1}^{N} u_{ij} > 0, \forall i \in \left[1,C\right] \right\}$$

(1)

The fuzzy memberships $U=\{u_{ij}\}_{i\in[1,C],j\in[1,N]}$ can be "hardened" by setting $u_{kj}=1$ for $k=\text{argmax}(u_{ij})_{i\in[1,C]}$, for any $j=[1,N]$, and $u_{ij}=0$ for any $i=[1,C]$, $i\neq k$. That is, object j is assigned to only one cluster, cluster k, for which its membership is maximum. Algorithms such as hierarchical clustering and Markov clustering produce hard partitions of the data.

Example 1. Consider N=3 gene products o_1, o_2 and o_3. Gene products o_1 and o_3 have known Gene Ontology annotations, GO_i i.e. $o_1=\{GO_1\}$ and $o_3=\{GO_2\}$, while o_2 is an unknown gene product. The question that we try to answer is: what are the functions of o_2? To find its function, we will need to annotate o_2 with Gene Ontology terms. All three gene products have known (amino acid) sequences. Using a sequence comparison algorithm, such as BLAST or Smith-Waterman (Smith and Waterman, 1981), we obtain a dissimilarity matrix D_3 that may look like:

$$D_3 = \begin{bmatrix} 0 & 0.4 & 0.9 \\ 0.4 & 0 & 0.6 \\ 0.9 & 0.6 & 0 \end{bmatrix}$$

Assume that, based on their dissimilarity matrix D_3, the three gene products are grouped in two clusters using a fuzzy clustering procedure (such as NERFCM, presented later in this chapter). The outcome of the clustering is a fuzzy partition U_{f23} of the kind given by (1) that may look like:

$$U_{f23} = \begin{bmatrix} 0.9 & 0.6 & 0.1 \\ 0.1 & 0.4 & 0.9 \end{bmatrix}.$$

In the above fuzzy membership matrix, o_2 belongs with degree 0.6 to cluster 1 and with degree 0.4 to cluster 2. The fuzzy membership matrix formalism allows us to describe gene product o_2 as a member, in some degree, of both cluster 1 and cluster 2. As a consequence, based on the "guilt by association" conjecture, we can infer both a GO_1 and a GO_2 functionality for o_2 with confidences of 0.6 and 0.4, respectively. A "hardened" version of U_{f23}, U_{h23}, is given below:

$$U_{h23} = \begin{bmatrix} 1 & 1 & 0 \\ 0 & 0 & 1 \end{bmatrix},$$

where, o_2 was assigned to the group in which it had the maximum membership (i.e. group 1, therefore $u_{21}=1$ and $u_{22}=0$). Since o_2 has been irrevocably assigned to cluster 1, any information about its GO_2 function is lost.

The eNERF algorithm requires that the elements of the dissimilarity matrix between N objects (also called relational matrix) $D_N = \left\{ d_{ij} \middle| i, j \in [1, N] \right\}$ satisfy the following conditions:

1. $d_{ii}=0$, for all $i\in [1,N]$,
2. $d_{jk}\geq 0$, for all $j,k\in [1,N]$,
3. $d_{jk}=d_{kj}$, for all $j,k\in [1,N]$.

If the dissimilarity matrix D_N was obtained by computing the distances between the objects represented in some feature space $FS \subset R^p$, then D_N is called Euclidean. In general, if D_N was obtained by employing a dissimilarity measure between objects, such as computing the sequence dissimilarity using BLAST (Altschul et al., 1990), it might not be Euclidean. In the mean time, if D_N is large, hence not loadable in the computer memory, we cannot apply regular fuzzy relational algorithms such as NERFCM (Hathaway & Bezdek, 1994). The eNERF algorithm was designed to handle large, non-Euclidean, relational data. The eNERF algorithm has three steps:

- **sampling**: the size of the dissimilarity matrix, D_N, is reduced in order to allow loading into memory and/or for speed-up of the clustering procedure. The size reduction is achieved by choosing only n objects of the total of N, n<<N, for further processing. The n sampled objects have to represent all the clusters present in the data and, most importantly, to allow the dissimilarity matrix D_n to be loaded in the memory. The sampling algorithm is discussed in more detail in the next subsection;

- **clustering**: given the dissimilarity matrix and the number of clusters, the fuzzy memberships of the n sampled objects in the C clusters, $U_n = \{u_{ij}\}_{i \in [1,C], j \in [1,n]}$, are computed. In this step, the regular non-Euclidean relational fuzzy c-means algorithm, NERFCM (Hathaway & Bezdek, 1994), is used. We briefly describe NERFCM in a following subsection;

- **extension**: given U_n and D_N, the fuzzy memberships U_N for all N objects are computed. The extension procedure is discussed later in this section.

Sampling Scheme

Two sampling schemes for relational data were tried in conjunction with eNERF: progressive sampling (Bezdek et al., 2006) and selective sampling (Wang et al., 2008). Both sampling schemes rely on selecting a set of h "distinguished features" from the set O of N objects, that is, a set of h<<N objects that are as far (dissimilar) from each other as possible. We note that the term "features" is a reminiscence of the fact that the sampling scheme for relational data was adapted from a similar scheme for object data. As a consequence, each row in the dissimilarity matrix D_N is considered an object that has as features the dissimilarities to all the other N-1 objects. In fact, the "distinguished features" (DF) algorithm is a feature selection algorithm that chooses the best features for sampling purposes (Bezdek et al., 2006). Although the choice of good objects as DFs will lead to a good partition (clustering) of O, the choice of DFs is not directly controlled by the clustering algorithm. The distinguished feature (DF) algorithm has the following four steps:

Step 1. Load in memory the dissimilarity matrix D_H for H candidate objects, where H is dictated by the available memory and n<<H<N. D_H is of size H×H.

Step 2. Choose the first row as the first distinguished feature (DF), $m_1 = 1$. Initialize a search array, δ^1, that will store the distances from the current distinguished feature to all the other H objects, $\delta^1 = \left\{\delta_k^1, k \in [1, H]\right\}$, which in this case is the first row of D_H.

Step 3. Compute the ith DF, with index m_i, as the object that is farthest away from the $(i-1)^{th}$ DF. The index of the farthest object, $m_i \in [1,H]$, is given by the index of the maximum element of the δ^{i-1} array. Note that each distinguished feature is an array of length H, which is in fact the m_i^{th} row of D_H.

Step 4. Recompute the search array δ^i by taking the minimum element-wise between δ^{i-1} and the m_i^{th} row of matrix D_H, that is, the kth element of the new search array is given by $\delta_k^j = \min\{\delta_k^{j-1}, d_{m_i k}\}$;

Figure 1. DF Algorithm

DF Algorithm: Select h distinguished features from D_N

Input: D_N, a N×N dissimilarity matrix
  h=number of distinguished features (DF)
  H=number of candidate rows that can be loaded
    in the memory, H<N
Step 1: Load into memory D_H
Step 2: Choose first row as the first DF, m_1=1;
  Initialize a search array: $\delta^1 = [\delta^1_1, .., \delta^1_H] = [d_{m,1}, .., d_{m,H}]$

for $i \in [2,h]$ **do**

  Step 3: $m_i = \arg\max([\delta^{i-1}_1, ..., \delta^{i-1}_H])$

  Step 4: $[\delta^i_1, .., \delta^i_H] = [\min\{\delta^{i-1}_1, d_{m,1}\}, ..., \min\{\delta^{i-1}_H, d_{m,H}\}]$

end
Output: a dissimilarity matrix, $D_{h \times H}$

Step 3 and 4 are repeated h-1 times.

We point out that the "distinguished features" chosen in step 3 of the above DF algorithm must come from the candidate rows still available after previous choices were made. For this purpose, a row availability list has to be maintained - a fact that, for simplicity, we omitted from the algorithm description. A summary of the distinguished features (DF) algorithm is given in Figure 1.

The number and the identity of candidate objects loaded in memory, H, depend on the available memory. The H objects are usually chosen by random sampling of the N objects to be clustered. However, even if we can fit into memory the dissimilarity matrix for H objects, its processing might still be prohibitive time-wise. For this reason, we would like to further choose n samples from the H available to apply the regular clustering on. In the progressive sampling scheme, the first n rows of the matrix D_H are loaded. Additional rows are added until the distribution of the dissimilarities for each distinguished feature approximates the distribution of the entire related row from D_H. Specific details about the progressive sampling procedure can be found in (Bezdek et al., 2006). It was found (Wang et al., 2008), that the progressive scheme is very conservative, often resulting in sample size n close to 50% of H, which still represent an intractable number in some cases. For this reason, in this work we used the selective sampling (SS) scheme described in (Wang et al., 2008).

In the selective sampling scheme, the final n objects are chosen by random sampling of the nearest neighbors of the DFs previously found. The main steps of the SS algorithm are:

Step 1: Load the dissimilarity matrix D_H for H objects chosen by random sampling of the unloadable D_N;

Step 2: Select h rows $\{m_1, ..., m_h\}$ from D_H as distinguished features using the DF algorithm given above. It is recommended (Bezdek et al., 2006) that h is chosen greater than the expected number of clusters, C. Intuitively, if h is too low, it might, indirectly, cause some clusters to be underrepresented mainly when n<<N. If h is too high, i.e. h $\cong$ n, it will increase the time necessary to complete the nearest neighbor search (next step). However, since we have the dissimilarities between objects already computed, the increase in computational time is small for an H of about 20,000 which is the limit imposed by the available memory in a 2009 desktop computer.

Figure 2. SS Algorithm

SS Algorithm: Select n samples from D_N

Input: D_N= an N×N dissimilarity matrix
   n= the desired sample size
   h= the number of DFs, which overestimates the number of clusters C
   H= the number of candidate objects with D_H loadable
Step 1: Obtain D_H = an H×H dissimilarity matrix by random sampling D_N;
Step 2: Select h distinguished features $\{m_1, ..., m_h\}$ from D_H using the DF
   algorithm;
Step 3: Group each of the H objects with its nearest DF:
   for i∈[1,H] **do**
      j= argmin($\{d_{m_1,i}, ..., d_{m_h,i}\}$)
      C_j=$C_j \cup \{i\}$
   end
Step 4: For each DF m_j, j∈[1,h], select a subsample of size $n_j = $ floor(n·| C_j | /H)

Output: D_n= an n×n matrix

Step 3: For each DF, m_j, j∈[1,h] find the set of rows C_j closest to it (i.e. its nearest neighbors). We note that, the neighborhood operations are performed in R^H, i.e. with distinguished features of length H. In (Wang et al., 2008) it is suggested that the DF be vectors in R^N, that is, the neighborhood operations be performed on the rows of the unloadable matrix D_N. While this strategy is possible, it increases the computational complexity of the algorithm, since the search procedure has to be conducted in blocks. In the example presented in this chapter, we did not deal with this problem since we were able to load the entire D_N matrix into memory, in other words, for us $H \equiv N$.

Step 4: From each set of rows C_j, j∈[1,h], choose at random n_j samples where n_j is given by the lower bound of n|C_j|/H and |.| is the number of rows from C_j. We note that, since we rounded off n_j, we might end up with slightly less samples than n. This might be corrected by taking n_h=n-(n_1+...+n_{h-1}). A summary of the SS algorithm is given in Figure 2.

NERFCM Clustering

NERFCM (Hathaway & Bezdek, 1994) is a clustering algorithm for relational data that assigns C labels to the n sampled objects by computing a fuzzy partition matrix $U \in M_{fCn}$ (Eq. 1). Similarly to FCM (Bezdek, 1981), NERCM is an iterative algorithm (alternative optimization) that has three main steps. In the first step, an initial guess, U_0, for the fuzzy partition matrix U=$\{u_{ij}\}_{i \in [1,C], j \in [1,n]}$, is used to compute C cluster centers, v_i, as

$$V_i = \left(\left(u_{i1} \right)^m, \left(u_{i2} \right)^m, ..., \left(u_{in} \right)^m \right) \bigg/ \sum_{j=1}^{n} \left(u_{ij} \right)^m , \; i \in [1,C]. \tag{2}$$

where $m \in (1, \infty)$ is a parameter ("fuzzifier") usually chosen to be m=2. A choice of m toward 1 results in harder (less fuzzy) partitions. The initial guess U_0 can be obtained by random initialization with numbers in [0,1] followed by column normalization. We point out that, unlike FCM that defines the cluster centers as a weighted average of the object vectors by their cluster memberships, NERFCM uses only the cluster memberships for this task. For this reason, the cluster centers in NERFCM are merely normalized memberships of objects in clusters, and they could be seen as a mixture of objects. For example, given the membership matrix U_{f23} from Example 1 and using Eq.(2), we get $\mathbf{v}_1$=(0.56 0.38 0.06). This cluster center may be interpreted as a virtual object that is 56% similar to o_1, 38% similar to o_2 and 6% similar to o_3.

The second step consists in computing the dissimilarity vector $\mathbf{d}_i$ between the ith cluster center and the n objects:

$$\mathbf{d}_i = (D_n \mathbf{v}_i^t) - 0.5(\mathbf{v}_i D_n \mathbf{v}_i^t), \ i \in [1,C],$$ (3)

where D_n is the dissimilarity matrix between the n sampled objects obtained in the previous section. Using again the distance matrix, D_3, from Example 1 and the cluster center, $\mathbf{v}_1$, shown above, we compute the dissimilarity vector of the first cluster center as to all objects as $\mathbf{d}_1$=(0.2 0.26 0.73)^t-0.13=(0.07 0.13 0.6).

Lastly, an updated fuzzy membership matrix, $U'=U_{ij}$ $i \in [1,C], j \in [1,n]$, is computed as:

$$u_{ij}' = \begin{cases} \left(\sum_{k=1}^{C} \left(\frac{d_{ij}}{d_{kj}} \right)^{\frac{1}{m-1}} \right) & if \quad d_{ij} >= \varepsilon \\ 1 & if \quad d_{ij} < \varepsilon \end{cases}$$ (4)

where $i \in [1,C]$ and $j \in [1,n]$. This equation is similar to the related one from FCM (Bezdek 1981). However, note that, since in Eq. (3) the dissimilarities are already squared, Eq. (4) does not have the usual "2" in the 1/(m-1) power exponent. If d_{ij} is smaller than a small value ε, $0<\varepsilon<<1$, u_{ij} is set to 1 and the rest of the memberships in cluster i are set to 0.

If D_n is non-Euclidean, some of the computed dissimilarities from Eq. (3) may be negative at this point and they can not be used as in Eq. (4). To address this problem, NERFCM uses a β-spread transform (Hathaway & Bezdek, 1994) that increments, at each iteration, the non-diagonal elements of D_n with a quantity $\Delta\beta$, given by

$$\beta = \max_{i,j}\{-2d_{ij} / \| \mathbf{v}_i - \mathbf{e}_j \|^2\}$$ (5)

where $\mathbf{e}_j = (0,...,1,...,0) \in R^n$ and e_{ij}=1.

Accordingly, the dissimilarities are modified using:

$$d_{ij} = d_{ij} + \left(\Delta\beta / 2\right) \cdot \|v_i - e\|^2, \ i \in [1,C], j \in [1,n].$$ (6)

The distances d_{ij} that are still negative after the above correction are set to 0. The summary of the NERFCM is given in Figure 3.

Figure 3. NERFCM Algorithm

NERFCM Algorithm: Cluster n samples in C clusters

Input: D_n=an n×n dissimilarity matrix, n<<N
C=the number of clusters,
U_0=an initial guess of the fuzzy membership matrix
MAXIT=maximum number of iterations
DEL=desired fuzzy membership matrix precision
Step 1: Initialize U=U_0, it=0, β=0, δ=BIG_NUMBER
   while δ<DEL and it<MAXIT
      Step 2: **for** i=1,...,C
            Compute v_i using Eq. (2)
         end
      Step 3: **for** i=1,...,C
            Compute d_i using Eq. (3)
         end
      if any d_{ij}<0
         compute correction $\Delta\beta$ using (5)
         modify distances d_{ij} using (6)
         if some d_{ij} are still <0, set d_{ij}=0
      end
      Step 4: re-compute fuzzy memberships U' using (4)
      it=it+1
      δ=||U'-U|| ; U=U';
   end
Output: U_{fcn}=a C×n fuzzy membership matrix
      $\{v_1, ..., v_c\}$=C 1×n cluster "centers"

Extension Scheme

After the fuzzy memberships for the n sampled objects, U_{fCn}, have been computed, an extension scheme is necessary to obtain the memberships in the C clusters for the rest of the (N-n) objects that were not part of the sample used in the clustering calculation. The initial extension scheme proposed in (Bezdek et al., 2006), consists in adding the (N-n) objects one-by-one and iteratively computing U_{fCn+1} using the Eqs. (2) through (6). Even by precomputing several variables, this method is extremely slow due to its iterative nature (Wang et al., 2008). Instead, we propose a simpler method that computes the dissimilarities in Eq. (3) between the (N-n) unsampled objects to the C cluster "centers" of dimension n, $\{v_i\}$, obtained in the previous step (see the output of the NERFCM algorithm above). More precisely, Eq. (3) becomes:

$$\mathbf{d}_i = (D_{N,n}\mathbf{v}_i^t) - 0.5(\mathbf{v}_i D_n \mathbf{v}_i^t), \ i \in [1,C], j \in [n+1,N], \tag{7}$$

Because the new extension algorithm is not iterative, it is at least one order of magnitude faster than the one proposed in (Bezdek et al., 2006). Moreover, although the previous extension algorithm is potentially more precise than one proposed here, they give similar results on our BLAST dataset for reasons that will become obvious in the next section. The proposed extension algorithm is summarized in Figure 4.

EXTENDED CORRELATION CLUSTER VALIDITY, ECCV

The Correlation Cluster Validity (CCV) (Popescu et al., 2008) is a validity measure for relational data sets. Assume we want to estimate the number of clusters for N objects, given the dissimilairty matrix D_N between them, where N is very large. To reduce the computational time, we employ the same sampling strategy as in eNERF. The resulting cluster validity is denoted as extended CCV (eCCV). eCCV consists of two steps: first, apply the SS sampling algorithm to reduce D_N to D_n (n<<N) and then estimate the number of clusters in D_n using CCV. For a fixed value of C, let U be the final fuzzy partition matrix obtained, say, by running NERFCM on D_n. The main idea of CCV is to define a reconstruction matrix U* as:

$$U^* = 1 - U^t U / (\max\{U^t U\}).$$
(8)

The assumption used in CCV to find the estimated number of clusters, C, is that the best grouping results in a maximum correlation between U* and D_n, that is,

$$C = \arg\max\left\{corr\left(U_k^*, D_n\right)\right\}$$
(9)

where U_k^* denotes the reconstruction matrix generated by the k×n fuzzy membership matrix obtained by grouping the n objects in k clusters. Here, the correlation between the two matrices will be computed using the Pearson correlation. The summary of the eCCV algorithm is given in Figure 5.

REFSEQ GENE PRODUCT DATASET

To test our clustering methodology, on September 12th 2008 we downloaded the RefSeq database (Pruit et al., 2007) build 36.3 in fasta format. RefSeq is a non-redundant, curated, sequence database intended to provide a solid foundation for genome annotation and gene characterization. The dataset consisted of 37,742 sequences of which about 60% belonged to known genes. About 40% of the human genes are either unknown or they have unknown function at this time.

Figure 4. Extension Algorithm

Extension Algorithm: Compute the fuzzy memberships $U_{C:(N-n)}$ for the rest of N-n unsampled objects

Input: $D_{N,n}$=a N×n dissimilarity matrix
$U_{C,n}$=a C×n fuzzy membership matrix
$\{v_1,...v_n\}$ cluster centers of the C clusters
Step 1: Compute d_{ij} using Eq. (7);
Step 2: Compute $U_{C,N}$ using Eq. (4)
Output: $U_{C,N}$ the fuzzy membership matrix for all N points in C clusters

The gene product similarity was computed using BLAST with the "-p" option (protein against proteins) and a cutoff E-score of 10. The similarity between gene products p_i and p_j, s_{ij}, was computed using the truncated E-score (Enright, Van Dongen & Ouzounis, 2002) as

$$S_{ij} = \begin{cases} 0 \: if \: E-score < 0 \\ 1 \: if \: E-score > 100 \\ E-score(i,j)/100 \: else \end{cases} \qquad (10)$$

We mention that the above E-score represents the confidence (so called, "p value") of the sequence similarity score, and not the score itself. For example, if two sequences, s_1 and s_2, have a BLAST score of 385 with a p-value of 0.0001, then the E-score $=-\log_{10}(0.0001)=4$. In addition, the score of s_1 vs. s_2 may differ from the score of s_2 vs. s_1, resulting in a non-symmetrical similarity matrix. Consequently, we set $s_{ij}=s_{ji}=0.5(s_{ij}+s_{ji})$. The resulting similarity matrix, S_{37000}, had about 1.5 million non-zero elements, that is, it was only 0.1% full (i.e., is a sparse matrix).

There are two characteristics of the RefSeq data set that represent a serious challenge for our clustering strategy. First, it is estimated that there are about 9,300 gene product families in our dataset (Finn et al., 2008). These families can be further grouped in 283 clans (groups of related families). The clan grouping was manually performed (Finn et al., 2008), so we consider it to be highly reliable. This information might suggest a value for the number of clusters we should use in our eNERF algorithm. Second, the distribution of the population in the above families is extremely unbalanced (Enright, Van Dongen & Ouzounis, 2002). About 30% of the families have only one member, 3% have more than 50 members, and only 0.3% have over 300 members. This distribution information suggests that the upper bound of the number of families that we can detect using a 1:10 sampling ratio is around 300, a number that is roughly equal to the number of clans. However, the family size distribution will seriously hinder any sampling strategy. To address the above challenges we preceded our analysis by a preprocessing step, described in the next section, aimed at removing the families with few members.

Figure 5. eCCV Algorithm

eCCV Algorithm: Estimate the number of cluster for N objects

```
Input: D_N=a N×N dissimilarity matrix
       n=sample size
       m=fuzzifier value
       [C_1,C_2]=an interval for searching the number of clusters
Step 1: Compute D_n using SS algorithm;
       for i∈[C_1,C_2] do
         Step 2: Run NERFCM on D_n with i number of clusters and
                 fuzzifier m, U_i=NERFCM(D_n, m, i).
         Step 3: Compute II using Eq. (8)
         Step 4: Cor(i)=Pearson(U_i', D_n)
       end
Step 5: C = argmax_{i∈[C_1,C_2]}{Cor(i)};
Output: C the estimated number of clusters
```

ENERF EXPERIMENTS ON THE REFSEQ DATASET

Preprocessing of the RefSeq Dataset

Because of its sparse nature, the entire S_{37000} matrix was easily loadable in memory (total size about 20 MB). However, when it was transformed into a dissimilarity matrix $D_{37000}=1-S_{37000}$ it required about 10 GB of data, memory still available on a high-end desktop system (Windows XP64 with 16 GB of memory). After this transformation, the rows and the columns of the D_{37000} dissimilarity matrix were rearranged using the *Visual Assessment of Cluster Tendency* (VAT) algorithm (Bezdek et al., 2002) which is essentially a version of the minimum spanning tree algorithm. The result of the reordering was

Figure 6. The VAT-reordered distance matrix between the first 2000 gene products of the DV_{37000} matrix (upper-left corner; black=0, white=1)

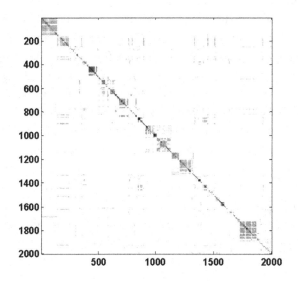

Figure 7. The number of gene products with similarity greater than 0 for each reordered gene product in the RefSeq dataset

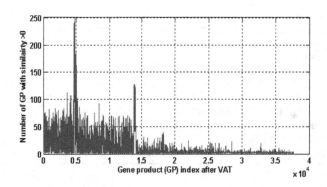

a distance matrix denoted DV_{37000}. The intention of the reordering was to separate the large clusters from the small clusters. The first 2000 reordered gene products from the upper-left corner of the DV_{37000} are shown in Figure 6.

In Figure 7 we plotted, for each of the 37,742 reordered gene products, the total number of gene products that were found to have some level of sequence similarity (as a result of Eq. (10)) to it.

If we assume that the family size is proportional to the number of non-zero similarities per gene products, we can see in Figure 7 that VAT did a reasonable job in arranging the large families (over about 20 members-see the cutoff at index 15,000) at the beginning (left side in Figure 7) of the [1, 37742] range. Consequently, we chose to continue our analysis using only the first 15,000 gene products (with indices between 1 to 15,000), which means that we used only the 15,000×15,000 upper-left corner of the rearranged matrix DV_{37000}, or, equivalently, DV_{15000}. The choice of further use only the gene products (i.e. DV_{15000} matrix) that had more than about 20 neighbors, was made in order to ensure that a 1 in 5 sampling rate would not drastically change the cluster structure.

Choosing the Fuzzifier, m and the Number of Samples, n

In order to choose the value of the fuzzifier m, we used the 360×360 upper-left corner of the DV_{37000}, denoted as DV_{360}. Since the value of m depends on the characteristics of the data and not on its size, we chose only a small portion of DV_{3700} to perform this experiment. By visual inspection we estimated that there are 3 clusters in DV_{360}: the first one with about 150 members and the other two with about 100 members each (see Figure 8).

The eNERF performance was estimated with a method similar to one used in *Correlation Cluster Validity* (CCV) (Popescu et al., 2008) by computing the correlation between the reconstruction matrix U^* (see Eq. (8)) and distance matrix (DV_{360} in this case). In Figure 8.b we show the reconstruction matrix U^* obtained from the fuzzy membership matrix U computed using eNERF with m=1.2 and n=60

Figure 8. a). The DV_{360} distance matrix. We assumed that there are 3 clusters in DV_{360}. b) The U^* matrix for m=1.2 and n=60. The Pearson correlation between a) and b) is 0.74

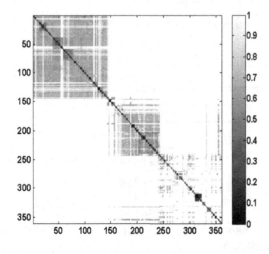
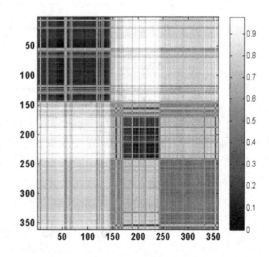

on the DV_{360} data. The resulting correlation between U^* and DV_{360} is 0.74, which is a reasonably high value. More correlation values for m={1.1, 1.2, 1.4, 1.6, 2} and n={60, 90, 120, 150, 180, 240, 360} are shown in Figure 9. From this figure, we conclude that eNERF is relatively resilient to down-sampling (i.e., choice of n), maintaining a relatively constant performance over sampling range from 1/1 to 1/6. Also, the maximum performance was obtained for m=1.2. Consequently, we use m=1.2 in all the subsequent experiments. Moreover, we will use a maximum down-sampling ratio of 1/5 throughout our experiments.

In the previous experiments, we observed that increasing the dynamic range of our data set (from [0,1]) might improve the clustering results. As explained in the previous section, our similarity score came from taking the logarithm of the sequence similarity confidence. As a consequence, we investigated the idea of using an exponential transformation to improve cluster separation. When the similarity SV_{360} data set was transformed to a dissimilarity using

$$DVL_{360} = 10^{(1-SV_{360})} - 1,$$ (11)

we obtained a correlation value between eNERF(DVL_{360}) and U^* equal to 0.83, which represents an increase of 10% versus the non-transformed version. For the experiments that follow we use the transform shown in Eq. (11) and denoted by "L".

eNERF Size Limit

Application of eNERF on the DVL_{15000} distance matrix with m=1.2, n=3000 and C=300 did not result in a correlation coefficient higher than 0.36. Comparing the two matrices, DVL_{15000} and resulting U^*, side by side (see Figure 10), we see that, except for the two big clusters around index 5000 and 14000

Figure 9. The variation of correlation index between U^* and DV_{360} for various numbers of samples, n, and fuzzifiers, m

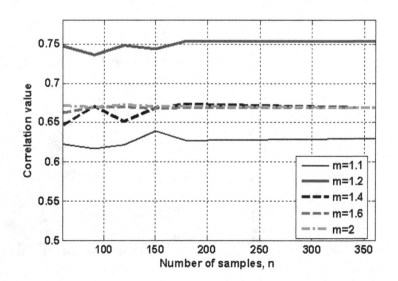

respectively, no other gene product groups are visible in the U* matrix. Further reduction in n (increase in sampling rate) decreases even further the correlation coefficient.

It seems that eNERF can not directly handle a 15000×15000 distance matrix. We suspect NERFCM performance, the imprecision in the number of clusters, the initial guess of the membership matrix, and the harsh nature of the data (as explained at the beginning of the results section) for this problem.

The question now is: what is the maximum size that can be handled by eNERF in these circumstances? To answer this question, we applied eNERF for various distance matrix sizes, N_s, selected from the upper-left corner of DVL_{15000}, which we denote as DVL_{N_s}. For each size N_s, the number of samples was kept at $n=N_s/5$. The number of clusters was determined by visual inspection of the DVL_{N_s} matrix (see Figure 11, row 2). The correlation results for various data sizes for both NERFCM and eNERF are given in Figure 11 and Figure 12.

In Figure 12, we see that both NERFCM and eNERF performance drop at about $N_s=1000$. As a consequence, we chose $N_s=1000$ as the largest data size that we directly run eNERF without a good estimate of the initialization matrix. Also, this result made us belive that, in fact, NERFCM is the primary reason for the eNERF failure (the nature of the data set being the second).

Since we are not able to process directly the entire set, DVL_{15000}, we propose a piece-wise eNERF initialization procedure that produces estimates for the number of clusters C and the membership matrix, U_0.

Piece-Wise Cluster Number and Membership Estimation Using eNERF

The DVL_{15000} dataset was divided in 15 non-overlapping blocks of size 1000×1000. The blocks were chosen on the main diagonal where the majority of the non-zero similarities were arranged by VAT (see Figure 12). For each block, b, we first estimate the number of clusters, C_b, $b \in [1,15]$, using the eCCV procedure previously described in this chapter (see Eq. (8) and (9)). Then, the eNERF algorithm is applied

Figure 10. a) The DVL_{15000} BLAST-derived distance matrix and b) the U^* matrix obtained by applying eNERF with m=1.2, n=3000 and C=300

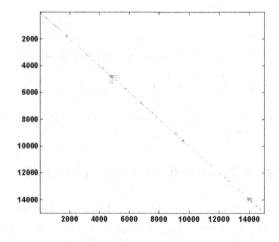
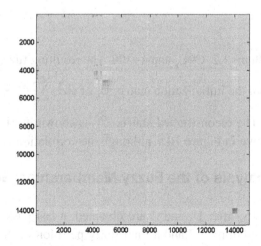

Figure 11. The correlation values for NERFCM and eNERF for various data sizes

Data size, N_t	250	370	400	500	650	1000	1200	1400	1700	2000
#clusters, C	3	4	5	7	9	12	15	17	20	25
NERFCM	0.83	0.74	0.79	0.81	0.79	0.75	0.66	0.35	0.33	0.41
eNERF	0.83	0.76	0.79	0.78	0.76	0.74	0.5	0.58	0.43	0.3

Figure 12. Correlation values for NERFCM and eNERF for various data sizes, N

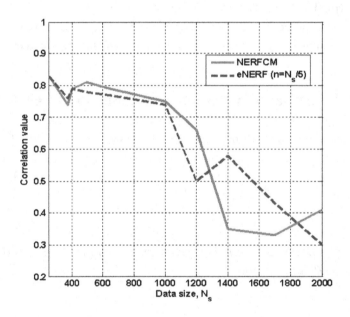

with m=1.2, C=C_b and n=200. The resulting fuzzy membership matrices $\{U_b\}_{b \in [1,15]}$ are concatenated to form the initialization matrix U_0 of size $\sum_{b=1}^{15} C_b \times 15000$ (see Figure 13). In our case $\sum_{b=1}^{15} C_b = 159$.

The reconstructed matrix U_0^* is shown in Figure 14.a. We see that U_0^* is closer to the data matrix shown in Figure 10.a, although the correlation is still low at 0.38.

Analysis of the Fuzzy Memberships Generated by eNERF on the RefSeq Data

Lastly, after U_0 and C are obtained, a last pass of eNERF was performed on the DVL_{15000} data with n=3000, m=1.2 and a final fuzzy partition of the data, U_N, was obtained. The resulting reconstructed

Figure 13. The initialization membership matrix (159 ×15000) generated using the piece-wise procedure

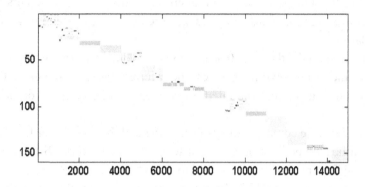

Figure 14. a) The reconstruction matrix, U_0^*], obtained using the piece-wise eNERF procedure; b) The reconstruction matrix, U_n^*, obtained using eNERF with C=159 and U_0 obtained using the piece-wise procedure

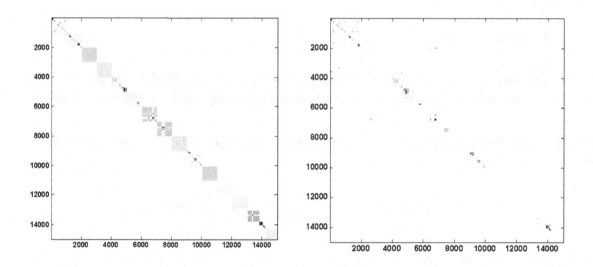

matrix, U_n^*, shown in Figure 14.b, has a correlation value of 0.6 for the original data matrix, DVL_{15000}. Although this value is lower than the "good" eNERF correlation values shown in Figure 12, it is 60% higher than the correlation obtained without the piece-wise procedure.

The fuzzy partition U_N can now be used to annotate or to summarize the RefSeq clusters using a procedure similar to the method shown in (Popescu et al., 2004). However, here we performed a simplified cluster analysis based on hardening the fuzzy partition matrix U_N (as explained in Example 1). After the hardening process, only about 25% (40) of the 159 clusters, more precisely { 3, 5, 8, 9, 10, 13, 14, 15, 16, 17, 18, 20, 21, 23, 28, 42, 46, 51, 52, 53, 54, 58, 64, 68, 73, 78, 83, 85, 94, 95, 98, 101, 103, 104, 116, 142, 144, 157, 158, 159}, were populated. One cluster had 11,314 members with max membership of 1/159. About 0.2% (3910) of the U_N fuzzy memberships were higher than 2/159, which is not surprising if we remember that the original similarity matrix had only 0.1% non-zero elements. The distance matrix for the 3704 gene products identified in the hardened clusters is shown in Figure 15. We see that the clustering procedure produced expected results by grouping gene products that had strong BLAST similarity.

Each hardened cluster contained about 20% unknown proteins (denoted as "LOCxxxxxxx" in Figure 16). The properties of these unknown proteins can be inferred based on the Gene Ontology functions of the known gene products using the computed fuzzy membership matrix as described in (Popescu et al., 2004).

The first cluster in Figure 16 contains numerous members of the zinc finger family and forkhead box family. These two families are both involved in transcription; the forkhead box members are transcription factors and the zinc finger members are related to DNA binding. Similarly, the two families listed in cluster no. 2, solute carrier and butyrophilin, have functions related to cellular membrane. In general, the computed clusters contain members of multiple families, which is what we intended. Fuzzy clustering is intended to group gene products with low degree of homology (sequence similarity under 40%) that have a common functions. However, further, more detailed, biological analysis is necessary to determine if the clustered gene products share protein domains (hence functions) (see an example of such analysis in (Enright, Van Dongen & Ouzounis, 2002)) or if they were mistakenly clustered together.

CONCLUSION

We presented a relational fuzzy clustering algorithm for large datasets, eNERF, and a related cluster validity measure, eCCV. The algorithm eNERF has been previously validated on large synthetic rela-

Figure 15. The distance matrix for the 3704 gene products assigned to clusters using the hardening procedure (Example 1)

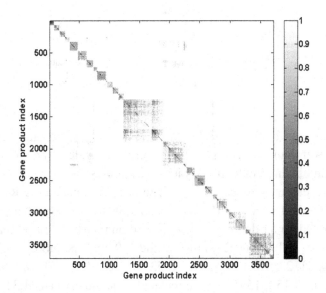

Figure 16. The gene products identified in the first 12 most populous clusters

Cluster no.	Cluster index	Cluster size	Gene products examples	Family examples
1	42	463	ZNF655, ZNF446, ZNF641, ZNF252, FOXD1, FOXI1, FOXN4	zinc finger, forkhead box protein
2	144	233	SLC12A6, SLC29A3, SLC25A35, BTNL2, BTNL8	solute carrier, butyrophilin
3	46	190	ABCD4, ABCG1, ABCG5, HOXA1, HOXC8	ATP-binding casette, homeobox domain
4	73	167	TMEM141, TMEM177, TMEM219, TMEM53, DLG1, DLG2	transmembrane proteins, channel associated protein
5	104	166	PPP1R9A, PPP2R2D, PPP2R5A, PPP2R5C, RAB3C, RAB7A	phosphoprotein phosphatase, RAS family
6	53	155	RNF38, RNF38, MAP7, MAPT	ring finger, microtubule associated protein
7	14	147	CD46, CD8B, IGH@, IGSF6	antigen, immunoglobulin related
8	18	145	OR10K1, OR11H12, OR4X1, OR51B4, CCDC15, CCDC86	olfactory receptors, coil-coil domain
9	98	129	TMEM151B, TMEM195, TMEM183A, OR10A7, OR10H3, OR4D10	transmembrane protein, olfactory receptors
10	78	121	KRT18P50, KRTAP5, GTF2A1L, GTF2IRD2B	keratin, general transcription factor
11	15	111	ZNF428, ZNF607, ZNF607, SLC18A3, SLC14A1	zinc finger, solute carrier
12	103	104	FBXW7, FBXO30, FRMD7, FRMPD2	F-Box domain, FERM domain

tional data sets obtained from a small number of balanced (the number of points in each cluster is about equivalent) Gaussian clusters. Here we examined eNERF's behavior on a large bioinformatics data set of about 37,000 sequences. The initial results were unexpected, partially due to the characteristics of the dataset (numerous, unbalanced clusters) and partially to reasons inherent to the eNERF algorithm, such as initialization and number of clusters. We overcame the algorithm shortcomings with a piece-wise procedure for finding a reasonable initialization for the fuzzy membership matrix, U_0, and by estimating the number of clusters with a cluster validity measure, eCCV. The clusters obtained after adapting the eNERF algorithm to the characteristics of the RefSeq data set showed reasonable similarity and correlation to the original distance matrix.

Our analysis raised several questions. Why is NERFCM failing for BLAST matrices larger than 1000×1000? Can NERFCM be defined on a similarity matrix instead of a dissimilarity one in order to take advantage of the sparseness of the former? Can fuzzy memberships be used for functional annotation of the 30% un-annotated human gene products? We hope to answer to all these questions in future work!

REFERENCES

Altschul, S. F., Gish, W., Miller, W., Myers, E. W., & Lipman, D. J. (1990). Basic local alignment search tool. *Journal of Molecular Biology, 215*(3), 403–410.

Benson, D. A., Karsch-Mizrachi, I., Lipman, D. J., Ostell, J., & Wheeler, D. (2008). GenBank. *Nucleic Acids Research, 36*(Database Issue), D25–D30. doi:10.1093/nar/gkm929

Bezdek, J. C. (1981). *Pattern recognition with fuzzy objective function algorithms.* New York: Plenum.

Bezdek, J. C., & Hathaway, R. J. (2002). VAT: A tool for visual assessment of (cluster) tendency. In *Proceedings of the International Joint Conference of Neural Networks* (pp. 2225-2230). Piscataway, NJ: IEEE Press.

Bezdek, J. C., & Hathaway, R. J. (2006a). Elastic control of subsample size in the geFFCM algorithm. In *Proceedings of 5th International Symposium on Intelligent Manufacturing Systems* (pp. 9-18).

Bezdek, J. C., Hathaway, R. J., Huband, J. M., Leckie, C., & Kotagiri, R. (2006). Approximate clustering in very large relational data. *International Journal of Intelligent Systems, 21,* 817–841. doi:10.1002/int.20162

Enright, A. J., Van Dongen, S., & Ouzounis, C. A. (2002). An efficient algorithm for the large-scale detection of protein families. *Nucleic Acids Research, 30*(7), 1575–1584. doi:10.1093/nar/30.7.1575

Finn, R. D., Tate, J., Mistry, J., Coggill, P. C., Sammut, J. S., & Hotz, H. R. (2008). The Pfam protein families database. *Nucleic Acids Research, 36*(Database Issue), D281–D288. doi:10.1093/nar/gkm960

Guha, S., Rastogi, R., & Shim, K. (1998). CURE: An efficient clustering algorithm for large databases. In *Proceedings of the ACM SIGMOD Int. Conf. on Management of Data* (pp. 73-84).

Hathaway, R. J., & Bezdek, J. C. (1994). NERF c-means: Non-Euclidean relational fuzzy clustering. *Pattern Recognition, 27,* 429–437. doi:10.1016/0031-3203(94)90119-8

Hathaway, R. J., Bezdek, J. C., & Huband, J. M. (2006). Scalable visual assessment of cluster tendency for large data sets. *Pattern Recognition, 39,* 1315–1324. doi:10.1016/j.patcog.2006.02.011

Havens, T. C., Keller, J. M., Rehrig, E. M., Appel, H. M., Popescu, M., Schultz, J. C., & Bezdek, J. C. (2008). Cluster analysis of bioinformatics data composed of microarray expression and gene ontology annotations. In *Proceedings of the Annual NAFIPS Conference,* New York.

Huband, J. M., Bezdek, J. C., & Hathaway, R. J. (2005). bigVAT: Visual assessment of cluster tendency for large data sets. *Pattern Recognition, 38,* 1875–1886. doi:10.1016/j.patcog.2005.03.018

Ouzunis, C.A., & Karp, P.D. (2002). The past, present and future of genome-wide re-annotation. *Genome Biology, 3*(2), comment2001.1-2001.6.

Popescu, M., Bezdek, J. C., Keller, J. M., Havens, T. C., & Huband, J. M. (2008). A new cluster validity measure for bioinformatics relational datasets. In *Proceedings of the World Congress on Computational Intelligence, WCCI2008,* Hong Kong (pp. 726-731).

Popescu, M., Keller, J. M., Mitchell, J. A., & Bezdek, J. C. (2004). Functional summarization of gene product clusters using gene ontology similarity measures. In M. Palaniswami, B. Krishnmachari, A. Sowmya, & S. Challa (Eds.), *Proc. of the 2004 ISSNIP* (pp. 553-559). Piscataway, NJ: IEEE Press.

Pruitt, K. D., Tatusova, T., & Maglott, D. R. (2007). NCBI reference sequence (RefSeq): A curated non-redundant sequence database of genomes, transcripts and proteins. *Nucleic Acids Research, 35*(Database issue), D61–D65. doi:10.1093/nar/gkl842

Smith, T. F., & Waterman, M. S. (1981). Identification of common molecular subsequences. *Journal of Molecular Biology, 147*, 195–197. doi:10.1016/0022-2836(81)90087-5

Stothard, P., & Wishart, D. S. (2006). Automated bacterial genome analysis and annotation. *Current Opinion in Microbiology, 9*, 505–510. doi:10.1016/j.mib.2006.08.002

Wang, L., Bezdek, J. C., Leckie, C., & Kotagiri, R. (2008). Selective sampling for approximate clustering of very large data sets. *International Journal of Intelligent Systems, 23*(3), 313–331. doi:10.1002/int.20268

Xu, D., Bondugula, R., Popescu, M., & Keller, J. (2008). *Applications of fuzzy logic in bioinformatics*. London: Imperial College Press.

Compilation of References

Aggarwal, C. C., Han, J., Wang, J., & Yu, P. S. (2003). A framework for clustering evolving data streams. In *VLDB '2003: Proceedings of the 29th international conference on Very large data bases* (pp. 81-92). VLDB Endowment.

Aggarwal, C. C., Han, J., Wang, J., & Yu, P. S. (2004). A framework for projected clustering of high dimensional data streams. In *VLDB '04: Proceedings of the Thirtieth international conference on Very large data bases* (pp. 852-863). VLDB Endowment.

Agichtein, E., Brill, E., & Dumais, S. (2006). Improving Web search ranking by incorporating user behavior information. In *Proceeding of the 29th Annual International ACM Conference on Research and Development in Information Retrieval (SIGIR '06)*, Seattle, Washington, USA (pp. 19-26). New York: ACM.

Agrawal, R., & Shafer, J. C. (1996). Parallel mining of association rules. *IEEE Transactions on Knowledge and Data Engineering, 8*(6), 962–969. doi:10.1109/69.553164

Agrawal, R., & Srikant, R. (1994). Fast algorithms for mining association rules. In *Proc. of the 20th Int. Conf. on Very Large Databases (VLDB 1994)*, Santiago de Chile (pp. 487-499). San Mateo, CA, USA: Morgan Kaufmann.

Agrawal, R., Gupta, A., & Sarawagi, S. (1995). *Modeling multidimensional databases.* Armonk, NY: IBM.

Agrawal, R., Imielinksi, T., & Swami, A. (1993). Mining Association Rule Between Sets of Items in Large Databases. In *Proceedings of the 1993 ACM SIGMOD international conference on Management of data* (pp. 207-216). New York: ACM.

Agrawal, R., Mannila, H., Srikant, R., Toivonen, H., & Verkamo, A. (1996). Fast discovery of association rules. In U. M. Fayyad, G. Piatetsky-Shapiro, P. Smyth, & R. Uthurusamy (Eds.), *Advances in knowledge discovery and data mining* (pp. 307-328). Cambridge, MA, USA: AAAI Press / MIT Press.

Alhajj, R., & Kaya, M. (2003). Integrating Fuzziness into OLAP for Multidimensional Fuzzy Association Rules Mining. In *Proceedings of the Third IEEE International Conference on Data Mining* (p. 469). Washington, DC: IEEE Computer Society.

Altera Corporation. (2002). *Excalibur device overview (ver 2.0, May 2002), data sheet.* Retrieved December 1, 2008, from http://www.altera.com/literature/ds/ds_arm.pdf

Altera Corporation. (2008). *NIOS II processor reference handbook (ver 8.1, Nov 2008).* Retrieved December 1, 2008, from http://www.altera.com/literature/lit_nio2.jsp

Altschul, S. F., Gish, W., Miller, W., Myers, E. W., & Lipman, D. J. (1990). Basic local alignment search tool. *Journal of Molecular Biology, 215*(3), 403–410.

Amdahl, G. M. (1967). Validity of the single processor approach to achieving large scale computing capabilities. In *Proceedings of the AFIPS spring joint computer conference* (Vol. 30, pp. 483-485).

Amirkhanzdeh, R., Khoei, A., & Hadidi, Kh. (2005). A mixed-signal current-mode fuzzy logic controller. [AEÜ]. *International Journal of Electronics and Communications, 59*, 177–184. doi:10.1016/j.aeue.2004.11.019

An, A., & Cercone, N. (2004). An Empirical Study on Rule Quality Measures. In *Proceedings of the 7th International Workshop on New Directions in Rough Sets, Data Mining, and Granular-Soft Computing* (LNCS 1711, pp. 482-491). Berlin, Germany: Springer-Verlag.

Angryk, R. A., & Petry, F. E. (2005). Mining Multi-Level Associations with Fuzzy Hierarchies. In *Proceedings of the 14th IEEE International Conference on Fuzzy Systems, 2005, FUZZ '05* (pp. 785-790). Washington, DC: IEEE.

Antoshenkov, G. (1994). *U. S. Patent No. 5363098.* Washington, DC: U.S. Patent and Trademark Office.

Anwar, T. M., Beck, H. W., & Navathe, S. B. (1992). Knowledge mining by imprecise querying: A classification based system. In *Proceedings of the International Conference on Data Engineering,* Tampa, USA (pp. 622-630).

Ascia, G., & Catania, V. (1998). A parallel processor architecture for real-time fuzzy applications. In A. Kandel, & G. Langholz (Eds.), *Fuzzy hardware architectures and applications* (pp. 182-196).

Ascia, G., & Catania, V. (2000). A pipeline parallel architecture for a fuzzy inference processor. In *Proceedings of the Ninth IEEE International Conference on Fuzzy Systems* (pp. 257-262).

Ascia, G., Catania, V., Ficili, G., Palazzo, S., & Panno, D. (1997). A VLSI Fuzzy expert system for real-time traffic control in ATM networks. *IEEE transactions on Fuzzy Systems, 5*(1), 20–31. doi:10.1109/91.554444

Asuncion, A., & Newman, D. (2007). *UCI machine learning repository – University of California, Irvine, School of Information and Computer Sciences.* Retrieved from http://www.ics.uci.edu/~mlearn/MLRepository.html

Atzmueller, M., Baumeister, J., & Puppe, F. (2004). Quality measures for semi-automatic learning of Simple diagnostic rule bases. In *Proceedings of the 15th International Conference on Applications of Declarative Programming and Knowledge Management (INAP 2004)* (pp. 65-78).

Aucouturier, J.-J., & Pachet, F. (2002). Scaling up music playlist generation. In *Proceedings of the IEEE International Conference on Multimedia and Expo (ICME'02)* (pp. 105-108).

Baader, B., McGuiness, D. L., Nardi, D., & Patel-Schneider, P. (Eds.). (2002). *Description logic handbook: Theory, implementation and applications.* Cambridge, UK: Cambridge University Press.

Baader, F., Brandt, S., & Lutz, C. (2005). Pushing the EL envelope. In *Proceedings of the International Joint Conference on Artificial Intelligence (IJCAI 05).*

Baader, F., Lutz, C., & Suntisrivaraporn, B. (in press). Is tractable reasoning in extensions of the description logic EL useful in practice? *Journal of Logic, Language and Information, Special Issue on Method for Modality (M4M).*

Babuka, R., van der Veen, P., & Kaymak, U. (2002). Improved covariance estimation for Gustafson-Kessel clustering. In *Proceedings of the FUZZ-IEEE Conference on Fuzzy Systems,* Honolulu, HI, USA (pp. 1081-1085).

Baker, Z. K., & Prasanna, V. K. (2005). Efficient parallel data mining with the apriori algorithm on FPGAs. In *Proceedings of the 13th IEEE Symposium on Field-Programmable Custom Computing Machines* (pp. 3-15).

Baldwin, J. F. (1992). The management of fuzzy and probabilistic uncertainties for knowledge based systems. In S. A. Shapiro (Ed.), *Encyclopedia of AI* (2nd ed., pp. 528-537). New York: John Wiley.

Baldwin, J. F. (1994). Mass assignments and fuzzy sets for fuzzy databases. In M. Fedrizzi, J. Kacprzyk, & R. R. Yager (Eds.), *Advances in the shafer dempster theory of evidence.* New York: John Wiley.

Baldwin, J. F., Martin, T. P., & Pilsworth, B. W. (1995). *Fril - fuzzy and evidential reasoning in AI.* UK: Research Studies Press.

Bandler, W., & Kohout, L. (1980). Fuzzy power sets and fuzzy implication operators. *Fuzzy Sets and Systems, 4,* 13–30. doi:10.1016/0165-0114(80)90060-3

Banfield, R. E., Hall, L. O., Bowyer, K. W., & Kegelmeyer, W. P. (2007). A comparison of decision tree ensemble creation techniques. *IEEE Transactions on Pattern Analysis and Machine Intelligence, 29*(1), 173–180. doi:10.1109/TPAMI.2007.250609

Banfield, R., Hall, L., Bowyer, K., & Kegelmeyer, W. (2005). Ensemble diversity measures and their application to thinning. *Information Fusion, 6,* 49–62. doi:10.1016/j.inffus.2004.04.005

Barwise, J., & Cooper, R. (1981). Generalized quantifiers in natural language. *Linguistics and Philosophy, 4*(2), 159–219. doi:10.1007/BF00350139

Basterretxea, K., Tarela, J. M., & del Campo, I. (2002). Digital design of sigmoid approximator for artificial neural networks. *Electronics Letters, 38*(1), 35–37. doi:10.1049/el:20020008

Basterretxea, K., Tarela, J. M., & del Campo, I. (2006). Digital Gaussian membership function circuit for neuro-fuzzy hardware. *Electronics Letters, 42*(1), 44–46. doi:10.1049/el:20063712

Basterretxea, K., Tarela, J. M., del Campo, I., & Bosque, G. (2007). An experimental study on non-linear function computation for neural/fuzzy hardware design. *IEEE Transactions on Neural Networks, 18*(1), 266–283. doi:10.1109/TNN.2006.884680

Baturone, I., Barriga, A., & Sánchez-Solano, S. (1994). Current-mode multiple-input maximum circuit. *Electronics Letters, 30*(9), 678–680. doi:10.1049/el:19940510

Baturone, I., Barriga, A., Sánchez-Solano, S., & Huertas, J. L. (1998). Mixed-signal design of a fully parallel fuzzy processor. *Electronics Letters, 34*(5), 437–438. doi:10.1049/el:19980392

Baturone, I., Barriga, A., Sánchez-Solano, S., Jiménez-Fernández, C. J., & López, D. R. (2000). *Microelectronic design of fuzzy-logic-based systems.* Boca Raton, FL: CRC Press LLC.

Baturone, I., Sánchez-Solano, S., Barriga, A., & Huertas, J. L. (1997). Implementation of CMOS fuzzy controllers as mixed-signal integrated circuits. *IEEE transactions on Fuzzy Systems, 5*(1), 1–19. doi:10.1109/91.554443

Bechhofer, S., van Harmelen, F., Hendler, J., Horrocks, I., McGuinness, D.L., Patel-Schneider, P. F., & Stein, L. A. (2004). OWL Web ontology language reference. *W3C Recommendation.*

Benson, D. A., Karsch-Mizrachi, I., Lipman, D. J., Ostell, J., & Wheeler, D. (2008). GenBank. *Nucleic Acids Research, 36*(Database Issue), D25–D30. doi:10.1093/nar/gkm929

Beringer, J., & Hullermeier, E. (2006). Online clustering of parallel data streams. *Data & Knowledge Engineering, 58,* 180–204. doi:10.1016/j.datak.2005.05.009

Bezdek, J. C. (1980). A convergence theorem for the fuzzy isodata clustering algorithms. *IEEE Transactions on Pattern Analysis and Machine Intelligence, 2,* 1–8. doi:10.1109/TPAMI.1980.4766964

Bezdek, J. C. (1981). *Pattern recognition with fuzzy objective function algorithms.* Norwell, MA, USA: Kluwer Academic Publishers.

Bezdek, J. C., & Hathaway, R. J. (2002). VAT: A tool for visual assessment of (cluster) tendency. In *Proceedings of the International Joint Conference of Neural Networks* (pp. 2225-2230). Piscataway, NJ: IEEE Press.

Bezdek, J. C., & Hathaway, R. J. (2006). Elastic control of subsample size in the geFFCM algorithm. In *Proceedings of 5th International Symposium on Intelligent Manufacturing Systems* (pp. 9-18).

Bezdek, J. C., & Pal, N. (1998). Some new indexes of cluster validity. *IEEE Transactions on Systems, Man, and Cybernetics, 28*(3), 301–315. doi:10.1109/3477.678624

Bezdek, J. C., Hathaway, R. J., Huband, J. M., Leckie, C., & Kotagiri, R. (2006). Approximate clustering in very large relational data. *International Journal of Intelligent Systems, 21,* 817–841. doi:10.1002/int.20162

Bezdek, J. C., Keller, J. M., Krishnapuram, R., & Pal, N. R. (1999). *Fuzzy models and algorithms for pattern recognition and image processing.* Boston, USA: Kluwer Academic Publishers.

Blake, C. L., & Merz, C. J. (1998). *UCI repository of machine learning databases.* Irvine, CA, USA: Dept. of Information and Computer Science, University of California. Retrieved from http://www.ics.uci.edu/~mlearn/MLRepository.html

Blischke, W. R., & Murthy, D. N. P. (1994). *Warranty cost analysis.* New York: Marcel Dekker.

Blischke, W. R., & Murthy, D. N. P. (1996). *Product warranty handbook.* New York. Marcel Dekker.

Bobillo, F., Delgado, M., & Gomez-Romero, J. (2006). A crisp representation for fuzzy SHOIN with fuzzy nominals and general concept inclusions. In *Proc. of the 2nd International Workshop on Uncertainty Reasoning for the Semantic Web (URSW 06).*

Bonissone, P. P., Cadenas, J. M., Garrido, M. C., & Diaz-Valladares, R. A. (2008). A fuzzy random forest: Fundamental for design and construction. In *Proceedings of the 12th International Conference on Information Processing and Management of Uncertainty in Knowledge-Based Systems (IPMU'08),* Malaga, Spain (pp. 1231-1238).

Bookstein, A. (1980). Fuzzy requests: An approach to weighted Boolean searches. *Journal of the American Society for Information Science American Society for Information Science, 31*(4), 240–247. doi:10.1002/asi.4630310403

Bordogna, G., Bosc, P., & Pasi, G. (1996). Fuzzy inclusion in database and information retrieval query interpretation. In *Proceedings of the 1996 ACM symposium on Applied Computing* (pp. 547-551).

Bordogna, G., Campi, A., Psaila, G., & Ronchi, S. (2008). A language for manipulating groups of clustered Web documents results. In *Proceeding of the 17th ACM Conference on Information and Knowledge Mining (CIKM08),* Napa Valley, CA, USA,(pp. 23-32).

Bordogna, G., Campi, A., Psaila, G., & Ronchi, S. (2008). An interaction framework for mobile Web search. In *Proceedings of the sixth International Conference on Advances in Mobile Computing and Multimedia (MoMM08),* Lintz, Austria (pp. 183-191).

Bordogna, G., Lucarella, D., & Pasi, G. (1994). A fuzzy object oriented data model. In *Proceedings of the IEEE Conference on Fuzzy Systems* (pp. 313-318).

Borgel, C. (2005). *Prototype-based classification and clustering (Habilitationsschrift).* Unpublished habilitation, Otto-von-Guericke-University of Magdeburg, Germany.

Borgelt, C. (2003). Efficient implementations of apriori and eclat. In *Proc. of the Workshop Frequent Item Set Mining Implementations (FIMI 2003, Melbourne, FL, USA), CEUR Workshop Proceedings 90.* Aachen, Germany: Sun SITE Central Europe / University of Aachen. Retrieved from http://www.ceur-ws.org/Vol-90/

Borgelt, C. (2005). An implementation of the FP-growth algorithm. In *Proc. of the Workshop Open Software for Data Mining (OSDM'05 at KDD'05)* Chicago, IL (pp. 1-5). New York, NY, USA: ACM Press.

Borgelt, C. (2005). Keeping things simple: Finding frequent item sets by recursive elimination. In *Proc. of the Workshop Open Software for Data Mining (OSDM'05 at KDD'05),* Chicago, IL (pp. 66-70). New York, NY, USA: ACM Press.

Bosc, P., & Bouchon-Meunier, B. (1994). Databases and fuzziness - introduction. *International Journal of Intelligent Systems, 9*(5), 419. doi:10.1002/int.4550090502

Bosc, P., & Kacprzyk, J. (Eds.). (1995). *Fuzziness in database management systems.* Heidelberg, Germany: Physica-Verlag.

Bosc, P., & Pivert, O. (1992). Fuzzy querying in conventional databases. In L.A. Zadeh & J. Kacprzyk (Eds.), *Fuzzy logic for the management of uncertainty* (pp. 645-671). New York: Wiley.

Bosc, P., & Pivert, O. (2001, Jul). *On some fuzzy extensions of association rules.* Paper presented at the IFSA world congress, Vancouver, Canada.

Bosc, P., & Prade, H. (1997). An introduction to the fuzzy set and possibility theory-based treatment of flexible queries and uncertain or imprecise databases. In A. Motro & P. Smets (Eds.), *Uncertainty management in information systems* (pp. 285-324). Amsterdam: Kluwer Academic Publishers.

Bosc, P., Dubois, D., Pivert, O., Prade, H., & de Calmes, M. (2002). Fuzzy summarization of data using fuzzy cardinalities. In *Proceedings of the 9th International Conference Information Processing and Management of Uncertainty in Knowledge-Based Systems (IPMU 2002),* Annecy, France (pp. 1553-1559).

Bosc, P., Lietard, L., & Pivert, O. (1995). Quantified statements and database fuzzy querying. In P. Bosc & J. Kacprzyk (Eds.), *Fuzziness in database management systems, studies in fuzziness* (pp. 275-308). Heidelberg, Germany: Physica-Verlag.

Bosteels, K., & Kerre, E. E. (2007). Fuzzy audio similarity measures based on spectrum histograms and fluctuation patterns. In *Proceedings of the International Conference on Multimedia and Ubiquitous Engineering (MUE07)* (pp. 361-365).

Böttcher, M., Spott, M., & Nauck, D. (2005). Detecting temporally redundant association rules. In *Proc. of the 4th Int. Conf. on Machine Learning and Applications (ICMLA 2005)*, Los Angeles, CA (pp. 397-403). Piscataway, NJ, USA: IEEE Press.

Böttcher, M., Spott, M., & Nauck, D. (2007). Framework for discovering and analyzing changing customer segments. In *Advances in data mining - theoretical aspects and applications* (LNCS 4597, pp. 255-268). Berlin, Germany: Springer.

Bouchon-Meunier, B., Rifqi, M., & Lesot, M. J. (2008). Similarities in fuzzy data mining: From a cognitive view to real -world applications. In J. M. Zurada, G. G. Yen, & J. Wang (Eds.), *Computational intelligence: Research frontiers* (pp. 349-367). Berlin, Germany: Springer.

Bouras, S., Kotronakis, M., Suyama, K., & Tsividis, Y. (1998). Mixed analog-digital fuzzy logic controller with continuous-amplitude fuzzy inferences and defuzzification. *IEEE transactions on Fuzzy Systems, 6*(2), 205–215. doi:10.1109/91.669017

Boutsinas, B., & Gnardellis, T. (2002). On distributing the clustering process. *Pattern Recognition Letters, 23*, 999–1008. doi:10.1016/S0167-8655(02)00031-4

Bradley, P. S., Fayyad, U., & Reina, C. (1998). Scaling clustering algorithms to large databases. In *Proceedings of the International Conference on Knowledge Discovery and Data Mining* (pp. 9-15).

Brazdil, P., & Torgo, L. (1990). Knowledge adquisition via knowledge integration. In B. Wielinga et al. (Eds.), *Current trends in knowledge acquisition.* Amsterdam: IOS Press.

Breiman, L. (1996). Bagging predictors. *Machine Learning, 24*, 123–140.

Breiman, L. (2001). Random forests. *Machine Learning, 45*, 5–32. doi:10.1023/A:1010933404324

Breiman, L., Friedman, J., Olshen, R., & Stone, C. (1984). *Classification and regression trees.* New York: Chapman and Hall.

Brin, S., Motwani, R., Ullman, J. D., & Tsur, S. (1997). Dynamic itemset counting and implication rules for market basket data. In *Proceedings of the 1997 ACM SIGMOD international conference on Management of data* (pp. 255-264). New York: ACM.

Bruha, I. (1996). *Machine learning and statistics.* John Wiley & Sons Inc.

Buell, D. A., & Kraft, D. H. (1981). Threshold values and Boolean retrieval systems. *Journal of Information Processing and Management, 17*, 127–136. doi:10.1016/S0306-4573(81)80004-0

Buell, D., & Kraft, D. H. (1981). A model for a weighted retrieval system. *Journal of the American Society for Information Science American Society for Information Science, 32*, 211–216. doi:10.1002/asi.4630320307

Buell, D., El-Ghazawi, T., Gaj, K., & Kindratenko, V. (2007). High-performance reconfigurable computing. *IEEE Computer*, 23-27.

Cabibbo, L., & Torlone, R. (1997). Querying multidimensional databases. In *Proceedings of the 6th International Workshop on Database Programming Languages* (LNCS 1369, pp. 319-335). Berlin, Germany: Springer.

Cabibbo, L., & Torlone, R. (1998). A logical approach to multidimensional databases. In *Proceedings of the*

Advances in Database Technologies – EDBT '98 (LNCS 1377, pp. 183-197). Berlin, Germany: Springer-Verlag.

Cabrera, A., Sánchez-Solano, S., Brox, P., Barriga, A., & Senhadji, R. (2004). Hardware/software codesign of configurable fuzzy control system. *Applied Soft Computing*, *4*(3), 271–285. doi:10.1016/j.asoc.2004.03.006

Calvanese, D., De Giacomo, G., Lembo, D., Lenzerini, M., & Rosati, R. (2005). DL-Lite: Tractable description logics for ontologies. In *Proc. of the AAAI*.

Calvanese, D., De Giacomo, G., Lembo, D., Lenzerini, M., & Rosati, R. (2007). Tractable reasoning and efficient query answering in description logics: The DL-Lite family. *Journal of Automated Reasoning*, *39*(3), 385–429. doi:10.1007/s10817-007-9078-x

Calvanese, D., De Giacomo, G., Lenzerini, M., Nardi, D., & Rosati, R. (1998). Description logic framework for information integration. In *Proc. of the 6th Int. Conf. on the Principles of Knowledge Representation and Reasoning (KR'98)*.

Cannataro, M., Congiusta, A., Pugliese, A., Talia, D., & Trunfio, P. (2004). Distributed data mining on grids: Services, tools, and applications. *IEEE Transactions on Systems, Man and Cybernetics . Part B*, *34*(6), 2451–2465.

Cannon, R. L., Dave, J. V., & Bezdek, J. C. (1986). Efficient implementation of the fuzzy c-means clustering algorithms. *IEEE Transactions on Pattern Analysis and Machine Intelligence*, *8*(2), 248–255. doi:10.1109/TPAMI.1986.4767778

Cantle, A. (2006). Scalable cluster-based FPGA HPC system solutions. *Xcell Journal*, (58), 35-37.

Canul-Reich, J., Shoemaker, L., & Hall, L. (2007). Ensembles of fuzzy classifiers. In *Proceedings of the IEEE International Conference on Fuzzy Systems*.

Cao, F., Ester, M., Qian, W., & Zhou, A. (2006). Density-based clustering over an evolving data stream with noise. In *Proceedings of the 2006 SIAM Conference on Data Mining* (pp. 328-339).

Card, S. K., Mackinlay, J. D., & Shneiderman, B. (2000). *Readings in information visualization: Using vision to think*. San Francisco, CA: Morgan Kaufmann Publishers Inc.

Castro, J. L. (1996). Fuzzy logic controllers are universal approximators. *IEEE Transactions on Systems, Man, and Cybernetics*, *25*(4), 629–635. doi:10.1109/21.370193

Chan, C.-y., & Ioannidis, Y. E. (1998). Bitmap index design and evaluation. In *Proceedings of the ACM SIGMOD 1998* (pp. 355-366). New York: ACM Press.

Chawla, N. V., Hall, L. O., Bowyer, K. W., & Kegelmeyer, W. P. (2004). Learning ensembles from bites: A scalable and accurate approach. *Journal of Machine Learning Research*, *5*, 421–451.

Chawla, N., Moore, T. E., Bowyer, K. W., Hall, L. O., & Kegelmeyer, W. P. (2001). Bagging is a small-data-set phenomenon. In *Proceedings of the International Conference on Computer Vision and Pattern Recognition (CVPR)* (pp. 68-69).

Chen, G., & Wei, Q. (2002). Fuzzy association rules and the extended mining algorithm. *Information Sciences*, *147*, 201–228. doi:10.1016/S0020-0255(02)00264-5

Chen, G., Liu, D., & Li, J. (2001). Influence and conditional influence – new interestingness measures in association rule mining. In Proceedings of the *IEEE International Conference on Fuzzy Systems (FUZZ-IEEE'2001)*, Vancouver, Canada (pp. 1440-1443).

Chen, G., Wei, Q., & Kerre, E. E. (2000). Fuzzy data mining: Discovery of fuzzy generalized association rules. In G. Bordogna & G. Pasi (Eds.), *Recent research issues on fuzzy databases* (pp. 45-66). New York: Springer-Verlag.

Chen, H., & Dumais, S. (2009). Bringing order to the Web: Automatically categorizing search results. In *Proceedings of the SIGCHI Conference on Human factors in computing systems* (pp. 145-152).

Chen, S. J., & Chen, S. M. (2000). A new method for fuzzy information retrieval based on geometric-mean averaging operators. In *Proceedings of the Workshop on Artificial Intelligence*, 2000.

Cheng, C.-S., & Wang, S.-S. (2003). A repulsive clustering algorithm for gene expression data. In *Proceedings of the IEEE International Symposium on Bioinformatic and Bioengineering* (pp. 407-412).

Cheng, T. W., Goldgof, D. B., & Hall, L. O. (1995). Fast clustering with application to fuzzy rule generation. In *Proceedings of the 4th IEEE International Conference on Fuzzy Systems*, Yokohama, Japan (pp 2289-2295). Piscataway, NJ: IEEE Press.

Cheng, T. W., Goldgof, D. B., & Hall, L. O. (1998). Fast fuzzy clustering. *Fuzzy Sets and Systems*, *93*, 49–56. doi:10.1016/S0165-0114(96)00232-1

Cheng, Y., Fayyad, U., & Bradley, P. S. (2001). Efficient discovery of error-tolerant frequent itemsets in high dimensions. In *Proc. of the 7th Int. Conf. on Knowledge Discovery and Data Mining (KDD'01)*, San Francisco, CA (pp. 194-203). New York, NY, USA: ACM Press.

Cho, K., Jo, S., Jang, H., Kim, S. M., & Song, J. (2006). DCF: An efficient data stream clustering framework for streaming applications. In *Database and expert systems applications* (pp. 114-122). Berlin, Germany; Springer.

Chortaras, A., Stamou, G., & Stafylopatis, A. (2006). Adaptation of weighted fuzzy programs. In *Proc. of the International Conference on Artificial Neural Networks (ICANN 2006)* (pp. 45-54).

Choudhary, A., Narayanan, R., Özisikyilmaz, B., Memik, G., Zambreno, J., & Pisharat, J. (2007). Optimizing data mining workloads using hardware accelerators. In *Proc. of the 10ᵗʰ Workshop on Computer Architecture Evaluation Using Commercial Workloads (CAECW)*.

Chowdhury, S. R., Chakrabarti, D., & Saha, H. (2008). FPGA realization of a smart processing system for clinical diagnostic applications using pipelined datapath architectures. *Microprocessors and Microsystems*, *32*(2), 107–120. doi:10.1016/j.micpro.2007.12.001

Chung, W., Chen, H., & Nunamaker, J. J. (2003). Business intelligence explorer: A knowledge map framework for discovering business intelligence on the Web. In *Proceedings of the 36th Annual Hawaii International Conference on System Sciences* (pp. 10-18).

Çilingiroglu, U., Pamir, B., Günay, Z. S., & Dülger, F. (1997). Sampled-analog implementation of application-specific fuzzy controllers. *IEEE transactions on Fuzzy Systems*, *5*(3), 431–442. doi:10.1109/91.618278

Coates, T., Connolly, D., Dack, D., Daigle, L., Denenberg, R., Durst, M., et al. (2001). *URIs, URLs, and URNs: Clarifications and recommendations, 1.0* (Tech. Rep. WWW Consortium, URI Planning Interest Group). Retrieved from http://www.w3.org/TR/2001/NOTE-uri-clarification-20010921/

Codd, E. F. (1979). Extending the database relational model to capture more meaning. *ACM Transactions on Database Systems*, *4*(4), 397–434. doi:10.1145/320107.320109

Cohen, L., Avrahami-Bakish, G., Last, M., Kandel, A., & Kipersztok, O. (2008). Real-time data mining of non-stationary data streams from sensor networks. *Information Fusion*, *9*(3), 344–353. doi:10.1016/j.inffus.2005.05.005

Cohen, M., DuBois, R., & Zeineh, M. (2000). Rapid and effective correction of RF inhomogeneity for high field magnetic resonance imaging. *Human Brain Mapping*, *10*, 204–211. doi:10.1002/1097-0193(200008)10:4<204::AID-HBM60>3.0.CO;2-2

Council, O. (n.d.). *The OLAP Council*. Retrieved from http://www.olapcouncil.org

Crockett, K., Bandar, Z., & McLean, D. (2001). Growing a fuzzy decision forest. In *Proceedings of the 10th IEEE International Conference on Fuzzy Systems*, Melbourne, Australia (pp. 614-617).

Cross, V. (1994). Fuzzy information retrieval. *Journal of Intelligent Information Systems*, *3*, 29–56. doi:10.1007/BF01014019

D'Amore, R., Saotome, O., & Kienitz, K. H. (2001). A two-input, one-output bit-scalable architecture for fuzzy processors. *IEEE J. Design Test Computation*, *18*, 56–64. doi:10.1109/54.936249

Dai, B.-R., Huang, J.-W., Yeh, M.-Y., & Chen, M.-S. (2004). Clustering on demand for multiple data streams. In *Proceedings of the Fourth IEEE International Conference on Data Mining, 2004. ICDM '04* (pp. 367-370).

Dameron, O., Gibaud, B., & Musen, M. (2004). Using semantic dependencies for consistency management of an ontology of brain-cortex anatomy. In *Proceedings of the First International Workshop on Formal Biomedical Knowledge Representation KRMED04* (pp. 30-38).

Datta, A., & Thomas, H. (1999). The cube data model: A conceptual model and algebra for on-line analytical processing in data warehouses. *Decision Support Systems, 27*, 289–301. doi:10.1016/S0167-9236(99)00052-4

Dave, R. (1991). Characterization and detection of noise in clustering. *Pattern Recognition Letters, 12*(11), 657–664. doi:10.1016/0167-8655(91)90002-4

Dave, R., & Krishnapuram, R. (1997). Robust clustering methods: A unified view. *IEEE transactions on Fuzzy Systems, 5*(2), 270–293. doi:10.1109/91.580801

Davies, D., & Bouldin, D. (1979). A cluster separation measure. *IEEE Transactions on Pattern Analysis and Machine Intelligence, 1*(2), 224–227. doi:10.1109/TPAMI.1979.4766909

De Micheli (Ed.). (1997). Special issue on hardware/software codesign. *Proceedings of the IEEE, 85*(3).

Dean, P., & Famili, A. (1997). Comparative performance of rule quality measures in an induction system. *Applied Intelligence, 7*, 113–124. doi:10.1023/A:1008293727412

del Campo, I., & Tarela, J. M. (1999). Consequences of the digitization on the performance of a fuzzy logic controller. *IEEE transactions on Fuzzy Systems, 7*(1), 85–92. doi:10.1109/91.746317

del Campo, I., Echanobe, J., Bosque, G., & Tarela, J. M. (2008). Efficient hardware/software implementation of an adaptive neuro-fuzzy system. *IEEE transactions on Fuzzy Systems, 16*(3), 761–778. doi:10.1109/TFUZZ.2007.905918

del Campo, I., Tarela, J. M., & Basterretxea, K. (2001). Quantisation errors in digital implementations of fuzzy controllers. In R. S. H. Istepanian & J. F. Whidborne (Eds.), *Digital controller implementation and fragility. A modern perspective* (pp. 253-274). Berlin, Germany: Springer.

Delgado, M., Marin, N., Sanchez, D., & Vila, M. A. (2003). Fuzzy association rules: General model and applications. *IEEE transactions on Fuzzy Systems, 11*(2), 214–225. doi:10.1109/TFUZZ.2003.809896

Delgado, M., Martin-Bautista, M. J., Sanchez, D., & Vila, M. A. (2003). On a characterization of fuzzy bags. In *Proceedings of the Fuzzy Sets and Systems – IFSA 2003* (LNCS 2715, pp. 119-126). Berlin, Germany: Springer.

Delgado, M., Sánchez, D., & Vila, M. (1999). Fuzzy cardinality based evaluation of quantified sentences. *International Journal of Approximate Reasoning, 23*(1), 23–66. doi:10.1016/S0888-613X(99)00031-6

Deliège, F., & Pedersen, T. B. (2006). Music warehouses: Challenges for the next generation of music search engines. In *Proceedings of the International Workshop on Learning the Semantics of Audio Signals* (pp. 95-105).

Deliège, F., & Pedersen, T. B. (2007). Using fuzzy song sets in music warehouses. In *Proceedings of the International Conference on Music Information Retrieval (ISMIR'07)* (pp. 21-26).

Demsar, J. (2006). Statistical comparisons of classifiers over multiple data sets. *Machine Learning, 7*, 1–30.

Diaz-Hermida, F., Losada, D. E., Bugarin, A., & Barro, S. (2005). A probabilistic quantifier fuzzification mechanism: The model and its evaluation for information retrieval. *IEEE transactions on Fuzzy Systems, 13*(5), 688–700. doi:10.1109/TFUZZ.2005.856557

Dick, S., Gaudet, V., & Bai, H. (2008). Bit-serial arithmetic: A novel approach to fuzzy hardware implementation. In *Proceedings of the Fuzzy Information Processing Society, 2008. NAFIPS 2008. Annual Meeting of the North American* (pp. 1-6).

Dietterich, T. (2000). An experimental comparison of three methods for constructing ensembles of decision trees: Bagging, boosting, and randomization. *Machine Learning, 40*, 139–157. doi:10.1023/A:1007607513941

Domingos, P., & Hulten, G. (2000). Mining high-speed data streams. In *Proceedings of the Sixth International Conference on Knowledge Discovery and Data Mining* (pp. 71-80).

Dubois, D., & Prade, H. (1982). A unifying view of comparison indices a fuzzy set-theoretic framework. In R. R. Yager (Ed.), *Recent development in fuzzy set and possibility theory* (pp. 3-13). New York: Pergamon Press.

Dubois, D., & Prade, H. (1988). *Possibility theory: An approach to computerized processing of uncertainty.* New York: Plenum Press.

Dubois, D., & Prade, H. (1992). Gradual rules in approximate reasoning. *Information Sciences, 61,* 103–122. doi:10.1016/0020-0255(92)90035-7

Dubois, D., & Prade, H. (1997). The three semantics of fuzzy sets. *Fuzzy Sets and Systems, 90,* 141–150. doi:10.1016/S0165-0114(97)00080-8

Dubois, D., Hullermeier, E., & Prade, H. (2006). A systematic approach to the assessment of fuzzy association rules. *Data Mining and Knowledge Discovery, 13*(2), 167–192. doi:10.1007/s10618-005-0032-4

Duda, R., & Hart, P. (1973). *Pattern classification and scene analysis.* New York: John Wiley.

Dunn, J. (1974). Well-separated clusters and optimal fuzzy partitions. *Cybernetics and Systems, 4*(1), 95–104. doi:10.1080/01969727408546059

Dunn, J.C. (1973). A fuzzy relative of the ISODATA process and its use in detecting compact well-separated clusters. *Journal of Cybernetics,* (3), 32-57.

Dutcher, B. (2006). Mining data without limits. *Xcell Journal,* (57), 64-66.

Echevarría, P., Martínez, M. V., Echanobe, J., del Campo, I., & Tarela, J. M. (2005). Design and HW/SW implementation of a class of piecewise-linear fuzzy system. In *Proceedings of the XII Seminario Anual de Automática, Electrónica Industrial e Instrumentación, SAAEI 05* (pp. 360-364).

Eichfeld, H., Klimke, M., Menke, M., Nolles, J., & Künemund, T. (1995). A general-purpose fuzzy inference processor. *IEEE Micro, 15*(3), 12–17. doi:10.1109/40.387677

Eichfeld, H., Künemund, T., & Menke, M. (1996). A 12b general-purpose fuzzy logic controller chip. *IEEE transactions on Fuzzy Systems, 4*(4), 460–475. doi:10.1109/91.544305

Eichfeld, H., Löhner, M., & Müller, M. (1992). Architecture of a CMOS fuzzy logic controller with optimized organisation and operator design. In *Proceedings of the First International Conference on Fuzzy Systems, FUZ-IEEE* (pp. 1317-1323). Washington, DC: IEEE Computer Society Press.

Elkan, C. (2003). Using the triangle inequality to accelerate k-means. In *Proceedings of the Int. Conf. Machine Learning* (pp. 147-153).

Enright, A. J., Van Dongen, S., & Ouzounis, C. A. (2002). An efficient algorithm for the large-scale detection of protein families. *Nucleic Acids Research, 30*(7), 1575–1584. doi:10.1093/nar/30.7.1575

Enrique, H. R. (1969). A new approach to clustering. *Information and Control, 15*(1), 22–32. doi:10.1016/S0019-9958(69)90591-9

Eschrich, S., Ke, J., Hall, L. O., & Goldgof, D. B. (2003). Fast accurate fuzzy clustering through data reduction. *IEEE transactions on Fuzzy Systems, 11*(2), 262–270. doi:10.1109/TFUZZ.2003.809902

Ester, M., Kriegel, H.-P., Sander, J., & Xu, X. (1996). A density-based algorithm for discovering clusters in large spatial databases with noise. In *Proceedings of 2nd International Conference on Knowledge Discovery and Data Mining (KDD-96)* (pp. 226-231).

Estlick, M., Leeser, M., Szymanski, J., & Theiler, J. (2001). Algorithmic transformations in the implementation of k-means clustering on reconfigurable hardware. In *Proceedings of the Ninth Annual IEEE Symposium on Field Programmable Custom Computing Machines 2001 (FCCM '01)* (pp. 103-110).

Eto, E. (2007). *Difference-based partial reconfiguration (ver 2.0, 2007), application note: Virtex architectures.* Retrieved December 1, 2008, from http://www.xilinx.com/support/documentation/application_notes/xapp290.pdf

Evsukoff, A. G., Costa, M. C. A., & Ebecken, F. F. (2005). Parallel implementation of a fuzzy rule based classifier. In M. Daydé et al. (Eds.), *Proceedings of the VECPAR 2004* (LNCS 3402, pp. 184-193). Berlin, Germany: Springer-Verlag.

Famili, A. (1990). Integrating learning and decision-making in intelligent manufacturing systems. *Journal of Intelligent & Robotic Systems, 3,* 117–130. doi:10.1007/BF00242160

Farnstrom, F., Lewis, J., & Elkan, C. (2000). Scalability of clustering algorithms revisited. *SIGKDD Explorations, 2,* 51–57. doi:10.1145/360402.360419

Fattaruso, J. W., Mahant-Shetti, S. S., & Barton, J. B. (1994). A fuzzy logic inference processor. *IEEE Journal of Solid-State Circuits, 29*(4), 397–402. doi:10.1109/4.280687

Fayyad, U. M., Piatetsky-Shapiro, G., Smyth, P., & Uthurusamy, R. (1996). *Advances in knowledge discovery and data mining.* AAAI/MIT Press.

Ferrara, A., Lorusso, D., Stamou, G., Stoilos, G., Tzouvaras, V., & Venetis, T. (2008). Resolution of conflicts among ontology mappings: A fuzzy approach. In *Proceedings of the International Workshop on Ontology Matching (OM2008),* Karlsruhe.

Finn, R. D., Tate, J., Mistry, J., Coggill, P. C., Sammut, J. S., & Hotz, H. R. (2008). The Pfam protein families database. *Nucleic Acids Research, 36*(Database Issue), D281–D288. doi:10.1093/nar/gkm960

fltoolbox. (2006). *The mathworks - fuzzy logic toolbox.* Retrieved from http://www.mathworks.ch/access/helpdesk r13/help/toolbox/fuzzy/fuzzy.html

Fred, A. L. N., & Jain, A. K. (2003). Robust data clustering. In *Proceedings of the IEEE Computer Society Conference on Computer Vision and Pattern Recognition (CVPR '03)* (pp. 2-128).

Freeman, M., & Jayasooriya, T. (2006). Hardware support for language aware information mining. In B. Gabrys, R.J. Howlett, & L.C. Jain (Eds.), *Proceedings of the KES 2006, Part III* (LNAI 4253, pp. 415-423). Berlin, Germany: Springer-Verlag.

Freund, Y., & Schapire, R. (1996). Experiments with a new boosting algorithm. In *Proceedings of the International Conference on Machine Learning* (pp. 148-156).

Frigui, H., & Krishnapuram, R. (1999). A robust competitive clustering algorithm with applications in computer vision. *IEEE Transactions on Pattern Analysis and Machine Intelligence, 21*(5), 450–465. doi:10.1109/34.765656

Galindo, J. (Ed.). (2008). *Handbook of research on fuzzy information processing in databases.* Hershey, PA: Information Science Reference.

Galindo, J., Piattini, M., & Urrutia, A. (2005). *Fuzzy databases: Modeling, Design and implementation.* Hershey, PA: IGI Publishing. *Intelligent sound.* (n.d.). Retrieved from http://www.intelligentsound.org

George, R., & Srikanth, R. (1996). A soft computing approach to intensional answering in databases. *Information Sciences, 92,* 313–328. doi:10.1016/0020-0255(96)00049-7

George, R., & Srikanth, R. (1996). Data summarization using genetic algorithms and fuzzy logic. In F. Herrera & J.L. Verdegay (Eds.), *Genetic algorithms and soft computing* (pp. 599-611). Heidelberg, Germany: Physica-Verlag.

Geurts, P., Ernst, D., & Wehenkel, L. (2006). Extremely randomized trees. *Machine Learning, 63*(1), 3–42. doi:10.1007/s10994-006-6226-1

Giannella, C., Dutta, H., Borne, K. D., Wolff, R., & Kargupta, H. (2006). Distributed data mining for astronomy catalogs. In *Proceedings of the 9th Workshop on Mining Scientific and Engineering Datasets, Proceedings of the SIAM International Conference on Data Mining.*

Goodman, I. R. (1982). Fuzzy sets as equivalence classes of random sets. In R. Yager (Ed.), *Fuzzy set and possibility theory* (pp. 327-342). New York: Pergamon.

Goodman, I. R., & Nguyen, H. T. (1985). *Uncertainty models for knowledge based systems: A unified approach to the measurement of uncertainty.* New York: Elsevier.

Gorry, G., & Morton, M. S. (1971). A framework for management information systems. *Sloan Management Review, 13,* 50–70.

Gray, J., & Szalay, A. (2004). *Where the rubber meets the sky: Bridging the gap between databases and science* (Tech. Rep. MSR-TR-2004-110). Redmond, WA: Microsoft.

Gray, J., Chaudhuri, S., Bosworth, A., Layman, A., Reichart, D., & Venkatrao, M. (1997). Data cube: A relational aggregation operator generalizing group-by, cross-tab, and sub-totals. *Data Mining and Knowledge Discovery, 1,* 29–53. doi:10.1023/A:1009726021843

Guha, S., Meyerson, A., Mishra, N., Motwani, R., & O'Callaghan, L. (2003). Clustering data streams: Theory and practice. *Knowledge and Data Engineering . IEEE Transactions on, 15*(3), 515–528.

Guha, S., Rastogi, R., & Shim, K. (1998). CURE: An efficient clustering algorithm for large databases. In *Proceedings of ACM SIGMOD International Conference on Management of Data* (pp. 73-84).

Guo, S., Peters, L., & Surmann, H. (1996). Design and application of an analog fuzzy logic controller. *IEEE transactions on Fuzzy Systems, 4*(4), 429–438. doi:10.1109/91.544303

Guo, Y., Pan, Z., & Heflin, J. (2005). LUBM: A benchmark for OWL knowledge base systems. *Journal of Web Semantics, 3*(2), 158–182. doi:10.1016/j.websem.2005.06.005

Gupta, C., & Grossman, R. (2004). GenIc: A single pass generalized incremental algorithm for clustering. In *Proceedings of the Fourth SIAM International Conference on Data Mining (SDM)* (pp. 22-24).

Gustafson, D., & Kessel, W. (1979). Fuzzy clustering with a fuzzy covariance matrix. In *Proceedings of the IEEE Conference on Decision and Control*, San Diego, CA (pp. 761-766).

Haines, S. (2006). *Pro Java EE 5 performance management and optimization.* Berkeley, CA: Apress.

Halgamuge, S. K., Hollstein, T., Kirschbaum, A., & Glesner, M. (1994). Automatic generation of application specific fuzzy controllers for rapid-prototyping. In *Proceedings of the IEEE International Conference on Fuzzy Systems* (pp. 1638-1641).

Hamzeh, M., Mahdiani, H. R., Saghafi, A., Fakhraie, S. M., & Lucas, C. (2009). Computationally efficient active rule detection method: Algorithm and architecture. *Fuzzy Sets and Systems, 160*(4), 554–568. doi:10.1016/j.fss.2008.05.009

Han, J. (1997). OLAP mining: Integration of OLAP with data mining. In *Proceedings of the 7th IFIP 2.6 Working Conference on Database Semantics* (pp. 1-11).

Han, J., & Fu, Y. (1999). Discovery of multiple-level association rules from large databases. *IEEE Transactions on Knowledge and Data Engineering, 11,* 798–805. doi:10.1109/69.806937

Han, J., Cai, Y., & Cercone, N. (1993). Data-driven discovery of quantitative rules in relational databases. *IEEE Transactions on Knowledge and Data Engineering, 5,* 29–40. doi:10.1109/69.204089

Han, J., Pei, H., & Yin, Y. (2000). Mining frequent patterns without candidate generation. In *Proc. of the Conf. on the Management of Data (SIGMOD'00),* Dallas, TX (pp. 1-12). New York, NY, USA: ACM Press.

Han, J., Pei, J., & Yin, Y. (2000). Mining frequent patterns without candidate generation. In *Proceedings of the 2000 ACM SIGMOD international conference on Management of data* (pp. 1-12). New York: ACM.

Harris, C. (2005). *Using programmable graphics hardware to implement the fuzzy c-means algorithm.* Unpublished honors dissertation, The University of Western Australia.

Hathaway, R. J., & Bezdek, J. C. (1994). NERF c-means: Non-Euclidean relational fuzzy clustering. *Pattern Recognition, 27,* 429–437. doi:10.1016/0031-3203(94)90119-8

410

Hathaway, R. J., & Bezdek, J. C. (2003). Visual cluster validity for prototype generator clustering models. *Pattern Recognition Letters, 24*(9–10), 1563–1569. doi:10.1016/S0167-8655(02)00395-1

Hathaway, R. J., & Bezdek, J. C. (2006). Extending fuzzy and probabilistic clustering to very large data sets. *Computational Statistics & Data Analysis, 51*(1), 215–234. doi:10.1016/j.csda.2006.02.008

Hathaway, R. J., Bezdek, J. C., & Huband, J. M. (2006). Scalable visual assessment of cluster tendency for large data sets. *Pattern Recognition, 39*(7), 1315–1324. doi:10.1016/j.patcog.2006.02.011

Havens, T. C., Keller, J. M., Rehrig, E. M., Appel, H. M., Popescu, M., Schultz, J. C., & Bezdek, J. C. (2008). Cluster analysis of bioinformatics data composed of microarray expression and gene ontology annotations. In *Proceedings of the Annual NAFIPS Conference*, New York.

Havens, T., Bezdek, J., Keller, J., & Popescu, M. (2008). Dunn's cluster validity index as a contrast measure of vat images. In *Proceedings of the 19th International Conference on Pattern Recognition (ICPR)* (pp. 1-4).

Hearst, M. A., & Pederson, J. O. (1996). Re-examining the cluster hypothesis: Scatter/gather on retrieval results. In *Proceedings of the 19th Annual International ACM SIGIR Conference* (pp. 76-84).

Hershtinkel, D., & Dinstein, I. (1996). Accelerated fuzzy c-means clustering algorithm. In *Proceedings SPIE Applications of Fuzzy Logic Technology III* (pp. 41-52).

Holi, M., & Hyvonen, E. (2006). Fuzzy view-based semantic search. In *Proceedings of the Asian Semantic Web Conference*.

Hölldobler, S., Nga, N. H., & Khang, T. D. (2005). The fuzzy description logic ALC_{FLH}. In *Proceedings of the International workshop on Description Logics*.

Hollstein, T., Halgamuge, S. K., & Glesner, M. (1996). Computer-aided design of fuzzy systems based on generic VHDL specifications. *IEEE transactions on Fuzzy Systems, 4*(4), 403–417. doi:10.1109/91.544301

Höppner, F. (2002). Speeding up fuzzy c-means: Using a hierarchical data organisation to control the precision of membership calculation. *Fuzzy Sets and Systems, 128*(3), 365–376. doi:10.1016/S0165-0114(01)00204-4

Höppner, F., Klawonn, F., Kruse, R., & Runkler, T. A. (1999). *Fuzzy cluster analysis*. Chichester, UK: John Wiley & Sons.

Hore, P., Hall, L. O., & Goldgof, D. B. (2007). A fuzzy c means variant for clustering evolving data streams. In *Proceedings of the IEEE International Conference on Systems, Man and Cybernetics,* Montreal (pp. 360-365).

Hore, P., Hall, L., & Goldgof, D. (2007). Creating streaming iterative soft clustering algorithms. In *Proceedings of the Fuzzy Information Processing Society, 2007. NAFIPS '07. Annual Meeting of the North American Fuzzy Information Processing Society* (pp. 484-488).

Hore, P., Hall, L., Goldgof, D., & Cheng, W. (2008). Online fuzzy c means. In *Proceedings of the Fuzzy Information Processing Society, 2008. NAFIPS 2008. Annual Meeting of the North American Fuzzy Information Processing Society* (pp. 1-5).

Horrocks, I., & Patel-Schneider, P. (2004). Reducing OWL entailment to description logic satisfiability. *Journal of Web Semantics,* 345–357. doi:10.1016/j.websem.2004.06.003

Hossain, A., & Manzoul, M. A. (1993). Hardware implementation of fuzzy replacement algorithm for cache memories using field-programmable gate arrays. *Cybernetics and Systems, 24*(2), 81–90. doi:10.1080/01969729308961701

Hu, X. J., Lawless, J. F., & Suzuki, K. (1998). Nonparametric estimation of a lifetime distribution when censoring times are missing. *Technometrics, 40,* 3–13. doi:10.2307/1271388

Hu, Y.-Ch., Chen, R.-Sh., & Tzeng, G.-H. (2002). Mining fuzzy association rules for classification problems. *Computers & Industrial Engineering, 43,* 735–750. doi:10.1016/S0360-8352(02)00136-5

Huband, J. M., Bezdek, J. C., & Hathaway, R. J. (2005). bigVAT: Visual assessment of cluster tendency for large data sets. *Pattern Recognition, 38,* 1875–1886. doi:10.1016/j.patcog.2005.03.018

Huertas, J. L., Sánchez-Solano, S., Barriga, A., & Baturone, I. (1993). A fuzzy controller using switched-capacitor techniques. In *Proceedings of the IEEE International Conference on Fuzzy Systems* (pp. 516-529).

Hung, D. L., & Zajak, W. F. (1995). Design and Implementation of a hardware fuzzy inference system. *Information Sciences-Applications, 3*(3), 193–207. doi:10.1016/1069-0115(94)00042-Z

Ikeda, H., Kisu, N., Hiramoto, Y., & Nakamura, S. (1992). A fuzzy inference coprocessor using a flexible active-rule-driven architecture. In *Proceedings of the IEEE International. Conference on Fuzzy Systems* (pp. 537-544).

Indue, T., Motomura, T., & Matsuo, R. (1991). New OTA-based analog circuits for fuzzy membership functions and maximum operations. *IEIC Transactions on Communication Electronics, 74*(11), 3619–3621.

Jain, A. K., & Moreau, J. V. (1987). Bootstrap technique in cluster analysis. *Pattern Recognition, 20*(5), 547–568. doi:10.1016/0031-3203(87)90081-1

Jain, A., & Dubes, R. (1988). *Algorithms for clustering data.* Englewood Cliffs, NJ: Prentice Hall.

Janikow, C. Z., & Faifer, M. (2000). Fuzzy decision forest. In *Proceedings of the 19th International Conference of the North American Fuzzy Information Processing Society (NAFIPS'00)* (pp. 218-221).

Jenkinson, M., Pechaud, M., & Smith, S. (2005). BET2: MR-based estimation of brain, skull and scalp surfaces. In *Proceedings of the Eleventh Annual Meeting of the Organization for Human Brain Mapping.*

Jensen, C. A., Mungure, E. M., Pedersen, T. B., & Sørensen, K. (2007). A data and query model for dynamic playlist generation. In *Proceeding of IEEE-MDDM* (pp. 65-74).

Jensen, C., Kligys, A., Pedersen, T., & Timko, I. (2004). Multimendional data modeling for location-based

services. *The VLDB Journal, 13,* 1–21. doi:10.1007/s00778-003-0091-3

Jin, R., Yang, G., & Agrawal, G. (2005). Shared memory parallelization of data mining algorithms: Techniques, programming interface, and performance. *IEEE Transactions on Knowledge and Data Engineering, 17*(1), 71–89. doi:10.1109/TKDE.2005.18

Jyh, S., & Jang, R. (1993). Anfis: Adaptive-network-based fuzzy inference system. *IEEE Transactions on Systems, Man, and Cybernetics, 23,* 665–685. doi:10.1109/21.256541

Kacprzyk, J. (2000). Intelligent data analysis via linguistic data summaries: A fuzzy logic approach. In R. Decker & W. Gaul (Eds.), *Classification and information processing at the turn of the millennium* (pp. 153-161). New York: Springer-Verlag.

Kacprzyk, J., & Yager, R. R. (2001). Linguistic summaries of data using fuzzy logic. *International Journal of General Systems, 30,* 133–154. doi:10.1080/03081070108960702

Kacprzyk, J., & Zadrożny, S. (1994). Fuzzy querying for Microsoft Access. In *Proceedings of the IEEE International Conference on Fuzzy Systems (FUZZ-IEEE'94) vol. 1,* Orlando, USA (pp. 167-171).

Kacprzyk, J., & Zadrożny, S. (1995). Fuzzy queries in Microsoft Access v. 2. In *Proceedings of the IEEE International Conference on Fuzzy Systems (FUZZ-IEEE'95), Workshop on Fuzzy Database Systems and Information Retrieval,* Yokohama, Japan (pp. 61-66).

Kacprzyk, J., & Zadrożny, S. (1995). FQUERY for Access: Fuzzy querying for a Windows-based DBMS. In P. Bosc & J. Kacprzyk (Eds.), *Fuzziness in database management systems* (pp. 415-433). Heidelberg, Germany: Physica-Verlag.

Kacprzyk, J., & Zadrożny, S. (1998). Data mining via linguistic summaries of data: An interactive approach. In T. Yamakawa & G. Matsumoto (Eds.), *Methodologies for the Conception, Design and Application of Soft Computing - Proceedings of IIZUKA'98,* Iizuka, Japan (pp. 668-671).

Kacprzyk, J., & Zadrożny, S. (1999). The paradigm of computing with words in intelligent database querying. In L.A. Zadeh & J. Kacprzyk (Eds.), *Computing with words in information/intelligent systems. Part 2. Foundations* (pp. 382-398). New York: Springer-Verlag.

Kacprzyk, J., & Zadrożny, S. (2000). On combining intelligent querying and data mining using fuzzy logic concepts. In G. Bordogna & G. Pasi (Eds.), *Recent research issues on the management of fuzziness in databases* (pp. 67-81). New York: Physica-Verlag.

Kacprzyk, J., & Zadrożny, S. (2000). Data mining via fuzzy querying over the Internet. In O. Pons, M.A. Vila, & J. Kacprzyk (Eds.), *Knowledge management in fuzzy databases* (pp. 211-233). New York: Physica-Verlag.

Kacprzyk, J., & Zadrożny, S. (2000). On a fuzzy querying and data mining interface. *Kybernetika, 36*, 657–670.

Kacprzyk, J., & Zadrożny, S. (2000). Computing with words: Towards a new generation of linguistic querying and summarization of databases. In P. Sinčak & J. Vaščak (Eds.), *Quo vadis computational intelligence?* (pp. 144-175). New York: Springer-Verlag.

Kacprzyk, J., & Zadrożny, S. (2001). Data mining via linguistic summaries of databases: An interactive approach. In L. Ding (Ed.), *A new paradigm of knowledge engineering by soft computing* (pp. 325-345). Singapore: World Scientific.

Kacprzyk, J., & Zadrożny, S. (2001). Computing with words in intelligent database querying: Standalone and Internet-based applications. *Information Sciences, 34*, 71–109. doi:10.1016/S0020-0255(01)00093-7

Kacprzyk, J., & Zadrożny, S. (2001). On linguistic approaches in flexible querying and mining of association rules. In H.L. Larsen, J. Kacprzyk, S. Zadrożny, T. Andreasen, & H. Christiansen (Eds.), *Flexible query answering systems. Recent advances* (pp. 475-484). New York: Springer-Verlag.

Kacprzyk, J., & Zadrożny, S. (2001). Fuzzy linguistic summaries via association rules. In A. Kandel, M. Last, & H. Bunke (Eds.), *Data mining and computational intelligence* (pp. 115-139). New York: Physica-Verlag.

Kacprzyk, J., & Zadrożny, S. (2001). Using fuzzy querying over the Internet to browse through information resources. In B. Reusch & K.-H. Temme (Eds.), *Computational intelligence in theory and practice* (pp. 235-262). New York: Physica-Verlag.

Kacprzyk, J., & Zadrożny, S. (2002). Protoforms of linguistic data summaries: Towards more general natural-language-based data mining tools. In A. Abraham, J. Ruiz del Solar, & M. Koeppen (Eds.), *Soft computing systems* (pp. 417-425). Amsterdam: IOS Press.

Kacprzyk, J., & Zadrozny, S. (2003). *Linguistic summarization of data sets using association rules.* Paper presented at the 2003 Fuzzy systems; Exploring new frontiers, St Louis, MO.

Kacprzyk, J., & Zadrożny, S. (2003). Linguistic summarization of data sets using association rules. In *Proceedings of the IEEE International Conference on Fuzzy Systems (FUZZ-IEEE'03),* St. Louis, USA (pp. 702-707).

Kacprzyk, J., & Zadrożny, S. (2005). Protoforms of linguistic database summaries as a tool for human-consistent data mining. In *Proceedings of the 14th Annual IEEE International Conference on Fuzzy Systems (FUZZ-IEEE 2005)* (pp. 591-596). Reno, NV, USA: IEEE.

Kacprzyk, J., & Zadrożny, S. (2005). Linguistic database summaries and their protoforms: Towards natural language based knowledge discovery tools. *Information Sciences, 173*, 281–304. doi:10.1016/j.ins.2005.03.002

Kacprzyk, J., & Zadrożny, S. (2009). Protoforms of linguistic database summaries as a human consistent tool for using natural language in data mining. *International Journal of Software Science and Computational Intelligence, 1*, 100–111.

Kacprzyk, J., & Ziółkowski, A. (1986). Database queries with fuzzy linguistic quantifiers. *IEEE Transactions on Systems . Man and Cybernetics SMC, 16*, 474–479. doi:10.1109/TSMC.1986.4308982

Kacprzyk, J., Pasi, G., Vojtaš, P., & Zadrożny, S. (2000). Fuzzy querying: issues and perspective. *Kybernetika, 36*, 605–616.

Kacprzyk, J., Yager, R. R., & Zadrożny, S. (2000). A fuzzy logic based approach to linguistic summaries of databases. *International Journal of Applied Mathematics and Computer Science, 10*, 813–834.

Kacprzyk, J., Yager, R. R., & Zadrożny, S. (2001). Fuzzy linguistic summaries of databases for an efficient business data analysis and decision support. In W. Abramowicz & J. Żurada (Eds.), *Knowledge discovery for business information systems* (pp. 129-152). Boston: Kluwer.

Kacprzyk, J., Zadrożny, S., & Ziółkowski, A. (1989). FQUERY III+: a 'human-consistent' database querying system based on fuzzy logic with linguistic quantifiers. *Information Systems, 14*, 443–453. doi:10.1016/0306-4379(89)90012-4

Kalbfleisch, J. D., & Lawless, J. F. (1988). Estimation of reliability in field-performance studies. *Technometrics, 30*, 365–388. doi:10.2307/1269797

Kalbfleisch, J. D., Lawless, J. F., & Robinson, J. A. (1991). Methods for the analysis and prediction of warranty claims. *Tecnometrics, 33*, 273–285. doi:10.2307/1268780

Kamber, M., Han, J., & Chiang, J. (1997). Metarule-guided mining of multi-dimensional association rules using data cubes. In *Proceedings of the KDD* (pp. 207-210).

Kampanya, N., Shen, R., Kim, S., North, C., & Fox, E. A. (2004). Citiviz: A visual user interface to the citidel system. In *Research and advanced technology for digital libraries* (LNCS 3232, pp. 122-133). Berlin, Germany: Springer.

Kandel, A., Pacheco, R., Martins, A., & Khator, S. (1996). The foundations of rule-based computations in fuzzy models. In W. Pedrycz (Ed.), *Fuzzy modelling, paradigms and practice* (pp. 231-263). Boston: Kluwer.

Kang, D., Xu, B., Lu, J., & Li, Y. (2006). Reasoning for fuzzy description logic with comparison expressions. In *Proceedings of the International Workshop on Description Logics (DL 06)*, Lake District, UK.

Karim, M. R., Yamamoto, W., & Suzuki, K. (2001a). Statistical analysis of marginal count failure data. *Lifetime Data Analysis, 7*, 173–186. doi:10.1023/A:1011300907152

Karim, M. R., Yamamoto, W., & Suzuki, K. (2001b). Change-point detection from marginal count failure data. *Journal of the Japanese Society for Quality Control, 31*, 318–338.

Karkkainen, I., & Franti, P. (2007). Gradual model generator for singlepass clustering. *Pattern Recognition, 40*(3), 784–795. doi:10.1016/j.patcog.2006.06.023

Karnik, N. N., Mendel, J. M., & Liang, Q. (1999). Type-2 fuzzy logic systems. *IEEE transactions on Fuzzy Systems, 7*(6), 643–658. doi:10.1109/91.811231

Kaya, M., & Alhajj, R. (2005). Fuzzy OLAP association rules mining-based modular reinforcement learning approach for multiagent systems. *IEEE Transactions on Systems, Man, and Cybernetics, 35*, 326–338.

kddcup08. (1998). *Kdd cup data*. Retrieved from http://kdd.ics.uci.edu/databases/kddcup98/kddcup98.html

Kim, D. (2000). An implementation of fuzzy logic controller on the reconfigurable FPGA system. *IEEE Transactions on Industrial Electronics, 47*(3), 703–715. doi:10.1109/41.847911

Kim, M. W., Lee, J. G., & Min, C. (1999). Efficient fuzzy rule generation based on fuzzy decision tree for data mining. In *. Proceedings of the IEEE International Fuzzy Systems Conference FUZZ-IEEE, 99*, 1223–1228.

Kimball, R. (1996). *The data warehouse toolkit*. John Wiley & Sons.

Klarner, M. (2004). Hyperbug - a scalable natural language generation approach. In R. Portzel (Ed.), *Proceedings of the 2nd International Workshop on Scalable Natural Language Understanding (ScaNaLu-2004)* (pp. 65-71). Boston, MA, USA: Association for Computational Linguistics.

Klawonn, F. (2004). Fuzzy clustering: insights and a new approach. *Mathware & soft computing, 11*(2-3).

Klawonn, F. (2006). Understanding and controlling the membership degrees in fuzzy clustering. In *From data and information analysis to knowledge engineering* (pp. 446-453).

Klawonn, F., & Höppner, F. (2003). What is fuzzy about fuzzy clustering? Understanding and improving the concept of the fuzzifier. In *Advances in intelligent data analysis* (LNCS 2779, pp. 254-264). Berlin, Germany: Springer.

Klawonn, F., & Höppner, F. (2003). An alternative approach to the fuzzifier in fuzzy clustering to obtain better clustering. In *Proceedings of the EUSFLAT Conf.* (pp. 730-734).

Klawonn, F., Chekhtman, V., & Janz, E. (2003). Visual inspection of fuzzy clustering results. In J. Benitez, O. Cordon, F. Hoffmann, & R. Roy (Eds.), *Advances in soft computing - engineering, design and manufacturing* (pp. 65-76). London: Springer.

Klawonn, F., Gebhardt, J., & Kruse, R. (1996). *Foundations of fuzzy systems*. New York: John Wiley and Sons.

Klir, G. J., & Yuan, B. (1995). *Fuzzy sets and fuzzy logic: Theory and applications*. Upper Saddle River, NJ: Prentice-Hall.

Koenigstein, N., Shavitt, Y., & Tankel, T. (2008). Spotting out emerging artists using geo-aware analysis of P2P query strings. In *Proceeding of the 14th ACM SIGKDD international Conference on Knowledge Discovery and Data Mining. KDD '08* (pp. 937-945). New York: ACM.

Kohavi, R., Bradley, C. E., Frasca, B., Mason, L., & Zheng, Z. (2000). KDD-Cup 2000 organizers' report: Peeling the onion. *SIGKDD Exploration, 2*(2), 86–93. doi:10.1145/380995.381033

Krishnapuram, R., & Freg, C.-P. (1992). Fitting an unknown number of lines and planes to image data through compatible cluster merging. *Pattern Recognition, 25*(4), 385–400. doi:10.1016/0031-3203(92)90087-Y

Krishnapuram, R., & Keller, J. (1993). A possibilistic approach to clustering. *IEEE transactions on Fuzzy Systems, 1*(2), 98–110. doi:10.1109/91.227387

Kubota, K., Nakase, A., Sakai, H., & Oyanagi, S. (2000). Parallelization of decision tree algorithm and its performance evaluation. In *Proceedings of the Fourth International Conference on High Performance Computing in the Asia-Pacific Region, Vol. 2* (pp. 574-579).

Kuncheva, L. I. (2004). *Combining pattern classifiers: Methods and algorithms*. New York; Wiley-Interscience.

Kung, Y.-S., & Tsai, M.-H. (2007). FPGA-based speed control IC for PMSM drive with adaptive fuzzy control. *IEEE Transactions on Power Electronics, 22*(6), 2476–2486. doi:10.1109/TPEL.2007.909185

Kuok, C., Fu, A., & Wong, M. (1998). Mining fuzzy association rules in databases. [New York, NY, USA: ACM Press.]. *SIGMOD Record, 27*(1), 41–46. doi:10.1145/273244.273257

Lalmas, M., & Murdock, V. (2008). Workshop on aggregated search. In *Proceedings of the ACM SIGIR 2008*. Retrieved from http://www.yr-bcn.es/sigir08

Landlot, O. (1996). Low power analog fuzzy rule implementation based on a linear MOS transistor network. In *Proceedings of the 5th International Conference on Microelectronics for Neural Networks and Fuzzy Systems* (pp. 86-93).

Last, M., & Kandel, A. (1999). Automated perceptions in data mining. In *1999 IEEE International Fuzzy Systems Conference Proceedings* (Part I, pp. 19-197).

Last, M., & Kandel, A. (2002). Perception-based analysis of engineering experiments in semiconductor industry. *International Journal of Image and Graphics, 2*(1), 107–126. doi:10.1142/S0219467802000512

Last, M., & Kandel, A. (2002). Fuzzy comparison of frequency distributions. In P. Grzegorzewski *et al.* (Eds.), *Soft methods in probability, statistics, and data analysis* (pp. 219-227). Heidelberg, Germany: Physica-Verlag.

Laurent, A. (2002). *Extraction de connaissances pertinentes à partir de baes de données multidimensionnelles*. Laboratoire d'Informatique de Paris 6.

Lawless, F. (1998). Statistical analysis of product warranty data. *International Statistical Review, 66*, 227–240.

Lawless, J. F., & Kalbfleisch, J. D. (1992). Some issues in the collection and analysis of field reliability data. In J.P. Klein & P.K.Goel (Eds.), *Survival analysis: State of the art* (pp. 141-152). Amesterdam: Kluwer.

Lawless, J. F., Hu, J., & Cao, J. (1995). Methods for the estimation of failure distributions and rates from automobile warranty data. *Lifetime Data Analysis, 1,* 227–240. doi:10.1007/BF00985758

Lawry, J. (2004). A framework for linguistic modelling. *Artificial Intelligence, 155,* 1–39. doi:10.1016/j.artint.2003.10.001

Lawry, J. (2006). *Modelling and reasoning with vague concepts.* Berlin, Germany: Springer.

Lawry, J. (2008). Appropriateness measures: An uncertainty model for vague concepts. *Synthese, 161*(2), 255–269. doi:10.1007/s11229-007-9158-9

Lawry, J., & Tang, Y. (2008). Relating prototype theory and label semantics. In D. Dubois, M. A. Lubiano, H. Prade, M. A. Gil, P. Grzegorzweski, & O. Hryniewicz (Eds.), *Soft methods for handling variability and imprecision* (pp. 35-42). Berlin, Germany: Springer.

Lawry, J., & Tang, Y. (2009). Uncertainty modelling for vague concepts: A prototype theory approach. *Submitted.*

Lazaro, J., Arias, J., Martin, J. L., & Cuadrado, C. (2003). Modified fuzzy c-means clustering algorithm for real-time applications. In *Field-programmable logic and applications* (pp. 2778). Berlin, Germany: Springer.

Lee, D. h., & Kim, M. H. (1997). Database sumarization using fuzzy ISA hierarchies. *IEEE Transactions on Systems, Man, and Cybernetics. Part B, Cybernetics, 27,* 68–78. doi:10.1109/3477.552184

Lee, J.-H., & Lee-Kwang, H. (1997). An extension of association rules using fuzzy sets. In *Proceedings of the 7th IFSA World Congress,* Prague, Czech Republic (pp. 399-402).

Lehn-Schiøler, T., Arenas-García, J., Petersen, K. B., & Hansen, L. K. (2006). A genre classification plug-in for data collection. In *Proceedings of the International Conference on Music Information Retrieval (ISMIR'06)* (pp. 320-321).

Lemaitre, L., Patyra, M. J., & Mlynek, D. (1993). Synthesis and design automation of analog fuzzy logic VLSI circuits. In *Proceedings of the IEEE Symposium on Multiple-Valued Logic* (pp. 74-79).

Lemaitre, L., Patyra, M. J., & Mlynek, D. (1994). Analysis and design of CMOS fuzzy logic controller in current mode. *IEEE Journal of Solid State Circuits, 29*(3), 317–322. doi:10.1109/4.278355

Leouski, A. V., & Croft, W. B. (1996). *An evaluation of techniques for clustering search results* (Tech. Rep. IR-76). Department of Computer Science, University of Massachusetts at Amherst.

Lesh, N., & Mitzenmacher, M. (2004). Interactive data summarization: An example application. In *Proceedings of the Working Conference on Advanced Visual Interfaces (AVI '04),* Gallipoli, Italy (pp.183-187). New York: ACM.

Lesot, M.-J., & Kruse, R. (2006). Data summarisation by typicality-based clustering for vectorial and non vectorial data. In *Proceedings of the IEEE International Conference on Fuzzy Systems* (pp. 547-554).

Leung, K. T., Ercegovac, M., & Muntz, R. R. (1999). *Exploiting reconfigurable FPGA for parallel query processing in computation intensive data mining applications* (UC MICRO Technical Report). University of California, Los Angeles, Computer Science Department.

Li, C., & Wang, X. (1996). A data model for supporting on-line analytical processing. In *Proceedings of the fifth international conference on Information and knowledge management* (pp. 81-88). New York: ACM.

Li, H., Liu, T. Y., & Zhai, C. X. (2008). Workshop on learning to rank for information retrieval. In *Proceedings of the Annual International ACM Conference on Research and Development in Information Retrieval (SIGIR2008).* Retrieved from http://research.microsoft.com/en-us/um/beijing/events/LR4IR-2008/

Li, T. H. S., Chang, S. J., & Chen, Y. X. (2003). Implementation of human-like driving skills by autonomous fuzzy behavior control on an FPGA-based car-like mobile robot. *IEEE Transactions on Industrial Electronics, 50*(5), 867–880. doi:10.1109/TIE.2003.817490

Li, Y., Xu, B., Lu, J., & Kang, D. (2006). Discrete tableau algorithms for FSHI. In *Proceedings of the International Workshop on Description Logics (DL 2006)*, Lake District, UK.

Liu, P., & Meng, M.-H. (2004). Online data-driven fuzzy clustering with applications to real-time robotic tracking. *IEEE transactions on Fuzzy Systems, 12*(4), 516–523. doi:10.1109/TFUZZ.2004.832521

Liu, Y., & Kerre, E. E. (1998). An overview of fuzzy quantifiers. (I). Interpretations. *Fuzzy Sets and Systems, 95*, 1–21. doi:10.1016/S0165-0114(97)00254-6

Losada, D. E., Diaz-Hermida, R., Bugarin, A., & Barro, S. (2004). Experiments on using fuzzy quantified sentences in adhoc retrieval. In *Proceedings ACM Symposium on Applied Computing* (pp. 1059-1066).

Louverdis, G., & Andreadis, I. (2003). Design and implementation of a fuzzy hardware structure for morphological color image processing. *IEEE Transactions on Circuits and Systems for Video Technology, 13*(3), 277–288. doi:10.1109/TCSVT.2003.809830

Lu, J., Kang, D., Zhang, Y., Li, Y., & Zhou, B. (2008). A family of fuzzy description logics with comparison expressions. In *Proceedings of the Third International Conference, Rough Sets and Knowledge Technology (RSKT 08)*.

Lui, C.-L., & Chung, F.-L. (2000). Discovery of generalized association rules with multiple minimum supports. In *Principles of data mining and knowledge discovery* (LNCS 1910, pp. 510-515). Berlin, Germany: Springer-Verlag.

Luo, T., Kramer, K., Goldgof, D. B., Hall, L. O., Samson, S., Remsen, A., & Hopkins, T. (2005). Active learning to recognize multiple types of plankton. *Journal of Machine Learning Research, 6*(Apr), 589–613.

Lutz, C. (2008). Two upper bounds for conjunctive query answering in SHIQ. In *Proceedings of the 21ˢᵗ International Workshop on Description Logics (DL 2009)*.

Mahalanobis, P. (1936). On the generalized distance in statistics. In *Proceedings of the National Institute of Science of India* (pp. 49-55).

Mailis, T., Stoilos, G., & Stamou, G. (2007). Expressive reasoning with horn rules and fuzzy description logics. In *Proceedings of the first international conference on web reasoning and rule systems (RR-07)*.

Mailis, T., Stoilos, G., Simou, N., & Stamou, G. (2008). Tractable reasoning based on the fuzzy-EL++ algorithm. In *Proc. of the 4th International Workshop on Uncertainty Reasoning for the Semantic Web (URSW 08)*.

Manaresi, N., Rovatti, R., Franchi, E., Guerrieri, R., & Baccarani, G. (1996). A silicon compiler of analog fuzzy controllers: From behavioral specifications to layout. *IEEE transactions on Fuzzy Systems, 4*(4), 418–428. doi:10.1109/91.544302

Manzoul, M. A., & Jayabharathi, D. (1994). CAD tool for implementation of fuzzy controllers on FPGAs. *Cybernetics and Systems, 25*(4), 599–609. doi:10.1080/01969729408902344

Manzoul, M. A., & Jayabharathi, D. (1995). FPGA for fuzzy controllers. *IEEE Transactions on Systems, Man, and Cybernetics, 25*(1), 213–216. doi:10.1109/21.362948

Marsala, C., & Bouchon-Meunier, B. (1997). Forest of fuzzy decision trees. In M. Mares, R. Mesiar, V. Novak, J. Ramik, & A. Stupnanova (Eds.), *Proceedings of the Seventh International Fuzzy Systems Association World Congress, volume 1*, Prague, Czech Republic (pp. 369-374).

Marsala, C., & Bouchon-Meunier, B. (1999). An adaptable system to construct fuzzy decision trees. In *Proc. of the NAFIPS'99 (North American Fuzzy Information Processing Society)*, New York, USA (pp. 223-227).

Marsala, C., & Detyniecki, M. (2005). University of Paris 6 at TRECVID 2005: High-level feature extraction. In *TREC Video Retrieval Evaluation Online Proceed-*

ings. Retrieved from http://www-nlpir.nist.gov/projects/tvpubs/tv.pubs.org.html

Marsala, C., & Detyniecki, M. (2006). University of Paris 6 at TRECVID 2006: Forests of fuzzy decision trees for high-level feature extraction. In *TREC Video Retrieval Evaluation Online Proceedings*. Retrieved from http://wwwnlpir.nist.gov/projects/tvpubs/tv.pubs.org.html

Marsala, C., Detyniecki, M., Usunier, N., & Amini, M.-R. (2007). High-level feature detection with forests of fuzzy decision trees combined with the rankboost algorithm. In *TREC Video Retrieval Evaluation Online Proceedings*. Retrieved from http://www-nlpir.nist.gov/projects/tvpubs/tv.pubs.org.html

Marshall, G. F., & Collins, S. (1997). Fuzzy logic architecture using subthreshold analogue floating-gate devices. *IEEE transactions on Fuzzy Systems*, *5*(1), 32–43. doi:10.1109/91.554445

Martin, T. P., & Azvine, B. (2003). Acquisition of soft taxonomies for intelligent personal hierarchies and the soft Semantic Web. *BT Technology Journal*, *21*(4), 113–122. doi:10.1023/A:1027391706414

Martin, T. P., & Azvine, B. (2005). Soft integration of information with semantic gaps. In E. Sanchez (Ed.), *Fuzzy logic and the Semantic Web*. Amsterdam: Elsevier.

Martin, T. P., & Shen, Y. (2008). Track - time-varying relations in approximately categorised knowledge. *International Journal of Computational Intelligence Research*, *4*, 300–313.

Martin, T. P., Azvine, B., & Shen, Y. (2007). *Finding soft relations in granular information hierarchies*. Paper presented at the 2007 IEEE International Conference on Granular Computing Fremont, CA, USA.

Martin, T. P., Azvine, B., & Shen, Y. (2007). Intelligent hierarchy mapping: A soft computing approach. In *Information technology and intelligent computing*.

Martin, T. P., Azvine, B., & Shen, Y. (2008). Granular association rules for multiple taxonomies: A mass assignment approach to. In M. Nickles (Ed.), *Uncertain reasoning in the Semantic Web*. Berlin, Germany: Springer.

Martin, T. P., Shen, Y., & Azvine, B. (2008). Incremental evolution of fuzzy grammar fragments to enhance instance matching and text mining. *IEEE transactions on Fuzzy Systems*, *16*, 1425–1438. doi:10.1109/TFUZZ.2008.925920

Martin-Bautista, M. J., Vila, M. A., Larsen, H. L., & Sanchez, D. (2000). *Measuring effectiveness in fuzzy information retrieval*. Paper presented at the Flexible Query Answering Systems (FQAS).

Mermoud, G., Upegui, A., Peña, C. A., & Sanchez, E. (2005). A dynamically-reconfigurable FPGA platform for evolving fuzzy systems. In *Computational Intelligence and Bioinspired Systems* (LNCS 3512, pp. 572-581). Berlin, Germany: Springer-Verlag.

Merz, C., & Murphy, P. (n.d.). *UCI repository of machine learning databases Univ. of CA., Dept. of CIS, Irvine, CA*. Retrieved from http://www.ics.uci.edu/~ mlearn/MLRepository.html

Michalski, R. (1990). Pattern recognition as rule-guided inductive inference. *IEEE Transactions on Patter Analysis and Machine Learning*, *PAMI-2*(4), 349–361. doi:10.1109/TPAMI.1980.4767034

Mika, P. (2005). Ontologies are us: A unified model of social networks and semantics. In *Proceedings of the 4th International Semantic Web Conference (ISWC 2005)*.

Miki, T., & Yamakawa, T. (1995). Fuzzy inference on an analog fuzzy chip. *IEEE Micro*, *15*(4), 8–18. doi:10.1109/40.400638

Modenesi, M. V., Costa, M. C. A., Evsukoff, A. G., & Ebecken, N. F. F. (2007). Parallel fuzzy c-means cluster analysis. In *Proceedings of the High performance computing for computational science – VECPAR 2006* (pp. 52-65). Berlin, Germany: Springer.

Moen, P. (2000). *Attribute, event sequence, and event type similarity notions for data mining*. Unpublished doctoral dissertation (Report A-2000-1), Helsinki, Finland: Department of Computer Science, University of Helsinki.

Molina, C., Sánchez, D., Vila, M. A., & Rodríguez-Ariza, L. (2006). A new fuzzy multidimensional model. *IEEE transactions on Fuzzy Systems, 14*, 897–912. doi:10.1109/TFUZZ.2006.879984

Monmasson, E., & Cirstea, M. N. (2007). FPGA design methodology for industrial control systems – a review. *IEEE Transactions on Industrial Electronics, 54*(4), 1824–1842. doi:10.1109/TIE.2007.898281

Muyeba, M. K., & Keane, J. A. (2000). Interestingness in attribute-oriented induction (AOI): Multiple-level rule generation. In *Principles of data mining and knowledge discovery* (LNCS 1910, pp. 542-549). Berlin, Germany: Springer-Verlag.

Nasraoui, O., Uribe, C., Coronel, C., & Gonzalez, F. (2003). Tecno-streams: Tracking evolving clusters in noisy data streams with a scalable immune system learning model. In *Proceedings of the Third IEEE International Conference on Data Mining, 2003. ICDM 2003* (pp. 235-242).

Neal, R. M., & Hinton, G. E. (1998). A view of the em algorithm that justifies incremental, sparse, and other variants. In *Learning in Graphical Models* (pp. 355-368).

Neumann, B., & Möller, R. (2006). On scene interpretation with description logics. In H.I. Christensen & H.-H. Nagel (Eds.), *Cognitive vision systems: Sampling the spectrum of approaches* (pp. 247-278). Berlin, Germany: Springer.

Nguyen, H. T. (1984). On modelling of linguistic information using random sets. *Information Science, 34*, 265–274. doi:10.1016/0020-0255(84)90052-5

NIST. (2006). *Guidelines for the TRECVID 2006 evaluation, National Institute of Standards and Technology*. Retrieved from http://www-nlpir.nist.gov/projects/tv2006/tv2006.html

O'Callaghan, L., Mishra, N., Meyerson, A., Guha, S., & Motwani, R. (2002). Streaming-data algorithms for high-quality clustering. In Proceedings of the 18th IEEE International Conference on Data Engineering (pp. 685-694).

Osinski, S. (2003). *An algorithm for clustering of Web search results*. Unpublished master's thesis, Department of Computing Science, Poznan' University of Technology. Retrieved from http://project.carrot2.org/publications/osinski-2003-lingo.pdf

Ota, Y., & Wilamowski, M. (1996). CMOS implementation of a voltage-mode fuzzy min-max controller. *Journal of Circuits . Systems and Computers, 6*(2), 171–184.

Ouzunis, C.A., & Karp, P.D. (2002). The past, present and future of genome-wide re-annotation. *Genome Biology, 3*(2), comment2001.1-2001.6.

Over, P., Kraaij, W., & Smeaton, A. F. (2007). *Guidelines for the TRECVID 2007 evaluation*. National Institute of Standards and Technology. Retrieved from http://www-nlpir.nist.gov/projects/tv2007/tv2007.html

Pagani, M., Bordogna, G., & Valle, M. (2007). G. Mining multidimensional data using clustering techniques. In . *Proceedings of the DEXA Workshop, FLEXDBIST-07*, 382–386.

Pal, N., & Bezdek, J. (2002). Complexity reduction for "large image" processing. *IEEE Transactions on Systems, Man, and Cybernetics . Part B, 32*(5), 598–611.

Pal, N., Pal, K., Keller, J., & Bezdek, J. (2005). A possibilistic fuzzy c-means clustering algorithm. *IEEE transactions on Fuzzy Systems, 13*(4), 517–530. doi:10.1109/TFUZZ.2004.840099

Pampalk, E. (2005). Speeding up music similarity. *Report on the Music Information Retrieval Evaluation EXchange (MIREX'05)*.

Pan, J. Z., & Thomas, E. (2007) Approximating OWL-DL ontologies. In *Proc. of the 22nd National Conference on Artificial Intelligence (AAAI-07)*.

Pan, J. Z., Stamou, G., Stoilos, G., & Thomas, E. (2008). Scalable querying services over fuzzy ontologies. In *Proceedings of the International World Wide Web Conference (WWW 2008)*, Beijing.

Pan, J. Z., Stoilos, G., Stamou, G., Tzouvaras, V., & Horrocks, I. (2006). f-SWRL: A fuzzy extension of

SWRL. *Journal on Data Semantics, 4090*, 28–46. doi:10.1007/11803034_2

Pan, J. Z., Thomas, E., & Sleeman, D. (2006). ONTOSEARCH2: Searching and querying Web ontologies. In *Proc. of WWW/Internet* (pp. 211-218).

Pan, J.-Y., & Faloutsos, C. (2002). VideoCube: A novel tool for video mining and classification. In *Proceedings of the International Conference on Asian Digital Libraries* (LNCS 2555, pp. 194-205). Berlin, Germany: Springer.

Park, J. S., Chen, M. S., & Yu, P. S. (1995). An effective hash based algoritm for mining association rules. *SIGMOD Record, 24*(2), 175–186. doi:10.1145/568271.223813

Patel-Schneider, P. F., Hayes, P., & Horrocks, I. (2004). OWL Web ontology language semantics and abstract syntax. *W3C Recommendation.*

Patyra, M. J., Grantner, J. L., & Koster, K. (1996). Digital fuzzy logic controller: Design and implementation. *IEEE transactions on Fuzzy Systems, 4*(4), 439–459. doi:10.1109/91.544304

Pauws, S., & Eggen, B. (2001). PATS: Realization and user evaluation of an automatic playlist generator. In *Proceedings of the International Conference on Music Information Retrieval (ISMIR'02)* (pp. 179-192).

Pavlov, D., Chudova, D., & Smyth, P. (2000). Towards scalable support vector machines using squashing. In *Proceedings of the sixth ACM SIGKDD international conference on Knowledge discovery and data mining* (pp. 295-299).

Pedersen, T. B., & Jensen, C. (2001). Multidimensional database technology. *IEEE Computer, 34*(12), 40–46.

Pedrycz, W. (2004). Associations and rules in data mining: A link analysis. *International Journal of Intelligent Systems, 19*, 653–670. doi:10.1002/int.20016

Pei, J., Han, J., Mortazavi-Asl, B., & Zhu, H. (2000). Mining access patterns efficiently from Web logs. In *Proc. of the Pacific-Asia Conf. on Knowledge Discovery and Data Mining (PAKDD'00)*, Kyoto, Japan (pp. 396-407). New York, NY, USA: Springer.

Pei, J., Tung, A. K. H., & Han, J. (2001). Fault-tolerant frequent pattern mining: Problems and challenges. In *Proc. of the ACM SIGMOD Workshop on Research Issues in Data Mining and Knowledge Discovery (DMK'01)*, Santa Babara, CA (pp. 7-12). New York, NY, USA: ACM Press.

Pelleg, D., & Moore, A. (1999). Accelerating exact k-means algorithms with geometric reasoning. In *KDD '99: Proceedings of the fifth ACM SIGKDD international conference on Knowledge discovery and data mining*, New York, USA (pp. 277-281).

Peters, L., Guo, S., & Camposano, R. (1995). A novel analog fuzzy controller for intelligent sensors. *Fuzzy Sets and Systems, 70*, 235–247. doi:10.1016/0165-0114(94)00221-R

Petersohn, C. (2004). Fraunhofer HHI at TRECVID 2004: Shot boundary detection system.(Tech. Rep.). In *TREC Video Retrieval Evaluation Online Proceedings, TRECVID*. Retrieved from http://www-nlpir.nist.gov/projects/tvpubs/tvpapers04/fraunhofer.pdf

Petry, F. E. (1996). *Fuzzy databases: Principles and applications*. Boston: Kluwer.

Popescu, M., Bezdek, J. C., Keller, J. M., Havens, T. C., & Huband, J. M. (2008). A new cluster validity measure for bioinformatics relational datasets. In *Proceedings of the World Congress on Computational Intelligence, WCCI2008*, Hong Kong (pp. 726-731).

Popescu, M., Keller, J. M., Mitchell, J. A., & Bezdek, J. C. (2004). Functional summarization of gene product clusters using gene ontology similarity measures. In M. Palaniswami, B. Krishnmachari, A. Sowmya, & S. Challa (Eds.), *Proc. of the 2004 ISSNIP* (pp. 553-559). Piscataway, NJ: IEEE Press.

Postgre, S. Q. L. (2008). *Postgresql manual*. Retrieved November 2008, from, http://www.postgresql.org/docs/8.3/interactive/storage-toast.html

Prade, H., & Testemale, C. (1984). Generalizing database relational algebra for the treatment of incomplete or uncertain information and vague queries. *Information Sciences, 34*, 115–143. doi:10.1016/0020-0255(84)90020-3

Provost, F., & Kolluri, V. (1999). A survey of methods for scaling up inductive algorithms. *Data Mining and Knowledge Discovery*, *3*, 131–169. doi:10.1023/A:1009876119989

Provost, F., Jensen, D., & Oates, T. (1999). Efficient progressive sampling. In *Proceedings of the Fifth International Conference on Knowledge Discovery and Data Mining* (pp. 23-32). New York: ACM Press.

Prud'hommeaux, E., & Seaborne, A. (2006). *SPARQL query language for RDF* (W3C Working Draft). Retrieved from http://www.w3.org/TR/rdf-sparql-query/

Pruitt, K. D., Tatusova, T., & Maglott, D. R. (2007). NCBI reference sequence (RefSeq): A curated non-redundant sequence database of genomes, transcripts and proteins. *Nucleic Acids Research*, *35*(Database issue), D61–D65. doi:10.1093/nar/gkl842

Punch, W., Jain, A. K., & Topchy, A. (2005). Clustering ensembles: Models of consensus and weak partitions. *IEEE Transactions on Pattern Analysis and Machine Intelligence*, *27*(12), 1866–1881. doi:10.1109/TPAMI.2005.237

Qao, Q., Lim, M. H., Li, J. H., Ong, Y. S., & Ng, W. L. (2006). A context switchable fuzzy inference chip. *IEEE transactions on Fuzzy Systems*, *14*(4), 552–567. doi:10.1109/TFUZZ.2006.876735

Qin, A., & Suganthan, P. (2004). Robust growing neural gas algorithm with application in cluster analysis. *Neural Networks*, *17*(8-9), 1135–1148. doi:10.1016/S0893-6080(04)00166-2

Radecki, T. (1979). Fuzzy set theoretical approach to document retrieval. *Journal of Information Processing and Management*, *15*, 235–245. doi:10.1016/0306-4573(79)90030-X

Rahimi, S., Zargham, M., Thakre, A., & Chhillar, D. (2004). A parallel fuzzy c-means algorithm for image segmentation. In *Proceedings of the IEEE Annual Meeting of the Fuzzy Information NAFIPS '04* (Vol. 1, pp. 234-237).

Raschia, G., & Mouaddib, N. (2002). SAINTETIQ: A fuzzy set-based approach to database summarization. *Fuzzy Sets and Systems*, *129*, 137–162. doi:10.1016/S0165-0114(01)00197-X

Rasmussen, D., & Yager, R. R. (1996). Using SummarySQL as a tool for finding fuzzy and gradual functional dependencies. In *Proceedings of the 6th International Conference Information Processing and Management of Uncertainty in Knowledge-Based Systems (IPMU'96)*, Granada, Spain (pp. 275-280).

Rasmussen, D., & Yager, R. R. (1997). Fuzzy query language for hypothesis evaluation. In T. Andreasen, H. Christiansen, & H. L. Larsen (Eds.), *Flexible query answering systems* (pp. 23-43). Boston: Kluwer.

Rasmussen, D., & Yager, R. R. (1997). A fuzzy SQL summary language for data discovery. In D. Dubois, H. Prade, & R.R. Yager (Eds.), *Fuzzy information engineering: A guided tour of applications* (pp. 253-264). New York: Wiley.

Rasmussen, D., & Yager, R. R. (1999). Finding fuzzy and gradual functional dependencies with summarySQL. *Fuzzy Sets and Systems*, *106*, 131–142. doi:10.1016/S0165-0114(97)00268-6

Rász, B. (2004). nonordfp: An FP-growth variation without rebuilding the FP-Tree. In *Proc. of the Workshop Frequent Item Set Mining Implementations (FIMI 2004), Brighton, UK, CEUR Workshop Proceedings 126*. Aachen, Germany: Sun SITE Central Europe / University of Aachen. Retrieved from http://www.ceur-ws.org/Vol-126/

Rász, B., Bodon, F., & Schmidt-Thieme, L. (2005). On benchmarking frequent itemset mining algorithms. In *Proc. of the Workshop Open Software for Data Mining (OSDM'05 at KDD'05)*, Chicago, IL (pp. 36-45). New York, NY, USA: ACM Press.

Raytchev, B., & Murase, H. (2001). Unsupervised face recognition from image sequences based on clustering with attraction and repulsion. In *Proceedings of the 2001 IEEE Computer Society Conference on Computer Vision and Pattern Recognition (CVPR 2001), Vol. 2* (pp. II–25-II–30).

Rehm, F., & Klawonn, F. (2005). Learning methods for air traffic management. In L. Godo (Ed.), *Symbolic and quantitative approaches to reasoning with uncertainty.* Berlin, Germany: Springer.

Rehm, F., Klawonn, F., & Kruse, R. (2006). Visualization of single clusters. In L. Rutkowski, R. Tadeusiewicz, L. Zadeh, & J. Zurada (Eds.), *Proceedings of the Artificial Intelligence and Soft Computing - ICAISC 2006.* Berlin, Germany: Springer.

Reiter, E. (1995). Building natural language generation systems. In A. Cawsey (Ed.), *Proceedings of the AI and Patient Education Workshop.* Glasgow, UK: University of Glasgow.

Ressom, H. W., Wang, D., & Natarajan, P. (2003). Adaptive double self-organizing maps for clustering gene expression profiles. *Neural Networks, 16*(5-6), 633–640. doi:10.1016/S0893-6080(03)00102-3

Reyneri, L. M. (2003). Implementation issues of neuro-fuzzy hardware: Going toward HW/SW codesign. *IEEE Transactions on Neural Networks, 14*(1), 176–194. doi:10.1109/TNN.2002.806955

Reyneri, L. M., & Renga, F. (2004). Speeding-up the design of HW/SW implementations of neuro-fuzzy systems using the CodeSimulink environment. *Applied Soft Computing, 4*(3), 227–240. doi:10.1016/j.asoc.2004.03.003

Robinson, J. A., & McDonald, G. C. (1991). Issues related to field relibility and warranty data. In G.E. Liepins & V.R.R. Uppuluri (Eds.), *Data quality control: Theory and pragmatics* (pp. 69-89). New York: Marcel Dekker.

Rojas, I., Pelayo, F. J., Ortega, J., & Prieto, A. (1996). A CMOS implementation of fuzzy controllers based on adaptive membership function ranges. In *Proceedings of the Fifth International Conference on Microelectronics for Neural Networks and Fuzzy Systems* (pp. 317-321). Washington, DC: IEEE Comp. Soc. Press.

Rosati, R. (2007). On conjunctive query answering in EL. In *Proceedings of the 2007 International Workshop on Description Logic (DL 2007).*

Rosch, E. (1973). Natural categories. *Cognitive Psychology, 4,* 328–350. doi:10.1016/0010-0285(73)90017-0

Rosenfeld, C., Doerman, D., & DeMenthon, D. (2003). *Video mining.* Amsterdam: Kluwer Academic Publishers.

Rovatti, R. (1998). Fuzzy piecewise multilinear and piecewise linear systems as universal approximators in Sobolev norms. *IEEE transactions on Fuzzy Systems, 6*(2), 235–249. doi:10.1109/91.669022

Rovatti, R., & Borgatti, M. (1997). Maximum-throughput implementation of piecewise-linear fuzzy systems. In *Proceedings of the Sixth IEEE International Conference on Fuzzy Systems. Vol. 2* (pp. 767-772).

Rovatti, R., Ferrari, A., & Borgatti, M. (1998). Automatic implementation of piecewise-linear fuzzy systems addressing memory-performance trade-off. In A. Kandel & G. Langholz (Eds.), *Fuzzy hardware* (pp. 159-179). Amsterdam: Kluwer Academic Publishers.

Rubenstein, W. B. (1987). A database design for musical information. In *Proceedings of ACM SIGMOD* (pp. 479-490).

Ruiz, A., Gutiérrez, J., & Felipe-Frenández, J. A. (1995). A fuzzy controller with an optimized defuzzification algorithm. *IEEE Micro, 15*(6), 76.40-76.49.

Salton, G., & McGill, M. J. (1983b). *Introduction to modern information retrieval.* New York: McGraw-Hill.

Salton, G., Fox, E. A., & Wu, H. (1983a). Extended Boolean information retrieval. *Journal of Communications of ACM, 26,* 1022–1036. doi:10.1145/182.358466

Sanchez, E. (1989). Importance in knowledge systems. *Information Systems, 14*(6), 455–464. doi:10.1016/0306-4379(89)90013-6

Sanchez-Solano, S., Cabrera, A. J., Baturone, I., Moreno-Velo, F. J., & Brox, M. (2007). FPGA Implementation of embedded fuzzy controllers for robotic applications. *IEEE Transactions on Industrial Electronics, 54*(4), 1937–1945. doi:10.1109/TIE.2007.898292

Sasaki, M., & Ueno, F. (1994). A novel implementation of fuzzy logic controller using new meet operation. In *Proceedings of the Third IEEE International Conference on Fuzzy Systems* (pp. 1676-1681).

Savasere, A., Omiecinski, E., & Navathe, S. (1995). An efficient algorithm for mining association rules in large databases. In *Proceedings of the 21st International Conference on Very Large Data Bases* (pp. 432-444). San Francisco: Morgan Kaufman.

Sebrechts, M. M., Cugini, J. V., Laskowski, S. J., Vasilakis, J., & Miller, M. S. (1999). Visualization of search results: A comparative evaluation of text, 2D, and 3D interfaces. In *Proceedings of the 22nd annual international ACM SIGIR conference on Research and development in information retrieval* (pp. 3-10).

Shankar, B. U., & Pal, N. R. (1994). FFCM: An effective approach for large data sets. In *Proceedings of the 3rd International Conference on Fuzzy Logic, Neural Nets and Soft Computing, Iizuka, Japan* (pp. 331-332).

Shen, L., & Shen, H. (1998). Mining flexible multiple-level association rules in all concept hierarchies (extended abstract). In *Proceedings of the 9th International Conference on Database and Expert Systems Applications* (LNCS 1460, pp. 786-796). Berlin, Germany: Springer.

Shen, L., Shen, H., & Cheng, L. (1999). New algorithms for efficient mining of association rules. *Information Sciences, 118*, 251–268. doi:10.1016/S0020-0255(99)00035-3

Shoemaker, L., Banfield, R., Hall, L., Bowyer, K., & Kegelmeyer, W. P. (2008). Using classifier ensembles to label spatially disjoint data. *Information Fusion, 9*(1), 120–133. doi:10.1016/j.inffus.2007.08.001

Shortliffe, E., & Buchanan, B. (1975). A model of inexact reasoning in medicine. *Mathematical Biosciences, 23*, 351–379. doi:10.1016/0025-5564(75)90047-4

Simou, N., Athanasiadis, Th., Stoilos, G., & Kollias, S. (2008). image indexing and retrieval using expressive fuzzy description logics. *Signal . Image and Video Processing, 2*, 321–335. doi:10.1007/s11760-008-0084-1

Simou, N., Stoilos, G., Tzouvaras, V., Stamou, G., & Kollias, S. (2008). Storing and querying fuzzy knowledge in the Semantic Web. In *Proceedings of the 7th International Workshop on Uncertainty Reasoning For the Semantic Web*, Karlsruhe, Germany.

Sinha, D., & Dougherty, E. R. (1993). Fuzzification of set inclusion: Theory and applications. *Fuzzy Sets and Systems, 55*, 15–42. doi:10.1016/0165-0114(93)90299-W

Smellie, A. (2004). Accelerated k-means clustering in metric spaces. *Journal of Chemical Information and Modeling, 44*(6), 1929–1935. doi:10.1021/ci0499222

Smith, T. F., & Waterman, M. S. (1981). Identification of common molecular subsequences. *Journal of Molecular Biology, 147*, 195–197. doi:10.1016/0022-2836(81)90087-5

Srikant, R., & Agrawal, R. (1995). Mining generalized association rules. (pp. 407-419). San Francisco: Morgan Kaufmann Publishers Inc.

Staley, E., & Twidale, M. (2000). *Graphical interfaces to support information search* (Tech. Rep.). Graduate School of Library and Information Science, University of Illinois. Retrieved from http://people.lis.uiuc.edu/~twidale/irinterfaces/bib-main.html

Stigler, S. M. (2002). *Statistics on the table: The history of statistical concepts and methods*. Boston: Harvard University Press.

Stoilos, G., Simou, N., Stamou, G., & Kollias, S. (2006). Uncertainty and the Semantic Web. *IEEE Intelligent Systems, 21*(5), 84–87. doi:10.1109/MIS.2006.105

Stoilos, G., Stamou, G., & Pan, J. Z. (2008). Classifying fuzzy subsumption in Fuzzy-EL+. In *Proceedings of the 21st International Workshop on Description Logics (DL 08)*, Dresden, Germany.

Stoilos, G., Stamou, G., Pan, J. Z., Tzouvaras, V., & Horrocks, I. (2007). Reasoning with very expressive fuzzy description logics. *Journal of Artificial Intelligence Research, 30*(5), 273–320.

Stoilos, G., Stamou, G., Tzouvaras, V., Pan, J. Z., & Horrocks, I. (2005). Fuzzy OWL: Uncertainty and the Semantic Web. In *Proceedings of the International Workshop on OWL: Experiences and Directions*.

Stoilos, G., Stamou, G., Tzouvaras, V., Pan, J. Z., & Horrocks, I. (2005). The fuzzy description logic f-SHIN.

In *Proc. of the International Workshop on Uncertainty Reasoning for the Semantic Web* (pp. 67-76).

Stoilos, G., Straccia, U., Stamou, G., & Pan, J. Z. (2006). General concept inclusions in fuzzy description logics. In *Proceedings of the 17th European Conference on Artificial Intelligence (ECAI 06)*, Riva del Garda, Italy.

Stothard, P., & Wishart, D. S. (2006). Automated bacterial genome analysis and annotation. *Current Opinion in Microbiology, 9*, 505–510. doi:10.1016/j.mib.2006.08.002

Straccia, U. (2001). Reasoning within fuzzy description logics. *Journal of Artificial Intelligence Research, 14*, 137–166.

Straccia, U. (2005). Towards a fuzzy description logic for the Semantic Web. In *Proceedings of the 2nd European Semantic Web Conference*.

Straccia, U. (2006). Answering vague queries in fuzzy DL-Lite. In *Proceedings of the 11th International Conference on Information Processing and Management of Uncertainty in Knowledge-Based Systems (IPMU-06)* (pp. 2238-2245).

Straccia, U. (2008), *fuzzyDL*: An expressive fuzzy description logic reasoner. In *Proceedings of the International Conference on Fuzzy Systems (Fuzz-IEEE 08)*.

Strehl, A., & Ghosh, J. (2002). Cluster ensembles – a knowledge reuse framework for combining partitionings. *Journal of Machine Learning Research, 3*, 583–617. doi:10.1162/153244303321897735

Suzuki, K. (1985). Estimation of lifetime parameters from incomplete field data. *Technometrics, 27*, 263–272. doi:10.2307/1269707

Suzuki, K. (1985). Nonparametric estimation of lifetime distributions from a record of failures and follow-ups. *Journal of the American Statistical Association, 80*, 68–72. doi:10.2307/2288041

Syeda, M., Zhang, Y.-Q., & Pan, Y. (2002). Parallel granular neural networks for fast credit card fraud detection. In *Proceedings of the 2002 IEEE international Conference on Fuzzy Systems* (pp. 572-577).

Tan, P. N., Steinbach, M., & Kumar, V. (2006). *Introduction to data mining*. Boston: Addison Wesley.

Tan, P.-N., & Kumar, V. (2000). Interestingness measures for association patterns: A perspective. *Future Generation Computer Systems, 13*(2-3), 161–180.

Thomas, E., Pan, J. Z., & Sleeman, D. (2007). ONTOSEARCH2: Searching ontologies semantically. In *Proceedings of OWL Experience Workshop*.

Timm, H., Borgelt, C., Döring, C., & Kruse, R. (2001). Fuzzy cluster analysis with cluster repulsion. In *Proceedings of the European Symposium on Intelligent Technologies, Hybrid Systems and their implementation on Smart Adaptive Systems*.

Togai, M., & Watanabe, H. (1986). Expert system on a chip: An engine for real-time approximate reasoning. *IEEE Expert, 1*(3), 55–62. doi:10.1109/MEX.1986.4306980

Tresp, C., & Molitor, R. (1998). A description logic for vague knowledge. In *Proc of the 13th European Conf. on Artificial Intelligence (ECAI-98)*.

Tsukano, K., & Inoue, T. (1995). Synthesis of operational transconductance amplifier-based analog fuzzy functional blocks and its application. *IEEE transactions on Fuzzy Systems, 3*(1), 61–68. doi:10.1109/91.366571

UCIrepository. (2006). *Uci machine learning repository*. Retrieved from http://www.ics.uci.edu/ mlearn/ MLRepository.html

Upegui, A. (2006). *Dynamically reconfigurable bio-inspired hardware*. Unpublished doctoral dissertation, École Polytechnique Fédérale de Lausanne, Switzerland.

Upegui, A., & Sanchez, E. (2005). Evolving hardware by dynamically reconfiguring Xilinx FPGAs. In *Evolvable systems: From biology to hardware* (LNCS 3637, pp. 56-65). Berlin, Germay: Springer-Verlag.

Vidal-Verdú, F., & Rodríguez-Vázquez, A. (1995). Using building blocks to design analog-fuzzy controllers. *IEEE Micro, 15*(4), 49–57. doi:10.1109/40.400633

Vidal-Verdú, F., Navas-González, R., & Rodríguez-Vázquez, A. (1998). Multiplexing architecture for mixed-signal CMOS fuzzy controller. *Electronics Letters*, *34*(14), 1437–1438. doi:10.1049/el:19980968

Vojtas, P. (2001). Fuzzy logic programming. *Fuzzy Sets and Systems*, *124*, 361–370. doi:10.1016/S0165-0114(01)00106-3

Wachs, J., Shapira, O., & Stern, H. (2006). A method to enhance the possibilistic c-means with repulsion algorithm based on cluster validity index. In A. Abraham, B. D. Baets, M. Köppen, & B. Nickolay (Eds.), *Applied soft computing technologies: The challenge of complexity*. Berlin, Germany: Springer.

Waller, W. G., & Kraft, D. H. (1979). A mathematical model of a weighted Boolean retrieval system. *Journal of Information Processing and Management*, *15*, 247–260. doi:10.1016/0306-4573(79)90031-1

Wang, C., Li, J., & Shi, S. (2004). A music data model and its application. In *Proceedings of the International Conference on Multimedia Modeling (MMM'04)* (pp. 79-85).

Wang, H., Ma, Z. M., Yan, L., & Cheng, J. (2008). A fuzzy description logic with fuzzy data type group. In *Proceedings of the International Fuzz-IEEE Conference*, Hong Kong.

Wang, H., Ma, Z. M., Yan, L., & Zhang, G. (2006). A fuzzy extension of ALC with fuzzy modifiers. In *Proceedings of the Knowledge-Based Intelligent Information and Engineering Systems*.

Wang, L., & Suzuki, K. (2001). Nonparametrc estimation of lifetime distribution from warranty data without monthly unit sales information. *The Journal of Reliability Engineering Association Japan*, *23*, 14–154.

Wang, L., & Suzuki, K. (2001). Lifetime estimation on warranty data without date-of-sale information-case where usage time distributions are unknown. *Journal of the Japanese Society for Quality Control*, *31*, 148–167.

Wang, L., Bezdek, J. C., Leckie, C., & Kotagiri, R. (2008). Selective sampling for approximate clustering of very large data sets. *International Journal of Intelligent Systems*, *23*(3), 313–331. doi:10.1002/int.20268

Wang, X., Borgelt, C., & Kruse, R. (2005). Mining fuzzy frequent item sets. In *Proc. of the 11th Int. Fuzzy Systems Association World Congress (IFSA'05)*, Beijing, China (pp. 528-533). Beijing, China: Tsinghua University Press.

Watanabe, H., Dettlof, W. D., & Yount, K. E. (1990). A VLSI fuzzy logic controller with reconfigurable, cascadable architecture. *IEEE Journal of Solid State Circuits*, *25*(2), 376–382. doi:10.1109/4.52159

Webb, G. I. (2007). Discovering significant patterns. *Machine Learning*, *68*(1), 1–33. doi:10.1007/s10994-007-5006-x

Webb, G. I., & Zhang, S. (2005). *k*-Optimal-rule-discovery. *Data Mining and Knowledge Discovery*, *10*(1), 39–79. doi:10.1007/s10618-005-0255-4

Weiwei, J., Dongming, J., & Xun, Z. (2004). VLSI design and implementation of a fuzzy logic controller for engine idle speed. In *Proceedings of the 7th International Conference on Solid-State and Integrated Circuits Technology* (pp. 2067-2070).

Weka. (2006). *Weka 3 - data mining with open source machine learning software in java*. Retrieved from http://www.cs.waikato.ac.nz/ml/weka/

White, R. W., Richardson, M., Bilenko, M., & Heath, A. P. (2008). Enhancing Web search by promoting multiple search engine use. In *Proceedings of the 31st Annual international ACM Conference on Research and Development in information Retrieval* (SIGIR '08), Singapore (pp. 43-50). New York: ACM.

Winkler, R., Rehm, F., & Kruse, R. (2009). Clustering with repulsive prototypes. In *Studies in classification, data analysis, and knowledge organization*. Berlin, Germany: Springer.

Wolf, W. (Ed.). (2003). A decade of hardware/software codesign. *Computer*, *36*(4), 38–43. doi:10.1109/MC.2003.1193227

Wu, H., & Meeker, W. Q. (2002). Early detection of reliability problems using information from warranty databases. *Technometrics, 44*, 120–133. doi:10.1198/004017002317375073

Wu, K., & Yang, M. (2005). A cluster validity index for fuzzy clustering. *Pattern Recognition Letters, 26*, 1275–1291. doi:10.1016/j.patrec.2004.11.022

Wu, K., Otoo, E. J., & Shoshani, A. (2006). Optimizing bitmap indices with efficient compression. *ACM Transactions on Database Systems, 31*(1), 1–38. doi:10.1145/1132863.1132864

Wu, X.-H., & Zhou, J.-J. (2006). Noise clustering using a new distance. In *Proceedings of the 2nd International Conference on Information and Communication Technologies (ICTTA)* (pp. 1938-1943).

Wynblatt, M. J., & Schloss, G. A. (1995). Control layer primitives for the layered multimedia data model. In *Proceedings of the ACM International Conference on Multimedia* (pp. 167-177).

Xilinx Inc. (2008). *Microblaze processor reference guide (ver 9.0, 2008)*. Retrieved December 1, 2008, from http://www.xilinx.com/support/documentation/sw_manuals/mb_ref_guide.pdf

Xilinx Inc. (2008). *Virtex-5 family overview (ver 4.4, 2008), data sheet*. Retrieved December 1, 2008, from http://www.xilinx.com/support/documentation/data_sheets/ds100.pdf

Xiong, X., Chan, K. L., & Tan, K. L. (2004). Similarity-driven cluster merging method for unsupervised fuzzy clustering. In *Proceedings of the 20th conference on uncertainty in artificial intelligence* (pp. 611-618). AUAI Press.

Xu, B., Lu, J., Zhang, Y., Xu, L., Chen, H., & Yang, H. (2003). Parallel algorithm for mining fuzzy association rules. In *Proceedings of the 2003 International Conference on Cyberworlds* (pp. 288-293).

Xu, D., Bondugula, R., Popescu, M., & Keller, J. (2008). *Applications of fuzzy logic in bioinformatics*. London: Imperial College Press.

Yager, R. R. (1982). A new approach to the summarization of data. *Information Sciences, 28*, 69–86. doi:10.1016/0020-0255(82)90033-0

Yager, R. R. (1986). On the theory of bags. *International Journal of General Systems, 13*, 23–37. doi:10.1080/03081078608934952

Yager, R. R. (1987). A note on weighted queries in information retrieval systems. *Journal of the American Society for Information Science American Society for Information Science, 38*(1), 23–24. doi:10.1002/(SICI)1097-4571(198701)38:1<23::AID-ASI4>3.0.CO;2-3

Yager, R. R. (1988). On ordered weighted averaging aggregation operators in multi-criteria decision making. *IEEE Transactions on Systems, Man, and Cybernetics, 18*, 183–190. doi:10.1109/21.87068

Yager, R. R. (1991). On linguistic summaries of data. In G. Piatetsky-Shapiro, & W. J. Frawley (Eds.), *Knowledge discovery in databases* (pp. 347-363). Menlo Park: AAAI Press/The MIT Press.

Yager, R. R. (1994). Aggregation operators and fuzzy systems modeling. *Fuzzy Sets and Systems, 67*, 129–145. doi:10.1016/0165-0114(94)90082-5

Yager, R. R. (1996). Database discovery using fuzzy sets. *International Journal of Intelligent Systems, 11*, 691–712. doi:10.1002/(SICI)1098-111X(199609)11:9<691::AID-INT7>3.0.CO;2-F

Yager, R. R. (1996). Quantifier guided aggregation using OWA operators. *International Journal of Intelligent Systems, 11*, 49–73. doi:10.1002/(SICI)1098-111X(199601)11:1<49::AID-INT3>3.0.CO;2-Z

Yager, R. R. (1998). Including importances in OWA aggregations using fuzzy systems modeling. *IEEE transactions on Fuzzy Systems, 6*, 286–294. doi:10.1109/91.669028

Yager, R. R. (2001). The power average operator. *IEEE Transactions on Systems . Man and Cybernetics Part A, 31*, 722–730.

Yager, R. R., & Filev, D. P. (1999). Induced ordered weighted averaging operators. *IEEE Transactions* on Systems, Man, and Cybernetics, 29, 141–150. doi:10.1109/3477.752789

Yager, R. R., & Kacprzyk, J. (1997). *The ordered weighted averaging operators: Theory and applications.* Boston: Kluwer.

Yager, R. R., & Kacprzyk, J. (1999). Linguistic data summaries: A perspective. In *Proceedings of the IFSA'99 Congress,* Taipei, Taiwan R.O.C. (pp. 44-48).

Yamakawa, T. (1988). High-speed fuzzy controller hardware system: The mega-FIPS machine. *Information Sciences, 45,* 113–128. doi:10.1016/0020-0255(88)90036-9

Yamakawa, T. (1993). A fuzzy inference engine in nonlinear analog mode and its application to a fuzzy control. *IEEE Transactions on Neural Networks, 4*(3), 496–522. doi:10.1109/72.217192

Yang, J. (2003). Dynamic clustering of evolving streams with a single pass. In *Proceedings of the 19th International Conference on Data Engineering, 2003* (pp. 695-697).

Yen, S.-J. (2000). Mining generalized multiple-level association rules., In *Principles of data mining and knowledge discovery* (LNCS 1910, pp. 679-684). Berlin, Germany: Springer.

Yosefi, G., Khoei, A., & Hadidi, K. (2007). Design of a new CMOS controllable mixed-signal current mode fuzzy logic controller (FLC) chip. In *Proceedings of the IEEE International Conference on Electronics, Circuits and Systems* (pp. 951-954).

Young, V. R. (1996). Fuzzy subsethood. *Fuzzy Sets and Systems, 77,* 371–384. doi:10.1016/0165-0114(95)00045-3

Zadeh, L. A. (1965). Fuzzy sets as a basis for a theory of possibility. *Information and Control, 8,* 338–353. doi:10.1016/S0019-9958(65)90241-X

Zadeh, L. A. (1965). Fuzzy sets. *Information and Control, 8,* 338–353. doi:10.1016/S0019-9958(65)90241-X

Zadeh, L. A. (1975). The concept of a linguistic variable and its application to approximate reasoning (part 1).

Information Sciences, 8, 199–249. doi:10.1016/0020-0255(75)90036-5

Zadeh, L. A. (1983). A computational approach to fuzzy quantifiers in natural languages. *Computers & Mathematics with Applications (Oxford, England), 9,* 149–184. doi:10.1016/0898-1221(83)90013-5

Zadeh, L. A. (1985). Syllogistic reasoning in fuzzy logic and its application to usuality and reasoning with dispositions. *IEEE Transactions on Systems, Man, and Cybernetics, SMC-15,* 754–763.

Zadeh, L. A. (1996). Fuzzy logic = computing with words. *IEEE transactions on Fuzzy Systems, 4,* 103–111. doi:10.1109/91.493904

Zadeh, L. A. (1997). Toward a theory of fuzzy information granulation and its centrality in human reasoning and fuzzy logic. *Fuzzy Sets and Systems, 90*(2), 111–127. doi:10.1016/S0165-0114(97)00077-8

Zadeh, L. A. (2002). A prototype-centered approach to adding deduction capabilities to search engines – the concept of a protoform. In *Proceedings of the BISC Seminar, 2002.* Berkeley: University of California.

Zadeh, L. A. (2002). From computing with numbers to computing with words – from manipulation of measurements to manipulation of perceptions. *Int. J. Appl. Math. Comput. Sci., 12*(3), 307–324.

Zadeh, L. A. (2006). From search engines to question answering systems - the problems of world knowledge relevance deduction and precisiation. In E. Sanchez (Ed.), *Fuzzy logic and the Semantic Web* (pp. 163-210). Amsterdam: Elsevier.

Zadeh, L. A., & Kacprzyk, J. (Eds.). (1992). *Fuzzy logic for the management of uncertainty.* New York: Wiley.

Zadeh, L., & Kacprzyk, J. (Eds.). (1999). *Computing with words in information/intelligent systems, 1. Foundations, 2. Applications.* New York: Physica-Verlag.

Zadrożny, S., & Kacprzyk, J. (1999). On database summarization using a fuzzy querying interface. In *Proceedings of the IFSA'99 World Congress,* Taipei, Taiwan R.O.C. (pp. 39-43).

Zadrożny, S., Kacprzyk, J., & Gola, M. (2005). Towards human friendly data mining: Linguistic data summaries and their protoforms. In *Proceedings of the Artificial Neural Networks: Formal Models and their Applications – ICANN 2005* (LNCS 3697, pp. 697-702). Berlin, Germany: Springer.

Zaki, M., Parthasarathy, S., Ogihara, M., & Li, W. (1997). New algorithms for fast discovery of association rules. In *Proc. of the 3rd Int. Conf. on Knowledge Discovery and Data Mining (KDD'97),* Newport Beach, CA (pp. 283-296). Menlo Park, CA, USA: AAAI Press. Mannila, H., Toivonen, H., & Verkamo, A.I. (1997). *Discovery of frequent episodes in event sequences* (Report C-1997-15). Helsinki, Finland: Department of Computer Science, University of Helsinki.

Zamir, O., & Etzioni, O. (1999). Grouper: A dynamic clustering interface to Web search results. In *Proceedings of the 8th International World Wide Web Conference* (pp. 1361-1374).

Zeira, G., Maimon, O., Last, M., & Rokach, L. (2004). Change detection in classification models induced from time series data. In M. Last, A. Kandel, & H. Bunke (Eds.), *Data mining in time series databases* (pp. 101-125). Singapore: World Scientific.

Zhang, Q., Chamberlain, R. D., Indeck, R., West, B. M., & White, J. (2004). Massively parallel data mining using reconfigurable hardware: Approximate string matching. In *Proceedings of the 18th Annual IEEE International Parallel and Distributed Processing Symposium (IP-DPS'04).*

Zhang, T., Ramakrishnan, R., & Livny, M. (1996). BIRCH: An efficient data clustering method for very large databases. In *Proc. of the ACM SIGMOD Int'l. Conf. on Management of Data* (pp. 103-114). New York: ACM Press.

Zhu, H. (1998). *On-line analytical mining of association rules.* Simon Fraser University.

Zhu, X., Wu, X., Elmagarmid, A. K., Feng, Z., & Wu, L. (2005). Video data mining: Semantic indexing and event detection form the association perspective. *IEEE Transactions on Knowledge and Data Engineering, 17*(5), 665–677. doi:10.1109/TKDE.2005.83

Ziv, J., & Lempel, A. (1977). A universal algorithm for sequential data compression. *IEEE Transactions on Information Theory, 23*(3), 337–343. doi:10.1109/TIT.1977.1055714

About the Contributors

Anne Laurent has been Assistant Professor at the LIRMM lab since September 2003. As a member of the TATOO group, she works on data mining, OLAP Mining, sequential pattern mining, tree mining, stream mining both for trends and exceptions detections and is particularly interested in the study of the use of fuzzy logic to provide more valuable results, while remaining scalable. Anne Laurent has numerous collaborations with companies, including small and big businesses. She serves as reviewer in the main conferences and journals related to data mining and fuzzy logic.

Marie-Jeanne Lesot obtained her PhD from the University Pierre and Marie Curie in 2005 and since 2006 she is an associate professor in the department of Computer Science of Paris 6 (LIP6) and member of the MAchine Learning and Information REtrieval (MALIRE) department. Her research interests include fuzzy machine learning, in particular fuzzy clustering, typicality and fuzzy prototypes, and similarity measures.

* * *

Koldo Basterretxea was born in Bilbao, Basque Country, Spain, in 1970. In 1994 he received the Licenciado degree in physics, with specialization in electronics and control, from the University of the Basque Country (UPV/EHU). In 2002 he received the Ph.D. degree in physics from the same university. He is currently a Senior Lecturer at the Department of Electronics and Telecommunications of the UPV/EHU. He has tought at the Schools of Industrial Technical Engineering of Eibar (1995-1998), and Bilbao (1998-2009), where he currently develops his teaching and research activities. His research interests include neural/fuzzy hardware design, hardware/software codesign, implementation of high-speed and real-time digital controllers on FPGAs , system on programmable chip (SoPC) implementations, and soft computing techniques.

Karishma Batra received the B.Sc. Statistics degree from Lady Shri Ram College for Women (LSR), University of Delhi, India, in 2005, and the M.Sc. Statistics degree from the University of Bangalore, India, in 2007. She has worked as a Research Associate in India Science Lab, General Motors Research and Development Centre for nearly two years. Her research interests include reliability analysis, non-parametric statistics and data mining. Ms. Batra is the recipient of the Central College Gold Medal and the Prof. R.R. Umarji Gold Medal from the University of Bangalore (2008), the GSK Scholar Award from GlaxoSmithKline (2006 and 2007), and the Best Student in Statistics Award from LSR (2004 and 2005).

Gloria Bordogna holds the position of senior researcher at the National Research Council Institute for the Dynamics of Environmental Processes and of contract professor at the Faculty of Engineering of Bergamo University, where she teaches IR and GIS. She received a laurea degree in Physics from the University of Milano. Her research interests concern soft computing techniques in the area of information retrieval, of flexible query languages and Geographic Information Systems. She was involved in several European projects such as Ecourt, PENG and IDE-Univers, edited three volumes and a special issue of JASIST in her research area, and participated in the program committee of several conferences such as FUZZ-IEEE, ACM SIGIR, ECIR, FQAS, CIKM, IEEE-ACM WI/IAT, WWW.

Christian Borgelt received his diploma (M.Sc.) in computer science from the University of Braun-schweig, Germany, in 1995. After spending a year at the Daimler-Benz Research Center Ulm, he became a Ph.D. student at the University of Magdeburg, Germany, and received his Ph.D. in computer science in 2000. He was awarded the Ph.D. Prize 2000 and the Research Prize 2002 of the faculty of computer science of the University of Magdeburg, Germany. In 2006 he received the venia legendi for computer science, again from the University of Magdeburg, Germany. Since April 2006 he is the principal researcher of the Intelligent Data Analysis and Graphical Models Research Unit of the European Center for Soft Computing, Mieres, Spain. His research interests include molecular and graph mining, (approximate) frequent item set mining, graphical models for diagnosis and planning, learning graphical models from data, prototypebased classification and clustering and many other intelligent data analysis methods.

Alessandro Campi is a researcher at the Politecnico di Milano. His works exploit the possibility of extending XQuery in several directions, more precisely, the possibility to add active rules, to execute fuzzy queries, to mine data and to draw the query without writing directly XQuery. Other research activities are related to investigating automatic construction and verification of data intensive Web site and on methodologies and tools for e-learning. He taught Programming languages, Data Structures and Algorithms, Database and Software Engineering at the Politecnico di Milano.

Inés del Campo was born in Buenos Aires, Argentina, in 1961. She received the Ph.D. degree in physics from the University of the Basque Country (UPV/EHU), Spain, in 1993. Currently she is a Senior Lecturer in the Electricity and Electronics Department of the Faculty of Sciences and Technology of the UPV/EHU. Her research interests mainly concern artificial neural networks, fuzzy systems, and genetic algorithms. She has an extensive experience in the design (methodologies and tools) of reconfigurable hardware (mainly FPGAs and SoPCs), and hardware description languages (HDLs). Her experience includes also hardware/software co-design techniques, finite wordlength analysis in digital systems, and high-performance design for real-time application with emphasis on scalable architectures.

Juana Canul-Reich received the BA degree in administrative informatics from Autonomous University of Tabasco (UJAT) and received the MSc in computer science from Monterrey Tecnological Institute (ITESM) and the MSc in computer engineering from University of South Florida (USF). She is currently working on the PhD degree in computer science and engineering at USF. Her research interests include, but are not limited to, support vector machines, feature selection and classification problems, microarray data analysis, machine learning.

Sugato Chakrabarty got his B. Tech from the Indian Institute of Technology, Kharagpur, his M.S. from the University of Delaware, Newark, Delaware and his Ph.D. from Texas A&M University, College Station, Texas all in Computer Science. He has worked in AT&T Bell Labs, Digital and other companies where he has gathered extensive industrial experience. Currently, he works in General Motors R&D, India Science Lab, where he is a Staff Researcher. He is interested in the areas of Machine Learning, Manufacturing Assembly Planning, Fuzzy Logic, Case Based Reasoning Text Analysis and Warranty Analytics and has published papers in these areas. He also holds several patents in these areas. He is also a reviewer in IEEE Transactions on Mobile Computing and the International Journal of Technology Management.

Weijian Cheng is currently a Masters student in Computer Science in University of South Florida, USA. He obtained his Bachelor of Science in Mathematics from Hefei University of Technology. China. His research interest includes data mining, video processing and artificial intelligence. His previous publications include fuzzy clustering system and automatic red tide detection by data mining methods. He is working with College of Marine Science in University of South Florida to improve the remote sensing based red tide detection methods through machine learning algorithms. He will be the Director of Technology for an online marketing firm iBayBiz.com from August 2009.

François Deliège is currently a Ph.D. student in computer science at Aalborg University, Denmark. He received his MS degree in computer engineering from the Université Libre de Bruxelles. In his Ph.D. project, he has developed data warehouse concepts and technologies that facilitate the management of vast amounts of musical audio features. During his master thesis, he developed a web service infrastructure for a Massively Multplayer Online Game. His research interests include multidimensional databases, data warehousing, data streams, and web services.

Marcin Detyniecki is a CNRS research scientist working at the Computer Science Laboratory (LIP6) of the University Pierre and Marie Curie (UPMC) in Paris, France. He received, from that same university, the Doctorate degree in Artificial Intelligence in 2000, and the Habilitation degree in 2006. His research interests include theoretical foundations of mathematical data fusion and artificial intelligence, and its application to multimedia retrieval and interaction. On these topics has edited three books and authored more than fifty publications in peer reviewed conferences and journals. He co-organizes AMR, the international annual workshop on Adaptive Multimedia Retrieval. He has been invited researcher at the University of California at Berkeley, University of Florence and Carnegie Mellon University.

Dmitry B. Goldgof has received Ph.D. degree from the University of Illinois. He is currently a Professor and Associate Chair of the Department of Computer Science and Engineering at the University of South Florida. Professor Goldgof research interests include Image and Video Analysis, Pattern Recognition and Bioengineering. Dr. Goldgof has graduated 14 Ph.D., and has published over 65 journal and 145 conference papers, 16 books chapters and edited 4 books. Professor Goldgof is a Fellow of IEEE and is an Associate Editor for IEEE Transactions on Systems, Man and Cybernetics and for International Journal of Pattern Recognition and Artificial Intelligence.

Lawrence O. Hall is a Professor and the Chair of the Department of Computer Science and Engineering at University of South Florida. He received his Ph.D. in Computer Science from the Florida

State University in 1986. He is a fellow of the IEEE. His research interests lie in distributed machine learning, extreme data mining, bioinformatics, pattern recognition and integrating AI into image processing. The exploitation of imprecision with the use of fuzzy logic in pattern recognition, AI and learning is a research theme. He has authored or co-authored over 65 publications in journals, as well as many conference papers and book chapters.

Frank Höppner received his Diploma and PhD in computer science from the University of Braunschweig in 1996 and 2003, respectively. He is full professor in Business Information Systems at the University of Applied Sciences Braunschweig/Wolfenbüttel in Wolfsburg (Germany). His main research interests focus on knowledge discovery in databases, especially clustering and the analysis of temporal and sequential data.

Prodip Hore received the B.Tech degree in Computer Science and Engineering from the Institute of Engineering and Management (IEM), Calcutta, University of Kalyani, India, 2002, and the Masters and Ph.D. degree in Computer Science from the University of South Florida, Tampa in 2004 and 2007 respectively. He is now working as a senior modeling scientist in Fair Isaac Corporation (also known as FICO), San Diego. His research interests include machine learning, data mining, and application of them to image processing. He has co-authored around 10 papers in reputed journals and conferences. He has also filed one US patent in collaboration with Fair Isaac.

Janusz Kacprzyk is Professor of CS at the Systems Research Institute, Polish Academy of Sciences, Warsaw, Poland. He is Member of the Polish Academy of Sciences and of Spanish Royal Academy of Economic and Financial Sciences. He is Fellow of IEEE and of IFSA. He was a visiting professor in the USA, Italy, China. His research includes: soft computing, fuzzy logic and computing with words, in decisions and optimization, control, database querying, information retrieval. He is the author of 5 books, (co)editor of 30 volumes, (co)author of 300 papers. He is the editor in chief of 4 book series at Springer, and of 2 journals. He received many awards, notably: 2005 IEEE CIS Pioneer Award in Fuzzy Systems, The Sixth Kaufmann Prize and Gold Medal for pioneering works on soft computing in economics. Currently he is President of IFSA and President of the Polish Society for Operational and Systems Research.

Frank Klawonn received his M.Sc. and Ph.D. in mathematics and computer science from the University of Braunschweig in 1988 and 1992, respectively. He is now the head of the Lab for Data Analysis and Pattern Recognition at the University of Applied Sciences in Wolfenbuettel (Germany). His main research interests focus on techniques for intelligent data analysis, especially clustering and classification. He is an area editor of the International Journal of Uncertainty, Fuzziness and Knowledge-Based Systems and a member of the editorial boards of the International Journals of Information Technology and Intelligent Computing, Fuzzy Sets and Systems, Data Mining, Modelling & Management, Hybrid Information Technology, Knowledge Engineering & Soft Data Paradigms as well as Mathware & Soft Computing.

Rudolf Kruse obtained his diploma (Mathematics) degree in 1979 from University of Braunschweig, Germany, and a PhD in Mathematics in 1980 as well as the venia legendi in Mathematics in 1984 from the same university. Following a short stay at the Fraunhofer Gesellschaft, in 1986 he joined the

University of Braunschweig as a professor of computer science. Since 1996 he is a full professor at the Faculty of Computer Science of the Otto-von-Guericke University in Magdeburg where he is leading the computational intelligence research group. He has carried out research and projects in statistics, artificial intelligence, expert systems, fuzzy control, fuzzy data analysis, computational intelligence, and data mining. His research group is very successful in various industrial applications. He has coauthored 15 monographs, 15 edited books, as well as more than 330 refereed technical papers in various scientific areas. He is associate editor of several scientific journals. He is a fellow of the International Fuzzy Systems Association (IFSA), fellow of the European Coordinating Committee for Artificial Intelligence (ECCAI) and fellow of the Institute of Electrical and Electronics Engineers (IEEE).

Mark Last is currently an Associate Professor at the Department of Information Systems Engineering, Ben-Gurion University of the Negev, Israel and the Head of the Data Mining and Software Quality Engineering Group. Prior to that, he was a Visiting Assistant Professor at the Department of Computer Science and Engineering, University of South Florida, USA (1999 – 2001). Mark obtained his Ph.D. degree from Tel Aviv University, Israel in 2000. He has published over 130 papers and chapters in scientific journals, books, and refereed conferences. He is a co-author of two monographs and a co-editor of seven edited volumes. Prof. Last serves as an Associate Editor of IEEE Transactions on Systems, Man, and Cybernetics (IEEE-SMC) and Pattern Analysis and Applications (PAA). His main research interests are focused on data mining, fuzzy logic, cross-lingual text mining, software testing, and security informatics.

Jonathan Lawry is Reader in Artificial Intelligence in the Department of Engineering Mathematics at the University of Bristol. He has a BSc. in mathematics from Plymouth Polytechnic and a PhD in mathematics from the University of Manchester. His research interests are in random set approaches to modelling vagueness and linguistic uncertainty in complex systems, and in particular the label semantic framework. Dr Lawry has published over 90 refereed articles in the area of approximate reasoning as well as four edited volumes and one book. He has received research funding from a number of bodies including EPSRC, the Tyndall centre, the Nuffield foundation and the Royal Academy of Engineering.

Nicolás Marín is a tenured associate professor in the Department of Computer Science and Artificial Intelligence at the University of Granada and a researcher in the Intelligent Databases and Information Systems Research Group. His research interests include database design, data mining, data warehousing, software modelling, and mathematical theory. He received his PhD in computer science from the University of Granada. He is a member of the IEEE Computer Society.

Christophe Marsala is Associate Professor in Computer Science at Université Pierre et Marie Curie - Paris (France). He obtained his PhD in Computer Science from Université Pierre et Marie Curie - Paris (France) in 1998. His dissertation was concerned with Artificial Intelligence and in particular with Fuzzy Decision Trees. His current research topics are concerned with data mining, and video mining.

Trevor Martin is Professor of Artificial Intelligence at the University of Bristol. Since 2001 he has been funded by BT as a Senior Research Fellow, researching soft computing in intelligent information management including areas such as the semantic web, soft concept hierarchies and user modelling. He is a member of the editorial board of Fuzzy Sets and Systems, and has served on many conference programme and organising committees, including programme chair (2007) and technical co-chair 2010) for the IEEE Fuzzy Systems Conference. He is a co-organiser of the URSW (Uncertain Reasoning for the Semantic Web) series of workshops, and is active in a W3C group investigating the same topic as well as chairing the IEEE Computational Intelligence Society's Semantic Web Task Force. He has published over 200 papers in refereed conferences, journals and books, and is a Chartered Engineer and member of the BCS and IEEE.

Yael Mendelson is currently a B.Sc. student in Information Systems Engineering at Ben-Gurion University of the Negev, Israel. Her main interest is in the data mining field. She has collaborated with GM – India Science Lab.

Carlos Molina received his M.S. degree in Computer Science in 2002 and his Ph.D. in Computer Science in 2005, both from the University of Granada. He is an assistant professor in the Department of Computer Science of the University of Jaén since 2004. His current main research interests are in the fields of Multidimensional Model, Data Mining and Soft Computing.

Jeff Z. Pan is a lecturer in Knowledge Technology in the Department of Computing Science in the University of Aberdeen. He received his PhD degree in computer science from the University of Manchester for his research on Description Logic Reasoning Support for the Semantic Web. Back in 2002, he was the first to propose a metamodeling architecture for Web ontologies languages RDF and OWL. He was later invited to review the Semantic and Abstract Syntax of the OWL Web ontology language by the W3C WebONT Working Group. His proposal on extending OWL with XML Schema datatypes was published as a W3C Note; this proposal was later implemented in the OWL 1.1 submission. He has published more than 50 paper, he has/had been involved in several European and national projects, such as Knowledge Web (IST-2004-507842), Wonder Web (IST-2001-33052), AKT (GR/N15764/01) and IPAS (TP/2/IC/6/I/10292), and in several W3C Standardisation activities.

Torben Bach Pedersen is a full professor of computer science at Aalborg University, Denmark. He received the MS degree in computer science from Aarhus University, Denmark, and the Ph.D. degree in computer science from Aalborg University. Before joining Aalborg University, he worked in the software industry for more than six years. His research interest includes Multidimensional databases, OLAP, data warehousing, federated databases, data streams, and location-based services. He has published more than 70 scientific papers on these issues in journals such as The VLDB Journal, Information Systems, and IEEE Computer and in conferences such as VLDB, ICDE, SSDBM, SSTD, IDEAS, ACM-GIS, ECIR, Hypertext, DOLAP, and DaWaK. He is a member of the editorial board of the International Journal on Data Warehousing and Mining and has served on more than 40 program committees including VLDB, ICDE, EDBT, SSDBM, and DaWaK. He is a member of the IEEE, the IEEE Computer Society, and the ACM.

Mihail Popescu is an assistant professor in the Department of Health Management and Informatics, School of Medicine at the University of Missouri (MU), Columbia. He also holds appointments in the MU Informatics Institute and in the Department of Computer Science at MU. His current research focus include medical decision making, fuzzy and ontological data mining algorithms and eldercare technologies. Dr. Popescu is a senior IEEE member.

Giuseppe Psaila is assistant professor at the Faculty of Engineering at University of Bergamo. He obtained the degree in Electronic Engineering from Politecnico di Milano, and the Ph.D. in Computer Engineering from Politecnico di Torino. His research interests are in the field of databases, in particular database models and languages, data mining, XML and workflow systems. He participated to several European funded research projects in the database field, such as the IDEA Project (development of an active, deductive and object oriented database system), Mietta (on Multilingual Information Extraction) and cInq (consortium on knowledge discovery by Inductive Queries).

Frank Rehm received his diploma degree (in Computer Science) from University of Applied Sciences Schmalkalden, Germany, in 2000 and M.Sc. and Ph.D. degrees (both in Computer Science) from University of Magdeburg, Germany, in 2003 and 2007, respectively. Since 2003, he is working at the German Aerospace Center as a Research Associate on the improvement of Air Traffic Management using modern data mining techniques.

Stefania Ronchi graduated cum laude in Computer Science Engineering, curriculum Information Systems, at the University of Bergamo in February 2008. She participated in the Italian regional research project "Dote Ricercatore" for the development of research projects in the technical-scientific area. She won a PhD grant in Information Engineering at the Department of Electronics and Information of Politecnico di Milano, where she currently carries out her research activity in the database area, dealing mainly with Web search, IR and Semantic Web. She authored two publications on her research topics in the proceedings of international conferences.

Daniel Sánchez received the M.S. and Ph.D. degrees in computer science, both from the University of Granada, Granada, Spain, in 1995 and 1999, respectively. Since 2001 he is Associate Professor in the Department of Computer Science and Artificial Intelligence of the University of Granada. He has participated and is currently a Member of the teams of several projects, and he has published more than 50 papers in international journals and conferences. He is co-coordinator of the DAMI Working group on Data Mining and Machine Learning of EUSFLAT (European Society for Fuzzy Logic and Technology). His current main research interests are in the fields of Semantic Computing, Data Mining & Knowledge Discovery, Approximate Reasoning and Fuzzy Set Theory, Soft Computing and Image Processing, Text and Web Mining, and Information Retrieval.

Yun Shen received the B.Sc. degree in computer science from Sichuan University, Chengdu, China, in 2000, and the Ph.D. degree in computer science from the University of Hull, Hull, U.K., in 2005. He is a Research Associate at the Artificial Intelligence Group, Department of Engineering Mathematics, University of Bristol, Bristol, U.K. His current research interests include intelligent text mining and data analysis, social networking mining and smart behavioural targeting advertisement.

Larry Shoemaker received the BS and MS degrees in computer science from University of South Florida in 2003 and 2005 respectively. His role as a graduate research assistant at University of South Florida included membership in the Avatar project research team from 2004 to 2008. He is currently pursuing the PhD degree in computer science and engineering at University of South Florida. His research interests are in data mining, machine learning, and knowledge discovery. He is a member of the IEEE.

Giorgos Stamou is a lecturer at the National and Technical University of Athens. Prior to that he was a research assistant professor at the Institute of Communication and Computer Systems, National Technical University of Athens. He is currently leading the Knowledge Technologies and Multimedia Annotation team of Image, Video and Multimedia Systems Laboratory. His research interest include knowledge représentation and reasoning, multimedia content archiving and retrieval. He is member of the RuleML Steering Committee, also co-chairing the Fuzzy RuleML Technical Group, W3C Advisory Committee Representative of NTUA, member of the SWBPD Working Group and co-chair of the Multimedia Task Force and member of the Steering Committee of the e-business forum on Emerging Information Technologies and Cultural Heritage of the Greek Ministry of Culture.

Giorgos Stoilos is a Research Assistant at the Image, Video and Multimedia Lab of NTUA. In 2008 he obtained his PhD degree from the School of Electrical & Computer Engineering, in the National and Technical University of Athens. His research interests include knowledge representation and reasoning, management of fuzzy knowledge and ontologies. He has designed several reasoning algorithms for fuzzy extensions of the popular ontology language OWL (a W3C standard) and the forthcoming OWL2 QL and OWL2 EL W3C standards. He has also worked in the area of semantic interoperability where he has proposed a popular string matching method called I-Sub. He has also participated in the W3C Rule Interchange Format (RIF) Working Group, the W3C OWL2 Working Group, the W3C Uncertainty Reasoning for the WWW Incubator Group, and the Fuzzy RuleML Technical Group, and in a number of EU funded projects, like X-Media (IP), K-Space (NoE), Knowledge Web (NoE) and BOEMIE (STREP).

Yongchuan Tang was born in Hubei, China, on December 5, 1974. He received the M.Sc. degree in applied mathematics and the Ph.D. degree from the Southwest Jiaotong University, China, in 2000 and 2003, respectively. He is currently an Associate Research Fellow with the College of Computer Science, Zhejiang University, Hangzhou, China. His research interests are in the mathematical representation of uncertainty, fuzzy computing, affective computing, and the study of uncertainty in complex systems.

M. Amparo Vila is full professor in the Department of Computer Science and Artificial Intelligence at the University of Granada, where she leads the Intelligent Databases and Information Systems research group. She holds a Ph.D. in Mathematics from the University of Granada. Her main research interests are in the fields of database design, data mining, and mathematical theory.

Xiaomeng Wang received her Bachelor's degree in Electronic Engineering from Hefei University of Technology, China, and the degree of Diplom-Informatikerin (Master's degree in Computer Science) from the Otto-von-Guericke University of Magdeburg, Germany. Currently she is working at SAP AG, Germany, alongside pursuing a Ph.D. at the Institute of Knowledge Processing and Language Engineering, Otto-von-Guericke University of Magdeburg, Germany.

Roland Winkler received his diploma degree in computer science from the University of Magdeburg in 2008. Since then, he is a Ph.D. student at the German Aerospace Center in Braunschweig, Germany. His scientific interests focus on the dimension problem of data analysis, especially in the domain of clustering and classification. He is also interested in exploiting connections between robust statistics and fuzzy clustering.

Ronald R. Yager, Director of the Machine Intelligence Institute and Professor of Information Systems at Iona College, has worked in the area of machine intelligence for over 25 years and published over 500 papers. Is among the world's top 1% most highly cited researchers. Recipient of the IEEE Computational Intelligence Society Pioneer award in Fuzzy Systems. Fellow of the IEEE, the New York Academy of Sciences and the Fuzzy Systems Association. Served at the National Science Foundation as program director. Editor and chief of the International Journal of Intelligent Systems. Serves on the editorial board of numerous technology journals.

Sławomir Zadrożny is Associate Professor (Ph.D. 1994, D.Sc. 2006) at the Systems Research Institute, Polish Academy of Sciences. His current scientific interests include applications of fuzzy logic in database management systems, data mining, information retrieval and decision support. He is the author and co-author of ca. 100 journal and conference papers. He has been involved in the design and implementation of several prototype software packages. He is also a teacher at the Warsaw School of Information Technology in Warsaw, Poland, where his interests focus on information retrieval and database management systems.

Index

G